THE FIRST TIME

a book of twentieth and twenty-first century music firsts

NICK HAMLYN

Copyright © 2018 Nick Hamlyn

Published by PPR Publishing,
19 Kingswell Road, Northampton NN2 6QB.

www.pprpublishing.co.uk

All rights reserved.

A CIP catalogue record for this book
is available from the British Library

ISBN 978 1 9164347 0 7

Edition 1.7

Printed and bound in Great Britain by IngramSpark / Lightning Source UK Ltd.

Dedicated to my parents, Eileen and Professor David Hamlyn,
who taught me to love music

Dedicated also to all the musicians who have created musical firsts
and to Catrin Vincent – one of the brightest hopes, with her band Another Sky, for music to come

CONTENTS

		Introduction	1
PART 1		INSTRUMENTS AND MUSICIANS	3
	1	Electric Guitar	4
	2	Bass Guitar	24
	3	Keyboard Instruments	32
	4	Electronics	48
	5	Drums and Percussion	58
	6	Orchestral Instruments	68
	7	World and Folk Instruments	78
	8	The PA System	90
PART 2		RECORDS AND RECORDINGS	93
	9	Formats	94
	10	Charts and Awards	106
	11	The Recording Studio	116
	12	Disc Jockeys	124
	13	Sampling	130
	14	The Remix	150
	15	Collecting Records	156
PART 3		MUSIC GENRES	163
	16	Rock 'n' Roll	164
	17	Blues	178
	18	Soul	188
	19	The Beatles	204
	20	Progressive Rock	216
	21	Heavy Metal	226
	22	Punk	240
	23	Funk	246

24	Disco and Dance Music	252
25	Rap	262
26	Ambient and Soundtrack Music	274
27	Musical Theatre	286
28	Jazz	292
29	Folk	312
30	Country	332
31	Reggae	344
32	World Music	358
33	Classical	366
	Bibliography	379
	Photo Credits	384
	Index of Firsts	386
	Index of Names	390
	About the Author	411

INTRODUCTION

The First Time is a song recorded by Adam Faith in late 1963 and it became a top five hit in the UK when issued as the A-side of a single. It was, as it happened, the first time that the singer worked with a new backing group, the Roulettes, in an attempt to move his music forward. The Roulettes were a beat group (with two members who later turned up in Argent) and they enabled Adam Faith to take on the sound and the style of the Beatles-inspired music that was rapidly making his brand of early sixties pop redundant.

Several other artists have also recorded songs called *The First Time*, including U2, Fanny, Brian Wilson, Andrew Lloyd Webber, and Ella Henderson. None of these is the same as the Adam Faith song and, more significantly as far as the thesis of this book is concerned, none is the first recording of a song with this title. That honour, such as it is, belongs only to Adam Faith.

The development of the recording industry during the twentieth century transformed the way in which music itself developed. In times before that, when music had to be propagated by means of live performance, with musicians able to travel from one venue to the next at a speed no greater than that of a trotting horse, change took place exceedingly slowly. The instrumental music categorised as classical took two hundred and fifty years to grow from the simple baroque dance music of Jean-Baptiste Lully to the extravagant symphonic composition of Gustav Mahler. A similar development within jazz, taking place in the era of recording, in the twentieth century, took forty years. Within rock music, from its emergence as a distinct genre to its adoption of symphonic ambitions, the time span was just fifteen years.

During the one and a quarter centuries since recording began, entirely new kinds of music have been invented and within those genres, different variations have been explored. At the beginning of the twentieth century, jazz, the blues, and country had barely started. Rock music was still more than fifty years away. For many people, the whole question as to who were the inventors and the innovators through the years within these and the other musical forms is a matter of intense interest. This book seeks to find the answers.

A cursory glance at the list of contents will reveal that the subject matter has been divided into three categories. The first is concerned with the various musical instruments. There have been several entirely new inventions in this area during the twentieth century, most of them involving the use of electricity. This is fertile ground for examining who and what was first. The second category is concerned with the recording industry and with the records themselves (and other formats). The third category explores in detail the music, as broken down into eighteen genres. The book attempts to find and describe the first, defining example of each genre, while recognising that in most cases, the origins developed gradually, rather than as the result of a single revolutionary process. It is perfectly possible for the reader to begin with the music that is their particular favourite, or else to read straight through from Part One, Chapter One: whatever works best for them. The reader will quickly discover, in either case, that the main argument proceeds through the right hand pages. The left hand, facing pages, contain pictures of records and artists, along with extra snippets of text that are intended to be interesting, but perhaps not essential to the thrust of the narrative.

Most of the chapters are concluded with a discography, setting out the necessary information about where the music referred to in the text can be heard. These are a little more than simple lists, as a small amount of extra information is included in places. The dates given alongside the various CD titles refer to the date of issue of the currently available CD and are usually not the dates of the first issue of the music.

The discussion that follows is inevitably centred on the music of America and Britain, with contributions from other nations only being considered in so far as they affect this. I have also employed a certain amount of editorial control over what is to be considered a significant musical first. Significance is primarily measured in terms of the amount of influence each new development has had on subsequent events. This is the reason why sales success is so often mentioned. It can be guaranteed that any music that is widely heard is likely to exert an influence. There is no mention, other than here, of idiosyncratic works such as Malcolm Arnold's *A Grand, Grand Overture*. This piece, included during the first Music Festival organised in November 1956 in London by the humorist Gerard Hoffnung, was scored for an orchestra supplemented by three vacuum cleaners, one electric floor polisher, and three rifles – required to 'put an end' to the noise of the appliances at the end of the performance. This was undoubtedly a musical first, but one without influence, being conceived entirely as a comic device. Unless, of course, one imagines that the incorporation of industrial machinery into the music of avant garde rock performers Einstürzende Neubauten in 1981 and afterwards was directly inspired by Malcolm Arnold's work.

I would like to offer my grateful thanks to the people who read my manuscript and offered helpful suggestions for its improvement, even if I did not always act on what they said: Michael J. Richards, Dave Skinner, Cliff Steele, and Phil Walker, as well as members of the Northampton Writers Group. And my wife, Liz, too, for putting up with my wittering about this book during the five years it took to write it!

Nick Hamlyn, Northampton UK, 2018

Postscript   February 2020

It is in the nature of Print on Demand books, such as this one, that they can be updated easily because there is no need to organise an expensive complete new edition. Since the first publication towards the end of 2018, I have made several small tweaks to the information contained in the book (and will doubtless continue to do so, as a result of new music discoveries). This is the reason why the book now contains a reference to some music made in 2019!

PART I

INSTRUMENTS AND MUSICIANS

THE FIRST TIME

The slide guitar style employed by Sam McGee and thousands of other guitarists before and since derives originally from Hawaii. It is said to have been invented in about 1894 by a school student called Joseph KeKuKu. Hawaiian music, complete with its now characteristic swooping guitar sound, rapidly caught on in America following the Pan-American Pacific Exposition in San Francisco in 1915 and remained widely popular for nearly half a century. The slide guitar technique was soon adopted by both blues and country musicians, at least in part as a guaranteed means of getting satisfactory intonation out of cheap, poorly constructed instruments. Blues guitarist Sylvester Weaver made *Guitar Blues* in November 1923 as the first slide guitar recording. The influential blues performer Blind Lemon Jefferson first recorded with the slide guitar on a song called *Jack O'Diamond Blues*, in May 1926. In October of the same year, Frank Hutchison made the first country record to feature the instrument, *Worried Blues,* retaining, unlike Jefferson, the Hawaiian preference for holding the guitar flat.

Orville Gibson founded a company to manufacture guitars and mandolins in 1902, in Kalamazoo, Michigan He was one of a few innovators to apply the principles of violin construction to the guitar, producing an instrument with an f-shaped aperture on either side of the strings, instead of a large central sound-hole. They were known as 'archtop' guitars and the Gibson company soon became the market leader, although its founder died in 1918.

Frying pan guitar in first Rickenbacker catalogue. To put the prices in context, the official report of the US Department of Labor shows that the average factory worker wage in 1932 was a little under $18 per week.

Lloyd Loar's electric harp guitar, with the pick-up device projecting from the side.

Lloyd Loar, a sound engineer working for the Gibson instrument company between 1919 and 1924, experimented with electrical amplification then. He made a prototype electric double bass in the early twenties, and in 1923 he built an electrically amplified harp guitar. This was an instrument that added ten extra strings alongside the six that passed above the fretboard, with acoustic versions dating back to the beginning of the nineteenth century. Unable to persuade Gibson to put his invention into production, Loar left the company. In 1933, he set up his own firm, called Vivi-Tone, which produced an electric guitar with a more conventional design.

Guitar pioneer Les Paul electrified *his* first guitar in 1928, using a record-player pick-up, a telephone mouthpiece, and a radio as an amplifier. His failure to turn the idea into an immediately successful business venture had, no doubt, something to do with the fact that he was a boy of twelve at the time. Working at a hamburger stand in the school holidays – and still using his given name of Lester Polfus – his ambition then extended no further than wanting to entertain his customers and be heard. No matter, for his time would definitely come later.

1 ELECTRIC GUITAR

The cultural and musical phenomenon that is rock music – defined as widely as anyone would wish – gains its strength and its power from a single musical instrument: the electric guitar. There have been, to be sure, a number of performers over the years, from Jerry Lee Lewis to Van Der Graaf Generator to the Pet Shop Boys, who have not relied on the electric guitar at all. These, however, are the exceptions – worthy of comment precisely for that reason. The fact remains that, as an icon for the popular music of the last sixty years, the electric guitar is the one.

It comes as a considerable surprise, therefore, to realise that the invention of the electric guitar is not quite the clear-cut event that one would imagine it should be. So confused are the early years of the instrument, that reference books find it necessary to qualify their descriptions of them by frequently adding the words 'probably' or 'maybe'. Despite which, the most widespread definite assertion, that the first electric guitarist was the jazz player Eddie Durham, does not actually stand up to close inspection.

In *The Guitar – The History The Music The Players,* Dan Forte mentions the occasion when the country player Sam McGee played at Nashville's Grand Ole Opry on a guitar equipped with a primitive pick-up of his own devising – holding the instrument flat on his lap and sliding a steel bar up the strings, in a style that was well established in the music even then. The conservative country audience was not impressed by the new technology and McGee, despite being a regular performer at the venue, was told not to play his guitar again. Forte gives a date of 1926, which would have made McGee a major pioneer. On his website, however, the artist and musician Brad Sondahl quotes Sam McGee's granddaughter as agreeing that her grandfather was the first person to play electric guitar at the Grand Ole Opry, but places the occasion as some time in the early forties.

The Chicago Musical Instrument catalogue for 1929 carried a full page advertisement for electrically amplified guitars made by the Stromberg company. Sadly, their chances of commercial success were destroyed by the Stock Market crash later the same year. It was left to the curiously named Ro-Pat-In company to try again with a commercially produced electric guitar in 1931. Known as the frying pan, due both to its appropriate shape and to the fact that it was made from cast aluminium, the A22 (together with its longer-necked sister, the A25) was made by a subsidiary of his established tool manufacturing concern by Adolph Rickenbacker. His engineers George Beauchamp and Paul Barth, had designed a prototype version of the guitar (made of wood) the previous year. The frying pan had a very high string action, making it difficult to finger the strings on the frets, but it was intended to be played as a lap steel guitar with a slide. (The technique, using an acoustic guitar, is demonstrated by Frank Hutchison on the LP cover shown opposite.) The action of a guitar refers to the distance between the frets and the strings passing above them – on an easily playable guitar this is very small.

The frying pan was followed later the same year by a second Ro-Pat-In production. This was an electrified hollow-body guitar known as the Electro Spanish, intended to be held upright and played in the fingered 'Spanish' style. Only a very small number of either guitar was sold, but a musician by the name of Gage Brewer presented the first public performance of the frying pan guitar on Halloween night 1932, at the Shadowland Pavilion in Wichita. Shortly afterwards, Jack Miller played one at Grauman's Chinese Theater in Los Angeles and subsequently went on tour with it, as a member of Orville Knapp's Orchestra. Hawaiian guitarist Sol Hoopii also played the instrument in live performance late in 1932, while Alvino Rey played one on his regular radio show in San Francisco. In February 1933, four tracks were recorded by Noelani's Hawaiian Orchestra, with an electric guitar given a prominent role. The tracks were issued on a pair of 78 rpm records, with *Dreams Of Aloha/Hawaiian Ripple* appearing first, miscredited to "Noi Lane's Hawaiian Orchestra". To judge by the song-writing credits, the guitarist was Joseph Lopes, possibly the husband or brother of singer Noelani Lopes. Orville Knapp's Orchestra first recorded in August 1934, with the sound

THE FIRST TIME

Milton Brown and his Musical Brownies – Bob Dunn plays slide electric guitar

Resonator guitars – as belatedly made famous by the picture of one model on the cover of the multi-million selling *Brothers In Arms* album by Dire Straits (see page 104) – represent a pre-electric attempt to make a louder guitar. Aluminium cones inside a wooden or metal body are designed to resonate in sympathy with the strings, giving a sound that is certainly loud, but rather harsh in comparison with a conventional acoustic guitar. Most players prefer to use a slide, although it is perfectly possible to play the guitar by fingering the frets. The resonator guitar was invented by John, Rudy, and Emil Dopyera in 1926 and subsequently sold through two companies – National and Dobro (an abbreviation of 'Dopyera brothers'). They are still being made today to the original designs. Tampa Red was the first to play the resonator guitar on record in 1928.

The photograph above, taken from the 1935 Rickenbacker catalogue, shows session guitarist Perry Botkin with a Model B Vibrola electric guitar, made of bakelite. Motorised pulleys inside the guitar body created a vibrato effect, but they made the instrument heavy enough to need supporting on a stand. It seems quite likely that Botkin would have used it on some of his sessions in the late thirties – in which case recordings by stars like Bing Crosby, Fred Astaire, Eddie Cantor, and Frank Sinatra contain some very early electric guitar playing, lurking within their arrangements.

The first performer to make a record featuring solo guitar, fitted with steel strings and played with a plectrum, was Nick Lucas (later famous as 'the crooning troubadour'). His acoustic guitar instrumentals, *Pickin' The Guitar* and *Teasin' The Frets*, were issued in 1922 on the Brunswick label. The following year, Gibson built the 'Nick Lucas Special' guitar for him, which became one of the company's most popular models.

Eddie Durham is shown at the top right on this cover of an mp3 compilation issued by Stardust Records in 2009. Anticlockwise from him, the other guitarists are Charlie Christian, Irving Ashby, Lonnie Johnson, and Django Reinhardt.

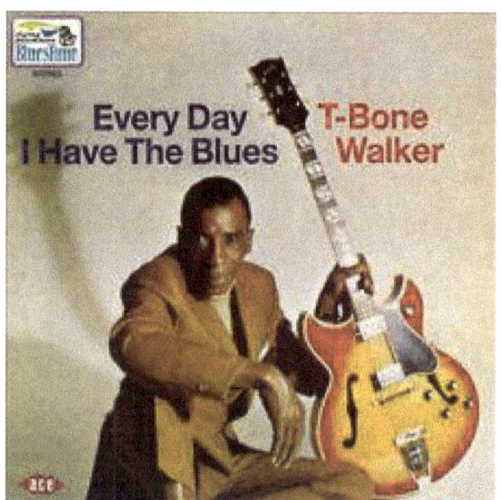

of Jack Miller's guitar clearly audible.

In late 1934, Bob Dunn joined Milton Brown and his Musical Brownies, a leading country group working out of Houston, Texas, and he recorded with them in January 1935. Dunn did not play a product of the Rickenbacker company (which had absorbed its guitar-making subsidiary by then) but rather an adapted acoustic guitar fitted with a pick-up. (Suggestions that Dunn needed to continually magnetise his strings in order for the pick-up to work are probably the result of a misunderstanding with regard to the metal bar he used as a slide.) According to fiddler Jimmy Thomason, as quoted in Cary Ginell's study, *Milton Brown and the Founding of Western Swing*, Dunn had taken the idea of amplifying his guitar from an unknown black guitarist he had met in New York. The energy and considerable virtuosity of his steel guitar playing makes it clear that Dunn was not only an electric guitar pioneer, but also the first to realise that his amplified instrument was an entirely new development and not just an acoustic guitar made to sound louder. As Nick Tosches puts it in *Country: The Twisted Roots Of Rock 'n' Roll*, his definitive history of the genre's roots, with perhaps a touch of entirely pardonable poetic licence:

> Great yelling dissonances burst from his bastard tool like glass against a stone wall. Three years before Django Reinhardt made his first records, Dunn had a style as subtle and involved as Reinhardt would be, but Dunn had a daring, febrile energy that neither Reinhardt nor the effete jazzbos who came in his wake could comprehend.

Django Reinhardt, of course, did not play the electric version of his instrument until right at the end of his career, so the comparison is not the best that Tosches could have made. But one gets his point.

A contemporary photograph of the Musical Brownies shows the musicians dressed in smart business suits, like stockbrokers deciding to enjoy an unusual lunchtime break from their normal routine. And there is Bob Dunn at the front, the wire joining the guitar that straddles his thighs to the tiny loudspeaker in front of him just visible. It is hard to imagine how this set-up could possibly manage to deliver the stinging tone heard on tracks like *Who's Sorry Now* and *Taking Off*, but the evidence is there that it did.

Despite the innovation and power of Dunn's playing, however, he was sadly not destined to maintain a high profile career. The Musical Brownies suffered a fatal set-back when Milton Brown died of injuries sustained in a car accident in April 1936. Dunn made a number of recordings with a new group of his own, the Vagabonds, and also with the Texas Wanderers, led by another former member of the Musical Brownies, Cliff Bruner. By 1940, however, he had stopped trying. He enlisted in the army and after the end of World War II, he retired to Houston, where he studied for a music degree and opened a successful music shop. When he died of cancer in May 1971, at the age of 63, there were no obituaries to mourn the passing of a remarkable and important musician.

Bob Dunn's contemporaries had been quick to follow his example. Another Houston guitarist, Ted Daffan, started to play electric steel with the Bar-X Cowboys, although he did not record with it until December 1939. Dunn allowed the young Leon McAuliffe to try out his guitar, and when McAuliffe joined the Texas Playboys in the spring of 1935, the group's leader, Bob Wills, bought him an electric steel guitar of his own. He recorded a number of tracks with it in September 1935, then a year later, made the influential *Steel Guitar Rag*, with much less skill than Bob Dunn, but with rather more of the steel guitar sound that has come to be associated with country music. Jim Boyd recorded *Hot Dog Stomp*, just after McAuliffe's first sessions, in his brother's band, Bill Boyd's Cowboy Ramblers. Al Dexter – later to make *Pistol Packin' Mama*, the first country record to climb to the top of the US pop charts (in 1943) – employed Bobby Simon to play electric guitar on his 1936 recordings. Simon had an instrument built to be played in the lap steel manner, but he chose to hold it upright and played it Spanish style on Dexter's *Honky Tonk Blues*.

Although blues guitarist T-Bone Walker was also from Texas, he moved to the West Coast in 1934 and may well have been unaware of the developments back in his home state. He began experimenting with an electric guitar in 1935 anyway, but neither he nor his fellow musicians had sufficient confidence in the results until 1942, when he

THE FIRST TIME

The slide guitar, played by moving something hard and smooth along the strings, rather than fretting them with the fingers, can also be referred to as a steel guitar or as a bottleneck guitar, depending on what is being used. The steel can be a specially made piece of metal or simply a short length of tubing, which might in reality be either steel or brass. The bottleneck is literally the long glass neck cut off a wine bottle. For the sake of eccentricity, the guitarists on Captain Beefheart's *Trout Mask Replica* album are credited as playing "glass finger guitar" and "steel-appendage guitar". For part of his solo on *All Along The Watchtower*, on the other hand, Jimi Hendrix simply grabbed whatever was near, which turned out to be a cigarette lighter. For his first LP, Bob Dylan borrowed his girlfriend's lipstick tube to do the same job. Sometimes too, a knife has been used.

The qualifications for becoming a successful band-leader in the thirties and forties did not include prowess on a particular instrument. Count Basie and Duke Ellington both directed their bands from behind the piano, which made some kind of sense. But Glenn Miller played the trombone, Benny Goodman the clarinet, and Alvino Rey, somewhat improbably, a steel guitar. Rey worked closely with Gibson in the production of their early instruments and when the company produced the first pedal steel guitar in 1939 – the Gibson Electraharp EH630 – it was Rey who pioneered the new development with his band. Country steel guitarists had begun to play lap guitars with as many as four necks so as to be able to play in different keys without retuning, but the new pedal design presented a far more streamlined solution to the problem. Alvino Rey was not a country performer, but it was country music that immediately took the pedal steel as its own, making its keening sound into the one that virtually defines the genre.

Replica of Les Paul's 'The Log' used in Epiphone advertising.

Slingerland Songster, manufactured by a company best known for its drum kits.

Merle Travis with the guitar built for him by Paul Bigsby

8

recorded the instrument in a band with pianist Freddie Slack. Nevertheless, as the first electric guitarist working in the blues field, he made an enormous impact. His showman tactics on stage, such as playing the guitar while held behind his head, did no harm to his reputation either. While Walker prevaricated, someone else became the first blues electric guitarist to record. This was a precocious white sixteen-year-old by the name of George Barnes, who backed Big Bill Broonzy on two tracks in March 1938.

Jazz guitarist Eddie Durham also began playing an electric guitar in 1935. He was yet another Texan, although in 1935 he was a member of the Jimmie Lunceford Orchestra and would have spent most of the time touring round the country. His recordings made on September 30th that year with Lunceford have often been cited as the first recorded appearance of the electric guitar (by people unaware of the earlier Lopes, Miller, Dunn, and McAuliffe recordings), but the aural evidence in any case is that the instrument on *Hittin' The Bottle* and its fellows is an acoustic guitar, amplified with a microphone. During an interview on YouTube with Durham's daughter, Topsy, she makes a clear distinction between her father's use of an 'amplified guitar' (i.e. a guitar playing very close to a microphone, which was a Durham innovation) and an electric guitar, fitted with a magnetic pick-up. Durham's solo on the August 1937 recording by the Count Basie Orchestra, *Time Out*, also sounds like an amplified guitar, not an electric.

As confirmed by his daughter, Eddie Durham first recorded his electric guitar in March 1938, with other Count Basie sidemen in the Kansas City Five, so he does at least retain the distinction of being the first *jazz* electric guitarist on record. *Good Mornin' Blues*, complete with group playing throughout and a solo, showed the way forward for other guitarists and several of them made recordings featuring the electric instrument during 1939 and 1940. There was Floyd Smith in Andy Kirk's Clouds Of Joy, Hurley Ramey with Earl Hines, and Al Norris with Jimmie Lunceford. Meanwhile, Muryel 'Zeke' Campbell of the Light Crust Doughboys and Eldon Shamblin, playing alongside Leon McAuliffe in Bob Wills' Texas Playboys, continued to wave the flag for Texas. Andy Kirk's *Take It And Git*, with a Floyd Smith solo, took the electric guitar into the charts for the first time – the record was the first number one in the *Billboard* 'Harlem Hit Parade' that started in 1942.

Most significantly of all, 1939 saw the first recordings by Charlie Christian, playing with both Lionel Hampton and Benny Goodman. At the age of twenty-three, Christian was comparatively uninterested in the guitar's established role as a harmonically based part of the rhythm section. For him, ever since being introduced to the electric guitar by a meeting with Eddie Durham in 1937, the instrument was a device for playing improvised solos, able to stand up against the naturally loud saxophones and trumpets as a result of its amplification. Fortunately, he was a fluent and inventive soloist as well as having a knack for making the right friends. He jammed in New York as their equal with many of the people who were to carry out the bebop revolution in jazz after the War. Sadly, Christian was not able to take part in the revolution himself as he died of tuberculosis in March 1942.

After Charlie Christian, the electric guitar was accepted as one of the major instruments of jazz, with a long line of significant (albeit effete!) names forming behind him. The measure of his influence can be gauged, perhaps, by the fact that Gibson, who had marketed since 1936 the ES150 electric guitar played by Christian, began to refer to the instrument as the Charlie Christian model.

In 1937, Les Paul started experimenting with designs for a solid electric instrument that would avoid the feedback problems associated with amplified hollow guitars. The Rickenbacker frying pan and Model B were solid guitars, and so was the Slingerland Songster, first produced in 1936 and aimed at the Hawaiian music market, but Paul had in mind something that would better suit jazz and blues players. His prototype, comprising a guitar neck fixed on to a four inch wide block of wood with pick-ups attached to it, and with body wings taken from a production Epiphone instrument, was christened 'The Log'. In 1941, he tried to persuade Gibson to produce a commercial version of his design idea, but the guitar company was unimpressed by "the kid with the broomstick" (Les Paul was 25). As a result, the kudos of being the first company to market the modern electric instrument went elsewhere. Country guitarist Merle Travis commissioned mechanical engineer Paul Bigsby to build a solid guitar to his design in

THE FIRST TIME

Fender Broadcaster

Gibson Les Paul

Fender Stratocaster

Gretsch guitar fitted with Bigsby vibrato

Bill Carson with Stratocaster

Leo Fender started working as an electrical repairman in 1938 in Fullerton, California. He became particularly interested in amplifiers and the instruments that drove them. In 1946 he decided to specialise in the manufacture of lap steel guitars and amplifiers, naming his company the Fender Electric Instrument Company.

The Stratocaster bearing the serial number 0001 has a white finish and a metal scratchplate and is owned by David Gilmour of Pink Floyd. Due to Fender's haphazard approach to numbering, however, this was not actually the first Stratocaster to leave the factory.

1947 and although no more than a dozen of these were made altogether, its striking appearance – reminiscent of a Gibson Les Paul with a Fender Stratocaster neck – marks it as a landmark development.

The following year, engineer George Fullerton joined the guitar company run by Leo Fender and within two years the two men had created what was to become the first mass production solid electric guitar. The Fender Broadcaster, first marketed in 1950, was swiftly renamed the Fender Telecaster, after complaints from Gretsch, who had a drum kit called a Broadkaster. The Telecaster name was chosen with a deliberate nod in the direction of another technological innovation rapidly becoming popular at the time – the television. Adopted immediately by country and blues musicians alike (though not the jazz players, who continued to prefer their hollow electrics), the Telecaster is still made today, its design hardly changed at all.

Gibson responded to the success of the Fender guitar by renewing contact with Les Paul, who had become a highly successful recording artist in the interim, and asking him to design a solid instrument for them. The first Gibson Les Paul guitar was launched in 1952 – as a craftsman built instrument that looked nothing at all like the Log and was something of a contrast too with the more basic Telecaster. During the next few years, changes were made to the pick-ups and bridge design, but in essence this second member of the great rock guitar triumvirate was then in place, with rock music barely started. The third member – and the guitar that is undoubtedly the most widely played and the most extensively copied of all – was a second product of the Fender company. The Stratocaster was first marketed in 1954 and was full of design subtleties introduced in response to suggestions directed at its predecessor, although in the event, the Telecaster continued to be sold alongside its updated sibling.

Just as in the case of the electric steel guitar and Bob Dunn, each of these three important guitars became an indispensable part of popular music as soon as they were adopted by significant musicians who drew attention to the particular guitar they had chosen to play. This happened during the sixties. The Telecaster, having acquired a reputation as the music's workhorse, capable of doing justice to any style, became particularly associated with the contrasting approaches of country-rockabilly ace James Burton and soul session supremo Steve Cropper. The Les Paul was taken up by Eric Clapton, Peter Green, and Mike Bloomfield, who discovered that the model was ideal for conveying the impact and emotionalism of their high-amplified versions of the blues. The Stratocaster was showcased by both Buddy Holly and the Shadows' Hank Marvin (the first UK musician to own one), but it gained a major boost when chosen by Jimi Hendrix as his main guitar and made to perform tricks undreamed of by Leo Fender.

The first guitar effect unit was invented before there was a suitable guitar for it to be used with. Doc Kauffman – subsequently a designer for Rickenbacker and also a business partner for a few months in 1945 with Leo Fender – patented a mechanical vibrato device in 1929, which he originally called a vibrola. A simple lever system attached to the bar that anchored the strings to the guitar body included a small metal arm that, when moved, made the strings go slightly sharp or flat. The vibrato effect (a wavering of the pitch of the played notes) that was thereby made possible would have been just about noticeable on an acoustic guitar, but could really come into its own when amplified by electricity. Many of the early Rickenbacker guitars were fitted with the device and so was Les Paul's Log, using a similar design of his own.

During 1946 to 1947, Paul Bigsby radically redesigned the vibrato arm, in an attempt to defeat its basic tendency to put the guitar permanently out of tune whenever it was used. The Bigsby vibrato – now transformed into a substantial piece of metalwork – was available as a factory-fitted optional extra on Gibson Les Paul and Gretsch guitars from the early fifties. Though still not entirely free of tuning problems, this device sufficiently impressed Leo Fender for him to make the decision to include a vibrato as an intrinsic part of his new Stratocaster guitar. He completed yet another radical redesign after his first attempt, modelled closely on the Bigsby unit, was rejected by guitarist Bill Carson, in his capacity as design consultant, due to its unfortunate side-effect of destroying much of the guitar's tonal sustain. The final result, however, involving a set of hefty springs fitted in the back of the guitar, to take the strain of the string tension, was so successful that the design has not been significantly altered since. Fender

THE FIRST TIME

A more elaborate version of the tremolo arm was the B-bender, invented in the late sixties by Clarence White, guitarist with the Byrds, and his colleague in the band, Gene Parsons. A system of levers fitted inside a Telecaster (as pictured on the left) enabled the pitch of the B string to be raised by pulling on the guitar's top strap button. A skilled player, like White himself, was then able to incorporate a pedal steel string-bending effect into his normal lead guitar work.

As befitted a man with a unique sound, Bo Diddley commissioned the Gretsch company to make him some unique guitars. One of these was covered in fake fur, but the one that drew the most attention was the rectangular guitar shown. Over the years, Bo Diddley used several different rectangular guitars, but the design was not adopted by anyone else – unlike his patent rhythm, which has turned up in the work of numerous different artists.

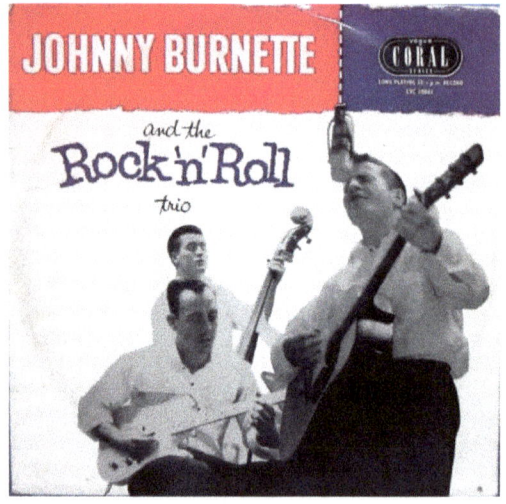

Jeff Beck playing his Telecaster with the Yardbirds

A year after the Rolling Stones recorded *Satisfaction*, Keith Richards got to hear a version of the song that was perhaps closer to his own original idea. It was included on Otis Redding's highly regarded *Otis Blue* album and subsequently became an essential ingredient in the singer's live performances. In both arenas – the studio and the stage – Redding's interpretation was enhanced by the trademark Stax brass sound: the one that had inspired Richards in the first place.

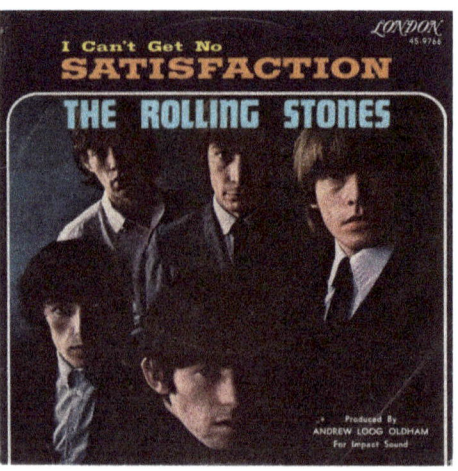

When *Keep On Running* by the Spencer Davis Group was released towards the end of 1965, complete with slashing fuzz guitar chords on the instrumental section that frames the song, the sound was still new enough for the pop music reviewer in the *Gramophone* magazine to assume that it was played by a saxophone with a split reed.

re-christened the device a 'tremolo' arm – technically a mistake, since the term tremolo actually refers to a variation in the loudness of a note rather than its pitch – but the name has stuck nevertheless. A modern attempt to use the name 'whammy bar' for locked string variations of the design, allowing for extravagant dive-bombing effects, has gained some foothold amongst heavy rock fans and players.

Through the forties and fifties, and following the example set by Bob Dunn, many Western swing, blues, and ultimately, rock 'n' roll players tried very hard to persuade their amplifiers to deliver a gritty, distorted sound that for them represented a peak of excitement and emotion. Some tried extreme measures – like Pat Hare, who turned all his amplifier controls to maximum when recording the blues with James Cotton; like Bo Diddley, who played through a full-on tremolo circuit designed to make the volume of his sound oscillate rapidly; like Paul Burlison, who made a virtue of a faulty amplifier valve when recording *Train Kept A Rolling* and other rockabilly titles with the Johnny Burnette Trio; or like Link Wray, who deliberately ripped his speaker cones in order to make them buzz.

In all cases, however, the guitarists' ambitions were very much hampered by the low power of the amplifiers available and by the fact that their manufacturers – with Leo Fender as the market leader – were incorporating design features specifically intended to *prevent* distortion. Fender employed working guitarists as consultants, but country players Eldon Shamblin and Bill Carson happened to prefer a clean tone. They were apparently unaware of, or uninterested in, blues guitarists like Buddy Guy and Magic Sam, who were making thrilling use of the Fender Bassman amplifier (introduced in 1955). The Bassman was more powerful and hence easier to make distort than its companion products, because it was really intended to amplify the less cutting frequencies of a bass guitar. Indeed, Leo Fender, who presumably shared the prevailing critical opinion of the late fifties that rock 'n' roll was never going to become more than a strictly temporary phenomenon, proceeded to move even further away from the preferences of the musicians who were potentially his best customers. As the newly invented transistor became available, he used this component to replace the valves in his amplifiers. More reliable it may have been, but the transistor did not lend itself to being overdriven to make a usable distorted sound.

The rival Gibson company showed more foresight at this point. Gibson was not a major manufacturer of amplifiers, but in 1962 it introduced its EB-OF bass guitar, which allowed a distorted fuzz tone to be switched on if required. It also incorporated the bass guitar's circuitry into a pedal, the Gibson Maestro Fuzztone. In the UK, Big Jim Sullivan used one of these to play a distorted solo on P.J.Proby's 1964 single, *Hold Me*. Meanwhile, in the US, session guitarist Red Rhodes came up with his own home-made fuzz device. The Ventures made use of this in their late 1962 recording, *The 2000 Pound Bee*, and the following year it was featured during a short guitar solo on Helen Shapiro's single, *Woe Is Me*, recorded in Nashville. This was played by Grady Martin, whose use of a faulty amplifier had enabled him to create notable low-toned fuzz solos on two records in 1961, *Don't Worry* by Marty Robbins and his own *The Fuzz*. None of these recordings, however, attracted the immediate attention of other guitarists and sales of Gibson's pedal were minimal. In 1965, however, Keith Richards of the Rolling Stones, who was recording with the group at the Chess studios in Chicago during May, decided to purchase one. The key riff that drives the song *Satisfaction* was originally intended to be played by a brass section. Keith Richards, however, decided to try out his new Fuzztone on it and although, reportedly, he did not really like the result, even after recording his part three times over, the sound of fuzz guitar was in place when the song was released on a US single in May.

In Britain, where *Satisfaction* remained largely unheard (its release being postponed until August), the proprietors of Macari's Musical Exchange in London were independently working on a similar fuzz unit at the instigation of guitarists Jeff Beck and Jimmy Page, who were two of the shop's customers. Their product, the Tone Bender, was first used by Jeff Beck at the recording session responsible for the Yardbirds' song, *Heart Full Of Soul*. As with *Satisfaction*, the fuzz guitar part was originally meant to be played by another instrument. In the Yardbirds' case, having featured a harpsichord on the hit single, *For Your Love*, they had decided to go one better and include a part for sitar on the follow-up, making them the first Western rock group to employ Indian instrumentation. In the event, the sitar riff sounded too weak for the crucial role in the song it was expected to take, especially when Jeff Beck was able to

THE FIRST TIME

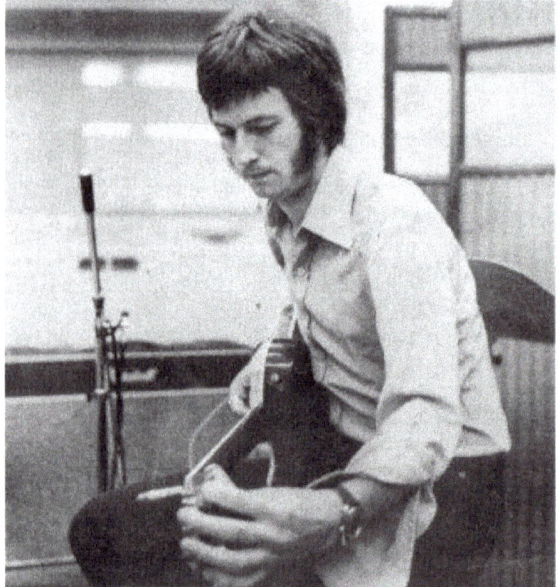

It was remarkable how three of the most influential guitarists of the sixties – Clapton, Beck, and Page – were to be found playing successively within the same group, the Yardbirds. Some of the most vital recordings of the time are, in consequence, scattered through the Yardbirds' work. Sadly, these share vinyl space with material that is frankly disappointing, since the members of the group were generally given too little studio time to develop their ideas properly.

Despite Eric Clapton's importance to the development of the electric guitar and notwithstanding his enormously impressive track record as a gifted and sensitive soloist within both his own and other people's music, he is a musician who very much prefers to work within the traditional rules of music as he sees them. He has stated in interview that he finds the acclaim generally accorded to his solo on Cream's *Crossroads* to be irritating, because as far as he is concerned, his playing is wrong, being a beat adrift from the song's rhythmic pulse. In fact, this displacement is a technique entirely familiar to jazz soloists as a device for heightening interest. On *Crossroads* it is precisely the factor that helps to make Clapton's playing sound so exhilarating.

Eric Clapton in the studio during the recording of the Bluesbreakers album. The amplifier next to him is the Marshall model 1962 combo, thereafter known as the Bluesbreaker.

The management at Vox believed the wah-wah to be a natural accompaniment for a trumpet, due to the similar effect already able to be produced on that instrument by the use of a mute. It was something of a signature sound for Clyde McCoy, which was the reason for the name and image of McCoy appearing on the first commercial wah-wah pedals, although, as Del Casher insists (in an interview recorded for the NAMM oral history website), the trumpeter had played no part in its invention or development. In 1970, however, jazz trumpeter Miles Davis did begin using a wah-wah pedal attached to his instrument via an electronic pick-up. The results can be heard on *Live/Evil* and all the albums recorded afterwards through the seventies by Davis. He was already a master of the muted horn; his wah-wah trumpet is something else again – a new, hard-edged sound that enabled Davis to play comfortably within the ferocious electric bands that he employed at that time. The guitarist Pete Cosey, who became a slightly belated replacement for John McLaughlin, emerged as a highly effective companion soloist for Miles Davis. He used wah-wah and fuzz continuously on an already overdriven guitar to produce a tremendously exciting sound. Cosey was also the lead guitarist on the controversial attempts to move the music of two venerable bluesmen into the psychedelic rock age of the late sixties – *Electric Mud* and *After The Rain* by Muddy Waters and *The*

The wah-wah sounds heard on Jimi Hendrix's *IDon't Live Today*, recorded in February 1967 for inclusion on the *Are You Experienced* LP, were achieved by the guitarist manipulating his tone controls. It is likely that he had heard the Vox promotional single, but would not have been able to buy the pedal in February. The film footage of Jimi Hendrix playing at the Monterey Festival in June makes it clear that the guitarist was not using a wah-wah or any other kind of effects unit during his performance then.

demonstrate a greatly superior alternative using his new Tone Bender. The result, with fuzz guitar lines presented by a group fast becoming only a little less influential than the Beatles, was released in June 1965.

The high profile of both the Rolling Stones and the Yardbirds meant that fuzz guitar sounds, whether played via Tone Bender or Maestro Fuzztone, became commonplace during the next year. A more radical and long-lasting approach to guitar tone, however, involving overall amplifier design, was even then taking shape. Another London music shop proprietor, Jim Marshall, developed an updated British version of the Fender Bassman amplifier, using valves to deliver a then unsurpassed 45 watts of power. Guitarist Eric Clapton, who had left the Yardbirds to join John Mayall's Bluesbreakers in order to explore his growing enthusiasm for the blues, discovered that the high output pickups of a late fifties Gibson Les Paul guitar were able to overdrive one of the new Marshall amplifiers set at maximum volume, to create a thick, wailing tone of unprecedented sustain and dramatic effect. The result was first heard on the John Mayall single, *I'm Your Witchdoctor*, recorded in June 1965 and released in October, and was subsequently refined on the album, *John Mayall's Bluesbreakers With Eric Clapton*, recorded in April 1966. The modern electric guitar starts here.

The sweeping tonal variation associated with the appropriately named wah-wah pedal derives from an innovation carried out by country guitarist Chet Atkins. He altered the circuitry in a pedal designed to increase and decrease volume, so that tone was affected instead. He showcased the result on a 1959 single called *Boo Boo Stick Beat* and on several other tracks included on the album that followed at the start of 1960, *Teensville*. The wah-wah sound is there, albeit lacking the power to startle due to Atkins' use of a guitar tone without sustain or distortion. In the UK, Big Jim Sullivan achieved a similar result on the Dave Berry single from 1964, *The Crying Game*.

Ampeg experimented with a commercial version of the idea in 1961, but a finished product did not emerge until the beginning of 1967, when the manufacturer's name stamped on it was Vox. Studio guitarist Del Casher, working with the engineering team at Thomas Organ, the company using the Vox trademark, developed the wah-wah pedal during 1966. Casher used a prototype on the Vic Mizzy soundtrack for the film *Did You Hear The One About The Traveling Saleslady* in 1966, although the film was not released until July 1968 and music from it did not appear on album until 2001.

In May 1967, Eric Clapton, recording in New York the songs that would make up Cream's *Disraeli Gears* LP, bought a new Vox wah-wah pedal from the city's leading instrument store, Manny's, and immediately used it on the song *Tales Of Brave Ulysses*. This was issued in the UK at the beginning of June, as the B-side of the single *Strange Brew*. Returning to the USA for the Monterey Festival in June, Jimi Hendrix would already have heard *Tales Of Brave Ulysses* when he purchased a wah-wah pedal of his own from Manny's and proceeded to employ it for the recording of the songs *The Burning Of The Midnight Lamp* and *The Stars That Play With Laughing Sam's Dice*. The resulting single, coupling the two songs, was issued in the UK in mid-August.

As far as most listeners were concerned – certainly in the UK – these records represented the debut of the new effect. Vox, however, had signed the Electric Prunes to a sponsorship deal at the start of the year and one result of this was the group, fronted by guitarist Ken Williams, recording an advertisement for the wah-wah pedal for radio broadcast. This was issued on a cardboard promotional single in February, which is therefore the first recording to feature the effect. In the words of Prunes drummer Preston Ritter, in an October 1997 interview with the organisers of an Electric Prunes fan website, "We were the first band in the world to use and record with the wah-wah pedal invented by Vox. We used the prototype on our second album, before it was mass produced and put on the market." The album in question, however, *Underground*, was recorded during the spring and early summer of 1967 and not released until August. The Vox advertisement claimed that the wah-wah pedal had already been acquired by Herman's Hermits, Paul Revere and the Raiders, the Seeds, and the Rolling Stones. But even if this was true, none of the groups seemed to be in any particular hurry to use the effect on record.

THE FIRST TIME

Each of the studio albums recorded by Jimi Hendrix during his lifetime contains examples of a sound collage approach to music. The resulting electronic pieces – the centre section of *Third Stone From The Sun* on the first album, *EXP* on the second, *And The Gods Made Love* and parts of the extended work *1983 A Merman I Should Turn To Be/Moon Turn The Tides... Gently Gently Away* on the third – would naturally be created by synthesizers today, but are here made up of sounds and textures generated almost entirely by the guitar. It is worth noting that the roadies responsible for setting up Hendrix's equipment on stage were reportedly unable to get anything other than electronic howl out of it if they tried to test the guitar set-up using his accustomed volume levels. Demonstrations of the remarkable control that Hendrix himself was able to exert on the set-up included his fondness for playing an intelligible "thank you" on his guitar in response to the audience applause. The lesson of *Electric Ladyland* for guitarists was absorbed by Brian May, who recorded textured layers of guitars on the albums made by Queen. He found it necessary to emphasise what he was doing by including the legend "no synthesizers" on the first five album covers.

Since Jimi Hendrix's untimely death, numerous candidates have been promoted as his musical heir. In the immediate aftermath, Robin Trower and Tony McPhee tried very hard to sound just like him, while Frank Marino insisted that he *was* Jimi Hendrix reincarnated, blithely ignoring the problems of timing and the fact that his actual playing rather gave the lie to his claim. In recent times the names of fleet-fingered players like Steve Vai and Joe Satriani have been mentioned by critics who seem to ignore the most obvious name: that of Vernon Reid, an extraordinary player who has managed to sound equally compelling whether playing angular avant-fusion jazz with Ronald Shannon Jackson, innovative hard funk-rock with Living Colour, or the various genre collisions of his solo albums. Even so, he lacks both Hendrix's compositional flair and his popular appeal. In truth, we are still waiting.

John McLaughlin on the back cover of Extrapolation

Larry Coryell generating feedback, in the studio with the Jazz Composer's Orchestra

Feedback occurs when an electric guitarist holds his guitar close to the amplifier. The sound coming out of the speaker is then received by the guitar pick-up and sent back to the amplifier, to be received again by the pick-up – and so on. The sound generated by this loop process very rapidly overloads the amplifier, resulting in a characteristic squeal. For a long time, feedback was considered to be a nuisance – particularly by jazz guitarists, whose hollow body instruments were particularly prone to it – one reason why those players kept their volume settings low. John Lennon was very proud of his idea for using feedback constructively on *I Feel Fine*, although it is likely he borrowed it from the Who, who had started to incorporate deliberate feedback into their live music in late 1964. The Who's studio debut of the effect, however, had to wait until May 1965 and the recording of the group's second single, *Anyway Anyhow Anywhere*. (There is even more feedback on the version of the song recorded for radio broadcast shortly afterwards – it can be heard on the Who's *BBC Sessions* CD.) Feedback is used on the *Fresh Cream* album (particularly on the track *Sweet Wine*), recorded during the summer of 1966, and here Eric Clapton manages to generate whistles that are in tune with the music, rather than using the random effect favoured by the Who's Pete Townshend. In November, Peter Green created an instrumental piece, *The Supernatural,* that uses tuned feedback as the primary ingredient in the melody – a remarkable demonstration of skill, given that the effect is achieved with guitar and amplifier alone. The invention of a sustain pedal easily able to reproduce the sound was still some years away.

Although Sonny Sharrock received considerable attention as the first avant-garde guitarist, the first player to employ his instrument purely as a sound generator was actually Keith Rowe, a founder member in 1965 of the free improvisation group AMM. Their first recording was the album *AMMusic*, which was edited from two sessions held in June 1966. As all of the five musicians are concerned with generating interesting sounds rather than specific notes – there is no melody as such to be heard anywhere on the album – it is sometimes quite hard to decide which of the noises are being made by a guitar!

INSTRUMENTS AND MUSICIANS

Jimi Hendrix made the wah-wah pedal an essential ingredient within his total sound. He also pioneered other effects. Most notable was the Octavia, designed by Roger Mayer and first used on *Purple Haze* (issued in March 1967), which generated extra notes an octave above those actually played. From early 1969, Hendrix used the Univibe, which produced a shimmering, warbly tone in simulation of the effect of a rotating Leslie organ speaker. Alongside an updated Mayer-designed fuzzbox (the Fuzz Face), these effects sent their extraordinary combined signals to linked 100-watt amplifiers – three at a time on stage – each sitting on top of a stack of two cabinets holding four speakers apiece. These had become available by the end of 1966, courtesy of Marshall's very rapid developmental work.

Only now did the jazz world, whose guitarists had been quite content to ignore the electronic sound possibilities of their instrument, begin to take notice. Larry Coryell, guitarist with the Gary Burton Quartet, introduced some quite gentle feedback-driven sustain on the track *General Mojo Cuts Up*, included on Burton's 1968 LP *Lofty Fake Anagram*. He received for his pains a critical response suggesting that he was not a very competent musician. Unabashed, Coryell repeated his modest experiment on Herbie Mann's *Memphis Underground* LP, which became one of the best selling jazz albums of the sixties. This time he was partnered by a second jazz guitar explorer. Sonny Sharrock did not use any kind of valve sustain, but he attacked his strings with such ferocity as to make it sound as though he did.

More cutting edge than either of these recordings, however, was Larry Coryell's contribution to the first Jazz Composer's Orchestra recording, which he made on May 8th 1968. The booklet that comes with the double album includes photographs of Coryell holding his guitar close to the amplifier in order to generate squealing feedback. The results can be heard on the lengthy solo that he plays during his spotlight feature, *Communications #9*.

Although Larry Coryell was able to use his innovations as the launching pad for a very successful career as a jazz guitarist, it was John McLaughlin who won the battle for using in jazz the same kind of tonal resources that Eric Clapton and Jimi Hendrix had discovered for rock guitar. In fact, McLaughlin maintains that he started to use feedback as long ago as 1962. While playing as a member of the Graham Bond Organisation, he commissioned a custom-made amplifier more powerful than anything else available at the time and he soon discovered that "feedback was nice". There is little recorded evidence available, but one track on the Graham Bond album *Solid Bond* is enough. *The Grass Is Greener* (not the Colosseum piece) is one of three tracks recorded at Klook's Kleek in June 1963. The Organisation at this time had yet to investigate R&B, and although the line-up contains some names familiar to rock listeners – Jack Bruce plays bass and Ginger Baker is the drummer – the music played by the group is straight ahead modern jazz, with Graham Bond himself playing only alto saxophone. But near the beginning of John McLaughlin's solo, he hits a note that sustains with the unmistakeable whine of feedback. Combined with McLaughlin's lightly amplified jazz tone, the effect is not at all startling. But it is there – predating not only Larry Coryell, but also the first constructive use of feedback in rock music, the introduction to the Beatles' *I Feel Fine*, recorded in October 1964.

During the several recording sessions that he completed in 1969 and the beginning of 1970, John McLaughlin brought jazz guitar completely up to date. On his album *Extrapolation*, recorded in January 1969, McLaughlin's tone has only a very slight buzz to distinguish it from the sound of his predecessors. His technical virtuosity, on the other hand, is obvious – he is already only a short distance away from being the fleetest fingered player of all. Moving to America, he played on Miles Davis' groundbreaking *In A Silent Way* album in February, still with a lightly amplified tone – indeed he played the acoustic guitar fitted with a pick-up that is pictured on the cover of *Extrapolation*. Then, in March, he jammed at the Record Plant studio with Jimi Hendrix. Whether or not he was directly affected by the experience, when McLaughlin recorded the double album *Emergency* with the Tony Williams Lifetime in May, he had started to use a noticeably distorted sound. He retreated a little from this for the Miles Davis *Bitches Brew* recordings in August, but turned up the power even further, adding both fuzz and wah-wah, for his own album *Devotion*, made at around the same time. As if to counter any objections from listeners who might have concluded from the overdriven guitar sound, matched to the powerful rhythms beaten out by drummer Buddy Miles, that *Devotion* was a rock LP and not jazz at all, McLaughlin made even wider use of its range of effects and sustain for his next sessions with Miles Davis, in November 1969 and in February to March 1970. The tracks were issued on the album *Big Fun*.

THE FIRST TIME

The Vox Guitar Organ, in which the frets were connected to a set of electric organ tone generators, was produced from 1965 until 1967. In effect, this was the immediate ancestor of the guitar synthesizer. A prototype was given to John Lennon in December 1964, but he does not appear to have ever used it in a recording. A YouTube video clip shows the instrument being played on an episode of the US TV show *I've Got A Secret*, broadcast in 1967. The instrument did not sell very well, although it inspired at least one imitator, the Guitorgan, which was manufactured in the US from late 1967.

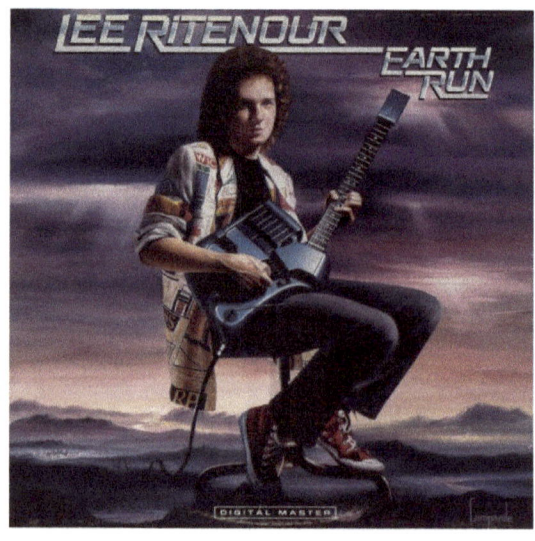

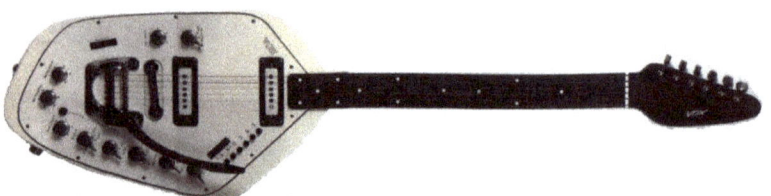

The 1984 Synthaxe, shown above in the hands of Lee Ritenour, was the first attempt to create from scratch a synthesizer that would appeal to guitarists, without suffering from the tracking problems associated with synthesizers triggered by actual guitars. The instrument contains two separate sets of strings, one for each hand, and the frets underneath the left-hand set are equally spaced. The result is an instrument that initially seems very strange for hands used to feeling their way around a guitar. Difficult to play in consequence and extremely expensive to buy, the Synthaxe was taken up by only two notable players – Allan Holdsworth and Lee Ritenour. Holdsworth in particular made several impressive showcase recordings using the Synthaxe, although his playing is delivered with such fearsome virtuosity as to leave little hope for anyone else to emulate it.

Jimmy Bryant

The first musician to apply distortion and other effects to the pedal steel guitar shared his name (apart from a small spelling difference) with a better known country performer, Glen Campbell. The steel guitarist first recorded as a member of the Misunderstood, whose December 1966 single, *I Can Take You To The Sun/Who Do You Love* served as a vital demonstration of his talents. Glenn Campbell took a revised version of the B-side song into the UK top twenty in March 1970 with his next band, Juicy Lucy.

George Harrison with Rickenbacker 12 string

INSTRUMENTS AND MUSICIANS

It was John McLaughlin who made the first recording with a guitar synthesizer, on his 1976 album *Inner Worlds*. Two different manufacturers were involved – Emulator and 360 Systems – but in both cases, the actual sound production was handled by a bank of Minimoog synthesizers, one for each guitar string. The novelty was the special guitar designed to send a signal to these whenever a string made contact with a fret. The instrument required extremely precise fretting in order to work, although this was no problem for McLaughlin, whose playing was renowned for exactly this quality. What was problematic was the speed of response of the Minimoogs to the signals from the guitar – they were simply not able to sound notes as rapidly as McLaughlin wanted to play them. The guitarist took the system on tour regardless, but he did not repeat the experiment until some years later, when the technology had caught up with his requirements.

Acoustic twelve string guitars, with the strings tuned in pairs, an octave apart in the case of the lower pitched strings, first appeared in the US at the beginning of the twentieth century. A catalogue published by the New Orleans manufacturer Grunewald in 1904 advertises a 'harp-guitar', describing the instrument as a new invention. The illustration included is of an ordinary guitar, but with twelve strings. Initially, the instrument was not taken seriously by professional musicians. Around 1912, however, Leadbelly bought a twelve string guitar manufactured by the New Jersey company Stella and made it an essential component of his music, although he was not recorded until 1933. Blind Willie McTell started playing the blues on a twelve string guitar in 1927 and began making records the same year. The twelve string instrument can be heard clearly on his first issued recording of 1928, coupling *Three Woman Blues* with *Statesboro Blues* for the Victor label.

In 1954, the little known Stratosphere guitar company produced a twin-necked electric instrument, on which one neck was fitted with twelve strings. It was intended to be unusually tuned, however, in order to allow a player to deliver harmonised lead guitar lines. As a result, the guitar was difficult to play and it was not a success, but the country player Jimmy Bryant used it for both sides of a 1954 single, coupling *Stratosphere Boogie* with *Deep Water*, with Speedy West playing along on pedal steel. (Twin-neck guitars, generally, date back to the seventeenth century).

The Danelectro Bellzouki was introduced in 1961, at the instigation of session player Vinnie Bell. It was a single necked twelve string electric guitar, modelled closely on the Greek bouzouki. Then, during 1963, Rickenbacker designed and built a small number of twelve string electric guitar prototypes. The first was given to country artist Suzi Arden; the second to George Harrison in early 1964, during the Beatles' first US tour. He played it on the February recording of *You Can't Do That* – and on many other Beatles recordings made during 1964. He can be seen with the guitar during several of the performances featured in the film *A Hard Day's Night*. Jim (later Roger) McGuinn bought one of the first production models the same year and proceeded to use it with his new group, the Byrds.

Guitars with various different string arrangements were tried during the nineteenth century. During the twentieth century, guitars with seven, eight, or nine strings were introduced at different times. The Rickenbacker frying pan guitar was issued in both six string and seven string versions. Blues player Big Joe Williams, who first recorded in 1930, played a nine string guitar of his own invention, doubling the top three strings in the manner of the twelve string instrument. Vox introduced its Mark IX electric guitar in 1965, but it attracted few enthusiasts. When John Mayall played a nine string electric guitar on his 1967 album, *The Blues Alone*, he followed the Big Joe Williams example and adapted a standard instrument himself.

Jazzman George Van Eps had a seven string guitar made for him by Epiphone in the late thirties. The seventh string was tuned five semitones below the standard low E string of the regular guitar, giving Van Eps a slightly wider range of notes to work with. The instrument was introduced to rock music by Steve Vai, who persuaded Ibanez to start producing a solid electric seven string guitar, the Ibanez Universe, in 1990. The Swedish heavy metal band Meshuggah began using eight string guitars in 2002. Paul Garthwaite has been playing a twenty-two string acoustic guitar since 2014, comprising fifteen and seven string instruments sharing a sound-box.

Moving in the other direction, towards greater simplicity, Keith Richards has favoured a five string guitar since

THE FIRST TIME

Marten Hagstrom of Meshuggah

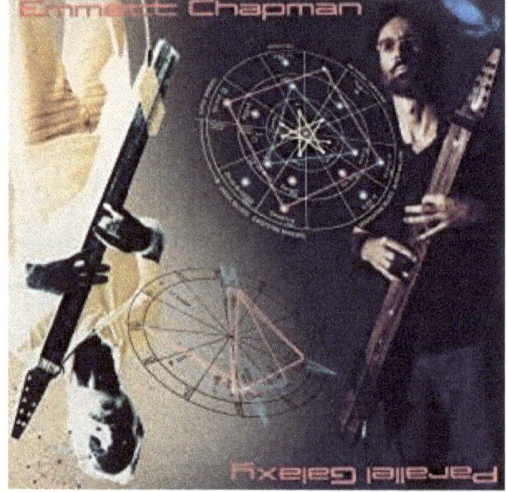

Jordan Rudess with harpejji

Hans Reichel with custom guitar

> There are several YouTube clips of Mathieu Terrade playing the harpejji. In one of them he chooses to perform an instrumental version of George Harrison's *While My Guitar Gently Weeps*. The result is undeniably impressive, but brings the harpejji into direct competition with the Chapman stick, because another YouTube video shows Bob Culbertson playing the same piece on a stick. Culbertson, who has issued more than a dozen albums, is a considerably more accomplished player, and makes the stick appear to be the superior, more expressive instrument. His version of the George Harrison song is a great performance, even if some of the YouTube commentators feel that he is let down by his facial expressions and by having failed to clean his fretboard!

1971, achieved by removing the bottom string from his vintage Fender Telecaster. Mark Sandman played a two-string bass guitar (for which he used a slide) and a hybrid instrument with a mixture of three bass and guitar strings. *Good*, the first album by Sandman's group, Morphine, was issued in 1992. He inspired the guitarists in the group Presidents of the United States of America, both of whom played six-string instruments fitted with both bass and guitar strings. Seasick Steve, catapulted to fame by his New Year's Eve 2006 performance on Jools Holland's UK television show, plays a variety of homemade guitars with just three or four strings.

Hammering-on (or using slurs, in the classical guitarist's vocabulary) is a playing technique long employed by acoustic guitarists of all kinds. It involves using fingers of the fretting hand to sound one or more notes by striking a string against the frets, in the aftermath of it being made to vibrate in the normal manner with a plectrum or finger of the playing hand. Aided by amplification, Jimi Hendrix extended the hammering-on process by playing lengthy phrases with his fretting hand alone. There are numerous examples on video showing Hendrix doing this.

The technique of making the guitar strings sound by tapping them on to the frets with *both* hands enables a skilled player to duet with himself and represents one of the most significant playing innovations since the original invention of the electric guitar. The spectacle of a modern virtuoso like Tosin Abasi casually incorporating the method into his high-speed playing of an eight string guitar is frankly jaw-dropping. It was Eddie Van Halen who first received acclaim for using a limited amount of two-handed tapping on his 1978 debut album, *Van Halen*, although Steve Hackett had already played this way on the Genesis album *Selling England By The Pound*, issued in 1973, and so did the avant-garde guitarist Fred Frith on his album *Guitar Solos*, issued in 1974. For *Guitar Solos 2*, recorded in December 1975 and January 1976, Frith invited three other inventive guitarists to contribute pieces to place alongside his own. Three tracks by Hans Reichel used two-handed tapping as the entire basis of his playing style – employing a guitar of his own construction, with a double neck but no body, and effectively turning the instrument into something akin to a fractious dulcimer. Stanley Jordan came to fame in the early eighties (via his privately pressed *Touch Sensitive* in 1982 and his major label debut, *Magic Touch*, in 1985) for doing exactly the same thing on a conventional instrument and in a jazz style that veered perilously close to easy-listening. There is a television clip on YouTube showing an Italian guitarist, Vittorio Camardese, using two-handed tapping on an acoustic guitar in 1965, but sadly he did not maintain a career in music, did not make any records, and failed to provide a lasting influence.

Meanwhile, Emmett Chapman produced a new instrument, derived from the guitar, that was intended to be played with precisely this two-handed tapping technique. The Chapman stick first appeared in 1974 and was used on record in that year by Tony Levin. Since Levin chose to employ the stick as a variety of bass guitar, further details of the instrument are given in the chapter devoted to the bass guitar.

A second instrument, with twenty-four or twenty-five strings stretched across a fretted board and needing to be played using two-handed tapping, was patented in 1985 by John D. Starrett. Only a very small number of StarrBoards were produced, but in 2010, a redesigned version of the instrument was launched by Tim Meeks, as the harpejji. The fretboard, designed to be laid flat on a stand rather than held like a guitar or a stick, is decorated with symbols which are intended to make it look familiar to keyboard players. Jordan Rudess, keyboard player with Dream Theater, added the harpejji to his equipment and first recorded with it for the *God Of War III* video game, released in 2010. The instrument has also been played on stage by Stevie Wonder.

TRACKING THE TRACKS

Complete Recorded Works Volume 1 by Sylvester Weaver (Document 1992) includes *Guitar Blues*. *The Rough Guide To Blind Lemon Jefferson* (World Music Network 2013) includes *Jack O'Diamond Blues*. Frank Hutchison's *Worried Blues* is on *Complete Recorded Works Volume 1 1926-1929* (Document 2009). *Bottleneck Guitar 1928-1937* by Tampa Red is on Yazoo (1992). *Pickin' The Guitar* by Nick Lucas is included on *Tip-Toe Thru' The Tulips* (Living Era 2000). Both this and *Teasin' The Frets* are on YouTube. A four CD boxed set on Proper Records, *Steelin' It – The Steel Guitar Story (2008)* provides an excellent overview of the work of the pioneers of the instrument. Both sides of the first record by Noi Lane's Hawaiian Orchestra can be heard on YouTube, as can two of the Orville Knapp Orchestra recordings from August 1934, *Blue Sky Avenue* and *Talkin' To Myself*. The work of Milton Brown and his Musical Brownies is given a comprehensive

THE FIRST TIME

overview on another four CD boxed set issued by Proper Records, called *Daddy of Western Swing* (2003). Bob Dunn plays on most of it. Recommended also is a third four CD boxed set on Proper called *Doughboys, Playboys and Cowboys – The Golden Years of Western Swing* (1999). Several tracks featuring Bob Dunn are included – both as a member of the Musical Brownies and afterwards – alongside songs that display the work of his immediate successors to good effect. There are a few tracks by Bob Wills and his Texas Playboys included in this set, but the group is important enough to deserve an album of its own. The best introduction to the music of the kings of Western swing is a French double-CD set on the Frémeaux and Associés label, *Bob Wills and his Texas Playboys 1932-1947* (1999). The playing of Leon McAuliffe dominates many of the tracks, while the album also draws attention to some of the talented guitarists who worked alongside him, including Junior Barnard and Eldon Shamblin. There is a four CD Proper boxed compilation for Bob Wills too, *Take Me Back To Tulsa* (2001).

Al Dexter's *Honky Tonk Blues 1936-40* is on Jasmine Records (2004). The early work of T-Bone Walker can be found on *The Beginning 1929-1946* (Epm 1997), while a good overview of his longer career is provided by *T-Bone Blues – The Essential Recordings Of T-Bone Walker* (Indigo 2000). For a more comprehensive look at Walker's music, there is a 5 CD boxed set, *The Ultimate Collection 1929-1957* (Acrobat 2014). A compilation of session work by George Barnes, including the tracks with Big Bill Broonzy, is provided by the double CD *George Barnes Vol.1 – Quiet! Gibson At Work 1938-1957* (El Toro 2014). Eddie Durham's *Hittin' The Bottle* and its companions are on *The Jimmy Lunceford Collection 1930-47* (Fabulous 2014). His first electric guitar recordings with the Kansas City 5 are on *Kansas City 5,6 and 7 1938-1944* (Jazz Chronological Classics 2000).

Andy Kirk & His Clouds Of Joy – *Jukebox Hits 1936-1949* (Acrobat 2011) includes *Take It And Git* and the Floyd Smith showcase, *Floyd's Guitar Blues*. Fifteen tracks on the download album *The Encyclopaedia Of Jazz Volume 034 – Earl Hines 1940-41* (Music Theme Licensing 2009) have Hurley Ramey in the band. Al Norris plays on every track of the Jimmie Lunceford compilation *Lunceford Special 1939-1940* (Sony 2001). Zeke Campbell plays on every track of *Light Crust Doughboys 1936-1941* (Krazy Kat 2007). The essential Charlie Christian recordings, all with bands led by Benny Goodman, are on *The Genius Of The Electric Guitar* (CBS/Sony 1987). Some surprisingly good quality live jam sessions, with the likes of Dizzy Gillespie, Thelonious Monk, Don Byas, and Kenny Clarke, working out how their bebop invention should be played, are to be found on *Live Sessions At Minton's Playhouse* (Jazz Anthology 1989). Alvino Rey and his Orchestra can be sampled on *King Of The Guitar – A Tribute* (Living Era 2004). The early work of Les Paul, with and without Mary Ford, is quite well represented on CD – *The Very Best Of Les Paul And Mary Ford* (EMI 2008) is as good as any.

The influential rock 'n' roll playing of James Burton can be found on Ricky Nelson's *25 Greatest Hits* (EMI 1998). A quarter-century later, his guitar is a vital ingredient within albums like *Aloha From Hawaii Via Satellite* by Elvis Presley (Sony 2003; original release 1973) or *Pieces Of The Sky* and *Elite Hotel* (both Rhino 2004; originally released 1975) by Emmylou Harris. He has only ever made one solo recording: *The Guitar Sounds Of James Burton* (Polydor 1997; original release 1971). The other wizard of the Telecaster, Steve Cropper, can be heard to greatest advantage on *The Best Of Booker T and the MGs* (Atlantic 2005), which inevitably includes the group's definitive take on a standard riff, *Green Onions*. 0Peter Green can be heard on *A Hard Road* by John Mayall and the Bluesbreakers (Universal/Decca 2006), which includes *The Supernatural,* and on *The Best Of Peter Green's Fleetwood Mac* (Sony 2002). Mike Bloomfield can be heard on *East West* by the Butterfield Blues Band (Warner 2013) and *Super Session* (Columbia 2003), where he is co-credited with Al Kooper and Steve Stills. *The Best Of Buddy Holly* is on Spectrum (2002). Hank Marvin's playing with the Shadows is on *20 Golden Greats* (EMI 1987).

Paul Burlison's playing with the Johnny Burnette Trio can be heard on *Rock 'n' Roll Trio – Tear It Up* (Beat Goes On 1993). These definitive rockabilly recordings are quite distinct from Burnette's later pop material like *You're 16,* which does not feature Burlison and has little resonance for today. Link Wray's guitar playing is the focus for the instrumentals collected on numerous CDs. *The Original Rumble* (Ace 1989) is as good as any, although there is rather more here than anyone who is not a dedicated fan is likely to want to own. The same comment probably applies to Chet Atkins' *Teensville* album (Hallmark 2011). Perhaps more surprising than the wah-wah effect is the idea that Atkins or his record company could really imagine that these tepid instrumentals would give Atkins credibility as a rock 'n' roll performer (especially when his work with Elvis Presley and the Everly Brothers did not appear to do the trick). The word 'patronising' comes to mind. Anyone with even a passing interest in the music of the fifties, however, should acquire something by Bo Diddley – *The Essential Bo Diddley* is on Spectrum (2000). Buddy Guy and Magic Sam both have good compilations of their most vital work – *Buddy's Blues* (Chess/Universal 2003) and *The Magic Sam Legacy* (Delmark 2008). Pat Hare can be heard playing with both James Cotton and Junior Parker on *Mystery Train* (Rounder 1990).

The Ventures' *2000 Pound Bee* is on *Walk Don't Run – The Best Of The Ventures* (EMI 1990). Helen Shapiro's *Woe Is Me* is on the two CD set *The Very Best Of Helen Shapiro* (EMI 2005). *Hold Me* is on *The Best Of P.J.Proby The EMI Years 1961-1972* (EMI 2008). The Rolling Stones' *Satisfaction* was included on the group's first Greatest Hits compilation, *Big Hits Volume 1 – High Tide And Green Grass*, and this is currently available on an Abkco CD (2006). A more comprehensive selection of sixties recordings by the Stones, including *Satisfaction*, is on a three CD set, *The Singles Collection – The London Years* (Abkco 1986). The set has a US bias in terms of track selection – indeed London was the group's US record label – but this is not inappropriate, given the fact that the Rolling Stones and their manager in the sixties, Andrew Loog Oldham, made the US market their priority. *The Crying Game* is on *The Very Best Of Dave Berry* (Spectrum 1998).

The Yardbirds' back-catalogue has long been in a somewhat chaotic state, but the group's most remarkable recordings with both Eric Clapton and Jeff Beck can be found on the double CD set, *Shapes Of Things – The Best Of The Yardbirds* (Music Club Deluxe 2010). The Spencer Davis Group's *Keep On Running* is on *The Best Of The Spencer Davis Group* (Universal/Island 1992). An excellent compilation of songs by the Electric Prunes is available as the two CD set *Too Much To Dream* (Rhino 2007), which includes the group's wah-wah radio advert and much else that is interesting, although the Prunes were not really major innovators of their time. *Bluesbreakers – John Mayall With Eric Clapton* has been reissued on CD including every track in mono and in stereo (the listener will struggle to hear the difference). A deluxe double CD includes other vital recordings, including *I'm Your Witchdoctor* (Decca 2006). Cream was in existence for only two years, but during that short time the group recorded four LPs, one of which was a double – and a further two LPs of live recordings were issued after the group split up. Conceived by and large as a blues group on overdrive, Cream soon evolved into interpreters of guitar-centred progressive song writing, on record at least (as documented on the magnificent *Disraeli Gears* and the studio half of *Wheels On Fire*). The CD *Very Best Of Cream* (Polydor 1995) provides a good set of studio highlights. Live, Cream was something else again – forgoing the studio subtleties in favour of using their blues songs as the starting point for extended high energy improvisation. *Crossroads* is the only live recording to be included on *Very Best Of Cream,* but despite being a master-class demonstration of Eric Clapton's ability to invent memorable guitar lines at speed, it is too short and too structured to be a typical live Cream track. The lengthy version of *Spoonful* contained on the live half of *Wheels Of Fire* is a prime example of how Cream was able to make improvisation work in a rock context, but the album as a whole is spoilt by the inclusion of the tediously long drum solo on the track *Toad*. All of Cream's original albums are available on CD, but there is also an excellent 4 CD boxed set, *Those Were The Days* (Polygram 1997), which contains everything the group recorded for its record company, Polydor, and is essential listening for anyone mystified, when hearing Eric Clapton's recent recordings, as to why he is held in such high regard.

The best demonstration of guitarist Pete Cosey's power in the Miles Davis group is the double CD *Agharta* (Columbia 1991), recorded live in 1975. His earlier session recordings are on the Muddy Waters albums *Electric Mud* (MCA 1997) and *After The Rain* (Universal 2011) and on *The Howlin' Wolf Album* (Universal 2011). The Jimi Hendrix catalogue has become very complicated in recent years, but the vital recordings are the four albums issued by Track in the guitarist's lifetime. These are *Are You Experienced* (the CD issue of which adds the six tracks comprising the first singles), *Axis: Bold As Love, Electric Ladyland,* and *Band Of Gypsies* (All MCA 1997). Two complementary live sets are also well worth investigating - *Live At Woodstock* (MCA 1999) and *Live At Winterland* (Sony 2011). There is some point in adding *The First Rays Of The New Rising Sun* (MCA 1997) to the list, this being the best of several attempts over the years to construct the album Jimi Hendrix might have released next if he had lived. There is a compilation, *Experience Hendrix – The Best Of Jimi Hendrix* (Sony 2010), but for an artist of Jimi Hendrix's stature, this is not really an adequate substitute for the original albums. The first, self-titled album by Queen, originally issued in 1973 and marking the first release for Brian May's remarkable playing, is on Universal/Island (2011). The most effective demonstration of Vernon Reid's talents is probably to be found on the album *Known Unknown* (Favored Nations 2004). The Beatles' *I Feel Fine* is on *1* (EMI 2000). The Who's *Anyway Anyhow Anywhere* is on the bargain priced three CD set, *The Ultimate Collection* (Universal 2002). The live BBC version is on the two CD set, *BBC Sessions* (Polydor 2000).

AMM's live recording from 1966 is on *AMMmusic* (Rér 1989). Guitarist Keith Rowe has a much more recent solo album that sounds like no other guitarist, indeed some would claim that the instrument does not sound like a guitar either – *The Room* (Erstwhile 2007). Sonny Sharrock's first exposure to the general public was on Herbie Mann's 1969 album, *Memphis Underground* (Atlantic 2002). The best of his solo albums is probably *Seize The Rainbow* (Enemy 1987). Larry Coryell's recordings with Herbie Mann and the Jazz Composer's Orchestra are both available on CD (Atlantic 2002 and ECM 2010 respectively). Gary Burton's *Lofty Fake Anagram* is available as half of a double CD package which also includes Burton's following album, *A Genuine Tong Funeral* (BGO Records 2006).

John McLaughlin's work with Graham Bond on the album *Solid Bond* was originally issued in 1970 some time after the Graham Bond Organisation had broken up. The most recent CD issue dates from 2008 (Rhino). *Emergency* by the Tony Williams Lifetime is on an Esoteric CD (2011), as is the band's follow-up *Turn It Over*, which is more startling (still!) and benefits from the addition of Jack Bruce to the line-up on some tracks. The key recordings from McLaughlin's subsequent work are *Extrapolation* (Polydor 1990) and *Devotion* (Charly 2005) in his own name; the Miles Davis albums *In A Silent Way, Bitches Brew, Jack Johnson, Big Fun,* and *Live/Evil* (all CBS/Sony 1999-2010); and the Mahavishnu Orchestra albums *The Inner Mounting Flame* and *Birds Of Fire* (both CBS/Sony 1998 and 2000). Many of McLaughlin's later recordings are well worth investigating too, but these are the ones that made his name. *Inner Worlds* is available on a Sony CD (1994), although the use of the guitar synthesizer apart, it is not one of McLaughlin's better efforts. Allan Holdsworth's astonishing virtuosity on both guitar and synthaxe can be sampled on *Against The Clock – The Best Of Allan Holdsworth* (Alternity 2005). There are two CDs, helpfully arranged with guitar on one and synthaxe on the other. Lee Ritenour's *Earth Run* is on Concord (2015).

Blind Willie McTell's *Ultimate Blues Collection* is a double CD on Not Now Music (2013). *Stratosphere Boogie – The Flaming Guitars Of Speedy West & Jimmy Bryant* is on Razor & Tie (1999). *A Hard Day's Night* (EMI 2009) by the Beatles includes *You Can't Do That* and many other examples of George Harrison's 12 string guitar playing. *The Essential Big Joe Williams* is a double CD on Not Now Music (2012). George Van Eps shares a CD with another guitarist, Johnny Smith, *Legends – Solo Guitar Performances* (Concord 1994). Steve Vai first played the Ibanez Universe on *Passion And Warfare* (Relativity 1993). Meshuggah unleashed the eight string guitars on *Nothing* (Nuclear Blast 2002). Paul Garthwaite's *22 String And Friends* is issued by himself (2021). *Good* by Morphine is on Rykodisc (1993). The self-titled first album by the Presidents of the United States of America is on Columbia (1996). The first album by Seasick Steve is *I Started Out With Nothin And I Still Got Most Of It Left* (Warner 2008).

Tosin Abasi is guitarist with Animals As Leaders. The first, self-titled album, which is a solo recording, is on Prosthetic Records (2009). There are also several live performance videos on YouTube. The first album by Eddie Van Halen is the 1978 album *Van Halen* (Warner Bros 2001). *Selling England By The Pound* by Genesis is on Virgin (2011). Fred Frith's *Guitar Solos* was given a CD release by Rér in 2002; *Guitar Solos 2* has not been issued on CD and the original 1976 LP on Caroline is scarce. Stanley Jordan's *Magic Touch* is on a Blue Note CD (2003). *Before The Dream Faded* by the Misunderstood (Cherry Red 2003) includes both sides of the 1966 single. The first (and best) album by Juicy Lucy is *Juicy Lucy* (Esoteric 2010).

THE FIRST TIME

Vernon Alley playing electric bass with the Lionel Hampton Orchestra in 1940

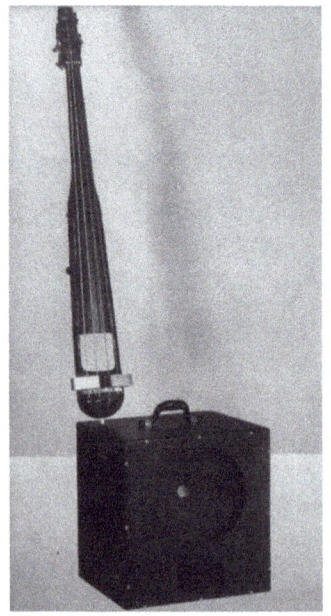

Rickenbacker electric bass

Lloyd Loar, engineer with Gibson, designed a prototype electric bass in 1924, but could not persuade the company to develop it further. In disgust, Loar resigned.

Mark Allen and his Orchestra

Gibson electric bass guitar, made for Wally Kamin in 1938. He was later the bass player with Les Paul. The instrument, one of two built, was designed to be played in the upright position.

Audiovox catalogue 1937

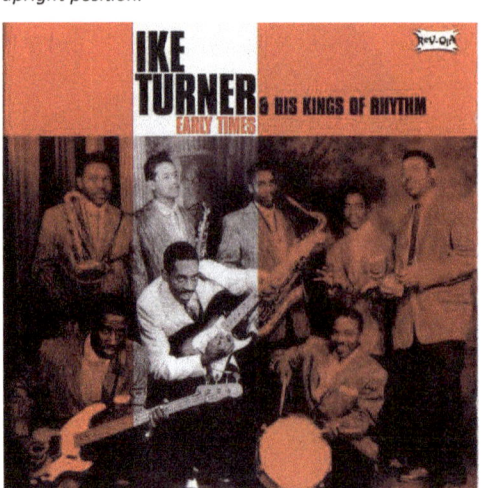

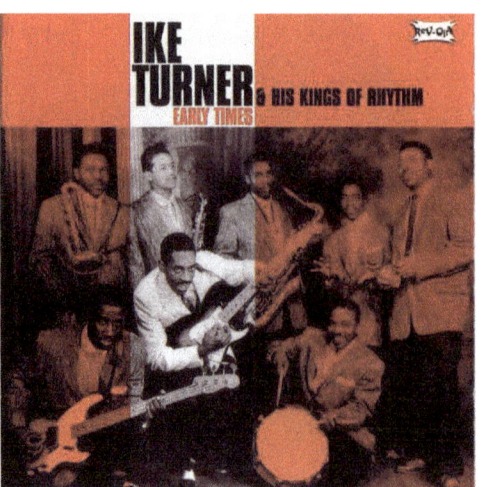

Jesse Knight Jr playing Fender bass with Ike Turner in 1956

Model 736—Bass Fiddle

This Electronic Instrument lends itself especially well to Orchestral use, giving Full Resonant Tones. Made of beautiful Black Walnut, inlaid position dots. Will take the place of 3 double basses. Compact! Length 42".

☆

Model 936

Powerful Amplifier—18 watts, at 3% distortion. Has heavy duty, High Fidelity, Concert Type, 12" Jensen Speaker. Supplied with Chrome chassis. Cabinet covered with Airplane Linen. Has 3 different tones. Complete with 2 inputs. Size: 13½"x17"x8".

2 BASS GUITAR

Jazz and country musicians playing the double bass in the twenties and thirties had to cope with the fact that their instrument was large and unwieldy, yet was also rather quiet, struggling to be heard at all when drums and loud brass instruments were involved. It was in order to provide a solution to these problems that several manufacturers came up with the idea of an electrically amplified bass during the late thirties, among them Regal, Rickenbacker, Vega, and Gibson. The otherwise unremarkable Mark Allen and his Orchestra were equipped with a complete set of Rickenbacker electric instruments in 1935, including a bass, and were featured in the company's catalogue. Allen's *If You Were Mine/Alone*, issued by Columbia in 1935, is the first record to feature an electric bass. A contemporary photograph shows the Lionel Hampton band playing in Seattle in November 1940, with bass player Vernon Alley clearly using an electric instrument. Alley first recorded with Hampton in December 1940, following which a 78 rpm record coupling *Lost Love* with *Smart Aleck* was the first to be issued in 1941. Presumably Vernon Alley is playing his electric bass on these tracks – certainly it sounds loud and clear.

As it happens, a Seattle musician and inventor, Paul Tutmarc, had already designed and built an electric double bass in 1933. Four years later, he made the first electric bass guitar (he called it a bass fiddle, but it was fretted), together with an amplifier designed to be used with it, and he advertised them both in the catalogue of his Audiovox company. Tutmarc's son, Bud, updated the design slightly and advertised it in 1947 as the Serenader. The soundtrack to the 1951 film, *The Day The Earth Stood Still*, recorded in August, includes a clearly audible bass guitar in places. Presumably, the uncredited player was using one of the Tutmarc instruments.

In October 1951, Fender, already established as a thriving electric guitar manufacturer, introduced the Precision bass guitar. It was a four string instrument, tuned an octave below the lowest four strings of the standard guitar, the same as a double bass. The company began manufacturing the Fender Bassman amplifier to go with it the following year. The Precision bass was not an immediate success, as is emphasized by the fact that a few years later, the leading rock 'n' roll performers were not using it. Elvis Presley, Bill Haley, and Buddy Holly all had bass players who still preferred the upright double bass. Nevertheless, for Presley's *Jailhouse Rock* in 1957, bass player Bill Black made the switch, while the group that Buddy Holly formed for his ill-fated 1959 tour included Waylon Jennings playing bass guitar. Some of the rhythm and blues bands were a little more willing to try something new – both Little Richard's band and Ike Turner's Kings Of Rhythm were early users of the Fender bass.

The first jazz musician to adopt the Precision was Roy Johnson, bass player with Lionel Hampton's band. Downbeat magazine published a feature about the new instrument in July 1952, complete with a photograph of Johnson. Unfortunately, he was not recorded playing it. Hampton made no recordings during 1952 and by the time he embarked on a European tour with some recording dates thrown in, at the end of September 1953, Johnson had moved on.

Country bass player Joel Price played the Fender Precision with Little Jimmy Dickens at the Grand Ole Opry in 1952, but did not record with it for another two years. It is often stated that the first Precision bass player to record was Monk Montgomery, who took over the bass position in Lionel Hampton's band. In July 1953, he recorded four tracks with Art Farmer. They were released as part of the LP *The Art Farmer Septet Plays the Arrangements and Compositions of Gigi Gryce and Quincy Jones*, but not until 1956. By this time the Little Jimmy Dickens records, *Take Me As I Am Or Let Me Go* and *We Could*, with Joel Price on bass guitar, had already appeared.

Meanwhile, the Treniers appeared on the Dean Martin/Jerry Lewis show on television (The Colgate Comedy Hour) in May 1954. They performed *Rockin' Is Our Bizness* with the house band, including John 'Shifty' Henry on bass

THE FIRST TIME

Shifty Henry (who clearly had the same careless attitude to spelling as did Shakespeare), playing his Fender Precision bass. He gets a name check – albeit recast as a fictional character – in the lyrics of the song Jailhouse Rock, written by Jerry Leiber and Mike Stoller for Elvis Presley.

Jet Harris with Fender VI and Tony Meehan

Monk Montgomery

Joel Price with the Little Jimmy Dickens band

Paul McCartney *John Entwistle (with Keith Moon)* *Larry Graham*

guitar. Henry played on the group's records too. *Hi-yo Silver*, issued in early 1953, but recorded the previous October, has Henry shifting to the bass guitar for the first time. To make the point that he is doing something new, he even gets to play a brief solo on the instrument. It is Henry, therefore, who is the first bass guitarist to be heard on record. Despite what many references maintain, Shifty Henry was not a member of Louis Jordan's band and did not record with him (unless his contribution has been omitted from the Jordan entry in Brian Rust's impeccable discography).

In July 1960, Duane Eddy had a big hit on both sides of the Atlantic with *Because They're Young*, which he played on a bass guitar. Probably, however, most purchasers of the record would not have realised this, since Eddy chose to perform on the six-string instrument that Danelectro had started selling in 1956, and for most of the song he played within the normal range expected of a standard guitar. No such confusion would have applied in the case of Jet Harris, who after his departure from the Shadows in 1962, managed to gain five UK chart hits during the next eighteen months. These included a UK number one hit, *Diamonds*, made in partnership with his former Shadows colleague, drummer Tony Meehan. Harris was well known as a bass player and it must have seemed a good idea to resist a switch to a standard guitar, even if he did want to play instrumentals. Jet Harris played the first Fender Precision to reach the UK while in the Shadows, but for his solo records he often preferred to follow the Duane Eddy example and use a six string bass. Happily, Fender had started to manufacture one, the Fender VI, in 1962.

During the sixties beat group era, there was a tendency to regard bass players as failed guitarists. As Paul McCartney explained in a July 1995 interview for *Bass Player* magazine, "It wasn't the number one job. We wanted to be up front. In our minds, it was the fat guy in the group who nearly always played the bass, and he stood at the back. None of us wanted that. We wanted to be up front singing, looking good, to pull the birds. Stu [Sutcliffe] said he was going to stay in Hamburg. He'd met a girl and was going to stay there with her and paint. So it was like, uh-oh, we haven't got a bass player. And everyone sort of turned round and looked at me. I was a bit lumbered with it, really. It was like, well... it'd better be you, then."

It was Paul McCartney, however, who became one of the major players responsible for raising the profile of the bass guitar in rock music. In particular, his powerful, inventive playing on the Beatles single *Paperback Writer/Rain*, recorded in April 1966, attracted much attention. Equally influential was the fluent playing of John Entwistle with the Who, who even managed a solo on the single *My Generation*, recorded in October 1965. By the end of the decade, virtuoso players like Jack Bruce (with Cream), Jack Casady (Jefferson Airplane), and Phil Lesh (the Grateful Dead) had changed the standing of their instrument for ever.

At the start of the seventies, a new style of playing the bass guitar was pioneered by Larry Graham, the bassist with Sly and the Family Stone. In a reference to the rock 'n' roll double bass players who would pull the strings and allow them to slap back against the neck, Graham's style became referred to as slap bass playing, although the essential part of it was the use of the side of the thumb to strike percussively against the strings. He can be heard doing it on the Family Stone single, *Thank You Falettinme Be Mice Elf Again*, issued in December 1969, and afterwards on the 1971 album, *There's A Riot Goin' On*. The approach became very influential very quickly, making slap playing an essential part of the bass guitarist's technique in funk and jazz fusion music.

Jaco Pastorius became famous in 1976 for the richness of his bass tone when playing with both Joni Mitchell and Weather Report. What made Pastorius' sound particularly distinctive was the fact that he played a fretless bass guitar, enabling the strings to resonate against the neck in the manner of a double bass. This was not as new as it appeared to be. As long ago as 1961, Bill Wyman had removed the frets from his bass guitar, one result being easily heard on the Rolling Stones tracks *I'm A King Bee* and *Nineteenth Nervous Breakdown*, which use a smooth bass slide only possible when there are no frets to get in the way. Ampeg marketed the first commercial fretless bass guitar in 1966 and it was played by Rand Forbes of the group United States Of America (it is pictured on the front cover of the group's 1968 album). Fender followed in 1970, its instrument being used (as well as an Ampeg) by Rick Danko on the Band's 1971 album, *Cahoots*, and the live album, *Rock Of Ages*, recorded the same year. The Pink Floyd track, *A Pillow*

THE FIRST TIME

The first album of solo bass playing was *Unaccompanied Barre* by Barre Phillips, which was released in 1968 and inspired numerous similar albums. This, however, was music by a double bass. Eberhard Weber plays an electric upright bass, an unusual instrument since the rise of the bass guitar, and he has a solo bass album, *Pendulum,* issued in 1993. Solo bass guitar albums are rare. The first is by Steve Lawson, from 2000, called *And Nothing But The Bass*. He uses a range of electronic units to create loops for himself to play over, effectively making his solo bass into several basses. He is, however, perfectly capable of playing the music live – and frequently has done.

Steve Lawson CD

Anthony Jackson with Fodera 6 string bass

Tony Levin playing the Chapman stick

Rick Danko

INSTRUMENTS AND MUSICIANS

Of Winds, on the 1971 album *Meddle*, employed a fretless bass guitar, although it is likely that this is played by David Gilmour, rather than the group's regular bass player, Roger Waters.

Modern bass guitars often come with five or six strings, extending the range of the instrument both upwards and downwards, and they have wide necks to enable players proper access to the strings. Early versions, like the Fender Bass VI and Fender Bass V, both manufactured in the early sixties, retained the same size neck as the four string version and simply set the strings closer together. The first of the new breed of six string bass (often called a contrabass guitar) was built by independent guitar maker Carl Thompson in 1975, at the request of session bass player Anthony Jackson, although the neck on this was nothing like as wide as those that later instruments by other makers would have. Jackson played his new bass on the title track of the 1975 Carlos Garnett album, *Let This Melody Ring On*.

Stanley Clarke came up with the idea of the piccolo bass and commissioned Carl Thompson to make one for him in the early seventies. Tuned up to an octave higher than a standard bass guitar, the piccolo version essentially turns the instrument into a guitar, except that the highest two strings are missing, the frets are a little more widely spaced than would be familiar to a guitarist, and the player would inevitably use his customary bass playing right hand technique. Clarke first played the piccolo bass on his 1975 album, *Journey To Love*, whose sleeve credits gleefully state that the instrument was "first used by Stanley Clarke". Ron Carter also developed something he called a piccolo bass, but his was an acoustic instrument derived from the double bass and therefore something like a cello. He first played this on the 1973 album *Blues Farm*. Joseph McCreary, known simply as Foley, played piccolo bass in Miles Davis' last touring band at the end of the eighties, alongside a regular bass guitarist. Foley was credited with playing 'lead bass' and he followed this role to the full, using a range of effects and playing high energy solos that sounded almost, though not quite, like the work of an electric guitarist.

The Chapman stick is a relatively new electric stringed instrument, put on the market in 1974 by its inventor, Emmett Chapman. It combines the range of guitar and bass guitar in one instrument, enabling it to be used as a kind of super bass. It is played by tapping with both hands, a technique that was pioneered by Chapman himself. The super bass was the role that Tony Levin gave it when playing on the 1981 King Crimson album, *Discipline*, and subsequently. Levin was a member of the group, but he has been a prolific session player and features on hundreds of albums by numerous artists. During an interview published on the Chapman stick website, Levin states that he first played the instrument on "the second album" by his friend, Gap Mangione, just a few days after acquiring it. Assuming that he means the second album he was involved with personally, then this must be *She And I*, which was issued in 1974. Undoubtedly, therefore, Tony Levin is the first musician to play the Chapman stick on record.

TRACKING THE TRACKS

If You Were Mine and *Alone* by Mark Allen and his Orchestra can be heard on YouTube.

Lost Love and *Smart Aleck* are included on the five CD set, *The Complete Lionel Hampton Victor Sessions 1937-1941* (Mosaic 2007), or the cheaper two CD set, *The Complete Lionel Hampton Vol 5/6 (1940-1941)* (RCA 2000).

A Soundcloud user named Geometro has uploaded a sound clip of himself playing the Tutmarc bass guitar. Despite the instrument's age and despite a slight intonation problem, it does sound like a modern bass guitar.

The soundtrack album for the film *The Day The Earth Stood Still*, with music composed by Bernard Herrmann, is on a Twentieth Century Fox CD (1993). The version issued on a Varese Sarabande CD is a re-recording – it is the same music, but cannot be definitive with regard to the instrumentation, although it does include a credited bass guitar.

The tracks recorded by Monk Montgomery with Art Farmer are the first four on the CD *Art Farmer Septet* (Original Jazz Classics 1993). *Take Me As I Am Or Let Me Go* and *We Could* by Little Jimmy Dickens are included on the CD *Country Giant* (Sony 1995). The early singles by the Treniers are on *This Is It! The Treniers In The '50s* (Rev-Ola 2008). *Rockin' Is Our Bizness* performed live on television can be seen on a YouTube video clip.

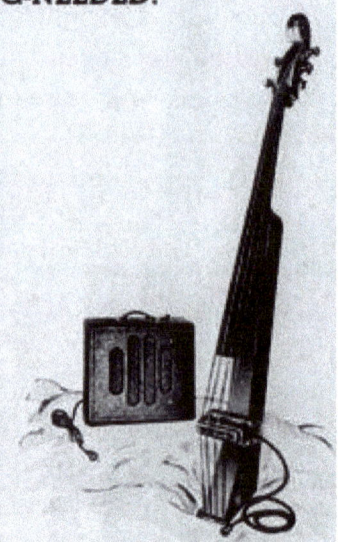

1936 advertisement for the Regal electric bass

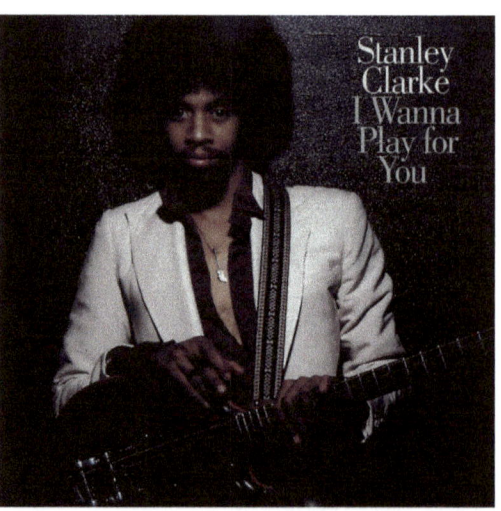

Bill Wyman, with the bass guitar from which he removed the frets.

INSTRUMENTS AND MUSICIANS

Because They're Young is on the Duane Eddy CD *Greatest Hits* (Not Now Music 2011). Jet Harris's hits are all on *The Best of Jet Harris and Tony Meehan* (Spectrum 2000). The Beatles' *Paperback Writer* and *Rain* are on the double CD *Past Masters* (EMI 2009). The Who's *My Generation* is on *My Generation – The Very Best Of The Who* (Polydor 1996).

Jack Bruce found fame as the bass player with Cream. His playing with that group can be sampled on *The Very Best Of Cream* (Polydor 1995). Jack Casady was bass player with Jefferson Airplane. The group's *Best Of* is on a Sony/BMG CD (2007). Phil Lesh was bass player with the Grateful Dead. This group's *Best Of* is a double CD (Rhino 2015). It should go without saying that these compilations are no more than a starting point for the work of these important musicians.

Dynamite! The Collection by Sly and the Family Stone (Sony 2011) includes the *Thank You* single and three tracks from the album *There's A Riot Goin' On*. *The Essential Jaco Pastorius (Sony 2007)* is a thoughtfully compiled double CD and includes key tracks by Joni Mitchell and Weather Report.

Nineteenth Nervous Breakdown is on all the compilations of the Rolling Stones' sixties material, such as *The Very Best Of The Rolling Stones 1964-1971* (Abkco 2013). *I'm A King Bee* is on the group's self-titled first album, which is most easily obtained on CD with its American track listing (Abkco 2002). The Band's *Cahoots* is on a Capitol CD (2000). It is less essential than the group's earlier albums, although this cannot be said about the live *Rock Of Ages* (Capitol double CD 2001). Pink Floyd's *Meddle* is on a Sony CD (2016).

Carlos Garnett's *Let This Melody Ring On* is on a Soul Brother CD (2014). Anthony Jackson has played on over five hundred albums, from the O'Jays to Chaka Khan to Al Dimeola to Madonna to Michel Petrucciani.

Stanley Clarke's *Journey To Love* is on Epic (1991). Ron Carter's *Blues Farm* is on CTI (2003). Foley is best experienced in a live context, such as on the Miles Davis DVD, *Live In Paris* (Warner 1990).

King Crimson's *Discipline* is on a DGM CD (2004). Gap Mangione's *She And I* was released on an A&M LP in 1974, but has not been reissued on CD.

In 2017, over fifty years after Paul McCartney demonstrated the vitality and importance of a bass guitar played imaginatively and skilfully in a rock music context, and regardless of the very numerous examples of other bass players doing the same in the years since, the following question appeared on the discussion website, *Quora*. "If Paul McCartney was the best musician in the Beatles, why did he play bass?" An answer provided by Abby Dees is too good to be consigned to the obscurity of a transitory list of comments.

"I have played guitar all my life and am comfortable with it. I'm no shredder but I think I have a great feel and sense of groove. So it would therefore be no big deal for me to switch over to bass, which is basically the same thing, with fewer strings and almost no chords to think about. And bass is all about groove, right?
Well, that has been a humbling experiment.
My bass playing is an exercise in frustration. Making it interesting and melodic while also keeping rooted in the groove is especially challenging. You can move around the drums parts on guitar, but doing that on bass is not for the faint of heart. I can't count the times that I went into a new song thinking I'd pull off some great counter melody or counter rhythm only to find myself scurrying safely back to the predictable tonics, hitting every quarter note. And even that isn't as easy as it seems if you want to truly support the tune. You need to hit those quarter notes with perfect feel every time. One slightly off little flourish or out-of-the-pocket note and you're playing on your own, the band a million miles away. And everyone will hear it — feel it — not just the band. You don't realize how free and easy you had it on guitar.
I am reminded of my own incredulity about what the big deal was about golf. You stand there and hit a ball that's sitting there. Surely this gets old and there is only a limited skill set you can possibly bring to bear. Yet every golfer I know describes an endless potential of joy and difficulty in that game and a limitless trajectory for what it takes to execute the perfect shot.
Paul McCartney taught us what was possible on bass and nothing has been the same since."

THE FIRST TIME

Reconstructed water organ from remains found in a Roman house

3 KEYBOARD INSTRUMENTS

All the traditional keyboard instruments – those relying on the movement of air across edges in pipes or reeds (the organ and the harmonium) and those relying on the striking or plucking of metal strings (the piano and the harpsichord) – were invented before the start of the twentieth century. In the case of the organ, it was long before then. An instrument recognisably the same kind of device, with differing water levels used to drive the air, was used by the ancient Greeks in the third century BC. Most recent is the harmonium, in which air is pumped by means of foot pedals. The instrument was patented in 1840 by a Frenchman, Alexandre Debain, although he had freely borrowed from a couple of earlier designs. Independently, something similar was developed in the US, differing only in preferring to move the air by suction rather than pressure.

The first electric instrument was the musical telegraph, a simple two octave keyboard device designed and built by the American Elisha Gray in 1874. Gray had discovered that an iron object placed near an electromagnet powered by an AC supply will vibrate and emit a sound. It was this same principle that lay behind the telharmonium (or dynamophone), which was patented in the US by Thaddeus Cahill in 1897. This was completed in 1906 as a huge machine weighing over two hundred tons – eventually three of them were built. Sound was generated by a series of dynamos mounted on twelve axles, whose speed of rotation corresponded to the frequency of each of the twelve notes of the chromatic scale. The sound was arranged to be transmitted through telephone lines, with paper cones attached to the receivers to make the volume loud enough for several people to hear it at one time. As if the instrument was not already complicated enough, Cahill decided to ignore the equal temperament tuning system, which has been used in Western music for several hundred years and blurs the slight frequency differences that physics describes for notes played in different keys. His keyboard provided thirty-six notes for each octave, providing something of a challenge for those wishing to play it. Cahill had hoped to be able to interest hotels and clubs in having the music of the telharmonium transmitted through their own telephone systems, which would have made it the source of the first background music later known as muzak. Unfortunately, the telharmonium did not succeed in attracting the interest of any of the public and in 1914, Cahill's company was declared bankrupt. Today, none of the instruments survive and if any recordings were ever made, they have not survived either.

From the mid 1920s, electric organs using a more efficient version of the dynamos used by the telharmonium (called tonewheels) were developed. The first of these was the Robb Wave organ, designed and built by Canadian Morse Robb in 1927, with a second version in 1934. Hampered by the economic problems of the thirties, the organ was a commercial failure and only thirteen were ever sold. A few other manufacturers developed different designs of organ during the thirties, but all of them ultimately succumbed to the success of the one built by the American Laurens Hammond in 1935.

The Hammond organ had more stable intonation than the competition, was capable of much greater tone variation due to having a system of drawbars, was a little cheaper, and employed a unique reverb device based on the action of a coiled spring. Marketing for the organ was targeted at churches (1750 of them bought Hammond organs during the first three years) and families, rather than professional musicians. Nevertheless, according to the company website, the first recording of the Hammond organ was by Milt Herth in the year of the instrument's launch. Three recordings from 1937 that can be heard on YouTube, *The Dipsy Doodle*, *Canadian Capers*, and *Toy Trumpet*, reveal Herth to be a pop performer in the area where jazz fades into easy listening. George Gershwin was another early customer of the Hammond company, but he died of a brain tumour in 1937 before he had managed to achieve much with his purchase. Fats Waller, who recorded jazz on a pipe organ as early as 1926, also started playing the Hammond organ in these early years. He recorded *Go Down Moses* and *Deep River* in 1938, becoming the first Hammond organist in jazz.

THE FIRST TIME

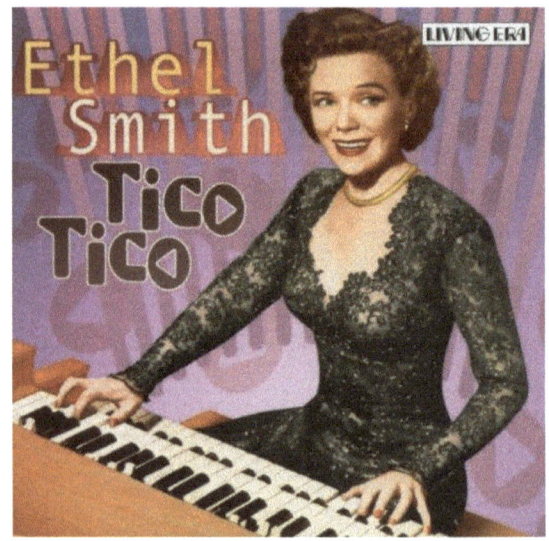

The mainstream media during the sixties, and clearly organ manufacturers too, were fond of referring to beat groups as 'combos', despite the fact that nobody else, whether fans or musicians, ever did (with the possible exception of Elvis Presley's bass player, who had several American hits between 1959 and 1962 with a group he called Bill Black's Combo).

Mike Ratledge

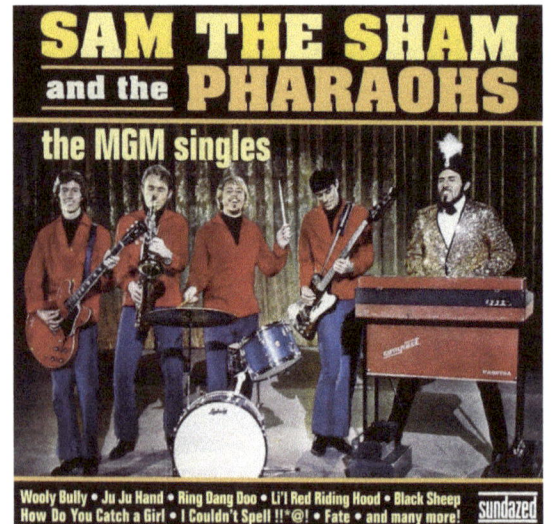

INSTRUMENTS AND MUSICIANS

Ethel Smith was a major populariser of the instrument in the forties – she performed the piece *Tico Tico* in the 1944 hit musical *Bathing Beauty* and sold nearly two million copies of the record worldwide. By now, the Hammond organ was being played in conjunction with a tone cabinet, manufactured by Leslie, and containing a rotating speaker to fully emphasise the vibrato effects of which the instrument was capable. Hammond had designed a cabinet themselves, but it was the Leslie version that became most successful.

Jimmy Smith, recording a series of successful records for the Blue Note label from 1956, was enormously influential in boosting the appeal of the Hammond organ in jazz and he inspired several imitators. In rock, Booker T Jones scored a major hit for the instrument in 1962 with his tune *Green Onions*, which inspired Georgie Fame to adopt the instrument. His influential *Rhythm and Blues At The Flamingo* album from 1963 and his January 1965 number one UK hit, *Yeh Yeh*, helped to spread the word. Soon afterwards, the rapid development of the music in 1966 to 1967 gave Hammond the same status as Fender and Gibson had acquired with the guitar. Records like *Gimme Some Loving* by the Spencer Davis Group (with Stevie Winwood playing the organ), the *John Mayall's Bluesbreakers with Eric Clapton* LP, and *A Whiter Shade Of Pale* by Procol Harum demonstrated the power of which the Hammond organ was capable. In 1967 too, the Nice began performing and recording, their organist Keith Emerson using his Hammond as a prop as much as an instrument and showing how a keyboard player could be as dynamic on stage as a lead guitarist.

The majestic organ part that dominates the 1964 hit, *The House Of The Rising Sun*, by the Animals, sounds like a Hammond, but was actually played by Alan Price on a Vox Continental. The design of this British built organ replaced the tonewheels of the Hammond with transistors, enabling the instrument to be much smaller and lighter. It was popular for a while with groups and was the instrument of choice for Ray Manzarek of the Doors, Mike Smith of the Dave Clark Five, Augie Meyers of the Sir Douglas Quintet, and John Lennon with the Beatles, but it lacked sufficient gravitas for the progressive rock bands, who preferred their Hammonds. Perhaps for this reason, the Vox Continental enjoyed a short revival during the new wave era, with Steve Naïve of Elvis Costello's Attractions and Mike Barson of Madness enjoying its characteristic thin sound (Alan Price's achievement notwithstanding).

Other organ manufacturers were popular too during the sixties, most notably Lowrey and Farfisa. Lowrey organs were as substantial as Hammonds but had built-in rhythm accompaniment, making them even more attractive for players at home. The company was indeed the largest of the time. The Lowrey organ was taken up by some professional musicians, including Garth Hudson, who played with the Band, and Mike Ratledge of Soft Machine, neither of whom much used the built-in rhythms. Ratledge did, however, connect a a guitar fuzzbox to his. The instrument was used too to produce the opening notes of the Beatles' *Lucy In The Sky With Diamonds* and what sounds like a synthesizer part on the Who's *Baba O'Riley*, for which one of the rhythm settings did prove to be very useful. Farfisa manufactured transistorised 'combo organs', similar to the Vox Continental. Spooner Oldham, a member of the session band at Muscle Shoals Sound Studio in Alabama, acquired one, with the result that it can be heard on several Atlantic soul hits, such as Percy Sledge's *When A Man Loves A Woman*. Other well-known users of the Farfisa organ included Sam The Sham and the Pharoahs, Pink Floyd, and Van Der Graaf Generator (until Hugh Banton managed to afford a Hammond in time to record the 1970 album *H To He Who Am The Only One*).

The first electric piano was built in 1929, as a joint production by the Bechstein and Siemens companies. Like a traditional piano, metal strings were struck by hammers, but the sound was amplified by means of electromagnetic pickups. At about the same time, the Vivi-Tone Clavier was designed and produced by Lloyd Loar, who had been the chief designer for the Gibson guitar company. For this instrument, the strings were replaced by metal tone bars. Neither of them got much further than the prototype stage, which was also true of the Selmer Pianotron, developed ten years later, and which was essentially a conventional upright piano fitted with electrostatic pickups.

In 1954, the Wurlitzer electric piano appeared, using metal reeds for its mechanism. This time, the instrument was manufactured commercially and slowly started to appeal to some professional musicians. Duke Ellington played one during two recording sessions in May 1955, but the five tracks concerned were not issued at the time. Eccentric

THE FIRST TIME

The tracks on which Duke Ellington played electric piano were small group performances where Ellington's own playing is much more prominent than it usually is when accompanying the full orchestra. They are *Coquette* from May 18th 1955 and *Discontented Blues, Once In A Blue Mood, Lady Be Good,* and *So Long* from May 19th. Other tracks recorded on May 18th were included on the LP *Duke Ellington Showcase,* but for these Ellington plays an ordinary acoustic piano.

The other *Super-Sonic Jazz* album tracks on which Sun Ra plays electric piano are *India, Advice To Medics, Sunology, Sunology Part II,* and *Springtime In Chicago.* The first of these is an atmospheric mood piece rather different from the other music Sun Ra was recording at this time and for which the electric instrument is well suited. The second of the tracks is a solo piano improvisation.

Ray Charles sings "what I say", but the Atlantic record company felt it was necessary to rewrite the black American phrase as though it was standard English, when printing the title on the records. The previous hit by Ray Charles, *Night Time Is The Right Time,* from earlier in the same year, but recorded in October 1958, also had Charles playing the electric piano, but somewhat buried in the mix. The song did very much less well in any case, reaching no higher than number ninety-five in the national charts.

The origins of the Fender Rhodes electric piano go back to the Pre-Piano, built by Harold Rhodes in 1946 as an educational instrument. Its toy piano sound made it unsuitable for professional use. The piano bass was produced in 1959, covering a similar range to that of the bass guitar, but persuaded few players of its worth, other than Ray Manzarek, who used it to play the bass parts, with his left hand, in the live music of the Doors. (A number of different bass guitar players were on the records). The full electric piano was unveiled in 1965.

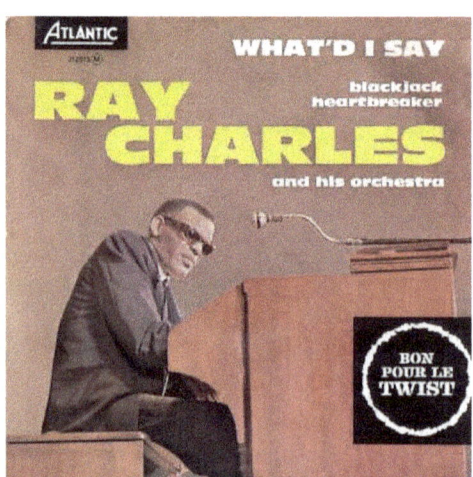

Ray Manzarek plays a Vox keyboard with the Doors, a Rhodes piano bass balanced on top.

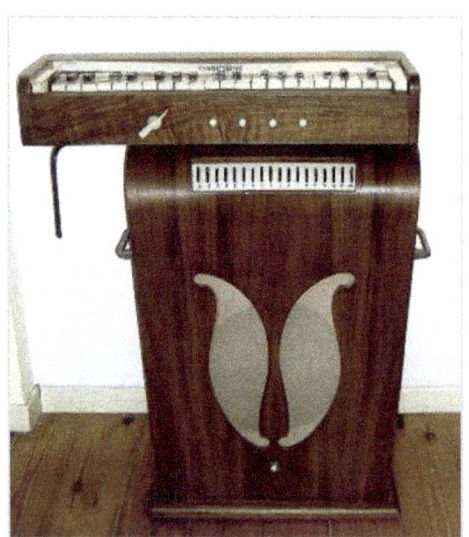

Ondioline

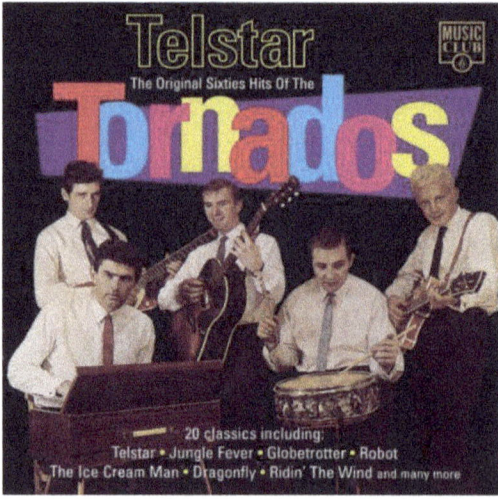

The Tornados, with clavioline

jazz bandleader Sun Ra produced seven tracks featuring the electric piano in 1956. Recorded in February, *Medicine For A Nightmare* and *A Call For All Demons* were issued on singles as part of a small batch making up the first releases on Sun Ra's newly set-up Saturn label. The first album on the label, recorded through 1956 and released in March the following year, was *Super-Sonic Jazz*, and this included the remainder of the tracks, together with an alternative take of the previously released *Medicine For A Nightmare*.

What Wurlitzer really needed to make sales of their instrument take off was for it to be played on a hit record. This was achieved in 1959, when the Ray Charles song, *What'd I Say*, went to number one in the American R&B charts and entered the top ten in the national charts – the first time that Ray Charles had managed to do this. Other electric piano records followed and, inspired by the success of Wurlitzer, other manufacturers opened for business during the sixties. These included Hohner, Baldwin, and the brand that soon became the market leader, Fender Rhodes.

The ondioline, an electronic keyboard that was an ancestor of the synthesizer, was invented by Frenchman Georges Jenny in 1938 and made commercially available in 1940. Electronic keyboard pioneer Jean Jacques Perrey became something of an ondioline specialist and he played it on the Charles Trenet record, *L'âme des Poètes*, which was a French hit in 1955. Perrey's first solo LP from 1957, *Prélude au Sommeil*, is made up entirely of ambient electronic music played on several ondiolines. He followed this up with a 1960 EP, titled *Mister Ondioline*. Recordings of the instrument are otherwise scarce, however. Kai Winding had a US hit with it in 1963, *More*; Tommy James and The Shondells mixed one into their 1967 single, *I Think We're Alone Now*; and Al Kooper soloed with it on his track with Mike Bloomfield, *His Holy Modal Majesty*, in order to emulate the sound of John Coltrane's soprano saxophone. But that is about it.

The instrument played on multi-million selling hit, *Telstar*, and other records by the Tornados, sounds like an ondioline, but is actually the similar clavioline, also invented in France, by Constant Martin in 1947, and licensed to Selmer in the UK, Gibson in the US. The Beatles used the clavioline in their 1967 recording, *Baby You're A Rich Man*. Legend suggests that John Lennon's unusual approach to playing it involved rolling an orange along the keyboard, but this has never been verified. The instrument that plays the solo on Del Shannon's 1961 hit, *Runaway*, was a clavioline modified with extra electronic circuitry by its player, Max Crook, who christened the result a 'musitron'.

The mellotron, which became a crucial ingredient within the progressive rock genre after being adopted by the Moody Blues, King Crimson, Barclay James Harvest, Genesis, and others, was first manufactured in 1963. Its origins, however, go back to an earlier instrument, the chamberlin. This was conceived by the American Harry Chamberlin in 1946 and brought into production a couple of years later. The sounds of various instruments (played by members of the Lawrence Welk Orchestra) were recorded on to magnetic tape, with the playback being triggered by the chamberlin keys. In essence, therefore, the instrument was employing the process of sampling to generate its music. Like the Hammond organ before it, the chamberlin was aimed at the domestic market – in this case it stayed there. Through the fifties, only around a hundred of the instruments were sold and it is unlikely that any of them were recorded – not even the one bought by Bobby Darin with the proceeds of his hit single, *Mack The Knife*, in 1959. There was considerable opposition to the professional use of the chamberlin from the American Federation of Musicians, who were concerned that an instrument capable of sounding like the playing of several different musicians would be likely to take work from the Federation's members.

Bill Fransen, previously employed as Harry Chamberlin's window-cleaner, or so it is said, was taken on as a salesman. He proceeded to travel to the UK with two of his boss's instruments and sought out an engineering company by the name of Bradmatic. He persuaded the three Bradley brothers, who ran the company, to begin production of an instrument like those he had brought with him. The Bradleys believed that they were the property of Fransen himself. The result was the mellotron, constructed with a few design improvements but sounding almost exactly the same. Eventually, Chamberlin found out what had happened. The Bradleys, realising they had effectively

THE FIRST TIME

Chamberlin

The essential point about a synthesizer is that it is a device that generates an electronic tone capable of being shaped and modified by further circuitry controlled by the user. The end result is a sound that has been 'synthesized', created by the player. Electric keyboards, such as the Hammond organ, the Fender Rhodes electric piano, or the clavioline, delivering a variety of preset sounds that cannot be significantly altered, are not synthesizers.

Robert Fripp of King Crimson, who had considerable experience of dealing with mellotrons on tour, once memorably stated, "tuning a mellotron doesn't!"

Mike Pinder playing the mellotron with the Moody Blues

Stylophone advert

The first Moog synthesizer

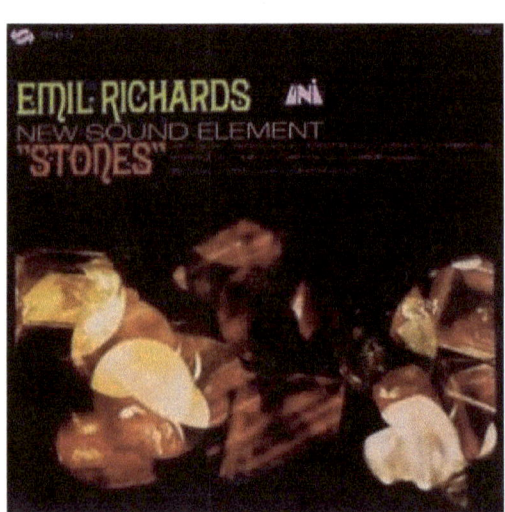

been conned, but reluctant to cease production of an instrument that was beginning to make some headway, reached an agreement whereby, on payment of a substantial sum of money, they could continue in the UK, leaving Chamberlin to cater to the American market.

In the UK, home music customers were also the original focus. Princess Margaret became one of the owners. Soon, however, professional musicians were also interested. The first mellotron on record was played by Graham Bond on both sides of his July 1965 single, *Lease On Love/My Heart's In Little Pieces*. He recorded two further tracks, *Hear Me Calling Your Name* and *Baby Can It Be True*, on the second LP by the Graham Bond Organisation, *There's A Bond Between Us*, released at the end of 1965. A mellotron makes a contribution to the maelstrom of sound on the Beatles' *Tomorrow Never Knows*, released in August 1966 as the last track on the LP *Revolver*. More obviously, Manfred Mann played one on the group's October 1966 hit, *Semi-Detached Suburban Mr James* and Paul McCartney played one on the Beatles' *Strawberry Fields For Ever*, released in February 1967. The Moody Blues, whose keyboard player, Mike Pinder, had worked for the Bradleys, testing the mellotrons when they were first being made, decided to make the instrument a central feature of their sound. It first appeared on the September 1967 single, *Love And Beauty*, which was not a hit, but was then used throughout the LP, *Days Of Future Passed*, which was.

In the US, the chamberlin remained at a lower profile. Producers Gary Paxton and Curt Boettcher owned two of the instruments, but the albums on which they used them during 1966-68, by the Gosdin Brothers, Jan And Dean, and Sagittarius, were not big sellers. In retrospect, it is apparent that the chamberlin was used by Brian Wilson on the LP *Wild Honey*, most obviously on the track *Country Air*, but nothing was made of this at the time and the Beach Boys, who were experiencing a lull in popularity, were rewarded with one of their worst selling albums. Through the seventies, the chamberlin was used by David Bowie on several albums (most notably on the instrumental track *Warszawa*) and even by the Moody Blues (on their album *Seventh Sojourn*) but by then, the mellotron had become so well known that it was assumed this was the instrument involved. Even today, the credits on Bowie's *Low* album reserve judgement by printing no more than 'synthetic strings'. The 1972 album by Herbie Hancock, *Crossings*, is more forthright. It credits Hancock with playing a mellotron, but given that he would have bought the instrument in the USA, it is much more likely that it was actually a chamberlin.

The stylophone was introduced in 1968 as a miniature, battery operated instrument, with a keyboard so small that it had to be played with a little stick (or stylus) rather than with the fingers. (The stylus was an essential item too in completing an electrical circuit when touching the metal keyboard and thereby generating the sound.) The stylophone was given a substantial advertising campaign, which centred on the sponsorship of entertainer Rolf Harris. It became viewed as a children's toy, rather than something for creating worthwhile music and it would not have been included in this chapter at all, were it not for the fact that David Bowie decided to use one as a major ingredient within the song that became his first big hit in 1969, *Space Oddity*.

The first synthesizer using a keyboard to play its sounds was developed by Robert Moog and Herbert Deutsch in 1964. The sounds were generated and treated electronically by transistor circuits – in principle any timbre imaginable or not could be created by such an instrument, although in practice synthesizer sounds are immediately recognisable as being produced by it. The Stearns Collection of Musical Instruments at the University of Michigan houses the first Moog synthesizer, built for New York choreographer Alwin Nikolais in October 1964. It follows the typical Moog design, whereby different modules can be connected together in different ways in order to send different signals to the keyboard. Herbert Deutsch composed the first piece for Moog synthesizer in September 1964, *Jazz Images – A Worksong And Blues*, but it was not recorded until 2012.

The first recording to feature the Moog synthesizer was the LP *Stones* by xylophone player Emil Richards, released in early 1967. Paul Beaver was employed to set up the synthesizer for Richards to play, although only two tracks do more than present a novelty easy-listening experience. *Emerald* and *Opal*, which are rather more experimental, show what the album could have been if Emil Richards had been bolder and are the most effective at demonstrating

THE FIRST TIME

> The release date of the *Stones* LP is variously given as 1966, 1967, or even 1968. It has the catalogue number 73008 on the UNI label, started by MCA in 1966 as a rock specialist. Eight numbers into the series is unlikely to have taken it into 1968 – in any case, LP number 73014 is *Incense And Peppermints* by the Strawberry Alarm Clock, which was definitely released towards the end of 1967. LP number 73006 is by Johnny Booth and titled *Country '67*, while 73005 is the soundtrack to the 1967 film *Privilege*. Emil Richards, quoted in the sleeve notes for the CD reissue of *The Zodiac Cosmic Sounds* is clear that *Stones* predated it, making early 1967 a reasonable estimate.

Robert Moog

Keith Emerson

> Rick Wakeman, of course, is famous for a great deal more than merely pioneering the Minimoog. In a career studded with musical highlights, he has, like Frank Zappa, never stopped his sense of humour from being allowed to exert an influence. Only Wakeman could have had the sheer bravado to present a live event at Wembley Arena in 1975, based on his album, *The Myths And Legends Of King Arthur And The Knights Of The Round Table*, and stage it *on ice*. He has also maintained that, during a gig with Yes at Manchester in 1973, he ordered and consumed a curry on stage, during the band's performance. Not so much an indication of his boredom with the music, perhaps, as an attempt to inject some timely comedy into the proceedings.

the potential of the new instrument. The fact that he was not bold is probably the reason so few people are aware of the record. Emil Richards and Paul Beaver were both involved in an album issued in May 1967. The title *The Zodiac – Cosmic Sounds* did not entirely make clear which was the name of the group, although the fact that the tracks were all named after signs of the zodiac was a clue. In fact, however, Cosmic Sounds was made up of various session musicians gathered specifically for the record by composer Mort Garson, at the instigation of Jac Holzman, the president of Elektra records. *The Zodiac* is rock music with a psychedelic edge, in which the synthesizer is a dominant feature.

In June 1967, Paul Beaver set up a display at the Monterey International Pop Music Festival to demonstrate the Moog synthesizer. More recordings followed – *Reflections* by Diana Ross and the Supremes in July, *Strange Days* by the Doors, released in September, three tracks on the Monkees LP, *Pisces Aquarius Capricorn And Jones Ltd*, released in November, and thereafter records by the Rolling Stones, the Byrds, the Electric Flag, Simon and Garfunkel, and Paul Beaver himself, in a duo with fellow synthesizer enthusiast Bernie Krause. In October 1968, Walter Carlos (or Wendy Carlos, as the musician is now called) issued an album of music by Johann Sebastian Bach played entirely on the Moog synthesizer, called *Switched-On Bach*. Perhaps surprisingly, the LP was an enormous hit, eventually selling over a million copies. It succeeded in raising the Moog profile more than any of the rock records had done and inspired numerous easy listening albums played by the synthesizer during the next few years (Jean Jacques Perrey's *Moog Indigo* from 1970 is typical). For once, the Beatles were behind the competition. George Harrison issued an album of synthesizer music under his own name in May 1969, although half of *Electronic Sound* was actually the work of Bernie Krause. *Abbey Road*, released in September 1969, included three tracks where the Moog synthesizer was played (by the former member of Manfred Mann, Mike Vickers), but by then this was no longer remarkable.

The first live performances of Moog synthesizer music were carried out by Herbert Deutsch. A select gathering at the Moog factory in August 1965 heard his piece *A Little Night Music, The Ithaca Journal, August 6, 1965*. Almost exactly four years later, Deutsch and Chris Swanson led quartets of synthesizer players in a concert held at New York's Museum Of Modern Art. In December 1969, jazz pianist Paul Bley and his wife Annette Peacock gave the first performance of their Bley-Peacock Synthesizer Show in New York. A recording of the group had to wait until 1971, however, when a live performance from March 1971 was issued as the LP *Improvisie*. Keith Emerson, who began touring with a Moog synthesizer in August 1970, with the group Emerson Lake and Palmer, was the first rock musician to do so.

Realising the potential for synthesizer sales, if more groups could be persuaded to tour with the instrument, Robert Moog designed a cut-down version, which he called the Minimoog, which was lighter and much more manageable. A prototype was given to jazz pioneer Sun Ra in 1969, following which the instrument was made commercially available in 1970. The chaotic nature of Sun Ra's huge record catalogue makes it hard to be sure about which were the first recordings featuring the Minimoog. However, various 1969 studio performances would appear to be included on the albums *My Brother The Wind, My Brother The Wind Volume II*, and *The Night Of The Purple Moon*, of which *My Brother The Wind* was released first, in 1970. The Minimoog was adopted by several rock players from 1970, following its public introduction at a live performance in August by Dick Hyman at New York's Museum Of Modern Art. Early players included Don Preston (working with Frank Zappa), Rick Wakeman, Jan Hammer, and Keith Emerson.

Rock groups made up entirely of synthesizer players started to appear during the early seventies. Mother Mallard's Portable Masterpiece Co., led by David Borden, who had worked with Robert Moog, started recording in 1970, although the results were not issued until 1973, on the group's self-titled first LP. By then, another all synthesizer rock album had already appeared – the 1971 *Zero Time* by Tonto's Expanding Head Band. 'Tonto' was intended to stand for 'The Original New Timbral Orchestra' by the two synthesizer players responsible, Malcolm Cecil and Robert Margouleff. They had succeeded in connecting several instruments together to create the first polyphonic synthesizer. (All the individual synthesizers available at this time were monophonic, that is, they were only

THE FIRST TIME

Oberheim advertisement
September 1976

Pink Floyd A Saucerful of Secrets

Kluster Klopfzeichen

Kluster, comprising Conrad Schnitzler, Hans-Joachim Roedelius, and Dieter Mobius, recorded two studio albums in 1970 and 1971. The group's bleak sound, full of percussive noises and electronic whine, created the music that has come to be labelled 'industrial' in more recent times.

Autobahn was not the first synthesizer music hit. That honour belongs to the novelty song, *Popcorn*, which became an international success for Hot Butter in the summer of 1972, although a drummer and a bass player lurk behind the synthesizers. Even this was beaten by the 1969 single, *The Minotaur* by Dick Hyman, but this was only successful in North America and did not make the top ten even there.

capable of playing one note at a time.) By this means they were able to create relatively elaborate music without needing to carry out the extensive overdubbing that an album like *Switched-On Bach* required. The record attracted enough attention for the pair to be employed by Stevie Wonder to play synthesizers on the four albums he made during 1972 to 1974, *Music Of My Mind, Talking Book, Innervisions,* and *Fulfillingness' First Finale,* after which Wonder felt he had learned enough to play the instrument himself. The first albums by Tangerine Dream, Kraftwerk, and Kluster date from 1970. They are heavily influenced by the Pink Floyd track, *A Saucerful Of Secrets,* and are master-classes in creating records that are informed by the aesthetics of electronic music, but they do not actually include any synthesizers. Not until 1973 to 1974, with the Tangerine Dream albums *Atem* and *Phaedra,* and the Kraftwerk albums *Ralf and Florian* and *Autobahn,* are these groups producing music in which synthesizers are the primary instrument, enabling the listener to say that this is synthesizer music. The title track of *Autobahn* was drastically edited to make it short enough for a single and became a substantial hit around the world.

During the seventies, other synthesizer manufacturers emerged to rival Moog. It was the company run by Tom Oberheim that produced the first commercially available polyphonic synthesizer in early 1975, made small enough to be no problem for a touring band, and capable of playing four notes at the same time. The instrument made its recording debut on the Herbie Hancock album *Man-Child,* released in August 1975. Close behind came Joe Zawinul, playing with Weather Report on the LP *Black Market* (released in March 1976) and Stevie Wonder, whose *Songs In The Key Of Life* finally appeared in September 1976. Wonder was the first purchaser of the Oberheim polyphonic synthesizer, but he believed in taking his time over the recording process.

The chart success of Kraftwerk's *Autobahn* in 1975 ultimately led to the development of two new genres of pop music based on the playing of synthesizers, especially since Kraftwerk themselves simplified the music and made it more obviously beat-based on subsequent albums. In July 1977, Giorgio Moroder and Pete Bellotte produced a record by Donna Summer, *I Feel Love,* which began a style of dance music using synthesizers, leading to the house music of the eighties and beyond. The Human League released their first record, *Being Boiled,* in June 1978. Their application of the 'anyone can play it' punk aesthetic to music played on synthesizers inspired Gary Numan's Tubeway Army, whose single, *Are Friends Electric,* became the first major hit in a style dubbed 'synthpop', in June 1979. The success of bands like Ultravox, Depeche Mode, and Soft Cell followed soon afterwards, with the last named band adopting a duo format, a singer and a synthesizer player, that became very popular through the eighties.

In 1979, the first synthesizer capable of digital sampling, and able to be employed as a complete electronic music workstation, was produced by a company based in Australia. This was the Fairlight CMI (for 'computer musical instrument'). Peter Gabriel was the first customer, but the first recording to use the instrument was the album *Never For Ever* by Kate Bush, released in September 1980. It was programmed by Richard Burgess and John Walters from the group Landscape, who were successful themselves a few months later with the single *Einstein A Go-Go*. The rival Synclavier was introduced as a digital synthesizer in 1977, but was upgraded to incorporate a similar specification to that of the Fairlight CMI in 1982. It became particularly associated with Frank Zappa, who produced music created and performed entirely on the instrument, most notably on the albums *Jazz From Hell,* from 1986, and *Civilization Phaze III,* the last new music made by Zappa before his death in 1993.

The home keyboards that started to become popular during the eighties, made by Yamaha, Casio, and other companies, were all in essence digital polyphonic synthesizers. The cheapest relied on a selection of preset sounds, while further up the quality scale increasing amounts of sound shaping – programming – became available, making the instruments useful to professional musicians too. Continuing developments in electronic technology enabled them to be small and inexpensive.

The melodica uses no electricity and appears to be a kind of recorder that just happens to have some piano keys in place of the customary holes. Essentially, however, the instrument is a miniature, portable harmonium, in which the air stream is provided not by pedals but by the player's lungs. The melodica was first manufactured by Hohner during

Mid eighties Casio advertisement for a short-lived attempt to make keyboard players look like guitarists

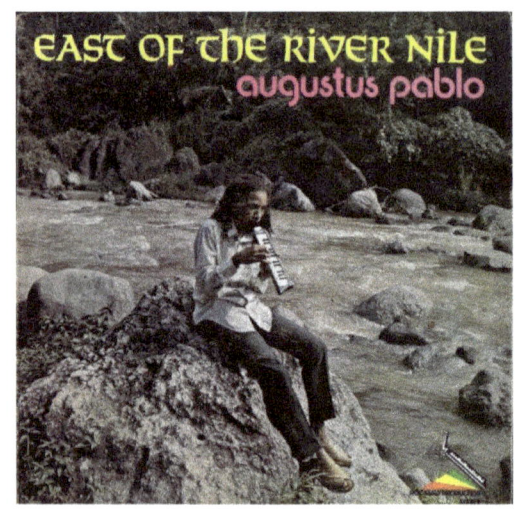

the fifties, although a very similar instrument called the harmoniphon, which consisted of a keyboard activated by blowing through a flexible tube, was invented in Paris in 1836. Two rather different pieces of music featuring the melodica were created in May 1966. Steve Reich's *Melodica* uses the instrument to play one of his phase-shifting experiments. Ray Davies, on the other hand, simply uses a melodica to add colour to his song, *A Sunny Afternoon*.

Reggae musician Augustus Pablo adopted the melodica as his instrument on a number of recordings, beginning with *East Of The River Nile*, released as a single in 1971. It was doubtless Pablo's example that persuaded a number of more recent artists to incorporate the melodica into some of their music, including Damon Albarn, New Order, The Gang Of Four, Depeche Mode, R.E.M., and Oasis. Despite the 'no electricity' claim made at the start of the previous paragraph, Korg did actually make an electric melodica (the pepe) for Joe Zawinul. He used it on his 1989 album, *Black Water*.

TRACKING THE TRACKS

The Fats Waller organ pieces *Go Down Moses* and *Deep River* are included on the 4 CD set *The Complete Recorded Works Volume 5 1938-1940* (JSP 2008). For anyone not wanting quite so much Waller, they are also available on the CD *London Suites* (Going For A Song 2000) or the CD *Fats Waller In London* (Disques Swing 1992).

Ethel Smith's *Tico Tico* is on the CD *Tico Tico – 28 Original Mono Recordings 1944-1952* (Sanctuary Living Era 2004). A clip of her performing the piece in the film *Bathing Beauty* can be seen on YouTube.

The recommended Blue Note album by Jimmy Smith is *The Sermon*, which was originally issued in 1958 (Capitol/Blue Note 1999)

There are several compilations of tracks by Booker T and the MGs and they all include *Green Onions*. *The Best Of Booker T & The MGs* (Atlantic 1991) is as good as any.

Georgie Fame's *Yeh Yeh* is on several compilations. The most recent is *Yeh Yeh – The Georgie Fame Collection* (Spectrum 2015), which also includes two tracks from the LP *Rhythm And Blues At The Flamingo*. The complete album is only available as an expensive Japanese import (Polydor 2014) although it is also included as part of the five CD boxed set that collects together all of the LPs that Fame recorded for UK Columbia in the sixties, together with numerous out-takes – *The Whole World's Shaking* (Universal 2015).

Gimme Some Loving is on the double CD by the Spencer Davis Group, *Eight Gigs A Week – The Steve Winwood Years* (Island 1996). On most other CD issues, the song is the version issued in the US. It is the same recording, but a different, inferior mix that boosts the piano part and the backing vocals at the expense of the Hammond organ. *Bluesbreakers – John Mayall With Eric Clapton* (Polygram/Deram 2000) includes both the mono and the stereo mixes of the original album, although the listener will struggle to hear the difference. *A Whiter Shade Of Pale* is included as a bonus track on the CD issue of Procol Harum's self-titled first album (Esoteric 2015).

The Nice *Live At The Fillmore East December 1969* is a double CD that acts an excellent showcase for Keith Emerson's Hammond organ playing, including the parts when he appeared to get a little carried away.

The House Of The Rising Sun is the first track on *The Best Of The Animals* (EMI 2000). *The Very Best Of The Doors* (which includes the track *Strange Days*) (Rhino 2007); *The Dave Clark Five – The Hits* (Universal 2008); and *Texas Fever – Best Of Sir Douglas Quintet* (Aim 1998) are good compilations. *I'm Down*, on which John Lennon plays a solo on the Vox Continental, is included on the Beatles' *Past Masters* double CD (EMI 2009). A video clip of the Beatles performing the song at Shea Stadium is on YouTube, although the quality is not great.

There is a nice promo video on YouTube of Elvis Costello and the Attractions performing *Radio Radio* in 1978, with Steve Naïve playing a Vox Continental.

Chest Fever, the track on which Garth Hudson demonstrates his prowess on the Lowrey organ, is on the 1968 Band album *Music From Big Pink* (Capitol 2000). An impressive longer live version, with the solo introduction given a separate title, *The Genetic Method*, is on the 1972 live Band double CD, *Rock Of Ages* (Capitol 2001). Mike Ratledge demonstrates his prowess on the live *Facelift* on the 1970 Soft Machine album *Third* (Sony 2007). *Lucy In The Sky With Diamonds* is on the 1967 Beatles album, *Sgt Pepper's Lonely Hearts Club Band* (EMI 2009). *Baba O'Riley* is on the 1971 Who album, *Who's Next* (Polydor 1999).

Percy Sledge's *When A Man Loves A Woman* is included with numerous other sixties Atlantic soul classics on the double CD *The Definitive Sound Of Atlantic Soul* (Warner 1999). *The Best Of Sam The Sham And The Pharoahs* is on a Spectrum CD (1999). Any of Pink Floyd's sixties recordings serve to highlight Rick Wright's Farfisa organ playing. *Relics* (EMI 1995) proves a good overview. Hugh Banton's Farfisa organ playing on *The Least We Can Do Is Wave To Each Other* by Van Der Graaf Generator (EMI/Virgin 2005) is remarkable.

THE FIRST TIME

Super-Sonic Jazz

The Duke Ellington electric piano tracks are unfortunately only available on the expensive 5 CD set, *The Complete Capitol Recordings* (Mosaic 1999). *Super-Sonic Jazz* by Sun Ra is on an Evidence CD (1991). The two tracks originally issued as singles, with other tracks recorded in 1956 and 1960, are on *Angels And Demons At Play,* which was originally issued as a Saturn LP in 1965. On CD (Evidence 1993) this is combined with another Saturn LP from 1966, which comprises tracks recorded in 1958-9, with Sun Ra playing electric piano on some of them. Even when reissued on CD, Sun Ra's catalogue continues to be chaotic. *What'd I Say* and *Night Time is the Right Time* by Ray Charles are on the double CD, *The Definitive Ray Charles* (Warner 2001).

Charles Trenet's *L'âme des Poètes* is included on the clumsily titled '*Le Fou Chantant*' – *La Mer – A Centenary Tribute – His 27 Finest 1937-1954* (Retrospective Records 2013). Jean Jacques Perrey's *Prélude au Sommeil* has not been reissued on CD. The original LP is extremely rare – only one copy has been sold on E-Bay in recent years (at nearly two hundred pounds). At the time of writing, however, the full album can be heard on YouTube. Perrey's *Mister Ondioline* was originally issued as a four track EP. Again, this is rare and is not available on CD, but it can be heard on YouTube. Its music, which is like a novelty soundtrack to a series of children's cartoons, is very different to the impressionistic music on the earlier album.

Kai Winding's *More* is on the CD *Soul Surfin'* (Verve 2012). *I Think We're Alone Now* by Tommy James and the Shondells is on *Anthology* (EMI 2007). *His Holy Modal Majesty* by Al Kooper and Mike Bloomfield is on *Super Session* (Sony 2003). *Telstar* and other hits by the Tornados are on *Telstar – The Original Sixties Hits Of The Tornados* (Music Club 1994). The Beatles' *Baby You're A Rich Man* is on *Magical Mystery Tour* (EMI 2009). Del Shannon's *Runaway* is on *Keep Searchin' And Other Great Hits Of The 60s* (Castle Select 2001), or *Runaway – The Very Best Of Del Shannon* (Universal 2010), or several other Del Shannon compilations.

Both sides of the Graham Bond 1965 single are included as bonus tracks on the CD *Love Is The Law* (Sunrise 2004). *There's A Bond Between Us* is packaged with Bond's first album, *The Sound Of 65*, on a double CD (Beat Goes On 1999). Manfred Mann's *Semi-Detached Suburban Mr James* is on *The Very Best Of The Fontana Years* (Spectrum 1997) or on several other compilation albums by the group. The Beatles' *Tomorrow Never Knows* is on *Revolver* (EMI 2009); *Strawberry Fields For Ever* is on *Magical Mystery Tour* (EMI 2009). The Moody Blues' *Days Of Future Passed* is on a Universal/Decca CD (2008). *Love And Beauty* is included as a bonus track.

Jan And Dean's *Save For A Rainy Day*, featuring the chamberlin, was recorded by Dean Torrence on his own while Jan Berry was recovering from a serious car accident. Columbia records decided not to release the album, leaving Torrence to issue it privately. It is available on a CD, however (Sundazed 1996). *Present Tense* by Sagittarius is on a Sony CD (2004). *Sounds Of Goodbye* by the Gosdin Brothers is on a Big Beat CD (2003). The Beach Boys' *Wild Honey* is combined with the *Smiley Smile* album on a Capitol CD (2001). David Bowie's *Warszawa* is on *Low* (EMI 1999). The Moody Blues' *Seventh Sojourn* is on a Universal/Decca CD (2008). Herbie Hancock's *Crossings* is on a Warner CD (2001).

David Bowie's *Space Oddity* is on the double CD *Best Of Bowie* (EMI 2002).

The two Herbert Deutsch tracks mentioned are included on the CD *From Moog To Mac* (Ravello 2012). Emil Richards' *Stones* is on an Omni CD (2012), which also includes the 1968 album *Journey To Bliss,* which does not use a synthesizer. *The Zodiac* by Cosmic Sounds is on an Elektra CD (2002). The Amazon catalogue entry for the album gets the title and artist name the wrong way round.

INSTRUMENTS AND MUSICIANS

The Nonesuch Guide To Electronic Music by Beaver and Krause (Collectors' Choice 2005) includes three or four short synthesizer pieces, but is mostly a demonstration of the basic techniques available to the instrument. As such, it is interesting but not designed for repeated listening. The albums that Beaver and Krause made in 1970 and 1971, *In A Wild Sanctuary* and *Gandharva,* are very good and are recommended, although the synthesizers are mixed in with other instruments. The albums are available combined on a single CD (Warner 1994).

Reflections is available on several different Diana Ross and the Supremes anthologies, such as *The Definitive Collection* (Universal/Motown 2009). The Monkees' *Pisces Aquarius Capricorn & Jones Ltd* is on a Rhino CD (2011).

Synthesizers can be heard on *The Notorious Byrd Brothers* by the Byrds (Columbia 1997), *A Long Time Comin'* by the Electric Flag (Sony 2013), *Bookends* by Simon and Garfunkel (Sony 2001), and *Abbey Road* by the Beatles (EMI 2009). The Rolling Stones bought a Moog synthesizer in September 1968 but seemed strangely reluctant to use it on record. It finally makes an appearance on the 1974 album, *It's Only Rock 'n' Roll* (Polydor 2009).

Switched-On Bach, now credited to Wendy Carlos, is most recently on an East Side Digital CD (2001), although this has become quite hard to find. Jean Jacques Perrey's *Moog Indigo* (Ace 1996) has acquired a cover upgrade from the basic design of the original vinyl release – now it appears to be inspired by P.P.Arnold (whose *Kafunta* album from 1968 has a similar cover design).

Paul Bley's *Improvisie* (Universal 2005) is one of three albums issued by his synthesizer show with Annette Peacock (four if we include Peacock's own *I'm The One*). ELP's *Pictures At An Exhibition* (Sony 2011) has Keith Emerson playing his synthesizer in concert.

The three Sun Ra Minimoog albums mentioned are hard to find. *The Night Of The Purple Moon* was issued on an Atavistic CD (2007), *My Brother The Wind Volume II* on an Evidence CD (1992). *My Brother The Wind* has not so far made it on to CD at all.

Don Preston first plays the Minimoog on the Mothers' album *Fillmore East June 1971* (Ryko 2006). Unfortunately, this is a candidate for Frank Zappa's worst album, although this is certainly not Don Preston's fault. Rick Wakeman first played his Minimoog on the Strawbs' 1971 album, *From The Witchwood* (A&M 1998). Jan Hammer first played his on the 1973 Mahavishnu Orchestra album, *Birds Of Fire* (Columbia 2010). Rick Wakeman's *The Myths And Legends Of King Arthur And His Knights Of The Round Table* is on A&M (2014).

There is a good compilation of music by Mother Mallard's Portable Masterpiece Co. on CD, *1970-1973* (Cuneiform 1999). *Zero Time* by Tonto's Expanding Head Band is on a Prog Temple CD (2012). The Stevie Wonder albums featuring synthesizers are *Music Of My Mind, Talking Book, Innervisions, Fulfillingness' First Finale,* and the double *Songs In The Key Of Life.* All are on Universal/Motown (2000).

The first Tangerine Dream album is *Electronic Meditation* (Esoteric 2012). *Atem* is also on an Esoteric CD (2011); *Phaedra* is on a Virgin CD (1995). The first Kraftwerk album is simply named after the group (Crown 2001), although it is preceded by the 1969 album *Tone Float* (Crown 1996, with Kraftwerk named on the front), credited to Organisation, which included the Kraftwerk founders, Ralf Hütter and Florian Schneider-Esleben. *Ralf & Florian* is on a Crown CD (2001); *Autobahn* is on an EMI CD (2009). The 1978 album *The Man Machine* (Mute 2009) finds Kraftwerk moving into proto-synth-pop territory. The first album by the less well-known Kluster is *Klopfzeichen* (Bureau B 2012).

Herbie Hancock's *Man-Child* is on a Columbia CD (1992); Weather Report's Black Market is also on a Columbia CD (2002).

Donna Summer's *I Feel Love* is on several compilations, such as the double CD *I Feel Love – The Collection* (Spectrum 2013). *Being Boiled* by the Human League is on several compilations too, such as *Greatest Hits* (Virgin 1988). *Are Friends Electric?* is on *Premier Hits* by Gary Numan/Tubeway Army (Beggars Banquet 2001). Ultravox, Depeche Mode, and Soft Cell all have greatest hits compilations: *Ultravox The Collection* (EMI 1990), *The Best Of Depeche Mode Volume 1* (Mute 2006), and *The Very Best Of Soft Cell* (Universal 2002).

Never For Ever by Kate Bush is on an EMI CD (1992). Landscape's *Einstein A Go-Go* is on *From The Tea-rooms Of Mars....* (Cherry Red 2002). Frank Zappa's *Jazz From Hell,* with only one track not performed on the Synclavier, is on Zappa Records (2012); *Civilization Phaze III,* which includes some of the most remarkable music made by a man who was indeed a thoroughly remarkable musician, is also on Zappa Records (1994).

Popcorn by Hot Butter is on the various artists compilation CD *Super Hits 1972* (King 2004). A whole album of the group, called *Popcorn*, is on Castle (2005), but it is deleted and becoming expensive. Dick Hyman's *The Minotaur* was originally issued on a 1969 LP called *Moog – The Electric Eclectics Of Dick Hyman.* The CD issue of this is deleted and expensive, but its tracks are combined with the earlier album, *Moon Gas*, on a CD entitled *Moon Gas* (Captain High 2015).

Steve Reich's *Melodica* can be heard on YouTube. Ray Davies' *A Sunny Afternoon* is on a number of Kinks compilations, such as *Kinks – The Ultimate Collection* (Sanctuary 2002). *East Of The River Nile* by Augustus Pablo is on a CD album with the same title (Shanachie 2002). Songs by the artists mentioned which include a melodica are *Clint Eastwood* (Gorillaz), *Your Silent Face* (New Order), *Ether* (The Gang Of Four), *Everything Counts* (Depeche Mode), *Find The River* (R.E.M.), and *Champagne Supernova* (Oasis). *Black Water* by The Zawinul Syndicate is on a CBS CD (1989).

THE FIRST TIME

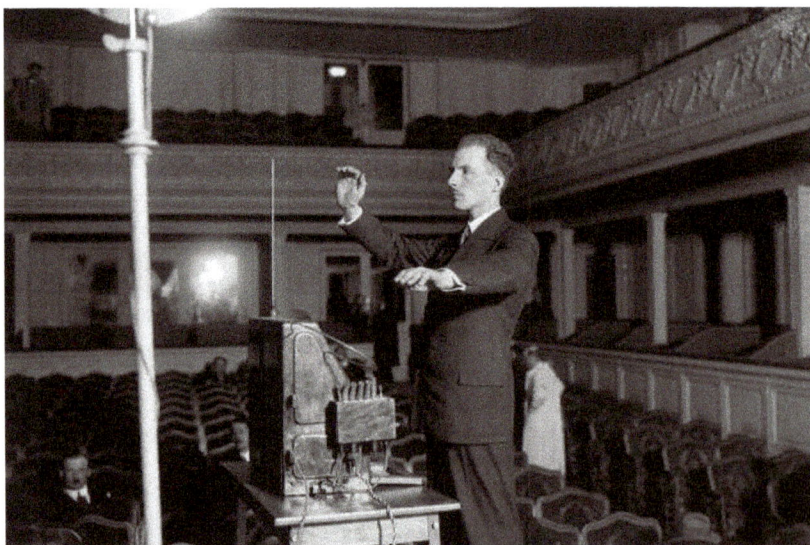

Leon Theremin with his invention

Barbara Buchholz playing a modern theremin

Mike Love playing the Moog ribbon controller

From the back cover of Presenting
Lothar and the Hand People

Ondes martenot

4 ELECTRONICS

Although electric keyboards and guitars have already been covered, there is much electronic music produced by other mechanisms and techniques. It is these that are the subject of this chapter. The first electronic instrument – one with no mechanical elements to help produce the sound – was the theremin, invented in 1920 by the Russian Leon Theremin (a Westernised version of his real name, Lev Termin). Two metal antennae sense the positions of the player's hands as they move around and convert the information into electronic sound. It is extremely difficult to exert any kind of accurate pitch control over this sound, although players like Lydia Kavina (the grand-daughter of Theremin's cousin), Clara Rockmore, and Barbara Buchholz seemed to manage it.

Joseph Schillinger wrote the first piece of music for the theremin in 1929, *First Airphonic Suite*. In 1935 the instrument was used in the soundtrack music for the film *Bride Of Frankenstein*, starring Boris Karloff. Several other films followed this example, finding the theremin ideal for conveying the required scary atmosphere in horror sequences. Miklos Roza, who used the instrument in his soundtrack for Alfred Hitchcock's 1945 film, *Spellbound*, was awarded an Oscar for his work. Lothar and the Hand People were formed in 1965 as a rock group using a theremin (the instrument was Lothar). The group issued three singles in 1967 and a first album, *Presenting Lothar and the Hand People*, in 1968. Since, however, the group also used a Moog synthesizer, it was not always clear what was theremin and what was synthesizer. The Rolling Stones album, *Their Satanic Majesties Request*, released in December 1967, uses a mellotron but not a synthesizer, making it easy to distinguish the brief theremin part that features during the track *2000 Light Years From Home*.

An instrument designed to replicate the sound of the theremin, but with the notes being controlled by a long slider (and therefore easier to use) was built by Paul Tanner and Bob Whitsell in 1958. Tanner was a trombonist with Glenn Miller and others, so knew all about slide mechanisms. He played his electro-theremin (or tannerin) with Andre Montero and his Orchestra on an LP called *Music For Heavenly Bodies*. When Brian Wilson wanted the sound of a tuned theremin on the 1966 Beach Boys songs, *Good Vibrations* and *I Just Wasn't Made For These Times*, he contacted Paul Tanner, whose instrument was still the only one to have been made. Tanner played on the records, although a contemporary film clip of the group performing *Good Vibrations* live shows Mike Love playing the Moog ribbon controller, a dedicated synthesizer built specifically to enable the group to play the song in concert.

The ondes martenot, an electronic instrument that also uses a slider control, was invented in 1927 by a French cellist, Maurice Martenot. The instrument initially had a dummy keyboard as well, intended as a marker for the slide, to enable it to be played with precision. Dimitrios Levidis composed the first work for the ondes martenot in the year of its invention, *Poème Symphonique* (a new arrangement of a piece written for violin the year before). Olivier Messiaen took advantage of the first model to include a functioning keyboard, designed to enable an unusually wide vibrato to complement the slide sounds. He composed *Fêtes des Belles Eaux* in 1937, employing six of the instruments. His celebrated *Turangalila Symphony*, which also has a prominent ondes martenot part, was completed in 1948. Over a thousand works have been composed with a role for the ondes martenot. In popular music, the earliest appearance for the instrument was in 1952 with the Edith Piaf song, *Je T'ai Dans La Peau*. It has not often been used in rock, whose musicians prefer their synthesizers, but it does feature on the 1975 albums, *Où Est Passée La Noce* and *Les Cinq Saisons* by the Canadian groups Beau Dommage and Harmonium. More recently, it was used in a few songs by Radiohead, starting with *The National Anthem* and *How To Disappear Completely* on the 2000 album, *Kid A*.

A third electronic instrument, the trautonium, was invented in 1930 in Germany by Friedrich Trautwein. Sounds were produced when a wire was pressed against a metal plate, with the notes being dependent on where the wire was

THE FIRST TIME

Trautonium

Magnetophon K1 tape recorder

The fascination that some musicians have for trains is evident in several blues songs, where a harmonica, played to an appropriate rhythm, is also used to replicate the train whistle. John Mayall's *Catch That Train* uses a recording of the real thing to accompany his harmonica playing. Later, his band improvised around the concept on a piece called *The Train*. In what may well have been a deliberate reference back to Pierre Schaeffer, Steve Reich used the sounds and the rhythms of trains as a major ingredient in his masterful 1988 work, *Different Trains*.

Although it is not in any way an electronic work, *Ionisation* by Edgard Varèse, composed in 1929-31, was enormously influential on the subsequent music that is. Scored entirely for percussion instruments, including sirens and a lion's roar, *Ionisation* presents music that consists of organised sound, with timbre and texture but no melodic content at all. As it happens, it is also an extremely powerful and moving piece of music. Later pieces by Varèse suggest that he was indeed simply waiting for the appropriate technology to arrive. His *Déserts*, composed between 1950 and 1954, is partly electronic; *Poème Electronique*, from 1957-8, is entirely so.

touched. It was not a commercial success, perhaps because it was too similar to the ondes martenot, but the composer Paul Hindemith wrote *Seven Pieces for Three Trautoniums* in 1930 and *Concert Piece for Trautonium and Strings* in 1931.

In 1930, composers Paul Hindemith and Ernst Toch presented a programme of short works as part of a festival of contemporary music in Berlin. The two Hindemith pieces, *Trickaufnahmen*, and the three Toch pieces, *Gesprochene Musik*, both employed pre-recorded music on discs that were then manipulated by playing at different speeds and used to create new recordings of the finished work. The two composers effectively invented the concept of turntables as instruments that was taken up again in a somewhat different context by Grandmaster Flash and others in the seventies.

The tape recorder, using plastic tape coated in iron oxide, which could be magnetised, was developed during the thirties, although its ancestor, a device that recorded by scratching a wave form on to a wax coated paper tape, was patented by Alexander Graham Bell in 1886. The Magnetophone K1, the first practical reel-to-reel machine, was made by the German company AEG in 1935, using tape manufactured by BASF. A recording of an unknown piano and cello sonata comprises the first tape recording, made on April 27th 1935, and it can be heard on YouTube.

The existence of tape recording made it possible to create music by processing and manipulating sounds deriving from a variety of sources. The tape could be varied in speed, played backwards, frequency filtered, edited, and so on. This was first done by the Egyptian composer Halim El-Dabh, with a 1944 piece called *Ta'abir al-Zaar (The Expression Of Zaar)*. The result sounds like an electronic work and had it been created twenty years later, the listener would have assumed that it was all produced by a synthesizer. In fact, the original sound sources are entirely acoustic. Working independently, the Frenchman Pierre Schaeffer produced similar pieces on tape, starting with *Etude aux Chemins de Fer* in 1948, which turned the sounds made by trains into music. He used the phrase 'musique concrète' to describe music produced in this way.

Through the fifties and beyond, a number of works were created by the techniques of magnetic tape treatment, using either acoustic sources, or sine wave tones generated electronically, or both. The classical music world chooses Karlheinz Stockhausen's *Gesang der Jünglinge* from 1955-6 as the first electronic masterpiece, without argument. It is a work that combines electronic sine wave tones and clicks with human voices and processes both. As far as the general public is concerned, the first significant electronic work comes a little later, with the theme music for the *Doctor Who* television series, produced in 1963 by Delia Derbyshire and the BBC Radiophonic Workshop. In between came *Song Of The Second Moon*, created in 1957 by Tom Dissevelt and Dick Raaijmakers (calling himself Kid Baltan) as the first piece of electronic pop music. Tape processing was used within the music of the Beatles, Pink Floyd, and other groups during the late sixties, but the first electronic rock album produced entirely in this manner would have been in 1967, if Paul McCartney had decided to release his *Carnival Of Light*. It remains unissued – the versions that can be heard on the internet are no more than ideas of what the music might have sounded like. As it is, the first album was *An Electric Storm*, issued in June 1969 and credited to White Noise, who turned out to be David Voorhaus and two members of the BBC Radio Radiophonic Workshop, Brian Hodgson and Delia Derbyshire.

Organs and pianos played by rolls of paper tape punched with holes were developed during the 1840s, but in 1930, the Frenchmen Edouard Coupleaux and Armand Givelet designed and built an organ, in which a paper tape controlled the timbre. The organ was installed in a number of French churches, but ultimately lost out commercially to the Hammond organ. Nevertheless, when RCA engineers Harry Olson and Herbert Belar were tasked at the start of the fifties with building an entirely electronic machine to compose and play music, they revived the punched paper tape idea. The resulting RCA Synthesizer Mark I comprised a huge collection of modules that filled an entire room. Having established that it worked, Olson and Belar proceeded to build the improved Mark II synthesizer in 1957. It was installed at the Columbia-Princeton Electronic Music Centre in New York. Milton Babbitt was hired to work with the Mark II and in 1961 he produced his *Composition for Synthesizer*. With the development of the Moog just three years later, the RCA instrument became obsolete. It had been used very little, although it was employed in 1968-69 by

Milton Babbitt and the RCA Mark II synthesizer on the cover of a CD issued on John Zorn's Tzadik label.

VCS3 synthesizer

Raymond Scott invented a number of electronic instruments during the fifties, including one he called the clavivox, which was essentially a theremin equipped with a keyboard. He had no interest in marketing his inventions, however, and none were taken up or recorded by anyone else. Scott himself produced electronic advertising jingles and a three LP set in 1964 titled *Soothing Sounds for Baby*. He began working on a device intended to generate melodies and rhythms, the electronium, which was bought by Berry Gordy of Motown, despite not being a finished product. It never appeared on any recording, mainly because Scott never did succeed in completing the work on it to his own satisfaction.

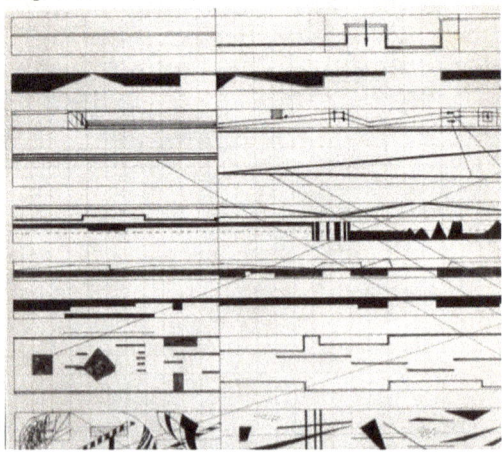

Delia Derbyshire and Peter Zinovieff start the computer at the Queen Elizabeth Hall

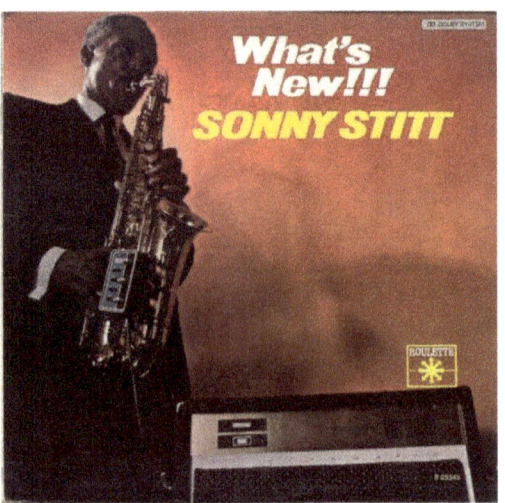

INSTRUMENTS AND MUSICIANS

Charles Wuorinen for *Time's Encomium*, which won a Pulitzer prize.

The instrument designed by Donald Buchla was the first commercially available synthesizer in 1966, beating the Moog to the marketplace. Morton Subotnick produced his *Silver Apples Of The Moon* on it in 1967. The first electronic work to be actually commissioned by a record company, this was released on an album by Nonesuch/Elektra the same year. Buffy Sainte-Marie's 1969 album, *Illuminations*, also used the Buchla synthesizer, but the instrument failed to generate any wider interest due to the fact that its inventor had decided to employ an innovative array of touch and pressure sensitive surfaces for its control, rather than a more user-friendly keyboard.

Another rival to the Moog synthesizer was the VCS3 (Voltage Controlled Studio version 3), manufactured by the Electronic Music Studios company, run by Peter Zinovieff. It was designed as a small, portable instrument that could reproduce some of what Zinovieff's extensive studio equipment was capable of, and it became available in 1969, a year before the Minimoog. Although it could be connected to a keyboard, the synthesizer could also be controlled using a joystick. It was the somewhat random nature of the resulting sounds, especially since they had a tendency to drift out of tune, that appealed to Brian Eno, who played the instrument with Roxy Music during 1972-3. The group's first album was released in June 1972. *The Unusual Classical Synthesizer* by Mike Hankinson was also released in 1972. It comprised interpretations of a number of classical music pieces, attempting to do for the VCS3 what *Switched On Bach* had done for the Moog. It did not manage this, if only because the bar for this kind of electronic classical music was seriously raised soon afterwards by the release of Tomita's collection of pieces by Debussy, *Snowflakes Are Dancing* (performed on a Moog). As far as being the first to use a VCS3 on record was concerned, both Roxy Music and Mike Hankinson were beaten by Hawkwind, whose Dik Mik (Michael Davies) played it. Hawkwind's self-titled first album was recorded in March and April 1970, released in August. The group's *Silver Machine*, which was a substantial chart hit during the second half of 1972 and highlighted the VCS3, was probably responsible for the adoption of the synthesizer by a number of other rock artists through the seventies. Peter Sinfield claims to have bought the first (or maybe the second) VCS3 around the time he became a member of King Crimson, although he did not get the opportunity to use it with the group until the recording of its third LP, *Lizard*, released in December 1970.

It was Peter Zinovieff who put together a compilation LP in 1968, *Cybernetic Serendipity Music*, designed to advertise the concept of music produced by computer. It was originally released to accompany an exhibition at the ICA in London with the same title. The first track was *Illiac Suite (Experiment 4)*, a 1957 piece for string quartet where, for the first time, the actual composition was completely carried out by a computer. It was programmed by Lajaren Hiller and Leonard Isaacson, who get the composing credit on the record. Curiously, the music sounds far more conventional than many purely human string quartets being produced at the time. *Composition 3* by Gerald Strang, produced in 1966 and also included on the LP, was both composed and performed by a computer and sounds much more satisfyingly bizarre, although it is barely more than two minutes long. Peter Zinovieff himself, who had long been interested in the use of computers for producing music and who also had a piece included on the LP, presented a concert at the Queen Elizabeth Hall in January 1968, where a computer was left alone on the stage to play music it was inventing itself (*Partita For Unattended Computer*).

With synthesizers becoming a major ingredient in several areas of music from the seventies onwards, it is not surprising that attempts were made to give access to the instrument's soundscape for musicians who were not keyboard players. The synthaxe and the guitar synthesizer, referred to in the electric guitar chapter of this book, achieved this for guitarists. Of course, guitars were already instruments that employed electricity. Saxophones were not, although Eddie Harris and Sonny Stitt pioneered the use of a dedicated electronic pickup for their instrument, the Varitone. Both men issued albums in 1966 featuring the device, somewhat discreetly – *What's New* by Sonny Stitt (recorded in June or July) and *The Tender Storm* by Eddie Harris (recorded in September). There is supposed to be a private recording of John Coltrane experimenting with the Varitone at this time, but it has not become generally available. Clark Terry used the device to amplify his trumpet on the 1967 album, *It's What's Happenin'*. The lyricon, a

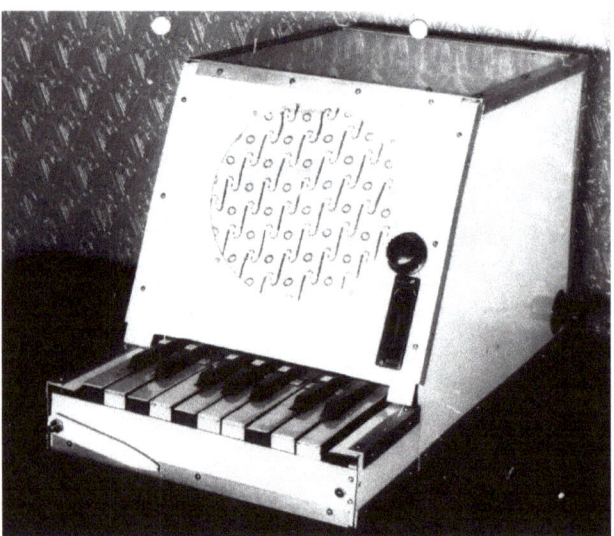
Rhythmicon (Theremin's third machine, built in the sixties)

Early 1981 advertisement for the Linn LM-1 drum machine

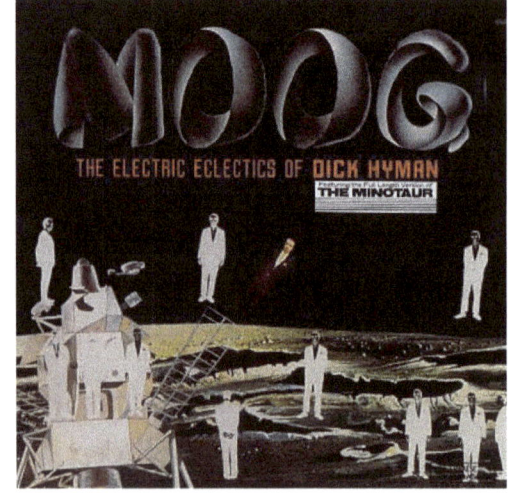

synthesizer controlled by something that looked and played like a saxophone, was developed in 1971, although it does not appear to have been recorded until late 1974, when Tom Scott used it on the L.A.Express album, *Tom Cat*.

The first drum machine was the rhythmicon, built by Leon Theremin in 1931, at the suggestion of composer Henry Cowell. Unlike the modern concept of such a machine, that it should play a regular pulse, this device was more concerned with delivering complicated rhythm patterns in odd time signatures, that would be difficult or impossible for a human musician to manage, because that was what Cowell wanted. The composer wrote a piece called *Rhythmicana* for the drum machine to play, but did not manage to finish it in time for a public rhythmicon concert in Paris at the beginning of 1932. Later Cowell renamed his work *Concerto For Rhythmicon and Orchestra*, because he decided to use the original title for something else. Only three rhythmicons were ever built.

In 1949 Harry Chamberlin built a drum machine that relied on the playback of pre-recorded tapes of real drumming – the same technology as he used in his Chamberlin keyboard instrument. He completed no more than ten machines and they never reached the marketplace, although about a hundred of an updated version were sold during the sixties. Wurlitzer offered an electronic drum machine, the Sideman, for sale in 1959. It provided a choice of twelve rhythm patterns in several tempos and was meant to be an accompaniment for the company's electric keyboards.

During the sixties, a number of machines with preset drum patterns were made by different manufacturers. Intended to provide rhythm in informal situations where a drummer was not available, it is not surprising that these early devices do not appear on record. The earliest drum machine recording that we do have is a memento of precisely one of these situations. It would not have been released at all, were it not for the fact that the artist concerned is Jimi Hendrix, a musician whose every note has become of interest to fans and collectors since his death. A demo version of *Angel*, recorded by Hendrix in November 1967, with his voice and guitar supported by only a drum machine, is included on the album *South Saturn Delta*, released in October 1997. In December 1967, the United States Of America group recorded its self-titled album, for release in early 1968. With electric instruments predominating and all the musicians credited with playing 'electric harpsichord', 'electric violin', 'electric bass', and the like, it was in keeping with the mood that Craig Woodson should be credited with 'electric drums'. What the listener hears, however, is a perfectly normal drum kit. If a drum machine was available in the studio, it seems that Woodson declined to use it.

The first commercial recordings to make use of a drum machine date from 1969. Dick Hyman's synthesizer album, *The Electric Eclectics of Dick Hyman*, and its hit single, *The Minotaur*, used one – and so did the solo album by Robin Gibb of the Bee Gees. *Saved By The Bell* was issued as a single in June 1969, with the album including it, *Robin's Reign*, following in early 1970. Gibb had fallen out with his brothers, temporarily as it turned out, but had perhaps become so disillusioned with the whole group experience as to decide not to bother with a real drummer for his album. *Somebody's Watching You*, a single by Little Sister and produced by Sly Stone, was issued in November 1970, after which recordings by four artists using drum machines were made in 1971. In order, these were *Peking O* by Can (included on the album *Tago Mago*), *'Til I Die* by the Beach Boys (included on the album *Surf's Up*), various tracks on *There's A Riot Goin' On* by Sly and the Family Stone, and various tracks on *Naturally* by J.J.Cale. Apart from their decision to use a drum machine in place of real drums, it would seem that these recordings have little in common.

During the seventies and eighties, steady advances in technology made drum machines increasingly attractive for record producers. The first programmable machine, the Eko ComputeRhythm, appeared in 1972. During the recording of the Steely Dan album, *Gaucho*, at the end of the seventies, engineer Roger Nicholls developed a device to process digital drum samples. By the time the album was released in November 1980, however, the Linn LM-1 drum computer had appeared on the market, doing the same thing. This was used on the Herbie Hancock album, *Mr Hands*, released in September. Later the same year, the Roland TR-808 tried to convince users that internally generated, deliberately unrealistic drum sounds could also be cool. The first MIDI equipped machine, enabling easy synchronisation with other electronic instruments, arrived in 1984 (the Sequential Circuits Drumtraks). Artists like Prince, Michael Jackson, Afrika Bambaata, New Order, Madonna, and the whole of the hip hop/dance music genre adopted drum machines in preference to human drummers.

THE FIRST TIME

TRACKING THE TRACKS

A performance of Joseph Schillinger's *First Airphonic Suite* can currently be seen on YouTube, introduced by Lydia Kavina, who plays the piece with Orchester Musikhochschule Karlsruhe. A CD by Lydia Kavina, *Music From The Ether*, has a version of the first part of the suite, arranged for just piano and theremin, and titled *Melody*.

The soundtrack to *Bride Of Frankenstein*, composed by Franz Waxman, is on a Silva Screen CD (1993). The music is played by the Westminster Philharmonic Orchestra, conducted by Kenneth Alwyn. The soundtrack to *Spellbound* is on an Intrada CD (2007), performed by the Slovak Radio Symphony Orchestra, conducted by Allan Wilson, with Celia Sheen playing the theremin. A Lydia Kavina CD called *Spellbound!* (Mode 2008) includes a six minute *Spellbound Suite*.

Presenting Lothar And The Hand People is on a Micro Werks CD (2010). *Their Satanic Majesties Request* by the Rolling Stones is on an Abkco CD (2002).

Music For Heavenly Bodies by Andre Montero and his Orchestra was originally issued on a scarce LP on the Omega Disk label. It has not been reissued on CD, although two people have uploaded the full album on to YouTube.

I Just Wasn't Made For These Times is on the Beach Boys album *Pet Sounds* (Capitol 2000). *Good Vibrations* is on *Smiley Smile*, issued together with *Wild Honey* (Capitol 2001). Some interesting out-take material is also included. Alternatively, the track can be heard on the CD *The Very Best Of The Beach Boys* (Capitol 2001).

Poème Symphonique by Dimitrios Levidis would not appear to have ever been recorded. Olivier Messiaen's *Fêtes des Belles Eaux* is on an Atma Classique CD (2008). There are several recordings of the *Turangalila Symphony* available. The one played by *Orchestre de l'Opéra Bastille* conducted by Myung-Whun Chung, with Messiaens' wife, Yvonne Loriod, playing the piano and her sister Jeanne playing the ondes martenot, is highly recommended (Deutsche Grammophon 2011). A second CD containing Messiaen's *Quartet For The End Of Time* is attached – this is another essential work, although the ondes martenot is not involved.

Edith Piaf's *Je T'ai Dans La Peau* is on the CD *Padam… Padam* (EMI 2000). *Ou Est Passée La Noce* by Beau Dommage is on an EMI CD (2008). This is hard to find, but the long track, *Un Incident A Bois-Des-Filion*, which includes an ondes martenot part, can be heard on YouTube. *Les Cinq Saisons* by Harmonium is on a Polydor CD (1991). This is also scarce, but again, the track with the ondes martenot, *En Pleine Face*, is on YouTube. Radiohead's *Kid A* is on an EMI CD (2000).

The Paul Hindemith works for trautonium are included on a CD by Oskar Sala, who plays the instrument and includes a much more recent work of his own, *Elektronische Impressionen*. The CD is called *Mixturtrautonium* (Erdenklang 1998), after the more sophisticated version of the trautonium developed by Sala himself.

Paul Hindemith's *Trickaufnahmen* can be heard on YouTube and there are also several versions there of the third part of Toch's *Gesprochene Musik*, titled *Fuge aus der Geographie*. With commendable virtuosity, the choirs involved perform the work live, rather than manipulating records as Toch did.

INSTRUMENTS AND MUSICIANS

A two minute extract from *The Expression Of Zaar* by Halim El-Dabh is on the CD *Crossing Into The Electric Magnetic* (Without Fear 2000). It is accurately, but unhelpfully given the title *Wire Recorder Piece*, for the full work was assembled on magnetic tape. *Etude Aux Chemins De Fer* is included with other works by Pierre Schaeffer and by Pierre Henry on *Panorama de Musique Concrète* (Cherry Red 2010).

John Mayall's *Catch That Train* is on *The Blues Alone* (Universal/Decca 2006). *The Train* is on the two CD set *The Diary Of A Band* (Universal/Decca 2007). Steve Reich's *Different Trains,* played by the Kronos Quartet, is on a CD sharing space, like the original vinyl release, with a multiple guitar work, *Electric Counterpoint*, played by Pat Metheny (WEA 1989).

Gesang der Jünglinge by Karlheinz Stockhausen shares space with a later electronic work, *Kontakte*, on the Deutsche Grammophon LP that was most recently issued in 1969. The CD, *Elektronische Musik 1952-1960* (Stockhausen-Verlag 2001) adds other works too, but is very hard to find. Fortunately, the music can be heard on YouTube.

BBC Radiophonic Workshop – 21 (Silva Screen 2016) includes forty-five pieces by various different members of the Workshop, one of which is the *Doctor Who* theme. The number in the title refers to the fact that the compilation was originally issued in 1979 to celebrate the twenty-first anniversary of the Workshop's founding.

Song Of The Second Moon by Tom Dissevelt and Kid Baltan is on a Fifth Dimension CD (2015).

Three YouTube uploads, all of them around fourteen minutes long, claim to be *The Carnival Of Light*. They are all different.

An Electric Storm by White Noise is on Island (2007).

A double CD is enough to contain everything Edgard Varèse composed. *The Complete Works* is on Universal/Decca (2004).

Milton Babbitt's *Composition For Synthesizer* was included on a 1964 Columbia LP called *Columbia-Princeton Electronic Music Center*, with electronic works by other composers. It has not been reissued on CD, but can be acquired as a paid-for mp3 download. Charles Wuorinen's *Time's Encomium* was issued on a Nonesuch LP in 1969. It has not been reissued on CD but can be heard on YouTube.

Raymond Scott's *Soothing Sounds For Baby Vols 1-3* is on three Basta CDs (2007). Morton Subotnick's *Silver Apples Of The Moon* is on a Wergo CD (1994) together with *The Wild Bull* from 1968. Buffy Sainte-Marie's *Illuminations* is on a Vanguard CD (2000).

The self-titled first album by Roxy Music, which includes the track *Virginia Plain*, is on a Virgin CD (1999). Mike Hankinson's *The Unusual Classical Synthesizer* was issued on Westminster Gold in 1972, but has not been reissued on CD. Two tracks can be heard on YouTube, but not the complete album. Tomita's *Snowflakes Are Dancing* is on a BMG CD (2000). Hawkwind's self-titled first album is on an EMI CD (2001). *Silver Machine* is included as a bonus track on the CD *In Search Of Space* (EMI 2001). King Crimson's *Lizard* is on DGM (2009).

Cybernetic Serendipity Music was originally issued on the ICA label in 1968. It was reissued in 2014 by The Vinyl Factory, but as an LP. It has not appeared on CD. *Illiac Suite* is on the CD *Computer Music Retrospective* by Lejaren Hiller (Wergo 1989). The Gerald Strang *Composition 3* can be heard on YouTube. A very short excerpt from *Partita For Unattended Computer,* included in an extract from a Peter Zinovieff documentary, is on YouTube. The event was a nice gimmick, although the reality of watching a computer run through a program is that it is akin to watching a CD player playing a CD and it is about as interesting.

Sonny Stitt's *What's New* was issued as a Pye or Roulette LP in 1966 and reissued by Roulette in 1976, with a new title, *Stardust*. It has not appeared on CD. A CD by Sonny Stitt called *What's New* is actually a different album. *The Tender Storm* by Eddie Harris is on an Atlantic/Collectables CD (2002). Clark Terry's *It's What's Happenin'* is combined with *The Happy Horns Of Clark Terry* for release on CD (Universal/Impulse 2011). *Tom Cat* by Tom Scott and the L.A. Express is on a Sony CD (1996).

According to Carol J. Oja's book, *Making Music Modern,* Henry Cowell's Rhythmicana (Concerto For Rhythmicon and Orchestra) was not performed until 1971. It does not appear to have ever been recorded (although two performances of a piano version can be heard on YouTube).

South Saturn Delta is one of the better collections of Jimi Hendrix out-takes. It is on an MCA CD (1997). The self-titled album by the United States Of America is on an Esoteric CD (2014).

Dick Hyman's *Moog – The Electric Eclectics Of Dick Hyman* was reissued on a 1997 CD that is now deleted and expensive, but its tracks are combined with the earlier album, *Moon Gas*, on a CD entitled *Moon Gas* (Captain High 2015). Robin Gibb's *Robin's Reign* is on Spectrum (1991). A three CD set on Rhino (2015), called *Saved By The Bell*, finds forty-six out-takes to add to the album. Little Sister's *Somebody's Watching You* is included on a compilation of tracks from Sly Stone's Stone Flower label, *I'm Just Like You – Sly's Stone Flower 1969-70* (Light In The Attic 2014). Can's *Tago Mago* is on a Spoon CD (2011). The Beach Boys' *'Til I Die* is on *Surf's Up* (Capitol 2012). *There's A Riot Goin' On* by Sly and the Family Stone is on Epic/Legacy (2007). J.J. Cale's *Naturally* is on Mercury (2011).

Steely Dan's *Gaucho* is on MCA (2003). Herbie Hancock's *Mr Hands* is on Columbia (1992).

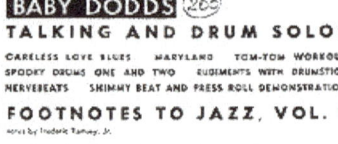

5 DRUMS AND PERCUSSION

The development of the drum kit took place rapidly during the early years of recorded jazz. The drums used by the Original Dixieland Jazz Band in 1917 comprised a large bass drum and a snare drum, adapted from their former incarnation as military band instruments. There was a small Chinese tom-tom, and there were a few other bits and pieces including a small suspended cymbal. During the next years, the set was gradually expanded by different drummers, with Baby Dodds, who worked with Louis Armstrong, being the major innovator. By 1930, the modern drum kit was essentially in place. Two or three large tom-toms were added, along with a ride cymbal and a high hat on a stand equipped with a pedal to open and close the paired cymbals, while the size of the bass drum was reduced. From that time, this remained the basic core drum kit, no matter what extra items some drummers decided to include.

Louis Bellson had the idea of adding a second bass drum to his kit at the end of the thirties, while he was still at school. As a professional musician, he continued to use it. This was not widely copied in jazz, although Sam Woodyard (playing with Duke Ellington) and the British drummer Eric Delaney were notable exceptions. Several rock music drummers, who appreciated the powerful sound it could deliver, also adopted the two bass drum set up. In an interview published by *Jazzwise* magazine in January 2010, Ginger Baker recounted how he and Keith Moon had seen Sam Woodyard playing with two bass drums at an Ellington concert in 1966 and had both decided to copy the idea. (The occasion must have been on February 16th when Duke's Orchestra played in Birmingham, on the only occasion during the Who/Graham Bond Organisation tour in the same period when Moon and Baker had a night off.) Keith Moon used the set-up for the Who's tour of Sweden in June, while Baker chose to wait for drum manufacturer Ludwig to make a double bass drum set with a double pedal specially for him, in time for the first gigs by the newly-formed Cream (which debuted in Manchester on July 29th).

Baker's memory is somewhat modified by the account in Martyn Hanson's biography of drummer Jon Hiseman, *Playing The Band,* of Baker acquiring a second bass drum in response to his discovery that Hiseman, his scheduled replacement in the Graham Bond Organisation, was already using a two bass drum set-up. Jon Hiseman maintains that he started playing like this in 1964, while a member of the Mike Taylor Quartet. He must have been doing it, therefore, on Taylor's album, *Pendulum,* which was recorded in October 1965. This is not a rock record, however.

It was Ginger Baker, as a member of the Graham Bond Organisation, who recorded the first improvised, extended drum solo in rock on the track *Oh Baby*, issued in early 1965 on the album *The Sound Of '65*. As a member of Cream during the following three years, Baker used his piece *Toad* as a similar showcase for his drum expertise. One studio version and a few live versions were recorded – his solo on the March 1968 Fillmore West performance, included on the four CD set *Those Were The Days*, lasts for more than thirteen minutes. This is not, as it happens, the longest recorded drum solo. John Bonham, playing with Led Zeppelin in California in June 1972, plays for over seventeen minutes on a version of *Moby Dick*. It appears on the three CD set, *How The West Was Won*.

The first recorded jazz drum solo was played by Gene Krupa on the 1937 Benny Goodman record *Sing Sing Sing*. The track is nearly nine minutes long and was split over both sides of the 78 rpm record. It is structured around its energetic drum beat and the several short drum breaks as well as the actual extended drum solo play without departing from that beat. The style was borrowed twenty years later by three chart hits – *Topsy Part II* by Cozy Cole (1958) and two pieces by Sandy Nelson, *Teen Beat* (1959) and *Let There Be Drums* (1961). Krupa himself left Benny Goodman in 1938 to form his own band, becoming the first drummer bandleader.

During the fifties, promoter Norman Granz had the idea of casting well-known jazz drummers as gladiators,

THE FIRST TIME

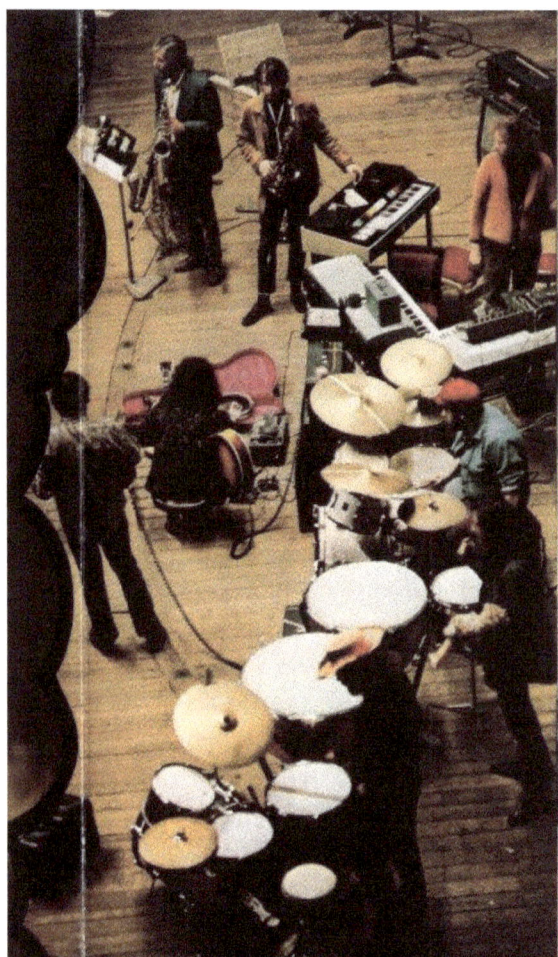

Artwork from the Mothers of Invention Burnt Weeny Sandwich LP. Three drummers are ready to play – Art Tripp, Jimmy Carl Black, and Billy Mundi.

Airto Moreira

Evelyn Glennie was a pupil of the acclaimed orchestral percussionist James Blades. It was Blades who made the sound of the gong at the start of Rank Organisation films from 1935, although he was not the man who could be seen on the screen, wielding the striker!

ready to do battle with each other, with their drum kits as weapons. Gene Krupa and Buddy Rich took part in the first drum battle, held at New York's Carnegie Hall in September 1952. It was recorded and issued on LP, as was a later studio meeting in 1955, although only one track on this actually had the two drummers playing together. Ginger Baker revived the drum battle idea in 1971 and presented a concert with Elvin Jones, the drummer who been a member of John Coltrane's quartet. A year later he did the same thing with Art Blakey. Opinions were divided as to who won the 'battles', but this was never the true point of the exercise.

In between, a number of bands incorporated two drummers into their permanent line-ups. In 1961, Ornette Coleman issued an album, *Free Jazz*, in which the music was improvised by a double quartet, including both Billy Higgins and Ed Blackwell on drums. The line-up did not perform live, but several years later, when Coleman was playing his idiosyncratic version of jazz fusion, he frequently played with two drummers. The Kenny Clarke-Francy Boland Big Band, co-led by a drummer (Clarke), added a second one, Kenny Clare, in 1968. Miles Davis, recording his landmark *Bitches Brew* album in 1969, used two drummers – and two percussionists as well. Meanwhile, in rock, Frank Zappa's Mothers of Invention and the Grateful Dead were using two drummers from 1966 and 1967 respectively. *Gloria*, a single B side by Them from late 1964 did the same, with the addition of a session drummer to the group.

There are several solo drum tracks to be heard, most notably those by Max Roach and Billy Cobham. The first to be recorded was *Drum Improvisation No.1* by Baby Dodds, in June 1946. There are also a number of complete albums featuring drums, sometimes with assorted percussion, but no other instruments. The earliest of these are *Milford Graves Percussion Ensemble With Sunny Morgan* (1965) and *What About?* by Andrew Cyrille (1969).

The Cuban Chano Pozo joined Dizzy Gillespie's big band as a percussionist in 1947, as an addition to Gillespie's drummer, Kenny Clarke. In the same year, another Cuban percussionist, Machito (a successful bandleader in his own right) recorded with Stan Kenton. *The Peanut Vendor* became a substantial hit. The following year, Machito recorded with Charlie Parker. Such collaborations gave birth to a genre known as Latin Jazz, where jazz improvisations are supported by rhythms originating in South America, played by drummers and percussionists working together. The style has continued ever since, but received a boost in 1963, when percussionist Mongo Santamaria scored a US top ten hit with his cover of a Herbie Hancock tune, *Watermelon Man*. The same year, saxophonist Stan Getz recorded a collaboration with Brazilian singer-guitarist Joao Gilberto. A track from the album was edited to highlight the vocal contribution from Gilberto's wife Astrud. *The Girl From Ipanema* was a big hit around the world and helped to launch a dance craze, the bossa nova. The track certainly had the right rhythmic feel, but it achieved this with minimal drumming and no additional percussion. According to a 2012 article in the Wall Street Journal, *The Girl From Ipanema* has become the second most recorded song after Paul McCartney's *Yesterday*.

Santana, a rock group using Latin American rhythms and employing two percussionists in addition to a drummer, was catapulted to fame by a performance at the Woodstock festival in 1969. Carlos Santana, the guitarist leader of the band, achieved the biggest success of his career thirty years later, still using percussionists playing Latin rhythms, with the album *Supernatural*. Many of the albums issued by the group in the early seventies, particularly *Caravanserai* and the live *Lotus*, contain music that is indistinguishable from jazz fusion. This is music that also greatly relies on the playing of percussionists, ever since Airto Moreira joined the Miles Davis group in late 1969. Airto subsequently played with both Weather Report and Chick Corea's Return To Forever, as well as leading bands of his own, becoming the first percussionist to achieve the same kind of recognition and influence as the masters of other jazz instruments. An equivalent figure within rock music is perhaps Ray Cooper, best known for his many contributions to the music of Elton John, although Cooper has never led a band of his own.

Stomu Yamash'ta, a Japanese virtuoso orchestral percussionist, began to attract attention at the start of the seventies. Adopting a spectacular and athletic approach to live performance, Yamash'ta's first albums were placed firmly within the world of avant garde classical music, with composers such as Hans Werner Henze and Peter Maxwell Davies writing works especially for him. For a while, he made this entire area of music interesting to the fans

Graeme Edge leading the Procession

'Vibes' is used for vibraphone and also for vibrations, meaning atmosphere or feeling (as in the Beach Boys song, *Good Vibrations*). The double meaning allowed some gentle humour on the sleeve credits for the Jimi Hendrix LP, *The Cry Of Love*. On side one, track two, Buzzy Linhart is credited with vibes; on track three Steve Winwood and Chris Wood are also credited with vibes. Only Linhart played the vibraphone!

of progressive rock, before deciding that he would like to play progressive rock himself. Much more recently, Evelyn Glennie has managed to fill the same slot for a longer time – that of a performer of frequently avant garde percussive music played with style, who manages to maintain a considerable level of popularity.

The vibraphone (occasionally vibraharp, more often vibes) is a twentieth century upgrade on the xylophone/marimba family of instruments. Although the tuned bars that make up the instrument mean that it plays melodically, the fact that the player strikes the bars with mallets is enough for the vibraphone to be classified as a member of the percussion category. Each of the horizontal bars of the vibraphone is paired with a vertical resonator tube, which increases both the volume and the sustain of the notes played. In addition, each tube is equipped with a motor-driven valve at its upper end. When made to spin, these give the notes a tremolo effect – a rapid oscillation in volume. It is this aspect that distinguishes the vibraphone from the earlier xylophone. The vibraphone was included in the works of a few classical composers, such as Ferde Grofé's *Grand Canyon Suite* from 1931, and Alban Berg's opera *Lulu*, which was completed in 1935. It has become far more widely used, however, in jazz. Drummer Paul Barbarin, who played in bands led by King Oliver and Luis Russell, among others, was the first jazz musician to play the vibraphone. He did so during the July 1929 sessions by trumpeter Henry Red Allen, on the tracks *Biff'ly Blues* and *Feeling Drowsy*. Lionel Hampton and Milt Jackson (known as Bags at one time) were the major players of the instrument during later years, but it was not until the sixties that Gary Burton developed the technique of playing with four mallets. Burton issued an album of solo vibraphone playing in 1971, *Alone At Last*.

Steel drums are another percussion instrument designed to play melody lines. They were invented in Trinidad by a musician who decided to take the name of the containers used for oil literally. According to the lyrics of a song by calypso star Lord Kitchener, *Tribute To Spree Simon*, this was Winston Spree Simon, in 1939. Turning the oil drums upside down, he hammered curved areas into the metal surface, each one being tuned to a different note. Steel drums have become an integral part of the Caribbean music once known as calypso, but now called soca. Every year, the Panorama competition is held in Trinidad to establish the champion steel band. Simon's own band, Destination Tokyo (named after a film) never managed better than second place, although its successor still plays, under the name Carib Tokyo. Victor Brady moved the music into R&B territory with the 1970 album *Brown Rain*, then the 20th Century Steel Band did something similar with the 1975 album, *Warm Heart Cold Steel*. This album has been extensively sampled. The application of the instrument to other kinds of music has been limited, although steel drums do turn up during two rock songs, *Emotions* by Family in 1969 and the 1967 hit by the Hollies, *Carrie Anne*. Stomu Yamash'ta plays them on his 1971 *Red Buddha* album and they feature too on two other albums from that year, *Happy Just To Be Like I Am*, by Taj Mahal and *The Mourning Of A Star* by Keith Jarrett. In 1979, two jazz albums belatedly followed suit – *Morning Dance* by Spyro Gyra and *Hidden Treasure* by Andy Narell, a man who made the steel drums his speciality through several further jazz albums. Narell's brother, Jeff, is a steel drums player too. He is less prolific, but started a little earlier – he can be heard on mid-seventies albums by Tom Fogerty and the New Riders of the Purple Sage.

The first electronic drums were made by Graeme Edge, in collaboration with Brian Groves, Professor of Electronics at Sussex University (who did most of the design work, one suspects). Edge played them on *Procession*, the first track of the Moody Blues album from 1971, *Every Good Boy Deserves Favour*. The first commercially produced electronic drum was the Syndrum, manufactured by Pollard Industries in 1976. It delivered a percussive sound effect rather than a definite drum beat and can be heard, used in precisely this way, on the 1978 hit by Rose Royce, *Love Don't Live Here Anymore* (produced by Norman Whitfield, famous for his earlier work with the Temptations). It also appears, played by Sly Dunbar, throughout the 1981 LP *Sinsemilla* by Black Uhuru. Dunbar uses the Syndrum as an addition to his regular drum kit. Probably the drum's first recording is on the 1976 LP *Automatic Man* by the group of the same name, led by Santana drummer Michael Shrieve.

Simmons started producing electronic drums in 1979 – one of them can be heard on the first, self-titled album by Landscape, issued the same year. With the SDS-5, produced with distinctive hexagonal drum heads in 1981, Simmons expanded its range to create the first complete electronic drum kit. Landscape used this on the second

THE FIRST TIME

Simmons SDS-5 drum kit

Bill Bruford

The original album including The Show

Neil Peart

album, *From The Tea-Rooms Of Mars*, issued in 1981. Bill Bruford became another early champion of the Simmons drums, using them with King Crimson and the jazz group, Earthworks, that he founded in 1986. Earthworks enabled him to further explore the possibilities of his electronic kit, including using the drums to play chords. Neil Peart, the drummer with Rush, also used Simmons drums, before switching to electronic drums manufactured by Roland, which he employed to trigger samples as well as play drum parts.

At the other end of the technology spectrum are the people who use their mouths to create percussion sounds. The approach has become particularly associated with rap and hip-hop, in which context it is known as 'beatboxing'. Doug E. Fresh issued *The Show* in 1985 as the first recorded example of the style, demonstrating his skill at mimicking drum machine and record scratching effects. The previous year, singer Bobby McFerrin made an album called *The Voice*, on which he delivered mainly jazz songs on his own, creating an array of tuned percussion sounds to accompany the melodies, in a dazzling display of vocal virtuosity. No instruments were used on the album and there was no overdubbing. Earlier still, in 1978, Vivian Fisher made a single, *Blaze Away*, where he created the sound of a brass band with his voice, complete with percussion, although here he did employ extensive overdubbing. The single was credited to 'Me, Myself & Me Again'. Vocal percussion effects are employed during two tracks on *The Piper At The Gates Of Dawn*, the 1967 debut album by Pink Floyd, (the tracks are *Pow R Toc H* and *Take Up Thy Stethoscope And Walk*), possibly inspired by something similar on the 1966 avant garde album made by Gruppo Di Improvviisazione Nuova Consonanza. Before that, the technique is found within folk music and the blues on occasion. The approach can be traced back to the traditional music of both India and Africa, with origins long before the beginning of the twentieth century.

TRACKING THE TRACKS

There are several compilations by the Original Dixieland Jazz Band available, such as the double CD *The Essential Collection* (West End 2006). Recordings by Baby Dodds are scattered across records by King Oliver, Louis Armstrong's Hot Seven, Jelly Roll Morton, and others. Not all of them show Dodds' playing to best advantage, due to the limitations of recording technology at the time. In 1946, Dodds recorded a series of reminiscences, with examples of his playing. These are available on the CD *Talking And Drum Solos* (Atavistic 2003). *Drum Improvisation No.1* can be heard on YouTube. There are two uploads of the track – one titled *Drum Improvisations* and the other *Trap Set Solo*. A double CD accommodates four LPs made by Louis Bellson in the early fifties under the title *Four Classic Albums Plus*. The albums in question are *Just Jazz All Stars, Concerto For Drums, At The Flamingo*, and *The Hawk Talks*.

The two albums made by the Graham Bond Organisation in 1965, *The Sound Of 65* and *There's A Bond Between Us*, are combined on a Beat Goes On CD (1999). *Pendulum* by the Mike Taylor Quartet is on Sunbeam Records (2007). *Those Were The Days* provides a comprehensive collection of the music of Cream (Polydor 1997). A very slightly abridged version of the same performance of *Toad* is on the double CD *Wheels Of Fire* (also Polydor 1997). Led Zeppelin's *How The West Was Won* is a three CD set on Atlantic (2003).

Benny Goodman's *Sing Sing Sing*, with Gene Krupa, is on *The Definitive/Ken Burns Jazz* (Sony 2000). Cozy Cole's *Topsy Part II* is included on the various artists double CD, *American Heartbeat 1958* (One Day Music 2014). Sandy Nelson's *Teen Beat* and *Let There Be Drums* are on the double CD *Teen Beat 1959-1961* (Jasmine 2013). The Gene Krupa – Buddy Rich drum battle is included on the CD *The Drum Battle* (Folio 2001), together with tracks by the Gene Krupa Trio. The studio collaboration is *Krupa and Rich* (Verve 1994).

Ornette Coleman's *Free Jazz* is on an Atlantic CD (2002). The Kenny Clarke-Francy Boland Big Band are not well served on CD, but *The Complete Live Recordings at Ronnie Scott's February 1969* (Rearward 2010) is recommended. Miles Davis's *Bitches Brew* is on a double CD (Columbia 1999). *Absolutely Free* by Frank Zappa's Mothers Of Invention, with Billy Mundi and Jimmy Carl Black playing drums, is on a Zappa CD (2012). *Anthem Of The Sun* by the Grateful Dead, with Bill Kreutzmann and Mickey Hart on drums, is on a Warner CD (2011). *Gloria* is included on the 3 CD set, *The Complete Them 1964-1967* (Sony 2015)

Max Roach's *Drums Unlimited* (Atlantic 2004) includes three typically musical solos. Billy Cobham's *Spectrum* (Atlantic 2002) includes three of his. *Milford Graves Percussion Ensemble with Sunny Morgan* is on an ESP CD (2008). *What About?* by Andrew Cyriile has been issued on LP three times, in 1969 (BYG), 1982 (Affinity), and 2001 (Get Back), but is not available on CD.

In Concert by the Dizzy Gillespie Big Band (including Chano Pozo) is on a GNP Crescendo CD (1993). *The Peanut Vendor* is on *The Best Of Stan Kenton* (Capitol 1995). Charlie Parker's recordings with Machito are on *The Complete Verve Latin Sides* (Verve 2001). Mongo Santamaria's *Greatest Hits* (Fantasy 1995) includes *Watermelon Man*. *The Girl From Ipanema* is included on *Getz/Gilberto* (Verve 2005) by Stan Getz and Joao Gilberto. Santana's performance at Woodstock is on the festival DVD (Warner 1999). *Caravanserai* is on a Sony CD (2003); *Lotus* is on a Columbia double CD (2008); *Supernatural* is on Arista (2010). The first Weather Report album, with Airto Moreira,

THE FIRST TIME

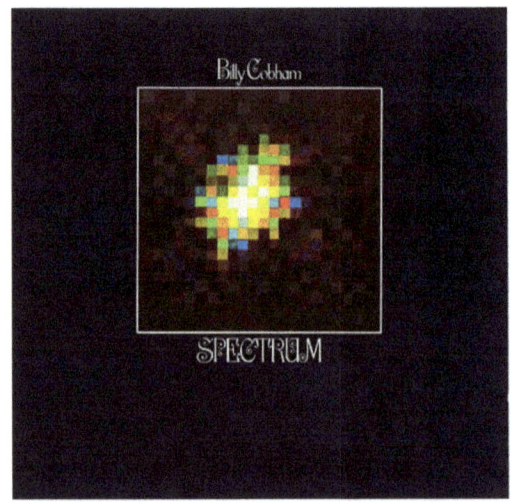

Sheila Chandra Zen Kiss

INSTRUMENTS AND MUSICIANS

is *Weather Report* (Columbia 2009). Airto drums on the first two albums by Chick Corea's Return To Forever – *Return To Forever* (ECM 2015) and *Light as a Feather* (Verve 1998. The first two albums in Moreira's own name are not available on CD, but the third, *Free* (Music On CD 2013), is – and it is one of his best.

Ray Cooper plays on numerous Elton John recordings and can be seen in action on the DVD *The Million Dollar Piano* (Eagle Rock 2013). The 1972 self-titled album by Stomu Yamash'ta (Universal/Decca 1990) has works by Henze, Maxwell Davies, and Takemitsu. *Red Buddha* (Spalax 1996) from 1971 has two works by Yamash'ta himself. *Freedom Is Frightening* from 1973 is progressive rock (Esoteric 2008) by a band that includes Gary Boyle on guitar and Soft Machine's Hugh Hopper on bass.

Grand Canyon Suite by Ferde Grofé is included on several CDs, with other works, such as one by the Bournemouth Symphony Orchestra on Naxos (1999). In order to hear the vibraphone playing in Alban Berg's *Lulu*, it is only necessary to listen to the shorter *Lulu Suite*. A number of recordings are available, such as the one played by the London Symphony Orchestra, conducted by Claudio Abbado, along with two other works by Berg (Deutsche Grammophon 2011). The vibraphone does not play much, but it is there.

The Paul Barbarin tracks with Henry Red Allen can be heard on a double CD by Allen, *Ride Ride Ride! – His 44 Finest 1929-1962* (Retrospecrive 2014). A similar compilation presents a good overview of Lionel Hampton's music – *Flying Home His 48 Finest 1930-1949* (Retrospective 2011). Milt Jackson has made several albums in his own name, but many more as part of the Modern Jazz Quartet. Another double CD, *Anthology – Bluesology – The Atlantic Years 1956-1988* (Warner 2009), provides a good overview. Gary Burton made his biggest impact with two late sixties albums that are now available together on a double CD – *Lofty Fake Anagram* and *A Genuine Tong Funeral* (Beat Goes On 2006). *Alone At Last* is on an Atlantic CD (1998).

There are numerous albums of steel band music. *Carnival Jump-Up – Steelbands of Trinidad and Tobago* (Delos 1989) is recommended, if it can be found. It includes a lengthy track by Carib Tokyo. *Brown Rain* by Victor Brady does not have an official CD reissue. *Warm Heart Cold Steel* by 20th Century Steel Band is on a Mr Bongo CD (2009). Lord Kitchener's *Tribute To Spree Simon* is on *Klassic Kitchener Volume Three* (Ice 2003). The song is covered by Van Dyke Parks (the lyricist for the Beach Boys *Smile* recordings) on his 1975 album *Clang Of The Yankee Reaper* (Bella Union 2012) and gets the full steelband treatment. *Emotions* by Family is on *Family Entertainment* (Pucka 2003). *Carrie Anne* by the Hollies is on *20 Golden Greats* (EMI 2000). *Happy Just To Be Like I Am* by Taj Mahal is on Columbia (1991), while the track with steel drums is also to be found on the double CD *The Essential Taj Mahal* (Sony 2005). *The Mourning Of A Star* by Keith Jarrett is on Wounded Bird (2001). *Morning Dance* by Spyro Gyra is on Sony (1994). Andy Narell's *Hidden Treasure* is on Traditions Alive 2010. The albums on which Jeff Narell can first be heard are the hard to find *Zephyr National* by Tom Fogerty (packaged with the album *Myopia* on Fantasy in 1999) and *Oh What A Mighty Time* by New Riders Of The Purple Sage (Beat Goes On 2007).

Every Good Boy Deserves Favour by the Moody Blues is on Threshold (2008). *Love Don't Live Here Anymore* is included on *Rose Royce Greatest Hits* (Whitfield Records 1990). *Sinsemilla* by Black Uhuru is on Island (2003). *Automatic Man* is on Lemon (2004). *Landscape* is on Cherry Red (2009). *From The Tea-rooms Of Mars…* is also on Cherry Red (2002). Much of King Crimson's 1982 album *Beat* (DGM 2005) is shaped by Bill Bruford's electronic dums. Bruford's Earthworks has a good compilation, *Heavenly Bodies* (Venture 1997). Neil Peart started using Roland electronic drums on the Rush album *Vapor Trails* (Atlantic 2013).

Doug E Fresh The Greatest Hits is on JTC Atlantic Partners (2011) and includes *The Show*. Bobby McFerrin's *The Voice* is on Elektra (1984). *Blaze Away* by Me Myself & Me Again can be found on its original vinyl or heard on YouTube. *The Piper At The Gates Of Dawn* by Pink Floyd is on EMI (2011). The self-titled album by Gruppo Di Improvvisazione Nuova Consonanza is on an Italian Sony/Schema CD. *The Zen Kiss* by Sheila Chandra (Realworld 1994) includes two remarkable Indian mouth percussion tracks.

Some people tell jokes about drummers, the way that some other people tell jokes about blondes:
"What do you call someone who hangs around with musicians? A drummer!"
"What's the last thing a drummer says in a band? Hey guys, why don't we try one of my songs?"
"A drummer, tired of being ridiculed by his colleagues, decides to learn to play a 'real' instrument. He walks into the shop and tells the assistant, 'I'd like to buy a Fender Stratoblaster, and a plectrum, and a set of strings.' The assistant stares at him for a moment, then says, 'You're a drummer, aren't you.' Crestfallen, the drummer agrees. 'But how did you know?' he asks. 'Easy,' the assistant replies, 'This is a fish and chip shop!'

On the other hand:
"An average band with a great drummer sounds great. A great band with an average drummer sounds average." (Buddy Rich)
"The greatest contribution jazz has made in music has been to replace the role of the conductor with a member of the ensemble who, instead of waving his arms to keep time and convey mood, is an active member of the musical statement. That person is the drummer." (Elvin Jones)
"I love being a drummer. Everyone thinks you're dumb. What they don't realise is that if it weren't for you, their band would suck." (Dave Grohl, former drummer with Nirvana; later guitarist, singer, and songwriter with the Foo Fighters)

THE FIRST TIME

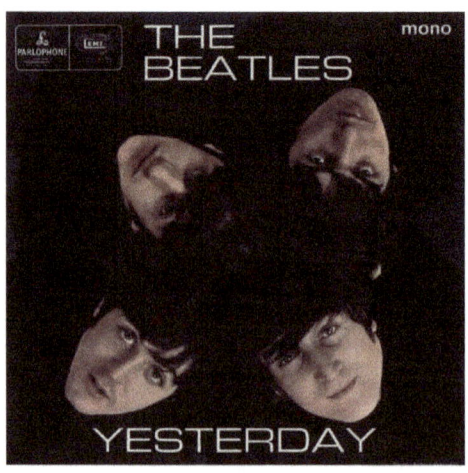
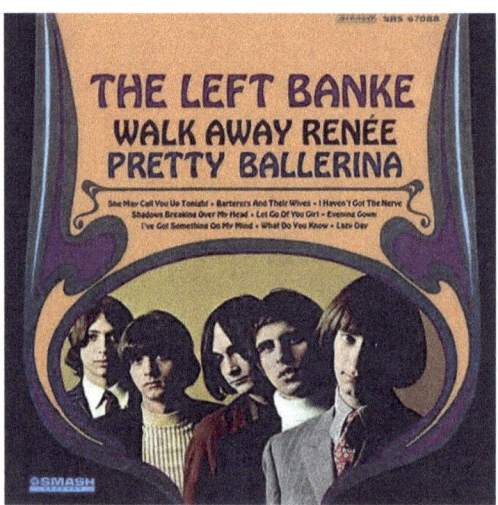
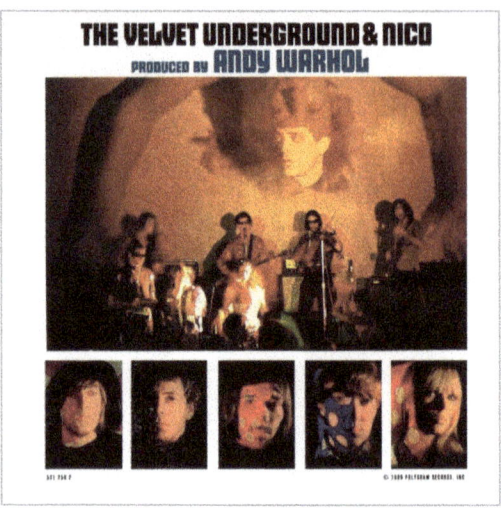

An electric violin, newly designed rather than simply being an acoustic violin with a pickup, was produced in 1930 by Ivan Makhonine. His instrument had a minimal body framework surrounding the neck and bridge and was used in a concert given in Paris by Cecilia Hansen. A similar instrument was included in the Rickenbacker catalogue for 1936. Much later, in 1958, a full solid body electric violin was manufactured by Fender. None of these electric violins were commercially successful.

The experimental performer Laurie Anderson invented an electronic variation of the violin in 1977. The usual horse-hair in the bow was replaced by a length of magnetic tape, which was then made to sound by being drawn across a playback head mounted in the bridge. The results can be heard on several tracks of Anderson's *United States Live,* a five LP set recorded in February 1983.

6 ORCHESTRAL INSTRUMENTS

The components of the classical orchestra were all in place by the end of the nineteenth century. As a result, orchestral accompaniment could be employed within numerous different styles of music from the earliest days of recording. Rock 'n' roll was presented and received as a musical rebellion, but even there, orchestral instruments eventually managed to find a way in. Four tracks were recorded in October 1958 by Buddy Holly, on which he was accompanied by the Dick Jacobs Orchestra. Arguably, *It Doesn't Matter Anymore*, *Raining In My Heart*, *Moondreams,* and *True Love Ways* were not really rock 'n' roll performances at all, although the first of these does at least have a beat. The previous year, Jackie Wilson's second hit, *To Be Loved*, used an orchestra, which was also organised by Dick Jacobs. This too is a ballad.

By 1965, a number of records, loosely describable as rock, had been made with the accompaniment of orchestras of various sizes. But the Beatles song *Yesterday*, issued in August as part of the LP *Help!*, broke new ground by employing a string quartet. The interest in classical music textures that this song inspired led to the US group, the Left Banke, incorporating them as a permanent feature of its music, beginning with the hit record, *Walk Away Renee*, in late 1966. The band did not have any string players in its line-up, but session violinist Harry Lookofsky, who was the manager, produced the records to include his own playing (he was also the father of the Left Banke's keyboard player, Michael Brown). Denny Laine, the original lead singer with the Moody Blues, formed his Electric String Band in December 1966, including string players alongside the guitars and drums. The band recorded two singles, *Say You Don't Mind* and *Too Much In Love*. In September 1969, Deep Purple became the first rock group to work with an entire symphony orchestra, when Jon Lord's *Concerto for Group and Orchestra* was performed with the Royal Philharmonic, conducted by Malcolm Arnold. Through the seventies, several other groups followed this example.

John Cale played viola with the Velvet Underground, whose first album, *The Velvet Underground & Nico*, was mostly recorded in April 1966, although it was not released until the following March. (The single, *Sunday Morning*, on which Cale's viola can be heard, was issued in December 1966.) The first bands to bring the violin to the fore and use it to play solos were the Blues Project and John Mayall's Bluesbreakers. The 1968 Blues Project album, *Planned Obsolescence*, featured violinist Richard Greene as part of a revised line-up – so revised, in fact, that subsequent recordings used a new band name, Seatrain. John Mayall's album, *Bare Wires*, also issued in 1968, gave a prominent role to trumpeter Henry Lowther's second instrument, the violin, on two tracks. The following year, 1969, a number of bands made albums in which the violin featured as a lead instrument. Simon House, playing with High Tide on the album *Sea Shanties*, used effects for the first time – wah-wah pedal and fuzz box.

The first violinist to use amplification was the jazz player Stuff Smith, who started recording in 1936. The first jazz violin playing, however, dates from ten years earlier. Joe Venuti recorded with guitarist Eddie Lang from 1926, while his first recordings were two years before that, as a member of the Jean Goldkette band. Country fiddler, Eck Robertson, made his first recordings in 1922. A 78 of *Sallie Gooden*, backed with *Arkansas Traveler*, on which Robertson was accompanied by a second fiddler, Henry Gilliland, was issued on the Victor label as the first ever country record.

The first use of the cello as a jazz instrument was in the hands of Oscar Pettiford, otherwise known as a bass player, who began recording with it in 1950. He never used a bow, however, preferring to treat the cello as a smaller version of a jazz double bass. The first jazz player to play cello with a bow was Fred Katz, recording with groups led by Chico Hamilton from 1955. In rock music, cellos were given a prominent role in the Beatles song *I Am The Walrus*, recorded in September 1967, and, a little before that, in the Spencer Davis Group song, *Time Seller*, which was released in July 1967. Jack Bruce, who had been trained as a classical cellist, played the instrument on some of the studio tracks

THE FIRST TIME

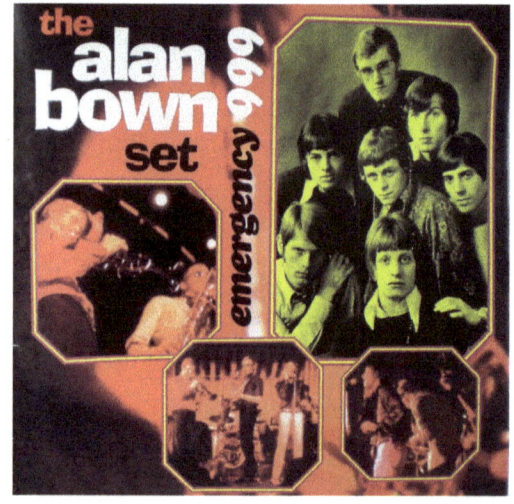
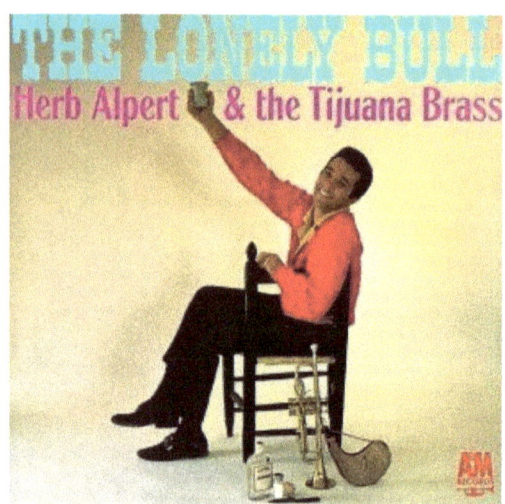
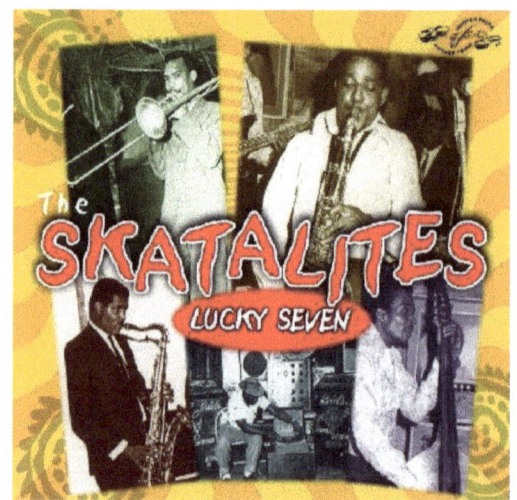

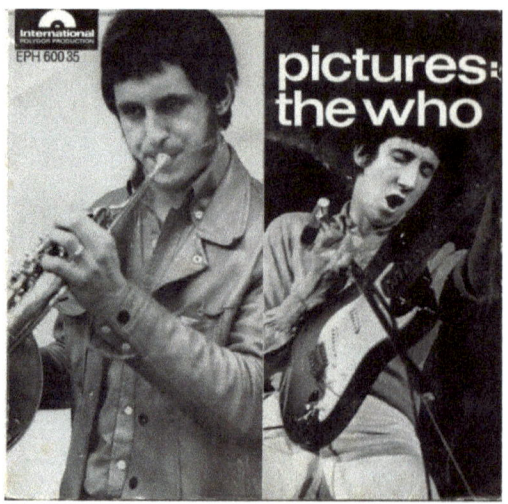

John Entwistle playing the French horn with the Who

on the Cream album, *Wheels Of Fire*, released in August 1968.

The primary instruments in the orchestral brass section, the trumpet and the trombone, were employed in jazz from the very beginning. Outside jazz and after the birth of rock 'n' roll, a video clip on YouTube shows Wanda Jackson performing *Hard Headed Woman* live in 1958, with a trumpet player adding a one verse solo half way through. John Barry formed a group, the John Barry Seven, in 1957, playing music at the interface between beat and easy listening, with his own trumpet an element in the sound, if not often a particularly major one. Eventually, Barry left his own band to concentrate on his increasingly successful composing career and the band gradually evolved into the Alan Bown Set, under the leadership of Barry's trumpet playing successor. For a couple of years, the Alan Bown Set was one of only two beat groups with a trumpet player (the other was the Mike Cotton Sound, which had originally played jazz), until Henry Lowther joined Manfred Mann and Mike Falana joined the Graham Bond Organisation, in 1966. The Beatles hit single, *Penny Lane*, issued in February 1967, included a trumpet solo, played on the high, piccolo version of the instrument by session musician David Mason. The high E note that ends the solo was previously thought to be unplayable, according to sound engineer Geoff Emerick.

Herb Alpert achieved his first hit in 1962, with *Lonely Bull*. As the most successful trumpet player outside jazz, he sold enough records during the next decades to turn the record company he founded with business partner Jerry Moss into one of the major industry labels – A&M Records.

So You Want To Be A Rock 'N' Roll Star, released as a single by the Byrds in January 1967, featured a trumpet part played by South African expatriate Hugh Masekela. Two notable American rock records from 1968 also included trumpet solos, although again, the instrument was not played in any of the other recordings by the groups concerned. *Alone Again Or* by Love, released in January, employed session player Ollie Mitchell. *Born Cross Eyed* by the Grateful Dead, released in April, was a solitary trumpet performance by the band's own Phil Lesh, who was classically trained on the instrument. In the UK, guitarist with Eclection, Mike Rosen, also played trumpet, and used it to deliver a memorable solo on the band's single, *Mark Time*, issued in June.

By this time, a number of bands had started to use brass sections – most notably the Butterfield Blues Band, John Mayall's Bluesbreakers, and the Electric Flag. (The Mar-Keys should be added to this list – actually formed considerably earlier than the rock bands, in 1958.) The first rock trombone player to achieve anything like star status was a member of a band operating in this jazz-rock area – James Pankow, who played in the band Chicago. The first album, *Chicago Transit Authority*, was released in April 1969. Prior to that, the only celebrated trombonist outside jazz was the Jamaican Don Drummond, who played as a member of the Skatalites from 1964 and also released records in his own name.

Other members of the orchestral brass section proved to be less popular in other kinds of music. A very small number of French horn players have made jazz records, with Claude Thornhill being the first bandleader to include the instrument in his arrangements. John Graas played with him from 1942. Julius Watkins was the first horn player to make a record in his own name. His 10" LP, *Julius Watkins Sextet*, was issued on the Blue Note label in 1955. In rock music, two French horn solos were played on record in 1966. The Beatles song, *For No One*, included on the group's *Revolver* LP, employed the classical player Alan Civil to play a solo. According to Mark Lewisohn, in his authoritative guide to the Beatles recording sessions, Alan Civil complained that the music was improperly tuned, being pitched in between B and B flat, but he managed anyway. John Entwistle of the Who played a French horn solo on *Disguises*, which made its debut on an edition of the *Ready Steady Go* TV programme devoted to the Who and subsequently appeared on an EP commemorating the fact, *Ready Steady Who*.

The tuba was sometimes used in preference to the double bass by early jazz groups. The Wolverines, led by trumpeter Bix Beiderbecke, first recorded in 1924 and the resulting *Fidgety Feet/Jazz Me Blues* 78 includes tuba playing by Min Leibrook. Tuba player Andy Kirk led his own band, the Clouds Of Joy, from 1929. Red Callender led a sextet for a 1957 album, *Callender Speaks Low*, functioning as a soloist on tuba. In rock music, bass player Herbie Flowers

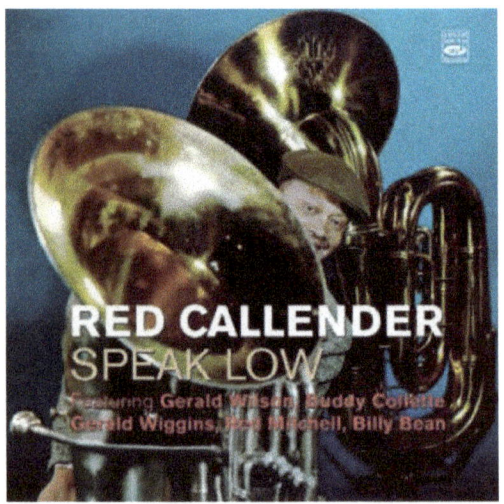

Taj Mahal with his Tuba Band

The Sax Bit by poet Ted Joans (included in *A Black Manifesto in Jazz Poetry and Prose*, 1971) is a tribute to Coleman Hawkins. Joans wonders why the saxophone even existed before Hawkins started playing it. He concludes, with a rare rhyming couplet:

"What tremors ran through Adolphe Saxe the day Bean grabbed his ax?"

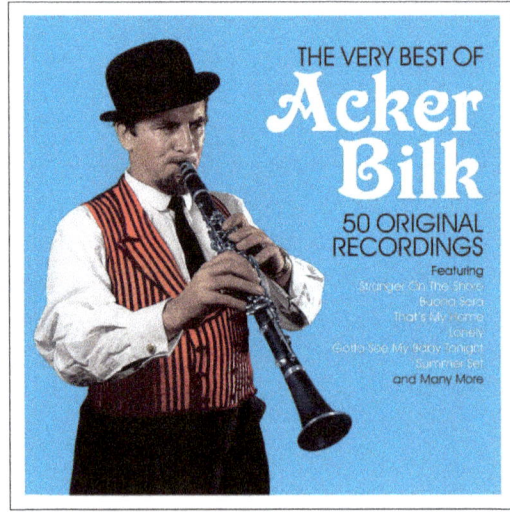

occasionally played tuba and did so on the track *Tuba Smarties* on the 1980 second album made by the band Sky, of which Flowers was a member. Earlier than this, trombonist Dave Bargeron joined Blood Sweat and Tears in 1970 and played tuba in addition to his main instrument. The 1976 live album, *In Concert,* includes Bargeron playing a tuba solo during a medley of *And When I Die* with *One Room Country Shack*. Earlier still, the Taj Mahal albums, *The Real Thing* and *Happy Just To Be Like I Am,* both issued in 1971, featured a band that included four tuba players, led by Howard Johnson.

The saxophone, a hybrid between a brass and a woodwind instrument, was patented by the Belgian Adolphe Sax in 1846. He designed several different-sized versions, from subcontrabass to sopranissimo, although only four have been in general usage – baritone, tenor, alto, and soprano. The saxophone was soon adopted by classical orchestras and chamber groups and also by military bands. Although the earliest jazz bands did not include the instrument, the success of Coleman Hawkins (known as 'Bean'), who first recorded with Fletcher Henderson in 1923, quickly led to it becoming ubiquitous. As one strand of jazz evolved into rhythm and blues and rock 'n' roll, so the saxophone followed along. A wailing saxophone solo was included in countless rock 'n' roll songs, being more common through the fifties than solos by guitar.

The technique of circular breathing, whereby the saxophonist breathes in through his nose while simultaneously pushing air out from his cheeks and into the instrument, was developed in jazz by Harry Carney, baritone saxophonist with the Duke Ellington Orchestra. Roland Kirk and Evan Parker became particularly associated with circular breathing and both recorded marathon solos which unfold continuously without any pause for breath. Kenny G decided to emphasise the record-breaking aspect of the method, rather than its musicality, when he set up a Guinness world record in 1997 for the longest held saxophone note. This was just under forty-six minutes and was mercifully not transferred to CD.

The clarinet was more popular in jazz than the saxophone in the early years, although it gradually lost appeal and did not cross over into rock 'n' roll, unless Elvis Presley's performances, supported by traditional jazz musicians, in the 1958 film *King Creole,* are counted. Acker Bilk achieved a million selling hit in 1962 with his easy-listening clarinet piece, *Stranger On The Shore,* but did not inspire a legion of copyists. Once again, it was the Beatles who introduced the instrument to rock, when they featured it on the song *When I'm 64,* included on the 1967 LP, *Sgt Pepper's Lonely Hearts Club Band.* Ian Underwood, who joined Frank Zappa's Mothers Of Invention in time for the 1968 album, *We're Only In It For The Money,* included clarinet in his sizeable instrumental repertoire, while Phil Shulman did the same with Gentle Giant, whose first album was released in 1970. Victor Hayden, also known as the Mascara Snake, played bass clarinet on Captain Beefheart's 1969 album, *Trout Mask Replica,* and was given a very prominent role.

The oboe family of instruments, using a double reed, has only occasionally made an appearance in either jazz or rock. Garvin Bushell played bassoon with the Louisiana Sugar Babes on a 1928 record, *Persian Rug/Thou Swell.* Though never a star, Bushell, who played all the reed instruments, was still performing in 1961, when he was included in the ensemble on John Coltrane's *Africa-Brass* album. Yusef Lateef was the first solo performer to use the oboe, which he originally added to his tenor saxophone and flute in 1958, with the live LP *Lateef At Cranbrook.* In 1964, he added bassoon, for the LP *Jazz Round The World.* The oboe has made intermittent appearances in rock music, beginning with *Don't Let The Sun Catch You Crying* by Gerry and the Pacemakers in 1964 and *I Got You Babe* by Sonny and Cher in 1965. The 1970 King Crimson LP, *Lizard,* included both oboe and its variant, the cor anglais, played by Robin Miller. Roy Wood played numerous instruments on the first LP by the Electric Light Orchestra in 1971, including both oboe and bassoon. Andy Mackay played oboe on several tracks while a member of Roxy Music, including the 1972 first single, *Virginia Plain,* and the first album that followed. Brian Gulland played bassoon (and also the medieval reed instrument, the crumhorn) as a member of Gryphon, whose first LP was issued in 1973. Terence Alan Wincott of Amazing Blondel played the crumhorn on the group's *Evensong* LP, from 1970. Lindsay Cooper joined the avant-rock band Henry Cow in 1973 and was featured playing oboe and bassoon on the 1974 album, *Unrest.*

THE FIRST TIME

The Amazing Blondel – Terence Alan Wincott holds a crumhorn

Andy MacKay

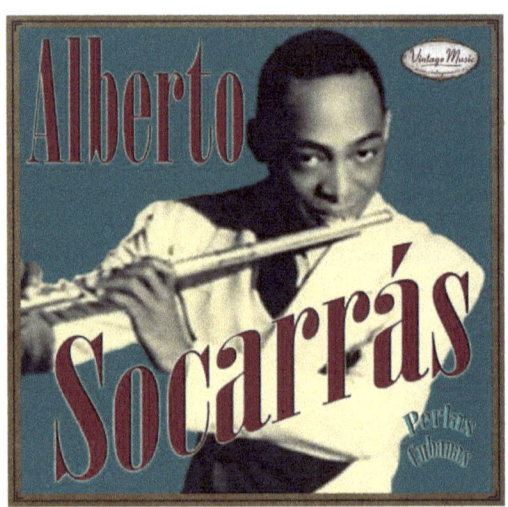

INSTRUMENTS AND MUSICIANS

The flute was first played on a jazz record when the Cuban musician Alberto Socarras recorded *Shooting The Pistol* with the Clarence Williams Orchestra in August 1927. Socarras led his own bands from 1935 and recorded the same year under his own name. The first rock group to use a flute was Manfred Mann. Mike Vickers played a short solo on *Without You*, the B-side to the single *5-4-3-2-1*, issued in January 1964. Ray Thomas of the Moody Blues played the flute during the closing section of the single, *From The Bottom Of My Heart*, issued in May 1965, although he did not deliver a proper solo until the group recorded *Nights In White Satin*, issued as a single and as part of the LP *Days Of Future Passed* in November 1967. Two flute solos were played on rock records in 1965 by session flautists who were not members of the groups concerned. The Beatles employed John Scott to play the closing section of *You've Got To Hide Your Love Away*, included on the *Help!* LP released in August. The Mamas and the Papas used Bud Shank on their single, *California Dreaming*, issued in December. Ian Anderson, who became internationally famous as a flautist, first played the instrument on several tracks of the first LP by Jethro Tull, *This Was*, issued in October 1968. Anderson's fondness for singing into the flute while he played it was a technique that he borrowed from the jazz musician Roland Kirk. The first recorded demonstration is the July 1961 track, *Funk Underneath*, included on the LP, *Kirk's Work*, and it is extended further the following month, on the track, *You Did It, You Did It*, on Kirk's LP, *We Free Kings*. The 1964 LP, *I Talk With The Spirits*, finds Kirk abandoning his main instrument, the tenor saxophone, in order to highlight the flute throughout. The first track is *Serenade To A Cuckoo*, which was adopted by Ian Anderson.

Although widely employed within renaissance and baroque music, the recorder has struggled to maintain credibility in more recent times, due to its adoption by schools as an ideal musical instrument for beginners. The first plastic recorders were manufactured in Germany in 1936 and became ubiquitous after World War II, being cheap to produce and relatively easy to play. It was not until 1967 that the instrument started to appear in pop and rock music. Significantly, the performers were all people whose main instrument was something else. Brian Jones used the recorder on *Ruby Tuesday*, issued by the Rolling Stones as a single B-side in January; Grace Slick played it on two tracks of the Jefferson Airplane LP, *Surrealistic Pillow*, issued in February; Jimi Hendrix played it on *If Six Was Nine*, included on his *Axis: Bold As Love* album from December; and Paul McCartney played it on *The Fool On The Hill*, from the Beatles *Magical Mystery Tour* set, issued in November in the US, December in the UK. Before any of these, however, Terry Kirkman, multi-instrumentalist with the American group, the Association, played a recorder solo on the group's first single, *Along Comes Mary*, which reached number 12 in the US charts in July 1966.

TRACKING THE TRACKS

The four tracks recorded by Buddy Holly with the Dick Jacobs Orchestra are included on several Holly compilations, such as *The Absolutely Essential 3 CD Collection* (Big 3 2016). Jackie Wilson's *To Be Loved* is on *The Very Best Of Jackie Wilson* (Ace 2004).

The Beatles *Help!* is on EMI (2009). The first Left Banke album, *Walk Away Renee/Pretty Ballerina,* is on Sundazed (2011). The four tracks recorded by Denny Laine's Electric String Band are not officially available on CD, although a bootleg release, *Memory Laine*, did include them, together with three live tracks recorded for the BBC. The entire album can be heard on YouTube. Jon Lord's *Concerto For Group And Orchestra,* recorded by Deep Purple with the Royal Philharmonic Orchestra conducted by Malcolm Arnold, was issued on CD by EMI in 2002.

The Velvet Underground & Nico is on Universal (2012). *Planned Obsolescence* by the Blues Project is on One Way Records (1996). *Bare Wires* by John Mayall's Bluesbreakers is on Decca (2007). *Sea Shanties* by High Tide is on Esoteric (2010).

The Complete 1936-1937 Sessions by Stuff Smith is on Hep (2008). A double CD, *The Joe Venuti and Eddie Lang Collection 1926-33,* is on Acrobat (2014). The Joe Venuti recordings with Jean Goldkette are on *Jean Goldkette Bands 1924-1929* (Timeless 2008). The Eck Robertson tracks are on *Old Time Texas Fiddler – Vintage Recordings 1922-1929* (County 1998).

United States Live by Laurie Anderson is a four disc set on CD (US Warner Bros 1991).

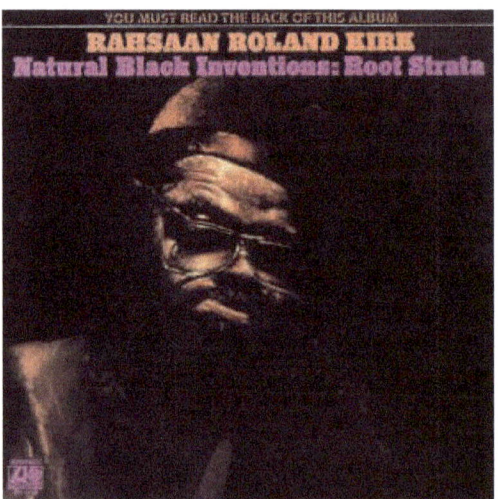
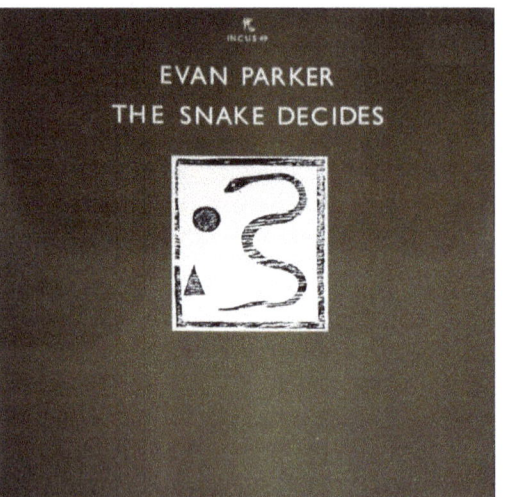

In A Cello Mood by Oscar Pettiford includes recordings from 1952-1954 and is on Fresh Sound (2007). *Complete Studio Recordings* by the Original Chico Hamilton Quintet (including Fred Katz) is on Phono (2016). The Fred Katz album shown is a double CD comprising three LPs from 1958 and 1959, issued in Katz's own name. They are *Soul Cello, 4-5-6 Trio,* and *Fred Katz and his Jammers*; the CD is on Fresh Sound (2013). The Beatles *I Am The Walrus* (and also *Penny Lane*) is on *Magical Mystery Tour* (EMI 2009). *Time Seller* by the Spencer Davis Group is included on *The Singles* (BR Music 2003). *Wheels Of Fire* by Cream is on Polydor (1997).

As already stated, the video of Wanda Jackson performing *Hard Headed Woman* in 1958 can be seen on YouTube. In addition to the trumpet player, Joe Maphis plays a solo on a rather splendid twin-necked electric guitar.

Hit And Miss is a good compilation of tracks by the John Barry Seven (C5 1989). The mid-sixties recordings by the Alan Bown Set are on *Emergency 999* (Sequel 2000). *The Mike Cotton Sound,* which includes the band's one original album with numerous bonus tracks, is on RPM (2015). Henry Lowther plays with Manfred Mann on Soul Of Mann (EMI 1999). Mike Falana plays on the Graham Bond Organisation single *St James Infirmary/Soul Tango*. It is included on *Love Is The Law* (Sunrise 2004). A later issue of the CD does not include these or the other bonus tracks.

The Very Best Of Herb Alpert (A&M 1991) includes *The Lonely Bull*.

So You Want To Be A Rock 'N' Roll Star by the Byrds is included on *Younger Than Yesterday* (Columbia 1996). *Alone Again Or* by Love is included on *Forever Changes* (Rhino 2008). *Born Cross Eyed* by the Grateful Dead is included on *Anthem Of The Sun* (Warner 2003). The author's copy of this CD has the single version of the song included, as a bonus track not mentioned anywhere in the booklet. *Mark Time*

INSTRUMENTS AND MUSICIANS

is included as a bonus track on the most recent issue of Eclection's self-titled album (Cherry Red 2016).

The Butterfield Blues Band added brass in time for the album *The Resurrection Of Pigboy Crabshaw* – included with the next album, *In My Own Dream,* on a Warner CD (2004). John Mayall's Bluesbreakers added brass for the album *Crusade* (Decca/Universal 2007). The Electric Flag album, *A Long Time Comin'*, is on Sony (2013). Of the many albums recorded by the Mar-Keys, *Otis Redding Live In Europe* (Volt 2014) is a definite highlight. *Chicago Transit Authority* is on Warner (2002), *Anthology* is a two CD compilation by the Skatalites (Primo 2007) and includes some tracks credited to Don Drummond.

The Claude Thornhill Collection 1934-53 includes Thornhill's early work with other bands as well as his own on a double CD (Fabulous 2015). The Julius Watkins Sextet *Volumes 1 and 2* is hard to find on CD, but is available as a download (Blue Note 1998). The Beatles *For No One* is on *Revolver* (EMI 2009). *Disguises* by the Who is included as one of several bonus tracks on the CD of *A Quick One* (Polydor 1995).

Fidgety Feet and *Jazz Me Blues* are included on the double CD *The Art Of Bix Beiderbecke* (Primo 2006). *Andy Kirk And His Twelve Clouds Of Joy 1929-1931* is on Jazz Chronological Classics (1994). It is hard to find and expensive on CD, but readily available as a download. *Red Callender Speaks Low* is part of the double CD set, *Red Callender – Four Classic Albums* (Avid Jazz 2016). *Sky 2,* which includes *Tuba Smarties*, is on Sanctuary (2005). Blood Sweat & Tears *In Concert* is a double CD on Wounded Bird (2012). Taj Mahal's *The Real Thing* is on SPV Recordings (2012). His *Happy Just To Be Like I Am* is on Columbia Mobile Fidelity (1991). Two tracks from each album are included on the double CD *The Essential Taj Mahal* (Sony 2005).

Coleman Hawkins can be sampled on *Body And Soul – Original Recordings 1933-49* (Naxos 2001), which includes his masterful demonstration of how to improvise, on *Body And Soul.*

Harry Carney played with Duke Ellington for virtually the whole of his career – forty-five years. Ellington died in May 1974 – Carney died just over four months later. *Rock Me Gently* is a rare album recorded, in 1960, without Ellington. It is included on CD with an album by two of Ellington's tenor saxophone players, *Two From Duke* by Paul Gonsalves and Harold Ashby (Vocalion 2012).

Roland Kirk's eccentric *Natural Black Inventions: Root Strata* from 1971 serves as a demonstration of the man's unusual playing abilities, including playing two or three instruments at the same time and playing without pauses for breath. It is combined with the album *The Inflated Tear* for release on CD (Rhino 2004).

On *The Snake Decides* from 1986, Evan Parker plays alone on soprano saxophone and constructs dense soundscape patterns of notes and riffs, using harmonics and circular breathing. The CD is on psi (2015).

Elvis Presley's *King Creole* is on RCA (1997). *The Very Best Of Acker Bilk* is a double CD on One Day Music (2015). The Beatles *Sgt Pepper's Lonely Hearts Club Band* is on EMI (2009). *We're Only In It For The Money* by the Mothers Of Invention is on Zappa Records (2012). Gentle Giant's self-titled first album is on Repertoire (2004). *Trout Mask Replica* by Captain Beefheart and his Magic Band is on Reprise (2004).

The two tracks by the Louisiana Sugar Babes can be heard on YouTube. They are also included on a 4 CD set by Fats Waller, who was a member of the group. This is *The Complete Recorded Works Volume 1 1922-1929* (JSP Records 2007). John Coltrane's *Africa/Brass* is on Essential Jazz Classics (2012). Yusef Lateef *Live At Cranbrook* has some studio recordings added for the CD *At Cranbrook And Elsewhere* (Cherry Red 2009). The original album is included on the double CD *Four Classic Albums* (Avid Jazz 2014) and is much cheaper. *Jazz Round The World* is not available on CD, but can be obtained as a download (Universe 2013).

The Best Of Gerry & The Pacemakers is on EMI (1992). *The Best Of Sonny & Cher – The Beat Goes On* is on Warner (2005). King Crimson's *Lizard* is on DGM/Panegyric (2009). The self-titled first album by the Electric Light Orchestra is on Harvest (2003). The self-titled first album by Roxy Music, including *Virginia Plain* is on Virgin (1999). The first album by Gryphon is on Talking Elephant (2007). *Evensong* by Amazing Blondel is on Edsel (1995). *Unrest* by Henry Cow is on ReR (2014).

Shooting The Pistol is on *Shake 'Em Up – Clarence Williams 1927 – 1929* (Frog Records 2000). The only available music by Alberto Socarras in his own name is an album called *Latin Impressions* (Vintage Music 2015), which was originally issued in 1956.

Manfred Mann's *Without You* is included on the compilation *A's B's & EP's* (EMI 2003) or else the first album by the group, *The Five Faces Of Manfred Mann* (Umbrella Music 2012). *From The Bottom Of My Heart* and *Nights In White Satin* are both included on the double Moody Blues CD, *The Singles* (BR Music 2001). *California Dreamin' – The Best of the Mamas and the Papas* is on Universal (2006). Jethro Tull's *This Was* is available as a double CD 'Collectors Edition', including both mono and stereo mixes and numerous radio session recordings and singles (EMI/Chrysalis 2008). Roland Kirk's *Kirk's Work* and *We Free Kings* are included in the double CD, *Four Classic Albums* (Avid 2014). *I Talk With The Spirits* is on Universal (1999).

Ruby Tuesday is included on the double CD, *Forty Licks* (Abkco/Virgin 2003) by the Rolling Stones. *Surrealistic Pillow* by Jefferson Airplane is on BMG (2003). *Axis: Bold As Love* by the Jimi Hendrix Experience is on Sony (2012). *Magical Mystery Tour* by the Beatles is on EMI (2009). *Greatest Hits* by the Association is on Warner Bros (2008).

George Harrison having a sitar lesson from master musician Ravi Shankar

Despite the cover picture, it was not John Mayer who played the sitar on the album

Moroccan street gimbri player

Sandy Bull playing the oud

7 WORLD AND FOLK INSTRUMENTS

During the making of the Beatles' second film, *Help!*, in April 1965, George Harrison became intrigued by the playing of some Indian musicians hired for one particular scene. He started learning to play the sitar himself and by October felt confident enough to add a part for the instrument to the recording of the song, *Norwegian Wood*. Released as the second track on the LP *Rubber Soul* in December 1965, the song marked the debut in rock music for the sitar. During the next few years, the characteristic drone and twanging sound of the instrument seemed to become ubiquitous in rock music, with groups like Magic Carpet and Cosmic Eye going so far as to include a sitar player as a permanent member of the line-up. *Norwegian Wood* very nearly failed to achieve its ground-breaking status. Earlier in 1965, the Yardbirds, who had already included the novelty sounds of harpsichord and tablas on their hit single, *For Your Love*, decided that the riff chosen to begin the song *Heart Full Of Soul* lent itself to being played on a sitar. The song was indeed recorded like this, but seemed to be lacking in drive. Jeff Beck then proved that he could generate a similar sound on his guitar, which was how the single was eventually released. According to the description by manager Giorgio Gomelsky, in the CD set, *The Yardbirds Story*, which includes both versions of the song, Jimmy Page, then a session guitarist working in the same studio, ended up buying the sitar from its original owner. He showed it to George Harrison – a second and equally plausible explanation as to how the Beatle ended up playing it on *Norwegian Wood*.

Indian-born violinist John Mayer joined forces with Jamaican-British alto saxophonist Joe Harriott at the instigation of the president of Atlantic records, Ahmet Ertegun. Fusing Mayer's quintet of classical Indian musicians with Harriott's jazz quintet, they produced an album called *Indo-Jazz Suite* in 1966, followed during the next two years by further albums, *Indo-Jazz Fusions* and *Indo-Jazz Fusions II*. The music, an unusual but highly successful amalgamation of different musical styles, marked the debut of the sitar in jazz. It was influential enough for Miles Davis to include the instrument within his own music during the latter part of 1969 and through 1972.

During their performances in 1967, the duo of Mike Heron and Robin Williamson would surround themselves with several exotic stringed instruments to add weight to their chosen name, the Incredible String Band. On the acclaimed album they made that year, however, *The 5000 Spirits Or The Layers Of The Onion*, they mostly contented themselves with playing acoustic guitars. An essential sitar featured on one track, although neither Heron nor Williamson played it. On another track, however, Williamson played an oud, while on another he played a bass gimbri, both of these being Arab stringed instruments. The appearance of the oud was not a first. The jazz bass player, Ahmed Abdul-Malik, incorporated the instrument during several ground-breaking albums that fuse jazz with world music, beginning with *Jazz Sahara* in 1958. The American group Kaleidoscope incorporated an oud into their line-up, played by Solomon Feldthouse, who also employed several other stringed instruments from different parts of the world, including the Turkish saz, the Greek bouzouki, and the Indian veena. All of these would be accessible to a musician trained on the guitar. The group's first album, *Side Trips*, was issued in June 1967, a month before the Incredible String Band LP. Two years earlier, folk pioneer Sandy Bull had his album *Inventions* released. He played guitar, bass, banjo, and oud, although the album made little impression at the time.

Kaleidoscope's use of the bouzouki was a first. Dave Dee, Dozy, Beaky, Mick & Tich sounded as though they were using one on their 1966 hit *Bend It*, but the instrument in question was actually an amplified mandolin. Cat Stevens included two bouzoukia on his *Teaser & The Firecat* album (they are extremely prominent on *Rubylove*), while what sounds like a guitar on the title track of the Jan Dukes De Grey album, *Mice And Rats In The Loft*, is an amplified bouzouki. Both of these records date from 1971. A duet by Jean Luc Ponty and Frank Zappa, with the latter playing bouzouki (included on the *Shut Up 'n Play Yer Guitar* set), was probably recorded in 1972. The same year, the Irish

THE FIRST TIME

Bouzouki

Balalaika

Ukulele

Mandolin

Pipa

Banjo

Vess Ossman

Luna Lee playing the gayageum

group Planxty was formed, with bouzoukia included in the line-up. The author of this book played a bouzouki during a student holiday to Greece in 1969 and wrote a song on it, but sadly this was never recorded.

The traditional Russian popular stringed instrument is the balalaika. Several of them can be heard on Van Dyke Parks' 1967 album, *Song Cycle*. Ian Anderson played one of them on two tracks of Jethro Tull's second album, *Stand Up*, in 1969. The Chinese pipa has been adopted by some Western musicians much more recently. The composer Lou Harrison wrote a Concerto for Pipa and String Orchestra in 1997. An earlier pipa concerto, *Little Sisters Of The Grassland*, written in a Western classical music style by a communist-approved committee of Chinese composers (Wu Zu Qiang, Wang Yan Qiao, and Liu De Hai) was first performed in 1977. The pipa features too on one track of the 2001 album, *Morning View*, by the Californian group Incubus, played by the group's guitarist.

The ukulele was developed in Hawaii at the end of the nineteenth century. It became very popular in the US during the twenties in both vaudeville and country music. Cliff Edwards, known as Ukulele Ike, recorded five songs for Columbia in 1919 as half of a duo with singer Pierce Keegan, but none of them was issued. In 1920, UK Columbia issued a record by the anonymous 'Hawaiian Guitars and Ukelele Trio' playing *La Paloma* and *Valse Bleue*. In 1922, Cliff Edwards recorded *Virginia Blues* with a jazz band called Ladd's Black Aces (whose pianist was the later Hollywood star, Jimmy Durante). The song was issued on a Gennett 78, coupled with the unrelated *You've Had Your Day* by the Mardis Gras Sextette. Edwards became a considerable star, gaining a number one hit in 1929 with *Singin' In The Rain*, and going on to become the voice of Jiminy Cricket in the 1940 Walt Disney film, *Pinocchio*. In the UK, George Formby made his first records, singing and playing the ukulele and the banjolele, in 1926. The Herman's Hermits 1965 hit, *Mrs Brown, You've Got A Lovely Daughter*, was deliberately reminiscent of George Formby, but what sounds like a lightly amplified ukulele is actually a guitar. A YouTube video of virtuoso ukulele player Jake Shimabukuro performing an instrumental version of *While My Guitar Gently Weeps* was uploaded in 2006 – ten years later it had attracted nearly fifteen million views. George Harrison himself became a fan of the instrument at the end of his life and played it on the Beatles 'reunion' single, *Free As A Bird*, in 1995.

The mandolin was widely popular from the end of the nineteenth century. It was then used in all kinds of music, although it eventually became most common within folk and country. There are numerous mandolin recordings made through the twenties in a variety of genres, but the earliest of all would appear to be *St Louis Tickle*, recorded by the Ossman-Dudley Trio (comprising banjo, mandolin, and harp-guitar) in 1906 and released on a Victor 78 in 1908. The first recordings by the Memphis Jug Band, the Dallas String Band, and the less well-known Aiken County String Band, all playing blues/country and all including a mandolin player, took place in 1927.

Vess L.Ossman, the banjo player in the Ossman-Dudley Trio, was an international star, known as 'The Banjo King', and successful from the eighteen nineties until the First World War. He first recorded in 1893, a cylinder of *Sousa's Washington Post March* being issued by the North American Phonograph Company. Many further Ossman recordings were released during the following years. The banjo was a particularly popular instrument at the time and even entered the world of classical music when Frederick Delius included it in his opera, *Koanga*, which he completed in 1897. Several players apart from Vess Ossman were recorded during the eighteen nineties. The first was Will Lyle, who had several cylinders issued during 1889.

The Japanese koto has rather more in common with a harp than a guitar. Nevertheless, a miniature version of the instrument was played by guitarist Brian May on the Queen track, *The Prophet's Song*, on the 1975 album, *A Night At The Opera*. The full sized instrument was played by David Bowie on the track *Moss Garden*, from his 1977 album, *Heroes*. It has been claimed that Brian Jones played the koto on two Rolling Stones tracks, recorded in 1966, but if he did, the instrument was placed so far down in the mix as to render it inaudible. The tracks in question are *Take It Or Leave It* and *Ride On Baby*. The Korean version of the koto, the gayageum, has been used by Luna Lee to play virtuoso interpretations of blues and rock material on the stage and on YouTube since 2009.

A West African instrument with some of the appearance of a guitar, but actually also played more like a harp, is

The kazoo is not so much an instrument as a cheap way of modifying the human voice. It makes no sound of its own but has to be sung or hummed into to achieve its novelty buzz. The kazoo was first patented in 1883, with the version still used today dating back to 1902, although similar devices are very much older than this. Its first appearance on record was for a solo on *Crazy Blues*, played in 1921 by the Original Dixieland Jazz Band.

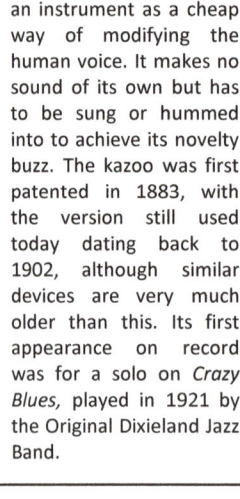

Washington Phillips

There is one set of earlier recordings by Jean Ritchie, on a series of children's records put together by record company executive Mitch Miller in 1948, under the title *Rounds And Roundelettes*. On these, however, Ms Ritchie sings but does not play her dulcimer. She explains all this in a lengthy interview published in the Winter 2003 issue of *Pass It On!* – the journal of the Children's Music Network.

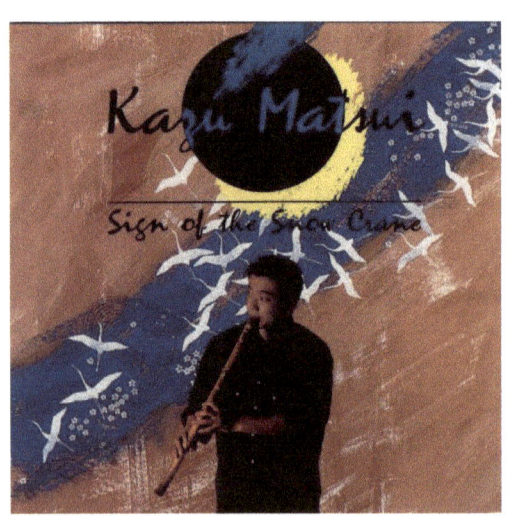

the kora. It has appeared in Western music as a result of African musicians being involved. The first of these was the Gambian kora player, Foday Musa Suso, who formed the band Mandingo Griot Society in Chicago and released a first album in 1978. Don Cherry, a jazz musician with a considerable interest in world musics, was a guest performer. Subsequently, Suso recorded with Herbie Hancock, including a 1985 album of keyboard and kora duets, *Village Life*. The French composer, Jacques Burtin, has become a kora specialist and has written a number of modern classical pieces to feature the instrument, beginning in 1986. A kora is included in the film soundtrack, *Powaqqatsi*, composed by Philip Glass in 1988 and is played by Foday Musa Suso.

The traditional Celtic harp was brought into the modern age by Breton musician Alan Stivell. He first attracted attention with the albums *Reflets* in 1970 and *Renaissance De La Harpe Celtique* in 1971, although he recorded four singles for the Breton label Mouez-Breiz between 1959 (when he was fifteen) and 1961, under his real name Alan Cochevelou, and a ten inch LP, *Telenn Geltiek – Harpe Celtique*, for the same label in 1961. The Swiss musician Andreas Vollenweider plays an electric harp of his own design, based on the Celtic harp. He made his first album, *Eine Art Suite In XIII Teilen*, in a progressive rock style, in 1979.

Gospel singer Washington Phillips was recorded during 1927 to 1929, accompanying himself on an ethereal sounding, tinkly instrument. It was long believed that this was a dolceola, a kind of zither whose strings were activated by means of a keyboard. A contemporary photograph, however, shows Phillips holding a pair of straightforward zithers. The instrument, played like a harp, but with a soundbox like a guitar, derives from Alpine Europe. It was prominently featured in the Johann Strauss II work, *Tales From The Vienna Woods*, composed in 1868, but achieved more modern fame when played by Anton Karas in the soundtrack music for the 1949 film, *The Third Man*. A simplified version of the zither, the autoharp, was invented in the eighteen eighties. It was played by Maybelle Carter, whose group the Carter Family began recording in 1927. She established a folk-country tradition, of which John Sebastian would have been well aware when playing an autoharp on the Lovin' Spoonful recordings of *You Baby* and *Younger Girl* in July and August 1965. Perhaps the same would not have been true of the British beat group, the Downliners Sect, whose singer Don Craine played autoharp on the group's first album, *The Sect*, issued in late 1964, nor of Pinkerton's Assorted Colours, whose February 1966 hit, *Mirror Mirror*, featured the instrument.

Another simplified version of the zither, with frets and only three or four strings, is the Appalacian dulcimer, which was first constructed in the Appalacian Mountain region of America at some time in the early nineteenth century. In the early decades of the twentieth century, Loraine Wyman became interested in the folk songs of the region and performed them in concerts held in New York, beginning in 1916. During the course of these, she demonstrated the dulcimer to her audiences, although she generally sang to the accompaniment provided by a pianist. She published the songs she had collected, complete with the piano arrangements, in two sheet music collections, but she made no recordings. It was not until 1952 that the Appalacian dulcimer appeared on record, with the release of a ten inch LP by folk singer Jean Ritchie, *Singing The Traditional Songs Of Her Kentucky Mountain Family* (the first folk record on the newly established Elektra label). The instrument made occasional forays within the folk music world after that, but it was nevertheless still treated as a novelty when Joni Mitchell used it to accompany four songs on her 1971 album, *Blue*. The Appalacian dulcimer made a rare appearance in rock when it was played by Brian Jones on the Rolling Stones songs, *Lady Jane* and *I Am Waiting*, included on the *Aftermath* LP in 1966.

The Japanese bamboo flute, the shakuhachi, which, unlike its Western counterpart, is blown across the end, reached Western music when the Japanese player, Kazu Matsui, recorded his first album in California in 1981. *Time No Longer* employs several well known jazz fusion musicians but is closer to progressive rock than jazz. The same year, Matsui played the shakuhachi on the Ry Cooder soundtrack, *Southern Comfort*, while in 1985, he played on another Cooder soundtrack, *Alamo Bay*, and on Joni Mitchell's *Dog Eat Dog* album. Ned Rothenberg, the first non-Japanese exponent of the shakuhachi, played it on his 1992 album, *The Crux*.

The nose flute, literally played by blowing air into it from the nostrils, originates in various parts of the world.

Roland Kirk

Charlie McMahon

Kathryn Tickell

Pete Hampton and Laura Bowman

The ocarina is one of the oldest instruments in the world, but does not feature much in modern music. Krzysztof Penderecki's use of several of them in his 1974 orchestral piece, *The Dream Of Jacob,* and the solo that appears in the middle of *Wild Thing* by the Troggs in 1966 are rarities.

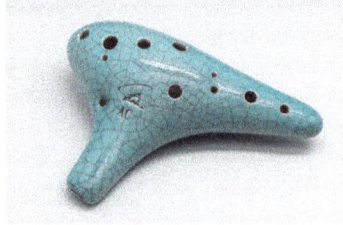

INSTRUMENTS AND MUSICIANS

Roland Kirk added the instrument to his arsenal, sometimes managing to play it at the same time as a conventional flute. He plays the nose flute on two occasions on the *Kirk In Copenhagen* LP from 1964 and, both times, members of the audience laugh.

Several recordings were made in 1910 by Pipe Major Willie Ross playing the Scottish bagpipes. Three pieces played by Tom Clough on the smaller and quieter Northumbrian pipes were issued by HMV in 1929. There is a surprising number of later instances of bagpipes of both kinds being played on recordings that are neither traditional nor military. Two rock records issued in 1968 include Scottish bagpipe playing – *Sky Pilot* by Eric Burdon and The Animals (included on the LP *The Twain Shall Meet*) and *Morning Dew* by the Jeff Beck Group (included on the LP *Truth*). Rufus Harley started playing the bagpipes as a jazz instrument in 1964 and made his first record the year after, the LP *Bagpipe Blues*. Harley was almost a lone voice, but Albert Ayler attempted to occupy the same territory, playing the bagpipes on his last album, *Music Is The Healing Force Of The Universe*, in 1969.

The Chieftains made their first, self-titled, album in 1964, on which the Uillean pipes (similar to the Northumbrian pipes) were highlighted. The subsequent success of other traditional groups, like Planxty and the Bothy Band, kept the pipes alive but it was not until 1981 that they appeared on a record that was not traditional – the LP *October* by U2. Two tracks on the 1982 Van Morrison LP, *Beautiful Vision*, are credited with including Uillean pipes, although they are only audible on *Celtic Ray*. More surprisingly, the pipes (played by Paddy Moloney of the Chieftains) are heard on one track on the first solo LP by former Eagle Don Henley, *I Can't Stand Still*, also released in 1982. A third album from the same year includes the Uillean pipes as well – *The Dreaming* by Kate Bush. The Northumbrian pipes, played by Kathryn Tickell, appear on two albums by Sting – *The Soul Cages* and *Ten Summoner's Tales* – from 1991 and 1993 respectively.

The Australian aborigine didgeridoo also appears on Kate Bush's *The Dreaming*, played by Rolf Harris. It was Harris who introduced the instrument to Western audiences, when he made it a major element of his 1962 hit single, *Sun Arise*, although the didgeridoo sound was actually mimicked by multiple double basses on this occasion. The 1966 LP, *Rolf Harris Again*, has a track called *That's What They Call A Didgeridoo*, on which someone – presumably Harris – does play the instrument. The first contemporary album by a band having a didgeridoo in its line-up was *Terra Incognita*, issued in 1984 by Charlie McMahon and Gondwanaland. The instrument is included in the Philip Glass soundtrack, *Naqoyqatsi*, composed in 2002.

The harmonica, also known as the mouth organ or, inaccurately, the mouth harp, was invented during the eighteen twenties, possibly by the German instrument maker, Christian Buschmann. The first harmonica player to be recorded was probably Pete Hampton, whose song, *Dat Mouth Organ Coon*, was issued on a cylinder in 1904. Hampton was himself African-American. The first recording of blues harmonica playing was on Clara Smith's *My Doggone Lazy Man* in 1924, with the instrument played by Herbert Leonard, although the previous year the white harmonica player Henry Whitter employed much the same style on *Rain Crow Bill Blues* and some other tunes, which were issued on the Okeh label. Whitter's *Lost Train Blues* established a blues harmonica style that later became ubiquitous. DeFord Bailey's *Pan American Blues* from 1928 raised the bar on playing that imitated the rhythms and the sound of a steam train to a level that is unlikely to be ever beaten.

The chromatic harmonica, equipped with a sliding bar to enable any note to be played, was first made in 1924 by the company founded in 1857 by Matthias Hohner. It was recorded the same year by the Dizzy Trio featuring Borrah Minevitch, playing *Hayseed Rag*. Larry Adler started to use the instrument to interpret classical pieces. His first recording, in 1934, was a version of *Smoke Gets In Your Eyes*, but two years later, Cyril Scott wrote a *Serenade* for Larry Adler to play with a pianist. During the fifties, a number of composers wrote full-blown harmonica concertos. The first of these was by Michael Spivakovsky in 1951, which was performed by Tommy Reilly. Adler was the recipient of concertos by Arthur Benjamin and Malcolm Arnold, in 1953 and 1954, while that by Heitor Villa-Lobos, in 1955, was written for John Sebastian (the father of the singer-guitarist who founded the Lovin' Spoonful).

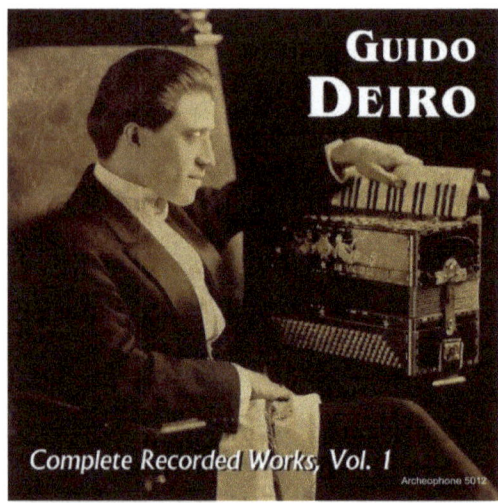
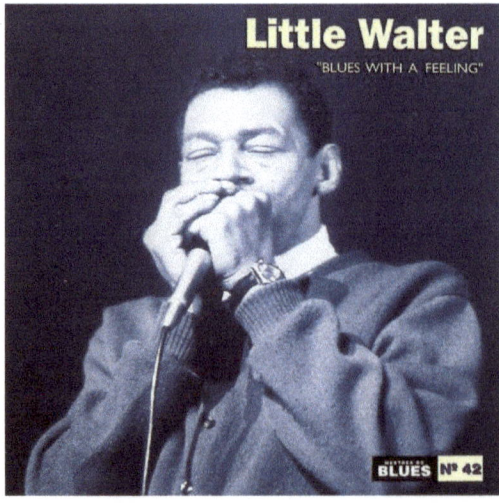

Joseph Falcon with Clemo Breaux

*The Basement Tapes (cover detail).
Rick Danko holds Garth Hudson's accordion;
Hudson holds a euphonium that he did not play.
Bob Dylan pretends he has not seen a mandolin before.*

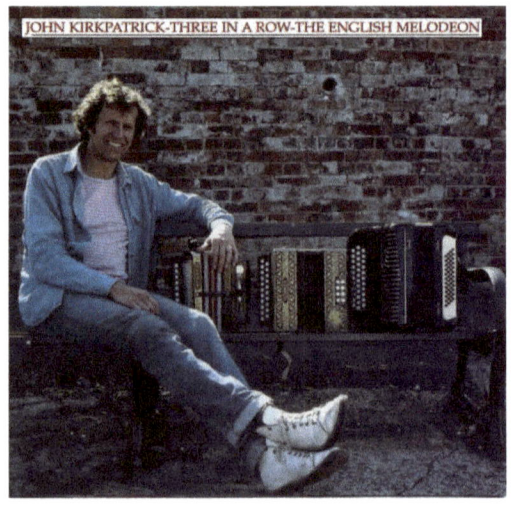

'Rock On' was already established as a cool phrase by 1972. It was the name of a record collectors' market stall in London and the title of a 1971 album made by Humble Pie. In the circumstances, the choice of title for an album made by various musicians, loosely working in the rock music area, but wanting to create some modernised English folk music, seemed obvious. *Morris On,* with its reference to traditional Morris dancing, was the one.

INSTRUMENTS AND MUSICIANS

Little Walter Jacobs pioneered the technique of cupping his hands round both harmonica and microphone in order to produce an effective electric instrument, complete with distortion overload when required. He first recorded in this way on *Country Boy* in July 1951, as a member of the Muddy Waters band. The first tune issued in his own name was *Juke*, recorded in May 1952, and a substantial hit, reaching number one in the Billboard R&B chart. William Russo incorporated this kind of blues harmonica playing into an orchestral work in 1973, *Three Pieces For Blues Band And Orchestra*. He chose the white Siegel-Schwall Band for the job, rather than someone like Little Walter. One suspects that this was because he wanted them to play in a routine, clichéd manner, to enable him to subvert their contribution with the unexpected and dissonant counter-melodies of the orchestra.

During 1962, three pop hits chose to include prominent harmonica parts. They were *Hey Baby* by Bruce Channel, *I Remember You* by Frank Ifield, and *Love Me Do* by the Beatles. Although John Lennon played the harmonica on a few more Beatles songs during the next two years, the fad was soon overtaken by the growing popularity of blues on the one hand and the rise of folk harmonica players like Bob Dylan and Donovan on the other.

Although considerably more complex in its construction, the accordion is essentially the same kind of instrument as the harmonica, producing its sound by the passage of air vibrating thin strips of metal. It is often credited with the same inventor, Christian Buschmann, at about the same time, although this remains unproven. The first big accordion star in vaudeville was Guido Deiro. His recordings of *Sharpshooters March* and *Ciribiribin Waltz* date from January 1911 and were issued on a Columbia 78. Though less successful, John J. Kimmel recorded a traditional tune called *American Clog* for the American Zonophone label in 1905, using the button accordion known as a melodeon. Before even that, around 1903, a Scottish shop-keeper, Peter Wyper, who sold music-related goods and had access to equipment with which he could record his own cylinders, began making recordings of traditional reels. Although the cylinders he produced did not have a wide availability, they were a commercial product.

A number of classical music composers included the accordion in their scores, of which the earliest, *Thème Varié Très Brillant* by Louise Reisner, dates from 1836. Peter Tchaikovsky wrote for the accordion in his *Orchestral Suite No.2*, in 1883. In the twentieth century, Paul Hindemith used the instrument in his 1921 *Kammermusik No.1* and this was the first work to feature the chromatic version of the accordion.

Clifton Chenier became a considerable star playing the accordion in the Louisiana blues music known as zydeco. He first recorded in 1954, with *Clifton's Blues*. The first zydeco recordings were made by Amede Ardoin in 1929, playing the accordion with fiddler Dennis McGee. *Taunt Aline* coupled with *Two Step De Mama* was the first 78 to be issued, on Columbia and Okeh. The first Cajun recording (essentially the same music, but played by white people) was made a year earlier by accordion player Joseph Falcon. *The Waltz That Carried Me To My Grave* backed with *Lafayette* was issued on a Columbia 78.

The accordion joined the rock music vocabulary when it was included, played by Garth Hudson, on the LP by the Band, *Music From Big Pink*, released in July 1968. Hudson had played it the year before on the Bob Dylan sessions that comprised *The Basement Tapes*, but these were not officially released until 1975. In the UK, Fairport Convention used the instrument (played by Richard Thompson) on the group's second LP, *What We Did On Our Holidays*, released in January 1969. Thompson was interested in Cajun music at this time, as was further evidenced by two tracks on the third Fairport Convention LP, the aptly titled *Cajun Woman* and a version of Bob Dylan's *If You Gotta Go*, performed in Cajun style and sung in French (the preferred language in Louisiana), as *Si Tu Dois Partir*.

John Kirkpatrick became the accordion player of choice within the UK folk and folk-rock world – the first accordion star in the country, if that is not over-stating his position. He was included on the 1972 album made by various people associated with Fairport Convention, *Morris On*, and made his own first record in the same year, the LP *Jump At The Sun*.

THE FIRST TIME

TRACKING THE TRACKS

The Beatles LP *Rubber Soul* is on EMI (2009). The self-titled Magic Carpet album, with Clem Alford on sitar, is on Magic Carpet Records (1995). *Dream Sequence* by Cosmic Eye, with Viram Jasini on sitar (and John Mayer on violin) is on Sound Edition (2013). Both versions of *Heart Full Of Soul* are on *The Yardbirds Collection* (Castle 1987) or on the 4 CD set *The Yardbirds Story* (Charly 2008). *Indo-Jazz Suite* by the Joe Harriott-John Mayer Double Quintet is on Atlantic (2014). The two volumes of *Indo-Jazz Fusions* are combined on a Universal CD (1998). The sitar playing in Miles Davis' music is most obvious and effective on some of the tracks included in the four CD set, *Bitches Brew – The Complete Sessions* (Columbia 1998).

The 5000 Spirits Or The Layers Of The Onion by The Incredible String Band is on Fledg'ling (2010). *Jazz Sahara* by Ahmed Abdul-Malik is on Universal/Riverside (2009). *Side Trips* by Kaleidoscope is on Sundazed (2007). *Inventions* by Sandy Bull is on Vanguard (2008) but is hard to find. Four of the six tracks are included on *Re-Inventions – Best Of The Vanguard Years* (Vanguard 1999).

Bend It by Dave Dee, Dozy, Beaky, Mick & Tich is included on *The Very Best Of* (Spectrum 1998). *Teaser And The Firecat* by Cat Stevens is on Island (2009). *Mice And Rats In The Loft* by Jan Dukes De Grey is on Mischief Music (2008). Frank Zappa's *Shut Up 'n Play Yer Guitar* is a double CD on Zappa Records (2012). *The Planxty Collection* is on Shanachie (1989). *Song Cycle* by Van Dyke Parks is on Bella Union (2012). *Stand Up* by Jethro Tull is on Chrysalis (2010).

Lou Harrison's *Concerto For Pipa With String Orchestra* is on the CD *For Strings* (Mode 2004). *Little Sisters Of The Grassland* by Wu Zu Qiang, Wang Yan Qiao, and Liu De Hai is played by the Boston Symphony Orchestra, conducted by Seiji Ozawa on a Universal/Decca CD (2013). The CD also includes works by Liszt and Sousa on which the pipa is not played. *Morning View* by Incubus is on Epic (2009).

The double CD *Fascinating Rhythm 1922-1935* by Cliff 'Ukelele Ike' Edwards is on Challenge Records (2011) and includes both *Virginia Blues* and *Singin' In The Rain*. There are a number of George Formby compilations, such as *Happy Go Lucky Me – The Best Of George Formby* (Music Digital 2013). The 1926 recordings are included on the four CD set, *Singles Collection Vol.1 1926-1937* (Real Gone Music 2016). *Mrs Brown You've Got A Lovely Daughter* is on the double CD *The Very Best Of Herman's Hermits* (EMI 2005). The Beatles *Free As A Bird* is available as a CD single (EMI 1995) and is also included on the double CD *Anthology 1* (EMI 1995).

There are no CDs available by Vess L. Ossman, although an LP, *Kings Of The Ragtime Banjo,* was issued in 1974 on the Yazoo label. Ossman shares space on the record with Fred Van Eps, but it does include *St Louis Tickle*. This track can also be heard on YouTube, together with several other Ossman tracks, though not Sousa's *Washington Post March*. Recordings by the Memphis Jug Band, the Dallas String Band, and the Aiken County String Band are available on YouTube. There are several CDs of the Memphis Jug Band, such as *The Best Of The Memphis Jug Band* (Yazoo 2001).

Delius's *Koanga* is on a double CD (EMI 2003), although it is deleted and copies turning up for sale are expensive. Videos of a 1995 performance made in Trinidad can be seen on YouTube. Nothing by Will Lyle would appear to be available, not even on YouTube.

A Night At The Opera by Queen is on Queen Productions (2011). *Heroes* by David Bowie is on EMI (1999). *Take It Or Leave It* and *Ride On Baby* are on the Rolling Stones album *Flowers* (Abkco 2002).

The self-titled first album by The Mandingo Griot Society is on Flying Fish (1992). *Village Life* by Herbie Hancock and Foday Musa Suso was released on vinyl in 1985. A Japanese Sony CD was issued in 1996, but is not currently available. The complete album can be heard on YouTube. *Le Chant Interieur* by Jacques Burtin is on a Discovery CD (2000). *Powaqqatsi* by Philip Glass is on Elektra/Nonesuch (1990).

The Alan Stivell albums *Reflets* and *Renaissance De La Harpe Celtique* are on Disques Dreyfus (1994). *Telenn Geltiek* is also on Disques Dreyfus (2000) but is much cheaper as a download. The singles are not currently available. Andreas Vollenweider's *Eine Art Suite In XIII Teilen* is not currently available but can be heard on YouTube. Many later albums are on CD, including a compilation, *The Essential Andreas Vollenweider* (Edel 2006).

All sixteen recordings made by Washington Phillips are on *The Key To The Kingdom* (Yazoo 2005). The Johann Strauss piece, *Tales From The Vienna Woods,* is included in several CDs, such as one named after it on Conifer (1987). *The Third Man (Harry Lime) Theme* played by Anton Karas is on *The Third Man And Other Classic Film Themes* (Naxos 2009).

The Best Of The Carter Family – The Millennium Collection is on MCA/Universal (2005). *You Baby* and *Younger Girl* by The Lovin' Spoonful are on *Do You Believe In Magic* (Buddha 2002). *The Sect* by Downliners Sect is on Repertoire (2005). *Mirror Mirror* by Pinkerton's Assorted Colours is remarkably hard to find on CD (a double CD compilation from 2004 is now selling for around a hundred pounds!). It can, however, be heard on YouTube, where it has been uploaded by several different users. *Jean Ritchie Singing The Traditional Songs Of Her Kentucky Mountain Family* is deleted on CD, but available as a Rhino/Elektra download. *Blue* by Joni Mitchell is on Reprise (2000). *Aftermath* by the Rolling Stones is on Abkco (2002).

Time No Longer by Kazu Matsui is on Cool Sound (2008). Matsui plays on five tracks on the double CD compilation of Ry Cooder soundtracks, *Music By Ry Cooder* (Warner Bros 1995). Joni Mitchell's *Dog Eat Dog* is on Geffen (1985). Ned Rothenberg's *The Crux* is on Leo (1992).

INSTRUMENTS AND MUSICIANS

Roland Kirk's *Kirk In Copenhagen* is on Universal (2004). *Crazy Blues* by the Original Dixieland Jazz Band is included on *The Essential Collection* (West End 2006).

Various recordings by Willie Ross can be heard on YouTube. Two tracks by Tom Clough are included on the various artists compilation, *The Northumbrian Small Pipes* (Topic 2009). *The Twain Shall Meet* by Eric Burdon and The Animals is on Repertoire (2011). Alternatively, *Sky Pilot* is included on *The Very Best Of Eric Burdon and The Animals* (Spectrum 1998). *Truth* by Jeff Beck is on EMI (2005). *Bagpipe Blues* by Rufus Harley is on Atlantic (2014). *Music Is The Healing Force Of The Universe* is combined with another Albert Ayler album, *New Grass*, on a Universal/Decca CD (2015).

The first, self-titled, LP by The Chieftains is on Claddagh (2000). *The Essential Chieftains* is a good overview on a double CD (Sony BMG 2006). *The Best Of The Bothy Band* is on Mulligan (2008). *October* by U2 is on Universal (2008). *Beautiful Vision* by Van Morrison is on Polydor (1989). *I Can't Stand Still* by Don Henley is on Asylum (1989). *The Dreaming* by Kate Bush is on Fish People (2011). *The Soul Cages* and *Ten Summoner's Tales, by Sting,* are on A&M (1998).

Wild Thing is on *The Troggs Greatest Hits* (Spectrum 2003). *The Dream Of Jacob* is on several compilations of Penderecki's music, such as the one on EMI Classics (2012).

Sun Arise and *That's What They Call The Didgeridoo* are both included on *The Best Of Rolf Harris* (EMI 2003). *Terra Incognita* by Gondwanaland is on WEA (1987); *Over Gondwanaland – Best Of* is on Destra (2000). *Naqoyqatsi* by Philip Glass is on Sony/BMG (2002).

Recordings by Pete Hampton comprise the first disc of the three CD set, *Over There! – Sounds And Images Of Black Europe* (Bear Family 2013). Clara Smith's *Complete Recorded Works In Chronological Order Volume 2* (Document 1989) includes *My Doggone Crazy Man.* The Henry Whitter collection on Doxy (2014), available as a download only, includes *Rain Crow Bill Blues* and *Lost Train Blues*. The first track can also be heard on YouTube. *Pan American Blues* is included on *The Legendary DeFord Bailey* (Tennessee Folklore Society 1998). *Hayseed Rag* by The Dizzy Trio can be heard on YouTube, uploaded by several different users. Larry Adler's performance of *Smoke Gets In Your Eyes* is included on several CD compilations of his early recordings, such as *Rhapsodies & Blues* (Newsound 2000, 2004). His performances of the harmonica concertos by Arthur Benjamin and Malcolm Arnold, with the Royal Philharmonic Orchestra conducted by Morton Gould, were issued on an RCA LP in 1968 but have not been reissued on CD. An earlier performance of the Benjamin concerto, with the London Symphony Orchestra conducted by Basil Cameron, is available as a download, courtesy of BNF Collection. A CD of Tommy Reilly playing the concertos by Spivakovsky, Arnold, and Villa-Lobos, with various orchestras, is on Chandos (1993). The Cyril Scott *Serenade,* performed by Wai Hang-hay with Rosalind But on the piano, can be seen and heard on YouTube.

A Little Walter CD, H*is Best – The Chess 50th Anniversary Collection,* is on Chess/MCA (2000). *Juke* is one of the tracks. The three CD set by Muddy Waters, *The Chess Singles Collection* (Not Now Music 2015), includes *Country Boy*. William Russo's *Three Pieces by Blues Band and Orchestra* are on a Deutsche Grammophon CD (2002), performed by the Siegel-Schwall Band with the San Francisco Symphony Orchestra, conducted by Seiji Ozawa. It is not easy to find, but the album can be heard on YouTube. Bruce Channel's *Hey Baby* is on a CD with the same title (Hallmark 2012). Frank Ifield's *I Remember You* is on *The Essential Frank Ifield Collection* (EMI 1997). The first LP by The Beatles, *Please Please Me* (EMI 2009) has John Lennon playing harmonica on four songs, including the title track and *Love Me Do.* Bob Dylan's harmonica playing is all over the hits compilation, *Dylan* (Columbia 2007). Donovan's playing is on *Catch The Wind* (Castle Pulse 2008).

Complete Recorded Works Vol.1 by Guido Deiro (Archeophone 2007) includes the accordionist's *Shapshooters March* and *Ciribiribin Waltz*. An LP of recordings by John J Kimmel, *Early Recordings Of Irish Traditional Dance Music,* was issued on the Leader label in 1977. It has not been reissued on CD, but many tracks from the LP, as well as other recordings by Kimmel, can be heard on YouTube. A small number of recordings by Peter Wyper can also be heard on YouTube, including one, with very poor sound quality, identified as the melodeon player's first. Five tracks are included on the Topic CD, *Melodeon Greats* (2011).

Louise Reisner's accordion composition, *Thème Varié Très Brillant,* can be heard on YouTube. Tchaikovsky's *Orchestral Suite No.2* is included on a Capriccio CD (1994) along with *No.1*. They are played by the Stuttgart Radio Symphony Orchestra, conducted by Sir Neville Marriner. Hindemith's *Kammermusik No.1* is included on a Universal/Decca double CD (2003) along with the other six *Kammermusik* pieces. They are played by the Royal Concertgebouw Orchestra, conducted by Riccardo Chailly. There are several other CDs available that include both the Tchaikovsky and the Hindemith pieces.

Clifton Chenier's *Rockin' Accordion* (Jasmine 2015) contains a selection of his recordings made from 1954 until 1960, including *Clifton's Blues*. *The Best Of Clifton Chenier* is on Arhoolie (2003). *Mama I'll Be Long Gone – The Complete Recordings Of Amede Ardoin 1929-1934* is on Tompkins Square (2011). Joseph Falcon's *Lafayette* (but not the other side of the original 78) is included on the various artists double CD compilation, *The Best Of Cajun & Zydeco* (Not Now Music 2010). A second Falcon track is there, as well as three by Amede Ardoin (one of which is *Taunt Aline)* and six by Clifton Chenier.

Music From Big Pink by The Band is on Capitol (2000). *The Basement Tapes* by Bob Dylan and The Band is on a double Columbia CD (2009). *What We Did On Our Holidays* and *Unhalfbricking* by Fairport Convention are both on Island (2003). *Morris On* by Ashley Hutchings, Richard Thompson, Dave Mattacks, John Kirkpatrick, and Barry Dransfield is on Fledg'ling (2009). John Kirkpatrick's *Jump At The Sun* was released as an LP on the Trailer label. It has not been reissued on CD, but one track is included on the compilation that serves as a 'Best of John Kirkpatrick', *The Dance Of The Demon Daffodils* (Fledg'ling 2009).

THE FIRST TIME

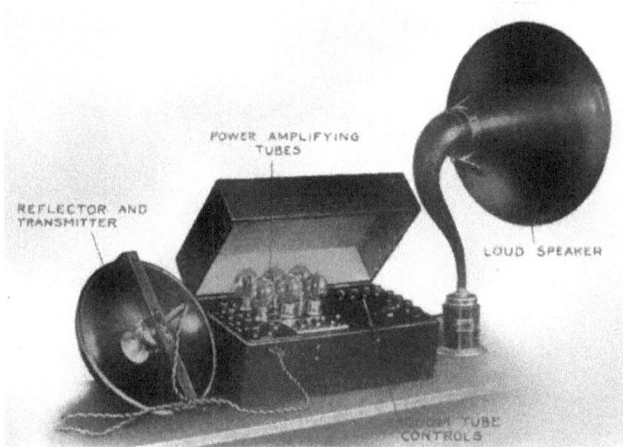
PA system from 1920. 10 watts of power

The Beatles at the Cavern. 25 watts of power

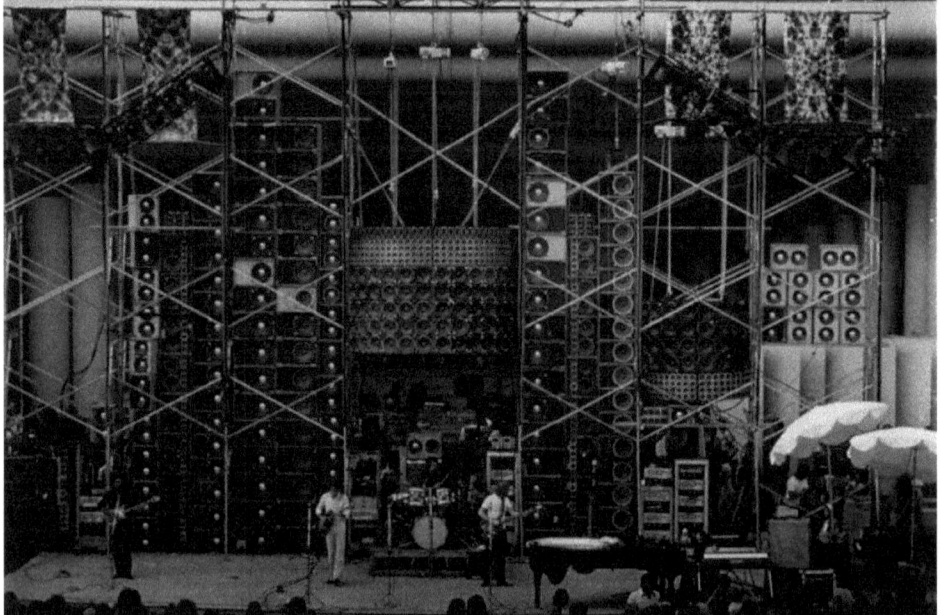
Grateful Dead Wall of Sound, Hollywood Bowl July 21st 1974. 28,800 watts of power. The sound system used at the Woodstock festival had a power of a little over 10,000 watts

The Newport Jazz Festival was started in 1954 in Rhode Island as the first large-scale music event. In the UK, the Beaulieu Jazz Festival was started in 1956. It faced problems with crowd violence in 1960 and did not continue, but was replaced by the National Jazz and Blues Festival in 1961, in Richmond, South West London. This eventually evolved, after changes in location and musical policy, into the Reading Festival, which still continues as an annual event. The first rock festival in the US was the Magic Mountain Festival, which was held in Marin County, California, in June 1967, a week before the much better known Monterey Festival. The Magic Mountain Festival had the Byrds, Jefferson Airplane, the Doors, and Captain Beefheart (who performed so badly that his guitarist, Ry Cooder, left the band). Monterey had Otis Redding and Jimi Hendrix, which, perhaps, made the difference.

The first occasion where on-stage monitoring was employed was a San Francisco concert given by Judy Garland in September 1961. Speakers at the side of the stage were turned towards the singer and her band by the McClune Sound Service, which had provided the PA system, although no attempt was made to create any kind of enhanced vocal mix for Garland's individual benefit. In the UK, where musicians were unaware of developments in the US, on-stage monitoring like this was first used at the National Jazz and Blues Festival in 1968, as a result of a spontaneous experiment by Charlie Watkins, who had provided the PA system.

Bill Hanley at Woodstock

8 THE PA SYSTEM

The first PA (public address) system was put together from components pioneered, in some cases, in the nineteenth century. The first microphone was invented by David Edward Hughes, an American music professor (though born in the UK), or by the American Thomas Edison, depending on whose dates are believed. For Hughes, the year is variously stated as 1866, 1875, or 1878. For Edison, it was 1877. The two men employed different technologies and it is Edison's use of a carbon diaphragm that survived in subsequent microphone designs. Claims are also made on behalf of the German Emil Berliner and the Scottish Alexander Graham Bell, who used the same carbon diaphragm technology in their telephone inventions, with patents dating back to 1876. A dispute between them was later resolved by the US Supreme Court, which declared Berliner's patents invalid.

The first moving coil loudspeaker, the ancestor of all speakers made since, was designed by the British physicist Oliver Lodge in 1898. He called his invention a bellowing telephone. The triode, a device that could amplify an electrical signal, was invented in 1906 by the American Lee DeForest, who called it an audion. Subsequently, various people began combining these different pieces of equipment. On December 24th 1915, Edwin Jensen and Peter Pridham demonstrated their pioneering PA system at San Francisco City Hall, where a Christmas carol concert was heard by a hundred thousand people. For several decades afterwards, there was no essential change in the way that music was amplified at live events and concerts.

For music fans who attended live performances in dance halls and clubs during the later sixties, when guitar amplifiers had become louder and more powerful to enable rock groups to make a greater impact, it became an accepted norm that the vocals would struggle to be heard or might even be completely inaudible. When the Beatles became the first rock act to play at a stadium – the Shea Stadium concert in New York in August 1965 – it became apparent that here too the amplification available was simply not up to the task. Although film of the event does not make this clear, from the stands the assembled fans could not hear the singing at all, especially when it had to compete with their own loud screaming.

The necessary work to improve the power and usefulness of the PA system for rock concerts was carried out as a response to the Shea Stadium experience. A number of sound engineers played their part in developing louder amplification – Charlie Watkins (whose company was called Watkins Electric Music, or WEM), Gene and Roy Clair (Clair Brothers), the McClune Sound Service (founded in 1932 by Harry McClune, to supply PA systems for dance bands), Bob Heil (who worked with the Grateful Dead in 1970, improving the clarity of the speakers and introducing feedback-cancelling measures), and Owsley Stanley (who designed the massive system used by the Grateful Dead in 1974). Two crucial developments were carried out by Bill Hanley, who had begun by providing the sound system for the Newport Jazz Festival in 1957. Hanley began lending his expertise to a number of rock bands in 1966, including the Remains, the Beach Boys, and Buffalo Springfield. Neil Young, with the last-named band, began using Hanley's equipment to provide himself with on-stage monitoring of his vocals, in the form of speakers placed on the stage in front of him and pointing at him, rather than at the audience. Subsequently, Bill Hanley was entrusted with building the sound system for the Fillmore East concert hall in New York, which opened in March 1968. He combined the cables feeding the speakers into a single bundle, the snake, which connected to a mixing desk placed at the back of the hall, with transformers to ensure no loss of signal. For the first time, a sound technician was able to properly balance and control the sound of the groups, hearing the same music as did the audience. Dinky Dawson was able to create a version of the snake to use on tour in 1969, with the group who employed him as road manager, Fleetwood Mac. Colosseum followed suit for concerts later the same year, the mixing desk manned by road managers Kenny Smith and Scott Thompson. Bill Hanley went on to organise the sound system for the Woodstock festival in August 1969.

THE FIRST TIME

PART 2

RECORDS AND RECORDINGS

THE FIRST TIME

Edison wax cylinder phonograph, turn of the century

Thomas Edison

The first flat disc record made by Emil Berliner, in 1889, contained a recording of himself reciting a poem by Friedrich Schiller. This was subsequently lost, but in 2012, Patrick Feaster, working at Indiana University, was able to use some remarkable computer technology to recreate a playable record from a photograph of the original printed in a magazine in 1890. The result can be heard on the website gizmodo.com.

The first novelty record appeared as early as 1912. *The Conundrum – What Will I Play Next*, was issued by Victor as the B-side to a record by comic narrator Mark Sheridan. It was made with four separate grooves, so that, depending on where exactly the needle was placed at the start, one of four different pieces of music would play. The band responsible and the singer who performs on three of the tracks are not credited. The idea was occasionally used again in later years, most notably on the *Jimmie Rodgers Puzzle Record* from 1931 and the Monty Python LP from 1973, *Matching Tie And Handkerchief*.

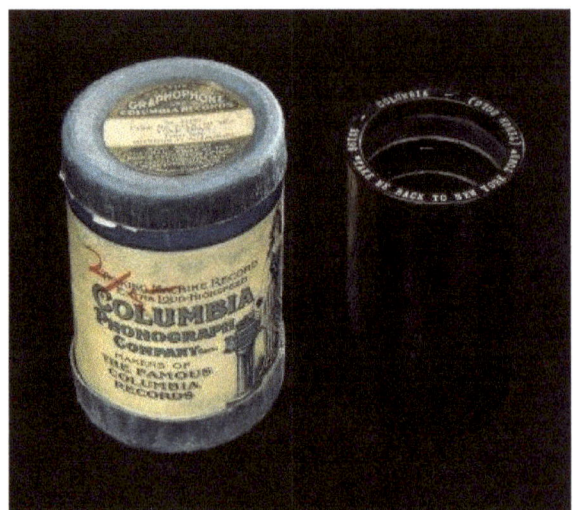

Columbia cylinder and case

Samuel Holland Rous, who recorded under the name S.H.Dudley. He claimed to be unaware of a popular black vaudeville singer by the name of Sherman Houston Dudley

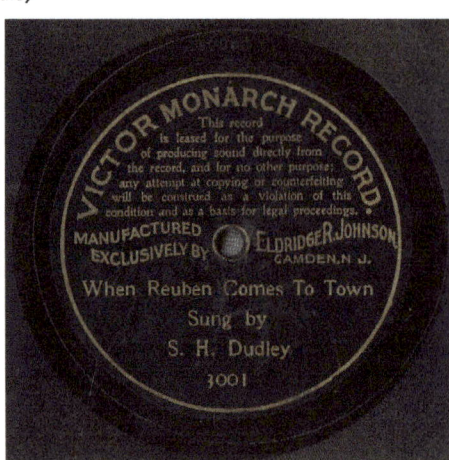

Francis Barraud painting, 'His Master's Voice', adopted as a logo by Emil Berliner

9 FORMATS

A kind of recording, dating from 1857, was patented by Frenchman Edouard-Léon Scott de Martinville. It consisted of a drawing of a waveform, captured by generating a scratch on a surface coated with soot. It was not possible to replay the recorded sound, but modern technology in 2008 has been able to convert a surviving drawing, made in 1860, into a twenty second fragment of a man singing a just recognisable French folk song, *Au Clair De La Lune*. This is the first recording we have, but it is not, perhaps, quite what we expect such a thing to be.

The American Thomas Edison invented a machine for recording sound and playing it back in 1877, calling it a phonograph. He described the first time he used the machine:

> I designed a little machine using a cylinder provided with grooves around the surface. Over this was to be placed tinfoil, which easily received and recorded the movements of the diaphragm … Kruesi (the machinist), when he had nearly finished it, asked what it was for. I told him I was going to record talking, and then have the machine talk back. He thought it absurd. However, it was finished, the foil was put on; I then shouted 'Mary had a little lamb,' etc. I adjusted the reproducer, and the machine reproduced it perfectly. I was never so taken aback in my life. Everybody was astonished. I was always afraid of things that worked the first time.

Edison lost interest in his new device, preferring to focus his attention on another of his inventions, the electric light bulb. It was left to Alexander Graham Bell to explore sound recording further and to develop the wax cylinder as the format of choice, enabling recordings that would survive repeat playbacks. The earliest known recording, carried out in this manner, was in 1888, when a performance of Handel's *Israel In Egypt* at Crystal Palace, London, by a four thousand-strong choir, was captured on a wax cylinder. A digitally restored (though still quite noisy) recording of the wax cylinder's contents was uploaded on to YouTube in 2011.

Cylinder recordings were sold to the public from 1890, when they were manufactured by the Columbia Phonograph Company. The first numbered Columbia cylinder is 32000, *Cupid's Arrow* by the banjo player Vess L. Ossman. This, however, was issued in 1903 – the earlier releases were not numbered. Several other companies made cylinders during the last years of the nineteenth century, including Edison's own. Different sizes were produced, with playing times of two, three, or four and a half minutes, although the shortest playing time was by far the most common version.

Emil Berliner started selling flat disc recordings in Europe in 1889, but the sound quality was inferior to that of the cylinders arriving soon afterwards. Nevertheless, Berliner founded Deutsche Grammophon in Germany and the Gramophone Company in the UK, in 1897. In the United States, the Victor Talking Machine Company was founded in 1901 by Berliner and gramophone manufacturer Eldridge Johnson. Initially the records were five or seven inches in diameter, but ten inch records were introduced on both sides of the Atlantic in 1901, followed by twelve inch discs in 1903. In 1904 records were introduced able to be played on both sides. Several different playing speeds were used – that of 78 rpm did not become the standard until 1925, long after the format battle with the cylinder had been won. Columbia and many other companies ceased the production of cylinders in 1912, although Edison carried on until 1929. The earliest ten inch record listed in the Discography of American Historical Recordings is *When Reuben Comes To Town*, performed by singer S.H.Dudley with piano accompaniment, recorded in January 1901 and issued on Victor with the number 3001.

In September 1931 RCA Victor, the company formed two years earlier when the Radio Corporation of America purchased the Victor Talking Machine Company, held the first demonstration of a long playing record, capable of delivering fifteen minutes of music on each side, while turning at a speed of thirty-three and a third rpm. In its

Specialist jazz label Dial issued the first LP by Charlie Parker, *The Bird Blows The Blues,* as a twelve inch disc in 1949, without an art cover, advertising it as being available by mail order. Subsequent LPs by Parker, also issued in 1949, were the ten inch records expected for popular releases at this time.

RCA long playing record and player, complete with second record waiting on automatic changer, as pictured in 1931 advertisement

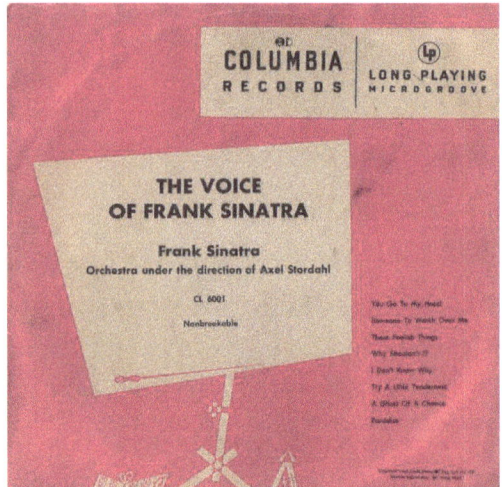

This album was reissued two years later with a blue cover

Mick Houghton's exhaustive history of Elektra Records, *Becoming Elektra,* includes a photograph of a record labelled as 'The very first LP' and dated 27th February 1946. This is a Columbia test pressing, made in advance of the 1948 press conference. It contains a recording of Nikolai Rimsky-Korsakov's *Scheherazade* by an uncredited orchestra. A recording of the work by Eugene Ormandy and the Philadelphia Orchestra was issued by Columbia in 1949, so this may well be that one.

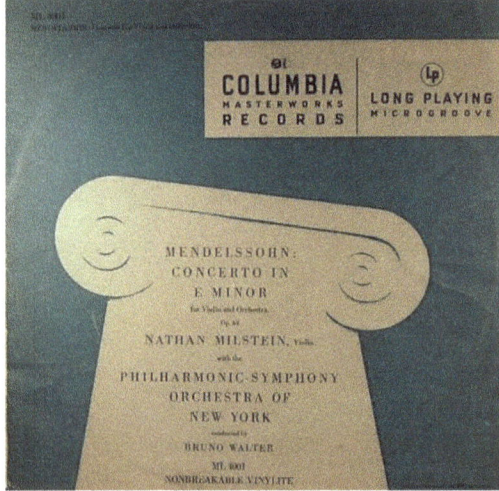

Arthur Crudup That's All Right

Spade Cooley Spanish Fandango

The long established company, Barnett Samuel and Sons, began manufacturing the first portable record player in 1914, using the trade name Decca. In 1929, stockbroker Edward Lewis, who had been hired as an adviser, bought the Decca Gramophone Company and switched to the manufacture of records, rather than players. Lewis began an American Decca company in 1934, but sold it three years later, thereby severing the connection between the two Decca labels.

subsequent advertising, the company referred to these records as 'program transcriptions'. It announced that thirty-four classical music recordings had already been made, the first of which was a performance of *Beethoven's Fifth Symphony*, conducted by Leopold Stokowski. Clearly the idea was a good one, but it was a commercial failure, due to the high prices charged for both the records and the equipment for playing them. The fact that the Great Depression was in progress did not help either.

Seventeen years later, Columbia Records decided to try again. At a press conference in June 1948, the company announced the release of 133 LP records (or albums, carrying on a term used to describe packaged sets of 78 rpm records featuring one artist or one classical work). This time, the company also promoted a cheap player. Designed to be attached to a radio, the record player was given away free with a purchase of five LPs. The great majority of the initial release comprised classical music on twelve inch discs. The first in the catalogue, given the number ML4001, was a recording of Mendelssohn's *Violin Concerto*, played by Nathan Milstein with the Philharmonic-Symphony Orchestra of New York, conducted by Bruno Walter. A much smaller number of popular recordings were contained on ten inch discs, of which the first in the catalogue, number CL6001, was *The Voice of Frank Sinatra*.

Capitol and Decca followed Columbia's example in 1949. RCA Victor, nervous about making the move for obvious reasons, decided to do so in January 1950. In the UK, EMI, formed in 1931 by the merger of the Gramophone Company with the UK arm of Columbia, prevaricated – and it was Decca which issued the first LPs in June 1950. The company's initial release sheet comprised fifty-three records, most of which were classical. The first in the catalogue were LXT2501, a recording of Bach's *Brandenburg Concertos numbers 4 and 6*, played by the Stuttgart Chamber Orchestra, conducted by Karl Munchinger; LF 1001, a ten inch LP by Ronnie Munro and his Orchestra, playing a selection of Chopin Waltzes; and LK4001, a recording of *Trial by Jury* by Gilbert and Sullivan, performed by the D'Oyly Carte Opera Company. The claims made on behalf of the new format by advertisers at the time will sound very familiar to those who remember the promotion of CDs nearly three and a half decades later. Superb sound quality, with 'almost silent' playing surfaces, negligible wear during play, unbreakability, and ease of storage were all cited as reasons for purchasing LPs, rather than albums of 78s.

RCA Victor introduced the 7" 45 rpm single in March 1949, intending the format to be a rival to Columbia's LP. 104 singles and 76 'albums' – boxed sets containing three or four records – were released simultaneously, most of them being reissues of music previously available on 78s. Seven different colours of vinyl were used, to indicate to which genre of music each record belonged. One single in each category was distributed to record shops for promotional purposes, in advance of the release date. These were a recording of excerpts from Tchaikovsky's *The Sleeping Beauty*, conducted by Leopold Stokowski ('Red Seal' music, red vinyl), *Because* by Dick Leibert (popular music, black vinyl), *The French Marching Song* by Al Goodman and his Orchestra (popular classics, midnight blue vinyl), *Spanish Fandango* by Spade Cooley (country & western, green vinyl), *That's All Right* by Arthur Big Boy Crudup ('blues and rhythm', cerise vinyl), *A Klein Melamedl* by Saul Meisels (International music, sky blue vinyl), and, presumably, as the record widely claimed as the first to be pressed, *PeeWee The Piccolo Song* by Paul Wing with Russ Case and his Orchestra (children's entertainment, yellow vinyl). It is likely, however, that other packages of coloured singles were also distributed, with different titles being used. The promotional sampler record giving the details to retailers and produced at the same time was uploaded on to YouTube by Verycoolsound in 2009. Two months after the official release date of the new format, *A – You're Adorable* by Perry Como, became the first record available on a 7" single (though on 78 too) to reach the top of the Billboard charts.

Columbia responded by issuing, in April 1949, a 7" version of their LP format, playing at 33 rpm, and with a small centre hole, in contrast to the large hole favoured by RCA. These records were not successful, but at the end of the year and into the beginning of 1950, other labels began to issue 7" singles playing at 45 rpm – including at the end of 1950, Columbia. What had been viewed as a battle of the formats had come to an end, with both sides being able to claim victory.

THE FIRST TIME

The three playing speeds used for records are related arithmetically, although there is widespread agreement that this is simply a coincidence. The website *straightdope.com* claims, however, that RCA, when developing the single, "told its engineers to come up with any old speed so long as it wasn't compatible with Columbia's system". The unspoken suggestion is that perhaps the RCA engineers chose 45 precisely because it was the result of subtracting Columbia's 33 from 78. *The Goldmine Price Guide to 45 rpm Records* by Tim Neely goes further than this. Its introduction quotes record producer George Avakian as saying, "in 1962, when I was at RCA, someone finally told me where 45 rpm came from. They apparently took 78 and subtracted 33 which left them with 45, which they went with out of spite".

A specialist US rhythm and blues label, Aladdin, issued many LPs from 1952 on both black and red vinyl, beginning with the second release in the catalogue, *Mood Music* by Charles Brown. Vinyl is clear when produced – black or any other colours have to be added.

A flexi disc is a record, usually the size of a 7" single, made of very thin, flexible vinyl. Such records were usually used as promotional releases or as free items attached to a magazine. Perhaps the first to be issued was a turquoise Cliff Richard record given away with *Serenade* magazine in 1960. Several 78 rpm records issued by Goodson from 1929 were also thin and pliable. The record numbered 101 was *Let's Pretend* by the Pennsylvania Melody Syncopators, coupled with *Just A Night For Meditation* by the Marathon Dance Orchestra, although there were a few earlier releases without numbers.

One of the last EPs to be issued in the UK in the sixties, *Something Else From The Move,* reclaimed the format's status as a miniature version of the LP and was manufactured to be played at thirty-three and a third rpm. In the US, Parkway Records tried the release of a 33rpm EP in 1961, with a record by Chubby Checker. A few other companies followed suit, but none persevered with the experiment.

The first batch of Decca LPs included a triple album of Bach's *The Art Of Fugue*, performed by the Radio Orchestra of Beromunster, conducted by Herman Scherchen. Columbia's catalogue from 1950 included a double LP set by Benny Goodman, *The Famous 1938 Carnegie Hall Jazz Concert,* but the two LPs were sold separately. The first double LP packaged as a single item in a gatefold sleeve was *Ella Fitzgerald Sings The Cole Porter Songbook*, released by Verve records in 1956. The following year, Elvis Presley's *Christmas Album* was released in a gatefold sleeve, despite being a single LP. The first double LP released by a rock artist (not including a couple of American Beatles albums put together in 1964 in order to make the most of what might have proved to be a short-lived phenomenon – *The Beatles vs The Four Seasons* and *The Beatles Story*) was the first album by the Mothers Of Invention, *Freak Out*, released on June 27th 1966. It was closely followed by Bob Dylan's *Blonde On Blonde*. A well-researched article by Jake Brown on the *gloriousnoise.com* website proves that the frequently quoted release date of May 16th for Dylan's album has to be incorrect, not least because overdubs were still being recorded for the track *4th Time Around* a month later than this.

In the UK, the 45 rpm single was not introduced until January 1953. EMI started to release singles on its HMV and Columbia labels. The Leroy Anderson pieces, *Blue Tango* and *Belle of the Ball*, performed by Ray Martin and his Concert Orchestra, were issued as the two sides of the first Columbia single and helped the record to reach number eight in the newly established New Musical Express chart. *I'm Yours/That's The Chance You Take* by Eddie Fisher was the first HMV release. Fisher's *Outside Of Heaven* reached number one at the end of January 1953, but the 45 rpm pressing was not issued until March. Many of the number one hit records during 1953 and 1954 were issued on the new format, but only some time after they had moved back down the charts. The first number one record where sales of the 7" singles would have contributed to its success was *Softly Softly* by Ruby Murray, issued in January 1955.

During 1952, RCA in America introduced the 7" EP – a record that still played at 45 rpm, but managed to contain two songs (sometimes more) on each side. A large number of records were issued that year. The format proved to be of limited popularity in the US, but was much more successful in the UK. The EMI labels, Columbia, HMV, and Parlophone, all issued EP records from April 1954. Alongside several classical music records, the first batch included a collection of four pieces by Eddie Calvert as the first release in Columbia's popular music series. It was issued in a generic record company sleeve – dedicated picture sleeves, like miniature versions of those used for LPs, did not become the norm until the following year.

Record players in the fifties and sixties had a fourth playing speed included. LPs made to be played at 16 (and two thirds) rpm were introduced in about 1950 and were used for spoken word recordings, often intended for the visually impaired. As it happens, the very first such release predated the LP. A set of shellac discs, playing at 16 rpm, was issued in 1935 in the UK by the Royal National Institute for the Blind. It was a recording of the Agatha Christie novel, *The Murder of Roger Ackroyd*, and it was the first audiobook.

During 1956-7, the specialist jazz record company, Prestige, issued a series of six LPs playing at the slow speed, each one containing two of the regular LP titles. The first of the series (PRLP 16-1) combined a self-titled record by the Milt Jackson Quartet with *Concorde* by the Modern Jazz Quartet. Vox issued a small selection of classical records at around the same time and a company called Dancetime issued a small number of light orchestral records by Will Kennedy and his Stereo Orchestra. Meanwhile, the French company Ducretet-Thomson was responsible for a much larger selection of light orchestral and other records.

At the annual Audio Fair held in New York in October 1957, the Westrex system – a method of cutting the groove on records so as to produce a double channel, stereophonic sound – was demonstrated. One company in America (Cook Records) had previously issued twin track stereo discs in 1952-3, using recordings of sound effects, but these had to be played with two pickups. During 1954, RCA in America and both Decca and EMI in the UK made stereo recordings. RCA issued the results commercially on pre-recorded reel-to-reel tapes, the first one being a recording of the Richard Strauss work, *Also Sprach Zarathustra*, performed by the Chicago Symphony Orchestra, conducted by Fritz Reiner. EMI did the same in the UK, issuing what it called 'stereosonic' tapes from April 1955 on its Columbia and HMV labels. The first to be issued were a recording of the Sibelius *Symphony No 2*, performed by the Philharmonia Orchestra, conducted by Paul Kletzki (on Columbia) and a recording of the Dvorak *Cello Concerto*, performed by Paul Tortelier with the Philharmonia Orchestra, conducted by Sir Malcolm Sargent (on HMV).

Towards the end of 1957, two small record companies in the US issued stereo demonstration records. Audio Fidelity's LP, intended as a promotional release, included six tracks by the Dukes of Dixieland on one side and a selection of railway engine sounds on the other. Bel Canto Records produced a similar item, pressed on multi-coloured vinyl. Side one presented a stereophonic tour of Los Angeles, while side two had six tracks by some lesser known jazz players, starting with Si Zentner. In March 1958, both companies issued a number of stereo LPs to the general public. The first releases were from Audio Fidelity, of which the lowest catalogue number was for *Mallet Magic* by Harry Breuer and his Quintet (AFSD 1825).

The first stereo issue used the mono cover with a gold 'StereoDisc' sticker on the front

Acetates are records made of metal with a thin vinyl coating. They were produced on occasions when only a very small number of records were required – maybe just one – and were made by cutting the recording wave form directly on to a blank disc, rather than going through the more complicated manufacturing process required for a mass produced general release. Song pluggers in the early sixties would often operate acetate disc-cutters to enable them to easily produce convenient demonstration recordings at a time when cassettes did not exist. Within recording studios, similar quickly produced acetates would be made in order to give the artist or some other interested party some idea of how the finished recording would sound. Various companies in the fifties and sixties offered a personal recording service with an acetate as the finished product. A famous early example is the record made by Elvis Presley, supposedly for his mother's birthday, coupling *My Happiness* with *That's When Your Heartaches Begin* on an acetate single, the year before his first studio recordings for Sun. The record was included in an auction of Elvis memorabilia held at his home, Graceland, in January 2015. Jack White of the White Stripes was the successful bidder, paying three hundred thousand dollars for the record.

The first *Greatest Hits* album is frequently claimed to be *Johnny's Greatest Hits* by Johnny Mathis, released on March 17th 1958 and beating *Elvis' Golden Records* by four days. At least three compilations of hits date from before this, however, even if they don't use the magic phrase 'Greatest Hits' in their titles. *The Best Of Elvis* was issued as a ten inch LP in the UK in October 1957. Its ten tracks were all UK or US hits – on the Mathis album only six out of the twelve tracks included were hit singles, with a further two being B-sides that achieved US hit status in their own right. Frank Sinatra's *This Is Sinatra* was released in November 1956 and included ten hits within its twelve tracks. Fats Domino's *Rock And Rollin' with Fats Domino,* issued in November 1955, included nine hits (from the Billboard R&B chart) out of its twelve tracks, although four were made into singles after the LP was released.

Embassy Records was founded in 1954 to sell cut-price singles in Woolworths shops in the UK, with cover versions of contemporary hits. In April 1961, a series of six-track EPs was started by the Cannon label in the UK, presenting compilations of similar hit cover versions. Several other companies adopted the same formula in subsequent years, most of which transferred it to LP records. The most successful of these was the *Top Of The Pops* series (unrelated to the BBC television show), begun in June 1968 for the budget Hallmark label by Alan Crawford, the man who had also started Cannon. Philip Kives went a stage further by licensing tracks issued by different record companies in order to release hit compilations on his own K-Tel label. These were the original versions and not sound-alike covers. His first release, in the US, was *25 Great Country Artists Singing Their Original Hits*, issued in 1966 on a label called Artistic. The first UK releases, on K-Tel, followed in 1972 – *20 Dynamic Hits* and *Believe in Music*, subtitled *22 Original Hits Original Stars*. The selection of tracks on these compilations tended to be a bit random, depending on those for which K-Tel had managed to complete a deal. The first *Now That's What I Call Music* album was issued in 1983 as a collaboration between Virgin and EMI, which allowed for a much better coverage of hit tracks.

The major record companies followed suit in August 1958, when a large number of stereo records, covering various kinds of music, were given a simultaneous release. In most cases, the catalogue numbers are of no help in determining the first issues, as the stereo records simply used a new prefix in front of the mono number, but were not released in the sequence this implied. Columbia, however, started two new stereo series. MS6001, the first of the company's 'masterworks', was a recording of the Respighi compositions *The Fountains of Rome* and *The Pines of Rome*, performed by the Philadelphia Orchestra, conducted by Eugene Ormandy. CS8001, the first of the pop series, was *'S Awful Nice* by Ray Conniff and his Orchestra. The first RCA classical record in what the company branded 'Living Stereo' was the Fritz Reiner recording of *Also Sprach Zarathustra*, which was given the number LSC 1806.

In the UK, Pye, EMI, and Decca all released records intended to demonstrate the system in mid 1958, the LPs comprising extracts from various light and classical pieces, together with assorted sound effect recordings. Commercial stereo LPs appeared in September. The first numbered LPs in the Decca catalogue were *Film Encores* by Mantovani (SKL 4002 – the previous number was taken by the demonstration record) and Tchaikovsky's *1812 Overture* with two other works, performed by the London Symphony Orchestra, conducted by Kenneth Alwyn (SXL 2001). For Columbia, the LPs were less logically numbered – *Waldteufel Waltzes* by Henry Krips and the Philharmonic Promenade Orchestra (SCX 3251) and Beethoven's *Emperor Concerto*, performed by Emil Gilels with the Philharmonia Orchestra, conducted by Leopold Ludwig (SAX 2252). For HMV, the first LP was Rimsky-Korsakov's *Scheherazade*, performed by the Royal Philharmonic Orchestra, conducted by Sir Thomas Beecham (ASD 251). Stereo recordings gradually increased in popularity during the sixties. All the major record companies had abandoned issuing new LPs in mono by the end of 1969, although many singles were still made in mono as late as 1974.

During the early seventies a number of quadraphonic LPs were issued. When played on a suitable system, incorporating a special decoder, such records enabled sounds to be heard from each of four speakers. These were intended to be arranged with two in front of the listener, as in stereo, and a further two behind the listener. The extra two speakers delivered ambient sound in the case of recordings designed to recreate the sound of a live performance; otherwise they could be essential ingredients in a surround-sound experience. The system was first made available to the public when Vanguard used it for a series of reel-to-reel tapes, issued in June 1969. The first release was a demonstration album comprising classical music extracts by Handel, Berlioz, and Mahler, together with one track each by Joan Baez, Buffy Sainte-Marie, and Jean Jacques Perrey. The first quadraphonic LPs were issued in 1971, using the SQ system developed by Columbia. This ensured compatibility with domestic stereo players, although the full surround sound experience could only be enjoyed by people who bought a proper quadraphonic system. The lowest catalogue number is for a recording of Tchaikovsky's *Swan Lake*, performed by the New York Philharmonic, conducted by Leonard Bernstein (MQ 30056), although it appears that this was not actually the first quadraphonic LP to be released. The Janis Joplin LP *Pearl* was given pride of place in Columbia's advertising at the time, so this may well be the one. Other companies issued LPs soon after Columbia did, but some decided to develop their own quad systems to avoid having to pay a royalty. The end result of having several different quadraphonic formats was that none of them became very popular.

A more sophisticated surround sound system, Ambisonic, was developed by Michael Gerzon and others from 1975, to provide a fully three dimensional soundscape. A number of LPs were issued, the first of which was a 1983 recording for the KPM music library, *Contact*, by Keith Mansfield and Richard Elen. The system is still used by the classical music specialist, Nimbus Records.

Half-speed mastered recording was an attempt to squeeze a little extra quality of sound from vinyl. The records were mastered at half the usual speed from a tape playing at half the usual speed, in order to create a superior sound quality when played back normally. Decca used this procedure on its classical records made from 1958 to 1967, which is the reason that these records are now so highly prized by aficionados. In 1977, Mobile Fidelity revived the process, licensing recordings originally issued by other companies. The first three releases, in 1978, were light orchestral LPs by the Mystic Moods Orchestra, the first of which, *Emotions*, had originally been issued by Philips in the US in 1968. The

The LP including the tracks released as a 12" single

Lincoln Mayorga had previously been a member of the Piltdown Men, who scored a few instrumental pop hits in 1960 and 1961. He co-produced and played piano on Ketty Lester's big hit of 1962, *Love Letters*, and his session work included playing on Frank Zappa's album, *Lumpy Gravy*. Doug Sax mastered the first album by the Doors and did the same for many well-known albums in the seventies, including *Eagles*, *Sticky Fingers* by the Rolling Stones, *Who's Next* by the Who, and *The Wall* by Pink Floyd.

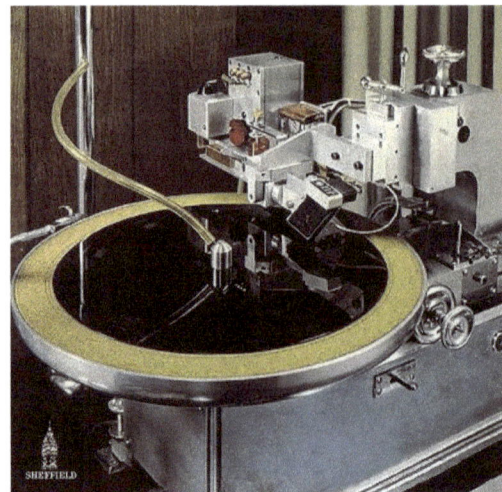

Lincoln Mayorga and Distinguished Colleagues. The cover art concerns itself with the recording technology rather than the musicians involved.

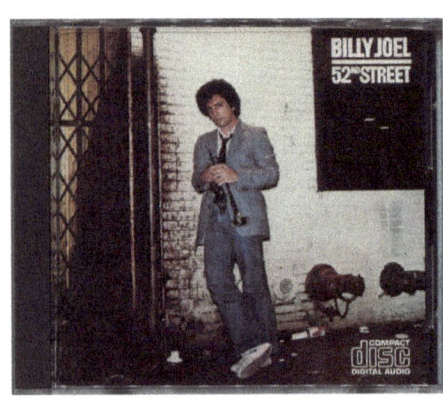

The last (1988) 8-track cartridge release by a major label

The first commercial digital recordings were made by Denon for the albums *Something* by Steve Marcus with J. Inagaki and Soul Media, and *Uzu* by Stomu Yamash'ta, as long ago as 1971. Both were released on Japanese Columbia. The first was not issued on CD until 2013; the second has not been issued on CD at all. Ry Cooder's *Bop Till You Drop* was promoted as the first digital recording when it was released in 1979, but it had been beaten by several other albums by then. It was, however, the first digital rock record. It was issued on CD in 1988.

fourth release was a sound effects record, *The Power and the Majesty*, but following that, Mobile Fidelity gained a considerable coup when it was allowed to release a half-speed mastered version of the Supertramp LP, *Crime Of The Century*. This had originally appeared in 1974, when it had been a top forty album in the US and had reached number four in the album charts in the UK.

An alternative route to high quality recording was followed by pianist Lincoln Mayorga and sound engineer Doug Sax, who set up the Sheffield Lab record company and issued a number of 'direct cut' recordings. These eliminated the use of tape recording altogether, effectively reverting to the method employed by studios before the invention of the tape recorder, whereby the sounds made by the musicians were fed directly to disc cutting equipment. The first album made in this way was *Lincoln Mayorga and Distinguished Colleagues*. This is given an issue date of 1971 by many sources, but the Sheffield Lab's own website refers to a date of 1968.

One further new format variation for vinyl was the introduction of the 12" single. The first of these was tried as an experiment in 1970 by Tower Records in San Francisco. As reported in *Billboard* in March, a few hundred copies of a single on the Cyclone label by jazz guitarist Buddy Fite, *Glad Rag Doll/For Once In My Life*, were pressed and sold at a bargain price in order to gauge the public response. The public cannot have been particularly impressed, because the experiment was not repeated at that time, although the fact that a fairly obscure artist had been chosen would not have helped. The standard 7" version of the single was not a hit. The rise of DJ culture later in the seventies inspired companies to try again and in 1975 a number of promotional records were issued as 12" singles. The first commercial record to use the format was released at the beginning of 1976, *Ten Per Cent* by Double Exposure, which was not a huge chart hit in the US, but sold well. The original song was remixed and extended in order to make use of the longer playing time available on the format. The first 12" single to be released in the UK appeared near the end of the year and was something of a surprising choice. *Substitute* by the Who, and two other sixties hits by the group on the other side, were issued in their original versions, without any attempt being made to extend them. The novelty was enough on its own, however, to propel the song back up to number seven in the UK singles chart.

Pre-recorded reel-to-reel tapes were introduced by EMI in the UK in 1952; RCA in America started selling them in 1954. The much more convenient cassette was launched by Philips in 1963 at the Berlin Radio Show (calling it the compact cassette), with pre-recorded versions coming on to the market in 1966. A four-track compilation, *Hits of The Walker Brothers*, was given the catalogue number MCP 1002, but the author has not been able to discover what MCP 1001 was. The same year, Mercury in the US (owned by Philips) issued an initial batch of forty-nine album titles by the likes of Johnny Mathis, Roger Miller, and the Four Seasons. The first cassette single was a song that eulogised the format, *C30,C60,C90,Go!* by Bow Wow Wow. This was issued in 1980, to take advantage of the new Sony Walkman portable player, which appeared on the market the previous year.

The eight-track tape cartridge was developed in 1964, as a side project for the Lear Jet Corporation. The format became popular for playing music in cars, and remained in production for a surprisingly long time, given the greater success of the cassette and CD alternatives, with some titles still being available to order from record clubs as late as 1989. Other alternatives to the cassette came and went, such as the Elcaset (developed in 1976), the digital audio tape (1987), the digital compact cassette (1992), and the MiniDisc (1992).

Research into the feasibility of the compact disc format began as early as the sixties, but it was not until March 1979 that Philips presented the first public demonstration of a prototype. In June 1981 a European press conference was held at which a CD test pressing of Richard Strauss's *Eine Alpensinfonie* performed by the Berlin Philharmonic, conducted by Herbert Von Karajan, was on show. The same year, a CD of the Bee Gees' *Livin' Eyes* was demonstrated on the BBC television programme, *Tomorrow's World*. The first generally available CDs were fifty titles issued by Sony in Japan in October 1982. The first number, 35DP 1, was given to the album *52nd Street* by Billy Joel, although the first to be pressed, at a factory established by Philips in Germany, were *The Visitors* by Abba and a recording of Chopin waltzes played by Claudio Arrau. A maximum playing time of seventy-four minutes was

THE FIRST TIME

The seventy-four minute playing time for CDs meant that the first CD issues of *Electric Ladyland* by Jimi Hendrix, in 1984, 1987, and 1989, had to be double disc sets. From 1990, with further technological advances making a longer playing time possible, the album could be accommodated on a single CD.

The jukebox, a machine designed to play a record when a coin is inserted, is as old as the records themselves. The first was invented in 1890 by Louis Glass and William S. Arnold and installed in the Palais Royal Saloon in San Francisco. The actual name 'jukebox' came into use in 1940. A juke (or juke joint) was an African-American word for a bar – celebrated in the Little Walter harmonica blues, *Juke*, which was recorded in 1952. As the formats for playing music have changed, so have the jukeboxes, although collectors of the machines are always likely to favour the models produced in what they consider to be the golden age, the fifties.

Luke Daniels with polyphon

Wurlitzer jukebox

104

supposedly chosen by Sony's vice-president, to please his wife, because this was the length of the longest recorded performance of Beethoven's *Symphony No.9* (conducted by Wilhelm Furtwangler in 1951). It was not until 1986, however, that a version of the symphony (conducted by Herbert Von Karajan) was released on CD and this was shorter. March 1983 saw the simultaneous release of some two hundred different titles in the US and the UK by all the major record companies. Appropriately enough, the first commercial CD to be manufactured in the US, in September 1984, was Bruce Springsteen's *Born In The USA*. The format received a major boost when Dire Straits became the first act to sell a million copies of a CD, the album *Brothers In Arms*.

CD singles crept on to the market rather more surreptitiously than the albums. A promotional single accompanying *Brothers In Arms* by Dire Straits became the first to be issued, in 1985. The first fully commercial release was *If You're Ready* by Ruby Turner, released in 1986 by Jive. The novelty did little to make the song a hit, however – it stalled at number 30 in the UK charts. The first UK number one single, available as a CD, was *I Wanna Dance With Somebody* by Whitney Houston, in May 1987. In the US, the song was only released as a promotional item on CD. Three inch CD singles were first issued in 1988, but were already disappearing by 1990.

The Super Audio CD, making what was already supposed to be a format with superior sound quality even more superior, was introduced in 1999. Meanwhile, the DVD was introduced in 1996. Originally intended to be a video format, the name stood for 'digital video disc'. When it was discovered that the disc had other possible uses, the 'v' part was changed to 'versatile'. In 2000, audio recording was introduced as one of these other uses.

The mp3 sound file format (developed by the Moving Picture Experts Group) was made available to the public in 1995. Suzanne Vega acquired a reputation as a major figure in the format's development, due to the fact that her recording of *Tom's Diner* was repeatedly used as a test piece. Mp3 enables the creation of a much smaller computer file than that derived directly from a CD, by eliminating audio information that has little effect on the overall sound. The resulting small size is essential in enabling the easy transfer and storage of computerised sound files and has revolutionised the way that music is acquired and listened to. The first song to achieve a million official downloads was *Hollaback Girl* by Gwen Stefani, in 2005. The first album to achieve a million official downloads was *Recovery* by Eminem, in 2011. In April 2006, *Crazy* by Gnarls Barkley became the first song to reach number one in the UK charts on the basis of download sales alone, although it achieved this with quite a modest number of sales, just over thirty-one thousand. The first single to be issued as a download only was *Telling Lies* by David Bowie, which he made available in three different versions on his own website in September 1996. It was not a hit, because download sales were not included in the UK singles chart until April 2005. It was claimed that over three hundred thousand people bought the David Bowie song. A CD containing all three versions was issued two months later.

A satisfying blend of old and new technologies was achieved in 2012 when a company called 8Dio made available a downloadable virtual polyphon instrument. The polyphon was originally a kind of musical box, invented in Germany in 1870. As described on the 8Dio website, it represented the first time that a device employed the basic principles of what would become the record player. It did this in so far as it used different large perforated metal discs to play its music, although no recording process was involved. The virtual polyphon was based on samples made from an original musical box. Two pieces using the software were posted on the SoundCloud website in 2013, produced by Pieter Schlosser and Troels Folmann. Something similar was carried out by folk singer songwriter Luke Daniels in 2016. His album, *Revolve And Rotate – The Polyphon Chronicles,* issued by Gael Music, included original music coaxed out of an old polyphon, with the help of both sampling and newly manufactured steel discs.

THE FIRST TIME

The July 19th 1913 chart published in Billboard lists the following songs, without giving any details with regard to the artists who may have recorded them.

Malinda's Wedding Day
When I Lost You
Snooky Ookums
Apple Blossom Time In Normandy
Great Big Blue Eyed Baby
Trail Of The Lonesome Pine
You Are All I Have
Floating Down The River
That's How I Need You
You Were All I Had

The *Billboard* 'Music Popularity Chart' of July 27th 1940 listed the following "best selling retail records" along with a list of the record shops that had provided the sales data – handy for those seeking to ensure their record a place in the subsequent charts.

I'll Never Smile Again – Tommy Dorsey
The Breeze And I – Jimmy Dorsey
Imagination – Glenn Miller
Playmates – Kay Kyser
Fools Rush In – Glenn Miller
Where Was I – Charlie Barnet
Pennsylvania 6-5000 – Glenn Miller
Imagination – Tommy Dorsey
Sierra Sue – Bing Crosby
Make Believe Island – Mitchell Ayres

The first specialist magazine relevant to the fledgling music industry was *The Phonoscope* – "A monthly journal devoted to scientific and amusement inventions appertaining to sound and sight". The first issue was published in New York on November 15th 1896 and is currently viewable on the website *archive.org*. Amongst the descriptions of a variety of ingenious devices, including an automatic banjo, driven by air, there is a listing of "the very latest popular songs published by the leading music publishers of the United States", which is divided into five categories ('Descriptive Songs and Ballads', 'Waltz Songs', 'Comic Songs', 'Coon Songs', and 'Miscellaneous'). On another page there is also an extensive listing of 'New Records for Talking Machines'. These could be construed to be the first music charts, except that they are just lists and make no attempt to put the songs in any kind of order.

The chart given the title 'Race Records' in 1945 was originally called 'Harlem Hit Parade' when started in October 1942. The number one record in the first chart was *Take It And Git* by Andy Kirk and his Clouds of Joy. The chart became 'Race Records' in February 1945 (with *I Wonder* by Cecil Gant at number one) and was then renamed 'rhythm and blues' in June 1949. *Trouble Blues* by the Charles Brown Trio was number one at the time of this change-over. The chart changed names several times after this. Since 2005, it has been known as 'hot r&b/hip-hop songs'.

Billboard October 5 1946, cover star Ella Fitzgerald

Cashbox September 10 1949, cover star Amos Milburn

An alternative chart to the one printed by *Billboard* was published by *Cashbox* magazine from the late forties. Like its established rival, the magazine produced a main listing alongside several subsidiary charts in different categories. It made a strategic error in the early years by combining different versions of the same song into the same chart position and although *Cashbox* undoubtedly had its followers, it never succeeded in supplanting *Billboard's* premier position. The magazine ceased trading in 1996, although it was revived as an internet-only concern in 2006. During its last years as a magazine, the *Cashbox* and *Billboard* charts had a few major discrepancies, which did not help *Cashbox's* reputation. Most notably, *The Letter* by Wayne Newton appeared in the *Cashbox* top hundred for thirty-one weeks and reached number one in December 1992, yet was never listed in the *Billboard* chart at all. Conversely, *Flava In Ya Ear* by Craig Mack reached number nine in the *Billboard Hot Hundred* in November 1994 and sold well enough to be awarded a Platinum Disc, yet never featured in the *Cashbox* chart.

10 CHARTS AND AWARDS

January 4th 1936 is widely mentioned on the internet and elsewhere as being the date on which the first music chart was published, in the American magazine, *Billboard*. Unfortunately, the 'fact' does not stand up to close scrutiny.

Billboard was first published on November 1st 1894 as the trade paper for the bill-posting advertising industry, which is the reason for the paper's name. Gradually, the focus was extended to cover the events that the posters advertised, including the music performed in the vaudeville theatres of the day. The issue for July 19th 1913 included a chart with the heading "last week's ten best sellers among the popular songs". Further information was provided that reports were received from a hundred and twelve music retailers and department stores in different parts of America and that these were then "carefully analysed and averaged". The chart was included alongside music news reports and song reviews, and is preserved on the archive website fultonhistory.com. Pages from the previous week's issue show no such chart, so it is probable that the one for July 19th was the first. The number one song, *Malinda's Wedding Day*, was recorded by the most successful duo of the era, Arthur Collins and Byron G. Harlan, and issued on a Victor record. The artist names are not given on the *Billboard* chart, because this was based on sales of sheet music. The following week, the number of retailers consulted had risen to three hundred and twelve. For the two weeks after that, it was over five hundred, but the chart did not then become a regular feature of the paper.

In the UK, *Melody Maker* started publication in 1926 and from 1935 printed occasional charts of the most popular sheet music, under the title 'Top Tunes'. During the thirties, *Gramophone* in the UK and *Variety* in the USA also printed occasional charts. *Billboard* did indeed try its earlier experiment again on January 4th 1936, in response to the rapid growth of the new jukebox industry. The chart was called 'The Hit Parade' and combined sales results for records and sheet music. The number one song was *Stop, Look And Listen*, recorded on Columbia by Joe Venuti and his Orchestra. It was not until 1940, however, that *Billboard* decided to make its hit parade into a permanent weekly event. The first regular music chart, therefore, dates back to the issue of the paper with a given date of July 27th 1940, although, in line with the practices of magazines then and since, the actual date of publication was July 20th. The number one record on this occasion was *I'll Never Smile Again* by Tommy Dorsey and his Orchestra, whose lead singer happened to be a young man by the name of Frank Sinatra.

By the end of 1945, *Billboard* had expanded its listings to fill three pages of the newspaper with a dozen different charts. These included an 'honor role of hits' in pride of place, which, as in 1913, gave song titles only, without any artist being mentioned. There were also separate charts for sheet music and for records (this time with the artists in place), and further break-downs into classical artists, jukebox records, jukebox folk records, and jukebox race records. There was even a list headed 'England's top twenty'. There were also two charts relating to music played on the radio, with the information being taken from John G. Peatman's 'Audience Coverage Index', a national survey of popular music broadcast on American radio networks. Peatman, a University professor with interests in psychology and statistics, had been carrying out his surveys and publishing the results in a chart of sorts since 1932. His research was officially adopted by *Billboard* on December 15th 1945.

The number of records included in the *Billboard* main chart varied between ten and thirty until November 1955, when a top hundred was introduced. At this point, *Billboard* was still breaking the chart down into subsidiary categories relating to physical record sales in shops, to radio plays, and to plays in jukeboxes, but these were phased out during the next three years. There were also a number of separate genre-specific charts such as rhythm and blues and country. On August 4th 1958, *Billboard* introduced its Hot Hundred – a chart combining all the other charts into one. The number one record was *Poor Little Fool* by Ricky Nelson. Genre charts continued, but now their records were also eligible for inclusion in the Hot Hundred. Although the details of how data was chosen and collected have varied

```
The New Musical Express chart of 14th November 1952

1     Al Martino – Here In My Heart
2     Jo Stafford – You Belong To Me
3     Nat King Cole – Somewhere Along The Way
4     Bing Crosby – Isle Of Innisfree
5     Guy Mitchell – Feet Up
6     Rosemary Clooney – Half As Much
7=    Vera Lynn – Forget Me Not
7=    Frankie Laine – High Noon
8=    Doris Day & Frankie Laine – Sugarbush
8=    Ray Martin – Blue Tango
9     Vera Lynn – Homing Waltz
10    Vera Lynn – Auf Wiedersehen
11=   Max Bygraves – Cowpuncher's Cantata
11=   Mario Lanza – Because You're Mine
12    Johnnie Ray – Walkin' My Baby Back Home
```

Top Of The Pops was the major exhibition arena for the glam rock groups in the early seventies and Slade, who achieved a run of twelve top-five hits, including six number ones, were the high priests

NME first issue

Melody Maker first issue

over the years since then, the Hot Hundred remains the definitive chart of song popularity in the United States.

The broadcasting of a pop music chart on American radio began in 1935 with a programme sponsored by Lucky Strike cigarettes, called *Your Hit Parade*. It continued until the beginning of 1953, but through the fifties, a television version of the programme was shown on NBC. Whether radio or television, the format involved a studio band and singers performing the hits of the day, which were sometimes a slightly idiosyncratic selection. The programme became less popular with the arrival of rock 'n' roll, for which easy listening big band cover versions were an unsatisfactory alternative to the original records, and it was moved to CBS in 1958 and cancelled a year later. There is a YouTube clip showing Snooky Lanson performing *Heartbreak Hotel* as though it were a dance band tune from the nineteen forties. A chart radio show using the actual records did not arrive until the beginning of July, 1970. Seven radio stations were involved initially, with the first broadcast being on KDEO in El Cajon, California. *American Top 40* was being syndicated to over five hundred stations by the early eighties and continues today. The chart used by the programme has always comprised the top forty records from the *Billboard* Hot Hundred or its predecessors.

In the UK, *Melody Maker* began printing a regular sheet music chart in July 1946, but it was not until 1952 that the first chart based on record sales appeared. Promoter Maurice Kinn bought a failing music paper called *Musical Express And Accordion Weekly* and relaunched it as *New Musical Express* in March 1952, with the intention of starting a UK pop record chart as soon as the necessary preparation was completed. This was in the *New Musical Express* for November 14th. The paper's advertising manager, Percy Dickins, phoned twenty major record shops and used a points system to aggregate their individual sales charts, rather than using actual sales figures. For successive charts, Dickins increased his list of record shops to fifty-three, choosing a different selection of between fifteen and twenty-five shops for his phone calls each week. The first chart, with the UK's first number one record, *Here In My Heart* by Al Martino, has been celebrated more recently by the release of all fifteen of its songs (in a top twelve!) on a Hallmark CD in 2004.

Other music magazines followed suit with their own charts during the next few years, using similar sampling methods. *Record Mirror* started in 1955, *Melody Maker* in 1956, and *Disc* in 1958. The last to join in was the industry trade paper, *Record Retailer*, on March 6th 1960. This last chart was retrospectively adopted by the company organising the charts today, the Official Charts Company, on its website and in the *British Hit Singles* books published by Guinness World Records. It was not the chart familiar to most record buyers in the sixties, however, who were much more likely to follow the *New Musical Express* chart, which was also broadcast on the popular music station, Radio Luxembourg, or else the chart used by the BBC. There were continual discrepancies between the *Record Retailer* chart and the others, most notably in the case of records by The Beatles. *Please Please Me* reached the number one place in every chart except the one printed in *Record Retailer*. Subsequently, both *New Musical Express* and *Melody Maker* showed eight Beatles' singles as entering the charts in the number one position, while *Disc* showed seven. For *Record Retailer*, this did not happen with any of them.

Pick Of The Pops, the radio programme started by the BBC in 1955, began presenting the charts from different music papers in September 1957, but from March 1958, it broadcast a specially prepared BBC chart, compiled as an average of the *New Musical Express, Melody Maker,* and *Disc* charts. The programme evolved into the *Chart Show* after September 1972 and has been broadcast on Radio One ever since. The *Pick Of The Pops* name has been revived, but as a programme playing records from archive charts only. The television show, *Top Of The Pops*, started in January 1964 and presented the BBC charts every week until its demise in July 2006. The Rolling Stones were the first act to appear on the first programme, performing *I Wanna Be Your Man*, while the number one record that closed the show was *I Want To Hold Your Hand* by The Beatles, on the fourth week of its five-week run at the top of the charts.

In 1969, an alliance between the BBC and *Record Retailer* created what was hoped would be a totally reliable official chart. For the first time, a professional polling organisation, the British Market Research Bureau, was given the task of collecting the sales data. A pool of three hundred record shops was used, which was more than the highest number used previously. The first official top fifty was published for the week ending February 12th, with Amen

Reissue of King Cole Trio on 1950 LP

RIAA Beatles Hello Goodbye gold disc

RIAA Michael Jackson Thriller album platinum disc

Corner's *If Paradise Is Half As Nice* at number one. There were inevitable problems with making sure the chart data was completely reliable, particularly during the early years, but eventually the official chart became accepted by everyone, although *New Musical Express* and *Melody Maker* did not abandon their own charts until May 1988.

Billboard introduced an album chart in 1945 with a list of five items and repeated the idea intermittently during the next few years. The 'albums' were collections of 78 rpm records, since the LP was not introduced until 1949. The first number one comprised the debut recordings by the King Cole Trio. At the start of 1955, both *Billboard* and *Cash Box* started weekly LP charts, both of which had Mario Lanza's soundtrack from the film *The Student Prince* as the number one record. As with the singles, the *Billboard* chart was the one that was most widely accepted. Gradually, the number of records listed was increased, until in May 1967 the total reached two hundred. Named *The Billboard 200*, the chart has been maintained ever since. In addition, *Billboard* introduced a second album chart in 1960 for back-catalogue records, which continued in various forms until becoming the 'Top Pop Catalog Albums' chart in 1991, which was for LPs more than eighteen months old that had dropped below position one hundred in the main chart.

In the UK, the first album chart, a top five, was published in *Record Mirror* on July 28th 1956, with Frank Sinatra's *Songs For Swingin' Lovers* in the top position. At the beginning of November 1958, *Melody Maker* published a top ten album chart, which supplanted the one in *Record Mirror*, by virtue of its longer listing and by its use of a larger sample of record shops. The number one album in the first *Melody Maker* chart was the soundtrack LP from *South Pacific*. *Record Retailer* started an LP chart in 1960, three weeks after its singles chart. Again, the chart has been retrospectively adopted by the Guinness books and the Official Charts Company, although the *Melody Maker* chart continued. *New Musical Express* started an LP chart at the beginning of June 1962, but continued its previous practice of listing LPs in the singles chart if their sales were large enough. The paper did not end this policy until near the end of the sixties – the last album to be included in the singles chart was the Beatles' *White Album*, which reached number twenty in the week it was released. In the seventies, with the boom in LP sales, there would have been more LPs than singles in the chart, if *New Musical Express* had still been combining different record formats.

The first million selling record was an aria from an opera by Ruggero Leoncavallo, *Vesti La Giubba (On With The Motley* or *On With The Play)*, sung by Enrico Caruso for the American Victor label. He recorded the song three times, in 1902, 1904, and 1907 – the cumulative sales of the three are estimated to have exceeded a million copies. The first UK million seller was *The Laughing Song* by Burt Shepard, recorded for Zonophone in 1910. The original recording of the song was by its composer, George Washington Johnson, who was the first black American to be recorded. It was a big selling cylinder during the early 1890s and was re-made as one of the first of the new flat records in 1895. Nevertheless, it was Shepard's cover version that ultimately became the bigger hit.

In 1905, violinist Marie Hall (who was later to give the first performance of Ralph Vaughan Williams' *The Lark Ascending*, a work dedicated to her) was presented with a charm bracelet by the Gramophone Company. Among the charms were seven miniature golden discs, representing her best-selling records. The first full-size gold disc ever awarded was in February 1942, when Glenn Miller was presented with a gold-laquered stamper by RCA Victor to celebrate sales of over 1.2 million copies of *Chatanooga Choo Choo*. RCA repeated the idea on at least two more occasions, awarding a gold disc to Elvis Presley in 1956 for a million sales of *Don't Be Cruel* and to Harry Belafonte in 1957 for a million sales of his album, *Calypso*. This was the first album by anyone to achieve the million sales figure.

In 1958, the R.I.A.A. (Recording Industry Association of America) introduced a formal system of gold disc awards, which were for records achieving a million dollars worth of retail sales, not including exports. Given the average cost of records at the time, this was equivalent to around 250,000 LPs or a million singles. The first gold disc to be awarded was in March, to Perry Como, for his single, *Catch A Falling Star*. The first gold disc for an LP came four months later, when the soundtrack album for *Oklahoma!* was the recipient.

In 1976, when sales of records generally had become much greater, the gold disc award was redefined to refer to

B.P.I Eric Clapton Tears In Heaven silver disc

RIAA Alanis Morissette Jagged Little Pill album diamond award

Taylor Swift's 2009 Grammy Award for Album of the Year

B.P.I. Rolling Stones Rolled Gold album gold disc

sales of five hundred thousand records (rather than a particular value). A new platinum award was introduced for sales of a million records. The first platinum discs were for the single *Disco Lady* by Johnnie Taylor and the LP *Their Greatest Hits 1971-1975* by the Eagles. Multi-platinum awards started being given in 1984, for records selling two or three million or more copies, while in 1999 a diamond award was created for sales of ten million copies. Several records had qualified by that time and were all given the award. As of 2014, the largest multi-platinum awards have been for the Eagles album and Michael Jackson's *Thriller*, which have both achieved twenty-nine times platinum status. In the UK, the music paper *Disc* started an awards system in 1959, with a silver disc being given for sales of two hundred and fifty thousand copies sold, while a gold disc was given for a million copies sold. The system depended on the co-operation of record companies and their willingness to supply accurate sales data, so that there were inevitable errors. The first single to earn a silver disc was *Side Saddle* by Russ Conway in May. In January 1961, Russ Conway was given a special silver award for combined LP sales, but the first individual LP to gain a silver disc was Elvis Presley's *G.I. Blues* in February 1962. The Shadows' *Apache*, which received a silver disc in September 1960, should have received a gold disc a little later, but was passed over for some reason. Instead, the first gold disc went to Elvis Presley's *It's Now Or Never*.

The B.P.I. (British Phonographic Industry) was formed in 1973 and immediately introduced a similar award system, insisting that record companies should submit audited sales figures. For singles, a silver disc was awarded for two hundred and fifty thousand copies sold, a gold disc for five hundred thousand, and a platinum disc for a million. The first platinum disc was earned by the Gary Glitter single, *I Love You Love Me Love* in January 1974. The qualifications were reduced in 1989 – a single earned a silver disc when it achieved only two hundred thousand sales; gold for four hundred thousand sales; and platinum for six hundred thousand sales. For albums, the awards were based on the value of sales and kept changing as prices rose. A silver disc was awarded for seventy-five thousand pounds worth of sales, rising to a hundred thousand pounds in 1975 and a hundred and fifty thousand pounds in 1977. A gold disc was awarded for a hundred and fifty thousand pounds worth of sales, rising to two hundred and fifty thousand pounds in late 1974 and three hundred thousand pounds in 1977. A platinum disc was awarded for a million pounds worth of sales. In 1979 the system was changed to match that used for singles, so that now the number of albums sold mattered, rather than their sales value. A silver disc was given for sixty thousand copies sold, a gold disc for a hundred thousand copies, and a platinum disc for three hundred thousand. These qualifications have not been changed again. Other countries have introduced similar award systems for their record sales, but the award thresholds vary considerably, depending on the size of the local record industry. Only the UK has a silver award.

The World Music Awards for outstanding achievements in the record industry were established in 1989 under the patronage of Albert II, Prince of Monaco. Using sales figures provided by the International Federation of the Phonographic Industry, a Diamond Award was introduced in 2001 for artists selling over a hundred million albums in total. As of 2014, only six of the awards have been made. Rod Stewart was the first – the others are Mariah Carey, Celine Dion, Bon Jovi, Michael Jackson, and the Beatles. However, these are not the only artists to sell over a hundred million albums – six glaring omissions are Elvis Presley, Garth Brooks, Pink Floyd, Led Zeppelin, Madonna, and Elton John.

The Grammy Award (for 'Gramophone Award', its original title) was introduced by the National Academy of Recording Arts and Sciences of the United States in 1959, to create for the recording industry an equivalent to the Academy Awards (Oscars) for the film industry. The main four categories of award were for album of the year, record of the year, song of the year, and best new artist. In addition, there were a number of categories relating to specific genres of music. The first main awards were to Henry Mancini for his album, *The Music From Peter Gunn*, and to Domenico Modugno for his song, *Volare*, which won in both the record and song of the year categories. No award was given for best new artist – the following year, it was Bobby Darin.

The worth of the Grammy awards in the eyes of many outside observers was reduced by the apparent dislike of the Academy for rock music. Not until 1968 did anything that could be called rock win a best recording category, when the Beatles' *Sgt Pepper's Lonely Hearts Club Band* was awarded album of the year. The Beatles were best new artist

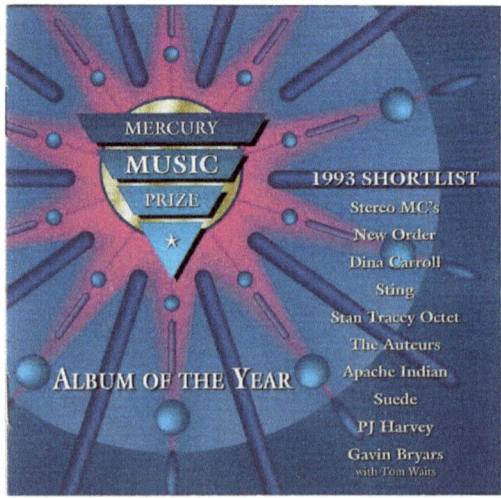

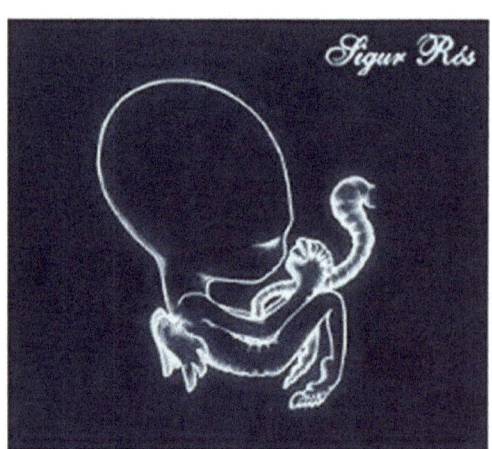

Queen's Bohemian Rhapsody, reissued as a limited edition on blue vinyl for the Silver Jubilee

in 1965 and *Michelle* was the song of the year in 1967. Apart from these, however, easy listening artists had the awards to themselves during the sixties. Even in the category of best rock and roll recording, winners included such unlikely recipients as pianist Bent Fabric, harmony duo Nino Tempo and April Stevens, and novelty vaudeville nostalgiacs the New Vaudeville Band. The nadir for the Grammys was widely considered to be the best new artist award in 1989, which was presented to the briefly successful duo Milli Vanilli and then withdrawn when it was discovered that the singers had not performed on their own records.

The American Music Awards were created by Dick Clark in 1974, as an alternative to the Grammy Awards. The results were determined by gathering votes from members of the public, so it might have been expected that there would be close agreement with the lists of best selling records during the year. In fact, the first award for Favourite Pop/Rock Album went to *Lady Sings The Blues* by Diana Ross, for a year in which the top entries in Billboard's list were *Goodbye Yellow Brick Road* by Elton John, *Dark Side Of The Moon* by Pink Floyd, and *The World Is A Ghetto* by War.

An attempt to entirely divorce an award from chart performance was made by the introduction of the Shortlist Prize For Artistic Achievement In Music by a panel of entertainment industry representatives. The first winner, in 2001, was Icelandic band Sigur Ros and their album *Ágætis Byrjun*, but the award has not been presented since 2007. Considerably more prestigious is the Pulitzer Prize, established in 1917 by provisions in the will of wealthy newspaper publisher and Congressman, Joseph Pulitzer. Since 1943, there has been a prize for the best composed work, the first winner of which was William Schuman, for his Secular Cantata No.2: A Free Song.

The B.P.I. introduced the Brit Award as a UK equivalent to the Grammy Awards in 1977, as part of the Queen's Silver Jubilee celebrations; then annually from 1982. The 1977 award winners, chosen from the music produced during the Queen's entire reign, were the Beatles' *Sgt Pepper* as best album and both Queen's *Bohemian Rhapsody* and Procol Harum's *A Whiter Shade Of Pale* as best singles. No doubt the panel could not resist picking a Queen single for the occasion, although it was a worthy winner regardless. The first annual award winners in these categories were *Kings Of The Wild Frontier* by Adam and The Ants and *Tainted Love* by Soft Cell. The Brit Awards have had their share of controversy too, though less as a result of the award choices than due to unfortunate events at the ceremony itself. The first of these was the shambolic presentation in 1989, when Samantha Fox and Mick Fleetwood were the hosts.

The Mercury Music Prize was established in 1992 as an alternative to the Brits, with just one category, that of Best Album. Originally sponsored by Mercury Communications, various sponsors have been involved since, but with the Mercury name being kept for the award name. The first winner was Primal Scream, for their album *Screamadelica*.

A large number of other music prizes have been established over the years, often sponsored by different music magazines. One of the more eccentric of these was the Festive Fifty, comprising songs chosen by listeners to John Peel's programme on BBC Radio One. The first of these, in 1976, had Led Zeppelin's *Stairway To Heaven* in the number one position. From 1982, Peel decided to restrict the choice to records released in the year in question. The number one record in 1982 was *Temptation* by New Order.

The Eurovision Song Contest was established in 1956, when the first event was held in Switzerland and won by the host country. The winning song was *Refrain* by Lys Assia. Seven countries participated on that occasion – the UK joined the next year, with the song *All* performed by Patricia Bredin. It was placed seventh out of ten entries. The first UK win was in 1967, with *Puppet On A String*, sung by Sandie Shaw.

There is no Nobel Prize for music, but in October 2016, Bob Dylan was awarded the Nobel Prize for literature, in recognition of his exceptional talent as a lyricist during over half a century of song writing. In keeping with his reputation for awkwardness, Dylan refused to attend the award ceremony and sent Patti Smith to collect the prize on his behalf. The Polar Music Prize, founded in 1989 by Stig Anderson, the manager of Abba, is considered by some as a music equivalent to the Nobel Prize, but it is much less well-known and offers a much smaller amount of prize money. Paul McCartney was the first winner.

Sidney Bechet's recordings were issued by RCA Victor. He, or whoever engineered the two tracks, may well have been aware of the fact that the company had earlier used a kind of overdubbing process when adding an orchestra to some recordings made by Enrico Caruso in 1904, when he was accompanied only by a piano. The company first did this in 1932. As with the recordings by Sidney Bechet, this was before tape recorders were available, so new direct-to-disc recordings of the orchestra playing along to the original records must have been made.

In the US, Patti Page was the best selling female artist of the fifties, with twenty-two top ten hits (plus one more in 1964), including four number ones. In the UK, she only managed one hit, the novelty song *How Much Is That Doggie In The Window,* although she returned to the top twenty in 1999, in spirit at least, courtesy of the duo Groove Armada. *At The River* samples lines from Page's song *Old Cape Cod,* which had been a US hit in 1957. Intriguingly, the credit on Groove Armada CDs does not mention Patti Page, but simply states that the song "contains a re-recorded sample of *Old Cape Cod*". The voice certainly sounds like that of Ms Page. She was aged seventy-one when *At The River* was recorded and might have re-done her vocal then, but it seems unlikely.

11 THE RECORDING STUDIO

The first recording studio was opened by the New York Phonograph Company in 1890. Recording was carried out by a mechanical process which involved feeding the voices and instruments straight to a lathe, which cut the sound directly on to a master cylinder or disc. Microphones giving sufficiently good sound quality to be used in recording were developed in 1923 and within two years, the recording studios were using them, thereby ushering in the era of electrical recording. The first electrical recording to be issued, by Victor in April 1925, was a medley of songs from a show called *Joan of Arkansas*, performed by the University of Pennsylvania Mask and Wig Glee Chorus. This had been recorded on March 16th. A few electrical recordings were made by both Victor and Columbia during the previous weeks, but the results were either issued later or not at all. The first would appear to be on February 25th, when singer Art Gillham recorded five songs for Columbia, including *You May Be Lonesome*, which was issued on a record in June. Gillham, dubbed the 'Whispering Pianist', pioneered the soft singing style made possible by the use of a microphone, which became known as 'crooning'.

The first practical reel-to-reel tape recorder was made in 1935, although the technology did not become generally available outside Germany until after the Second World War. Quickly adopted by the recording studios, magnetic tape removed the need for recordings to be made straight to disc.

Even before the introduction of recording on tape, jazz musician Sidney Bechet came up with the idea of turning himself into a band by means of a studio technique that later became known as overdubbing. In the process, he became the first musician to create music that only existed in the recording studio. In April 1941 he recorded two tracks that were issued as being by Sidney Bechet's One Man Band. For *Blues Of Bechet* he played four times, using clarinet, soprano saxophone, tenor saxophone, and piano, and combined the four parts into one. For *Sheik Of Araby*, he added bass and drums to give six parts that he combined into one – and did this twice to create two finished takes.

The first US hit by Patti Page, *Confess*, was recorded and issued in 1948. It features a double-tracked lead vocal by the singer, dueting with herself. It has been variously suggested that the reason for this was that there was a strike of backing singers at the time or that it was a cost-cutting measure. The most likely explanation is simply that the result sounds very effective. The engineer responsible for carrying out the recording was Bill Putnam. Moving from jazz-slanted material to country, Ms Page's recording of *Tennessee Waltz* had a closely harmonised twin vocal which became her trademark sound. The song was Patti Page's second number one, in late 1950, and went on to sell over six million copies (three million in the first year), making it one of the biggest hits of its era. It also achieved over one million sheet music sales, the last hit record to do this.

During the early thirties, while still a teenager, Les Paul worked out the details of his multi-guitar recordings. He signed to Capitol in 1948 and presented his new sound with the record *Lover*, which came complete with four or five guitar parts, some speeded up, and bass and drums too, all played by Les Paul himself. Subsequent records added echo and delay to the mix and most also had Paul's wife, Mary Ford, singing, with her voice recorded multiple times too, though not speeded up. The duo achieved twenty-eight US hits through the fifties, including four million-sellers.

The first recording to apply reverberation (reverb) to its sound was in 1947, when the engineer Bill Putnam recorded the Harmonicats, playing *Peg O' My Heart*, in the toilet of the Universal Recording studio he had founded himself. With four harmonica players, a double bass, and an electric guitar, the recording session must have been a bit of a squash! An electro-mechanical device to achieve the same effect, the plate reverb, was developed by the German company EMT in 1957, in time for Hank Marvin to use it on his records with Cliff Richard and the Shadows. From 1955, engineer Robert Fine, working for Mercury records, started recording classical orchestras in a large room where

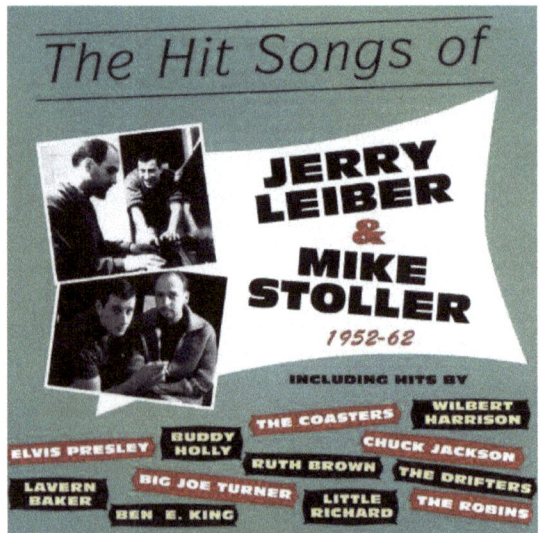

Mike Stoller is on the left in the top picture, on the right in the bottom picture

Denis Preston

Compilation of late sixties British jazz, recorded at Lansdowne Studios, "under the personal supervision of Denis Preston".

> The LP that Joe Meek intended as his masterwork remained unreleased at the time of his death in 1967, although four tracks were issued on an EP in 1960. *I Hear A New World,* credited to the Blue Men, is a showcase for the special effects and studio tricks that Joe Meek had at his disposal, unfortunately applied to forgettable pop music that is simply not worthy of the attention being lavished on it. Although the music is mostly instrumental, there are some passages of speeded-up vocals, in the manner of Ross Bagdasarian's 1958 hit, *The Chipmunk Song.* Applied to a science fiction theme rather than to comedy, however, the results are a little embarrassing.

he used three microphones to capture the natural reverberation in stereo. The resulting Living Presence records are still prized for the excellence of their recording quality.

Jerry Leiber and Mike Stoller started out as songwriters, with a preference for the blues. Their songs were recorded by Jimmy Witherspoon, Amos Milburn, and the Robins (the group that evolved into the Coasters) in 1950 and 1951. The songwriting duo achieved its first R&B hit in early 1952 with *Hard Times*, recorded by Charles Brown. Scoring several more R&B hits, including *Hound Dog* by Big Mama Thornton, *Kansas City* by Little Willie Littlefield, and *Riot In Cell Block Number Nine* by the Robins, Leiber and Stoller decided to form their own label, Spark, in 1953. For the recording of *Hound Dog*, the duo controlled the session, including swapping the Johnny Otis Band drummer for Otis himself, in order to achieve the sound they wanted for the song. They were taking the role of record producers, although it was a role that did not officially exist at that time. When, however, Atlantic records bought Spark at the beginning of 1956, Leiber and Stoller were retained in that capacity, with the agreement that they would also be able to carry out production work for other labels.

In the UK, the equivalent figure was George Martin, although he did not start to work independently of a record company until 1965. He is particularly associated with the music of the Beatles, but during the fifties he supervised the Dick James hit, *Robin Hood*, and signed the first skiffle group to emerge in the wake of Lonnie Donegan's success, the Vipers. Unfortunately, he passed on the group's original lead singer, who subsequently found solo success as Tommy Steele. George Martin produced big hits by Matt Monro and the Temperance Seven (whose primary novelty was that there were nine of them), as well as the distinctive *Sun Arise* by Rolf Harris. He was also behind numerous comedy recordings for Parlophone, including those by Peter Sellers, Bernard Cribbins, and the duo of Michael Flanders and Donald Swann. Such comic masterpieces as *Balham Gateway To The South*, *Right Said Fred*, *The Hippopotamus Song*, and *I'm A Gnu* are therefore his responsibility.

Denis Preston worked as an independent record producer in the UK from as early as 1950, even though the term was not yet in use. The Josh White record, *T.B.Blues*, carries the legend "supervised by Denis Preston" on its label, while *Nora – Calypso* by Lord Kitchener states "direction – Denis Preston". He established his Lansdowne Studios in London in 1957, which became particularly well known for its British jazz recordings through the sixties. One of Preston's first productions there was *Bad Penny Blues* by Humphrey Lyttelton, which managed to scrape into the charts in July. He also produced Acker Bilk's clarinet with strings opus, *Stranger On The Shore*, which became the biggest hit of 1962 and the first British record to reach number one in the US charts.

Denis Preston's engineer at Lansdowne, the man who actually operated the recording controls, was Joe Meek. At the end of 1959, Meek left the studio in order to set himself up as a producer in his own right. He established his own record company, Triumph, although he was also prepared to sell his productions to other companies. The Michael Cox single, *Angela Jones*, was a UK top ten hit in 1960 and was released on the Triumph label, but Meek's biggest success was on Decca – *Telstar* by the Tornados – which reached number one in 1962 in both the UK and the US. Joe Meek employed the full range of studio effects that had been developed by Les Paul. He became the first record producer in the UK to achieve a celebrity on a par with that of his most successful artists. The legend 'RGM sound' on a label (for Robert George Meek, his real name) was enough, for a year or so, to immediately give the record a certain cachet.

In the US, Phil Spector achieved a similar reputation. Girl groups the Ronettes and the Crystals gained a number of hits with records that benefited from Spector's 'wall of sound'. The producer hired a large number of backing musicians for his sessions, including up to three drummers and pianists, in order to achieve a particularly dense sound. The Phil Spector Christmas album, *A Christmas Gift For You*, was first released in 1963. It featured all the artists associated with the producer, but it was Phil Spector's own name that was placed most prominently on the LP cover.

If Joe Meek and Phil Spector came close to releasing records in their own names, the first producer to go all the

Arguably, the greatest record to benefit from Phil Spector's production was *River Deep Mountain High*. Spector himself certainly believed this to be the case, according to his biographer, Mark Ribowsky. Although the credited artists were Ike and Tina Turner, it has become the stuff of legend that Spector paid Ike Turner to stay at home when the record was being made. It was a number three hit in the UK in June 1966, but mysteriously failed completely in the US.

Reissue of Phil Spector's Christmas Album, showing the producer dressed as Santa Claus

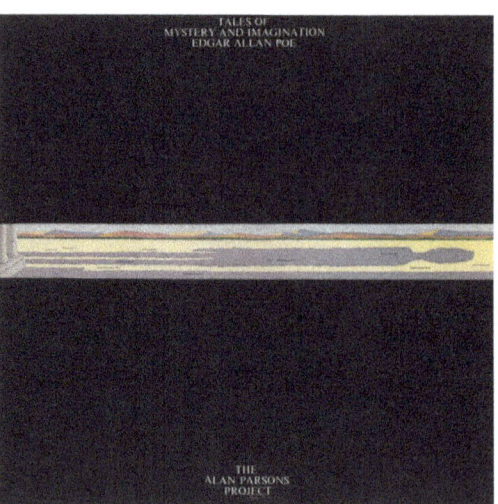

Recording Studio (Rock Factory, Hadley, Massachusetts)

way was Alan Parsons. Previously known for engineering the album *Dark Side Of The Moon* (produced by the members of Pink Floyd themselves) and producing two albums by Cockney Rebel, Parsons recorded the first of several albums issued under the name of the Alan Parsons Project, in 1976. Like its successors, *Tales Of Mystery And Imagination* appeared to be the work of a group but was really a studio creation, played by session musicians. No live performance was undertaken until 1990.

The opposite procedure, whereby a recording artist began working as a producer of his own records, was begun by Brian Wilson of the Beach Boys in 1963. He had previously proved his worth with production for two songs by Rachel and the Revolvers (actually session singer Betty Willis) in 1962. The Rolling Stones produced their own 1967 LP, *Their Satanic Majesties Request*. The group's earlier records had manager Andrew Oldham credited as producer, although a quote supposedly taken from the band's website can be read in several places on the internet: "Accounts regarding the value of his musical input to the Stones recordings vary, from negligible to absolute zero". In which case, the Rolling Stones themselves were responsible for the production work on the group's recordings going back to the first single, *Come On*, in May 1963. Phil Spector was present during the recordings for the first album (called *The Rolling Stones* in the UK, but *England's Newest Hitmakers* in the US, with a few differences to the track listing). He is credited with playing maracas on one track, but it would be surprising if his production expertise was not also called upon.

The development of recording technology led to increasing numbers of studio tracks being available to producers, but different studios upgraded their equipment at different times. The key manufacturer involved in the development of multi-track recording was Ampex, short for 'Alexander M. Poniatoff excellence', after the company's 1944 founder. Ampex moved very quickly. In 1949 came the first two-track recorder, followed a year later by the first four-track recorder. This machine could only record with the four tracks being used at the same time – during the next year, Ampex developed heads that could simultaneously record and playback, avoiding the small time lags made inevitable by having separate heads. The result enabled Les Paul to carry out the first multi-track recording in 1952, using the four available tracks to record parts separately. Paul himself started work on the design for an eight-track recorder in 1953 – Ampex installed the first finished product in the guitarist's home studio in 1957. A second eight-track recorder was sold to Atlantic records in 1958, where Tom Dowd worked as producer. Multi-track recording made it possible to build up the music one part at a time, even when no actual overdubbing was required. If one musician in a group made a mistake, then his part could be redone on its own, without affecting the recording of the rest of the group.

In the UK, the EMI Abbey Road studios in London introduced recording on magnetic tape in 1946 and converted to two-track recording during the fifties. Working in that studio, George Martin placed the Beatles' vocals on one track and the instruments on the other for the group's early recordings, mixing them together for the mono releases. The stereo issues of *Please Please Me* and *With The Beatles* over the years simply used the two master tracks as they were, giving a stereo image that sounds a little peculiar. Abbey Road bought a four-track machine in 1959, but it was only used for classical recordings until late in 1963, when the Beatles used it to record *I Want To Hold Your Hand*. Even the recording showcase that was the LP *Sgt Pepper's Lonely Hearts Club Band* was a four-track recording, albeit using two machines linked together. The first eight-track recorders in the UK, built by Scully rather than Ampex, were installed in the London Advision and Trident studios in 1968. Both studios upgraded to sixteen-track recording the following year – the first Ampex machine was bought by the Mirasound studio in New York in 1967, while TTG studio in Los Angeles acquired a twenty-four-track machine (manufactured by MCI – Music Center Incorporated) in 1968. Thirty-two-track recorders were developed at the end of the seventies, but by then analogue tape machines were starting to become superseded by digital recorders. These also offered thirty-two tracks, although the recordings could not be edited by the established method of cutting and joining bits of tape.

The Tascam Portastudio, which enabled good quality home recording to be carried out, with four tracks available on cassette, was introduced in 1980. The large number of independently produced new wave records that appeared on the market in the early eighties was made possible by this device. The growth in processing power and popularity of

THE FIRST TIME

The studio effect known as phasing was invented by an engineer at Olympic studios in West London, George Chkiantz, who was working as an assistant to producer Glyn Johns in July 1967. They used it the same afternoon on the recording of the Small Faces song, *Itchycoo Park,* where the whooshing sound managed to perfectly encapsulate the psychedelic imagery of the song's lyrics. Subsequently, the effect found notable applications on the Jimi Hendrix track, *Bold As Love,* and on much of the second album by Captain Beefheart and his Magic Band, *Strictly Personal.* Don Van Vliet (the Captain) was reportedly unhappy at producer Bob Krasnow's use of phasing, although in the days when it was still a novelty, the effect did succeed in giving the music extra impact and it well suits a record that epitomises the period particularly strikingly.

Artificial double tracking was a technique for enhancing the lead vocals on a record, involving combining the vocal recording with a slightly delayed copy of it. Ken Townsend, an engineer at Abbey Road, developed it in 1966 at the instigation of John Lennon. Previously, double tracked vocals were achieved by the singer recording his part twice and attempting to make a close match. The Beatles proceeded to use artificial double tracking throughout the *Revolver* LP on many of the instrumental parts as well as the vocals. Subsequently, the effect became a standard addition to the recording vocabulary for other artists.

Recording music and then reversing the tape so that the music is heard backwards (a technique later known as 'backmasking' when applied to the hiding of supposedly secret messages within a recording) was widely used within musique concrète and other electronic music produced from the late forties – as soon, in fact, as recording on magnetic tape began. Its first use as a deliberate effect in pop or rock music would appear to be on the Beatles song, *Rain,* recorded in April 1966. It was then used in several places on the *Revolver* LP, most notably for George Harrison's backwards guitar solo on *I'm Only Sleeping. Rain* employed a second studio effect as well, whereby the rhythm track was slowed a little in order to give it a rather different tonal quality.

In 1956, pianist Lennie Tristano introduced the Les Paul approach to jazz. The first four tracks on his self-titled album featured the overdubbing of extra piano parts and tape speed manipulation. Bass and drums were added for two tracks, but the other two had no other involvement than that of Tristano himself. The music was not influential – not until 1963 did anyone else try anything similar. In that year, however, Bill Evans issued *Conversations With Myself*, where the pianist recorded three separate parts for each track. Thereafter, Miles Davis adopted the full panoply of studio editing techniques, under the guidance of producer Teo Macero. The John Mayall album of 1967, *The Blues Alone,* had a title intended to be taken two ways. Every track was a blues and, apart from drumming by Keef Hartley on eight of the tracks (out of twelve), all the instruments were played by Mayall himself. The record was produced by Mike Vernon and John Mayall. In 1970, two rock albums were issued that were also created by means of extensive overdubbing. These were the first solo LPs by the American singer-songwriter, Emitt Rhodes, and by Paul McCartney. In both cases, the artist played all the instruments, although Linda McCartney added a few vocals to her husband's record, preventing it from being an entirely solo work. Both records were produced by the artist too, although Rhodes had help from Harvey Bruce.

A good demonstration of the effectiveness of reverb applied in the studio is provided by the recording of a John Mayall track, *Double Trouble.* Originally issued as a single in June 1967, much of the song's impact is due to the cavernous sound of Peter Green's guitar playing, to which producer Mike Vernon had applied a huge amount of reverb. When reissued on the retrospective compilation LP, *Looking Back,* however, John Mayall decided to remove almost all of the effect. The result is to rob the performance of ninety per cent of its power, even though the notes played by Peter Green are exactly the same.

Software called Auto-Tune, designed to automatically correct the pitch of wayward singers, was developed in 1997. When employed too aggressively, it gives an electronic edge to the vocals. The effect was used deliberately on Cher's 1998 hit, *Believe,* and inspired other artists to do the same, although the sound robs the singer of a chance to demonstrate any natural soul they may have.

Since 2014, when she was sixteen, Amy Slattery has been making recordings at home of Beatles songs (and some other material too), in which she sings all the vocal lines and plays all the instruments. She has made videos of her performances, so that she has been able to upload the finished results on to YouTube. Musically, her versions of the songs are profoundly impressive, while the professional sound quality that she achieves is a stunning testament to what can be managed in the twenty-first century with recording software available for use on ordinary domestic laptop computers.

The first songs composed entirely by A.I., with no human input, in 2016, were called *Daddy's Car* and *Ballad Of Mr Shadow,* using the Beatles and the classic American songwriters as templates. The released versions, however, on a 2018 Sony 7" single, were arranged by François Pachet and Benoît Carré, who were given the composing credits. An entire A.I. produced album, *I Am AI,* was released by singer Taryn Southern in 2018, with a preview single, *Break Free,*

issued the previous year. The album is available via YouTube or streaming services. Southern placed her vocals, with her own lyrics, over the A.I. music.

personal computers during the nineties led to a vast increase in the number of commercial releases being produced at home. They were recorded and edited on computers using software developed for the purpose. The majority of the established recording studios survived regardless, employing the expertise of their engineers and producers, along with more sophisticated computer technology than most home computer users could afford.

TRACKING THE TRACKS

Joan Of Arkansas and Art Gillham's *You May Be Lonesome* can be heard on YouTube.

The Sidney Bechet One Man Band recordings are included on the double CD, *The Essential Collection* (Avid 2009). *Patti Page The Complete US Hits 1948-62* includes all the tracks mentioned on a three CD set (Acrobat 2015). *At The River* is on *The Best Of Groove Armada* (Sony 2007). *Les Paul with Mary Ford – The Best Of The Capitol Masters 90th Birthday Edition* is on Capitol (2005).

Jerry Murad & his Harmonicats – Peg O' My Heart – Their 32 Finest is on Nimbus/Retrospective (2014).

The Shadows *20 Golden Greats* is on EMI (1987).

The Mercury Living Presence Collector's Edition is a fifty-one CD set on Decca/Universal (2012). Many individual Mercury Living Presence albums are also available on CD.

There are a number of CD sets dedicated to Leiber and Stoller songs, and all four of the recordings mentioned can be found between them, although none has all four. The most helpful selection is provided by *The Hit Songs Of Jerry Leiber & Mike Stoller 1952-62*, a double CD on Acrobat (2015). This includes *Hard Times* by Charles Brown, *Hound Dog* by Big Mama Thornton, and *Riot In Cell Block Number Nine* by the Robins, together with the hit version of *Kansas City* by Wilbert Harrison.

A good account of George Martin's career is provided by the DVD *Produced By George Martin* (Eagle Rock 2016). *The Best Of Sellers* by Peter Sellers (Hallmark 2011) includes *Balham – Gateway To The South*. *The Very Best Of Bernard Cribbins* (EMI 2004) includes *Right Said Fred*. *At The Drop Of A Hat* by Michael Flanders and Donald Swann (Hallmark 2011) includes *The Hippopotamus Song* and *I'm A Gnu*.

T.B.Blues by Josh White is included on the two CD set, *From New York To London – The Classic Recordings* (Jasmine 2002). *Nora* by Lord Kitchener is on *Klassic Kitchener Volume One* (Ice 1993). *The Best Of Humphrey Lyttelton* (EMI 2002) includes *Bad Penny Blues*. *Very Best of Acker Bilk* (One Day Music 2015) is a double CD including *Stranger On The Shore*.

There are several compilations of Joe Meek material on CD. The three CD set, *Telstar – Anthology* (Not Now Music 2013) includes *Angela Jones* by Michael Cox, *Telstar* by the Tornados, and four tracks by the Blue Men. There are several CD compilations by Phil Spector too. *Wall Of Sound – The Very Best Of Phil Spector 1961-1966* lives up to its title. *A Christmas Gift For You From Phil Spector* is on Sony (2009).

Tales Of Mystery and Imagination by the Alan Parsons Project is on Mercury (1992).

Pet Projects – The Brian Wilson Productions (Ace 2003) comprises non-Beach Boys material from the sixties. His finest Beach Boys material can be found on *The Smile Sessions* (EMI 2011), *Pet Sounds* (Capitol 2001), and *Today!/Summer Days* (Capitol 1990).

The finest Rolling Stones material of the sixties is to be found on the singles. Most of these are compiled on *The Very Best Of The Rolling Stones 1964-1971* (Abkco 2011). The UK version of the first album, *The Rolling Stones,* is on London (2000). The US version, *England's Newest Hit Makers,* is on Abkco (2002). *Their Satanic Majesties Request* is also on Abkco (2002).

The Beatles CDs are listed at the end of the Beatles chapter in this book. In particular, *Revolver* is on EMI (2009) and *Rain* is included on *Past Masters* (EMI 2009).

Itchycoo Park by the Small Faces is included on the double CD, *Ultimate Collection* (Sanctuary 2008). *Axis: Bold As Love* by the Jimi Hendrix Experience is on Sony (2012). *Strictly Personal* by Captain Beefheart and his Magic Band is on Liberty (1994).

The John Mayall recording of *Double Trouble* without added reverb is on Decca (2000). The recording with added reverb is included as a bonus track on *Crusade* (Decca 2007). *The Blues Alone* is on Decca (2006).

Lennie Tristano is on Rhino (2003). Bill Evans *Conversations With Myself* is on Verve (2006).

Emitt Rhodes is on One Way Records (1993). *McCartney* is on Universal (2011). Cher's *Believe* is included on the album of the same title (WEA 1998) and can also be found on *The Greatest Hits* (WEA 1999). Amy Slattery can be seen and heard on YouTube.

Christopher Stone

Martin Block

LP compiled by Jocko Henderson

12 DISC JOCKEYS

On Christmas Eve 1906, Reginald Fessenden, a Canadian engineer working in the USA, made a radio broadcast from Brant Rock, near Boston, Massachusetts, to prove that it could be done. It was received by a number of ships, equipped with the only radio receivers in the area. Fessenden included some music by Handel, played on a record, and in the process became the first disc jockey. The first person to regularly play records for radio was Ray Newby, a student in California, in 1909. The principal of his college, Charles Herrold, had given crystal sets to people living nearby so that they could receive the broadcasts he made. According to Newby, speaking as a guest on the CBS television show, *I've Got A Secret*, in 1965, the records he played were mostly by Enrico Caruso, who was very popular at the time.

The first licensed radio station, KDKA, began broadcasting in Pittsburgh in late 1920 – two years later there were well over five hundred stations. In the UK, in November 1922, the BBC was formed, becoming the first national broadcaster. Christopher Stone eventually managed to persuade the BBC to allow him to host a programme in which he played records and, in July 1927, he became the first British disc jockey, on *Time For A Tune*. A photograph of Stone in evening dress and operating a twin turntable during his broadcast is locked away in the BBC archive library, but is widely displayed on the internet.

Walter Winchell, employed as the first gossip columnist by the New York Daily Mirror newspaper, was also a regular radio commentator and used the phrase 'disc jockey' for the first time in 1935, referring to presenter Martin Block. In 1941, the term was printed in *Variety* magazine, with a reference to someone singing along to the records he played. It seems likely, therefore, that the 'Gilbert' mentioned was also the first rapper!

Martin Block was the first star disc jockey, hosting a show called *Make Believe Ballroom* on WNEW in New York, from 1935. The idea was that Block pretended he was at a live concert, although in reality he was playing records. Initially, these were records he had bought himself, as the radio station did not have any. Within four months, four million listeners were tuning in to the programme.

The chapter on rock 'n' roll in this book describes the crucial part played by radio DJ Alan Freed in popularising the music. Freed began his rhythm and blues programme, *The Moon Dog House*, in 1951 in Cleveland. The same year, Maurice 'Hot Rod' Hulbert began broadcasting in Baltimore. He adopted an extravert approach, using catch phrases and rhymes, which inspired New York DJ, Douglas 'Jocko' Henderson, to do the same in his successful *Rocket Ship Show*, beginning in 1954.

Murray Kaufman, known as Murray the K, broadcasted in New York, filling the gap left by the disgraced Alan Freed in 1958. It was Kaufman who introduced radio jingles, among other gimmicks, and coined the phrase, 'blast from the past'. He became the best known American DJ during the sixties, especially when his enthusiastic support for the Beatles led him to adopt the title of 'the fifth Beatle'.

Kaufman's broadcasting style was the inspiration for the DJs on the UK pirate radio ships, starting in 1964, the most successful being Radio Caroline, which was the first, and Radio London. These stations took advantage of a loophole in the British radio regulations that allowed them to operate because they were based offshore. Their DJs, who included Tony Blackburn, Dave Lee Travis, Tommy Vance, Simon Dee, Emperor Rosko (Michael Pasternak), Kenny Everett, and John Peel, provided a huge contrast with the sedate presentation of the BBC's Light Programme (Alan Freeman apart). When new government legislation closed the pirate radio stations in 1967, the BBC reorganised its programme structure. The Light Programme was divided into Radio 1 (for contemporary pop) and Radio 2 (for

The theme tune chosen by Tony Blackburn for his *Daily Disc Delivery* programme was a piece by John Dankworth called *Beefeaters*. A small segment of this was played before the Move song and was therefore technically the first record to be played on Radio 1. Arguably, *Beefeaters* was a strange choice, as it had already been used by ITV in 1964 as the theme for its programme, *Search for a Star.* The BBC's own website suggests that George Martin's specially commissioned *Theme One* was played even before this, but a sound clip uploaded on to YouTube enables the beginning of Radio 1 to be heard and *Theme One* is not played.

Terry Noel

Tony Blackburn made a number of recordings as a singer

Roger Eagle at the Twisted Wheel

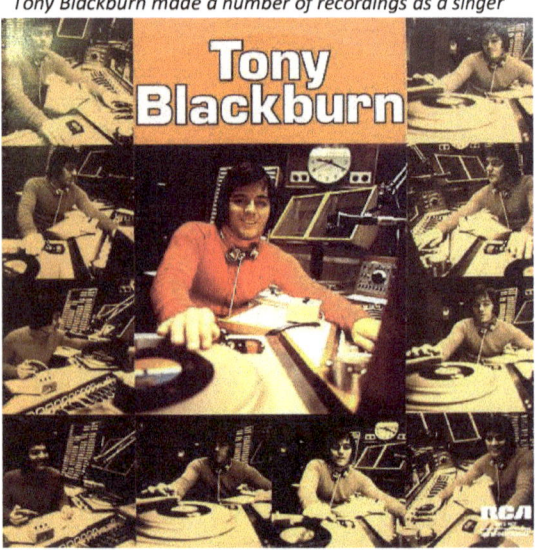

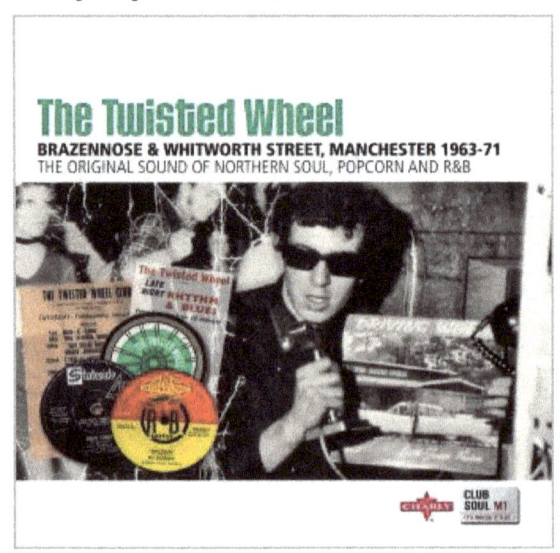

Ian Samwell with Cliff Richard and drummer Terry Smart

easy listening) and many of the pirate radio DJs were employed. Tony Blackburn was in charge of the first programme to be broadcast on Radio 1, on September 30th. Just before he started, a couple of jingles were played – never previously heard on the BBC – and then Tony Blackburn began by playing a record by the Move, *Flowers in the Rain*.

From the beginning of the service until his death in 2004, John Peel was a DJ on Radio 1. Known for championing styles of music that other presenters would not touch, Peel was a major influence in the initial success of progressive rock, punk, indie rock, and drum and bass – anything that he felt was genuinely attempting something new. He started his own label, Dandelion, in 1969, with the intention of releasing music by artists that would otherwise remain unheard. He is no longer the longest serving Radio 1 DJ, having been beaten by Annie Nightingale.

In 1943, a young man in the UK who had stopped working as a miner due to back injury came up with the idea of hiring a function room and charging people a shilling to hear records being played. The man's name was Jimmy Savile. Subsequently, Savile was hired by Mecca to repeat the performance at various of its ballrooms. He started using two turntables in 1946, in order to eliminate the gaps between records – although as the BBC archive photograph of Christopher Stone makes clear, this was already being done by at least one radio station. The first discotheque – a club for dancing where records were played rather than a live band being used – was the Whiskey A Go-Go, opened in Paris in 1947. In New York, Le Club, with Peter Duchin playing the records, opened on New Year's Eve 1960, as the first American discotheque.

Terry Noel, DJ at the New York club, Arthur, owned by Richard Burton's first wife, Sybil, came up with the idea of blending two records together, using two turntables and a mixer to control the sounds fed to each of four large speakers. This is the technique that became known as 'mash-up' in the early years of the twenty-first century, but Noel was doing it in 1965. As he explained in an interview given for the DJHistory website: "I got to the point where I would play two records at the same time. I'd mix them. You'd be hearing like *Foxy Lady* by Hendrix, and you'd hear the lyrics from the Beatles". Given that the stereo editions of the early Beatles albums were mixed with the vocals entirely on one side of the stereo and the instruments on the other, it is eminently believable that Terry Noel could have done this. It has been suggested that these mixes were somewhat primitive compared to what has been achieved more recently, but Noel gained a considerable celebrity locally, with a clientele including the major music stars of the time. It is unlikely that they would have been impressed by rubbish.

There are two candidates for the first discotheque in the UK. In 1961, French actress and socialite, Hélène Cordet, opened the Saddle Room as an upmarket nightclub in London's Mayfair. It established itself as an important part of the promotion machine for EMI and Decca, playing demo copies of the companies' new single releases. During this period, the 'needle-time' restrictions of the BBC made it difficult to get radio exposure. One such record was *I'm Just A Baby*, which became a top twenty hit in the summer of 1962, sung by Hélène Cordet's daughter, Louise. Meanwhile, also in 1961, the songwriter Ian Samwell (responsible for Cliff Richard's first hit, *Move It*) was employed by the Lyceum in London to play records for Tuesday lunch-time dance sessions. His collection comprised classic rhythm and blues singles on the Atlantic and Chess labels, together with the early releases on Tamla – all of these being acquired during regular visits to New York. He set the style and the sound of the music to dominate the clubs thereafter.

A club called The Twisted Wheel opened in Manchester towards the end of 1963. It was there that resident DJ Roger Eagle started the Northern soul scene during 1965 to 1966, before quitting out of boredom with no longer being able to play a wider range of musical styles. By the end of the sixties, several clubs playing the music were flourishing in various towns in the north of England and as far south as Northampton. The term 'northern soul' was first used by soul enthusiast Dave Godin, writing about The Twisted Wheel in *Blues and Soul* magazine in June 1970. 'Northern' refers to the north of England. The music could be made anywhere, but consists of records that are either products of the Tamla Motown label or sound as though they should be. None of them, however, could be at all well known. A DJ's success depended on his skill, or luck, in finding records that had the right sound and the right beat,

TRACKING THE TRACKS

Ray Newby describing his status as the first person to play records regularly on the radio is on a YouTube clip from the TV show *I've Got A Secret*.

Christopher Stone made a small number of recordings and two of them can be heard on YouTube. *Christopher Stone's Medley* fills two 78 rpm discs, on which he introduces several pieces of music in the same way as he must have done on the radio. *The Decca A.B.C.* is effectively a promo for Decca records – Stone introduces a number of recordings issued by that company, in alphabetical order. The first set was recorded in June 1932; the second dates from the end of 1933. Over the years, many DJs have wanted to see their name on records, as well as just playing them. Christopher Stone was the first.

Six short films were made in 1948 of Martin Block interviewing musicians for his *Musical Merry-Go-Round* show. One involving Ray Noble and Buddy Clark and another with Les Brown and Tex Beneke are available on YouTube. There is also a short excerpt from a 1940 broadcast, in which Martin Block presents Glenn Miller with an award for being America's number one dance band. A short interview from 1954 has Block talking about the differences between broadcasting on radio and television. Half an hour from a 1954 Martin Block show can be heard on www.radioechoes.com.

There are excerpts from radio broadcasts by Alan Freed on YouTube, dated 1953, 1954, 1955, and 1957. Twenty-three broadcast extracts from Freed's *Rock 'n' Roll Dance Party* in 1956, each around twenty-four minutes long, can be heard on www.radioechoes.com. A compilation taken from these was issued on CD in 1991, but this is hard to find and has lower sound quality than the radioechoes recordings. A CD of recordings by the Alan Freed Rock 'n' Roll Big Band, playing instrumental versions of various hits, was issued by Ace in 2008, under the title *A Stompin' Good Time*.

There is a three minute extract from Maurice Hulbert broadcasting on WWIN in Baltimore. There are two rather longer extracts from Douglas Jocko Henderson broadcasting on WOV New York in 1957. Henderson also recorded a single on the Wand label. He speaks the lyrics on *A Little Bit Of Everything*, but sings on the other side, *Blast Off To Love.* All of these can be heard on YouTube.

Murray the K had two various artist LPs issued on his own Brook-lyn label. *Murray The K's Greatest Holiday Show Live from the Brooklyn Fox* (1964), which includes introductions from Murray himself, and *Murray the K Presents* (1968) which does not. A slightly earlier Murray the K live show was issued in 1963, on the KFM label, as *Murray the K Live from the Brooklyn Fox in his Record Breaking Show*. This one can be heard on YouTube. A CD presents different material from these, *Murray the K's Holiday Revue – Live at the Brooklyn Fox December 1964* (Magnum 2008). Murray's interviews with the Beatles in 1964 were issued as an EP, *The Beatles and Murray the K As It Happened.* There was also a promotional 7" recording issued, including numerous Murray the K jingles. Both of these records can be heard on YouTube. The DJ issued a music single on the Red Bird label in 1965, *It's What Happenin' Baby/The Sins Of A Family.* He sings though not very well. A TV special, also called *It's What Happenin' Baby,* with Murray the K introducing a number of specially filmed music videos by well-known artists was shown on US television in June 1965. It can be seen, divided into three parts, on YouTube.

but were not being played by any of his competitors. Northern soul DJs became avid record collectors, pushing the prices of hard-to-find records ever higher. The first DJ to adopt this approach, actively seeking rare records as exclusives, was Farmer Carl Dean, who worked at a club called the Catacombs, in Wolverhampton. Eventually, the Northern soul clubs did start to expand their musical policies, incorporating the early disco records being played in New York, together with music from the developing jazz-funk genre. The Blackpool Mecca was the first club to make the change, where Ian Levin and Colin Curtis were the resident DJs.

The roll call of disc jockey firsts is not quite complete here, but the crucial work of the New York club DJs Kool Herc and Grandmaster Flash and the subsequent success of people like Coldcut and DJ Shadow, making records out of records, is described in the next chapter of this book, Sampling.

There are a few compilation CDs that make reference to the pirate radio stations as their selling point, but they are simply collections of sixties hits. A three CD set, Radio Caroline Calling – 60's Flashback (Disky 2001) claims to include original jingles, but there are only three of these. The set also manages to avoid including the song Caroline by the Fortunes, that was used as the station's theme tune. More to the point is the CD Pirate Radio Jingles from the Sixties (Jumbo 2007). There are a few extracts from original broadcasts by Radio Caroline and Radio London on YouTube, including the last hour in the life of Radio London.

As already stated, a recording of the opening of Radio 1 can be heard on YouTube. John Dankworth's Beefeaters is on the double CD Let's Slip Away – Film and TV 1960-1973 (Universal 2009). George Martin's Theme One is on Produced by George Martin – Highlights from 50 Years in Recording (EMI 2006). A rather splendid version of the piece was recorded by Van Der Graaf Generator and is included as a bonus track on the CD of Pawn Hearts (Virgin 2005).

Tony Blackburn made several records as a singer. Those released as singles are on The Singles Collection 1965-1980 (Cherry Red 2012). The three CD set, Tony Blackburn Presents Soul Classics (Universal 2013) tells us which records the DJ likes, but his contribution to the set, as with many other such compilations, extends no further than the selection of the music and his picture on the front.

John Peel made many contributions to records. John Peel Presents Top Gear was issued by BBC Records in 1969. Alongside some exclusive recordings by Bridget St.John, Ron Geesin, Sweet Marriage, and White Noise, a recording of John Peel's own voice, treated by the BBC Radiophonic Workshop, is included. The record is hard to find and has not been reissued on CD, but can be heard on YouTube. Even harder to find is John Peel's Archive Things, issued by BBC Records in 1970. The LP is a compilation of short world music extracts that were included in Peel's wide-ranging Night Ride programme. Peel is not included himself, but the record is nevertheless entirely representative of him. This too can be heard on YouTube. John Peel made cameo appearances on several records. Among many others, he was credited as producer of the Liverpool Scene album, Amazing Adventures Of, and the Bridget St.John album, Ask Me No Questions. He read children's stories on My People Were Fair and Unicorn by Tyrannosaurus Rex, played jew's harp on Alchemy by the Third Ear Band, played a plastic pipe twirler on Nurses Song With Elephants by David Bedford, and spoke a line on Soundtrack by Principal Edwards Magic Theatre. His own Dandelion label is well represented by The Dandelion Sampler 1969-1972 (See For Miles 1996).

There are numerous tracks on different CDs from the various live sessions that John Peel supervised on his programmes over the years, including several complete albums of Peel Sessions. His introduction to the concert by Soft Machine on the CD BBC In Concert 1971 (Hux 2005) is marked as a separate track. Peel supervised his only mix album in 2002, as part of the Fabriclive series of DJ mix CDs. Fabriclive.07 plays like one of his later programmes, although his own commentary is missing. The inclusion of a fragment from a Liverpool football match within Joy Division's Love Will Tear Us Apart is a typically eccentric touch. Since John Peel's death in 2004, two double compilation albums have been issued by way of a tribute to him, although, again, his own voice is not included. They are Right Time Wrong Speed 1977-1987 (Warner 2006), which concentrates on Peel's more recent music choices and John Peel – A Tribute (Warner 2005), which attempts to represent the DJ's entire career. A few complete John Peel programmes – or lengthy extracts – can be heard on YouTube, including Peel's last ever broadcast, on October 14th 2004.

There are several compilation albums of northern soul tracks, such as the double CD The Story Of Northern Soul (Sanctuary 2001). Club Soul Volume 2 – The Twisted Wheel is on Charly (2013).

A fascinating series of LPs was issued by Increase Records, starting in 1970. Cruisin' 1955, Cruisin' 1956, and so on, up to Cruisin' 1970, were intended to present a history of American rock 'n' roll radio during those years. They did this by selecting a particular station for each LP and using a mixture of original adverts and announcements with re-creations by the original DJs involved and a selection of music that would have been played at the time. The covers, representing the social changes year by year by means of cartoons involving a red-headed man called Eddie and the women in his life, are particularly memorable in themselves. The LPs have been reissued on CD, but with several changes that spoil the original concept a little. The original LPs can be heard (and indeed downloaded) on www.archive.org.

The 1949 gospel record sampled by Moby for his track Run On. *The song has also been recorded by Elvis Presley and by Johnny Cash, without any sampling being involved.*

As far as orchestral versions of rock anthems are concerned, an interesting special case is provided by Mike Oldfield's *Tubular Bells*. This presented a rock slant on the minimalist approach of Steve Reich, a composer working at the cutting edge of post-war classical music. The work was subsequently orchestrated by David Bedford, an inspired cutting edge composer in his own right. Doubtless, the orchestration seemed appropriate for a work that was already half in the classical world, but the results prove the importance of timbre. Whereas the original easily outstrips the achievements up to that point of Reich himself, emerging as a genuinely great work, the orchestral version, using all the same notes in the same order, but with a different, and in classical terms, a more conventional instrumentation, struggles to avoid sounding dull.

Meanwhile, the author has heard a recorded version of Queen's *Bohemian Rhapsody* played on a music box. With the themes of the original version completely intact, but with none of the instrumental timbre remaining, Freddie Mercury would have received his royalties regardless. The power and distinction that Mercury created, however, is completely lost, to be replaced by a comic effect that was none of his intention.

Two honourable omissions from the list of uninspired orchestral rock albums are both the responsibility of conductor/arrangers with experience of working directly in the rock music world. Darryl Way, a founder member of Curved Air, leads the LSO on *Fortress – The London Symphony Orchestra Performs The Music Of Sting*. Hermann Weindorf, keyboard player with Passport in the early eighties, leads the RPO on *The Royal Philharmonic Orchestra Plays Hits Of Pink Floyd*. Both were originally issued in 1994 and are vital additions to the catalogues of the rock artists concerned.

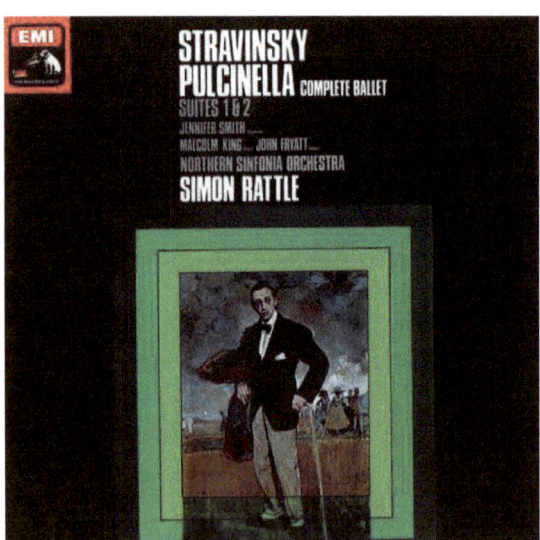

13 SAMPLING

During the nineties, the technique known as sampling became an essential tool for the record producer. Sampling is the employment, within a piece of music, of previously recorded material that has been removed from its original context. The sample might be used as flavouring within a piece whose arrangement is essentially complete without it, or it might have a more significant role within the structure of the new music.

Moby's 1999 *Play* album, for example, which reached number one in the UK album charts, gained a platinum award in the US, and included music that became widely used within television advertising during the following years, uses vocals taken directly from old gospel and blues recordings. Moby makes these into centre-pieces within musical settings that bear little relation to the originals. The timbre of the voices, recorded decades earlier than Moby's own material, is distinctive and evocative in a way that would be difficult to reproduce in a modern recording studio. To make the attempt, to use contemporary singers to deliver the lines, would be to ruin the effectiveness of the music, whether or not the vocals could be artificially aged. The songs on *Play* derive their power from the juxtaposition of turn-of-the-millennium synthesised textures with voices that not only sound old, but actually are old.

Igor Stravinsky is quoted as saying that lesser artists borrow, while greater artists steal. (The quote is also attributed to Pablo Picasso and T.S.Elliot – at this distance it is impossible to tell who was stealing from whom.) In Stravinsky's case, the reference is to the fact that it is commonplace in the field of classical music for composers to employ musical themes written by others. Their justification – apart from any claim to greatness, and however much the champions of modern copyright law might disagree – is that the mere slinging together of notes into a theme is a tiny and not particularly significant part of the overall business of creating music. What matters is what is done with the theme, in terms of its development and variation, its arrangement, instrumentation, harmonic structure, and so forth. If the composer succeeds in creating music that is memorable, innovative, and moving in ways not achieved or imagined by the person who first ordered the notes of the theme, then this has indeed been stolen, rather than merely borrowed. It has been made the composer's own.

Viewed like this, a theme should be treated as a resource or ingredient for music-making – no different from the timbre and note range available from the various musical instruments. The choices made with regard to the latter resources are, of course, generally very important themselves to the success of the finished music. The point is succinctly made by the albums presenting orchestral versions of rock anthems, which nearly always, in the course of the translation, lose most of the qualities making the anthems memorable.

Regardless of the success or otherwise of the result, we, as listeners and critics, are entirely happy with the idea of a composer, in whatever musical genre, selecting his timbres from a pre-existing fixed palette. Although we may be excited if they do, we do not expect composers to continually invent new instrumental sounds for their works. Composers of the Stravinsky persuasion are equally happy with the idea of them selecting the order of the notes they use from a pre-existing palette.

Stravinsky certainly followed his own maxim, stealing melodic material if he felt that this was appropriate for his art. His 1920 ballet, *Pulcinella*, for example, reworked themes by the operatic composer Pergolesi, transforming the two hundred year old material with twentieth century harmonies, rhythms, and instrumental combinations in much the same way of working as Moby. This is sampling, which in Stravinsky's case is achieved by using quotations from written scores rather than from sound recordings, since before the invention of the modern record or CD player, a written score was the means by which music was recorded. The technology is different, but the sampling principle is the same.

THE FIRST TIME

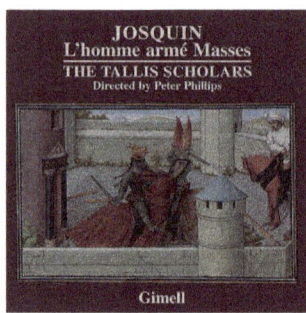

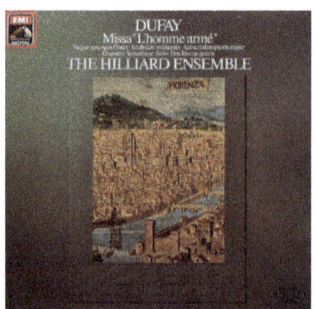

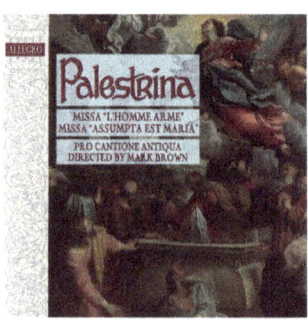

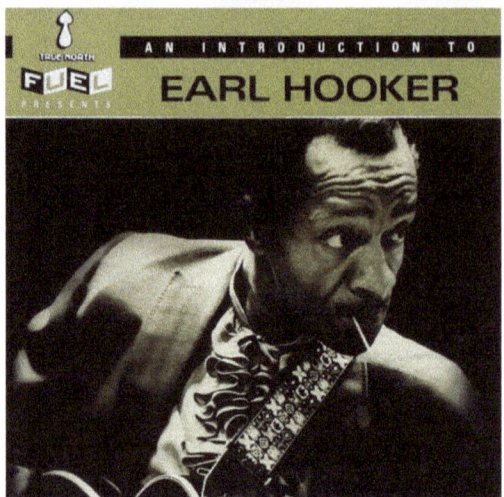

The fact that Willie Dixon is the credited writer of *You Shook Me* is itself an example of the lax approach to these things in the blues. In May 1961, slide guitarist Earl Hooker recorded tracks with his band that included an instrumental he called *Blue Guitar*. At the instigation of label owner Leonard Chess, Muddy Waters overdubbed a vocal part directly on to the instrumental a year later, using lyrics written by Willie Dixon. When the result, now titled *You Shook Me*, was released as a single in 1962, the Earl Hooker writing credit that had appeared on *Blue Guitar* was gone. The same thing happened with *You Need Love*, which again began life as an Earl Hooker instrumental, recorded in July 1962. This time, the original Earl Hooker track, which may have been recorded specifically for the purpose of having Muddy Waters sing on top of it, was unreleased. Hooker died in 1970, long before Willie Dixon's settlement with Led Zeppelin, but his name was again mysteriously absent from the writing credits for *You Need Love*.

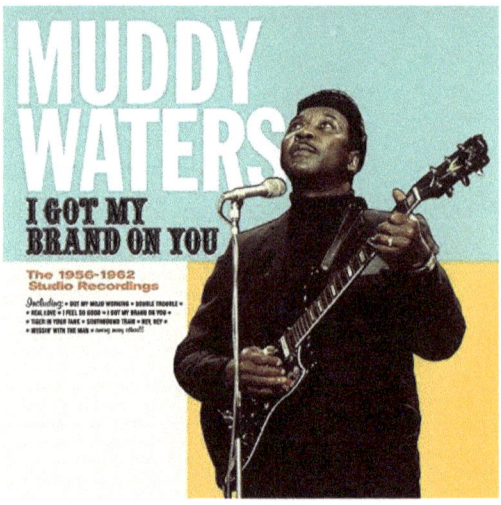

The back cover of the first Led Zeppelin album shows Jimmy Page taking the traditional tune Black Water Side as his own and giving it a new title, while the medley of well-known blues pieces, beginning with Howlin' Wolf's *How Many More Years*, is claimed as a group composition with a slightly reworded title. *Dazed and Confused* – a song not part of the blues tradition but written in 1967 by Jake Holmes and recorded by him then – is credited to Jimmy Page, who had merely re-arranged the song. Holmes received an out-of-court settlement in 2012. Similarly, *Babe I'm Gonna Leave You* was composed by folk singer Anne Bredon, although to be fair, the Joan Baez *In Concert* album which was the source of the song for Led Zeppelin also claimed that the song was traditional. Like Holmes, Anne Bredon is given her credit on recent issues of the album.

Stravinsky was by no means the first classical composer to work in this way, as is made very clear by the large number of works by various composers, from Johann Sebastian Bach onwards, with titles along the lines of *Variations on a theme of...*. As early as the fifteenth century, when the primary role of a composer was to produce music for use in the church, the dominant form was the parody mass, in which themes taken from Gregorian chant or else from secular madrigals or other songs were incorporated into the music. Josquin Desprez, for example, who is considered by many to be the greatest composer of the period, wrote two masses based on a song called *L'homme Armé*. Indeed, many of his contemporaries did the same, for over thirty different versions of a *L'homme Armé* mass have survived.

The earliest known examples of the parody mass are those composed by two Italians – Antonio Zacara da Teramo and Bartolomeo da Bologna – both dating from before 1420. Indeed, the *Gloria* from Bartolomeo's mass takes the melody of a secular song, *Vince con Lena,* and inserts it in the middle without any further adaptation. Tentatively, therefore, we can claim that the technique of sampling begins here.

Within popular music too, the stealing of musical and lyrical material has long been commonplace, only becoming an issue when large sums of money are involved. Perhaps noticing that classical composers regularly stole themes from each other, and certainly aware that copyright problems would never arise, song-writers have often sought inspiration from the same source. The well-known *Stranger In Paradise* (originally from the 1953 musical *Kismet*, but recorded by a large number of artists, including Tony Bennett and Bing Crosby) takes a theme from Borodin. The Shangri-Las' mournful narration on their dramatic song, *Past, Present And Future*, from 1966, is laid over Beethoven's *Moonlight Sonata*. The Manfred Mann Earth Band 1973 hit, *Joybringer,* uses themes from Holst's *Planets Suite*. In more recent times, the group Lamb, on its 1996 debut album, incorporates a section from Gorecki's *Third Symphony*, in a song titled, appropriately enough, *Gorecki* (although this uses an actual sample from a recording of the work, which is itself a modern composition, from 1976). The list could go on and on – Wikipedia gives over a hundred examples of songs like this, written between 1891 and 2012, and could have found many more. In the progressive rock era, various groups employed re-workings of huge amounts of classical music in their attempts to emphasise that the music they were playing was to be considered as Art. Keith Emerson's groups, the Nice and Emerson Lake and Palmer, were particularly prolific in this respect, while the first album by Renaissance (issued in 1969), which saw the Yardbirds' singer, Keith Relf, trying to prove that he could be responsible for music as vital as that being played by his former guitarists (Eric Clapton, Jeff Beck, and Jimmy Page), inserted classical motifs into the music as often as it could manage.

In the blues, the practice of stealing material has been positively encouraged, with the songs sharing a song structure and numerous phrases and lines being viewed as part of a tradition to be maintained. When the members of Led Zeppelin recorded a number of blues performances on their first albums, they saw themselves as merely following in this tradition. They had no problems with crediting themselves as the song writers, in the way that blues artists had always done. Only *I Can't Quit You Baby* and *You Shook Me*, with clearly attributed Willie Dixon authorship on versions recently recorded by John Mayall and Jeff Beck respectively, could not avoid being treated differently. *Whole Lotta Love*, though clearly an interpretation of another Willie Dixon song, *You Need Love* (albeit with a riff that was Jimmy Page's own), could. In 1985, an out-of-court settlement was made in favour of Dixon. An earlier version of the song by the Small Faces, titled *You Need Loving*, without the Page riff, did not credit Willie Dixon either, but did not earn the huge sums of money that were achieved by Led Zeppelin.

When Brian Wilson of the Beach Boys set new lyrics to the music of Chuck Berry's *Sweet Little Sixteen*, for the 1963 song that became the group's first big hit, *Surfin' USA*, Berry's music publisher protested. Chuck Berry, with a background in the blues tradition and used to recycling his own music through several similar songs, was presumably not much perturbed by any artistic license taken. He just wanted the credit and the royalties – which he got. When John Lennon took just one line from the Chuck Berry song, *You Can't Catch Me*, and recast it as the opening to the Beatles song, *Come Together*, in 1969, Berry's publishers were considerably more outraged – more money was at stake! Four years previously, Lennon had taken a line from an Elvis Presley song, "I'd rather see you dead than to be with

Morris Levy, owner of Roulette Records, sued John Lennon over the use of the Chuck Berry line, in his role as music publisher. An out-of-court settlement included Lennon's agreement to record three Levy-owned songs on his 1975 album of fifties covers, *Rock 'n' Roll*. With the album delayed for various reasons, Levy sued again, this time for breach of contract. He had meanwhile obtained unmastered recordings from John Lennon, intended for the *Rock 'n' Roll* album, and proceeded to issue these as a mail order LP called *Roots*. Both Lennon and EMI records countersued Morris Levy, who lost the case and ended up some $150,000 out of pocket. Ironically, singer Tommy James, who had a series of major hit records for Roulette during the sixties, maintained in his 2010 autobiography that Levy's company was little more than a front for organised crime and continually failed to pay royalties due to its artists.

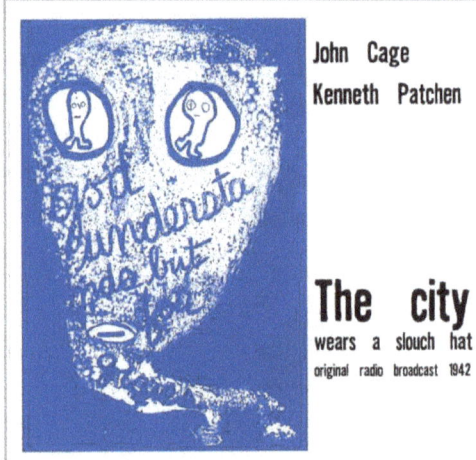

Morris Levy proved to be less than adept at running a mail order business. Surviving copies of the *Roots* album are seriously scarce, with copies selling to collectors in recent years for around £250 – a value that would undoubtedly be higher were it not for the existence of near-perfect bootleg facsimiles, issued in much greater numbers than the originals.

Jack Jackson

James Tenney (seated)

another man", and used it within his own *Run For Your Life,* without anyone apparently noticing. Bluesman Arthur Gunter, the writer of the line, which occurs originally in the song *Baby Let's Play House,* did not have the financial clout of Chuck Berry.

The earliest known recording was of a performance of Handel's *Israel In Egypt* at Crystal Palace, London, by a four thousand-strong choir, in 1888. The work includes music recycled from Handels' own previous compositions and also re-worked pieces by other composers. If we accept that this is a kind of sampling, then the first recording was also the first recorded use of sampling

In 1939, American avant-garde composer John Cage supervised the performance of a piece he called *Imaginary Landscape No.1,* "for records of constant and variable frequency, large Chinese cymbal and string piano", according to the published score. The records, test recordings of electronic tones, were played on two variable-speed record players. In 1942, Cage upped the game by using records of various classical pieces by other composers (chosen at random by the performers, but with suggestions by Cage) within a work that Cage called *Credo In Us.* If either of these compositions had been recorded at the time, they would have become the first records to employ sampling in the modern sense – that of incorporating a previously recorded musical extract within a new work. In fact, the first recording of *Imaginary Landscape No.1* was as part of a 1959 three LP set, attributed to no particular record company, entitled *The 25-Year Retrospective Concert Of The Music Of John Cage,* which was a live recording made in New York in May 1958. *Credo In Us* had to wait until 1972 and the release of a 4 LP set in Germany by Ensemble Musica Negativa, which also included a recording of *Imaginary Landscape No.1.*

Meanwhile, a collaboration between John Cage and writer Kenneth Patchen, with Cage including previously recorded sound effects (and live effects too), accompanying a radio play, was broadcast on the CBS network in May 1942, as *The City Wears A Slouch Hat.* The sampling here does not include any previously recorded *musical* extracts, but the work does qualify as a recording in so far as it has been issued on CD.

From 1948, Pierre Schaeffer experimented with what he called 'musique concrète', whereby he manipulated tape recordings of different naturally created sound effects, varying the speed, playing them backwards, and so on. Other composers tried the same techniques, but it was not until 1961 that James Tenney applied them to a previously recorded piece of music. His *Collage No.1 (Blue Suede)* subjects a recording of Elvis Presley's *Blue Suede Shoes* to extreme treatment. For most of the piece's three and a half minute duration it is not possible to determine the source of the apparently electronic sounds being heard, but every now and then a second or two of unadulterated Elvis pushes through. The piece received a belated release in 1992, when it became the first track on a CD compilation of Tenney's music, *Selected Works 1961-1969.*

In 1956, Buchanan and Goodman issued a novelty single called *The Flying Saucer.* A news report, delivered as if by a radio announcer, describes the sighting of a flying saucer and uses frequent fragments of recent rock 'n' roll hits, with lyrics fitting into the narration, to give it a humorous effect. *Blue Suede Shoes* is one of the songs used here too, though it is the version recorded by its composer, Carl Perkins. Whether the simple placing of unaltered musical extracts, one after the other, into something that has no other music can really be described as sampling is debatable, however. Radio presenter Jack Jackson used to do much the same during his programmes for the BBC Light Programme (later Radio One and Radio Two) and Radio Luxembourg. Broadcasting from 1948 until 1977, Jackson evolved a fun approach to playing records, where the gaps between them were filled by fragments of comedy and music, that he skilfully edited and joined together.

In 1967, Frank Zappa recorded and released the third album with his group, the Mothers of Invention. It was the first time that Zappa had full control over his own music. Tom Wilson, who had produced the previous LPs by the group was now credited as 'executive producer', which meant that he did not actually do anything. Frank Zappa was the producer. *We're Only In It For The Money* was a tour de force demonstration of the recording studio's possibilities. It

THE FIRST TIME

For the first vinyl release of *We're Only In It For The Money,* Verve decided to use this picture for the *inside* of the gatefold sleeve, to avoid any court action. The CD restores it to its rightful place. Note the presence of Jimi Hendrix, in person, on the right. *We're Only In It For The Money* has been subjected to a certain amount of censorship over the years, with various of its more risqué lines being edited out for different issues of the album. It has been suggested that Frank Zappa, for reasons of increased publicity, was not necessarily averse to this being done and may even have been responsible for it himself. Certainly, the editing that was carried out was done with an expertise that few producers other than Zappa himself could have managed. This includes the addition of an excised verse from the track *Mother People* to the end of side one, with the music reversed and edited into a short passage of processed whispering. This is actually referred to on the sleeve, so the edit must have been done before the album's artwork was finalised.

AMM, whose music is characterised by making timbre and incident of central importance and avoiding melody (or even recognisable notes) altogether, was adopted for a while by Pink Floyd's management, who must have imagined that a group capable of being viewed as even more psychedelic than the Floyd's most far-out moments might just become a commercial success. The LP was issued on that coolest of sixties labels, Elektra. It did not happen, although AMM's extraordinary guitarist Keith Rowe, saxophonist Lou Gare, and percussionist Eddie Prevost have continued with a similar musical philosophy (separately for the most part) ever since. Only pianist Cornelius Cardew made the decision to abandon the avant garde. A CD of his piano music was issued in 1991, ten years after his death in a car accident, and comprises, for the most part, pieces simple enough to be used for mid-grade tutorials. AMM was formed in 1965. A group with a similar approach to making music, Il Gruppo, was formed in Italy the previous year and had its first album, *The Private Sea Of Dreams,* issued in the US in 1967. It attracted even less attention than AMM, and perhaps the most remarkable aspect of the Italian group, whose full name was Gruppo di Improvvisazione Nuova Consonanza, was that one of its members was Ennio Morricone, best known for his many acclaimed film soundtracks.

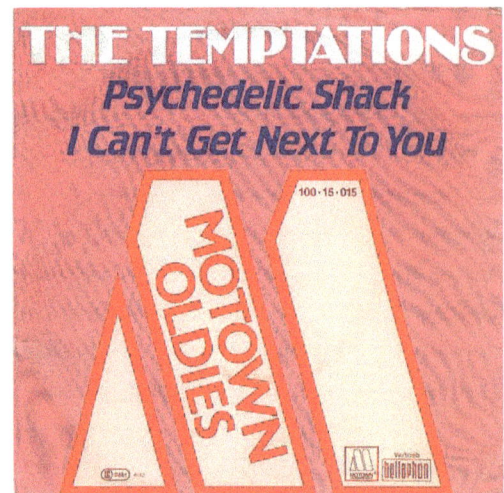

King Crimson In The Wake Of Poseidon

136

used huge amounts of tape manipulation in the manner of Pierre Schaeffer's musique concrète, it included the precise editing of hundreds of musical fragments, taken from several different sessions, and it contained one clear, unequivocal musical sample. And all this on an LP that was supposed to be a pop music record – one that had a set of memorable tunes played by musicians who knew how to rock if they had to, but were flexible enough to cope with more diverse and more complex material. Naturally, the whole affair was shot through with Zappa's ironic humour, with lyrics that poked fun at the hippy culture of the time (despite the followers of this culture being Zappa's most likely customers) and a cover that mocked the Beatles' *Sgt Pepper's Lonely Hearts Club Band*, which was released just before Zappa started his recording. The sample is referenced off-handedly on the album's cover as 'a little bit of surf music', but the music was used with the full agreement of its creator, who happened to be Frank Zappa himself. It was an eighteen second segment from the start of the 1964 single *Heavies* by the Rotations, who were Zappa and his privately-owned studio colleagues, Paul Buff and Dave Aerni.

The Beatles, who were also fond of adopting an experimental approach to recording, had nevertheless not employed any samples beyond a few sound effects and bits of speech (unless one counts the cut-up pieces of fairground organ sound used to flavour the song *Being For The Benefit Of Mr Kite*, which perhaps one should). Opinions are divided with regard to the brass instruments heard on *Yellow Submarine*, but Mark Lewisohn's carefully researched book on the subject refers to the use of session musicians. The single, *All You Need Is Love*, recorded just after the release of *Sgt Pepper's Lonely Hearts Club Band*, came close, but the extracts used in the song, the French National Anthem (*The Marseillaise*), the Joe Loss signature tune, *In The Mood*, and the Beatles' own *She Loves You*, were performed live in the studio and not taken from existing recordings.

The Beatles' track, *I Am The Walrus*, which made its debut in the group's 1967 television show, *Magical Mystery Tour*, included during its closing section the sound of a radio sweeping through the stations, pausing for a few moments whenever it found anything interesting. On the day that the recording was made, all the radio stations seemed to be broadcasting spoken word programmes rather than music. The idea of using radios as a sound source originated with John Cage, whose composition *Imaginary Landscape No.4* from 1951 was for twelve radios and nothing else. The free improvisation group AMM used radios too, as part of the instrumental arsenal they employed during their performances, two of which can be heard on the 1966 LP *AMMmusic*. When the American group Silver Apples decided to copy the Beatles' idea in 1968, their radio managed to find more interesting programmes and the appropriately titled *Program* includes samples of various pieces of vintage and classical music as a result. The track is included on the group's eponymous first album.

There are just a handful of sampling incidents that struggle to fill the fourteen-year gap between Frank Zappa's *We're Only In It For The Money* and the appearance of the first track to be made up entirely of samples, which was released in 1981. One of them is indeed another recording by the Beatles, since *Revolution 9* includes a number of small classical music samples within its sound collage. An even tinier sample on a 1969 Temptations track must have seemed of little significance at the time, but has turned out to be of some historical import. The applause and spoken introduction to the group's December 1969 single, *Psychedelic Shack*, repeats the introduction used on the previous single, *I Can't Get Next To You*. It is the same piece of recording, but rather than take it from the original master tape, producer Norman Whitfield chose to record the single as it played – the sound of the crackle as the stylus hits the vinyl can be heard quite clearly.

The pioneering progressive rock band, King Crimson, samples itself during the maelstrom that forms the end section of the track *The Devil's Triangle* on the 1970 album, *In The Wake Of Poseidon*. Briefly emerging like flotsam from the torrent of sound, a few bars of *In The Court Of The Crimson King*, from the band's previous album, can be heard. The track was itself based on Holst's *Mars* (from the *Planets Suite*), that the band played to bring its live sets to a final climax, but rewritten enough to avoid copyright problems. Gustav Holst died in 1934, so that, according to British copyright law, his family still had the right to refuse permission for the work to be adapted. Presumably, the group Sands, who incorporated an interpretation of *Mars* into their song, *Listen To The Sky*, in 1967, without so much as

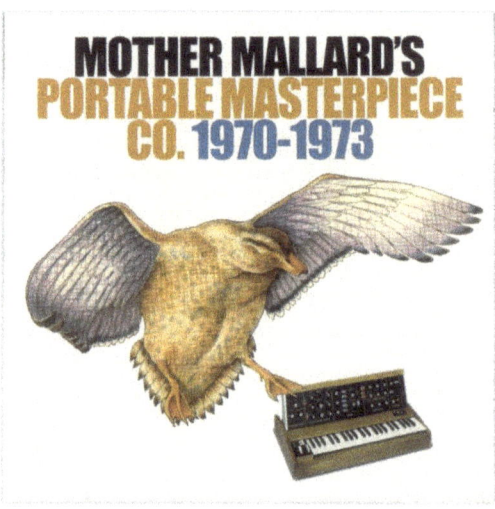

According to the sleevenotes for his compilation CD package *Plunderphonics 69-96*, John Oswald played a turntable in a band in 1964, sampling records by the Beach Boys and the Dave Clark Five for inclusion in the band's versions of the songs. The band was called the Grebs, but if Oswald recorded any of the music, he has not made it available to the general public.

Some copies of the Pink Floyd album, *Dark Side Of The Moon,* on different formats over the years, include a brief part of an orchestral version of the Beatles' *Ticket To Ride,* mixed into the final seconds of the album's last track, *Eclipse*. Opinions are divided over whether the extremely quiet extract is some kind of peculiar mastering mistake or a deliberate use of the sampling technique, but it cannot be heard on every CD or LP. The track was recorded in January 1973. *Fearless* on the 1971 Pink Floyd album, *Meddle*, includes a live recording of football fans singing *You'll Never Walk Alone*, intended as a sound effect rather than a specifically musical sample, in the same manner as the crowd noise on Chicago's *Someday*.

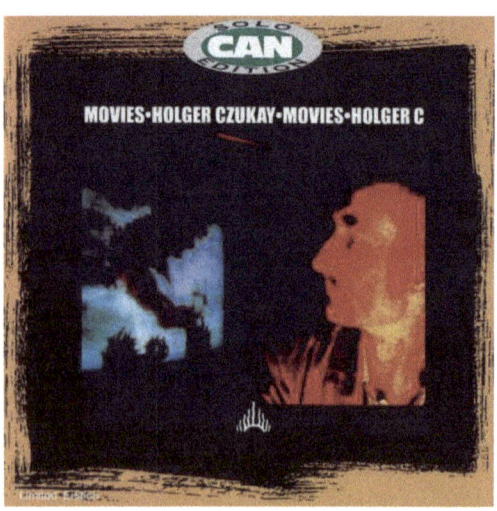

giving Holst a name-check, were too far under the radar to be noticed.

One of the early seventies groups to use synthesizers to play its music, Mother Mallard's Portable Masterpiece Co., uses a sample of the song *Music! Music! Music! (Put Another Nickel In)* to introduce its own piece, *Music*, and thereafter to provide a rhythmic underpinning via an electronic repeating of the 'music' bit. It was an out-take from the group's eponymous first album from 1973 and included on the CD reissue in 1999. The sample is sung by an unknown female singer, though she may be a slightly speeded up Theresa Brewer, who recorded the original hit as well as several later versions. Melanie also recorded a song about putting a nickel in, but her 1971 *Nickel Song* does not quote directly from Theresa Brewer and definitely does not sample her, whatever Wikipedia might believe.

Rikki Don't Lose That Number, the track that opens Steely Dan's 1974 album, *Pretzel Logic*, is driven by a piano riff that has been stolen directly from a jazz piece, *Song For My Father*, by Horace Silver. The item is significant because the riff is used as part of the new song's structure and is not there merely for flavouring. It is intended, moreover, that the jazz reference should be noticed – if the chord choices throughout the album were not telling enough, then Steely Dan's jazz interests are further made apparent by the reference to Charlie Parker in another track and in the cover of a piece by Duke Ellington. Strictly speaking, however, the piano riff is not a sample – it is played as nearly identically to Horace Silver as he could manage by session player Michael Omartian.

Also in 1974, James Brown asked Maceo Parker and Fred Wesley to overdub new horn parts on to the rhythm track from his record, *Soul Power*, turning it into an instrumental. *Soul Power '74* was given extra impact by including a sample of Martin Luther King's "I have been to the mountain top" speech over the closing part of the music, with the noise of the crowd being sampled at the beginning as well, when the listener does not know what is to follow later. The track is included on the album *Us* by Maceo. Speech samples were also used on records by the Electric Flag *(Killing Floor)* and Chicago *(Someday – August 29, 1968)* in the late sixties, but were perhaps less an intrinsic part of the music than is the case with *Soul Power '74*.

It is hard to tell exactly what is going on during many of the eccentric records by the Residents, but the introduction to *Let's Twist Again* used at the start of *Swastikas On Parade* on the 1976 album, *The Third Reich 'n' Roll*, definitely samples the drumming and the opening two bars of band accompaniment from the original version of the song by Chubby Checker. Later in the same track, during a section that is supposed to be a German language interpretation of *Papa's Got A Brand New Bag*, a recognisable horn stab sampled from James Brown's recording appears twice. In 1977, the Residents issued a single with the overall title, *The Beatles Play The Residents And The Residents Play The Beatles*. The A-side, *Beyond The Valley Of A Day In The Life*, is a collage created by jumbling together pieces of Beatles songs, sampled from the original recordings, but frequently made to sound low-fi in the process. The group's first album, *Meet The Residents* (1974), with its cover and title also making reference to the Beatles, includes a number of instrumental flourishes that may be unidentifiable samples, but it is impossible to be sure.

The first album to include tracks whose whole point was the sampling they contained was Holger Czukay's *Movies*, which was released in 1979. Czukay was the bass player with the experimental German group Can during the seventies, but left the group in order to pursue his interests in studio production. All four of the tracks on *Movies* contain samples taken from short wave radio broadcasts and film soundtracks. Some are in the form of speech, but some are musical, with *Persian Love* making the singing of an unnamed Iranian singer into the central focus of the track. In the album's sleeve notes, Czukay writes, "I had an exciting time finding out how the different worlds of film or radio could meet in a piece of music as if they would have belonged together from the very beginning."

A similar approach was used by Brian Eno and David Byrne on their collaborative effort, *My Life In The Bush Of Ghosts*, recorded in 1979-80 and released in 1981. At its core, the music did not make a particularly big leap away from the self-conscious rock of Byrne's main band, Talking Heads, being fashioned along the same lines as the arty, skeletal dance music of New York's Material, which was making its first recordings at the same time (and whose bass player,

An album from 1975 contains music that seems to make it a better candidate for the first record with tracks having sampling as their whole point than Holger Czukay's *Movies*. The Gavin Bryars LP that was issued as the first record on Brian Eno's Obscure label has a piece called *Jesus' Blood Never Failed Me Yet* occupying the whole of its side two. For this, Bryars used a field recording of a tramp singing the hymn of the title as the basis for an extended work. The tramp's song – just a single chorus – is looped so as to be heard over and over again within the unfolding music. The result is surprisingly moving, to the extent that Bryars felt justified in re-recording the work and making it nearly three times longer for its release on CD in 1993. As the tramp's song, however, was not itself taken from a record, but was on an unused section from a film made by a friend of Bryars, with the sound edited by Bryars himself, it does not really count as being a sample. Its first appearance on record (or anywhere) is as part of the *Jesus' Blood* work.

Scratching, whereby a record is manipulated back and forth by hand while the stylus remains in the groove, was invented during the mid seventies by a teenager called Theodore Livingstone. He became a DJ, using the name Grand Wizard Theodore, under the initial tutelage of Grandmaster Flash. The technique, which effectively transformed a turntable into an instrument in its own right, was first recorded during Grandmaster Flash's *The Adventures Of...* session. It became a more widely heard sound on record, following its use on Herbie Hancock's hit dance track, *Rockit*, in 1983. Producer Bill Laswell was seeking out musicians to accompany the keyboard player, who liked to experiment with all the most advanced electronic instruments available, and was recommended to employ the skills of Derek Showard, a turntable performer who had learned his skills watching Grandmaster Flash and who used the name Grand Mixer D.St. Showard's contribution to the rhythm section on *Rockit* is vital and he also plays an extended solo break. There are brief samples to be heard on *Rockit* too, most notably the powerful guitar chord near the start, but it is likely that these are delivered by Hancock's keyboards, with built-in sampling technology, rather than by Grand Mixer D.St.

The man responsible for operating the turntables on the 1972 Ensemble Musica Negativa recording of John Cage's *Imaginary Landscape No.1* and *Credo In Us* was Johann Nikolaus Matthes. He was not, however, required to do any scratching.

Tribute murals to Kool Herc in The Bronx, New York

Clive Campbell (DJ Kool Herc) was born and brought up in Jamaica, where DJs had been an important part of the music since 1970. It was then that U Roy made his first recordings, the singles *Wake The Town* and *Wear You To The Ball,* on which the original vocal parts were stripped off previously recorded tracks and replaced by the DJ's own ranting (known as toasting). No sampling is involved, but the influence on the American DJ scene that led to *The Adventures Of Grandmaster Flash On The Wheels Of Steel* is clear.

Bill Laswell, plays on one track). In addition, however, *My Life In The Bush Of Ghosts* adds a wealth of sampled material to the mix, some of it in the form of spoken word extracts, taken from short wave radio, but some taken from LPs of esoteric world music field recordings. The samples give the whole album an exotic flavour, although, in truth, they are not crucial to the music's structure in the manner of *Persian Love*.

One night in 1973, August 11th, at his sister's party in the Bronx, New York City, DJ Kool Herc (short for Hercules – Clive Campbell was six foot six inches tall, with a physique to match) tried an experiment. Realising that there were certain parts of particular records that had the greatest effect on the crowd's dancing, he decided to play just these parts, one following quickly after another, as he faded out one song and faded in the next. He was already using two turntables to keep the music playing without a break. The result was so successful, that he made it a regular part of his set from then on, calling it the 'Merry-go-round'. He also discovered that, by using two copies of the same record, and switching back and forth between the two records on the two turntables, he could extend the length of the passages that were his audiences' favourites. His skill at doing this was good enough, but could not compare with that of a DJ who learned from DJ Kool Herc and practised hard to take the technique further. This was Joseph Saddler, who used the name Grandmaster Flash for his performances, to underline his expertise with the turntables. He became able to switch from record to record so precisely that no-one would even notice a switch had been made. His extended versions of tracks were seamless and he could edit together the music from different records without dropping a beat.

Although he refused some early requests to record a performance, feeling that no-one would be interested in buying a record of other people's records, Grandmaster Flash finally relented after the first hip hop records appeared and he realized that he could become a part of the genre's success. *The Adventures Of Grandmaster Flash On The Wheels Of Steel* was issued in 1981 and demonstrated exactly why the DJ was so highly rated in the club community where he worked. Using three turntables and two mixers, Grandmaster Flash took three hours to get the recording right, determined to do it as a single live performance, without any studio editing. Over the course of seven minutes, he took the listener on an aural tour of the clubs' favourite dance tracks, with the classic bass-line from Chic's 1979 hit song, *Good Times* (already made doubly familiar by its underpinning of the break-through rap single, *Rapper's Delight*, by the Sugarhill Gang) acting as a recurring motif to link the whole thing together. *The Adventures…* became the first record to be made up entirely of samples, assembled together to make a cohesive and valid musical work in its own right.

The record inspired Radio Luxembourg DJ Tony Prince to begin broadcasting a programme called the *Disco Mix Club Show* and by 1984, he was issuing records containing 'megamixes' in the manner of Grandmaster Flash, using several different turntable experts. The impact of these amongst the music-loving general public – or even amongst other musicians – was reduced by the fact that the *Disco Mix Club* records were issued to accredited DJs only, who had to pay a membership fee. The idea was, that if a DJ had not managed to become skilful enough to deliver a fully mixed set on two turntables, then he could simply play a DMC record, where the mixing had already been done. There were some remarkable tracks to be heard, including an Alan Coulthard construction called *The Heartbrobs*, created by interweaving hit songs by Howard Jones and Nik Kershaw, another Alan Coulthard track called *Megasisters*, that achieved a similar effect with songs by Sister Sledge, and, best of all, *The Adventures Of Sanny*, from January 1985, a virtuoso turntable performance from Sanny X to rival Grandmaster Flash.

Meanwhile, towards the end of 1983, Tommy Boy Records held a competition to promote a single release, *Play That Beat, Mr. D.J.* by G.L.O.B.E. and Whiz Kid, in which contestants were invited to create a remix of the song. Working together, sound engineer Douglas DiFranco and advertising copywriter Steve Stein, adopting appropriate DJ names, Double Dee and Steinski, rather exceeded their brief. They delivered a lengthy megamix in which the original single merely served as a jumping-off point for a parade of twenty-four samples, taken not just from hip-hop and disco records, but from well-known tracks by Little Richard, the Supremes, and Culture Club, as well as film dialogue by Humphrey Bogart. The duo won the competition and, although their mix, titled *Lesson One (The Pay-off Mix)*, could

Double Dee and Steinski

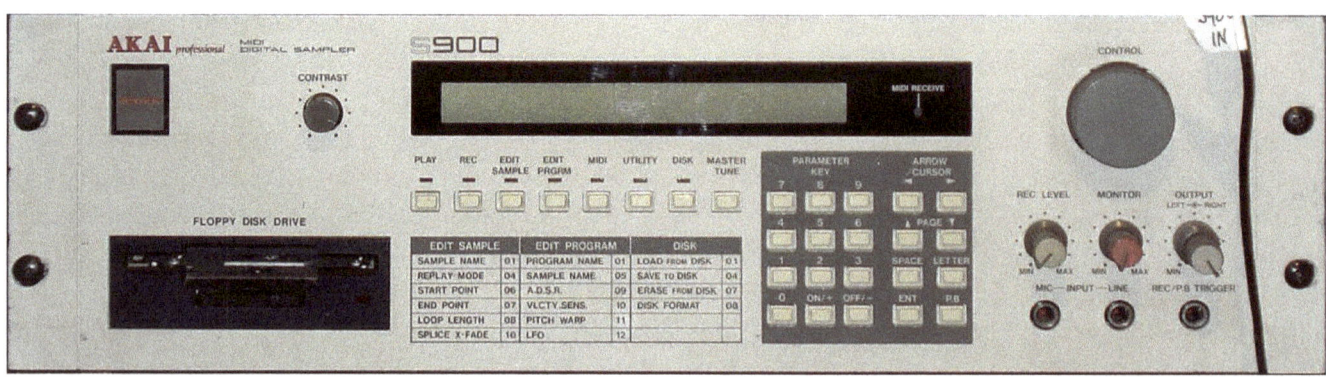

Akai S900 sampler

Record Without a Cover – the embossed lettering on the black vinyl made legible with the help of a bottle of liquid paper

not be given an official release due to the enormous copyright problems that would have ensued, the music was widely heard nevertheless. Double Dee and Steinski consolidated their influence by making two more megamixes during the next two years, which they called *Lesson Two* and *Lesson Three*.

As it happened, there were two different lessons to be absorbed from these recordings. Matt Black and Jonathan More, DJs working together as Coldcut, realised that it was acceptable to use a much wider range of music in their mixes than just what was conceived as dance music. They made a recording that was issued as a 12" single, *Say Kids (What Time Is It)*, in 1987, by which time the enormously useful Akai S900 sampler had become available – an electronic unit capable of recording and editing up to sixty-three seconds of sound. Building the music entirely out of samples, in the manner of Grandmaster Flash, Coldcut gleefully combined Walt Disney samples with James Brown and Grandmaster Flash himself. The record is frequently claimed as the first UK megamix record, although in reality it was preceded by the Disco Mix Club releases. Coldcut applied the same maverick approach to sample choice when asked to remix a rap song, *Paid In Full*, by Eric B and Rakim. The samples, which included a memorable extract from Israeli singing star Ofra Haza, threatened to overwhelm the rappers' own performance, but emerged nevertheless as one of the most remarkable recordings of 1987. It was not the first remix hit, but is certainly one of the best. In 1989, Coldcut were in a position to issue the first DJ fronted album, *What's That Noise*, which did not include either *Say Kids (What Time Is It)* or *Paid In Full*, but did have the hit songs *People Hold On* (featuring Lisa Stansfield) and *Doctorin' The House* (featuring Yazz and the Plastic Population).

Bill Drummond and Jimmy Cauty learned another lesson. Double Dee and Steinski had not created their works by becoming expert manipulators of turntables – they had assembled them in the studio by cutting and sticking together pieces of magnetic tape. To Drummond and Cauty, this meant that anyone could produce 'turntable' music and in 1987 they made and released an album, named after the year of its release (*1987 – What The Fuck Is Going On*), which sought to apply this punk aesthetic. Glorying in the name of Justified Ancients Of Mu-Mu (later renamed The KLF – Kopyright Liberation Front), the record borrowed huge chunks from some well-known tracks. The JAMMS were hoping, perhaps, that the artists would be no more concerned than Queen had been, when their music was sampled by Grandmaster Flash, or more likely they just did not care. In the event, the songwriters from Abba did strongly object, and the album was ordered to be withdrawn from sale, with all remaining copies destroyed. The albums already sold became instant collectors' items and if the value of these has remained on the low side (around £60) this is likely to be a result of the record, declared to be an illegal bootleg, itself being frequently bootlegged. The JAMMS responded by issuing a version of the record in which all the samples were removed – it filled a twelve inch single. On the back, the duo gave detailed instructions as to how the purchaser could recreate the original album, using three turntables and a pile of selected discs. Suggesting that any music fan could easily perform a turntable mix for themselves was in line with the 1977 punk fanzine quote, that anyone who learned two chords on the guitar knew enough to start a band. In fact, even given that the editing on the JAMMS albums very much lacked the skill and finesse of Grandmaster Flash, the duo was being disingenuous, for the edits had been achieved using studio technology and not turntables.

Christian Marclay is a turntable player working out of a different tradition. Employed by cutting-edge jazz composer John Zorn to contribute to some tracks on the albums *The Big Gundown* and *Spillane* (from 1985 and 1987), Marclay was as likely to use classical or bluegrass records as anything else, and manipulated the samples he chose in an extreme form of the scratching technique. The two solo albums he made during the eighties highlighted his skills. The one-sided *Record Without A Cover* (1985) was exactly that – it was intended that the record should become damaged in order to add to the montage of percussive scratching (in the traditional sense of the term) already recorded on the vinyl. The abstract mélange of rapidly changing classical and easy listening samples that makes up the rest of the sound on the record is a world away from either of *The Adventures Of…* recordings or the *1987* album, and not just because it is impossible to dance to. *More Encores*, issued in 1989 as a ten inch vinyl album, (with an implied exclamation mark after the first word in the title, since there was never a record called *Encores*), is arguably more

The cover art from the front and back of the Endtroducing album, showing a vinyl record shop in Sacramento, California. It has been turned into a poster, which is available for purchase from DJ Shadow's website djshadow.com

U.F.Orb contains an edited version of the track *Blue Room*. Previously, the song, extended to just under forty minutes – a timing chosen because the organisers of the chart had announced that a single qualifying for inclusion had to have no more than that amount of music in total – was released to become the hit single with the longest ever playing time. The great majority of LPs made in the days before CDs, including *Sgt Pepper's Lonely Hearts Club Band* and *Bridge Over Troubled Water,* were shorter than this. The Orb appeared on the BBC TV show *Top Of The Pops,* wearing space suits and playing a game of chess, while the music sounded.

Two particularly interesting sample-based albums were issued in 1993 and 1994. *Hand On The Torch* is by rappers Us3, but sounds rather different from the hip-hop norm due to the fact that all its samples are taken from the Blue Note catalogue of fifties and sixties jazz. A few of the rhythms are emphasised a little, but for the most part the album has the sound of a thrilling jazz-rap fusion. It was itself issued on the Blue Note label. For *If 60s Were 90s,* the Beautiful People created a set of impressive tracks, at the point where ambient and dance musics meet, out of a skilful and inspired assembly of Jimi Hendrix samples. *The Sea... Eventually,* which brings the album to a close with a reworking of phrases from *Hey Baby (New Rising Sun), Pali Gap,* and *1983 A Merman I Should Turn To Be,* amongst others, is something of a masterpiece and an easy demonstration of the worth and power of the whole sampling process.

interesting, and certainly more listenable, for the way in which it presents musical portraits of a number of artists, from Maria Callas and Johann Strauss to Jimi Hendrix, by means of a collage of carefully selected sampled fragments of their music. Marclay creates his collages in the same manner as Grandmaster Flash, by playing bits of the original records, except in the case of his *John Cage* track. For this, he literally cut up records of John Cage music and glued the pieces together to form a new record, which he then played. The sounds of the stylus hitting the joins becomes part of the resulting music.

The fact that it became possible to deliver live samples via electronics (samplers) meant that the use of turntable players within groups did not become very widespread, although the most influential rap group, Public Enemy, whose first records appeared in 1987, felt it was absolutely necessary to include one, to deliver various scratching sounds. Terminator X was described as 'the assault technician' or as 'the track attacker'. Public Enemy used samples within their music – it was a rare hip hop or dance group that did not – but it was not necessarily Terminator X's turntables that delivered them. Nevertheless, the first mainstream album to be made up entirely of samples was issued by a musician who had practised the art of playing turntables to the point where he could be described as 'the Jimi Hendrix of the turntable', in acknowledgement of his unequalled skill and innovation on his chosen instrument. DJ Shadow (Josh Davis) was able to perform the intricately compiled music on his album, *Endtroducing* (1996), live. To emphasise his virtuosity and absolute technical command of turntables and other equipment used simultaneously, he also managed to include sampled visual material, to play at the same time as the music. Crucially, he undertook concert tours, in the manner of a rock group, rather than playing the music of *Endtroducing* in clubs. For the most part, it was too slow to be used as dance music. The Hendrix comparison breaks down when the relative influence of the two artists is considered. Jimi Hendrix introduced new sounds and ways of playing the guitar that have remained a major inspiration to guitar players ever since. DJ Shadow, on the other hand, set the bar so high that no artist since has attempted to create an extended work of sampled music as he did, by using turntables (apart, it has to be said, from DJ Shadow himself, although his subsequent music has generally made less of an impact.) Not for nothing did DJ Shadow incorporate the word 'end' in the name he chose for his album.

In 1989, a computer programme, Sound Tools, allowing recording to be carried out on a computer and stored on its hard disc, was developed. By 1992, personal computers with sufficient processing power to run the programme properly had appeared. The first recording to take advantage of the new system was probably the second album by the Orb, *U.F.Orb,* the music being heavily reliant on the use of samples, most of them obscure and manipulated beyond the point of recognition. By 1997, Sound Tools had been refined and extended, and was now known as Pro Tools. With computers having become more powerful too, the recording studios all abandoned recording based on magnetic tape in favour of Pro Tools. Numerous records based around sampling appeared, now that the process had become much easier to carry out. Vital albums by the Avalanches, Cinematic Orchestra, Fatboy Slim, Goldie, Groove Armada, Kinobe, Morcheeba – and Moby – were all released before the turn of the century.

TRACKING THE TRACKS

The LP recording of Stravinsky's *Pulcinella* pictured at the start of the chapter was chosen for the sake of the portrait of the young Stravinsky himself on the cover. This Simon Rattle performance was issued on CD in 1993, alongside a ballet by Kurt Weill, but with a different cover. As usual with the recording of classical works, there are numerous different performances available, with little reason to choose any particular one other than listener preference. The CD *Stravinsky Conducts Stravinsky – The Mono Years 1952-1955* includes the complete *Pulcinella* ballet and is presumably performed as the composer wanted it to be heard, although the early recording date and the lack of stereo image inevitably makes the music a little lacking sonically.

Of the vast number of other classical works, where the composer is stealing themes from another, one of the most interesting is the *Concerto For String Quartet and Orchestra* by Arnold Schoenberg, composed in 1933. For this work, Schoenberg started with a *Concerto Grosso* composed nearly two hundred years earlier by George Handel, and 'improved' it by adding new, twentieth century harmony and structuring, while stripping out what he felt were the substandard parts, to the point where Handel's music is left poking through a mass of new composition, exactly like a series of samples. As in the case of the Stravinsky, the work is available on several different CDs.

The two Josquin Desprez *L'homme Armé* masses are on a Gimell CD issued in 1996, in performances by The Tallis Scholars. The masses by Antonio Zacara da Teramo and Bartolomeo da Bologna do not appear to be currently available on CD.

Mike Oldfield's *Tubular Bells* was originally issued in 1973 as the first release on Richard Branson's new Virgin record label. The album has been reissued on CD on several occasions, but for some of these, Mike Oldfield has not been able to resist tinkering with the music and changing some of the details, including making a complete re-recording in 2003, which replaced Vivian Stanshall's narration at the end of the first part with one by John Cleese. The CD that is simply the original work with improved sound quality is the one remastered in 2000. *The Orchestral Tubular Bells* was originally issued on Virgin in 1975. It has also been reissued several times – the most recent CD dates from 2003 and has a newly designed cover, but the music is the same.

The CD containing *Bohemian Rhapsody* on a music box is not currently available. Two recreations of the sound can be heard on YouTube at the time of writing, although one has a grandeur and depth of sound like no actual music box the author has ever heard. An American company advertising on the internet will produce a music box containing a tune of the customer's choice, which could presumably be *Bohemian Rhapsody*. Or you could just imagine it.

Fortress – The London Symphony Orchestra Performs The Music Of Sting is on Angel (1994). The orchestral Pink Floyd album was reissued as *The Royal Philharmonic Orchestra Plays The Music Of Pink Floyd* (Emporio 1996).

Stranger In Paradise is on a number of Tony Bennett compilation CDs, such as *The Essential Tony Bennett* (Columbia 2005). A new version of the song, performed by Bennett in a duet with Andrea Bocelli, is on *Duets II* (Columbia 2011). *Past, Present And Future* is on *The Best Of The Shangri-Las* (Polygram 1997). *Joybringer* is on the two CD set *World Of Mann* (Universal 2006), which includes hits by the original Manfred Mann group, as well as by Manfred Mann's Earth Band. *The Best Of Manfred Mann's Earth Band Remastered* (Creature Music 1999) is better, concentrating on just the Earth Band, but it has been deleted. The 1987 album, Masque (CD on Creature Music 1999), completes a Holst music project that the Earth Band hoped to complete in 1973, but could not gain permission from Holst's family (compare King Crimson, elsewhere in this chapter). It includes *Joybringer*, alongside other pieces based on themes taken from *The Planets Suite*. Lamb's *Gorecki* is on *Lamb* (Fontana 1996).

The best of the four original LPs made by The Nice is *Ars Longa Vita Brevis* from 1968. This was expanded to a double CD on Castle in 2003, by including BBC session tracks, but it is not easy to find now. The compilation album, *Diary Of An Empty Day* (Repertoire 2010) is a good alternative. Emerson Lake and Palmer are well served by a two CD anthology, *The Essential Emerson Lake & Palmer* (Sony 2011). Most of the available albums by Renaissance are the work of a later, more successful group than that fronted by Keith Relf (though they are linked – one evolved into the other as personnel changed). The 1969 album made by the Relf group is *Renaissance* (Repertoire 2008).

The first two Led Zeppelin LPs, which are the most blues-oriented of the group's albums, were issued by Atlantic as newly remastered double CDs in 2014, with assorted demos and live tracks filling the second discs. The Small Faces *You Need Loving* is on the two CD *Ultimate Collection* (Sanctuary 2008). Earl Hooker's *Blue Guitar* is on *An Introduction To Earl Hooker* (Fuel 2006). The Muddy Waters songs, *You Shook Me* and *You Need Love*, are on *I Got My Brand On You – The 1956-1962 Studio Recordings* (Hoodoo Records 2013).

The Beach Boys' *Surfin' USA* is on all of the group's Greatest Hits compilations. *20 Golden Greats* is one of the few to organise its tracks in chronological order, which means that *Surfin' USA* plays first. The LP was issued in 1976; the CD is from 1987 (EMI). Chuck Berry's *Sweet Little Sixteen* is on *The Best Of Chuck Berry* (Spectrum 2000). It is also on the three CD set *The Ultimate Chuck Berry* (Spectrum 2007), which includes *You Can't Catch Me*. The Beatles' *Come Together* is on *Abbey Road* (EMI 2009 – original LP 1969); *Run For Your Life* is on *Rubber Soul* (EMI 2009 – original LP 1965). Elvis Presley's *Baby Let's Play House* is on *Elvis At Sun* (BMG 2004).

One of the CDs in EMI's *American Classics* series is dedicated to John Cage and includes both *Imaginary Landscape No.1* and *Credo In Us* (EMI 2008). These are the recordings made by Ensemble Musica Negativa in 1972. All five of the *Imaginary Landscape* pieces are on a Hat Hut CD (1995) in performances by the Maelstrom Percussion Ensemble, directed by Jan Williams. *The City Wears A Slouch Hat* is on two CD releases (Mode 1999 and Cortical Foundation 2000), though neither is very easy to find. Helpfully, as is often the case on these occasions, a few different YouTube subscribers have uploaded recordings of the original radio broadcast on to the website.

Works by Pierre Schaeffer, many of them produced in collaboration with fellow musique concrete pioneer, Pierre Henry, are to be found on *Panorama De Musique Concrète* (El/Cherry Red 2010) This compiles recordings made in 1956-7 and originally issued on a pair of very scarce LPs. James Tenney's *Collage No.1 (Blue Suede)* is available on an American CD, *Selected Works 1961-1969* (Frog Peak/Artifact 1992).

Buchanan and Goodman's *The Flying Saucer* is included on an American CD, *Everything You Always Wanted To Know About Buchanan and Goodman But Forgot To Ask* (Sting Music 1993), along with some follow-up singles that use the same formula. Easier to find is the compilation CD, *25 All-Time Novelty Hits* (Varese Sarabande 2002), which places *The Flying Saucer* at the front of a parade of novelty single releases extending to 1981. The other tracks have nothing to do with sampling.

There are several CDs available by Jack Jackson, in his role as dance band leader, in the years before he became a radio presenter. For a taste of his radio programme, we must make do with a solitary YouTube upload playing just under seven minutes of broadcasting, with the records taken out. The excerpt has been taken from near the end of Jackson's career in the seventies and lacks, perhaps, some of the energy of his earlier work.

There are several different LP and CD issues of Frank Zappa's *We're Only In It For The Money*. In 1984, Zappa remixed the album, restoring all the material that had been deleted on various vinyl issues, but replacing the original bass and drum parts with new recordings made by his current band members. Many listeners regard the new instrumental parts as sounding out of place. The Rykodisc CD from 1995 restores the original mix: the Universal CD from 2012 is a reissue of this. They have the same deleted sections as on the original 1968 LP. The *Heavies* single by The Rotations is included on an American CD that compiles Frank Zappa's previously released work from the early sixties, *Cucamonga* (Del-Fi 1991).

The Beatles' *Being For The Benefit Of Mr Kite* is a track on the album *Sgt Pepper's Lonely Hearts Club Band* (finally remastered for CD in 2009, EMI). *All You Need Is Love* and *I Am The Walrus,* similarly remastered for CD in 2009, are on *Magical Mystery Tour* (EMI). *Revolution 9* is on *The Beatles (The White Album)* (EMI, 2009).

AMMmusic by AMM was reissued on CD in 1989 by Rér. It contains the complete 1966 performances, out of which the music comprising the original LP was edited, but includes those edits too, as separate tracks. The listener therefore has the means of hearing the original LP, exactly as it was issued, if that is their choice. Cornelius Cardew's *Piano Music* is on B&L Records (1991). *The Private Sea Of Dreams* is reissued on an Italian CD that reverts to the album title used on the original 1966 release in Italy, *Gruppo Di Improvvisazione Nuova Consonanza* (Italian Sony/Schema 2016). The eponymous Silver Apples CD comprises the group's first two albums from 1968 and 1969 (MCA 1997).

Several people have uploaded the last section of Pink Floyd's *Eclipse* on to YouTube, with the equalisation adjusted to make the *Ticket To Ride* sample sound more clearly. *Meddle* is on a Pink Floyd Records CD (2016).

The Temptations' singles, *I Can't Get Next To You* and *Psychedelic Shack*, are included on the two CD compilation, *At Their Very Best* (Universal/Motown 2001). Alternatively, they can be heard on an interesting two CD compilation that focuses on the group's Norman Whitfield productions, *Psychedelic Soul* (Universal/Motown 2003).

The other tracks mentioned as containing seventies samples are included on CD as follows:
King Crimson *In The Wake Of Poseidon* (Discipline 1999)
Mother Mallard's Portable Masterpiece Co *1970-1973* (Cuneiform 1999)
Steely Dan *Pretzel Logic* (MCA/Universal 1999)
Maceo *Us* (Japanese People 2003)
The Residents *Third Reich 'n' Roll* (Mute 2005; US MVD 2012)
The Residents *Meet The Residents* (US MVD 2011)
Holger Czukay *Movies* (Revisited 2007)
Brian Eno and David Byrne *My Life In The Bush Of Ghosts* (Virgin 2006)

Listen To The Sky by Sands is included on the box sets *Nuggets II* (Rhino 2001) and *Acid Drops, Spacedust & Flying Saucers* (EMI 2001). These would be expensive ways of getting to hear one track, but both sets include a wealth of vital psychedelic music from the late sixties and, for that, are well worth it. Melanie's *Nickel Song* is on *The Best Of Melanie* (BMG 20003). *Killing Floor* by The Electric Flag is on *A Long Time Comin'* (Sony 2013). *Someday (August 29, 1968)* by Chicago is on *Chicago Transit Authority* (Rhino 2002). The Residents' track *Beyond The Valley Of A Day In The Life* is not available on CD but has been uploaded on to YouTube by five different subscribers. The early recordings by Material are compiled on a useful (and cheap) three CD boxed set, *Bill Laswell & Material* (Golden Stars 2005).

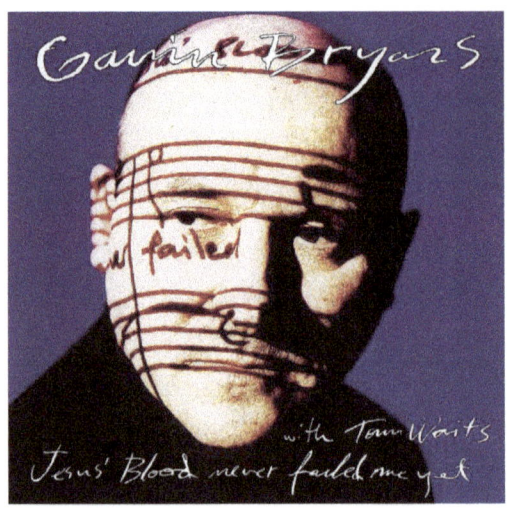
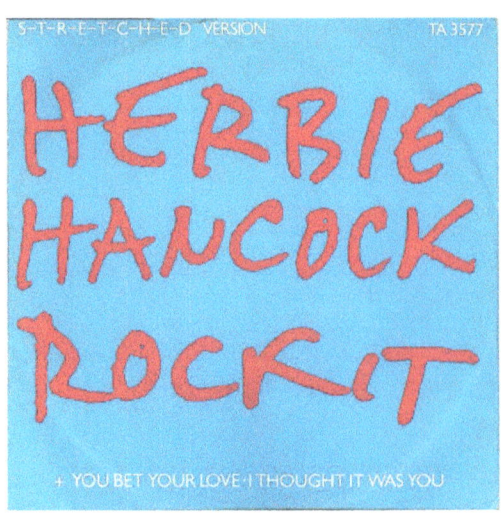

Both versions of *Jesus' Blood Never Failed Me Yet* by Gavin Bryars are on CD. Virgin was responsible for a straight reissue in 1998 of the original 1975 LP, which had *Jesus' Blood..* on one side and *The Sinking Of The Titanic* on the other. The longer, reworked version of the track fills the 1993 Point Music CD.

A 4 CD boxed set issued by Sony in 2014 and titled *The Grandmaster Flash Collection* manages to include fifty-six tracks, mostly inspired by, rather than performed by Grandmaster Flash, but without including *The Adventures Of Grandmaster Flash On The Wheels Of Steel*. It is a fine collection, but spoilt by the omission of that track. A various artists double CD compilation, *The Best Hip Hop Anthemz... Ever* (Virgin 1998), is a vastly better proposition. It has Grandmaster Flash's *The Adventures...* and also *The Message* and *White Lines (Don't Do It)*. It has Herbie Hancock's *Rockit* and the Sugarhill Gang's *Rapper's Delight*. It has the Coldcut remix of Eric B and Rakim's *Paid In Full*. It has the seminal *Planet Rock* by Afrika Bambaata and Public Enemy's best-known track, *Don't Believe The Hype.* It has Coolio's updating of Stevie Wonder, *Gangsta's Paradise*, it has Run D.M.C.'s collision between hip hop and hard rock, *Walk This Way* (featuring Aerosmith), and it has twenty-eight other near-essential tracks. In short, to use a slightly over-worked phrase that is nevertheless completely apposite, the compilation 'does what it says on the tin'.

Herbie Hancock's long career is distinguished by numerous musical high points, of which *Rockit* is just one. The track is included on his album, *Future Shock* (Columbia 1992), alongside music from the same sessions that has less immediate impact, but is still very interesting.

Original DJ (Virgin 1995) is a compilation of tracks by U Roy and presents a fine overview of his career in the seventies, even if some of the dates given in the booklet are not reliable. *Version Galore* (Trojan 2002) covers similar ground, but includes a second CD with the original tracks that U Roy used for his toasting.

The Disco Mix Club tracks mentioned are to be found on the vinyl LPs *September 84 Mixes* (Alan Coulthard's *The Hearthrobs)* and *January 85 Mixes* (Alan Coulthard's *Megasisters* and Sanny X's *The Adventures Of Sanny*). Frustratingly, they have not been reissued on CD and the LPs are hard to find. At the time of writing, however, Megasisters can be heard on YouTube, while The *Adventures Of Sanny* is on two websites – YouTube and Mastermix.org.

The Double Dee and Steinski *Lesson* tracks have been uploaded several times to YouTube.

The Coldcut album, *What's That Noise,* was issued on CD in 1989 on the Ahead Of Our Time label. It is not currently available, but is commonly found second-hand. *Say Kids (What Time Is It)* has not made it on to CD, but can be heard on the YouTube or SoundCloud websites.

Two of the tracks from the JAMMS *1987* album (*Don't Take Five* and *All You Need Is Love*) are included on the American CD *The History Of The Jams* (TVT Records 1989). Inevitably, the complete album can be heard on YouTube.

The John Zorn albums including contributions from Christian Marclay are *The Big Gundown* (Nonesuch 1986; reissued 2000 on Tzadik with extra tracks), a re-imagining of the music of soundtrack composer Ennio Morricone, and *Spillane* (Nonesuch 1990). Marclay's *More Encores* has been reissued on CD by Rér (2003), but *Record Without A Cover*, whose whole point is that it is a vinyl record, is not available on CD. The record is hard to find – an abridged version of the music, cut down to half its length, can be heard on YouTube, while a couple of sites offer a (not strictly legal) download of the full work, converted to mp3 format.

The essential Public Enemy album is the group's second, originally issued in 1988, *It Takes A Nation Of Millions To Hold Us Back* (Def Jam 2000). It is a powerful political manifesto that also happens to be great, inspiring music. There is also an excellent 'Best Of' anthology – *Power To The People And The Beats: Public Enemy's Greatest Hits* (Def Jam 2005).

DJ Shadow's *Entroducing* is on the Mowax label (1996). It was reissued as a double, deluxe CD in 2005 (Universal/Island), the extra disc being filled with out-takes, alternative versions, and part of a live set. A package comprising a CD and a DVD, *In Tune And On Time – Live!* (Universal Island 2004) provides a fascinating addition to the 1996 album, showing how DJ Shadow is able to deliver the same music live (and newer tracks too – the live set is from 2002) with a bank of turntables, samplers, beat boxes, and mixers.

The Orb's *U.F.Orb* is on Big Life/Wau! Mr Modo (1992). The 'short' version of *Blue Room* (seventeen and a half minutes) is on the album, but for the full effect, the first CD single is needed (Big Life/Wau! Mr Modo). It is deleted and the few unplayed copies on offer are expensive, but second-hand copies are cheap and easy enough to find.

The classic end-of-century albums using samples are as follows: The Avalanches *Since I Left You* (Modular/XL 2000) / Cinematic Orchestra *Motion* (Ninja Tune 1999) / Fatboy Slim *You've Come A Long Way Baby* (Skint 1998) / Goldie *Saturnzreturn* (ffrr 1998) double CD / Groove Armada *Vertigo* (Jive Electro 1999) / Kinobe *Soundphiles* (Zomba 2000) / Morcheeba *Big Calm* (China 1998) / Moby *Play* (Mute 1999) / Beautiful People *If 60s Were 90s* (Continuum 1994) / Us 3 *Hand On The Torch* (Blue Note 1993)

The original 7" single of *Relax* was supplemented by a 12" single including a sixteen and a half minute *Sex Mix*, which employed the rhythm of the original issue and not much else. This was soon replaced with a shorter *US Mix* and then this was replaced by an even shorter *New York Mix*. A cassette version was issued (at a time when cassette singles sold well), with the title *Relax's Greatest Bits* and consisting of extracts from the other mixes already used. The follow-up single, *Two Tribes*, played the remix game more extensively. Again, an original 7" single was joined by a 12" single, with the *Annihilation Mix*. A month later, a second 12" single appeared, with the *Carnage Mix*, followed by a third 12" single, with the *Hibakusha Mix*. Different mixes were used on the cassette single and the American release, while a version prepared by Alan Coulthard for the Disco Mix Club, titled *Frankie Goes To High Bronski*, melded *Two Tribes* with two other records, *High Energy* by Evelyn Thomas and *Smalltown Boy* by Bronski Beat. When the single tracks eventually appeared on the Frankie Goes To Hollywood LP, the mixes were different again. Many further remixes of *Relax* and *Two Tribes* were made by various DJs during the next years. With regard to the later Frankie Goes To Hollywood singles, a particularly striking remix (the *Attack Mix*) of *Warriors Of The Wasteland* was created by employing guitarist Gary Moore to solo over much of the song and turn it into heavy metal.

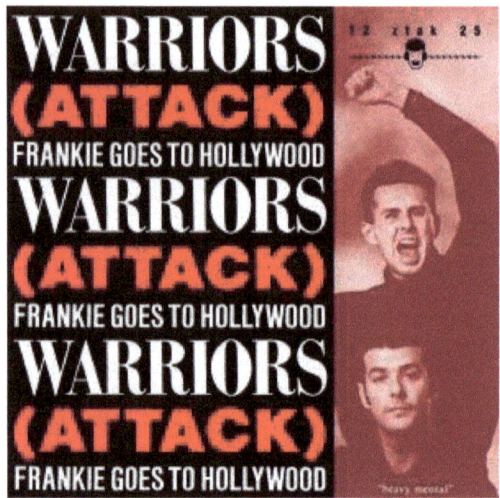

Revolution 1 and *Revolution 9* are both included in Rutherford Chang's remix of the entire Beatles *White Album*, which was issued on vinyl in 2013. Chang collects original numbered copies of the *White Album* – as of July 2017 he had 1774 of them, while by February 2018 the number had risen to 1947. He is particularly interested in discovering what has happened to the minimalist covers – how they have worn over the years and how they might have been defaced or decorated by the original owners. His remix was created by simultaneously playing a hundred copies of the album and recording the sound. As each side proceeds, the records move out of synchronisation, until by the end, nothing is recognisable. His limited edition release has a cover design (shown above) consisting of a collage of some of the more interesting decorated covers in his collection. The Rutherford Chang *White Album* is an example of the plunderphonics approach, described later in this chapter.

Eclection with Kerrilee Male

Dorris Henderson

14 THE REMIX

From the beginning of 1984 through to the end of 1986, Frankie Goes To Hollywood achieved six hit singles. The publicity surrounding a BBC ban on playing the first of these, *Relax*, helped to turn the group into one of the biggest pop acts of the mid eighties. A major factor in the chart success of the singles was the fact that each of them was issued in several different remixes, with fans being encouraged to buy them all. Although this was not the first time that songs were treated in the studio in this way, it was the first time that the creation of several different versions of songs was used as a deliberate marketing tool. Its success opened the floodgates for the release of remixes by other artists.

The essential point of a remix is that it involves going back to the original recording studio mastertapes of a song and removing some of the individual tracks while adding other new ones. In this way, a link is maintained with the recording that was issued first, even if the overall effect is to make the song sound very different. Simply recording more than one version of a piece does not constitute making a remix. In 1968, the Beatles issued a song called *Revolution* as the B-side to the single *Hey Jude*. The song was loud and aggressive, in keeping with its title. When the double LP, *The Beatles* was released (known as *The White Album*, although this was never the record's actual title) it contained a track called *Revolution 1*. This was the same song, but played more gently, with an acoustic guitar delivering the rhythm. Although the term was not in use at the time, this was clearly not a remix, but a completely new recording. A longer track, called *Revolution 9*, began life as an extended coda to the recording of *Revolution 1*. This was turned into a melange of found sounds and effects in the manner of the older musique concrète style, and in the process of applying the overdubs, the original recording disappeared, apart from a solitary call of "alright!". This was enough for John Lennon to feel justified in retaining the *Revolution* title, but the music was not a remix. If *Revolution 9* had included a few significant traces of the original single, then the Beatles could have added the invention of the remix to their list of accomplishments, but, as it happened, the group failed to make this essential connection. Curiously, when *Revolution* was included on *Love*, the album of Beatles remixes produced in 2006, the only remixing it received was in the sense of being mixed again. The balance of instruments was changed a little and the track was made shorter, but nothing was removed and no new elements were added, as they were on other tracks on *Love*. As a result, *Revolution* on this album is not a remix in the modern sense.

Also in 1968, Eclection (two of whose members later joined the ever-changing roster of Fairport Convention) issued a single called *Please*. When, shortly afterwards, lead singer Kerrilee Male was replaced by Dorris Henderson, producer Ossie Byrne stripped Male's vocals from the mastertape and remixed the single, using the original instrumental tracks, but a new vocal recorded by Henderson. The single was reissued, with a new catalogue number, as *Please Mk.II*. This is a remix in the modern sense.

During the later sixties, as mono recordings were gradually giving way to stereo, albums were issued in both formats. Recording techniques were becoming more complicated, with music being built from layers of overdubs, but until the end of the decade there were generally only four studio tracks available for producers to use. In consequence, mono and stereo mixes had to be recorded separately once the basic first layer of recording had been completed. Subsequent overdubs would often be different, depending on whether it was the mono or the stereo mix that was being created. Whichever was done first, mono or stereo, the other was a remix.

The second album by the Yardbirds, often known as *Roger The Engineer* after the title given to the cartoon shown on the front cover, was issued in July 1966. Contrary to what might be expected, the mono version has a fuller sound. The stereo version adopts, for many of its tracks, the rushed, easy solution found on early Beatles LPs. The lead vocals are heard on the left channel and everything else is on the right channel. The result makes the music sound

THE FIRST TIME

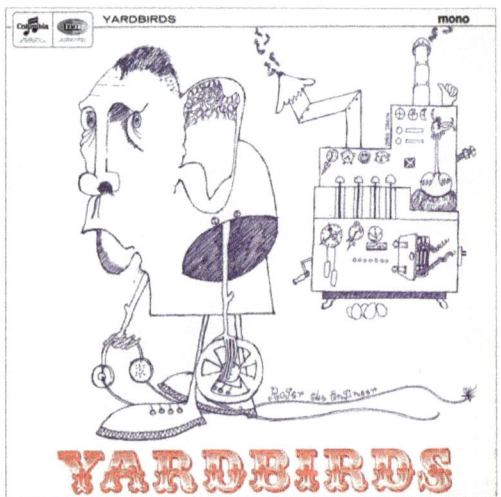
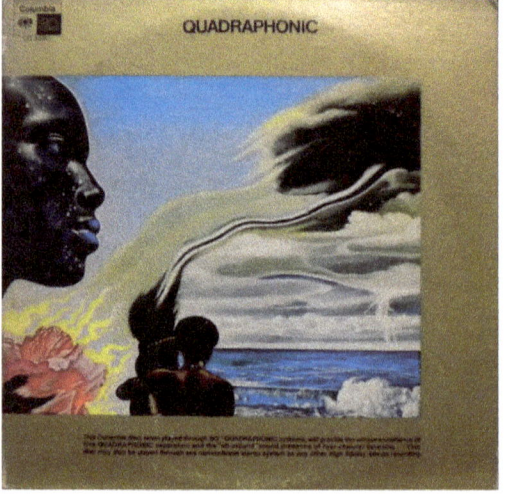

After Buddy Holly died in 1959, some of his recordings were given overdubs by producers Jack Hansen and Norman Petty before being released. The same thing happened with Jimi Hendrix, when producer Alan Douglas completed some of his recordings using session musicians. Although the results may be different to how the artists would have made them if they had lived, they are not remixes. The original recordings are on studio mastertapes, not finished pieces of vinyl. In January 1962, the theme song from Cliff Richard's film, *The Young Ones,* was issued as a single, complete with a prominent orchestral string section overdubbed on to the album version from the previous December. Effectively. therefore, this *was* a remix. although nothing was removed from the original recording. In June 1965, Tom Wilson added extra instrumentation to the Simon and Garfunkel song, *The Sound Of Silence*, previously released on the duos's first album, *Wednesday Morning 3am*. The result, which was a similar kind of remix, became a substantial hit single.

During the late sixties, dub reggae was developed by King Tubby and others in Jamaica. The intention was to create new pieces of music out of the rhythm tracks of songs already on record. It is a kind of remixing technique, although it was not really presented as such and the original songs were not usually credited. The Jacob Miller song, *Baby I Love You So,* for example, became *King Tubbys Meets Rockers Uptown* when its rhythm track was used as a resource. Dub reggae is discussed further in this book in the chapter on reggae.

Tom Moulton is credited as the 'father of the disco mix' as a result of his idea of programming the three tracks on the first side of Gloria Gaynor's January 1975 LP, *Never Can Say Goodbye,* to play without gaps in between them. The accolade seems somewhat overstated, as no mixing takes place to blend the tracks into each other and the fact that the rhythms are synchronised is due to the three tracks all having the same beat anyway. The concept of segueing songs on an LP was carried out eight years earlier on the Beatles LP, *Sgt Pepper's Lonely Hearts Club Band.* Moulton does not actually get a mention on the sleeve credits for the Gaynor album.

unfinished. On two tracks, *Hot House Of Omagararshid* and *He's Always There*, Jeff Beck plays typically exciting guitar solos towards the end of the mono versions. For the stereo versions, the solos are either much shorter (*He's Always There*) or missing altogether. It seems likely that, throughout the album, the unsatisfactory stereo version was done first, with the better sounding mono tracks, complete with the extra guitar playing, essentially being remixes.

There are numerous small differences between the mono and stereo versions of the Beatles album *Revolver*, issued in August 1966, though nothing as dramatic as a complete missing guitar solo. Like the Yardbirds album, however, the mono version sounds fuller. The stereo mix places the vocals in the centre and nearly everything else on the left. The right channel is reserved for occasional extras like additional percussion or guitar solos. According to the website, *The Usenet Guide To Beatles Recording Variations*, the superior mono mixes were done first, so that for this album, the stereo tracks are the remixes.

During the early seventies, various record companies attempted to make popular a stereo upgrade called quadraphonic, which enabled records to deliver a surround-sound experience when they played. Several albums were newly mixed to take advantage of the new format, but in the case of one, *Bitches Brew* by Miles Davis, the process went a little further than this. For the 1971 quadraphonic remix, much of the album is treated with huge amounts of extra echo, which doubles all the keyboard phrases on *Pharoah's Dance*, gives the lonely trumpet a ghostly partner on *Sanctuary*, and turns a trumpet, already electronically enhanced on the album's title track, into an electronic whirlwind. All of this is easily heard on a player only capable of ordinary stereo.

The procedure whereby New York club DJs during the seventies developed the technique of extending the length of popular singles, by manipulating copies of the records on two turntables, was eventually recognised by a recorded equivalent. An extended version of *Ten Percent* by Double Exposure was issued on a twelve inch single in 1975, with the necessary remixing (called disco blending on the label) carried out by Walter Gibbons. By looping and repeating sections of the original three minute seven inch single, Gibbons managed to extend the length of the track to nearly ten minutes. The record is claimed as the first commercially released twelve inch single, although it was preceded by a number of limited edition issues. It became a minor US chart hit, but proved to be enormously influential. During the next years, every record aimed at the dance market was given one or more extended remixes.

The idea of a favourite single being available in a longer form crossed over to the indie market too. During the early eighties, it became normal for hit singles to be issued in both seven and twelve inch formats. The extended versions of songs like *Papa's Got A Brand New Pigbag* by Pigbag, *Say Hello Wave Goodbye* by Soft Cell, or *Everything Counts* by Depeche Mode, however, were not so much remixes as naturally long pieces of music. They sounded as though they were then edited to create a song short enough to be played on the radio. For Frankie Goes To Hollywood it was different, with the procedure being carried out the other way round.

In 1985, composer John Oswald presented a paper to the Wired Society Electro-Acoustic Conference in Toronto. Titling his thesis *Plunderphonics, or Audio Piracy as a Compositional Perogative*, Oswald explained the artistic benefits that could be derived from treating records as a resource for further experimentation. Four years later, he issued a CD, *Plunderphonic*, to further illustrate what he meant. Every track on this album was the result of treating and manipulating records. He did things like gradually slowing Dolly Parton's voice until she became male, pairing Elvis Presley with an avant garde jazz group, and making Michael Jackson sound as though he was taking part in a Steve Reich composition. All of these are remixes, but of a particularly radical kind, and carried out without the permission or involvement of any of the artists or producers concerned. Although Oswald gave all copies of the CD away and made no profit from the exercise, threatened court action by the Canadian Recording Industry Association forced him to destroy all the remaining copies of the CD. It has been suggested that the real concern was not so much the music as the image of an apparently naked (and female) Michael Jackson on the cover.

It took until 2001 for one of the lessons of *Plunderphonic* to be absorbed, that interesting results could be obtained

John Oswald is a fascinating musician, the kind of maverick figure who is essential to the process of music development, even if the industry does not know how to deal with him. In 1975 he produced a track called *Power*, in which the ranting of a preacher was placed over samples of Led Zeppelin, somewhat in the manner of the Brian Eno and David Byrne album, *My Life In The Bush Of Ghosts*, released six years later. The track might have been an important influence on both sampled music and rap, except that it was not released until ten years later. Although the *Plunderphonic* CD is no longer available, all but three of its twenty-four tracks were included on a box set of John Oswald music, issued in 2001 as *69 Plunderphonics 96* and still available. In the late nineties, John Oswald was employed by Phil Lesh to apply his plunderphonics techniques to the creation of a Grateful Dead compilation of performances of the group's magnum opus, *Dark Star*. The result was issued in 1999 on a double CD called *Grayfolded*.

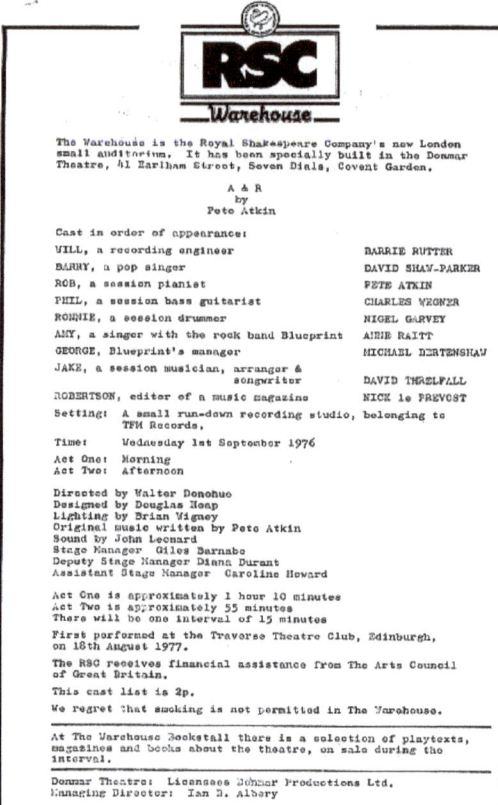

In 1987, in an effort to show that the Pet Shop Boys had stolen the music from Cat Stevens' *Wild World* for their song *It's A Sin,* Jonathan King recorded a single of *Wild World* on which he sang Cat Stevens' words over a replica of the Pet Shop Boys' music. The Pet Shop Boys did not see the joke and sued, winning an out of court settlement. King's recording was almost a mash-up – to be completely one, he would have needed to place Cat Stevens' own vocals over the Pet Shop Boys' synthesizers. Of course, with only a finite number of chords for songwriters to use, there have been numerous songs over the years that have used the same chord sequences (which was what the Pet Shop Boys had done with regard to the Cat Stevens song). The point was made rather neatly during Pete Atkin's musical play, *A&R*, which was performed by Atkin himself and the Royal Shakespeare Company in London's Covent Garden in 1978. Playing the part of a session pianist in a recording studio, Atkin performed a medley of well-known fifties songs that all happened to employ the same four chords in the same order. One was *All I Have To Do Is Dream,* originally recorded by the Everly Brothers. This moved smoothly into such songs as *Teenager In Love* (Dion), *Take Good Care Of My Baby* (Bobby Vee), and others, all without changing the accompaniment. If something similar had been done using the original records, it would have been the first mash-up. The Australian rock comedy group, Axis Of Awesome, made the same point as Pete Atkin in the 2009 piece, *Four Chords.* This comprised a medley of thirty-eight familiar songs, all based on an identical sequence of four chords – the ones used by Atkin, as it happens, though in a different order.

by combining two different records playing at the same time. In January of that year, Richard X produced an unofficial single, *I Wanna Dance With Numbers/Being Scrubbed*, credited to Girls On Top. The A-side mixed Whitney Houston's *I Wanna Dance With Somebody* with Kraftwerk's *Numbers*. The B-side pushed *Being Boiled* by the Human League and *No Scrubs* by TLC together. In August, Richard X tried again, with another Girls On Top record he titled *We Don't Give A Damn About Our Friends*. This one merged Adina Howard's *Freak Like Me* with Gary Numan's *Are 'Friends' Electric*. Richard X was asked to make an official version of the track, with the result that the Sugababes took the first example of a technique that had become known as a 'mash-up' to the top of the charts. The Sugababes' single was titled *Freak Like Me*, but was still produced by Richard X in exactly the same manner as he had done before.

TRACKING THE TRACKS

Two compilations provide, between them, as extensive a range of Frankie Goes To Hollywood remixes as any but the most ardent collector could need. The double CD *Twelve Inches* (ZTT 2001) has the *Relax Sex Mix*, *Two Tribes Hibakusha Mix*, and *Warriors Of The Wasteland Attack Mix*. The CD *Reload* (ZTT 2000) has the *Relax New York Mix* and *Two Tribes Carnage Mix*. *Frankie Goes To High Bronski* can be heard on YouTube.

The Beatles (White Album) is on EMI (2009). The Rutherford Chang *White Album* is no longer available. Second hand copies are on sale, but with increasingly high prices. The first side of the album can be heard on Chang's website, rutherfordchang.com/white.html, or on Soundcloud. The Beatles *Love* is on EMI (2006).

Simon and Garfunkel's *Wednesday Morning 3am* is on Columbia (2001). The new version of *The Sound Of Silence* is on *Sounds Of Silence* (Columbia 2001). Cliff Richard's *The Young Ones* soundtrack album is on Hallmark (2012); the single version of the title track is on many different Cliff Richard compilation albums, such as *The Best Of The Rock 'n' Roll Pioneers* (Parlophone 2019). Eclection's *Please* singles are included as bonus tracks on one issue of the band's self-titled album, on Flawed Gems (2011). The Collectors' Choice edition of the album from 2001, without any bonus tracks, should be avoided due its extremely poor sound quality.

The CD issue of *Yardbirds (Roger The Engineer)* has both the mono and the stereo versions, together with several bonus tracks (Repertoire 2016). The Beatles *Revolver* is on EMI (2009) in stereo only. The mono version can only be heard as part of an expensive box set of all the albums, *The Beatles In Mono* (EMI 2009), or by acquiring the vinyl LP, although this was reissued as recently as 2014.

The quadraphonic version of *Bitches Brew* by Miles Davis was issued by Columbia in 1971 but has not been reissued. The seven inch and twelve inch versions of *Ten Percent* by Double Exposure are both included on the CD *Ten Percent* (Big Break Records 2012).

Buddy Holly recorded six tracks on his own in December 1958. After he died, they were overdubbed by producer Jack Hansen. They are included on *The Buddy Holly Story Vol.2* (Hallmark 2011). The two posthumous Jimi Hendrix albums with overdubs by producer Alan Douglas are *Crash Landing* and *Midnight Lightning*. They were both issued on vinyl in 1975 – they have been issued on CD, though not in the UK. German releases date from 1993 and 1989.

King Tubbys Meets Rockers Uptown is the title track of a 1976 album by Augustus Pablo. It is on a Shanachie CD (2004).

Gloria Gaynor's *Never Can Say Goodbye* is on Big Break Records (2010), but on this release the first three tracks are given a DJ mix.

Pigbag's *Volume One – Dr Heckle & Mr Jive* (Fire Records 2010) has the short and long versions of *Papa's Got A Brand New Pigbag* included on a double CD. The long version of Soft Cell's *Say Hello Wave Goodbye* is on the 3 CD set *The Twelve Inch Singles* (Mercury 2000). The short version is on *The Very Best Of Soft Cell* (Universal/Mercury 2002). The short and long versions of *Everything Counts* by Depeche Mode are available on a CD single (Mute 2004).

John Oswald's 2 CD set *69 Plunderphonics 96* is on Seeland (2001). It includes *Power* and almost the whole of the *Plunderphonic* album. The John Oswald/Grateful Dead double CD *Grayfolded* is on Snapper (1999).

The Girls On Top singles are no longer available, but they can be heard on YouTube. The Sugababes' *Freak Like Me* is on *Overloaded – The Singles Collection* (Universal Island 2006).

Jonathan King's *Wild World* can be found on a 7" single or on YouTube. Cat Stevens' original is on *The Very Best Of Cat Stevens* (Universal/Island 2006). The Pet Shop Boys' *It's A Sin* is on *Discography – The Complete Singles Collection* (EMI 1991).

Axis of Awesome can be seen performing *Four Chords* at the 2009 Melbourne International Comedy Festival on YouTube. The song is included on their download album, *Infinity Rock Explosion* (2010).

THE FIRST TIME

> During the eighties, there were over 2200 record shops in the UK. By 2000 this had fallen to 700, with an all-time low of 269 being reached in 2009. There has been a slight revival since then and by April 2016 there were 342 record shops. In the US, there were 3329 record shops in 2003 – ten years later this had fallen to 1590.

1948 second edition

One of four compilations issued in 2005 to celebrate the 30th anniversary of Ace Records, the label that describes itself, with every justification, as "the leading reissue record company in the UK".

Contemporary record fair (organised by VIP Record Fairs)

156

15 COLLECTING RECORDS

There have been record collectors for as long as there have been records. The first record shop in the world opened its doors in 1894. This was Spillers Records in Cardiff. Remarkably, when the number of record shops in the UK has plummeted in recent years, Spillers Records is still trading. The first shop selling records in the US was Rinehart's Music in Kirksville, Missouri, which opened in 1897. This too is still trading. George's Song Shop in Johnstown, Pennsylvania, claims on its website to be the oldest record shop in the US, having started trading in 1932. Its claim can only be justified by the fact that it is a record specialist, whereas Rinehart's Music stocked other music items as well, such as sheet music, pianos, and record players.

A shop catering to collectors, selling second-hand records, opened in 1906 in Islington market in London under the name of Music Exchange. It changed its name to Gramex seventy-two years later and is still trading, under new ownership and in new premises. The shop specialises in the music it has always sold – classical music. Dobells, specialising in collectable jazz records, opened within the family bookshop in London's Charing Cross Road in 1946. It became a shop selling records only in 1955. The Vintage Record Centre, specialising in collectable rock 'n' roll and describing itself in later advertising as 'England's first genuine oldies store', opened in Roman Way in North London in 1972. Ted Carroll's Rock On, perhaps the most well-known collectors' record shop of all, started as a market stall in Portobello Road market in 1971, but did not make the upgrade to an actual shop (in London's Camden Town) until 1975. In the US, the Times Square Record Shop opened in 1959, selling collectable doo-wop records from the fifties, which were already being described as 'oldies'. None of these shops continue, although Rock On has an internet presence and Ted Carroll was still trading at record fairs well into the twenty-first century (as well as running his successful Ace record reissue label). The Times Square Record Shop and the reissue record company it ran were bought by Relic Records as long ago as 1965. The Relic Record Shoppe still trades in Hackensack, New Jersey.

According to Roy Shuker, the author of *Wax Trash & Vinyl Treasures – Record Collecting As A Social Practice*, the first record collectors fair to be held in the US (where such events were referred to as swap meets) was in the early 1950s in a car park behind the Palms Bar in West Hollywood. At some point at the end of the 1960s, the Los Angeles record swap meet began running outside the RCA Records building. Soon afterwards, it moved to the parking lot of Capitol Records in Hollywood, continuing as a weekly event for several years. Curiously, given a product whose condition needed to be inspected in good light, the Capitol Records swap meet was regularly opened at midnight.

The first record fair in the UK took place in Liverpool, at the Concert Hall, Bluecoat Chambers, in October 1976. It was advertised in *Record Mart*, a trading magazine for record collectors that had been published monthly since April 1968. It was followed by fairs in Manchester and Nottingham in June and July 1977 and by a September fair at the Ivanhoe Hotel in Russell Square, in the centre of London, which ran periodically for several years. Rob Lythall's VIP Fairs, which became the most successful organiser of collectors record fairs in the UK, started in October 1980, with an event in Leicester.

The first comprehensive record listing was published in 1934 by French jazz enthusiast and co-founder of the Hot Club de France, Charles Delaunay, who invented the term 'discography' for his publication. It was translated into English two years later as *Hot Discography*, by which time a rival publication had already appeared – *Rhythm on Record* by Hilton R.Schleman.

Pricing information for collectable records was provided in a sporadic fashion by Goldmine magazine in the US, which started in September 1974, and by Record Collector magazine in the UK which started in September 1979. The first published price guide was in 1976 in the US – *Record Collectors' Price Guide* by Jerry Osborne and Bruce Hamilton.

The fifth edition of Nick Hamlyn's price guide from 2000 (now titled *The Penguin Price Guide for Record & CD Collectors*) included, for the first time, a number of record-collecting charts. The rarest record, with a listed value of £12,000, was the initial stereo pressing of Bob Dylan's *Freewheelin'* LP with four different tracks to the familiar version. Number two was the Beatles *White Album*, or more precisely, any of the first ten copies, with a printed number on the front cover between 0000001 and 0000010. The listed value for these was £5000. In December 2015, the copy with 0000001 on the front rather exceeded this value when it was put up for sale at Julien's Auctions in Los Angeles by Ringo Starr. The record sold for $790,000 – the highest price achieved by a commercially released record sold at auction up to that date. The artist with the largest number of rare records, as listed in Nick Hamlyn's Guide, was the Beatles.

Hip-hop group, the Wu-Tang Clan, came up with a unique marketing strategy when the double CD album, *Once Upon A Time In Shaolin,* was pressed in a limited edition of just one copy. This was sold at auction in 2015 for two million dollars, making it the most valuable recording to date, albeit one that could not quite be described as being fully commercially released. The purchaser was the controversial millionaire Martin Shkreli, who was reported as wanting to "keep it from the people". Not that the Wu-Tang Clan, two million dollars better off, would have been too upset about this. In September 2017, Shkreli placed the album for sale on E-Bay, where the winning bid was a little over a million dollars. Just to put the matter in context, it should be noted that Bob Dylan's original handwritten lyrics for *Like A Rolling Stone* sold for just over two million dollars in 2014, while the most expensive musical instrument, a Stradivarius viola, was sold for forty-five million dollars in the same year.

The LP *Magical Love* by Saturnalia was also issued as a picture disc, with many reference books (including the first version of this one) claiming a 1969 release date. Interviews carried out by Austin Matthews with musicians from the band Horse, who subsequently formed Saturnalia, make it clear, however, that the Saturnalia album could not have appeared in 1969 because the group did not exist then. It was in fact released in 1973. The recording sessions for the album, with Keith Relf producing, took place in the Island studios in October 1972. The interviews form the basis of sleeve notes written by Matthews for reissues of the Horse and Saturnalia albums on the Rise Above Records label.

The 1978 second edition gave a clearer idea of the contents with its modified title, *Popular and Rock Records 1948-1978*. 'Records' in this context meant singles. A price guide published by Goldmine, *Price Guide to Collectible Record Albums* appeared in 1989 and was followed by *Rock 'n' Roll 45 rpm Record Price Guide* in 1990. Both were written by Neal Umphred. In the UK, a number of small specialised price guides were compiled during the eighties, starting with *Collectable 45's: Price Reference Guide to Singles: A-K, January 1950-December 1964*, published by the Vintage Record Centre in 1981. The first price guide aiming to be a comprehensive listing of all collectable records (apart from classical) was the 1990 *Music Master Price Guide for Record Collectors* by Nick Hamlyn. Record Collector's own *Rare Record Price Guide 1993*, restricted to UK issues only and ignoring most promotional releases, followed in 1992 (!). The earlier *Record Collector 1987 Rare Record Price Guide* focussed on just a small number of 'important' collectable artists. A *Rare Classical Record Price Guide* was published in 2004, written by Barry Browne, including records from just three UK companies.

Record companies were slow to appreciate the existence of record collectors, as opposed to people who simply bought records they had heard and liked. It was not until 1969 that a record was produced with the intention of appealing directly to the collectors' market. The German Metronome company released a various artists compilation called *Hallucinations Off II – Psychedelic Underground*, which included tracks by Love, the Doors, the MC5, the Incredible String Band, and other Elektra artists. This was issued in the form of a picture disc, in which the artwork that would normally only be used on the cover was apparently imprinted on to the vinyl itself. In fact, a thin layer of plastic was used to cover a piece of card with the picture on it. One result was that the record had a very poor sound quality and deteriorated further each time it was played. The low sales of this record might just about have excused Warner Brothers from making a big fuss in 1970 when they released the debut album by Curved Air, *Airconditioning*, as a limited edition picture disc, alongside a normal black vinyl version. As it happens, neither of these records was actually the very first picture disc of all. A number of barely playable 78 rpm records were issued in a picture disc form during the thirties, including a few records promoting Adolf Hitler. The first of the picture 78s was a recording of *Cowhand's Last Ride* by Jimmie Rodgers, issued by RCA Victor in the US in 1933, with *Blue Yodel No.12* on the other side. The title of the record was sadly appropriate, since Rodgers died nine days after making it and never saw the finished product.

In 1979, A&M Records in the US upped the ante a little when they issued a single by the Police as a picture disc cut into the shape of an American police badge. Fortunately, the grooves themselves remained circular – the record played *Roxanne* on one side and *Can't Stand Losing You* on the other. It took a year or two for other record companies to follow suit, but eventually, during the eighties, shaped picture discs became an established limited edition format, aimed at record collectors.

The inclusion of a small poster inside the sleeve of early copies of the 1967 Jimi Hendrix LP, *Axis: Bold As Love*, might be considered to be a feature to attract collectors (and, of course, it has been in more recent times). Unfortunately, however, Track records never thought to tell anybody about it. Jimi Hendrix was, in any case, at the height of his popularity, and the record sold perfectly well without the help of such exclusive additions. Special inserts in the covers of the Beatles albums *Sgt Pepper's Lonely Hearts Club Band* and *The White Album* were not limited editions, but the same was not true in the case of a special version of the Beatles' LP, *Let It Be*, issued in 1970, which included a substantial book of photographs and was packaged inside a thin cardboard box.

The second album by Spooky Tooth, *Spooky Two*, issued in 1969, was made available in a choice of five or six differently coloured covers. If the intention was to persuade fans to buy all of them (and further variations produced by the vagaries of printing) it was not successful. The LP failed to enter the album charts. Led Zeppelin tried something similar in 1979, with the album *In Through The Out Door*. This was issued in six different sleeves, presenting different views of the same bar scene. As the record was sealed inside a brown paper bag at the point of purchase, however, it was impossible for collectors to determine which version of the sleeve they were getting.

THE FIRST TIME

In late 1968, the London magazine, *Time Out,* printed a review of a group called Heavy Jelly. Invented as a joke to tantalise collectors, Heavy Jelly was entirely fictitious. Nevertheless, hoping to gain a little momentum from the review, two different groups, both of them adopting the name, issued records. *I Keep Singing That Same Old Song* flopped as a single, but gained considerable exposure when included on the Island records sampler, *Nice Enough To Eat,* released near the end of 1969. This Heavy Jelly was eventually revealed as being the group that had previously issued singles and an album under the name of Skip Bifferty. A second Heavy Jelly, featuring singer Jackie Lomax from the Merseybeat group, the Undertakers, and including members of the Aynsley Dunbar Retaliation, followed with a single on the Head label. This was given the appropriate title, *Time Out (The Long Wait).* The band recorded tracks for an album, but this was abandoned when Lomax was signed to Apple Records as a solo artist. In the US, *Rolling Stone* magazine tried a similar ploy with a Greil Marcus review of an album by the Masked Marauders in October 1969. This time, the recording was claimed to be a super session, featuring Bob Dylan and members of both the Rolling Stones and the Beatles. The magazine then decided to extend the joke by employing uncredited session musicians to record an actual album, which was released by Warner Bros. The ridiculous track-listing should have been enough to alert record buyers as to the true nature of the record, yet somehow it managed to sell an incredible hundred thousand copies regardless. A few other fictitious artists have been the subject of collectors' wants lists, articles, or even record releases since then, but perhaps none has been as celebrated as these sixties originals.

The first rock bootleg record appeared in 1969 – a double LP titled *Great White Wonder* by Bob Dylan. The album included some informal live recordings from 1961, alongside several later out-takes, some of which comprised music played with the Band that was not properly released until 1975 (as part of *The Basement Tapes*). The existence of bootleg records – making available live performances or studio out-takes that the official record companies did not want to release – depended entirely on the activities of collectors, who were desperate to obtain more music by their favourite artists. Such records had long been a feature within the worlds of classical music and jazz. According to music enthusiast Michael Gerzon, in conversation with the author of this book, when the Metropolitan Opera House in New York was stripped, prior to its demolition in 1967, an extra microphone was found, one that no-one could account for. Meanwhile, Charlie Parker fan, Dean Benedetti, would hide his newly acquired reel-to-reel machine at various venues where his hero was playing during 1948 and record for posterity the incandescent solos of a master musician in his prime. One album of his recordings, *Bird On 52nd Street*, has been issued several times over the years by different legitimate record companies, presumably without paying royalties to Parker (or his estate), Benedetti, or anyone else. It should be mentioned that bootleg records are quite different from pirate records, which are simply unauthorised, counterfeit copies of record company releases.

Record collectors are concerned with tracking the different issues over the years of the titles in which they have an interest. Details of label design, in conjunction with the matrix numbers and other information scratched in the area of vinyl between the grooves and the label enable them to identify which pressing is which. Usually, it will be the first pressing that they want. Many will concentrate on particular record companies or on particular label designs issued by those companies. The Island pink label albums, issued between 1967 and 1970, provide one example. The Vertigo black and white 'swirl' label (often inaccurately referred to as 'spiral'), issued between 1969 and 1973, is another. The first label to receive serious attention from collectors in the UK was London, owing to its policy of issuing the best of American rock 'n' roll and rhythm and blues records during the fifties. Many collectors have tried to obtain complete runs of London singles, at least up until the mid-sixties, when the rise of British beat effectively put an end to the label's importance. Their task in this respect was hindered by the extreme rarity of some of the issues, but they were also safe in the knowledge that a complete collection would contain remarkably few dud recordings. The earliest London singles have gold writing on a black label and these 'gold label' singles are the most highly prized and the most valuable. (Within the record industry itself, the colour was actually referred to as 'bronze', the responsible dye being known as 'bronzing powder'.) Where gold label singles were reissued as later 'silver label' pressings (silver writing on a black label), these are generally only worth around half the value of the first issues. Unfortunately, the London label did not appear to be particularly systematic in its procedures, so that during the early months of 1957, some records were issued on gold labels and some on silver. The first gold label London single was *Caribbean/Weep Away* by the country singer, Mitchell Torok. This was given the catalogue number HL8004. The record was issued in October 1954, having been a US Country number one, the previous year. Earlier numbers in the series (and several after this one) were for records that were issued only on the 78 rpm format. Generally, these generate a much lower level of collectors' interest. It is one of the curiosities of record collecting that a seriously rare and expensive record such as *Earth Angel* by the Penguins, issued in January 1955 – a gold label London single that has sold for as much as £1250 – is worth very much less (typically around £75) on the American label, Dootone, which was the record's original issue.

The whole business of collecting records was transformed as soon as records began to be advertised for sale on the internet. No rare record shop or collectors fair could ever hope to compete with the power of a search engine. Ebay began trading in 1997 and the same year, MusicStack, the first specialist record trading website, also started. Popsike, a website devoted to listing the prices achieved by sales of records on Ebay, was founded in 2004. Discogs was set up at the end of 2000, with the intention of creating a database of every record ever released, throughout the world. As of the end of 2016, 8,000,000 items had been listed, an estimated 50% of the record issues that exist. From late 2005, Discogs also allowed collectors to sell records to each other via the website.

THE FIRST TIME

PART 3

MUSIC GENRES

THE FIRST TIME

Johnny B Goode was Chuck Berry's twelfth hit single in the US, and his sixth million seller. Remarkably, however, it fared very poorly in Britain. Berry tried very hard over the years to desecrate his own image. He liked to perform short-measure concerts with under-rehearsed pick-up bands – giving every impression that his only real motivation was the money. And his biggest hit was not a rock 'n' roll song at all, but a dire piece of schoolboy smut called *My Ding-A-Ling*. Some of his attitude was doubtless a reaction to knocks taken when he was still struggling for success. His song *Maybellene* carries to this day a co-writing credit to disc-jockey Alan Freed, whose actual role in the creation of Berry's first hit record was restricted to his agreeing to play it on his influential radio programme.

The wackily effective legs akimbo pose adopted by Chuck Berry on the album sleeve shown above was expanded into a fully-fledged 'duck walk' on stage. By adopting more or less the same pose a couple of decades later on the cover of his first album, Elvis Costello was able to make an affectionately ironic reference to all three of the major rock 'n' roll icons at the same time. Chuck Berry's stance is combined with Elvis Presley's name and Buddy Holly's appearance.

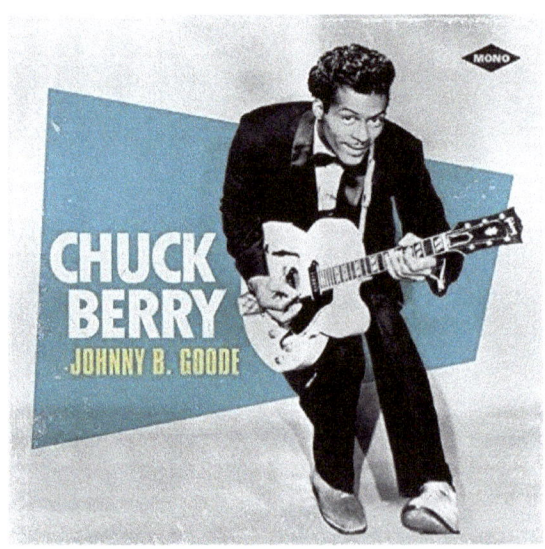

The Voyager I and Voyager II spacecraft, launched towards interstellar space in 1977, contained a record designed for the benefit of any extra-terrestrial life-forms who might happen to come across it. Amongst the sounds intended to convey an idea of the diversity of Earth culture in the late twentieth century was a recording of Chuck Berry's *Johnny B Goode*.

16 ROCK 'N' ROLL

The quest for the elusive very first rock 'n' roll record is one that can never achieve its goal. A couple of titles are frequently mentioned in this context, but the fact is that to select Bill Haley's *Rock Around the Clock* or Jackie Brenston's *Rocket 88* or any other record as the first is to make an essentially arbitrary decision. One can point to a time when there was no rock 'n' roll; equally, the large number of rockin' records from the second half of the Fifties is testament to the time when the music had definitely arrived. But the boundary between these two conditions is no more precise than that between day and night.

Johnny B Goode by Chuck Berry was issued in 1958 and is beyond consideration. It is, however, the defining example of the rock 'n' roll genre; the song most likely to be selected for a spontaneous jam by rock musicians old enough or aware enough to be in touch with the music's roots. On record, covers of *Johnny B Goode* have been tackled by artists as diverse as Jimi Hendrix and the Beach Boys, Dr. Feelgood and Meat Loaf, the Grateful Dead and Tom Jones. Peter Tosh has transported the song to Jamaica, Buck Owens to Nashville; the Sex Pistols tried to trash it; Status Quo have based virtually their entire career on it. John Lennon, who played *Johnny B Goode* during the early days of the Beatles (it is on the group's *Live at the BBC* CD compilation), said "If you tried to give rock and roll another name, you might call it Chuck Berry."

In the 1985 film *Back To The Future*, the character Marty McFly, played by Michael J. Fox, travels back in time thirty years from the mid Eighties. During his subsequent adventures, he has the chance to play guitar with a local R&B band and naturally chooses to play *Johnny B Goode*. The other musicians do not know the song – for them it has not yet been written – but they do know the chord changes and they proceed to tackle them with enthusiasm. A delightfully irreverent sequence shows one of them ringing his cousin, none other than Chuck Berry himself, to allow him to hear over the telephone line a sound that he can adopt as his own! McFly dumbfounds everyone, however, and succeeds in bringing the proceedings to a complete halt, by launching into a post-Van Halen guitar break quite alien to his Fifties audience.

In truth, Chuck Berry's own original version of *Johnny B Goode* does sound rather dated – weak even – to ears accustomed to hearing more modern renditions. But in 1958, it was definitely state-of-the-art. Berry's tale of the teenager who hopes to make it big as a guitar player encapsulates every rock 'n' roll fan's secret ambition. It is not surprising that a song whose lyrics are actually about the rock 'n' roll dream establishes a particularly firm foothold within the music. The simple tune sits squarely on the standard twelve-bar chord changes that underpin the whole of rhythm and blues: changes that are conveyed by two crucial instruments – a piano, played percussively in the upper register to ensure that its sound cuts through, and Chuck Berry's own lead electric guitar, which frames the entire song and effectively acts as the voice of Johnny B Goode himself. A second guitarist plays the actual chords, but quietly, and the bass is not an electric instrument, but an enthusiastically plucked double bass.

It is entirely significant that the creator of *Johnny B Goode* is black, since the arrival of rock 'n' roll marked the commercialisation within white America of a music that had essentially been played by black musicians for several years previously. To properly explore the roots of rock 'n' roll, it is necessary to travel back over twenty years before *Johnny B Goode*.

During the course of five sessions held in November 1936 and June 1937, singer-guitarist Robert Johnson recorded twenty-nine songs that provide, between them, the basic instruction manual for playing the blues. Although he did not invent the music, he formalised both its structure and the patterns of its lyrics into a shape that rapidly became definitive. Since Johnson, the term blues has primarily referred to a very specific kind of song. It is one whose

THE FIRST TIME

During his recording sessions, which took place in a hotel room rather than an actual studio, Robert Johnson was apparently so nervous that he performed his songs in the corner of the room facing the wall, so that he could pretend the various onlookers were not really there. By all accounts, his guitar playing was nothing special when he started his career, but he improved so rapidly that stories began to circulate about how he had gone down to the crossroads at midnight in order to make a pact with the devil. This was not the first time that a story of this kind had been told in reaction to the astonishing virtuosity of a musician – something very similar happened in the case of the violinist, Niccolo Paganini. In his case the story was given extra credence by his gothic appearance – he seemed to be ready and waiting to join some early nineteenth century forerunner of the Sisters Of Mercy. Robert Johnson was quite happy to capitalise on his rumours, making reference to them in his songs *Cross Road Blues* and *Hellhound On My Trail*. If there was any truth in them, then the devil was not long in exacting payment, for Johnson died a year after his last recording session – poisoned by one of the many women sharing his chaotic lifestyle, at the age of just twenty-seven. The 1986 film, *Crossroads*, directed by Walter Hill and featuring Steve Vai as the devil's guitar-playing representative, presented the Robert Johnson legend as a contemporary fantasy.

Niccolo Paganini by Hetty Krist

John Lee Hooker was always a highly idiosyncratic performer and his original recording of *Dimples* is actually more complicated than a straight ten-bar blues. He adds an extra bar in between some of the verses, and adds six bars after the instrumental break, which is itself structured around twelve bars, rather than ten. Since he was inclined to make these kinds of changes to a song at random whenever he performed, Hooker was a notoriously difficult musician to accompany. His first single, *Boogie Chillen*, recorded when he was thirty-one, became the best selling rhythm and blues single of 1949 and allowed him to give up his factory job to become a professional musician. Forty-two years later, his album *Mr Lucky* reached number three in the UK charts (it did less well in the US) making John Lee Hooker, at seventy-nine, the oldest artist to achieve a top three LP hit. (A record that was beaten in 2017, when Vera Lynn, having just celebrated her hundredth birthday, saw her latest album become a best-seller).

The Andrews Sisters' huge hit of 1941, *Boogie Woogie Bugle Boy Of Company B*, typified the public's fascination at the time for all things boogie woogie, even if the link between this song and Meade Lux Lewis was a little tenuous. The integration of a driving left-handed bass line with improvised right-handed explorations of the treble keys would, after all, be a little hard to reproduce on a single bugle!

The lindy-hop evolved out of a Charleston variant known as the Breakaway and was named, somewhat improbably, after Charles Lindbergh's solo flight across the Atlantic in 1927. Star dancer Shorty Snowden was apparently asked by a reporter what he was doing, and with memories of newspaper headlines proclaiming "Lindy hops the Atlantic" fresh in his mind, gave an appropriate answer.

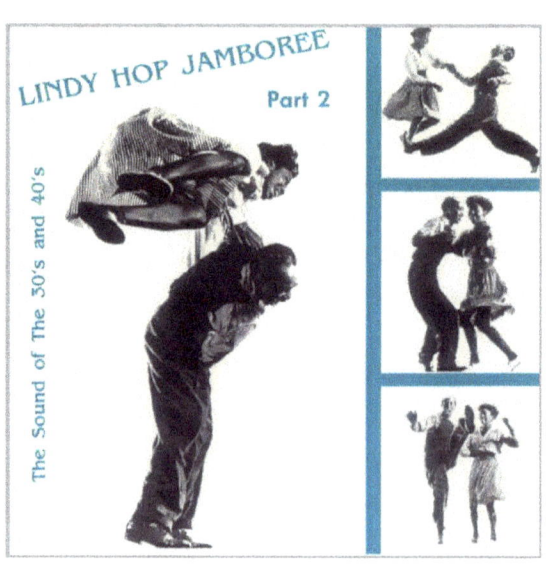

verse has exactly twelve bars. The first four of these float a line of lyrics over the root chord (or tonic) of the piece. In a guitar blues, this is most often an A, B, or E chord, since these are keys that come easily to fingers coping with the normal tuning of a guitar. They allow the frequent use of open, unfretted strings, which tend to ring out more powerfully when struck.

> "I went down to the crossroads, fell down on my knees."

Robert Johnson sings this over a repeated B chord that is the tonic in his song, *Cross Road Blues*. The line of lyrics is then repeated, for emphasis, over two bars based on the chord of the fourth step of the scale (or subdominant) – an E chord in this case – followed by two more bars of the tonic.

> "I went down to the crossroads, fell down on my knees."

Finally, by way of a response to the song's double opening call, a rhyming line of lyrics is sung over one bar based on the fifth step of the scale (or dominant) – an F# chord in this case – followed by one bar based on the subdominant and, to finish the verse, two more bars based on the tonic.

> "I asked the Lord above for mercy, hey boy help me please."

Johnny B Goode has this same structure (although Chuck Berry, despite using no saxophones that would appreciate it, chooses a jazz key, Bb) and so do the great majority of the rhythm and blues songs that precede it. Even the exceptions, like Muddy Waters' *Mannish Boy*, which sticks resolutely to the same A chord throughout, or John Lee Hooker's *Dimples*, which leaves out the two-bar return to the tonic and is turned into a ten-bar blues, are essentially the results of their creators playing games with a form that both they and their audiences view as being standard. *Cross Road Blues* and its companions, therefore, provide a basic ingredient for rock 'n' roll, even though they are not rock 'n' roll themselves.

In 1929, pianist Montana Taylor recorded a piece he called *Detroit Rocks*. The powerfully rhythmic playing style of this blues instrumental had been unveiled just a couple of years previously with the release of Meade Lux Lewis's first recording of *Honky Tonk Train Blues* and it was christened boogie woogie in 1928 via the Clarence 'Pinetop' Smith recording *Pinetop's Boogie Woogie*. A number of pianists made boogie woogie records during the next few years, but without any of them managing to achieve more than minority appeal. In 1938, however, impresario John Hammond organised a showcase concert of blues, gospel, and jazz, staging it at New York's Carnegie Hall under the title of *Spirituals To Swing*. The concert was a huge success and achieved Hammond's goal of bringing these black music forms to the attention of mainstream America. The surprise hit of the show turned out to be a trio of furiously pounding boogie woogie pianists performing together – Meade Lux Lewis, Pete Johnson, and Albert Ammons. The music moved overnight from cult to mass market, expanding beyond its traditional unaccompanied piano instrumentation and becoming in the process a central part of the developing rhythm and blues band sound. There is little difference between the boogie woogie playing of Montana Taylor or Meade Lux Lewis and the rock 'n' roll playing of Little Richard, Jerry Lee Lewis, or Johnnie Johnson, pianist with Chuck Berry on *Johnny B Goode*.

At the time Robert Johnson made his recordings, big band jazz was in the ascendant. Bandleaders like Count Basie and Duke Ellington were packing out the black clubs in Harlem and elsewhere with a music they called swing. In his *Autobiography*, Malcolm X describes the dancing that audiences would do to this music. It was called the lindy-hop.

> If you've ever lindy-hopped, you'll know what I'm talking about. With most girls, you kind of work opposite them, circling, side-stepping, leading. Whichever arm you lead with is half-bent out there, your hands are giving that little pull, that little push, touching her waist, her shoulders, her arms. She's in, out, turning, whirling, wherever you guide her. With poor partners, you feel their weight. They're slow and heavy. But with really good partners, all you need is just the push-pull suggestion. They guide nearly effortlessly, even off the floor and into the air, and your little solo manoeuvre is done on the floor before they land, when they join you, whirling, right in step.

THE FIRST TIME

Blues singer Trixie Smith recorded a song with the title *My Daddy Rocks Me (With One Steady Roll)* in 1922 and at least four cover versions were made and released during the remainder of the twenties. From 1929, several other songs with titles making reference to rocking or rolling were recorded – one, in 1930, used both terms, Bob Robinson's *Rocking And Rolling*, although this was not issued at the time. In the autumn of 1934, first the Boswell Sisters and then Joe Hayne released a song called *Rock and Roll*. None of these songs were actually rock 'n' roll music – indeed their terminology did not refer to music at all. This is less obviously the case, however, with the songs made from 1939 and through the forties: titles like *Rockin' The Blues* by the Port Of Harlem Jazzmen, *I Want To Rock* by Cab Calloway, *Good Rockin' Tonight* by Wynonie Harris, *Rock The Joint* by Jimmy Preston, and several others. One cannot insist with any degree of certainty either that the last titles, issued in 1948 and 1949, are not actually rock 'n' roll music, especially as they were covered during the fifties by Elvis Presley and Bill Haley, without either artist making any significant changes to the songs' formats.

From *The Fat Man* to *Walkin' To New Orleans*, in 1960, twenty-three of the singles released by Fats Domino sold over a million copies each, an achievement only bettered during this period by Elvis Presley. His first LP, *Rock And Rollin' With Fats Domino*, included the first five of these million sellers, along with four more songs that became million sellers afterwards. The LP has twelve tracks altogether. It was the fourth release in Imperial's new 9000 series of twelve inch records, started in 1956 – previously Imperial's LPs had all been of the ten inch variety. *Rock And Rollin' With Fats Domino* was given the catalogue number LP-9004. Later in the same year, a second Fats Domino LP was issued, with the catalogue number LP-9009. This was called *Rock And Rollin'* and included an entirely different set of twelve tracks. Only one of these, *I'm In Love Again*, was a million selling single, although a second track, *When My Dreamboat Comes Home*, was also a substantial hit. The similar titles of the two LPs, both issued in 1956, has caused much confusion elsewhere, this being exacerbated by the fact that, in the UK, the LPs were released the other way round, both in 1957. LP-9009 came first, as London HAU 2028 and with the same title as the US Imperial release. LP-9004 came second, as London HAP 2041, and re-titled *Carry On Rockin'*.

A list of significant milestones on the road to rock 'n' roll begins in 1945 with a typically driving piano boogie by Albert Ammons, *The Boogie Rocks*, and with an equally powerful boogie played on guitar (with backing from a second guitar and a bass) by a country musician with a jazz background, Arthur Smith. *Guitar Boogie* sold well in the South and did even better when re-released towards the end of 1948. The single became a successful national hit in both the country and popular charts, ultimately enabling Smith to start his own country music show on television, which ran for over thirty years. He was also the composer of the banjo piece used in the 1972 film *Deliverance* under the title *Duellin' Banjos* and subsequently a number two hit in the Billboard Hot 100 chart, although he had to sue Warner Brothers to get his royalty payments. *Early In The Morning* was first recorded by John Lee 'Sonny Boy' Williamson in 1937, when it was a slow blues. He re-recorded the song in 1945 as *New Early In The Morning* with piano and drums in accompaniment and played much faster – just like a rock 'n' roll record in fact. It should be noted here that the better-known Sonny Boy Williamson, who toured the UK in the 1960s, is a different person (his real name was Rice Miller). He was often referred to as Sonny Boy Williamson II to help avoid confusion.

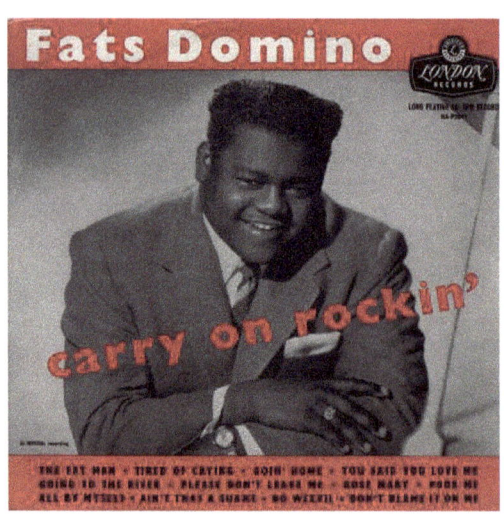

Arthur Smith, guitarist, is shown posing with a fiddle!

MUSIC GENRES

Following Cab Calloway's million selling hit of 1939, *Jumpin' Jive*, the lindy-hop metamorphosed into the jive – sometimes too it was known as the jitterbug – but the dance was the same. As the music changed, young dancers found that their moves still fitted: teenage audiences jived to *Johnny B Goode* without even thinking about it.

In 1942, in recognition of the growing economic importance and influence of black music in America, Billboard magazine introduced a specialist black music chart, published alongside its established popular music hit parade (which began in January 1936). The 'Harlem Hit Parade', as it was called, featured as its first number one *Take It And Git* by Andy Kirk and his Clouds of Joy – a swing big band. Through the 1940s, a variety of songs appeared in which the beat was emphasized more and more strongly and the jazz content, the rhythmic bounce and the improvisation, became reduced. By 1948-49, the transformation was complete, with a number of records having a sound more or less indistinguishable from that of rock 'n' roll records made in the 1950s. Of these, *Good Rockin' Tonight* by Wynonie Harris was a number one hit in the Billboard black music chart (now called 'Jukebox Race Records') and has the distinction, therefore, of being the first record sounding like rock 'n' roll to become a big hit.

Later the same year, *Chicken Shack Boogie* by Amos Milburn also reached the number one spot with the same rhythm and a similar sound, while *We're Gonna Rock, We're Gonna Roll* by Wild Bill Moore was also a hit in 1948, though without getting to number one. Bluesman Muddy Waters entered the charts with his second single, *I Can't Be Satisfied*. Accompanied only by the slapping double bass of Big Crawford and his own incisive electric slide guitar playing, Waters delivered a performance that is pure rock 'n' roll. It is the bass playing too that gives the country recordings of the Maddox Brothers and Rose their power, especially on their cover of Hank Williams' *Move It On Over*. Moving through into 1949, more rockin' records were produced, with differing approaches to the same kind of rhythm, among them *Drinkin' Wine Spo-dee-o-dee* by Stick McGhee, *Rock The Joint* by Jimmy Preston, *Rock And Roll Blues* by Erline Harris, *Rock Awhile* by Goree Carter, and *Do The Boogie* by John Lee Hooker.

The first million selling rockin' record followed only a little while later. *The Fat Man* was the first single by Fats Domino, issued at the end of 1949. Although it only reached number two in the chart that Billboard had renamed a second time, earlier in the year (now it was the 'Rhythm and Blues' chart), it also achieved some success in the main hit parade. Selling steadily over a period, the record had achieved a million sales by 1953. In 1956, following a few more million-selling singles, Domino released his first LP. This was called *Rock and Rollin' With Fats Domino*. There was no question by then that this was the genre of music that Fats Domino was playing. The first track on the LP was *The Fat Man*, now happily included as a rock 'n' roll song.

The increasing emphasis on rhythm during the 1940s within the music that had come to be known as rhythm and blues was paralleled by a similar development within country music, even if the accompanying dance of choice was less likely to be the lindy-hop or jive than a two-step. In June 1951, guitarist and singer Bill Haley, leading a Western swing band he called Bill Haley and the Saddlemen, had the idea of recording a cover version of a contemporary rhythm and blues hit. He chose *Rocket 88*, which was at the top of the Rhythm and Blues chart at the time, performed by Jackie Brenston and his Delta Cats. There are a few differences in instrumentation in the two versions – Haley uses a pedal steel guitar in place of Brenston's saxophone and he has no drummer. Instead the rhythm is driven by a bass player, whose slap of strings against fingerboard gives all the percussive beat that is needed. On Brenston's version the bass is inaudible, if it is there at all, although its usual role is carried most effectively by Willie Kizart's guitar. Haley also adds the roar of a car engine at the start and ending of the song, which may or may not be that of an actual Rocket 88 car.

Bill Haley continued with his new sound on subsequent singles, including a cover of Jimmy Preston's *Rock The Joint*, on which Haley's lead guitarist, Danny Cedrone, plays a solo identical to the one he later used on *Rock Around The Clock*. In 1953, Haley's perseverance paid off when his fifth single for the Essex label, *Crazy Man Crazy*, (written by Haley and his bass player Marshall Lytle) became the first rock 'n' roll song to enter the Billboard pop charts, reaching number fifteen. By now, the Saddlemen had been renamed the Comets and Haley had added a drummer to the line-

THE FIRST TIME

Arthur Crudup's *That's All Right Mama* was issued in 1946, as one of the first batch of the new 45 rpm single format, introduced by RCA Victor. Backed by an energetic double bass, though with under-recorded drums, Crudup's original version of this song is a little rougher, a little harder than Elvis Presley's cover made eight years later, but it has exactly the same beat. Louis Jordan's *Choo Choo Ch'Boogie* from the same year was one of his biggest hits and epitomises the jump blues style that Jordan played – a kind of halfway house between swing and rock 'n' roll. From 1944 until 1950, Louis Jordan achieved fifteen number one hits in the rhythm and blues chart and some of them were successful in the national chart too, including *Choo Choo Ch'Boogie*, which reached number seven. The song was co-written by Milt Gabler, Jordan's recording engineer, who was later responsible for recording Bill Haley's *Rock Around The Clock*. Jordan's *Ain't That Just Like A Woman* was also released in 1946 and is introduced by a guitar figure, played by Carl Hogan, that is nearly the same as the one played later by Chuck Berry on *Johnny B Goode*.

Roy Brown's *Good Rockin' Tonight* was a race records hit in 1947, although it did not manage to reach the number one spot. It is very much in the style of Louis Jordan. It was the cover version by Wynonie Harris the following year that tightened up the beat, became a number one hit, and presumably attracted the attention of the young Elvis Presley at some point, before his own recording of the song in 1954. *Big Mama Jump* by blues singer and guitarist Lightnin' Hopkins was issued in 1947 too. Backed by a drummer, the song has all the drive of a rock 'n' roll song, although a little faster than most. Dancers would have struggled to keep up with this one! Country artists were also heading towards rock 'n' roll in 1947. Hank Williams presented a song, *Move It On Over,* whose melody line and tempo make it a fore-runner of *Rock Around The Clock*, for all that it is dominated by fiddle and pedal steel guitar. One of the biggest stars of Western swing, Spade Cooley, recorded *Boggs' Boogie*, featuring his pedal steel guitarist Noel Boggs, which builds up the momentum of a steam train, although the music is as close to its dance band roots as that of Roy Brown.

Significant rockin' records from 1950 include the rhythm and blues hits *Cool Down Mama* by Long John Hunter, *Rock And Roll* by Laverne Ray, *That Ain't The Way To Do It* by B.B.King, and *We're Gonna Rock* by Cecil Gant, as well as the country recording *Birmingham Bounce* by Hardrock Gunter. In 1951, apart from the records by Jackie Brenston and others mentioned elsewhere in this chapter, there were *Train Kept A-Rollin'* by Tiny Bradshaw, *Rock-a-bye Baby* by Roy Brown, *How Many More Years* by Howlin' Wolf, and *Get Rich Quick* – one of the first recordings by Little Richard, but not a hit.

  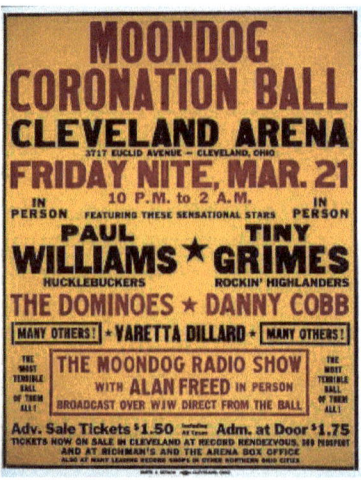

up, although he retained the pedal steel guitar. In 1954, Bill Haley signed to the Decca label and issued a single called *Thirteen Women* to moderate success. A second Decca single presented a version of a contemporary rhythm and blues song, Joe Turner's *Shake Rattle And Roll*. It proceeded to sell a million copies, reached number seven in the pop charts, and even managed to reach number four in the most widely accepted British chart, that published in New Musical Express. Both chart feats marked a first time achievement for a rock 'n' roll artist. In 1955, the B-side of *Thirteen Women* was chosen as theme song for the film *The Blackboard Jungle*. The record was flipped, re-released, and went on to become a bigger hit than *Shake Rattle And Roll*. *Rock Around The Clock* stayed at number one in the Billboard charts for eight weeks and reached number one in the UK as well, where it became the first rock 'n' roll million seller. It is estimated that the record has now sold in excess of two hundred million copies worldwide – beaten only by Bing Crosby's *White Christmas*. In its wake, Bill Haley and the Comets became the first rock 'n' roll act to appear on Ed Sullivan's influential TV show and, in 1956, starred in the first two rock 'n' roll films, *Rock Around The Clock* and *Don't Knock The Rock*. Billboard magazine uses the year of the record's first success as a dividing line for its music industry statistics. 1955 onwards is, for them, the rock era.

The moment that rhythm and blues and the rhythmic country played by the likes of Bill Haley became known as 'rock 'n' roll' is well documented. DJ Alan Freed was working on Cleveland radio station WJW-AM from 1950, presenting an evening music programme – classical music, according to Freed himself, on a YouTube video clip of his appearance on the fifties television show *To Tell The Truth*.. In any event, at some point early in 1951, Freed was invited to visit a Cleveland record store, Record Rendezvous, run by Leo Mintz, who was keen to draw the DJ's attention to the fact that a large number of white teenagers were buying rhythm and blues records. He persuaded Alan Freed to begin a radio show, immediately following the one he was already hosting, in order to highlight the rhythm and blues music. Freed was quickly won over and on July 11th began broadcasting a show he called *The Moon Dog House*. It was during 1952 that the crucial moment occurred. It was recalled by Bill Haley's bass player, Marshall Lytle, during a 1994 interview for the Las Vegas Sun:

> "I was there when Alan Freed coined the phrase 'rock 'n' roll'. It was 1952 and the Comets were in Cleveland to promote *Rock The Joint* on Freed's show." As the song played, with its four times repeated chorus line "we're gonna rock, rock this joint", Freed began pounding on the table and shouting 'rock and roll, rock and roll!' for all his radio listeners to hear, as he had left the microphone switched on. Afterwards, Lytle said, "The people kept calling up and saying, 'will you play that rock 'n' roll song again?' He played it twelve times. That's the night rock 'n' roll was invented."
>
> (Quoted on the Rockabilly Hall Of Fame website)

Rock The Joint was released on April 26th, so we can presume that the event Marshall Lytle describes took place round about then. Alan Freed renamed his show *Moondog's Rock 'n' Roll Party* soon afterwards. He tried to copyright the phrase 'rock 'n' roll', but it was not long before it became part of the everyday language and Freed's attempt failed.

Freed had already helped to organize a dance concert in Cleveland in March, along with Leo Mintz from the record shop and local promoter Lew Platt. The event, advertised as the *Moondog Coronation Ball*, would have been the first rock 'n' roll concert, but it did not go well. The ice hockey arena booked to hold the event could cope with ten thousand people. More than twenty thousand turned up. A riot began and the police responded by shutting down the concert. Just one song had been performed, by Paul Williams and his Hucklebuckers. The incident became the talk of Cleveland, outraging the established community, but boosting the popularity of Alan Freed's radio show (which was fortunate, as the management of WJW had originally wanted to fire the DJ). In May, Freed's *Moondog Maytime Ball* was held at the same arena, but featuring three shows to handle the crowds. It was a success and became the first of numerous events promoted by Freed.

In August 1954, Alan Freed moved to a radio station in New York, WINS, and *Alan Freed's Rock 'n' Roll Party* was syndicated to over forty other radio stations across the USA. The listeners of all these stations discovered quickly that the music they liked was called rock 'n' roll and by early 1956, the music industry too had accepted the term and

THE FIRST TIME

Alan Freed took the name Moon Dog from Louis Hardin, an eccentric blind musician and composer who wandered the streets of New York and called himself Moondog. He had made some recordings and Freed used one of these, *Symphony No.1 Timberwolf,* as the theme tune for his show. The music is entirely percussive, with occasional wolf cries – it has nothing to do with rhythm and blues but is somehow appropriate anyway. In due course, Louis Hardin protested at the unauthorised use of his name and sued Alan Freed in 1954, after which Freed was no longer allowed to use the Moondog name. Hardin has an album issued on CBS in 1968, *Moondog,* at a time when the explosion of new sounds in rock music allowed record companies to believe that anything a little different from the norm might prove to be a commercial success. *Moondog* actually sold quite poorly, but it contains one track, *Bird's Lament* (a tribute to jazz saxophonist Charlie Parker) that has achieved some resonance, especially since being incorporated into the 1999 hit dance track *Get A Move On* by Mr.Scruff.

Sadly, Alan Freed's career did not end well. The US government decided in 1959 to investigate alleged corruption in the music industry, whereby radio DJs were paid to promote particular songs. The practice, given the name 'payola', undoubtedly did occur, but was considered by many to be an acceptable business practice. Nevertheless, when Alan Freed was asked by ABC to sign an affidavit that he had not accepted payola, he refused to do it and was fired from the TV show he was then hosting. In May 1960, Freed was arrested and charged with benefiting from commercial bribery. In December 1962, he pleaded guilty to two counts of bribery, out of the twenty-six he was charged with, and received a suspended sentence and a small fine. He never worked again and in January 1965 was admitted to hospital, suffering from cirrhosis of the liver. He died twenty days later, at the age of forty-three.

The earliest recordings by Bill Haley gave no indication of his later musical choices. In January 1946, the Down Homers, in which Haley was one of two guitarists, recorded tracks that were issued on two Vogue singles. The singer was Kenny Roberts, who favoured a yodelling cowboy approach and later became a successful solo artist, still yodelling. When Bill Haley formed his own band in 1947, the Four Aces of Western Swing, with himself as singer, he followed Roberts' example with at least two songs in his repertoire – *Yodel Your Blues Away* and *A Yodeller's Lullaby.* The band was also responsible, however, for a song called *Rovin' Eyes,* recorded in 1948, which would be claimed as a rock 'n' roll performance were it not for the prominent accordion playing throughout.

Maybe it is the fact that *Rocket 88* was covered by Bill Haley that makes the Jackie Brenston song so frequently cited as the first rock 'n' roll record, or maybe it is the fact that Willie Kizart's electric guitar sounds a little distorted, though no more so than that heard on several blues performances – such as Joe Hill Louis' *Boogie In The Park* from 1950 (itself a rockin' record, albeit driven only by a guitar, with no band in support). The citation was originally made by studio owner Sam Phillips, who had something of a vested interest in it, given that he was the producer of the single. Its success, moreover, gave Phillips the finance necessary to start his own label in 1952, the legendary Sun Records. Ike Turner, who had assembled the band heard behind singer Jackie Brenston in 1950, had expected to see his own name on the credits when the single was released. As far as Chess records were concerned, however, it was the singer they had under contract and not the band. Following the success of *Rocket 88,* the band stayed with Brenston and left Ike Turner behind. With no further hits forthcoming, Jackie Brenston joined Ike Turner's new band as a saxophonist and occasional singer in 1955. It is said that Turner did not allow him to sing *Rocket 88.*

Rock 'n' roll revisionists have a tendency to downgrade Bill Haley's significance within the history of the music. Haley certainly did not have the glamour and charisma of Elvis Presley, but neither was he 'middle-aged' as is often claimed. When Alan Freed played *Rock The Joint* and labelled it as being rock 'n' roll, Bill Haley was 26 years old, the same age as Elvis when his song *Wooden Heart* reached number one in the UK charts. During the international success of *Rock Around The Clock,* Bill Haley celebrated his thirtieth birthday – making him just a year older than Chuck Berry and the same age as B.B.King.

was using it in its advertising.

Sam Phillips, the owner of Sun Records in Memphis, is quoted as saying, "If I could find a white man who had the Negro sound and the Negro feel, I could make a million dollars". In an interview given to Richard Buskin near the end of his life and published in *Sound On Sound* magazine in 2003, Phillips modified his statement, though only a little:

> "I had felt all along that, as long as the artists were black, you were going to get a limited amount of play on the air. In fact, I had found that out and I knew that, because I had been in radio myself since the forties, and I had thought that if there was a way for some white person to perform with the feel of a black artist... I did not want anybody who did not have a natural feel, but I said to myself – and this is true – Man, if I can find a white person who can give the feel and the true essence of a blues-type song, black blues especially, then I've got a chance to broaden the base and get plays that otherwise we couldn't. And man, did that prove to be a phenomenal philosophy!"

When the eighteen year old Elvis Presley came to the Sun Studios in order to record two songs for his mother, using the studio's custom recording service, Sam Phillips believed that he had found the person he had been seeking. After several weeks of trying out material during the summer of 1954 with guitarist Scotty Moore and bass player Bill Black, Elvis picked up his acoustic guitar and delivered a note-perfect version of Arthur Crudup's blues from eight years previously, *That's All Right Mama*. Moore and Black joined in.

"What's that you're doing?" Sam Phillips asked, according to the sleeve notes for the *Elvis at Sun* compilation CD. "We don't know," came the response. "Well back up and do it again."

Inspired by that performance, the musicians worked on a version of the country ballad *Blue Moon Of Kentucky*, gradually transforming it into something more like the rockin' *That's All Right Mama*. An out-take from the sessions, with the song getting close to its final version, captures Sam Phillips exclaiming, "Hell, that's fine! That's different! That's a pop song now, nearly 'bout!". *Sound on Sound* magazine quotes local musician Jim Dickinson commenting later that this was "what it sounded like ten minutes before rock & roll was invented". With Bill Haley recently at the top of the charts, the comment was something of an exaggeration. *Blue Moon Of Kentucky* was undoubtedly the first rockabilly song – a name created to describe precisely this small group fusion of rhythm and blues and country. But to have said that this was "what it sounded like ten minutes before *rockabilly* was invented" would not have had quite the same grandeur.

The five Elvis Presley singles issued by Sun sold well locally but were not national hits. Presley's new manager, Colonel Tom Parker, was keen for his client to be signed to a major record company and, somewhat reluctantly, Sam Phillips eventually agreed. RCA Records paid $35,000 for Elvis Presley's contract, a huge sum for a largely unknown artist. The company asked Phillips to continue working with the singer, but he felt committed to the other artists on his own label and refused. Elvis Presley's first single for RCA, *Heartbreak Hotel*, was released on January 27th 1956 and climbed slowly up the Billboard Hot Hundred chart, entering the top twenty on March 24th, and finally reaching number one on May 5th, where it stayed for seven weeks. (It was supplanted by Gogi Grant's *The Wayward Wind*). The record became Presley's first million seller. Curiously, *Heartbreak Hotel* is not a rockin' record at all (and it's B-side, *I Was The One*, is definitely a ballad), although it does manage to convey the energy of rock 'n' roll regardless. The follow-up, *I Want You I Need You I Love You*, is another smouldering ballad (reaching number three in the charts), but the third RCA single, *Hound Dog*, is unequivocal rock 'n' roll. *Hound Dog* climbed to number two in the charts, but was then prevented from reaching the top by the fourth Elvis Presley single, *Don't Be Cruel* (also a rock 'n' roll performance) nipping into the number one position ahead of it. Clearly, RCA was determined to make the most of its new star while it still could.

As we know, the record company need not have worried. Elvis Presley's popularity continued and he never signed to another label. He became the first rock 'n' roll superstar, the appellation for once being bestowed on someone worthy of it.

THE FIRST TIME

According to the Rockabilly Hall of Fame website, the surviving members of the Comets are understandably bitter that they were paid only session fees for *Rock Around The Clock* – $47.50 each. Their request for a $50 raise on their $225 weekly pay in 1956 was turned down by Bill Haley, on the grounds that he could not afford it, despite the group earning up to $50,000 a week at the time. Three of the five Comets left the group as a result. It might have helped if Haley had not been so profligate in other areas. Rival group leader, Boyd Bennett, in the sleeve-notes to his *Tennessee Rock 'n' Roll* compilation CD, states that the Comets would arrive at gigs in five gold Cadillacs, one for each member of the group.

Arguably, an artist meeting Sam Phillips' prescription had already been discovered as early as 1951. In May, Charlie Gracie recorded two songs he had written himself, *Boogie Woogie Blues* and *Rockin' 'n' Rollin'*, which are hardly less rockin' than Bill Haley's version of *Rocket 88*, recorded a month later, albeit with a few jazz and mainstream pop touches that dilute their impact just a little. Gracie's voice was well up to the task and he played skilful lead guitar on the songs too. And he was only fifteen years old. No doubt Charlie Gracie had less charisma than Elvis Presley, but perhaps the timing was simply wrong, for the singles, released on the New York Cadillac label, were not successful. Eventually, Charlie Gracie did achieve considerable chart success, but the hit singles *Butterfly, Fabulous,* and *Wandering Eyes,* all from 1957, for all that they are attractive songs, represent a considerable dilution of the rock 'n' roll ethic. They move the music towards pop in the manner of a Guy Mitchell, when Elvis Presley was still rock 'n' rollin' with the likes of *All Shook Up* and *Jailhouse Rock*.

For the first rock 'n' roll record issued in the UK and recorded by a British artist, there is a choice of two. Tommy Steele's *Rock With The Caveman* (complete with a suitably rousing tenor saxophone solo by jazzman Ronnie Scott, who probably thought that he was slumming it) was issued in October 1956. It reached number thirteen in the *NME* chart. By this time there had already been several rock 'n' roll hits by American artists, most of them by Elvis Presley and Bill Haley. Tommy Steele did not continue with rock 'n' roll for very long – by the end of the decade he was starring in musicals and singing about "a little white bull". Also issued in October 1956 was Tony Crombie's *Teach You To Rock*. Crombie was a jazz drummer trying to get a hit and his single is close to being a jazz performance despite its title. It just failed to reach the top twenty. Arguably, the first British record able to realistically compete with American rock 'n' roll was Cliff Richard's first single, *Move It*, which was released in August 1958.

Although classified as skiffle rather than rock 'n' roll, the first records made by Lonnie Donegan pre-date Tommy Steele and have just as much rhythmic energy. Donegan's first record was a cover of the Leadbelly folk-blues song, *Rock Island Line*, which he recorded in July 1954 (just a few days after Elvis Presley's first recording sessions at Sun), while working as banjo player in Chris Barber's traditional jazz band. It was Barber's habit to feature Donegan playing folk and blues songs on guitar during breaks in the band's sets. Originally issued as part of Chris Barber's *New Orleans Joys* ten inch LP in 1954, *Rock Island Line* was chosen for release as a single and reached number eight in the *NME* chart in January 1956. Donegan's skiffle music was enormously influential and persuaded a number of future professionals to take up the guitar. These included John Lennon, who formed his own skiffle group, the Quarrymen (named after his school, Quarry Bank), in November 1956.

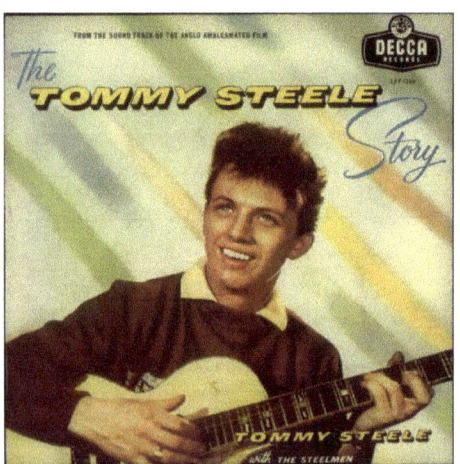

MUSIC GENRES

To sum up, the following records are candidates for consideration as the 'first rock 'n' roll record', depending on how one wishes to define this. You can take your pick.

Trixie Smith – My Daddy Rocks Me (With One Steady Roll) (1922).
    First record with an appropriate title.
Montana Taylor – Detroit Rocks (1929).
    First record with an appropriate title and with an appropriate beat.
Boswell Sisters – Rock And Roll (1934).
    First record to use the exact wording.
Albert Ammons – The Boogie Rocks (1945).
    First record sounding something like rock 'n' roll.
Arthur Crudup – That's All Right Mama (1946).
    First record with a rockin' beat and rockabilly instrumentation.
Wynonie Harris – Good Rockin' Tonight (1948).
    First big rockin' hit.
Fats Domino – The Fat Man (1949).
    First rockin' million seller.
Jackie Brenston – Rocket 88 (1951).
    First rock 'n' roll record according to Sam Phillips.
Bill Haley – Rocket 88 (1951).
    First rockin' cover of a rhythm and blues song by a country artist.
Bill Haley – Rock The Joint (1952)
    Record inspiring the first use of the phrase 'rock 'n' roll' to describe the music.
Bill Haley – Crazy Man Crazy (1953)
    First rockin' record to enter the national charts in the US.
Bill Haley – Shake, Rattle And Roll (1954)
    First international rock 'n' roll hit
Elvis Presley – That's All Right Mama/Blue Moon Of Kentucky (1954)
    First rockabilly record and first record by the first rock 'n' roll superstar.
Bill Haley – Rock Around The Clock (1955)
    First rockin' record to reach number one in the national charts.
Elvis Presley – Heartbreak Hotel (1956)
    First number one in the national charts by the first rock 'n' roll superstar.
Elvis Presley – Don't Be Cruel (1956)
    First rockin' record by the first rock 'n' roll superstar to reach number one in the national charts in the US.

Phew**!!!**

> "Rock and roll is a means of pulling the White Man down to the level of the Negro. It is part of a plot to undermine the morals of the youth of our nation."
>
> Secretary of the North Alabama White Citizens Council c.1956
>
> "Rock 'n' roll. The most brutal, ugly, desperate, vicious form of expression it has been my misfortune to hear."
>
> Frank Sinatra c. late 1950s

THE FIRST TIME

The difficulty in choosing a first rock 'n' roll record also applies to the choice of the first rock 'n' roll LP and for the same reasons. The transition from uptempo rhythm and blues to undisputed rock 'n' roll is a gradual one. The first rockin' LPs all date from the fifties and their tracks would have been played on Alan Freed's show, even if many of those tracks were originally issued as singles somewhat earlier. These are the first six relevant album releases – all as ten inch LPs.

Significantly, the first five are on relatively small, independent labels.

Rhythm And Blues (Savoy MG15008. 1952)
 The tracks by various artists represent the jazzier end of the rhythm and blues spectrum.
Earl Bostic And His Alto Sax Volume One (King 295-64. 1953)
 So do these.
Tiny Bradshaw Off An On (King 295-74. 1954)
 Includes his 1951 rhythm and blues hit *Train Kept A-Rollin'* (covered as rockabilly in 1956 by the Johnny Burnette Trio and as high energy psychedelic rock in 1966 by the Yardbirds).
The Midnighters Sing Their Hits (Federal 295-90. 1954)
 Doo-wop – some rockin', some slow.
Billy Ward And His Dominoes (Federal 295-94. 1955)
 More doo-wop.
Bill Haley Shake Rattle And Roll (Decca DL 5560. 1955)

Doo-wop is discussed further in Chapter 18 of this book, 'Soul'.

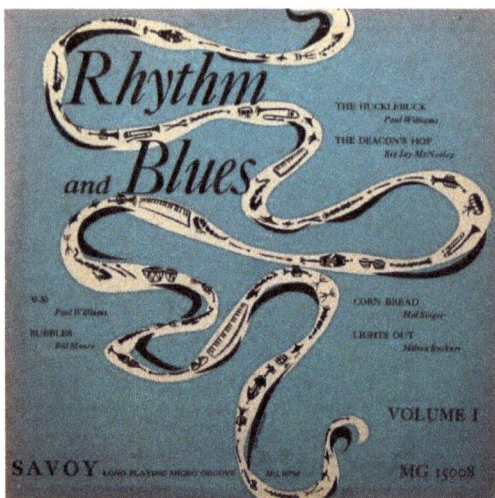

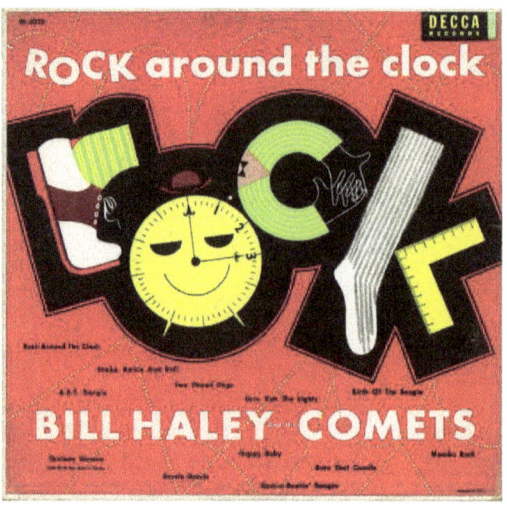

MUSIC GENRES

> "Viewed as a social phenomenon, the current craze for Rock-and-Roll material is one of the most terrifying things ever to have happened to popular music… Musically speaking, of course, the whole thing is laughable."
>
> Steve Race, writing in *Melody Maker,* May 1956
>
> "Rock and roll will be gone by June." *Variety* magazine, 1955
>
> [Rock and roll is] "inspired by what has been called race music, modified to stir the animal instinct in teenagers. Its chief characteristics now are a heavy, unrelenting beat and a raw, savage tone. The lyrics tend to be nonsensical or lewd, or both. Rock and roll might best be summed up as monotony tinged with hysteria."
>
> Vance Packard, author of *Hidden Persuaders,* 1958
>
> [Rock & roll] "It's not music; it's a disease." Mitch Miller, 1950s
>
> "I always felt rock and roll was very, very wholesome music." Aretha Franklin
>
> "Rock and Roll has no beginning and no end for it is the very pulse of life itself." Larry Williams
>
> "Rock and roll music, if you like it, if you feel it, you can't help but move to it. That's what happens to me. I can't help it."
>
> Elvis Presley

TRACKING THE TRACKS

Most, if not all of the songs mentioned in this chapter can be heard on YouTube, although it is necessary to be wary of accompanying misinformation. A recording of *Rock And Roll* by Wild Bill Moore that was uploaded a little while ago had an attached date of 1947. Much discussion appeared as to whether or not it might be the first rock 'n' roll record – discussion that would have been curtailed if it had been realized that in fact the record was made in 1949 – a year after the same artist's *We're Gonna Rock, We're Gonna Roll*.

The author has found the following compilation CDs to be useful:

Atlantic R&B Volume 1 1947-1952 (Rhino/Warner 2006)
The Best Of Jump & Jive (Prism Leisure 1999)
The First Rock And Roll Record (3 CD set) (Famous Flames 2011)
From Spirituals To Swing (3 CD set) (Vanguard 1999) Hard to find – original vinyl issues much easier!
The Road To Rhythm & Blues And Rock 'n' Roll Volumes 1 & 2 (Flapper 1997)
Rocket 88 – The Original Rock 'n' Roll Pioneers (Prism Leisure 2001)
We're Gonna Rock We're Gonna Roll (4 CD set) (Proper Records 2005)

Individual artist CDs come and go where this period is concerned, but the following were available at the time of writing:

Chuck Berry – *The Ultimate Collection* (Spectrum 3 CD set 2007)
Fats Domino – *The Complete Hits 1950-62* (Acrobat 3 CD set 2015)
Lonnie Donegan – *Puttin' On The Style – The Greatest Hits* (Sanctuary 2003)
Charlie Gracie – *Cool Baby! The Singles And More 1951 To 1957* (GVC 2009)
Bill Haley – *The Singles Collection 1948-60* (Acrobat 2 CD set 2016)
John Lee Hooker – *The Very Best Of John Lee Hooker* (Not Now Music 2CD set 2016) and *Mr Lucky* (Silvertone 1991)
Tommy Steele – *The Best Of Tommy Steele* (Spectrum 1999)
Ike Turner & His Kings Of Rhythm – *Rhythm Rockin' Blues* (Ace 1995)
Muddy Waters – *His Best 1947-1955* (Chess/Universal 1999)
Elvis Presley – *Elvis At Sun* (BMG 2004) and *30 #1 Hits* (BMG 2002)
Robert Johnson – *King Of The Delta Blues Singers* (Sony 1999)
Louis Jordan – *Choo Choo Ch'Boogie* (ASV Living Era 1999)
Moondog – *The Viking Of Sixth Avenue* (Honest Jon's Records 2008)

17 BLUES

The beginnings of the blues, the original folk music of black America, remain something of a mystery. *Savannah Syncopators,* Paul Oliver's masterful study of the subject, tries very hard to persuade us that there are clear musical links between the blues and the music of West Africa. The recorded evidence, however, is not very convincing. The problem, as with jazz, is that the roots of the music are lost in the time before recording began; lost too within a culture that was not at all interested in studying the habits of its most disadvantaged people. There is much in common between the playing of someone like Ali Farka Touré, the late Malian singer and guitarist, and the blues. But at this point in time, it is impossible to say whether that similarity is due to the influence of his own African tradition, or whether he has simply heard the blues of today and is himself influenced by it.

Several recordings were made in the thirties and again in the late forties by John and Alan Lomax at various prisons in the Southern states of America. They believed that the music performed by long-stay prisoners was likely to be relatively free of contemporary influences and might, therefore, give some clues as to how the roots of the blues might have sounded. The various spirituals, work songs, and hollers do not have the structure or the instrumentation of the blues, but they do have its sound, its feeling. The similarity with an early blues recording like *Levee Camp Moan*, recorded by Texas Alexander and Lonnie Johnson in 1927, is striking. This song does not have the familiar blues structure either.

The first piece of published music using the definitive blues chord progression was *I Got The Blues* in 1908. The composer of what is otherwise a ragtime piano tune, Anthony Maggio, later admitted that his inspiration had been an elderly black musician he had heard playing the guitar in New Orleans. The first blues recording was from an unlikely source – the Victor Military Band, whose version of W.C.Handy's *Memphis Blues* was laid down for posterity in July 1914. Handy claimed to have discovered the blues when hearing a slide guitar player in 1903, although his own approach to the music was to make it rather more complicated than what he must have heard then. Morton Harvey recorded a vocal version of *Memphis Blues* in October 1914.

The first blues recording by an African-American singer was *Crazy Blues* by Mamie Smith, in August 1920, released on the Okeh label. Smith had recorded for the same company in February, but then the songs she sang were much closer to jazz-cabaret. *Crazy Blues* too is a jazz performance, with a full band in support. The record was extremely successful, selling close to a million copies. Bessie Smith, unrelated to Mamie, and who eventually became known as 'the Empress of the Blues', made her first record in February 1923. *Down Hearted Blues* was a second near-million seller, in a similar jazz blues style, though with only pianist Clarence Williams in support, and it gave Columbia records its first pop hit. One line from the song, "I've got the world in a jug, the stopper's in my hand", would become very familiar through its use in many later blues songs. The words were composed by singer Alberta Hunter (assuming that Lovie Austin was responsible for the music). She recorded the song herself in July 1922, accompanied by a jazz band, for release on Paramount.

At the beginning of November 1923, Sara Martin, singing in a similar style to both Smiths, recorded *Roamin' Blues*, on which she was accompanied by a single acoustic guitar, played by Sylvester Weaver. The duo recorded *Longing For Daddy Blues* two days earlier, but this was released later. At the same November session, Weaver recorded a guitar instrumental called *Guitar Blues* and this time he held a knife in his left hand, sliding it along the strings. He thereby became the first musician to play the slide guitar on record. In the spring of 1924, Ed Andrews sang and played guitar on *Barrel House Blues* and *Time Ain't Gonna Make Me Stay*. These recordings were also released on the Okeh label, which had established a category it called 'race records' in 1921. Some of the illustrations used in the company's advertising would not be acceptable in today's more politically correct world.

THE FIRST TIME

The Five Royales are the inspiration behind a particularly fine piece of writing about rock music. *Dedicated To You* by Ed Ward is about the group, but with a twist that readers will have to discover for themselves. The piece is included in Greil Marcus's anthology *Stranded – Rock And Roll For A Desert Island,* published in 1979. As Marcus himself writes, later in the same book, "a black vocal group, with a guitar player. Once upon a time, Eric Clapton would have paid to hold his coat".

The first seriously influential country blues performers were Charley Patton and Blind Lemon Jefferson. Between the end of 1925 and 1929 (the year he died, at the age of just thirty-two), Jefferson made seventy-nine records for Paramount, most of which were best-sellers. Nearly all the songs were self-composed, making Jefferson one of the first singer-songwriters, and all of them were enhanced by his obviously skilful, intricate guitar playing. His first recording, an atypical gospel song from December 1925, was *I Want To Be Like Jesus In My Heart*. In March the following year, he reverted to his main style, with *Got The Blues*. His song, *Matchbox Blues*, recorded for a rare departure to Okeh in 1927, was updated in the rock 'n' roll era by Carl Perkins, whose interpretation was later covered in turn by the Beatles. Charley Patton made his first record, *Pony Blues*, in June 1929. Paramount viewed him as a natural successor to Blind Lemon Jefferson. Whereas most country blues players at the time were itinerant musicians, playing where they could, Patton was booked in advance for paid gigs at bars and clubs. He was a considerable showman, using his guitar as a prop, including playing it behind his head. His fame locally meant that he was regarded as the undisputed king of the Mississippi Delta blues. Like Jefferson before him, however, he died young, in 1934, at the age of about forty-three.

In April 1924, a pianist by the name of Jimmy Blythe recorded a piece called *Chicago Stomp*, which was issued on a Paramount 78 in June or July. Many listeners consider this to be the first example of the rhythmic blues piano style known as boogie woogie. Blythe was employed by Columbia to produce piano rolls and he specialised in the blues, though playing in several other styles as well. *Chicago Stomp* attracted the attention of ragtime pianist and publisher, Axel Christiensen, who published the music in April 1927, with a composing co-credit for himself, as *The Walking Blues*. Given the walking bass line played by Blythe's left hand, this is perhaps a better title. Certainly, the piece lacks the drive of boogie woogie performances recorded at the end of the twenties, such as *Honky Tonk Train Blues* by Meade Lux Lewis (1927) or *Pinetop's Boogie Woogie* by Pinetop Smith (1928). To employ a term that was barely in use at the time, the later pieces rock, but *Chicago Stomp* does not. (Montana Taylor's appropriately titled *Detroit Rocks* dates from 1929). Arguably, the Blythe piece is a piano blues, but not boogie woogie. Jelly Roll Morton recorded a solo piano blues the previous July, called *New Orleans Joys*. A similar walking bass line to that employed by Blythe can be heard on *Weary Blues* by the Louisiana Five, recorded in 1920, and it is unlikely that it was being played for the first time even there.

The story of the blues from the thirties to the fifties is intimately bound up with the development of its more overtly commercial manifestations, rhythm and blues and rock 'n' roll. These are explored during the previous chapter of this book. In particular, the music of Robert Johnson is discussed and used to explain the chordal structure of the blues generally. Johnson's music, recorded during 1936 and 1937, served to describe the form and the vocabulary of the blues so authoritatively that it has remained the standard exemplar ever since. Rock 'n' roll stars like Chuck Berry and Bo Diddley were essentially blues players who had found a way to make their music reach a wider audience than was ever managed by Robert Johnson. Lowman Pauling, playing lead guitar lines within the music of the doo-wop group, the Five Royales, showed that the blues was intrinsic to that music too.

The development of the electric guitar in the late thirties and forties meant that blues performers on the instrument could play in noisy clubs and be easily heard; meant too that they could lead blues bands. T Bone Walker started to play electric guitar in 1935 and recorded with it for the first time in 1942, in a band that he co-led with pianist Freddie Slack. Muddy Waters took up the electric guitar in 1944 and recorded with a band in Chicago in 1946. From 1951 and right through the fifties, he led a band made up of musicians good enough to also run bands of their own, including Little Walter on harmonica, Jimmy Rogers on guitar, Otis Spann on piano, and, sometimes, Willie Dixon on bass. The success of a song recorded by B.B.King in 1951, *Three O'Clock Blues,* two years after his very first session, enabled him to form a band too and go on tour with it. Waters, a musician who had started as a country blues player, favoured what was essentially an electrified version of it, full of rough edges. King, however, preferred a sophisticated sound delivered by around a dozen players. Both men eventually issued live albums as the perfect demonstration of their art – *Muddy Waters at Newport 1960* and *B.B.King Live at the Regal* (recorded in 1964).

THE FIRST TIME

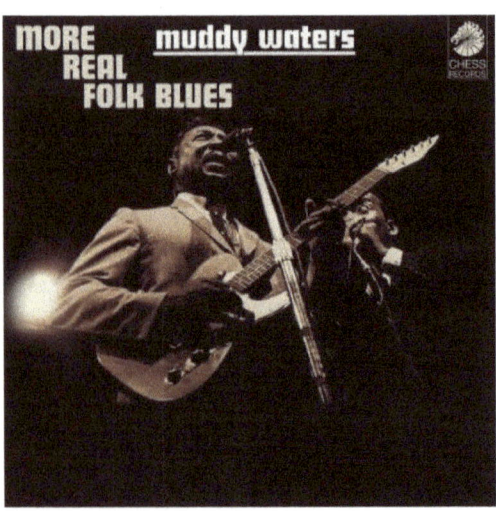
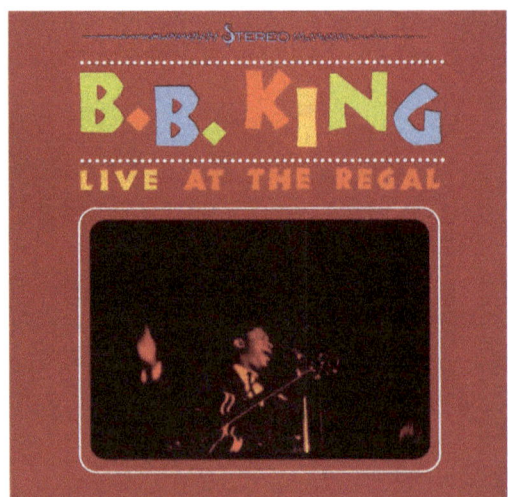

The parochial audiences at Muddy Waters' first British tour in 1958 were expecting a rustic individual arriving straight from the Mississippi Delta, equipped with a cheap acoustic guitar. They were the same people who believed trad to be the 'purest' form of jazz and who viewed skiffle as inherently superior to commercial rock 'n' roll. What they got was a sharp-suited musician brandishing a Telecaster – accustomed, after all, to delivering powerful electric blues in a downtown Chicago club. Like the electric Bob Dylan a decade later, Muddy Waters was not appreciated.

Howlin' Wolf with guitarist Hubert Sumlin

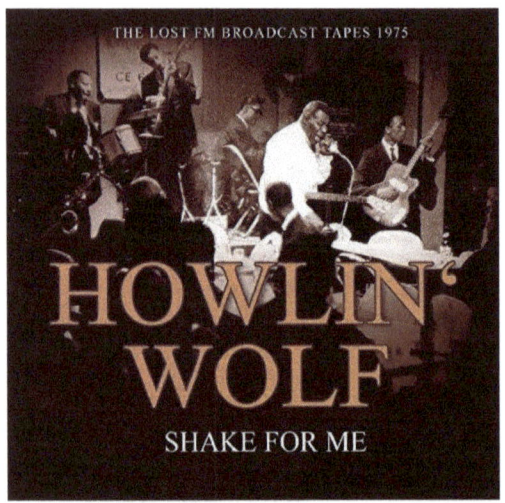

According to the author Lee Child, writing in *Killing Floor* (a novel named after a song by Howlin' Wolf and giving the real-life blues musician Blind Blake a significant cameo role), the frequently recorded sound of John Lee Hooker's tapping foot was achieved by pushing beer bottle tops into the sole of his shoe. Child is a surprising blues authority to be quoting, but his statement rings true.

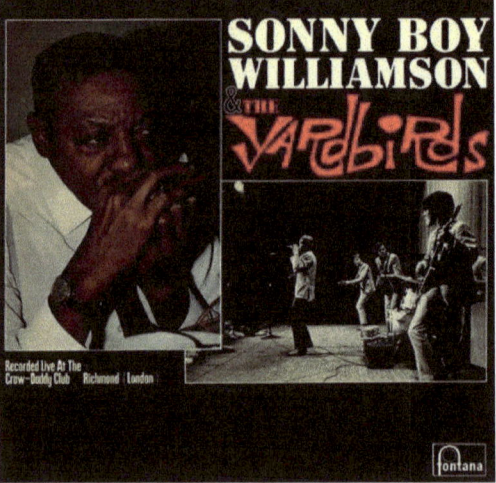

Poor research on Fontana's part resulted in a cover picture showing Jeff Beck playing with the Yardbirds, when it was Eric Clapton who was on the record.

Howlin' Wolf was an older man than either Waters or King. He had heard Charley Patton play and learned the guitar from him. Like Waters, he was a country blues musician who amplified his music when that became possible. He formed a band in 1948 and through the fifties maintained a spirit of rivalry with Muddy Waters. Wolf scored fewer chart hits, but the two men were equally influential. Meanwhile, John Lee Hooker recorded two songs in 1948 that eventually became million selling records. *I'm In The Mood* and *Boogie Chillen* feature nothing more than Hooker's electric guitar and amplified foot, yet manage to make as much impact as if they were played by an entire band.

In the UK, where the small black population had a different musical tradition to the Americans and for whom 'blues' referred to another kind of music, players like Blind Lemon Jefferson and Robert Johnson were largely unknown. A Greek-Austrian immigrant became an unlikely evangelist for the blues. Alexis Korner played with Chris Barber in 1949, recorded skiffle with Ken Colyer in 1955, and formed his own blues band, Blues Incorporated, in 1961. Over the years, the band proved to be a hugely influential force and a training ground for many musicians going on to form other bands of their own, including such diverse talents as the Rolling Stones, the Graham Bond Organisation, Cream, and the Pentangle. The Rolling Stones managed to take the blues to number one in the charts in 1964, with a cover of a Howlin' Wolf/Willie Dixon song, *Little Red Rooster*, complete with a prominent slide guitar part, played by Brian Jones.

Guitarist Eric Clapton, inspired by Korner, although never a member of Blues Incorporated, tried hard to push his own band, the Yardbirds, in a blues direction. They covered songs by Howlin' Wolf, John Lee Hooker, and Billy Boy Arnold, and, when blues harmonica legend Sonny Boy Williamson was invited to perform in the UK in 1963, the Yardbirds became his backing band. The results were recorded for a live LP, *Sonny Boy Williamson and the Yardbirds*. Subsequently, Clapton left the band, in protest at the decision to release a pop single (even though he managed to squeeze a blues instrumental of his own on the B-side and despite *For Your Love* climbing to the top of the UK charts). He joined the band led by the similarly uncompromising John Mayall. In the same manner as Alexis Korner's band, John Mayall's Bluesbreakers changed personnel frequently and served as a school for British musicians wanting to play the blues. Mayall and his former sidemen became responsible for the British blues boom that was a major feature of the rock music scene in the late sixties. A record label, Blue Horizon, was established in 1966 to cater for this and it made a point of releasing records by British blues musicians, but also by some of the American bluesmen who were their inspiration. Peter Green's Fleetwood Mac (three of whom had been members of John Mayall's Bluesbreakers) achieved a UK number one single for the label in 1968, *Albatross*, and two top ten albums.

In the US, Paul Butterfield's Blues Band served a similar function to John Mayall's Bluesbreakers, with the added advantage that Butterfield (who played harmonica) and his guitarists, Elvin Bishop and Mike Bloomfield, were able to learn the blues at source by jamming in Chicago clubs with the likes of Muddy Waters – and were good enough to do so. The original rhythm section of the Butterfield Blues Band comprised former members of Howlin' Wolf's band.

It was the renewed interest in the blues on both sides of the Atlantic that was at least partly responsible for the success of the most innovative and incendiary guitarist of them all, Jimi Hendrix. Much of Hendrix's music was not blues at all, even if it bore its influence plainly, but when he did choose to play the music straight, as on *Red House*, *Voodoo Chile*, or *Hear My Train A-Comin'*, then his performances were definitive.

It was easy in the late sixties to make fun of middle class white boys from Britain or America, who had decided that the music of Robert Johnson and Blind Lemon Jefferson was part of their own heritage. Indeed, the Bonzo Dog Doo-Dah Band did just that, with its song *Can Blue Men Sing The Whites*, and so did the Liverpool Scene, with *Fleetwood Mac Chicken Shack, John Mayall Can't Fail Blues*. The fact of the matter is, however, that ever since Jimi Hendrix, an African-American bluesman who decided that he wanted to play rock (and took it over), the blues has become a legitimate form for all kinds of musician to explore if they so wish. In the late twentieth century and beyond, Robert Cray and Keb' Mo' (and John lee Hooker, a best-selling international star in his eighties), or Stevie Ray Vaughan and Joe Bonamassa, have delivered their own interpretations of the blues and have been accorded equal respect.

THE FIRST TIME

Peter Green had the distinction of being the one British guitarist of the sixties to impress B.B.King, who was reported as saying, "He has the sweetest tone I ever heard; he was the only one who gave me the cold sweats". The two men shared an approach to playing in which the tone and the emotional impact of the notes played were more important than how many of them were squeezed into each bar. Peter Green's Gibson Les Paul was examined and discussed by aficionados who ignored the fact that he sometimes played other instruments yet still achieved the same tone. The guitar eventually ended up with Gary Moore – another fine player, yet one who sounded different even on the same guitar. Green began a return to music in the late seventies after a breakdown and several years without playing. He could still play the guitar, but sadly he could no longer play it like *that*.

Eventually, the sheer staying power of Eric Clapton must have impressed B.B.King too, for the guitarists made an album together, *Riding With The King,* in 2000. The CD artwork included a photograph of the two men jamming together in about 1968. Clapton already had a history at this point of wanting to contribute to the music of the people that inspired him. His playing with Otis Spann on the 1964 track, *Pretty Girls Everywhere*, is exemplary and he makes a telling contribution to the Aretha Franklin track, *Good To Me As I Am To You* (a contribution that the album sleeve notes rather smugly refer to as a guitar 'obbligato').

Peter Green with Willie Dixon

Don Van Vliet, who performed as Captain Beefheart and was blessed with a gruff, sometimes roaring voice, like that of Howlin' Wolf, used the blues as a launching pad for music that was more abrasive, more avant garde than the blues ever normally attempted. On the album *Mirror Man,* that was intended to be their second, in late 1967, Captain Beefheart's Magic Band use a Robert Johnson piece, *Terraplane Blues*, as a bare framework for a lengthy jam, *Tarotplane.* The musicians play individual spiky riffs and patterns, fighting each other's rhythms, yet managing, seemingly against the odds, to integrate into a distinctive and powerful overall sound. For *Trout Mask Replica,* issued in 1969, the process was stretched as far as it could go without falling apart. Too different to exert much influence on its contemporaries, the impact of Beefheart's music could be heard ten years later, in the sound of post-punk terrorists like the Fall, Pere Ubu, and the Gang Of Four.

The blues has remained an essential part of the vocabulary of jazz musicians throughout the music's history. Many of Louis Armstrong's performances were straight blues interpretations; the same was true for Charlie Parker. John Coltrane recorded an album made up entirely of blues tunes (*Coltrane Plays The Blues*) and so did Miles Davis (*Kind Of Blue* – although this does stretch the blues format a little). Even avant garde jazz performers would sometimes use the blues as a way of reminding listeners that their unsettling music still had the familiar roots. The Albert Ayler track *Drudgery*, on which the Canned Heat guitarist Henry Vestine also plays, is a blues. So, almost, is Archie Shepp's *My Angel*, where his wayward tenor saxophone battles with a pair of blues harmonica players.

The bluesmen visible on the Hendrix album cover are, in order: Albert King, BB King, Chuck Berry, Hubert Sumlin, Howlin Wolf, John Lee Hooker, Curtis Mayfield, Robert Johnson, Muddy Waters, Albert Collins, Earl Hooker, Jimmy Reed, Buddy Guy, T-Bone Walker, Ike Turner, Lightnin' Hopkins, Freddie KIng, Robert Lockwood Jnr, Sonny Boy Williamson, Lonnie Johnson, Clarence Gatemouth Brown, Son House, Elmore James, Otis Rush.

MUSIC GENRES

TRACKING THE TRACKS

DJ Mike Raven, who hosted a specialist blues programme on pirate radio and then BBC Radio 1 during the late sixties, issued two LPs presenting an overview of the music with his own helpful comments introducing each track. *The Mike Raven Blues Show* and *The Mike Raven Blues Sampler* have not made it to CD, but vinyl copies do turn up sometimes and are well worth looking out for. Eight out of the twelve tracks on the first LP can be heard on YouTube.

A double CD compilation called *The Story Of The Blues* (Sony 2003) provides a good overview. It is not the same as the a double LP issued in 1969 with the same title, although there are a few tracks in common. A three CD set, *Bluesology* (Not Now Music 2016) is a good anthology of mostly electric blues tracks. There are many other useful blues compilations

A record was issued by CBS in 1970 to go with Paul Oliver's book, also called *Savannah Syncopators.* It is not available on CD. A double LP, *African Journey – A Search For The Roots Of The Blues* was issued by Vanguard in 1975. This covers similar territory, though without making direct comparisons between African and American performances as *Savannah Syncopators* does. It is not available on CD either. There are many CDs available by Ali Farka Touré. *Niafunké* is on World Circuit (1999).

The Lomax prison recordings from the late forties are on two CDs, *Prison Songs Volumes 1 and 2* (Rounder 1997). A majority of the tracks are on *Negro Prison Blues and Songs* (Collectables 2007), which is a little easier to find. The more interesting thirties recordings were originally on a Library Of Congress LP, *Afro-American Spirituals, Work Songs, and Ballads.* This was reissued on a Rounder CD in 1998. Texas Alexander's *Levee Camp Moan* is on the *Mike Raven Blues Show* LP, or else *The Country Blues Volume Two* (Smithsonian Folkways 2007). The track is also included on *Texas Alexander Volume One 1927-1928* (Document 2009).

Two different modern piano recordings of Maggio's *I Got The Blues* can be heard on YouTube, along with a version of it played by string quartet. Both of the 1914 recordings of *Memphis Blues* can also be heard on YouTube. *Memphis Blues* is included with several other Handy compositions on *Louis Armstrong Plays W.C.Handy* (Columbia 2009), which was originally issued in 1954.

Crazy Blues – The Best of Mamie Smith is on Columbia (2004). *Downhearted Blues – Original 1923-1924 Recordings* is on Naxos (2003). A good overview of Bessie Smith's subsequent career is provided by the double CD *Anthology* (Not Now Music 2010). *Complete Recorded Works Volume 1* by Alberta Hunter (Document 2009) includes her recordings of *Downhearted Blues.*

Complete Recorded Works Volume 1 by Sylvester Weaver (Document 1992) includes *Guitar Blues.* The recordings with Sara Martin are on *Sara Martin in Chronological Order Volume 2* (Document 1995). *Guitar Blues* and *Roamin' Blues* are both also included on an expensive Japanese CD called *Guitar Blues* (P-Vine 2002) or can be heard on YouTube. The Ed Andrews tracks are included on *Country Blues Collector's Items 1924-1928* (Document 2009) and can be heard on YouTube.

There are several good compilations of music by Blind Lemon Jefferson, such as *The Rough Guide To Blues Legends – Blind Lemon Jefferson* (World Music Network 2013). Most do not include *I Want To Be Like Jesus In My Heart*, but this one does. *The Rough Guide To Blues Legends – Charley Patton* (World Music Network 2012) is again one of several possible alternatives.

Anthology of the Boogie Woogie Piano (Primo 2007) is a good compilation of all the essential recordings on a double CD. It does not include *Chicago Stomp* by Jimmy Blythe. This is included on another compilation, *Boogie Woogie Blues* (Biograph 1991). *Weary Blues* by the Louisiana Five can be heard on YouTube.

Robert Johnson – The Complete Recordings is a double CD on Sony (2008). *The Best Of Chuck Berry* and *The Essential Bo Diddley* are both on Spectrum (2000). *The Very Best Of The Five Royales*, which includes the group's original recordings of *Think* and *Dedicated To The One I Love* (later covered by James Brown and the Mamas and the Papas respectively), is on Collectables (2004).

The early work of T-Bone Walker can be found on *The Beginning 1929-1946* (Epm 1997), while a good overview of his longer career is provided by *T-Bone Blues – The Essential Recordings Of T-Bone Walker* (Indigo 2000).

Muddy Waters *The Chess Singles Collection* fills a three CD set at a bargain price (Not Now Music 2015). *Muddy Waters At Newport 1960* is on Hallmark (2015). A good collection of B.B.King's fifties recordings can be found on the three CD set *Nothin' But Bad Luck* (Not Now Music 2016), again at a bargain price. *Live At The Regal* is on MCA (1997). King's successful career took him way past the fifties. The best of his later music is well represented by the double CD *His Definitive Greatest Hits* (Universal/Island 1999). The album recorded with Eric Clapton, *Ridin' With The King,* is on Warner Bros (2000).

Howlin' Wolf also has a cheap three CD set, *The Absolutely Essential 3CD Collection* (Big 3 2015). *The Very Best Of John Lee Hooker* is a double CD on Not Now Music (2016). The album that launched his renewed success in 1989 is *The Healer* (Silvertone).

The best introduction to the work of Alexis Korner is the double CD *Kornerstoned – The Alexis Korner Anthology 1954-1983* (Sanctuary

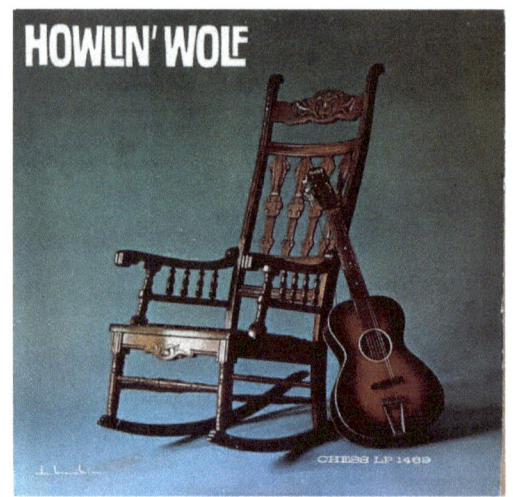

MUSIC GENRES

2008). It is becoming hard to find – a reasonable alternative is *Alexis Korner And... 1961-1972* (Castle 1994). The Rolling Stones *Little Red Rooster* is on the group's definitive three CD collection, *Singles Collection – The London Years* (Abkco2002).

The Very Best Of The Early Years (Union Square Music 2016), credited to Eric Clapton, includes live and studio tracks by the Yardbirds, including *For Your Love* and its B-side *Got To Hurry*, as well as several recordings with Sonny Boy Williamson. The original *Sonny Boy Williamson and the Yardbirds* album is on Repertoire (2007).

The album made by John Mayall and Eric Clapton is *Bluesbreakers – John Mayall With Eric Clapton.* All the CD reissues include the tracks in both mono and stereo, although there is little difference between them. The double CD Deluxe Edition (Universal/Decca 2006) is worth it, for the sake of the bonus tracks, most of which are live. All the albums made by John Mayall during the sixties are highly recommended. There is a decent compilation CD, *The Best Of John Mayall and the Bluesbreakers* (Decca 1997), but it includes almost nothing from Mayall's two best albums, *Bare Wires* and *Blues From Laurel Canyon.*

There is an excellent three CD compilation of tracks from the Blue Horizon label, *The Blue Horizon Story Volume 1 1965-1970* (Sony 2006). It includes the Fleetwood Mac track, *Albatross*. The first LP by Peter Green's Fleetwood Mac, simply titled *Fleetwood Mac* is on Columbia (2004). The greatly inferior second album, *Mr Wonderful,* is also on Columbia (2004). The tracks led by Peter Green are very good, but the album is spoilt by the tracks led by Jeremy Spencer, who delivers several different versions (albeit with different titles and different lyrics) of the same song, Elmore James' *Dust My Blues. The Best Of Peter Green's Fleetwood Mac* (Columbia 2002) includes several non-album singles, one of which is *Albatross.* A little confusingly, the CD also includes Chicken Shack's greatest hit, *I'd Rather Go Blind*, presumably on the grounds that the singer, Christine McVie (then called Christine Perfect), was later a member of Fleetwood Mac; and a much later ambient version of *Albatross,* which has nothing to do with Fleetwood Mac other than the fact that it employs Peter Green to play the notes of his original recording. *The Best Of Peter Green Splinter Group* (Snapper 2002) presents the music of a damaged guitarist thirty years on.

Pretty Girls Everywhere by Otis Spann with Eric Clapton was originally issued on a 1967 compilation LP called *Raw Blues.* A 1987 reissue of this on a London CD is scarce. The track is also included as a bonus on a double CD reissue of two Otis Spann albums, *The Blues Of Otis Spann* and *Cracked Spanner Head* (BGO 2005). *Good To Me As I Am To You* is on Aretha Franklin's *Lady Soul* (Rhino 1995).

The first two albums by the Paul Butterfield Blues Band, the self-titled first LP and *East West*, were issued as a two CD set in 2001 (Warner).

The Jimi Hendrix CD, *Blues* (Sony 2015), gathers together some of Jimi's performances in that genre, including two versions of *Red House*, two versions of *Hear My Train A-Comin'* and an alternate take of *Voodoo Chile* to the one heard on *Electric Ladyland*.

Mirror Man by Captain Beefheart & His Magic Band has been extended for CD. *The Mirror Man Sessions* is on Buddha (1999). *Trout Mask Replica* is on Reprise (2004).

Coltrane Plays The Blues is on Essential Jazz Classics (2011). *Kind Of Blue* by Miles Davis keeps being reissued – it is the best selling jazz album ever made. The most recent issue at the time of writing is on vinyl (Not Now Music 2016). The CD is on Vintage Pleasure (2012). Clearly the album has passed out of Columbia's copyright control. *Drudgery* is on the 1969 Albert Ayler album, *Music Is The Healing Force Of The Universe* (Impulse 2003). *My Angel* is on the 1969 Archie Shepp album, *Blasé* (Charly 1996).

Can Blue Men Sing The Whites is on the Bonzo Dog Doo-Dah Band album, *The Doughnut In Granny's Greenhouse* (Liberty 2007). Fleetwood Mac, Chicken Shack, John Mayall *Can't Fail Blues* is on the double CD, *The Amazing Adventures of The Liverpool Scene* (Esoteric 2009).

Strong Persuader by Robert Cray is on Virgin (1991). The self-titled album by Keb' Mo' is on Okeh/Epic (2004). *Texas Flood* by Stevie Ray Vaughan is on Epic (2013). *Blues Of Desperation* by Joe Bonamassa is on J&R Adventures (2016). All four musicians have made several other albums too.

The blues are the roots and the other musics are the fruits. It's better keeping the roots alive, because it means better fruits from now on. The blues are the roots of all American music. As long as American music survives, so will the blues. *Willie Dixon*

The blues? It's the mother of American music. That's what it is – the source. *B.B.King*

When all the original blues guys are gone, you start to realise that someone has to tend to the tradition. I recognise that I have some responsibility to keep the music alive, and it's a pretty honourable position to be in. *Eric Clapton*

Blues is easy to play, but hard to feel. *Jimi Hendrix*

Fisk Jubilee Singers 1871

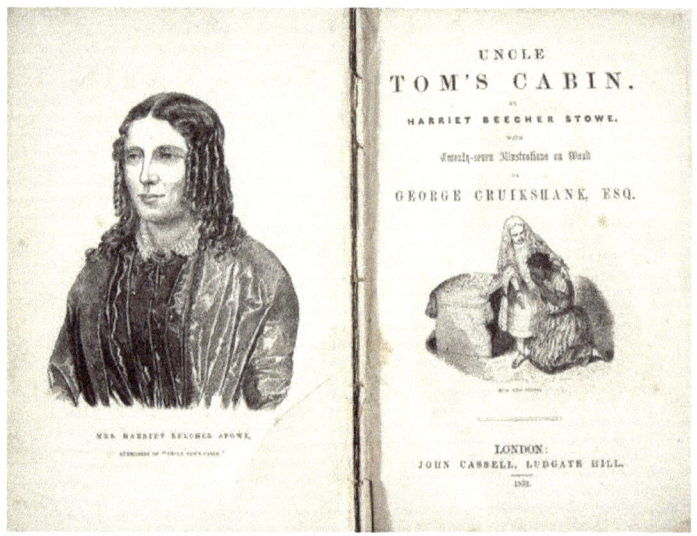

Thomas A. Dorsey also performed as a blues pianist, using the name Georgia Tom. He led a band backing singer Ma Rainey and, working with guitarist Tampa Red, he recorded a huge selling hit in 1928, *It's Tight Like That*. During the thirties, he moved over entirely to gospel music. He was responsible for tutoring singer Mahalia Jackson, who eventually became one of gospel's biggest stars, known as 'the Queen of Gospel'. Her 1947 single, *Move On Up A Little Higher,* sold two million copies.

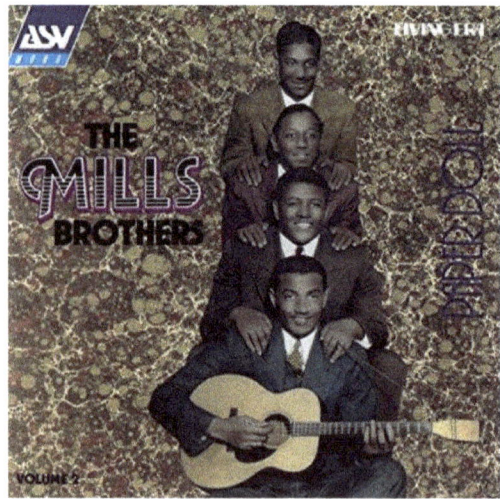

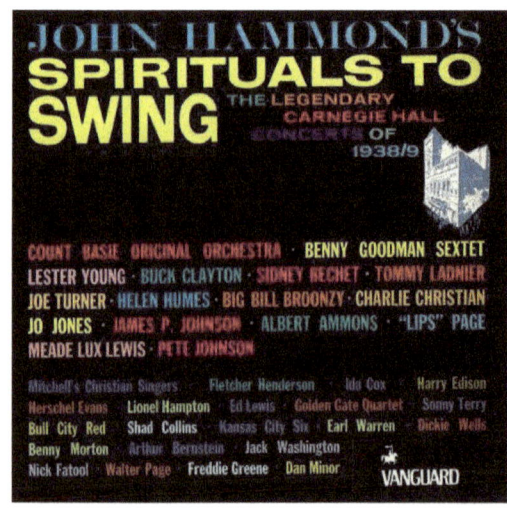

18 SOUL

The religious songs known as spirituals were developed by African-Americans during the time of slavery in the eighteenth and nineteenth centuries. They were first described in the pages of Harriet Beecher Stowe's novel, *Uncle Tom's Cabin,* which was published in 1852 with the aim, in part at least, of drawing her society's attention to the iniquities of slavery. In 1871, a choir of eight black singers and a pianist, the Fisk Jubilee Singers, gave a concert in Cincinnatti, Ohio and included a number of spirituals. They went on to have a very successful career, including a brief performance at the White House and a tour of the UK, which included singing for Queen Victoria. They eventually got to make a record, when four of them performed *Swing Low Sweet Chariot* in 1909.

During the last years of the nineteenth century, barbershops became established within African-American communities as places where men could meet socially. The phenomenon of the barbershop quartet began in this context, with spirituals serving as one of the main kinds of music to enter the repertoire. The Dinwiddie Colored Quartet, based in Virginia, was recorded by Victor in 1902 performing a selection of five spirituals. These were the first gospel music recordings. The Unique Quartette made a number of recordings during the previous decade, beginning in 1890. The sound of the music was similar, but the songs this group performed were not spirituals.

Paul Robeson began performing spirituals in the twenties – his first recording, for Victor in 1925, was *By 'n By (I'm Goin' To Lay Down Dis Heavy Load).* He became a big star as a singer in concert and in musicals, although his anti-racism stance caused him trouble in the US, leading him to having his passport withdrawn for a decade up to 1958. Ironically, he received a Grammy lifetime award twenty-two years after his death in 1976 and was honoured with a postage stamp bearing his image.

The songwriter Thomas A. Dorsey wrote his first religious song in 1922 and was later responsible for some very well-known material, including *Precious Lord Take My Hand* and *Peace In The Valley.* During a 1976 interview with the writer Steve Turner (transcribed in Turner's *An Illustrated History Of Gospel*), Dorsey claimed to be the person who first referred to such compositions as being gospel songs, to distinguish them from hymns. In 1874, however, the white songwriter Philip Bliss had put together a collection he titled *Gospel Songs.* It was undoubtedly Dorsey, however, who made sufficient impact with his songs to justify his frequent appellation as 'the father of gospel music'.

Music entrepreneur John Hammond organised a concert of black American music, *From Spirituals To Swing,* held at New York's Carnegie Hall, just before Christmas 1938. Advertised with the slogan, 'the music that nobody knows', the concert did indeed manage to bring black music to the attention of white America, even if recordings of the event had to wait for twenty years before becoming available. Three gospel acts were included in the line-up – Sister Rosetta Tharpe, whose energetic singing accompanied by her own resonator guitar (electric later) made her a significant influence on the R&B artists to follow, and two quartets, Mitchell's Christian Singers and the Golden Gate Quartet. The concert stage was a new kind of venue for the gospel singers, who made a considerable impact. It was noticeable, however, that Sister Tharpe failed to be included on the LP package when it finally appeared and when a second concert was presented at Carnegie Hall a year after the first, none of the gospel performers were included.

The Mills Brothers were a vocal quartet who chose not to include gospel songs in their repertoire, even though they had sung in church choirs while growing up. As it happened, the boys' parents did indeed own a barbershop, in Piqua, Ohio, where the brothers frequently performed. Signed to Brunswick records in 1930, the Mills Brothers were immediately successful with their first record, *Tiger Rag,* which eventually became a million seller. It began a remarkable run of seventy-one hit records, through to 1968, including four more selling over a million copies each. The biggest hit, *Paper Doll* from 1942, was claimed to have sold eleven million copies by 1959. John Mills died from

THE FIRST TIME

The first record on which the singers utter the phrase "doo-wop, doo-wop" is described on the website of the Doo-Wop Society (part of www.electricearl.com) as being *Never*, issued in 1954 by the otherwise unremarkable Dundees. The first hit record using the phrase is claimed as being *When You Dance* by the Turbans, which reached number three in the R&B chart at the end of 1955. The Turbans, it must be mentioned, stayed absolutely true to their chosen name in their choice of dress for publicity photographs. *Let The Boogie Woogie Roll* by Clyde McPhatter and the Drifters pre-dates both of these records, as it was recorded in 1953, but it was unfortunately not released until 1960. Meanwhile, however, what sounds suspiciously like "doobie doobie doo a-doo-wop" can be heard on the Clovers record *Good Lovin'*, which did manage to get released in 1953 – and reached number two in the R&B charts. The first time that 'doo-wop' appeared in print, in reference to a style of music, was in 1961, when Chuck Davis, writing in the *Chicago Defender,* used it to describe *Blue Moon,* the record by the Marcels.

The soundtrack album to the 1973 film *American Graffiti,* which is concerned with an eventful day in the lives of a group of American teenagers at the beginning of the sixties, includes nineteen doo-wop songs in its collection of forty-one tracks, played on the radio during the film and chosen to define the era. One suspects that a real radio station of the time would not have played so many oldies, as most of the songs would have been for real teenagers, but the film does serve to underline how doo-wop was a fundamental part of rock 'n' roll. This may have come as a surprise to rock 'n' roll fans in the UK, where doo-wop made very little impression, apart from a few hits by the Platters and the Coasters.

One doo-wop song included in *American Graffiti* emerges as one of the most sublime pieces of music of its era – or any era. *I Only Have Eyes For You* by the Flamingos shows off the art of the genre to perfection, as the high tenor voice of Nate Nelson is cushioned by the layered harmonies of the rest of the group. The song reached number three in the R&B chart in the summer of 1959 and was a big national US hit too. When Art Garfunkel decided to cover the song, taking it into the top twenty in the *Billboard* Hot Hundred in 1975, and to number one in the UK, he modelled his own vocal on that of Nate Nelson. Sadly, however, the vital "d'-bub-sh'-bub"s and the soaring falsetto counterpart of the Flamingos version were missing.

To be fair, the Beach Boys owed as much to the Four Freshmen for their vocal harmonies as they did to doo-wop. The Four Freshmen were a group of white singers inspired by modern jazz rather than by R&B and they worked extensively with band-leader Stan Kenton during the fifties. Their 1960 arrangement of *Their Hearts Were Full Of Spring* was copied by Brian Wilson for the Beach Boys recording of *A Young Man Is Gone i*n 1963.

Berry Gordy outside the Motown headquarters in Detroit

The first release by the Miracles was *Got A Job,* recorded in January 1958. The song was conceived as an answer to the Silhouettes' big hit of the time, *Get A Job*. The hit original is something of a doo-wop classic and the Miracles' response is itself very much in the doo-wop style. Berry Gordy, who produced *Got A Job* for very little return, was advised by lead singer Smokey Robinson to start his own label, which Gordy proceeded to do.

The elevation of Diana Ross to lead singer of the Supremes had the effect of relegating Florence Ballard to support singer in the group she had been responsible for starting. Suffering from depression, she was ousted from the group altogether in 1967. A solo career was not a success, and in 1976, reduced to a state of poverty, she died of a heart attack, aged thirty-two. The sad story is told in detail in Stuart Cosgrove's book, *Detroit '67 – The Year That Changed Soul.*

pneumonia in 1936 and was replaced in the group by his father, also called John. A similar vocal quartet achieved considerable success in the wake of the Mills Brothers – the Ink Spots gained a pair of million selling hits during 1946, following an earlier record as successful as this, *Into Each Life Some Rain Must Fall,* issued in 1944, where the group sang in support of Ella Fitzgerald. Their biggest hit of all, however, was *If I Didn't Care,* issued in 1939 as one of their first 78s, and becoming the tenth best selling single ever, as of May 2017, with sales of around nineteen million. According to Wikipedia, Decca paid the group less than five thousand dollars out of the resulting revenue.

The Ravens made their first recordings in 1946 and, although these were not immediately successful, the group scored several top ten hits in the R&B charts between 1948 and 1952. Clearly taking the Mills Brothers as their inspiration, the Ravens nevertheless changed the vocal group formula by bringing their bass singer, Jimmy Ricks, to the fore. There was a humorous quality to Ricks' voice, quite different to the sedate tones of Paul Robeson, especially when set against the falsetto singing of Maithe Marshall and the sprightly jump-jazz rhythms that the group favoured. In this way, the Ravens created the template for a vocal group music that came to be called doo-wop. A vital extra ingredient was the group's introduction of choreographed dance steps, performed on stage while they sang. The Ravens' doo-wop version of *White Christmas,* an R&B hit in 1948, directly inspired a similar treatment of the song by Clyde McPhatter and the Drifters, an R&B hit in 1954. The Drifters' interpretation, arguably more distinctive than that of the Ravens, was closely followed by Elvis Presley, when he recorded the song in 1957.

The success of the Ravens inspired a rash of other vocal groups to name themselves after birds and in September 1948, one of these, the Orioles, scored a number one hit in the R&B charts with a doo-wop ballad, *Too Soon To Know.* It was a sound that proceeded to dominate American pop music through the fifties, being accepted as an essential part of rock 'n' roll, even if its approach was not at all similar to that of Chuck Berry, Bill Haley, or Elvis Presley's rockabilly.

The more extreme vocal mannerisms characteristic of doo-wop became smoothed out as the fifties drew to a close, to the point where the genre could be heard to have evolved in the sixties into two new styles of music altogether. On the one hand were the Four Tops and the Supremes, the Shirelles, the Crystals, and the Impressions – vocal groups signed to the Motown label or appealing to much the same market. Many of these were groups of female singers, who had not much featured in doo-wop or the gospel music that preceded it. On the other hand were the Four Seasons and the Beach Boys, both of which retained a rather greater fondness for doo-wop vocal effects, at least in their early years.

The Motown record company was founded in Detroit by songwriter Berry Gordy in January 1959, using an eight hundred dollar loan from his parents. He had proved his musical worth by writing three big hits for Jackie Wilson – *Reet Petite, To Be Loved,* and *Lonely Teardrops* – but the royalties had yet to materialise. Berry released a local issue of *Come To Me* by Marv Johnson (subsequently a national hit on the United Artists label) as the first record on a label he called Tamla. The name was chosen, surprisingly, as a reference to the song *Tammy,* which had been a hit for Debbie Reynolds in 1957. Success followed quite quickly. *Money* by Barrett Strong was issued in August 1959 as a joint venture with the Anna label run by Gordy's sister, Gwen, and reached number two in the R&B chart, number twenty-three in the national chart. *Shop Around* by the Miracles was issued in October 1960 and reached number one in the R&B chart, number two in the national chart. *Please Mr. Postman* by the Marvelettes was issued in August 1961 and reached number one in both charts.

Gordy's response was to start another label, named Motown after the parent company. The first release was *My Beloved* by the Satintones, in September 1961, although this was not a hit. The first records by the Supremes were on the Motown label. Several singles were released without much success, until *Where Did Our Love Go,* issued in June 1964, hit number one in the R&B chart. The group was formed by Florence Ballard in 1958 as a quartet called the Primettes, intended as a sister act to a male quartet called the Primes. In due course, the Primes became the Temptations and both groups were signed by Berry Gordy in 1961.

THE FIRST TIME

The Marvin Gaye LP is not a typical Motown release, as it features a selection of jazz tunes. They include some rather eccentric instrumental work in places, such as the chaotic drumming on *Love For Sale,* which comes courtesy of Marvin Gaye himself. He made two more LPs in the same style after this, *Hello Broadway* (1964) and *A Tribute To The Great Nat King Cole* (1965), before being persuaded that his own soul music was better!

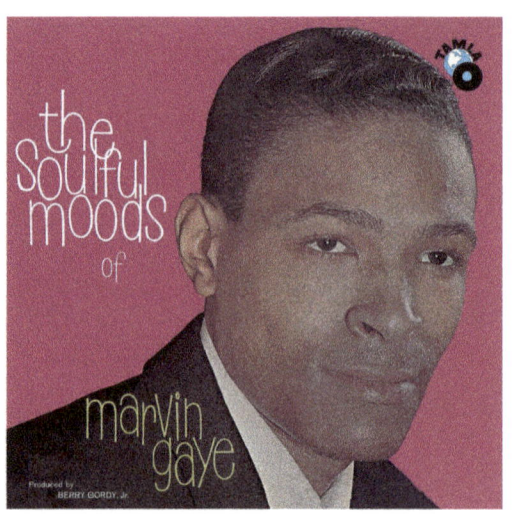

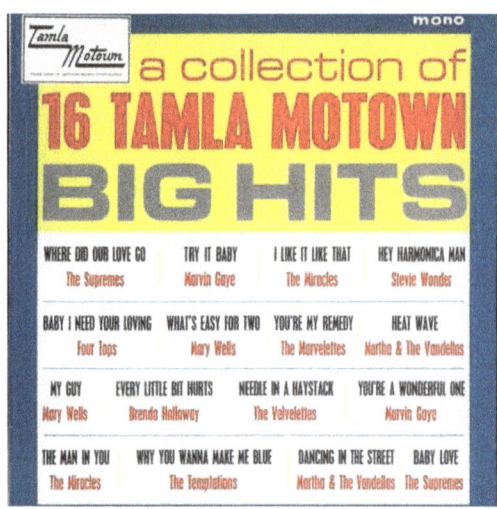

When Sam Cooke was shot dead in a motel room he had booked with a prostitute, there were those who thought that this was his retribution for turning his back on gospel music. Towards the end of 1957, Little Richard moved in the opposite direction, recording gospel music and preaching sermons. In 1962, he returned to playing rock 'n' roll, having discovered that he still had a considerable following, but nobody attempted to shoot him.

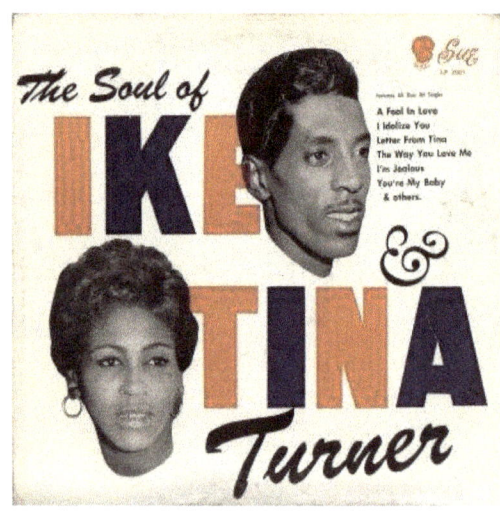

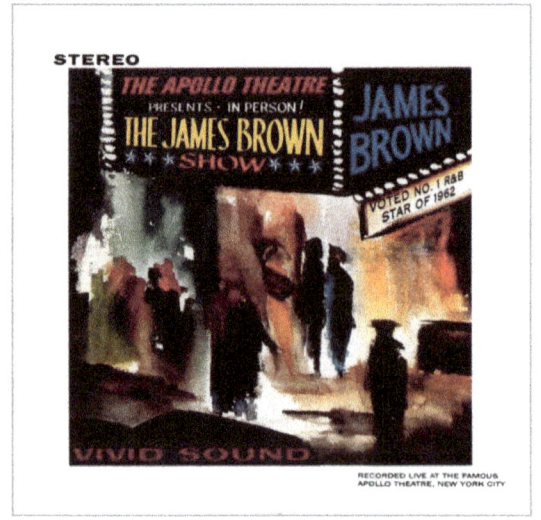

MUSIC GENRES

The first Tamla LPs were issued in June 1961 – *Hi! We're The Miracles* and *The Soulful Moods Of Marvin Gaye* – although the sales were not spectacular. Nevertheless, by the end of 1963, Motown had the third highest singles sales in the US, behind RCA and CBS, a remarkable achievement for a company that was only five years old.

In the UK, the Beatles included three Motown songs on their late 1963 second LP, *With The Beatles,* one of which was a powerful version of *Money*. Motown records were issued on different labels – London, Fontana, and Oriole – and when the company gained its first hit, *My Guy* by Mary Wells, which entered the chart in May 1964, this was on Stateside. Two more Stateside hits followed towards the end of 1964, by the Supremes. *Where Did Our Love Go* reached number three and *Baby Love* came closely behind and went to number one. In March 1965, the company finally set up its own UK label, calling it Tamla Motown, with the single *Stop In The Name Of Love* by the Supremes and the various artists LP, *A Collection Of 16 Tamla Motown Big Hits,* as the first releases.

Back in 1954, it was Ray Charles who came up with the idea of rewriting old spirituals and gospel songs, taking out the overtly religious references, but still singing them in the inspirational style used in the African-American churches. Thus *Talkin' 'Bout Jesus* became *Talkin' 'Bout You*, *This Little Light Of Mine* became *This Little Girl Of Mine, You Better Leave That Liar Alone* became *You Better Leave That Woman Alone*, and *How Jesus Died* was completely retitled, as *Lonely Avenue*. *I Gotta Woman,* created in this way (from I've Got A Saviour – Way Across Jordan), was released as a single in January 1955 and was a number one hit in the R&B chart. Further hits in the same style followed, though not all derived from actual gospel songs – *Drown In My Own Tears, Hallelujah I Love Her So,* and *Lonely Avenue*, all of them doing well in the R&B chart through 1956. The biggest hit of all was *What'd I Say*, driven by the novel sound of the electric piano, with Charles trading ecstatic lines with his backing singers, the Raelettes. Split over two sides of a single, the song got to number one in the R&B charts in the summer of 1959 and became Ray Charles's first big national hit too, reaching number six. Meanwhile, James Brown, adopting the same preaching style of singing, gained a big R&B hit in 1956 with *Please Please Please* and an even bigger one in 1958 with *Try Me*. Little Richard employed the same kind of singing too, on his numerous rock 'n' roll hits through the fifties, beginning with *Tutti Frutti* at the end of 1955.

An LP issued in 1958 by Ray Charles and Milt Jackson was titled *Soul Brothers,* although this was a jazz album, with Charles playing piano and alto saxophone and not singing. Obviously 'soul' was a term very familiar to gospel music singers. The lead singer of the highly regarded Soul Stirrers, Sam Cooke, decided to take advantage of the market he could see had been opened up by Ray Charles and left the group. Cooke's singing was less histrionic than that of Ray Charles or James Brown, but no less heartfelt. His first solo single, *You Send Me,* was a number one hit in both the R&B and the national charts. In this context it is not surprising that 'soul' began to be used as a term for the music, although it would appear that this did not happen until 1961. *The Soulful Moods of Marvin Gaye* was released in that year and so was an LP called *The Soul Of Ike And Tina Turner.*

In May 1963, King records released an album of music taken from a James Brown live performance at the Apollo Theatre in Harlem, New York. Brown had been trying for some time to persuade Syd Nathan, the boss of King records, that a live recording would be a good idea. Faced with Nathan's continued intransigence, Brown decided to finance a recording himself. He selected the performance due to take place on Wednesday October 24th 1962 as the best choice. This was the last show in a run that had started the previous Friday, with five performances per day, and it was likely that the momentum would produce something special. Hearing the tape, with music that was dominated by a nearly eleven minute version of one of Brown's biggest hits, *Lost Someone,* delivered as if it was a rapturous sermon, Nathan relented. The resulting LP carried the wording *The Apollo Theatre Presents – In Person! The James Brown Show* on the front cover, *James Brown 'Live' At The Apollo* on the back. Driven by listener requests, the black radio stations took to playing the entire album, as if it was a single, something that had never happened before. *Live At The Apollo* stayed in the national pop LP chart for an astonishing sixty-six weeks, peaking at number two. The sleeve notes shouted, "This is without a doubt one of the most exciting albums ever recorded at a live performance", and it appeared that millions o f record buyers agreed.

THE FIRST TIME

The Rolling Stones covered *You Better Move On* and so did the Hollies, while another of Arthur Alexander's songs, *Anna,* was recorded by the Beatles. Yet another, *Every Day I Have To Cry,* was covered by Dusty Springfield. Since Alexander's own version of *Anna* was his only substantial hit, one would imagine that the songwriting royalties came in very useful, although Alexander did spend the whole of the eighties working as a bus driver.

Otis Redding at Monterey with the MGs

The first record issued by the musicians who became the Who was a single coupling *Zoot Suit* with *I'm The Face*, issued in 1964, and credited to the High Numbers. Written by the group's manager, Peter Meaden, both tracks were very thinly disguised re-writes of original soul songs. A reissue of the single scraped into the bottom of the top fifty in 1980 – the original sold hardly at all.

MUSIC GENRES

Towards the end of 1961 and in the summer of 1962, a pair of rhythm and blues instrumentals became huge hits in the R&B and the national charts. Both *Last Night* by the Mar-Keys and *Green Onions* by Booker T and the MG's (the rhythm section of the Mar-Keys) were little more than riffs, but played with drive and with feeling. The musicians involved were session players at the Stax studios in Memphis. The Stax record company was started in 1959, using the name Satellite Records and primarily covering country music. It began to shift to rhythm and blues and, following a distribution deal with Atlantic in 1961, it switched almost entirely to that music. Towards the end of 1961, Satellite changed to Stax, after objections were raised by an established Californian company that was also using the original name. The Memphis recording studio was set up in 1960 and first used to make the single *Cause I Love You* by the father and daughter act, Rufus and Carla Thomas. This was not a national hit, but sold well locally.

Otis Redding recorded *These Arms Of Mine* for Stax at the beginning of 1963, having previously made a couple of singles for other companies without any success. The Stax single was issued on a new subsidiary label, Volt, and Redding was rewarded with a top twenty R&B hit. Gradually increasing his popularity and impact from record to record, Otis Redding achieved his biggest success at this time with an album, *Otis Blue*. Released in the autumn of 1965, the LP reached number one in the R&B chart and was a big seller in the UK too, reaching number six in the album chart. He was added to the line-up of the Monterey Pop Festival in June 1967, as the first soul act to achieve major cross-over success. He finally achieved a number one hit single in the national chart in early 1968, reaching number three in the UK, with *The Dock Of The Bay*. Sadly, the achievement was posthumous. Otis Redding died in a plane crash in December 1967 – the recording session responsible for *The Dock Of The Bay* was his last.

Wilson Pickett recorded his first big hit, *In The Midnight Hour*, at the Memphis studio in May 1965, but his later records were made in Alabama, at the FAME studio in Muscle Shoals. FAME (for Florence Alabama Music Enterprises) was founded in the town of Florence but moved to Muscle Shoals in 1961. It followed a similar path to the Stax studio, beginning with country and moving to R&B and soul. The change of direction was confirmed when local singer Arthur Alexander recorded *You Better Move On* and had a small hit with it, in late 1961.

In January 1967, Aretha Franklin was signed to Atlantic records and brought to the Muscle Shoals studio to record. *I Never Loved A Man* was issued as a single and became a huge hit, kick-starting Ms Franklin's career as the most acclaimed female soul singer of all. The daughter of a well-known preacher in Detroit, Rev.Cecil L.Franklin, Aretha had a background singing gospel music. She recorded an album, *Songs Of Faith*, in 1956, when she was fourteen. She was signed to Columbia in 1960 by John Hammond, who tried to turn her into a jazz-pop artist, but with limited success. Her re-launch as a soul singer with Atlantic seemed like a dramatic new direction, but it was in reality a return to the music of her roots. A live double LP recorded by Aretha Franklin in 1972, *Amazing Grace*, comprising a complete set of gospel songs, proved once again how soul and gospel were, in musical terms, two aspects of the same style. *Amazing Grace* became not only Aretha Franklin's biggest selling album, but also the biggest ever selling gospel album.

In the UK, a number of fashion-conscious young people in London in the mid sixties, the mods, discovered that they rather liked soul music. When two mod groups made their first recordings in 1965, it was inevitable that they would attempt some soul covers. The debut LP by the Who, *My Generation*, included two James Brown Songs. They were by far the weakest tracks on the album, because singer Roger Daltrey was unable to match Brown's histrionics. With Pete Townshend's song writing becoming ever more accomplished, the group did not try to do anything similar again (although a few years later, Daltrey had developed into a much more powerful singer and could have handled it). The Small Faces were more convincing, because in Steve Marriott, the group had a singer with a genuinely soulful voice. The group covered Sam Cooke on the self-titled debut album in early 1966 and included versions of two Motown songs and two from Memphis, on the collection of hits and left-overs released as *From The Beginning*. Many of the group's own songs sounded like products of the Memphis or Muscle Shoals studios when sung by Marriott, most notably the group's first success, *What'cha Gonna Do About It* (with a riff borrowed from Atlantic soul singer

THE FIRST TIME

Sly Stone had previously worked as a producer. Among his clients were the Beau Brummels, one of the most notable American responses to the British beat invasion. Stone was very familiar, therefore, with the methodology of rock music.

Producer Jimmy Miller, who worked with the Spencer Davis Group in the mid-sixties, had the idea of pretending that one of his productions was a rare soul import from America. *Incense* was credited to the Anglos, and released on one of the subsidiary labels run by Chris Blackwell, the proprietor of Island Records. Miller employed Stevie Winwood, the singer with Spencer Davis, to deliver the impassioned lead vocal. Winwood was happy to go along with the deceit and denied any involvement in the recording, for years afterwards, when asked. He did, however, use the pseudonym of Steve Anglo when recording with John Mayall and others. The aural evidence is unmistakeable, despite attempts over the years by various scribes to deny the obvious. These soul fans could not believe that such a soulful performance could possibly be the work of a white teenager from Birmingham. Winwood's brother, Muff, however, the bass player with the Spencer Davis Group and subsequently a producer, was unequivocal when quoted in the sleeve notes to a CD compilation of music by his former band, *Eight Gigs A Week*. He states that Stevie Winwood definitely was the lead singer on *Incense*. The subterfuge was in vain, however. The single was a success in the clubs, but despite numerous reissues on different labels through the sixties, somehow managed to avoid the charts.

When John Peel played a track from the newly released LP by Big Brother and the Holding Company, *Cheap Thrills*, on his influential BBC Radio programme, in August 1968, he was clearly unaware that the singer, Janis Joplin, was white. Impressed by the apparent blend of hard rock with soul, he commented that it was a pity other soul singers did not sound like that.

Vanilla Fudge was best known for an extravagant cover version of the Supremes' hit, *You Keep Me Hangin' On*. The group transformed the Motown dance tune into a psychedelic extravaganza, slowing the music down and shaping it around a moody Hammond organ part and a driving rock riff. Edited for release as a single in 1967, a year after the Supremes' original, the song was a big hit, though not quite as big as its predecessor. Had Vanilla Fudge been a black group, then its recording might have been hailed as taking Motown back into the church. It is not too great a stretch to imagine that Vanilla Fudge's music was an influence on the similarly ambitious arrangements carried out by Isaac Hayes a couple of years later on his albums *Hot Buttered Soul, The Isaac Hayes Movement,* and *To Be Continued.* Undoubtedly too, the group's approach would have been noted by Joe Cocker when deciding to make a distinctive cover version of the Beatles' *With A Little Help From My Friends*.

A much later blending of traditional Irish music with Southern, Memphis soul was achieved by Dexys Midnight Runners on their 1982 album, *Too-Rye-Ay*. The music was worthwhile, though representing a less visionary fusion than that of Van Morrison. It was also achieved at some cost to the strengths of the original Dexys band, which had presented a particularly powerful updating of the Otis Redding style, driven by an extremely dynamic brass section.

Solomon Burke) and the number one hit, *All Or Nothing*.

Of course, the mod groups were not the only ones to be influenced by soul music – indeed there was hardly a UK group in the mid sixties that was not. The term 'blue-eyed soul', however, was first used in the US with reference to the music of the Righteous Brothers. The duo achieved a massive first hit at the beginning of 1965 with a single produced by Phil Spector, *You've Lost That Lovin' Feelin'*, but had already issued an album titled *Some Blue-Eyed Soul.*. Just to confuse the issue, the hit single also reached number three in the R&B chart.

The lead singer with a successful Northern Irish beat group, Them, decided to try a solo career towards the end of the sixties. Van Morrison's album, *Astral Weeks,* released in November 1968, presented a unique fusion. Jazz rhythms and instrumentation were combined with folk guitar playing, while Morrison's voice glided over the top, adopting an emotional, improvised approach, with lyrics following the Bob Dylan school of poetic surrealism. The result was spiritual and soulful, albeit a kind of soul that had little to do with the sound of Memphis or Detroit. *Astral Weeks* was a critical but not a commercial success, but subsequent albums built on its achievements, while experimenting with the instrumental detail, and all became steady sellers. A typically free-floating track from 1970 was titled *Caledonia Soul Music*. Although this was not released other than on a bootleg recording, Morrison kept the name for the band he formed in 1973, the Caledonia Soul Orchestra. It was most appropriate. (Strictly speaking, 'Caledonia', deriving from the Romans, refers to Scotland, but Morrison was choosing to extend the name to all the Gaelic peoples, which include Ireland).

The influences flowed in the other direction as well. Sly and the Family Stone added a flavour of rock music to the LP *Stand!* issued in May 1969 and got to play a set at the Woodstock festival in August. Meanwhile, the Temptations, under the guidance of producer Norman Whitfield, also experimented with rock guitars and a harder sound. The process was begun with *Cloud Nine,* issued as a single in February 1969 and distinguished by driving bass and drums and a wah-wah guitar owing much to the playing of Jimi Hendrix. It climaxed with the LP *Masterpiece,* issued in February 1973, and presenting a dazzling pot pourri of wah-wah guitar, swirling orchestral strings and brass, and multiple vocal lines. It was an impressive achievement, although in truth the real masterpiece had been made a few months earlier, with the magnificent *Papa Was A Rollin' Stone*, a thoroughly justified number one US hit.

Stevie Wonder's first Motown record, *I Call It Pretty Music,* was issued in the summer of 1962, when Wonder was just twelve years old. Reaching the age of twenty-one in 1971, his contract had to be renegotiated and he was able to gain unprecedented artistic freedom for himself. There followed a run of five albums, one of them a double, that presented a body of songwriting and performance that was amongst the finest to be found in any genre of music. *Music Of My Mind,* issued in March 1972, *Talking Book* (October 1972), *Innervisions* (August 1973), *Fulfillingness' First Finale* (July 1974), and *Songs In The Key Of Life* (a double LP with an additional bonus single, September 1976) were put together like the best of the Beatles' LPs, with a variety of song structures and moods and an attention to detail in the arrangements, in order to make each song as distinctive as it could be. Stevie Wonder's ambition on these records did nothing to hinder their commercial success – all except the first sold a million copies or more, with the last of the series achieving ten million sales. Several tracks were released as singles, of which five reached number one in the US national charts, with a further three appearing in the top ten. These sales were achieved because Stevie Wonder's records were appealing as much to the rock audience as to his soul music following.

Guitarist Jeff Beck was invited to play a solo on a track from *Talking Book, Lookin' For Another Pure Love.* In return, Stevie Wonder gave his song *Superstition,* also included on the LP, to Beck, in the sense that he agreed to allow the guitarist to release it as a single first. The song appeared on the album made by a new group formed with the rhythm section of Vanilla Fudge, *Beck Bogert Appice,* in 1973. Berry Gordy, however, who knew a hit record when he heard one, insisted that Stevie Wonder should release *Superstition* and forget about his promise. The single shot to the top of the national charts, giving Wonder his first number one since his debut hit, *Fingertips,* back in 1963.

THE FIRST TIME

Some of the tracks on the two live LPs made by Kool and the Gang in 1971 flirt with jazz, but sound very tame compared to what was happening in the real thing at the time. The funk groups, of course, following the example of James Brown, were used to playing instrumental solos. Motown artists were not. Much later, in 1990, Maceo Parker, the saxophonist famous for his crucial role within the James Brown bands, recorded a vibrant jazz album he titled *Roots Revisited,* where Parker originals rubbed shoulders with Charles Mingus and jazz-era Ray Charles.

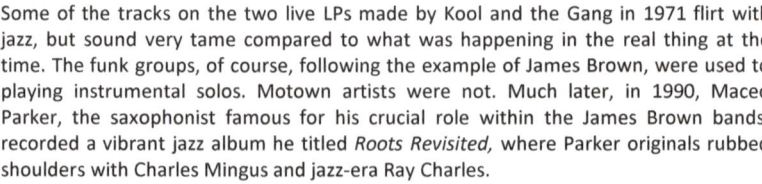

If this was a history of soul music, rather than an account of musical firsts, it would be necessary to examine the rise of Philadelphia soul in the seventies. The fact of the matter is, however, that artists like the O'Jays, Harold Melvin and the Blue Notes, and the Three Degrees occupied an identical position in the music of the seventies as the Four Tops, Smokey Robinson and the Miracles, and the Supremes had done in the music of the sixties. The orchestral arrangements of Gamble and Huff, though a little more lush, were from the same mould as those of Holland-Dozier-Holland before them.

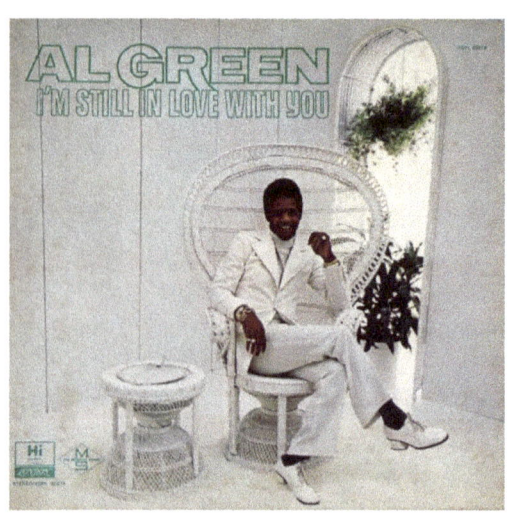

Quincy Jones had first produced a pop record in the spring of 1963. *It's My Party* by Lesley Gore became a number one hit in the US, top ten in the UK. Several other hits for Lesley Gore followed, all of them produced by Quincy Jones.

Herbie Hancock was the star guest on *Songs In The Key Of Life,* providing more than a touch of jazz fusion on the song, *As.* No doubt inspired by this, Wonder made an uncompromising jazz fusion track without Hancock, the instrumental (bar a few lines of wordless backing vocals), *Contusion,* in which guitarist Mike Sembello was given a starring role. Several jazz musicians had previously dabbled with soul music, but this was arguably the first time that a soul artist had moved so definitely in the other direction.

Even before Stevie Wonder, Marvin Gaye had taken his own music into the territory of what might be described, by analogy with similar developments in rock music, as progressive soul. His album *What's Going On* was released in May 1971 and presented a unified song cycle, with tracks linked together musically and intended to provide a commentary on the problems of contemporary American society. The music had an attractive lightness in its rhythms, the polar opposite of funk, and it had a spacious quality to its arrangements, which were dominated by the sound of Marvin Gaye's voice – singing lead and supplying some of his own backing vocals. Gaye had to contend with some resistance from Berry Gordy before the album could be issued, but it became his first top ten album, eventually selling over two million copies, and it was hailed as a masterpiece by the critics. Three tracks released as singles were also substantial hits, although neither album nor singles managed to do much business in the UK.

For Marvin Gaye, the social theme of *What's Going On* was a project, one that did not need to be repeated. His next album, *Let's Get It On,* released in 1973, concerned itself with sex. It was another very successful record as far as sales were concerned, but it was much less interesting. It was left to Curtis Mayfield to continue making records with a conscience, such as his albums *Back To The World* from 1973 and *There's No Place Like America Today* from 1975. He had previously been responsible for the soundtrack to a gritty 1972 thriller, *Superfly,* set in the ghetto, where the serious message in the lyrics of his songs stood in noticeable contrast to the escapism of the film itself. Earlier still, as a member of the Impressions in the sixties, Mayfield had been responsible for black power anthems like *People Get Ready, Keep On Pushing,* and *Mighty Mighty Spade And Whitey.*

The Southern, Memphis soul was brought back into prominence in the seventies by the success of Al Green. The singer slowed the music down and favoured songs that strung a melody line out over the groove and chords that did not change much, in the manner of James Brown. Al Green scored a significant hit with *Tired Of Being Alone* and a number one with *Let's Stay Together,* both of them in 1971, but he did as well with albums like *I'm Still In Love With You* (1972) and *Call Me* (1973). Just as his career began to falter, he made the opposite move to Sam Cooke and began working as a preacher, while making only gospel music records..

Towards the end of the seventies, the primary focus for black music moved away from soul and towards the realms of rap, hip hop, and house. Two notable artists, however, bucked the trend and became the most successful of all. As an eleven year old, Michael Jackson sang with his brothers in the Jackson Five, achieving a number one hit with their first Motown release, *I Want You Back,* at the beginning of 1970. He gained some solo success in the following years, then in 1979, at the age of twenty-one, he hired the veteran jazz musician and producer, Quincy Jones, to produce an album. *Off The Wall* emerged as an attractive pop record, varied, but with many of the tracks based on dance rhythms. Without being startlingly innovative, the LP nevertheless sounded utterly contemporary and it proceeded to become an enormous success, eventually selling an estimated twenty million copies. The two albums that followed, *Thriller* in 1982 and *Bad* in 1987, were also produced by Quincy Jones and employed the same danceable pop formula. *Thriller* became the best-selling album of all time, with estimated sales of sixty-five million copies. *Bad* could not manage to match this astonishing statistic, but sold over thirty million copies nevertheless. The several tracks from these albums that were chosen to be released as singles were all big hits too, ten of them reaching number one in the US. It was Michael Jackson, therefore, who turned black music into the dominant pop music form that it has since become.

Prince Rogers Nelson, known simply as Prince (apart from a few years in the nineties when he decided that an unpronounceable symbol should be his name) issued his first record in April 1978, the album *For You.* He made an

THE FIRST TIME

Prince placed considerable emphasis on his Hendrix-inspired guitar playing. It was the Isley Brothers who first introduced this kind of extrovert guitar into soul music, unless we consider that this was really done by Jimi Hendrix himself on his album *Band Of Gypsys*. Younger brother Ernie Isley joined the band in time for the 1973 album, *3 + 3*, and used his guitar to greatly increase the impact of songs like *That Lady* and *Summer Breeze*. Jimi Hendrix had played with the original trio during 1964 and 1965. *Testify*, recorded in March 1964, is a quite startling fusion of rock and soul predating by several years the forays of the Temptations and Sly and the Family Stone into this territory. It was not a hit, however, and failed to attract attention at the time.

Seal is a British singer. Two other singers from Britain are particularly impressive soul performers, but struggle somewhat to find the world acclaim their talent deserves. Both have achieved some success, however, and have managed to maintain lengthy careers. Heather Small was lead singer with M People, who gained a number of big hits during the nineties. She almost stole the show with her contribution to the various artists charity single from 1997, *Perfect Day*. Beverley Knight has had several hit albums and singles since her debut in 1995, but nothing higher than a number seven (the 2002 album, *Who I Am*). Touring in support of Morcheeba in 1998, she also stole the show.

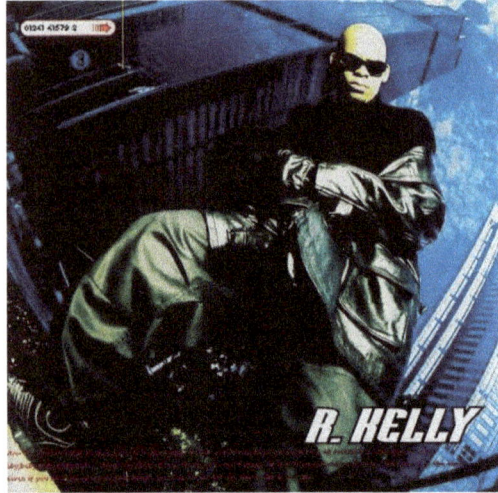

Beyoncé's sprawling masterpiece of an album from 2016, *Lemonade*, displays an ambition and an emotional and musical depth not often found in the work of artists marketed as pop. It draws on a wide range of genres, from blues and gospel to poetry, rap, and the avant garde, in the way that the Beatles used to do. It is presented as a thoroughly twenty-first century artefact, however, complete with a bonus DVD that delivers a visual package as the most satisfying way of experiencing the album. Half a century on from *Sgt Pepper*, the popular music world has become far more compartmentalised than it ever was in the Beatles' time. *Lemonade* was the best selling album of 2016, and yet it is probably too much to hope that it will acquire a similar status to that of its illustrious predecessor. But it deserves to.

album per year after that, increasing his sales and his popularity with each one, until his breakthrough as an international success was achieved with *Purple Rain,* issued in 1984. The album was accompanied by a film, which provided a useful source of promotional videos, and it was surprisingly inventive for such a popular record. The title track, in particular, was an impressive fusion of gospel-styled preaching with hard rock rhythms and guitar. It had an anthemic chorus and a thrilling lead guitar solo and was extended to nearly nine minutes by the addition of a partly synthesized orchestral coda. To all intents and purposes, this was a piece of progressive rock, capable of standing proud next to the work of King Crimson and Genesis.

In 1982, the specialist Billboard chart that had used the title 'Soul Singles' since 1969, was renamed as 'Black Singles'. Then, in 1990, it was renamed again as 'R&B Singles' – reverting to the name that had been applied in the years before soul music was invented. This was no more than an acknowledgement of the fact that the music of Michael Jackson, Prince, and their contemporaries was not really soul music at all, despite its roots within the genre. Black music stars in the twenty-first century, like Beyoncé and R.Kelly, are referred to as R&B artists, not soul singers, and when someone like Seal decides to issue an album such as *Soul* (in 2008), it is presented as a deliberate tribute to a past golden age.

TRACKING THE TRACKS

Early recordings by the Fisk Jubilee Singers are to be found on the CD *In Bright Mansions* (Curb Records 2003). *Swing Low Sweet Chariot* is not included. This can be found on a CD of the same name, which comprises the group's recordings made in 1909 to 1911. It is hard to find on CD, but available as a download. The spirituals recorded by the Dinwiddie Colored Quartet are included on *The Earliest Negro Vocal Quartets 1894-1928* (Document 1991). *Mama's Black Baby Boy,* recorded by the Unique Quartette in 1893, can be heard on YouTube. There are also some later recordings, from 1921, which are spirituals.

There are several compilations of Paul Robeson songs available, but few of them include *By 'n By*. One that does include the song is *Negro Spirituals (And More)* (Discmedi Blau 2010). *Precious Lord – Recordings Of The Great Gospel Songs Of Thomas A.Dorsey* is on Sony (1994). *It's Tight Like That* is included on a various artist compilation of early country blues tracks – *A Handful Of Riffs – Blues Guitar Pioneers* (Catfish 1999).

Gospel – The Absolutely Essential 3CD Collection (Big 3 2011) provides a superb overview of gospel music's founding artists, including Sister Rosetta Tharpe, the Soul Stiirrers, the Golden Gate Quartet, and Mahalia Jackson's *Move On Up A Little Higher*.

The *Spirituals To Swing* recordings have been issued on CD a few times, but they are not currently available other than as very expensive collectors' items. Vinyl issues from 1972 on Vanguard turn up second-hand reasonably often and are very much cheaper.

The Very Best Of The Mills Brothers is on Universal/Spectrum (1997). *The Ultimate Collection* by the Ink Spots, a double CD on One Day Music (2011) contains all the essential tracks.

There is only one compilation by the Ravens available, called *Be I Bumble Bee Or Not* (indigo 2008). *The Dawn Of Doo-Wop* is a typically well put together anthology by Proper Records, on 4 CDs (2002). It includes tracks by the Mills Brothers, the Ink Spots, and the Ravens, as well as *Too Soon To Know* by the Orioles and much else besides. *The Very Best Of Doo-Wop,* a double CD on One Day Music (2015) has *Blue Moon* by the Marcels, *I Only Have Eyes For You* by the Flamingos, and *Get A Job* by the Silhouettes, alongside much else that is essential. *Doo-Wop – The Absolutely Essential 3 CD Collection* is on Big 3 (2011) and has the Marcels, the Silhouettes, and also *Too Soon To Know* by the Orioles. Both sets would be the ideal purchase, although there would be quite a bit of overlap. The other doo-wop tracks mentioned can be heard on YouTube.

Money Honey by Clyde McPhatter and the Drifters is a double CD (Great Voices Of The Century 2009) containing all the group's important recordings, alongside tracks by McPhatter on his own. The Drifters is the same group as the one that had several big hits at the end of the fifties and through to the seventies, though with numerous changes in personnel along the way. Elvis Presley's version of *White Christmas* is on *The Classic Christmas Album* (RCA/Sony 2012).

The *American Graffiti* soundtrack is a double CD on Universal/Island (1999). It is a very good compilation, although the majority of its tracks are also included on CDs mentioned elsewhere in this book. The film itself is available on a Universal DVD.

Art Garfunkel's version of *I Only Have Eyes For You* is included on his *Simply The Best* (Sony 1998).

THE FIRST TIME

The Shirelles are well served by a double CD named after their greatest hit, *Will You Love Me Tomorrow* (Not Now Music 2012). *Da Doo Ron Ron – The Very Best Of The Crystals* is on Sony (2011). *People Get Ready – The Best Of Curtis Mayfield's Impressions* is a double CD on Spectrum (2013). *The Definitive Frankie Valli & The Four Seasons* is on Rhino (2001). *The Very Best Of The Beach Boys* is on Capitol/EMI (2001), although it is not an adequate representation on its own of a particularly important group (albeit not for soul fans, probably). *A Young Man Is Gone* is on *Little Deuce Coup* – packaged together with the album *All Summer Long* on Capitol/EMI (2001). *It's A Blue World – Their 30 Finest 1951-1960* by the Four Freshmen is on Retrospective (2013) and includes *Their Hearts Were Full Of Spring*.

The Very Best Of Jackie Wilson (Ace 1987) has the three Berry Gordy songs as its first three tracks. A three CD set called *Tamla Motown Gold* (Universal 2001) claims to have "all the hits from the 60's" and it does. *Come To Me* is included on *Marvelous Marv Johnson* (Hallmark 2012). *Hi We're The Miracles* is also on Hallmark (2012). *Got A Job* is included with a comprehensive selection of other Miracles tracks on a double CD, *The Best Of Smokey Robinson & The Miracles* (Motown 1995). *Tamla Motown – The Singles Collection Volume One* includes Marv Johnson and the Satintones, alongside *Shop Around* by the Miracles, *Money* by Barrett Strong, and a large number of other singles that will only be familiar to Motown specialists, on a four CD set (Real Gone 2014). Marvin Gaye's *Soulful Moods* is on Hallmark (2012). *Hello Broadway* is on US Motown (1990); *A Tribute To The Great Nat King Cole* is on Motown (2015). *A Collection Of 16 Tamla Motown Big Hits* has not been reissued on CD, although most of its tracks are included on *Tamla Motown Gold*.

With The Beatles is on EMI (2009).

Ray Charles The Ultimate Collection is a three CD set on Not Now Music (2013). *Soul Brothers* is on Jazz Best (2013). James Brown's early hits are included on the four CD set, *Star Time* (Universal/Polydor 2007), which is essential for the comprehensive coverage it gives to Brown's subsequent career as the inventor of funk. *Live At The Apollo* is on Universal/Polydor (2004). *The Very Best Of Little Richard* is on Universal (2008).

The Soul Of Ike & Tina Turner is on Hallmark (2016). *Portrait Of A Legend 1951-1964* by Sam Cooke is on Universal (2013).

Last Night and *Green Onions* are both included on a CD combining early recordings by the Mar-Keys and by Booker T and the MGs, *Soul Fingers* (Delta 2013). *Cause I Love You* is on the Rufus Thomas CD, *Walking The Dog* (Atlantic 1991).

The Dock Of The Bay – The Definitive Collection by Otis Redding (WEA 1987) includes *These Arms Of Mine* and the title track. *Otis Blue* is on Atco (1992). *Historic Performances Recorded At The Monterey International Pop Festival* was issued on vinyl in 1970, with Jimi Hendrix on one side and Otis Redding on the other, but it has not been reissued on CD. The Otis Redding tracks are included, however, on the various artists four CD set, *Monterey International Pop Festival* (Union Square 2013). *The Very Best Of Wilson Pickett* is on Warner (2005).

The Greatest by Arthur Alexander is on Ace (2006). The Rolling Stones version of *You Better Move On* is on *December's Children* (Abkco 2002); the Hollies version is on *Stay With The Hollies* (EMI 1997). The Beatles play *Anna* on *Please Please Me* (EMI 2009). Dusty Springfield sings *Every Day I Have To Cry* on *A Girl Called Dusty* (Mercury 1997). The album includes several other soul covers. In September 1968, Dusty Springfield recorded an album in the American Sound studio in Memphis (not the Stax studio, but with a similar reputation for producing quality soul, alongside other kinds of music). *Dusty In Memphis* has become widely rated as one of the great soul albums, remarkable for a white singer from London. The currently available CD is on Mercury (2002).

MUSIC GENRES

Respect – The Very Best Of Aretha Franklin is a double CD on Warner (2003). The album *I Never Loved A Man The Way I Love You* is on Rhino (1995). *Songs Of Faith* is on a French Vogue CD (1987). *Amazing Grace – The Complete Recordings* is a double CD on Rhino (1999).

My Generation by the Who is on Polydor (2012). *Zoot Suit* is included on the double CD, *The Who Hits 50* (Universal/Polydor 2014). Both sides of the High Numbers single are on the four CD set by the Who, *Thirty Years Of Maximum R&B* (Polydor 1994). The 40th Anniversary Edition of the first album by the Small Faces is on Universal/Decca (2006). It includes *What'cha Gonna Do About It*. *From The Beginning* includes both *What'cha Gonna Do About It* and *All Or Nothing*. It is on Decca (2003). *Incense* by the Anglos is included on the Spencer Davis Group CD, *The Singles* (BR Music 2003). *The Essential Collection* by the Righteous Brothers is on Spectrum (2013). *Some Blue-Eyed Soul* has not been reissued on CD, although it is available as a download via TP4 Music (2015).

Van Morrison's *Astral Weeks* is on Warner Bros (2015). In 2008, unexpectedly, Morrison gave a very well received live performance of the album's music, with a couple of extras, and released the result on a CD, *Astral Weeks Live At The Hollywood Bowl* (EMI 2009). *Caledonia Soul Music* can be heard on YouTube, slightly speeded up from its original sound on vinyl.

*Stand! b*y Sly and the Family Stone is on Epic (2007). Just over fifteen minutes of the group's performance at Woodstock is included on the double CD, *Woodstock – Music From The Original Soundtrack And More* (Rhino 2009). *Introducing The Beau Brummels,* released in April 1965 and including the Beatles-inspired hit single *Laugh Laugh,* is on a Repertoire CD (1998).

Cheap Thrills by Big Brother And The Holding Company is on Columbia (1999).

The best of the Norman Whitfield productions for the Temptations are included in the double CD *Psychedelic Soul* (Motown 2003). *Masterpiece* and one other track from the album of that title are included. The complete *Masterpiece* album is on Motown (1986).

Stevie Wonder's *I Call It Pretty Music* is on the double CD, *Introducing Stevie Wonder* (Not Now Music 2013). The albums mentioned are *Music Of My Mind, Talking Book, Innervisions, Fulfillingness' First Finale,* and *Songs In The Key Of Life* (all Universal/Motown 2000). *Fingertips* is included in *Tamla Motown Gold.*

Beck Bogert Appice is on Repertoire (2005). The debut, self-titled album by Vanilla Fudge (Atco 1997) includes the full version of *You Keep Me Hanging On*. *Hot Buttered Soul* by Isaac Hayes is on Universal/Stax (2009). *The Isaac Hayes Movement* is on Universal/Stax (2006); *To Be Continued* is on Stax (1991). *With A Little Help From My Friends* is on Joe Cocker's *The Life Of A Man – The Ultimate Hits 1968-2003* (Sony double 2015)

Too-Rye-Ay by Dexys Midnight Runners is on Mercury (2011). The power of the original line-up is demonstrated on the live BBC set from 1981 that makes up most of the CD *The Projected Passion Revue* (Universal/Mercury 2007).

Kool And The Gang *Live At The Sex Machine* is on US Mercury (1996). *Live At P.J.'s* is on US Mercury (1999). Maceo Parker's *Roots Revisited* is on Minor Music (2000).

Marvin Gaye's *What's Going On* is on Universal/Motown (2010), expanded to a double CD set with alternate mixes and live recordings. *Let's Get It On* is on Universal/Motown (2002).

Curtis Mayfield's *Back To The World* is on Charly (2006). *There's No Place Like America Today* is on Charly (2001). The soundtrack to *Superfly* is on Charly (2005). *Mighty Mighty Spade And Whitey* is not included on the Impressions compilation mentioned earlier. It is included on the Impressions album *The Young Mods' Forgotten Story*, which is packaged together with *This My Country* on Charly (2008).

A double CD, *Love Train – The Ultimate Sound Of Philadelphia* (Sony 1998) provides an excellent overview of Philadelphia soul.

Al Green Greatest Hits is a double CD on Fat Possum (2014). *I'm Still In Love With You* and *Call Me* are on the same label (2009 and 2014).

The Best Of Michael Jackson And The Jackson 5ive – The Motown Years is on Universal/Motown (2001). Michael Jackson's *Off The Wall, Thriller,* and *Bad* are on Sony (2015). *The Essential Collection* by Lesley Gore is on Spectrum (1998).

For You by Prince is on Warner Bros (1987). *Purple Rain* is also on Warner Bros (2011). The film is available on a Warner DVD (1999).

3 + 3 by the Isley Brothers is on Epic (1997). *Testify* is included on the four CD set by Jimi Hendrix, *West Coast Seattle Boy* (Sony 2010). Hendrix's *Band Of Gypsys* is also on Sony (2010).

Soul by Seal is on Warner Bros (2008). *Ultimate Collection* by M People Featuring Heather Small is on Sony (2005). *The Collection 1995-2007* is a double CD by Beverley Knight on Music Club Deluxe (2012). *Perfect Day* is available on a CD single that also includes the video (EMI 2000).

R.Kelly's self-titled CD is on Jive (2001). *Dangerously In Love* by Beyoncé is on Sony (2003). *Lemonade* by Beyoncé is on Sony (2016).

THE FIRST TIME

Not everyone agreed with William Mann, at least as far as establishment critics were concerned. The review of the Beatles *Help!* that was published in the specialist classical music magazine, *The Gramophone*, when the LP was first released, seemed to have been included with the sole intention of dismissing the group as being beneath the contempt of all those interested in 'proper' music. The LP includes the song *Yesterday*, which was voted the best song of the twentieth century in a 1999 poll conducted by BBC Radio 2.

William F. Buckley, noted American conservative, wrote in the *Boston Globe* in September 1964:

> The Beatles are not merely awful; I would consider it sacrilegious to say anything less than that they are god awful. They are so unbelievably horribly, so appallingly unmusical, so dogmatically insensitive to the magic of the art that they qualify as crowned heads of anti-music, even as the imposter popes went down in history as 'anti-popes'.

Classical pianist Glenn Gould, during a CBC radio broadcast that he made in December 1967, extravagantly praising the hit recordings of pop singer Petula Clark, said of the Beatles:

> The indulgent amateurishness of the musical material, though closely rivalled by the indifference of the performing style, is actually surpassed only by the ineptitude of the studio production method. *Strawberry Fields* suggests a chance encounter at a mountain wedding between Claudio Monteverdi and a jug band.

Although from an earlier date, it is worth mentioning again the comment made by Decca executive Dick Rowe when rejecting the Beatles in 1962, as reported by Brian Epstein and quoted in Hunter Davies' 1968 book, *The Beatles: The Authorized Biography*:

> We don't like their sound. Groups of guitars are on the way out.

Decca signed Brian Poole and the Tremeloes, a group of guitars, albeit one without any of the Beatles' power, at the same time as it rejected the Beatles. The group's first single, *Twist Little Sister*, was issued in May but was not a hit. It was the group's fifth single that finally did the trick, entering the charts in July 1963, after the Beatles had already scored two massive hits. The song, *Twist And Shout*, was one that had already become associated with the Beatles, as the closing track on the group's first LP and the title of a hit EP including four of the LP tracks.

In contrast to the comments above, there have been numerous positive statements over the years about the Beatles, from their fellow musicians. These include the Ozzy Osbourne quote printed two pages further on and one from Jimmy Page in 1985, looking back on his years with Led Zeppelin, during a guest appearance on the US radio show, *Scott Muni's Ticket To Ride*. "If it hadn't been for the Beatles, there wouldn't have been anyone like us around."

The film *Just For Fun*, made for teenagers, was issued in the UK in 1963, but with music dating from the previous year. It acts like a collection of period pop videos and provides an excellent overview of the music scene into which the Beatles burst, like a bunch of rowdy gate-crashers arriving at a sedate dinner party. The likes of Bobby Vee, Freddy Cannon, Johnny Tillotson, the Tornados, and the Crickets (disastrously reduced in stature and energy by the tragic absence of Buddy Holly) present a music that has replaced the excitement and drive of rock 'n' roll with a sanitised, satin-suited pop glitz, on which the firm restraining hand of the music industry establishment clearly rests. Despite Alan Freeman's passionate introductions to the performances, it is hard to understand why the teenage audiences in the film should be finding anything to be enthusiastic about. The music is a product that realistically differs little from the easy-listening fare of their parents. The film soundtrack was issued by Decca, with the LP sleeve crediting Dick Rowe as the producer for all the music. It is clear why Rowe and Decca were nervous of a seemingly raucous guitar group that might upset the cosy music world the company was overseeing. Four years earlier, they had also turned down Cliff Richard, but perhaps they made up for these errors when later they signed the Moody Blues, John Mayall's Bluesbreakers, and the Rolling Stones.

The template for the Beatles' music was set by Buddy Holly and the Crickets, who established the classic rock line-up of two guitars, bass, and drums, and who also wrote much of their own material. The Holly group's name too was an obvious inspiration for the Beatles' decision to use an insect as the basis for their own name. In February 2016, the Crickets, with drummer Jerry Allison from the original line-up still on board, gave what they announced was their final performance, after an amazing fifty-nine years.

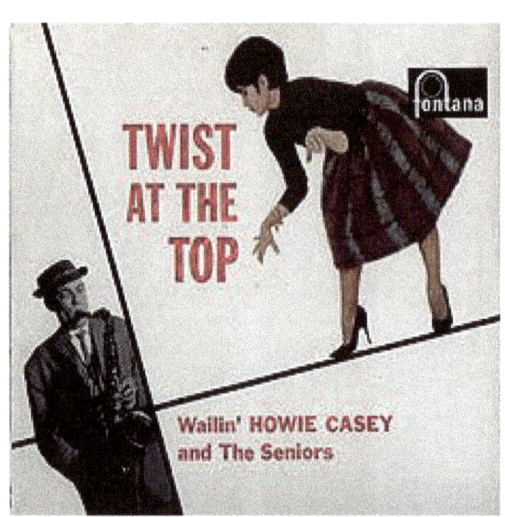

A demonstration copy of Love Me Do – one of the first records off the press. The spelling of Paul's name was corrected for the full release.

19 THE BEATLES

To anyone who, like the author, grew up during the sixties, the rock music created and played during the period 1963-1976 seems like that of a golden age. It was a period during which the squalling infant, rock 'n' roll, matured into a young adult; a period of such creativity that it seemed every month brought ideas and sounds that were new; and a period that in the process saw rock music being accorded the status of an art form. This was typified by the Times music critic William Mann's comparison between the Beatles and Schubert in his sixties column and the overblown but significant study of the Beatles, *The Twilight Of The Gods* (1973) by the music professor at York University, Wilfred Mellers.

There are problems in deciding the total sales figures of records issued during this period.. Record companies frequently exaggerated sales in their reports for reasons of status and advertising. Often, however, record companies during the sixties did not keep reliable accounts of the sales of individual records – a situation that resulted in a number of more recent court actions initiated by artists dissatisfied with their royalty payments (including the Beatles). The R.I.A.A. (Recording Industry Association of America) introduced a system of certification awards (the gold records) in 1958. In the UK, the BPI (British Phonographic Industry) did the same, but not until 1973. Other countries followed even later. Certified sales figures, based on these awards, are accurate for records released in recent years, but do not even exist for UK records issued in the sixties. As a result, sales figures for Beatles records are largely a matter of guesswork. Nevertheless, estimates agree that the Beatles must have sold over six hundred million records worldwide, with the certified figures reaching nearly two hundred and sixty five million records as of 2013. Both figures put the group considerably ahead of the second placed artist, Elvis Presley, leaving no doubt that the Beatles are the most successful artists of all time.

Within this global accounting, there are several other achievements to note, such as the fact that, as at 2014, the Beatles have the most number one hits in the American Hot Hundred chart, and have the most number one album hits in the UK. In the US album charts, the Beatles have four out of the all-time top ten albums, based on chart success, including the number one (*Sgt Pepper's Lonely Hearts Club Band*). At the height of the group's popularity in 1964, the Beatles had the top five singles in the Hot Hundred chart for April 4th, the first and only time such an achievement has happened. Further down the chart, seven more Beatles songs were placed – and the following week these were joined by two more – making a total of fourteen Beatles songs in the chart. In the UK, the previous year had seen the single *She Loves You* achieving the fastest sales of any record up to that time and it remained the biggest selling single in the country until 1978, when it was overtaken by (Beatle) Paul McCartney's *Mull Of Kintyre*.

In February 1962, the first UK LP by a Liverpool group was issued by Fontana. This was *Twist At The Top*, by Howie Casey and the Seniors. It was followed by three singles, the first of which was *Double Twist*. None of these records was particularly successful, although Howie Casey's group (as Derry and the Seniors) had managed to become the first from Liverpool to play in Hamburg, to be followed by the Beatles. (Both were beaten by an ad hoc London outfit, the Jets, featuring singer and guitarist Tony Sheridan). It was while they were in Hamburg, that the Beatles, with Pete Best on drums, recorded several tracks as a backing group for Tony Sheridan, in June 1961. *My Bonnie* was issued as a Polydor single in Germany in October, but credited to 'Tony Sheridan and the Beat Brothers'. It was a modest chart hit. A German LP followed in January 1962, with the 'Beat Brothers' credit still in place. The same month, *My Bonnie* was released in the UK, and this time the Beatles were properly credited. It made no difference, the single disappeared, almost without trace.

When the Beatles' first single for Parlophone, *Love Me Do*, was released in October 1962, it benefited from EMI's better promotion and reached number seventeen in the UK charts, becoming the first hit in a genre that was soon

THE FIRST TIME

The estimated sales of *Please Please Me*, based on the number of records shipped by the record company to record outlets, according to the website *beatlelinks.net*, amount to 310,000 copies. *Billboard* magazine printed in its International News Report that advance orders alone for the Frank Ifield single exceeded 250,000. It seems likely, therefore, that Frank Ifield did outsell the Beatles on this occasion, a conclusion further supported by the fact that second-hand, original copies of *The Wayward Wind* are in much greater supply than original copies of *Please Please Me*. This was Frank Ifield's third number one single and he was to gain one more, before finally succumbing to the tidal wave of Merseybeat.

The name order for the songwriting credit had yet to be settled

Album sales before the Beatles were not huge. In 1961, EMI was proud to announce the company's first LP to sell over a hundred thousand copies in the UK (*The Black And White Minstrel Show* by the George Mitchell Minstrels). The Beatles' second album, *With The Beatles*, achieved sales of 270,000 even before it was released. A week after release, it had gone over half a million and the LP was being listed in the singles charts. The million sales figure was eventually reached in 1965, making *With The Beatles* the highest selling LP in the UK up to that time.

 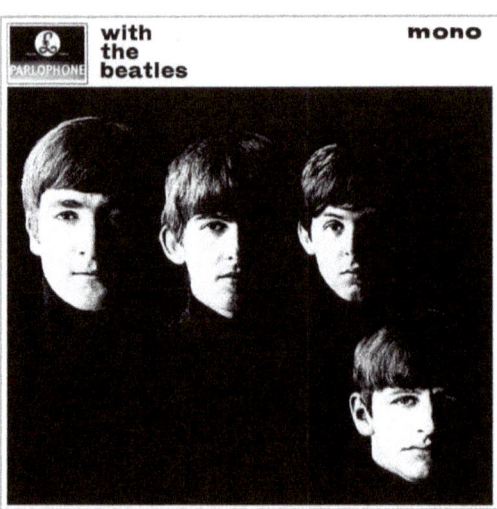

"That song changed my life. *She Loves You* had such an impact on me. I remember exactly where I was. I was walking down Witton Road in Aston, I had a blue transistor radio and when that song came on I knew from then on what I wanted to do with my life. This was so brand new and it gave me a great feeling. Then I became an avid Beatles fan – they were great. I owe my career to them because they gave me the desire to want to be in the music game." Ozzy Osbourne, quoted on the *Classic Rock* magazine website, December 2017.

Two of the albums by Soft Machine entered the album charts – the double LP, *Third,* which reached number eighteen, and *Fourth*, which reached number thirty-two. They were presented as being the work of a rock group, although they will sound little different to jazz to modern ears. Presentation is crucial. There was no question in marketing Miles Davis' landmark album, *Bitches Brew*, a record which changed the face of modern jazz after its release in 1970, as anything other than a jazz work. It did eventually sell a million copies worldwide, but reached no higher than number seventy-one in the UK charts.

named Merseybeat. The second single, *Please Please Me*, was issued in January 1963 and climbed rapidly to the top of the charts, becoming the first Merseybeat number one. The statistic has become subject to a little confusion in the years since. As far as the listening public was concerned, the chart that mattered at the time was the one broadcast in the BBC programme, *Pick Of The Pops*, which was presented by Alan Freeman on Sunday afternoons. For those who preferred a chart that was written down, the one printed in *New Musical Express* was the most widely followed, partly because it had been the first chart to be published in the UK. On both of these charts, *Please Please Me* went to number one. In a chart included in the trade paper, *Record Retailer*, and not seen by ordinary members of the public, *Please Please Me* stalled at number two, being kept at bay by Frank Ifield's *The Wayward Wind*. This is the chart that has been adopted by the Official Charts Company, which is responsible for the contemporary charts, and it is also used by the compilers of *The Guinness Book Of British Hit Singles*. By their reckoning, the first Merseybeat number one was *How Do You Do It* by Gerry and the Pacemakers, which reached the position in April. Ironically, George Martin had wanted the Beatles to issue that song as a single, and the group did record it, but managed to persuade Martin that their own *Please Please Me* was better.

That William Mann and Wilfred Mellers should have chosen the Beatles' music in particular to be the subject of their scholarly analyses was appropriate, not because of the group's high public profile, but because of the way in which the Beatles acted as a catalyst for the entire development of rock music during the sixties. The phenomenal rise to popularity of the Beatles in the early part of the decade was due in part to their talents as musicians and songwriters, but as much to skilful marketing and as much again to luck. In this respect, the group was no different to the likes of Frank Sinatra and Elvis Presley before them, or to Madonna and Michael Jackson afterwards. Unusually, however, once established, the Beatles were revealed as being musically restless, preferring always to try a slightly new approach rather than merely to repeat a successful formula. In their dual role as superstars and as experimenters, the Beatles were able to create a climate in which fans and fellow musicians alike would eagerly await the group's next record release in order to find out how rock music should now sound.

At the same time, because the Beatles were so popular, they attracted the attention of listeners and critics who had previously been unaware of, or at least apathetic towards the music (William Mann, for example). And because the Beatles' music was manifestly produced with care and with intelligence, rock music in general began to acquire an artistic credibility, so that other worthy musicians also began to receive attention that they might otherwise not have. Meanwhile, the record companies were encouraged to equate innovation with commercial success, so that even after the Beatles' influence began to wane – in the aftermath of the climactic album, *Sgt Pepper's Lonely Hearts Club Band* – the onus remained on rock musicians to continually expand the frontiers of their style. It was a happy reversal of the rules that have more often been applied to the creation of music intended to be commercial. Certainly, the music made in the wake of punk did not place a high premium on instrumental virtuosity, on structural and melodic complexity, or on esoteric sounds and textures. Yet here in the Beatles years was a group, to take the Soft Machine as an extreme but symptomatic example, that was fond of extended instrumental works, using elements of avant garde jazz and process music, often with unusual time signatures, strange voicings, and melodies that were impossible to whistle, yet signed to a major company (CBS) and selling records in sufficient numbers to gain a good placing in the albums charts.

The genesis of the approach that made the Beatles' 1967 recordings (which include *Sgt Pepper*) as satisfying as they continue to be, is to be found as early as on the *Beatles For Sale* album of 1964. The writer of the sleeve notes took great delight in listing such details as Ringo Starr playing a packing case in place of his drums on one track (*Words Of Love*) and George Harrison thumping an African drum on another (*Mr Moonlight*). While the use of such instruments hardly constitutes an innovation of landmark proportions, it is significant that the Beatles were interested in introducing this kind of modest novelty at a time when the LP would have been commercially successful whatever it had sounded like. The effects are important because they show how the Beatles were beginning to search for new sounds in an effort to give each song a distinct character of its own.

THE FIRST TIME

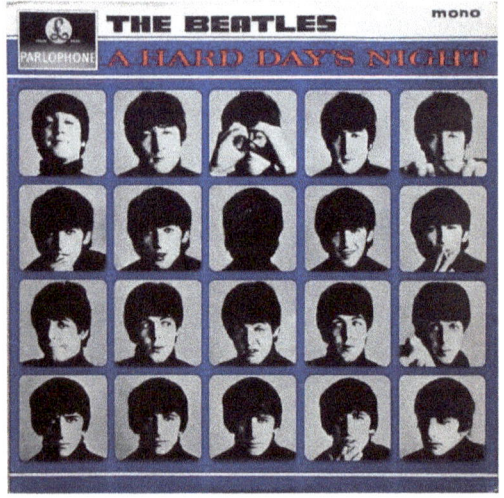

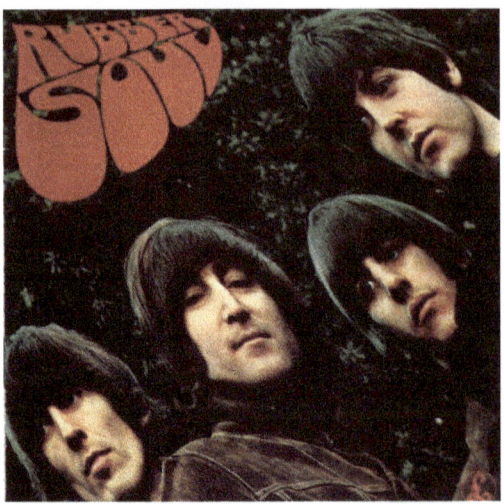

Modern critics have apparently swallowed wholesale the Beatles' insistence, not wanting to incur any further wrath from the establishment at the time, that the lyrics of *Lucy In The Sky With Diamonds* have nothing to do with drugs. It is impossible to imagine, however, that John Lennon was not aware of the fortuitously initialled title of the painting by his son that was his first inspiration. In a song as complex as this, with its shifting key centres, we do not have to be satisfied that it is only about one thing!

The recording for *Sgt Pepper's Lonely Hearts Club Band* was carried out after the Beatles had announced that they would not be making any more live performances. It is probably the case, therefore, that the album represented the first time a record was produced in a studio purely as a record, with no intention or expectation that any of its music would ever be performed again.

This search became most apparent when the group stopped recording other people's songs. The two albums from 1965, *Help!* and *Rubber Soul*, reveal how the Beatles were becoming masters of the three minute song. In particular, both records are object lessons in how to utilise a basic group line-up so as to produce music that is both varied and stimulating. The songs already have distinct personalities by virtue of their differences in mood and tempo, but these differences are further emphasised, within each album, by giving each song just one musical sound that is not found on any of its fellows. In this respect, the Beatles were also aided by their rapidly improving instrumental skills. They had always been competent instrumentalists, without being especially outstanding, but now they displayed a craftsmanship that enabled them to achieve musical effects that had not been available to them earlier.

During the recording of the LP *Revolver*, the Beatles began to exploit the facilities available in the recording studio, as well as further extending the individualised arranging of songs already carried a long way on *Rubber Soul*. They used a backward guitar effect on *I'm Only Sleeping* to enhance the dream-like quality implicit in the song's title (and the song also includes a beautifully recorded yawn, heard just once in the middle of the mix). They employed Alan Civil to interpolate a French horn solo into the music of *For No One*, where the sprightly tune somehow manages to underscore all the more effectively the pathos of the lyrics. There are strings on *Eleanor Rigby*, brass on *Got To Get You Into My Life*, and a whole range of sound effects on *Yellow Submarine*. Most impressive of all is the final track on the record, *Tomorrow Never Knows*, where the weird sounds supplied by a pre-recorded tape loop, together with the unnatural quality of John Lennon's voice – achieved by singing through a rotating organ loudspeaker – create aurally exactly the drug-induced sensations described in the words of the song. Significantly, however, the standard of the song writing throughout *Revolver* is such as to prevent any of these effects and additions sounding like buttresses for poor quality compositions. The songs come first, by virtue of their interesting melody lines, harmonies, and lyrics – everything else is a bonus.

The achievement represented by *Revolver*, although considerable, was soon eclipsed by what is probably the most famous rock record of all – *Sgt Pepper's Lonely Hearts Club Band*. Much has been made of the presumption that the record is intended to be listened to as a continuous work, this being made all the easier by the fact that the ending of one song often blends into the beginning of the next. However, apart from the obvious link between the first two songs and the reprise of the title track towards the end of the second side, there is little thematic continuity. Mr Kite is at a different show to Billy Shears! The record is better viewed as being a musical collage, where sound follows sound in a kind of aural feast. The record was a comparatively long time in the making – certainly by the standards of the time, where the norm had always been to bash out a rock album in a matter of days – and the benefit derived is apparent in the tremendous attention to detail within every song. There is the final development of the Beatles' instinctive ability to create maximum effect with the minimum of resources, such as the comb and paper sound which occurs early in *Lovely Rita* and retains its novelty unspoilt by being omitted from later repeats of that part of the tune. Where on *Help!* each song was given a distinct musical colour by the addition of one particular instrumental sound, here this technique is expanded to create for every song a complete palette of musical colours. It suffices to mention the combination of Lowrey organ and helium-altered singing on *Lucy In The Sky With Diamonds*, which forms the perfect accompaniment to the world of childish fantasy conjured up by the words of the song; the culmination of George Harrison's dalliance with the sitar in his employment of only Indian musicians to play the music of *Within You, Without You*; and the extraordinary tension and release generated by the string crescendos in *A Day In The Life*.

Two songs that were originally intended to be included within the *Sgt Pepper* album were instead released as a single (for the Beatles, these were alternatives – they did not generally release album tracks as singles in the UK). Even more than the LP, they stand together as the Beatles' masterpiece. *Penny Lane* is an affectionate portrait of the Beatles' Liverpool, in which a succession of clever and imaginative word images are clothed in a joyfully uplifting melody and rounded out by a lively, upper register trumpet solo, courtesy of classical musician Philip Jones. This conveys all the jollity of the Northern brass bands, but within a single voice. For *Strawberry Fields Forever*, John Lennon went a little further than the somewhat obtuse imagery of Bob Dylan and produced a pattern of words that manage to sound

THE FIRST TIME

There has been a notable critical retreat in the UK in recent years from granting *Sgt Pepper's Lonely Hearts Club Band* the accolade of best album or even best Beatles album. A chart of the all-time best, printed in the American *Rolling Stone* magazine in 2012, kept *Sgt Pepper* in the number one position. Similar charts published in Britain, in *New Musical Express*, *Q* magazine, or *Pop Vortex*, a website claiming to produce a definitive chart based on combining the results from a wide range of other charts, tell a different story. In these, *Sgt Pepper* is overtaken by both *Revolver* and *The White Album*. It is not too difficult to work out why this critical rethink has taken place. Certainly, the music itself has not changed. The arrival of punk ten years later, however, brought with it a revised, narrower definition of what was to be counted as rock music. Another thirty to forty years on, within a musical climate that is still inclined to take the release of *Anarchy In The UK* as its ground zero, *Sgt Pepper* simply does not conform with the contemporary audience's idea of what rock music is supposed to sound like. It must be remembered too, that the idea of rock and pop being different kinds of music, with rock being superior, was not one that applied in 1967. It was all pop then, even if a year or two later, with the arrival of groups like Led Zeppelin, for whom singles and chart success were an irrelevance, a distinction started to be made.

Mark Lewisohn, in his meticulously researched *The Complete Beatles Recording Sessions*, quotes Jerry Boys, who was a tape operator at Abbey Road studios at the time the Beatles were recording *Sgt Pepper*. "If you listen to the album now, there are noises which are still impossible to make, even with today's computerised 48-track equipment and all the microchips imaginable. It's a very very clever record. In terms of creative use of recording it has been one of *the* major steps forward".

The Bonzo Dog Doo Dah Band's first album, *Gorilla*, painted its comedy on to a musical backcloth made up of traditional jazz and music hall nostalgia. The band made a guest performance in the Beatles' *Magical Mystery Tour* film and acquired a whole set of new influences in the process. Singer songwriter Neil Innes emerged from the band a few years later with his affectionate Beatles pastiche, *The Rutles*. Originally a sketch on Eric Idle's TV show, *Rutland Weekend Television*, the Rutles concept was expanded into a television film of its own, *All You Need Is Cash*, which was accompanied by a soundtrack album. Neil Innes managed to tread a clever line, where original Beatles songs were recalled without ever being actually quoted. Later, in response to the release of the Beatles *Anthology* albums, Neil Innes responded with his own mock version, still using the Rutles name, and with the album title *Archaeology*. Again, he succeeded in writing songs that sounded like the Beatles but were his own originals.

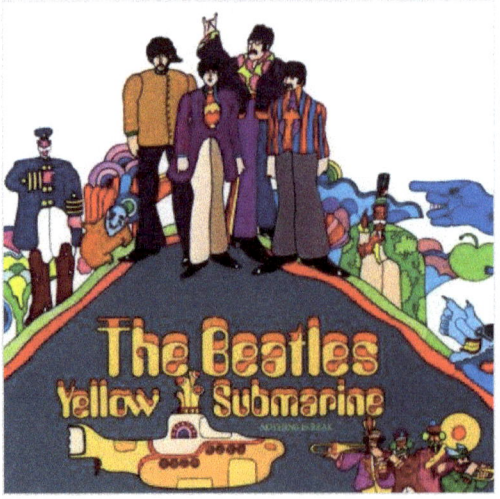

Fakin' It, on the Simon and Garfunkel album *Bookends*, achieves a direct link with the Beatles by beginning with a reproduction of the musical train that departs at the end of *Strawberry Fields Forever*. The two songs could be easily welded together into a neat megamix, although the author does not know if any DJ has ever done this within his set.

The tracklisting for *The Great Lost Beatles Album Of Spring 1968* (more logically titled *Magical Mystery Tour*), using music recorded as early as February 1967, but essentially undertaken the day after *Sgt Pepper* was declared to be finished and extending through to the following February, would be something like this:

Magical Mystery Tour	Across The Universe
Only A Northern Song	Your Mother Should Know
All Together Now	Hey Bulldog
Lady Madonna	The Inner Light
It's All Too Much	I Am The Walrus
The Fool On The Hill	Hello Goodbye
Baby You're A Rich Man	All You Need Is Love
Flying	You Know My Name (preferably edited)
Blue Jay Way	

The sides are then both a little under half an hour, with the last track on side two presented as a bonus. It is long for a sixties album, but not impossibly so.

In June 2017, *Sgt Pepper* was re-released in a 50th anniversary edition, after being given a new remix by George Martin's son, Giles. For some listeners, this was a controversial thing to do, akin to desecrating a work of art, but for others the procedure was a revelation, giving the album the impact of a brand new twenty-first century release. It went to number one in the UK charts, marking a new first time achievement for the Beatles. No other album had ever reached number one on occasions separated by a time span as long as fifty years.

absolutely right together, yet which are ultimately meaningless. Hence the unreality described as being the major feature of the Strawberry Fields. The pattern of words is laced through with a similar pattern of musical sounds, from the dawn chorus of mellotron flutes, through the unsettling lurch as the guitar plunges down into the Strawberry Fields, to the departing train driven across the end of the song by the drums and the brass.

Some interesting insight into the way in which the Beatles created their music at this time is provided by the inclusion of various early versions of both *Strawberry Fields Forever* and *A Day In The Life* on the second of the three *Anthology* sets, issued in 1996, and on the fiftieth anniversary *Sgt Pepper's Lonely Hearts Club Band* sets, issued in 2017. These recordings reveal the Beatles to be gradually feeling their way forwards to the finished versions and using the recording studio itself as a tool to help in the creation of these. The first take of *Strawberry Fields Forever* is very different from the familiar performance of the song. All the details of the arrangement, including the basic parts played by the Beatles themselves, and even the song's final structure, were worked out in the studio during the course of successive recordings, with each change and addition being made as a direct response to the sound of the previous recorded take. This approach to recording is much more complex than the simple transfer of performance to tape that was the norm for all kinds of music before this time.

Sgt Pepper's white-hot level of inspiration set a new standard for song writing and performance that the Beatles' contemporaries felt was essential to try to reach. Certainly, few albums released during the next year were untouched by its blend of attention to detail and eclectic instrumentation, whether the background of the artists concerned was in folk (Donovan's *Sunshine Superman*, for example), blues (John Mayall's *Bare Wires*), garage punk (Love's *Forever Changes*), musical comedy (the Bonzo Dog Doo Dah Band's *The Doughnut In Granny's Greenhouse*), or pop (the first LP by the Bee Gees and *Odyssey and Oracle* by the Zombies).

Those groups who felt themselves to be in closest competition with the Beatles were quick to produce their own versions of *Sgt Pepper*. The Rolling Stones' *Their Satanic Majesties Request*, the Hollies' *Butterfly*, the Byrds' *Notorious Byrd Brothers*, Simon and Garfunkel's *Bookends*, and the Beach Boys' *Smile* recordings are all collections in which the art of the arranger has been elevated to be on a par with that of the composer. In each case, it is obvious how considerable care has been applied to the task of making each song totally distinctive. The range of sounds employed, unusual by virtue of their timbre or their context, is remarkable, especially considering the relatively low level of recording technology available at the time.

As for the Beatles themselves, when the time came for them to produce a follow-up to *Sgt Pepper*, they were faced with a considerable problem, which they never really managed to solve. More than ever before, they found themselves in the invidious position of having a reputation to maintain. Audiences had become used to each record being an advance on the previous one and were waiting with a collective bated breath for the record that would represent a progression from even *Sgt Pepper*. It became suddenly clear as well that the Beatles were no longer the only artists, or even the best, to be producing records worthy of consideration as works of art. A new generation of rock musicians had been steadily improving their skills and many of these people had developed an instrumental virtuosity, compared to which the Beatles were completely outclassed. These players had also been listening hard to other kinds of music – especially the jazz of innovators like John Coltrane – with which the Beatles had no sympathy. It was no accident that the Beatles had earlier recorded the Chuck Berry song, *Rock and Roll Music*, with its declaration of disinterest in modern jazz and symphonic music. The first two albums by Stevie Winwood's Traffic, *Axis: Bold As Love* and *Electric Ladyland* by Jimi Hendrix, *Music In A Doll's House* by Family, *In Search Of The Lost Chord* by the Moody Blues, *Disraeli Gears* and *Wheels Of Fire* by Cream, and *A Saucerful Of Secrets* by Pink Floyd – these were amongst the most remarkable rock LPs to be released during 1967 and 1968. All of them had clearly absorbed the lessons of *Revolver* and *Sgt. Pepper* and were making bold statements to the effect that this rock music was Art. Sgt Pepper's Lonely Hearts Club Band had expanded to include a membership of several score.

That the Beatles lost their position of importance, however, was at least in part their own fault. Aware of the

THE FIRST TIME

It is not hard to find old reviews of the *White Album* that do share the author's opinion of it. *Rolling Stone*'s review, preserved on the magazine's website, tries very hard to praise the record, but concludes that it is not as good as *Sgt Pepper*. According to the *White Album Project* website, the magazine's later Album Guide states that the record has "loads of self-indulgent filler". Nik Cohn, writing in the *New York Times* in 1968, describes the album as "boring almost beyond belief". Peter Altman, writing in the *Minneapolis Star* at the same time, says that it is "hardly their most exciting or most persuasive album". A contemporary review from the student newspaper of the University of San Francisco, reprinted on *Flashback* magazine's Facebook page in May 2017, states "not the masterpiece one has come to expect from the Beatles". Alan Smith headed his review in *New Musical Express* with "The Brilliant, the Bad, and the Ugly" – two of those adjectives being a remarkable about-turn when applied to the music of a group it was previously considered could do no wrong. The newspaper's *Illustrated Encyclopaedia Of Rock*, published in 1976, refers to the album as "the work of a disintegrating unit", while a year by year guide, published by W.H.Smith in 1980 as *25 Years Of Rock*, makes its opinion clear by omitting any reference to the record altogether. Even as late as 1999, the Parragon *Encyclopaedia Of Albums* was still maintaining that "there was a notable absence of cohesive atmosphere or continuity to this patchy epic".

George Harrison returned Eric Clapton's favour by playing on a track on Cream's album, *Goodbye*, recorded later in 1968. Harrison is listed as guitarist under the name of L'Angelo Misterioso on *Badge* but gets the co-writing credit, with Clapton, in his own name. The friendship between the two men was tested when Eric Clapton fell for George Harrison's wife, Patti, who did eventually become Clapton's wife, though not until 1979. She became, along the way, the subject of three particularly well-known songs – Harrison's *Something* and both *Layla* and *Wonderful Tonight* by Eric Clapton.

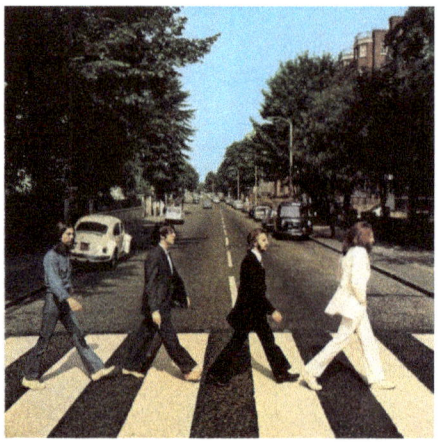
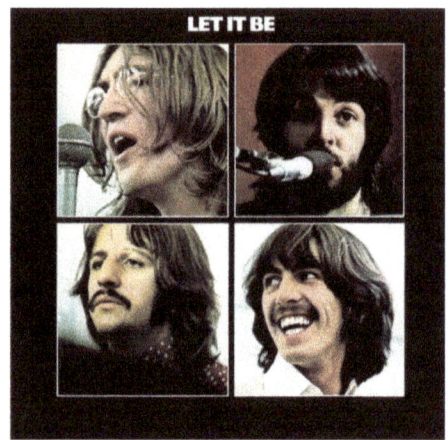

The "Ten Beatles Innovations" are claimed as:
1. The seven and a half minute single *Hey Jude* was a catalyst in the move from AM radio dominance to FM in the US.
2. The Beatles were the first artists to abandon touring.
3. *Sgt Pepper* had the lyrics of the songs printed on the sleeve.
4. The Beatles pioneered or popularised various studio techniques, including artificial double tracking, back masking, tuned feedback, spliced audio loops, distortion, equalisation, stereo effects, multi-tracking (overdubbing), compression, phase shifting, and innovative use of microphones.
5. The Beatles achieved unparalleled chart success.
6. The group was the star turn during the first ever live global satellite television broadcast, in June 1967.
7. The group was the first to start its own record label.
8. The group was the first to play a concert at a sports stadium.
9. *Sgt Peppers Lonely Hearts Club Band* was the first 'concept' album.
10. The Beatles were responsible for the first dedicated music video, for *Paperback Writer* in 1966.

5 is definitely true. Ripostes on the *listverse.com* website point to the others as being untrue or of little significance or both.

Free As A Bird was issued along with a promotional video that incorporated a large number of Beatles references, mainly taken from their song lyrics. It is included at the end of the last *Anthology* DVD, issued to accompany the *Anthology* CD sets. The single was produced by Jeff Lynne, chosen because of his connection with George Harrison in the Traveling Wilburys and because George Martin declined the opportunity, blaming hearing problems. For Lynne this must have had the feeling of completing a circle. In 1971, he formed the Electric Light Orchestra with Roy Wood, specifically to continue the style of Beatles songs like *Strawberry Fields Forever* and *I Am The Walrus*. On the group's self-titled first album, it is very obvious that this is what they are doing. At some point in the mid-seventies, John Lennon remarked that if the Beatles had continued playing, they would probably have sounded like the Electric Light Orchestra, which had become a very successful band on the back of albums like *Out Of The Blue*. This was interpreted as a put-down by some commentators, although it is more likely that Lennon was simply being realistic.

difficulties involved, they hesitated and eventually let their next recordings be issued in dribs and drabs, wherein their impact was considerably lessened. The music they created during the rest of 1967 and early 1968 would have made a formidable LP. *I Am The Walrus*, *Blue Jay Way*, *Only A Northern Song*, and *Hello Goodbye* in particular are achievements to rival any of the songs of the previous months, showing precisely the same kind of imagination and detailed sound structure as the earlier songs. The other music, while being on the whole somewhat simpler, nevertheless displays a wide variety of styles and the same assuredness of touch, sufficient to well complement the four more complex pieces. A *Magical Mystery Tour* LP, including the five new *Yellow Submarine* songs and *Hello Goodbye*, and segueing from one track to the next as on *Sgt Pepper*, would have been a record to rival its predecessor. We can at least listen to the separate songs.

The LP that did eventually emerge, *The Beatles* (known as *The White Album*), turned out to be not one, but two records – and something of a disappointment. It was acclaimed regardless by many of the critics, but it remains a very inferior collection of songs compared to what had gone before. Gone is the attention to detail and the rich tapestry of sounds. The album does have several redeeming features – not least in George Harrison's *While My Guitar Gently Weeps*, where the guitar seems to do just that (even if Harrison did decide to call on an uncredited Eric Clapton to play a part he ought to have been quite capable of playing himself), in John Lennon's smouldering *Dear Prudence* and *Cry Baby Cry*, and in the powerful *Helter Skelter*, where Paul McCartney sings of climbing up, with a tune that similarly climbs, only to be pulled down again by crashing guitars that remain firmly fixed to the earth. Overall, however, the album provides only a pale shadow of the group's former glory.

It should be emphasised in all this, that although the Beatles were very widely viewed as style leaders and major innovators for five years or so, they were seldom, if ever, the inventors of the sounds and techniques they used – although they usually adopted them so rapidly and so publicly as to make it seem as though they were. The point is made succinctly, if unintentionally, by a listing made in 2012 on the website *listverse.com*. The 'Ten Beatles Innovations That Changed Music' are all challenged by people outraged at the inaccuracy of the list. They are right, because the items mentioned are mostly not Beatles innovations at all, but it is true that most people do believe them to be and it is equally true that, having been adopted by the Beatles, they did, as a result, profoundly influence the music made afterwards.

TRACKING THE TRACKS

Ideally, it is necessary to listen to all of the core studio recordings made by this remarkable group. These were remastered for a second time in 2009, with noticeable sound improvements over the previous 1987 CD issues. They are, in order of original release, *Please Please Me, With The Beatles, A Hard Day's Night, Beatles For Sale, Help!, Rubber Soul, Revolver, Sgt.Pepper's Lonely Hearts Club Band, Magical Mystery Tour, The Beatles* (always referred to as *The White Album* because of its plain white cover), *Yellow Submarine, Abbey Road*, and *Let It Be* (all on EMI). Insightful reviews of each album are to be found on the website *pitchfork.com*, written by Tom Ewing, Scott Plagenhoef, and Mark Richardson. In May 2017, *Sgt.Pepper's Lonely Hearts Club Band* was reissued as a double CD on Universal/Apple. The second disc comprises early takes of the songs, which are interesting, but the first disc comprises the original album, given a thorough remix for stereo by Giles Martin, and is a revelation.

The songs featured in the TV show, *Magical Mystery Tour*, were originally issued in the UK in the form of a double seven inch EP package. The CD reproduces the original US release, which expanded the music into an LP by adding tracks from singles, including *Penny Lane* and *Strawberry Fields Forever*. The *Yellow Submarine* album contains tracks recorded, just after the *Sgt Pepper* sessions, for the cartoon film of the same title. It also includes orchestral music written for the film by George Martin, so is effectively only half a Beatles album. A 1999 issue called *Yellow Submarine Songtrack* adds Beatles songs used in the film in place of the George Martin music, but all of these were previously issued on other albums. *Abbey Road* contains the last music recorded by the Beatles, even though it was not released last. It takes its place alongside many other albums that set a classic rock agenda for the seventies, which, as far as the Beatles were concerned, was built on by the various solo albums that followed. *Let It Be* presents the best of earlier sessions which found the group members arguing with each other and struggling to create an album of decent material. The songs chosen were remixed by Phil Spector without reference to the Beatles, and much to Paul McCartney's displeasure. The CD *Let It Be.. Naked* from 2003 removes the Spector additions, puts the tracks into a different order, and omits John Lennon's brief rendition of the Liverpool folk tune, *Maggie Mae*, altogether. It makes little difference to what remains the Beatles' least essential album. The double CD, *Past Masters*, needs to be added to the list,

THE FIRST TIME

The Quarrymen, comprising John Lennon, Paul McCartney, George Harrison, pianist John Lowe, and drummer Colin Hanton, recorded two songs at a Liverpool sound recording service in July 1958. These were pressed on to an acetate record, playing at 78 rpm. The songs were a cover of Buddy Holly's *That'll Be The Day* and a composition by Paul McCartney and George Harrison called *In Spite Of All The Danger.* This, the first record involving the Beatles, was passed around the group members for a while, but eventually settled with John Lowe. He attempted to auction it in 1981, but it was Paul McCartney who ended up paying to take possession of it. He pressed around fifty copies of the acetate, some on 78 rpm records and some on 45 rpm singles, which he gave as presents to friends. It is reasonable to suppose that these would be substantial collectors' items if they ever came on to the market, but so far none has. As for the original pressing, it is probably the most valuable record ever made, but as it is never likely to be sold, the value can only be a matter of speculation. An even earlier recording, on a reel-to-reel tape dating from July 1957, when the only Beatle member of the Quarrymen was John Lennon, was auctioned at Sotheby's in 1994 and bought by EMI for £78,500. The company decided not to use the recording due to a sound quality that has been described as 'appalling'.

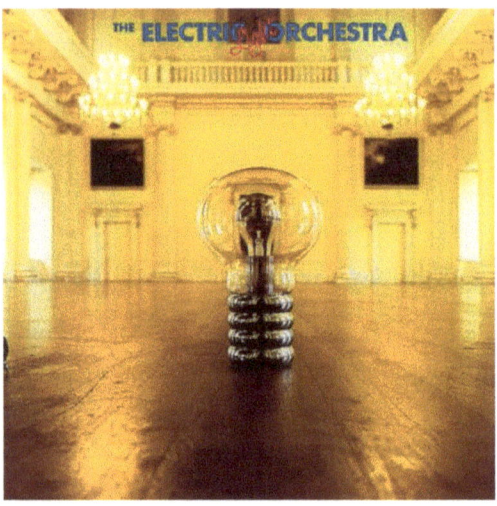

The careers of the Beatles and the Beach Boys were linked, after a fashion, when their first UK singles were released on the same day. Eventually, Brian Wilson of the Beach Boys felt that he had to prove himself by capping each Beatles album release with a 'better' one of his own. Like the Beatles, he gave up playing live in order to concentrate on work in the recording studio, although the rest of the group continued to tour without him. *Pet Sounds* was intended as a response to *Rubber Soul*; the planned album *Smile* would be one to beat *Revolver*. Sadly, after *Sgt Pepper* appeared, Wilson felt that he had lost the battle and would not be able to compete with it. He suffered a mental breakdown and left *Smile* unfinished. The final completion of his song cycle in 2004 made it clear that Wilson had always had a clear idea of how the music was supposed to sound. It makes a remarkable album, with recurring musical themes that give it an overall structure, linking the songs together in a way that *Sgt Pepper* might have intended at one time, but did not carry through. If only Brian Wilson could have finished *Smile* in the sixties, it would undoubtedly be an album held in as much regard as *Sgt Pepper*. As it is, the 2004 recording cannot quite match the brilliance and vitality of the original versions of *Good Vibrations, Heroes And Villains, Cabinessence,* and *Surf's Up*. It is a shame too that *Good Vibrations* is given a different set of words, mainly as a consequence of Brian Wilson falling out with Beach Boys lead singer, Mike Love, who wrote the original. It should be remembered in all this, that the Beach Boys, though very popular, were nevertheless a long way behind the Beatles in their sales. *Pet Sounds* was the group's most successful album in the UK, apart from compilations of hits, but still only managed to reach number two in the album charts. In the US, the album did less well than earlier Beach Boys releases, peaking at number ten.

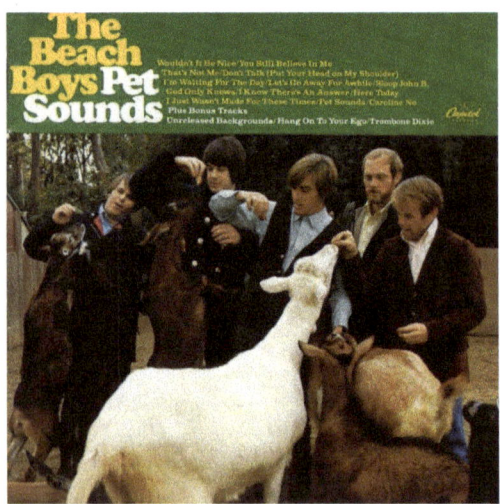
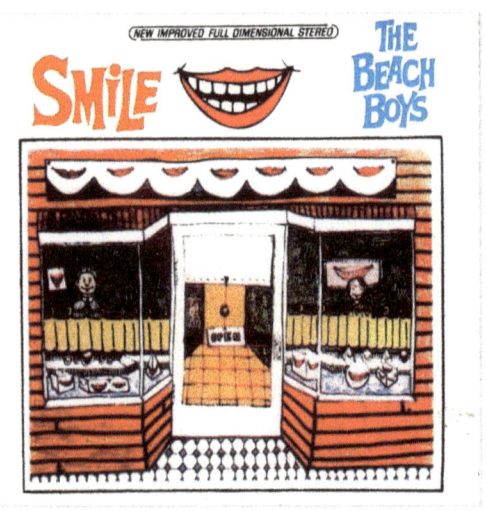

comprising all the tracks not otherwise available on the CD albums. Most of these are the songs that were issued as singles. The Hamburg recordings are available on a double CD, *The Beatles' First* (Universal 2004), rather unnecessarily providing mono and stereo versions.

As an alternative for anyone who does not really want to hear that much Beatle music, there are two double CD compilations, originally issued on vinyl during the seventies, and released with the new remasters in place in 2010. *1962-1966* and *1967-1970* present as many career highlights as could be crammed into the space available and choose the right tracks on the whole. Attempting to cover the Beatles phenomenon with a single CD, the hit collection, *1*, loses too much, especially as it fails to keep to its own brief. The inclusion of a couple of tracks that were not singles (at least not in the UK) and the failure to include a couple that were is just annoying – especially when one of the missing tracks is the magisterial *Strawberry Field Forever* (part of a double A-side to be sure, but so was *We Can Work It Out*, which is on the album). A far more interesting and worthwhile attempt to condense the Beatles music into a single CD is provided by *Love*, issued in 2006. For this, George Martin and his son Giles carried out an extensive remix project, making familiar songs sound fresh by incorporating parts originally recorded for quite different songs. All the music is taken from the original recordings by the Beatles, with the exception of a new string arrangement, written by George Martin to accompany George Harrison's original demo recording of *While My Guitar Gently Weeps*. The album is not intended as a historical document of the Beatles' music; instead it makes the group sound utterly contemporary.

The set of three *Anthology* double CD packages, issued in 1995 and 1996, comprises early recordings, out-takes, unfinished bits and pieces, and a little live material. Some of the music makes for slightly uncomfortable listening, showing that sometimes the Beatles playing in the studio simply did not sound very good. Others are fascinating, such as the Sgt Pepper demos referred to earlier, and there are also important historical recordings, including the only two existing performances by the Quarrymen (featuring John, Paul, and George), five of the songs included on the rejected Decca audition tape, and a number of unreleased songs that the Beatles never managed to finish properly. Most remarkable of these is perhaps George Harrison's powerful *Not Guilty*, driven by his guitar playing, and which should have been part of *The White Album* (where it would have been one of the highlights). Also included on the first two *Anthology* albums are what are effectively two brand new Beatles recordings. *Free As A Bird* and *Real Love* were created by adding new material to unfinished demos made by John Lennon in 1977. They would never have been able to live up to the weight of expectation heaped on them, but they are worthy additions to the Beatles catalogue and both did well in the charts when issued as singles. *Free As A Bird*, which is the more striking of the two songs, reached number two in the UK charts, but could not defeat the might of Michael Jackson's *Earth Song*, at number one. R*eal Love* reached number four, being undoubtedly hampered by the decision of BBC Radio One to exclude the record from its playlist.

There are two volumes of recordings made by the Beatles for the BBC, which present the full catalogue of song influences the group knew well, from playing them live in Hamburg and Liverpool. These are heard alongside efficient renderings of the early hits. The CDs, issued in 1994 and 2013, are interesting but not essential. A live album, *The Beatles At The Hollywood Bowl*, featuring performances from 1964 and 1965, was issued on vinyl in 1977, but has not been reissued on CD. Five songs from a concert in Stockholm in 1963 are included on the first *Anthology* set. They prove what a great live band the Beatles was in the early days, before the problems of audiences who would rather scream than listen and amplification that was inadequate for the large venues made necessary by the group's popularity put the Beatles off the whole live experience. *Eight Days A Week – The Touring Years* is a DVD issued in 2016 and provides film footage of some significant Beatles performances.

Twist At The Top by Howie Casey And The Seniors waited a long time for a release on CD, but has one now (US Bearsville 2010). The *Just For Fun* soundtrack album has not made it to CD, but the film itself is available on a Sony DVD issued in the US.

The albums by other artists, mentioned in the text as being inspired by the Beatles and, in some cases, moving further on are as follows: Donovan – *Sunshine Superman*. The UK version of the album combined tracks taken from two different US albums, but is stronger for this. A double CD issued by EMI in 2011 presents the original mono UK album (it was not issued in stereo) alongside newly discovered stereo mixes of the original US album with the same title and a number of extra tracks. John Mayall – *Bare Wires* (Decca/Universal 2007). Love – *Forever Changes* (Elektra 2001). The Bonzo Dog Doo Dah Band – *The Doughnut In Granny's Greenhouse* (EMI 2007). The Bee Gees – *1st* (Reprise 2007 – this is a double CD with both mono and stereo versions of the original album and a large number of out-takes). The Zombies – *Odessey And Oracle* (Big Beat 2007). The Rolling Stones – *Their Satanic Majesties Request* (Abkco 2002). The Hollies – *Butterfly* (EMI 2000). The Byrds – *The Notorious Byrd Brothers* (Columbia 1997). Simon And Garfunkel – *Bookends* (Sony 2001). Traffic – *Mr Fantasy* and *Traffic* (both Universal/Island 1999). The Jimi Hendrix Experience – *Axis: Bold As Love* and *Electric Ladyland* (both Sony 2012). Family – *Music In A Doll's House* (Pucka 2012). The Moody Blues – *In Search Of The Lost Chord* (Universal 2008). Cream – *Disraeli Gears* and *Wheels Of Fire* (both Polydor 1998). Pink Floyd – *A Saucerful Of Secrets* (EMI 2011)

The Beach Boys *Smile* recordings have a complicated history and only a few, including the singles *Good Vibrations* and *Heroes And Villains* were issued at the time. There are now two alternative albums presenting the material. The double CD, *The Smile Sessions* (EMI 2011) has the intended album on one disc and some interesting out-takes on the second. It should be stressed that the album on the first disc has several tracks that are unfinished, with the lead vocal lines missing. They make an essential comparison, however, with Brian Wilson's own *Brian Wilson Presents Smile* (Nonesuch 2004) which has the complete finished work, using all new recordings carried out by Wilson with members of the group Wondermints. No one is pretending that the Soft Machine albums *Third* and *Fourth* (both Sony 2007) sound remotely like the Beatles – just that their acceptance by the rock buying public owed everything to the way the Beatles had made experimentation seem cool.

THE FIRST TIME

The symphonies of Gustav Mahler are the flowering of a form developed by Haydn and Mozart a hundred years earlier. Mahler delighted in excess – all his symphonies are long works, with the third lasting for over an hour and a half and intending to represent six increasingly complex stages of creation from micro-organisms through to the angels. The eighth, subtitled *Symphony Of A Thousand,* to describe, with only a little exaggeration, the number of people required to perform it, was supposed to represent the resolution of the conflict between the 'eternal masculine' and the 'eternal feminine'. The underpinning of *Tales Of Topographic Oceans* by four classes of Hindu scripture, the 'shastras', seems to be of a kind with Mahler's approach. It is interesting to note that although Mahler is revered today as one of the finest symphonic composers of all time and is even quite popular, after the use of some of his music in the 1971 film, *Death In Venice,* he was not highly rated as a composer during his lifetime (he died in 1911), nor for forty years after that. Ralph Hill, in his book *The Symphony*, published by Penguin in 1949, does include a chapter devoted to Mahler, which would not have happened if the book had been written a few years earlier, but he is inclined to damn the composer with faint praise. He concludes, "Mahler's aim undoubtedly was 'expression', but it is doubtful whether what he wanted to express was always worth the trouble he took over it." Such changes over time in critical opinion regarding the 'great' classical composers are by no means uncommon. Antonio Vivaldi, the creator of the now hugely popular *Four Seasons*, fell out of favour towards the end of his life. His music was completely ignored for nearly two hundred years until its rediscovery in the 1920s.

 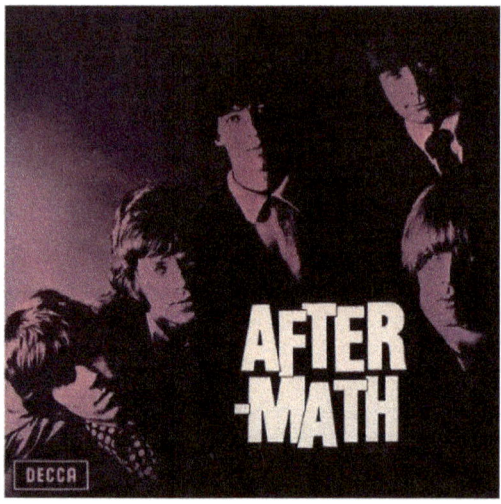

EMI established a specialist label to cater for progressive rock at about the same time as Decca issued its compilation album. *The Book Of Taliesyn* by Deep Purple was the first release on the new Harvest label in June 1969. Phonogram followed in November with a progressive rock label called Vertigo, issuing *Valentyne Suite* by Colosseum as its first LP release. The rapidly growing Island records moved to an almost entirely progressive rock policy during 1969, and accordingly had no need to create a separate label. B&C Records, set up as a rock music adjunct to the reggae specialist, Trojan, began issuing progressive rock records on a new Charisma label, starting with the self-titled LP by Rare Bird in November 1969. The Decca subsidiary, Deram, made the same move as Island, despite which Decca tried yet another progressive label, Nova. Confusingly, records were issued as being either Decca Nova or Deram Nova, but with a single catalogue number sequence. *In From The Cold* by Ashkan, attributed to Decca Nova, was the first release in January 1970. The company's most successful progressive band, however, Caravan, had its first album for Decca retained by the parent label, rather than Nova, which ceased operation soon afterwards, at the end of 1970.

20 PROGRESSIVE ROCK

In December 1973, the group Yes released a double LP called *Tales From Topographic Oceans*. The previous five albums had presented music that was becoming increasingly ambitious – this one contained a single work divided into four parts, one for each side of the record. The structure and scope of the work would have seemed familiar to Gustav Mahler, who completed nine symphonies between 1894 and 1910, although he would not have met the instrumentation used and the rhythms. *Tales Of Topographic Oceans* is symphonic, but it is played by a basic rock group line-up of guitar, bass, drums, and vocals, with a battery of state-of-the-art keyboard instruments (for 1973) adding orchestral texture and complexity. It is rock music, but of a kind that has become inspired and influenced by the aesthetics of classical music.

By 1973, the music played by Yes and many other similar groups was being referred to as 'progressive rock'. When the term first began to be used, during the late sixties, it was actually applied rather more widely than this. Chris Welch uses the word 'progressive' in an October 1968 edition of the music paper, *Melody Maker,* to describe the music of the Yardbirds, whose music was rooted in the blues, albeit frequently tugged into new directions by the spectacular playing of guitarist Jeff Beck. The edition of the American *Billboard* magazine for July 13th 1968 uses the phrase 'progressive rock' in a way that suggests its use as the name for a type of music was already well established. The groups Procol Harum, the Crazy World Of Arthur Brown, and the Who are specifically mentioned. The Decca compilation LP, *Wowie Zowie – The World Of Progressive Rock* was issued in the summer of 1969 and included tracks from the previous two years. They are an eclectic assortment, but none is particularly influenced by classical music. Three tracks are British blues – even if they are a little removed from the American blues that is their original inspiration. They are *Where Did I Belong* by John Mayall, *Train To Nowhere* by Savoy Brown, and *Not Foolish Not Wise* by the Keef Hartley Band. Two tracks are jazz, one being jazz of a particularly impressionist kind – this is *Voodoo Forest* by Johnny Almond. The other is *Go Away, Come Back Another Day* by the John Cameron Quartet, which had previously been employed providing some of the backing for Donovan's *Sunshine Superman* and *In Concert* albums. *Computer Lover* by William R Strickland is an eccentric offering by a solo performer who supposedly improvised his songs at the time of recording. *Nights In White Satin* by the Moody Blues is included, as the only track to have troubled the singles charts, which leaves three tracks of inventive, left-field rock – *Down At Circe's Place* by Touch, *Communion* by East Of Eden, and *In The Beginning* by Genesis, from the group's first, overlooked album.

What these pieces of music have in common is that they are all the work of people trying to be as inventive and as creative as they can. Their priority was to make satisfying music displaying depth and innovation. None of them were thinking in terms of hit singles, although we can be sure that both they and their record company were hoping to sell respectable numbers of LPs. The idea that rock music should be continually innovative – should, in fact, be treated as a form of art – derived from the Beatles. As described in the chapter devoted to the group, the Beatles were concerned with adding new sounds and new techniques to their music, to the point where rock musicians, listeners, and record companies alike were persuaded to equate innovation with success. The LP, *Sgt Pepper's Lonely Hearts Club Band*, received as the Beatles' most innovative work of all, became hugely influential on both the group's contemporaries and the large number of new groups emerging in the album's wake. Although the word 'underground' was tried for a while as a description for the rock music played at this time, this became somewhat untenable when many of the groups were clearly achieving considerable commercial success. 'Progressive rock' worked much better – and the first progressive rock record was clearly the Beatles' *Sgt Pepper's Lonely Hearts Club Band*, released in June 1967.

The Rolling Stones album, *Aftermath*, was issued the year before, in April (June in the US, with a different track listing and three fewer tracks). Both versions of the album included a track called *Goin' Home*, recorded the previous

THE FIRST TIME

A willingness to produce longer pieces of music than can be accommodated on a 7" single implies an increased level of skill on the part of the musicians involved. Following *Goin' Home*, seven more tracks lasting over ten minutes were issued during the next year. *Sad Eyed Lady Of The Lowlands* occupied the whole of side four on the double LP, *Blonde On Blonde*, released by Bob Dylan at the start of July 1966 (see page 98). It is a short side, as the song lasts for less than eleven and a half minutes. *Goin' Home* is only a few seconds shorter and shares the space on its album side with four or five other songs. Dylan's song is only as long as this, however, because it has a large number of musically identical verses. It is, in effect, a short song made to last a long time by means of multiple repetitions. The other six long tracks are all the results of jam sessions. *The Return Of The Son Of Monster Magnet*, fills the fourth side of Frank Zappa's Mothers Of Invention first album, *Freak Out* (released in June 1966), only a little better than did Bob Dylan, but provides the 'freak out' of the album's title. *East West* by the Paul Butterfield Blues Band is the title track of the group's second album, issued in August 1966. Solos by the band's two guitarists and by Butterfield himself on harmonica create an improvised piece that would be jazz if the rhythms were different. Live versions were often even longer than the eleven and a quarter minutes here – a performance recorded in California early in 1967 and available on CD lasts for over twenty-eight minutes. *Up In Her Room* by the Seeds was released in October 1966 on the album *A Web Of Sound*; *Revelation* on the Love LP *Da Capo* and *Two Trains Running* on the Blues Project LP *Projections* were both released in November, with the former track weighing in at an impressive nineteen minutes. *The End* is the eleven minutes, forty seconds final track on the first, self-titled LP by The Doors, which was released in January 1967. All of these tracks are by American artists. In the UK, John Mayall's Bluesbreakers were playing songs as long as these in live performance, but nothing was released on record until the two LP set, *The Diary Of A Band*, which comprised live material from late 1967. A live recording by Cream from October 1967 has been issued on a bootleg CD, with six of the ten tracks included being over ten minutes long and one of them, *Spoonful*, lasting for twenty-two minutes. *Virgin Forest*, an eleven minute avant garde sound collage with some rock music elements, and made up, not of a single performance, but from several separate recordings jammed together, was included on the self-titled album by the Fugs, issued a couple of weeks before the Rolling Stones' *Aftermath*. *Desolation Row*, another Bob Dylan song made to last a long time by means of repetition, dates from August 1965 (it is included on the *Highway 61 Revisited* album), but its determinedly folk treatment (with no drums) prevents it from stealing *Goin' Home*'s thunder.

A young Mick Jagger sings with Alexis Korner's Blues Inc. Jack Bruce (later with Cream) plays bass and Dick Heckstall-Smith (later with John Mayall and Colosseum) plays tenor saxophone.

In February 1966, a single of unprecedented power was released, with a guitar that used high amplification and controlled feedback to give itself a sustaining sound only previously heard on the John Mayall/Eric Clapton single, *I'm Your Witchdoctor*. *Shapes Of Things* by the Yardbirds launched a style of rock music that was identified and given a name much later, when journalist Phil Smee coined 'freakbeat' for a retrospective CD issued in 1989. The various groups that, lacking a Jeff Beck to play cutting-edge guitar, applied an assortment of slightly weird studio sounds to their beat music, were considerably upstaged as soon as the Beatles presented *Tomorrow Never Knows* on the *Revolver* LP in August. In the US, an LP called *Psychedelic Moods* was issued in October by a group called the Deep, comprising music that would be called freakbeat if it was British. This was the first time that the term 'psychedelic' appeared in a descriptive record title, although there is a rival claim from the Thirteenth Floor Elevators, whose first album was issued the same month, with "Psychedelic Sounds" printed on the back cover but not on the front or the labels. Its debut in a lyric was earlier than this, in the song *Hesitation Blues*, on the 1964 first album by the folk duo, the Holy Modal Rounders. Meanwhile, *Eight Miles High* by the Byrds, issued seven months before the Deep LP, initiated a psychedelic music of rather more lasting significance.

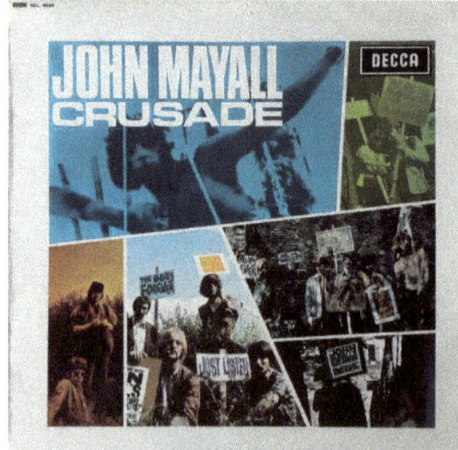  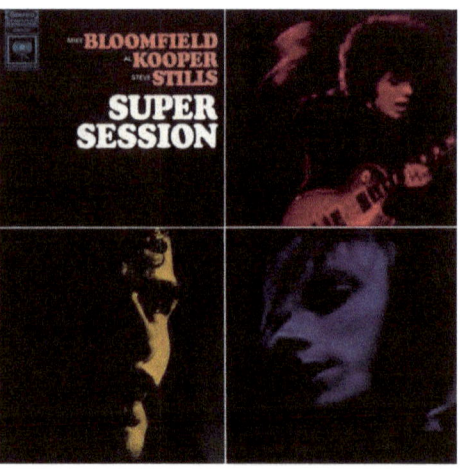

December, which made available the results of the band jamming in the studio. The song was extended to well over eleven minutes as a result, becoming the longest rock song on record up until then. The track attracted even more attention when part of it was adopted by the influential UK television show, *Ready Steady Go*, as its last theme tune. The music of the Rolling Stones had always been perceived as being tougher, less pop, than that of the Beatles. Whereas the Beatles were primarily influenced by rock and roll and early soul music, the Stones, whose name was taken from a song by Muddy Waters, liked early soul too, but were most interested in the blues. They had even achieved a number one hit with a faithful rendering of a Howlin' Wolf song, *Little Red Rooster*, complete with slide (bottle-neck) guitar playing, which was a considerable novelty in the UK at the time. The original Rolling Stones line-up (with Dick Taylor, later of the Pretty Things, on bass) had come together via jam sessions at the Ealing Jazz Club, hosted by Alexis Korner's Blues Incorporated, with whom Charlie Watts was the drummer for a short time in 1962. The Stones had therefore come into contact with musicians like Dick Heckstall-Smith and Jack Bruce, who had a background in jazz and were comfortable with an improvisational approach to playing blues-based music. It is not surprising that the Rolling Stones liked to jam in the studio. In contrast, the Beatles had a background that involved working out versions of rock 'n' roll songs to play at the Cavern or in Hamburg, rather than improvising on the blues. Amongst the wealth of Beatles studio out-takes, released over the years on numerous bootleg records and CDs, there is little jamming and nothing like *Goin' Home*.

Alexis Korner's Blues Incorporated was one of two UK blues bands to act as a training school for musicians destined to exert significant influence on the development of rock music during the sixties, the other being John Mayall's Bluesbreakers. Both bands adopted an improvisational approach to their music, in which instrumental skill was paramount. John Mayall's own sleevenotes on his LP, *A Hard Road*, released in February 1967, praised the individual talents of the members of his band, suggesting that new guitarist Peter Green should be considered as the equal of the established blues guitar greats, Jimi Hendrix, Buddy Guy, Otis Rush, and Eric Clapton (Green's predecessor in the Bluesbreakers). The next LP, *Crusade*, was intended to have its title taken literally, presenting itself as an audio manifesto for the superiority of blues-rock music over other forms of pop, where instrumental skill was not important. Mayall complained on the back cover, "Radio and television stations everywhere daily churn out synthetic sounds while the musical papers relay the fairy tales and extol the virtues of performers only fit for the screams of children". He listed the key that each song on the LP was played in, to emphasise that they were all different and that some were quite difficult. In the US, the Paul Butterfield Blues Band and the Blues Project were similarly concerned with playing music that relied on instrumental prowess, although these bands did not have the huge turnover of musicians that both Alexis Korner and John Mayall presided over.

Musicians involved in the two American bands (along with guitarist Stephen Stills from Buffalo Springfield, drafted in to replace an ailing Mike Bloomfield) were responsible for the influential *Super Session* album, issued in July 1968 as something of another manifesto for the rock musicians wanting to be taken seriously as skilled exponents of their instruments. The instigators were Al Kooper and Mike Bloomfield, who had previously played together in support of Bob Dylan. The music was presented as the recorded result of after-hours jam sessions, making the point that these rock players were more than capable of behaving in the same way as jazz players had done during the previous thirty years or more. They were even confident enough to reference John Coltrane, the leading cutting-edge jazz performer of the time, in a convincing modal improvisation in the Coltrane manner, entitled *His Holy Modal Majesty*. *Super Session* was a surprise hit, entering the album charts on both sides of the Atlantic and qualifying for a gold disc award in the US. Clearly its time had come.

The combination of Beatles-inspired adventure in songwriting and arrangement with more sharply honed instrumental skills produced some remarkable albums during the late sixties, all of them worthy of the description 'progressive rock', even if they were not actually called that at the time. Steve Winwood left the hit-making Spencer Davis Group in April 1967 in order to create more wide-ranging music with musicians he had met jamming in a Birmingham club called The Elbow Room. The resultant *Mr Fantasy* album, released in December and credited to

THE FIRST TIME

Pink Floyd was the first group to think in terms of long composed works that were not extended by means of passages of improvised soloing, The title track of the 1968 album, *A Saucerful Of Secrets,* presented the first of these. It was constructed in three movements, in the manner of classical music, although the influences from that musical world were much more contemporary than those adopted by the likes of Keith Emerson. *Ummagumma* and the three albums that followed included further explorations of the style. The music was taken as a starting point by a number of German performers – Tangerine Dream, Kluster (later reborn as Cluster), Kraftwerk, Klaus Schulze, and others. These increasingly incorporated electronics into their version of progressive rock, including synthesizers, as soon as these became easily available. The term 'Krautrock' was adopted for these artists, which, luckily, no-one appeared to find insulting. In the US, Frank Zappa frequently followed a similar approach throughout his career, although the results were rather different, being less concerned than the Floyd with timbre, texture, and impressionism.

The version of the album *Forever Changes* currently available on CD includes both sides of a single that was originally recorded and released a few months later. The album benefits greatly as a result – and it was already close to being essential. *Laughing Stock* revisits Love's high energy garage roots, as displayed on the driving earlier recording *Seven And Seven Is*, but is filtered through the improved musicianship the group had developed since. *Your Mind And We Belong Together* caps an unusual song structure with a ferocious guitar solo – more dramatic by far than those included on *A House Is Not A Motel* and *Live And Let Live*.

By incorporating improvised solos alongside quotes from classical music within complicated segmented works, Frank Zappa anticipated the methods of progressive rock on his album with the Mothers Of Invention, *Absolutely Free*, released in May 1967. Initially sidelined as an interesting, but essentially unimportant novelty artist (the acclaim that greeted the guitar playing on Zappa's 1969 album, *Hot Rats*, indicated that his similar playing on *Absolutely Free* had not been noticed), Zappa had little immediate influence on the bands subsequently developing progressive rock. But his later master works, climaxing with the last album he completed, *Civilization Phaze III*, succeeded in outclassing most of them.

These days, progressive rock music is often referred to using the short-hand term 'prog', which was not employed during the seventies when the genre was most popular. It is not entirely clear when this name began to be used. In the sleevenotes to the archive compilation CD set by King Crimson, *Epitaph,* issued in 1997, Robert Fripp refers to the term 'prog' as though it was a fairly new invention. Three years earlier, a survey of the genre published in *Vox* magazine was headlined as a 'Prog Rock Special'. Earlier than that, the trail runs cold, although the author is assured that copies from the late eighties of the Genesis fanzine, *The Waiting Room,* use the term 'prog rock dinosaur', presumably ironically.

Traffic, was one of the more highly acclaimed examples of the new movement. It took its place alongside such influential albums as *Disraeli Gears* by Cream, *Axis: Bold As Love* by the Jimi Hendrix Experience, the self-titled *Procol Harum*, *Forever Changes* by Love, *A Piper At The Gates Of Dawn* by Pink Floyd, and *Their Satanic Majesties Request* by the Rolling Stones, all of which were released towards the end of 1967 and shared a similar aesthetic. Not that the music was without its critics. Writers in the newspapers *NME* and *Melody Maker* were puzzled at Procol Harum's lack of movement on stage. They did not understand that Gary Brooker and company believed their colourful clothing to be sufficient compromise in the presentation of music intended to overwhelm audiences on its own merits. Meanwhile, it is *still* widely held that the music of *Their Satanic Majesties Request*, with its kaleidoscopic instrumental timbres and textures, is an unfortunate aberration, rather than a rare example of the Rolling Stones demonstrating an ambition that, for once, could not be encompassed within the comfortable slogan, "it's only rock 'n' roll". Pink Floyd would certainly never have accepted such a limited point of view. Their own approach to music making was rather summed up by the photograph used for the back cover of their 1969 album, *Ummagumma*. The equipment laid out in front of the group's van is modest by modern standards, but at the time it seemed that the quantity of it was extraordinary. Clearly the band was ploughing the proceeds of its record sales straight back into the music. Pink Floyd was, at this time, the only band presenting a surround sound experience to its audiences, with speakers placed strategically around the entire venue and controlled by a device mounted on the keyboards and christened the 'azimuth co-ordinator'.

For a long time, the classical music establishment did not look very favourably on the pop music upstart. Although rock and pop were responsible for developing new instruments (such as the electric guitar) and new ways of using the resources of the recording studio, these were largely ignored by classical composers and musicians until well into the nineteen seventies. The first electric guitar concerto, written by a composer with an appropriately academic training (the Royal Academy of Music), did not arrive until 1974 – decades after the instrument's invention. Even then, David Bedford, who named his concerto *Star's End* and employed Mike Oldfield to play it, remained something of a maverick. He had, after all, chosen to play in a rock group for a while (Kevin Ayers and the Whole World). One of the earliest employments of an electric guitar within a composed 'classical' work is actually the responsibility of a man who was self-taught and is primarily known as a rock musician. A piece performed by the Pomona Valley Symphony Orchestra in 1961 was intended as the soundtrack for the low-budget independent film *The World's Greatest Sinner*. It is essentially a modern orchestral work with a rock element introduced at the start and it was composed by Frank Zappa. It has never received an official release on record or CD, although it is included on a bootleg album issued in 1983 called *Serious Music*.

In September 1967, the struggling Moody Blues were asked by their record company, Decca, to consider recording a rock version of Dvorak's *New World Symphony*, with an orchestra. Later recordings by the likes of Louis Clark *(Hooked On Classics)* suggest that this might not have turned out very well, but in the event the Moody Blues decided to use the allotted studio time to record their own songs, with Peter Knight agreeing to provide orchestral accompaniment and linking material. Decca, who had been thinking in terms of a demonstration record to highlight the quality of their improved stereo recording (which they branded 'Deramic Sound System') decided to release the record anyway – with a mono version issued too, despite this rather making a mockery of the whole project. The concept of combining popular music with an orchestra was hardly new, as the likes of Frank Sinatra, the Drifters, and Gerry and the Pacemakers would have testified, and neither did the presence of an orchestra necessarily make the songs have anything to do with classical music. Some of the songs on the Moody Blues' *Days Of Future Passed* are rather good, but the orchestral links threaten to turn the whole thing into the soundtrack for a TV soap. Nevertheless, the album has managed to acquire the kudos of a landmark recording regardless and a significant element in the birth of progressive rock. The key track *Nights In White Satin* was a much smaller hit in the UK than people remember (it reached no higher than number 19 in the charts, although a reissue five years later, when the Moody Blues had become big stars, and following the record's belated climb to the top of the US charts, did a little better at number 9).

The idea of making rock versions of classical pieces was taken up by keyboard player Keith Emerson. He filled

THE FIRST TIME

The sleeve-notes of David Chesky's 2010 *Concerto for Electric Guitar and Orchestra* attempt a potted history of the form and can only come up with the name of Frank Zappa prior to 1980. Zappa's *Revised Music For Guitar And Low-Budget Orchestra* was recorded in 1975 and first issued on the album *Studio Tan*. There are others that could have been mentioned – apart from David Bedford's *Star's End*, there are works by Patrick Gowers (*Rhapsody for Guitar, Electric Guitars, and Electric Organ* – also from 1974, though not recorded until 1977) and John Buller (Proenca, 1979). The electric guitar also features prominently in two other early works – William Russo's *Three Pieces For Blues Band and Symphony Orchestra* from 1968 and Jon Lord's *Concerto for Group and Orchestra* from 1969, although neither composer usually worked in the classical music world. A handful of other works, such as Leonard Bernstein's Mass from 1971, incorporate electric guitar into their instrumentation, but without making anything of its potential, or giving it any kind of prominent role. This proviso applies equally to the very first use of electric guitar in a classical piece, if works by Karlheinz Stockhausen can be so categorised. His *Gruppen*, first performed in 1958 (and therefore predating the Frank Zappa piece), has an electric guitar, apparently equipped with a volume pedal, included within the ranks of one of the three orchestras needed to perform the work. It can be heard delivering a few crisp notes in a couple of places, but in such an understated manner as to be easily missed. As with the Bernstein Mass, one feels that an acoustic guitar could have served equally well – as indeed it has done during some live performances of *Gruppen*.

Liquid light shows, in which lights were shone through coloured oils placed on top of overhead projectors, or else held within photographic slides, were pioneered by Bill Ham in 1965 at the Red Dog Saloon in Virginia City, Nevada and used in particular with the music of the Charlatans. Ham called his company Light Sound Dimension, doubtless deliberately selected to echo the initial letters of the recreational drug of choice at the time. In 1966, Ham moved to San Francisco and provided the light show for the Avalon Ballroom, where the likes of Jefferson Airplane were regular performers. In the UK, as a separate parallel development, a light show operated by Mike Leonard and others was used by Pink Floyd from early 1966.

Although different versions of King Crimson have performed and made records ever since 1969, under the leadership of guitarist Robert Fripp, the original band sadly broke up at the end of the year, following an exhausting American tour. Greg Lake, the singer and bass player, co-founded the band Emerson Lake and Palmer and went on to achieve enormous success. Ian McDonald, the mellotron and wind instrument player, eventually joined Foreigner, which was also a highly successful band. Drummer Michael Giles contented himself with session work and appeared on many albums. Lyricist Peter Sinfield continued to write (and produce) for a variety of artists including Roxy Music, Emerson Lake and Palmer, PFM, and Procol Harum's Gary Brooker. Some of his later work was surprising, including as it did, songs for Bucks Fizz and Celine Dion, At the start of the new century, McDonald and Giles reunited to play again the original King Crimson material, as the Twenty-First Century Schizoid Band. Other Crimson alumni were involved too, together with guitarist Jakko Jakszyk, who managed the difficult task of handling the lead vocals at the same time as reproducing Robert Fripp's tricky guitar parts. Fripp himself was apparently not interested in looking backwards at that time and did not join the band. A King Crimson tour in late 2015, however, with Jakko Jakszyk and saxophonist Mel Collins included in the line-up, did revisit early material.

King Crimson would have liked to include *Mars* on the album, but was unable to gain the necessary permission from Gustav Holst's daughter, who retained the copyright. A version of the music eventually appeared on the second album credited to King Crimson, changed enough to avoid copyright problems and retitled *The Devil's Triangle*.

It is Robert Fripp who was responsible for the thought-provoking aphorism, in 1980, "Music is the cup that holds the wine of silence", slightly misquoted in an episode of the ITV series, *Rosemary And Thyme*. *The Wine Of Silence* was used as the title for an album of orchestral arrangements of Fripp soundscapes, issued in 2012.

Since the seventies, a number of bands have adopted a progressive rock style, using as template the work of the three seen as particularly embodying the music – King Crimson, Yes, and Genesis. The first of the late arrivals to achieve success was Marillion, whose debut album, *Script For A Jester's Tear*, was issued in March 1983. King Crimson itself has departed considerably from the classic sound, with albums like *The ConstruKction Of Light*, from 2000, deliberately seeking new musical territory and thereby continuing to be 'progressive' despite sounding quite unlike *In The Court Of The Crimson King*. One of the few more recent bands to create progressive rock in this sense is Radiohead. Initially seen as a one trick pony after the success of the single *Creep* in 1993, the band chose to continually find new approaches to songwriting and performance and, miraculously, it kept its popularity intact while doing this. The album *OK Computer* from 1997 has often appeared at the top of lists of all time great albums.

some of the second LP by his group the Nice (*Ars Longa Vita Brevis*, issued in November 1968) with this kind of music, alongside a group composition (with a little input from Bach), divided into movements in the classical manner. An orchestra was employed in places, but Emerson's virtuosity on the Hammond organ and piano was enough to make the classical fusion work quite well in any case. Subsequently, he expanded the approach with Emerson, Lake, and Palmer – devoting a whole album to a rock music reworking of Mussorgsky's *Pictures At An Exhibition* in 1971 and eventually writing a convincing piano concerto of his own (included on the 1977 ELP album, *Works Volume 1*).

In May 1969, the first music to be heard by a new group, King Crimson, was broadcast on John Peel's BBC radio programme, *Top Gear*, which had become recognised as the showcase for all the latest developments in rock music. The three songs that were played made a huge impression. *21st Century Schizoid Man*, *I Talk To The Wind*, and *In The Court Of The Crimson King* were powerful compositions, complex in the manner of classical music, yet with highly memorable melodies and strong rhythms, and delivered with an easy virtuosity that seemed incredible for a previously unknown band. It transpired that the musicians had been continually rehearsing their material since January – and it showed. The use of the mellotron to create orchestral sounds recalled the Moody Blues, who had pioneered the instrument as a central part of their own sound, but it seemed to be even more dramatic and forceful when employed by King Crimson. Its player also performed on alto saxophone and flute, proving himself to be highly skilled on all his instruments. The guitarist contented himself for the most part with adding character and colour – rhythm guitar would have been an inadequate description for what he managed to achieve. But when he soloed, which he did on *21st Century Schizoid Man*, he was adept, innovative, and surprising. The singer was powerful and compelling, while anchoring the proceedings with his well chosen bass guitar lines. Meanwhile, the drummer, adopting the decorative approach of an orchestral player, but combining it with the rhythmic sophistication of a jazzman, was revealing himself to be one of the most talented percussionists of his generation. Unusually, the band also had a fifth member, who was not heard on the BBC session because he did not play anything. He was in charge of the band's light show on stage – an essential addition to live performances at the time – and he also wrote the lyrics for all the songs.

A second Peel session followed in early September, with the band reprising *In The Court Of The Crimson King*, but adding two new pieces as distinctive as those already heard – *Epitaph* and an inspired cover of a Donovan song, *Get Thy Bearings*. The band was gigging hard in London and elsewhere, building a loyal following, and in July was one of the acts supporting the high-profile Rolling Stones performance in London's Hyde Park. Though playing for just half an hour, many observers felt that King Crimson had rather stolen the show. The result of all this activity was that the first album, which eventually appeared in October on the Island label, was highly anticipated, especially when endorsed by the Who's Pete Townshend, who described it as "an uncanny masterpiece" in a series of newspaper advertisements. The album, called *In The Court Of The Crimson King – An Observation By King Crimson*, after the band's signature song, had apparently been recorded quite quickly, due to the group's familiarity with the music. It presented the key songs from the live performances alongside a new piece, *Moonchild*. This incorporated some of the relatively gentle free improvisation with which the band liked to intrigue audiences during the lead-up to the powerful version of Gustav Holst's *Mars* that brought the live set to a fitting final climax. *Moonchild* was over twelve minutes long. The other tracks were a little shorter than this, but there were still only five of them in total. In each case, the music was sufficiently extended to justify the use of subtitles for sections within each song. The title track, for example, had become *In The Court Of The Crimson King inc. The Return Of The Fire Witch and The Dance Of The Puppets*. Only *I Talk To The Wind* managed to keep its title unadorned. It was the shortest track, but still lasted for over six minutes.

The album sold well, reaching number 5 in the UK charts and number 28 in the USA, where it was awarded a gold disc. Its success, combined with the powerful impact of its music, meant that it became hugely influential on other bands. The combination of extended song-writing, with voicings that were frequently orchestral in sound, and virtuoso musicianship, made it into a blueprint for a genre of music to follow – progressive rock. As Peter Sinfield's own words to the song *In The Court Of The Crimson King* proclaim, as if describing a race organiser with a starting pistol, "The pattern juggler lifts his hand, the orchestra begin".

THE FIRST TIME

TRACKING THE TRACKS

Tales Of Topographic Oceans by Yes is available on a Warner double CD (2003), which includes two bonus studio run-throughs not on the original vinyl. The uncommitted listener should probably first try one or more of the previous three albums, the music on these being in the same style, but split into slightly smaller chunks and more accessible. These are *The Yes Album*, *Fragile*, and *Close To The Edge* (all Warner, 2003).

Wowie Zowie – The World Of Progressive Rock has not been issued on CD, although copies of the original LP are not scarce. Its individual tracks have all been issued on the parent album CDs by the various artists involved, although the CD by the John Cameron Quartet is no longer easily available, with second-hand copies being hard to find and quite expensive. *Sgt Pepper's Lonely Hearts Club Band* by the Beatles was remastered for CD in 2009 (EMI) and given a full remix for stereo in 2017 (EMI).

Both versions of *Aftermath* by the Rolling Stones were remastered for CD release in 2002. Bob Dylan's *Sad Eyed Lady Of The Lowlands* is on *Blonde On Blonde* (Sony, 2004). Frank Zappa's *Freak Out*, credited to the Mothers Of Invention, is on Rykodisc (1995). *East West* by the Butterfield Blues Band is available as part of a double CD, which also includes the first album, *The Paul Butterfield Blues Band* (Warner, 2001). Three live versions of the title piece, including the one that lasts twenty-eight minutes, are on *East-West Live* (Winner 1996).

The Seeds' *A Web Of Sound* is packaged with the group's first album on a double CD (Edsel 2001). *Da Capo* by Love is on a Warner CD (2002) which includes the album in both mono and stereo. *Two Trains Running* by the Blues Project is most easily obtained on the double CD compilation, *The Blues Project Anthology* (Polygram, 1997). The whole of the *Projections* album is included. The 40th Anniversary edition of the self-titled first album by the Doors is on Rhino (2007). *The End* is also included on the compilation CD, *The Best Of The Doors* (Warner, 2000). *The Fugs* is on an Ace CD (1993) with various bonus tracks.

Shapes Of Things is included on several compilations of Yardbirds hits, such as the double CD *The Best Of The Yardbirds – Shapes Of Things* (Demon 2010). *Psychedelic Moods* by the Deep is on Pilot (2012). *The Psychedelic Sounds of the Thirteenth Floor Elevators* is on Charly (2010). The first two albums by the Holy Modal Rounders are combined on a single CD on Fantasy (1999). There are several good compilations of freakbeat available – such as the four CD set, *Nuggets II* (Rhino 2001).

The John Mayall albums *A Hard Road*, *Crusade*, and *The Diary Of A Band* are all available as Decca/Universal CDs (2006-7). *Diary* was issued as two separate LPs on vinyl and is still a double disc set on CD. The live recording by Cream from October 1967 was issued as a double CD called *Sun Vanishes* and can be heard on YouTube.

Alexis Korner made a lot of albums (though not as many as John Mayall, who at the age of 84 in 2018 is still making them) and the majority are on CD. *The Roots Of UK Rock 'n' Roll* (Delta 2013) is a good compilation of his early recordings and includes the complete *R&B From The Marquee*, Korner's live showcase originally issued in 1962.

Super Session, credited to Mike Bloomfield – Al Kooper – Steve Stills, is on a Sony CD from 2003 and includes two tracks that were not on the original LP, along with alternate versions of two that were. (They lack the horns that Al Kooper overdubbed after the original recordings were completed. It is clear, however, that Kooper knew what he was doing.)

Mr Fantasy by Traffic was issued on CD by Island in 1999. The complete UK stereo version of the album is included, alongside the complete US mono version. This US edition adds the two singles, *Paper Sun* and *Hole In My Shoe*, which were not included on the UK release. The mono and stereo mixes of the tracks that have the same titles differ by more than their spatial separation, with completely different guitar solos and other very noticeable variations in some cases.

Disraeli Gears by Cream is available as a two CD deluxe edition (Universal/Polydor 2004) which comprises the mono and stereo versions of the album, along with numerous out-takes and BBC session recordings. *Axis: Bold As Love* by The Jimi Hendrix Experience is on a CD issued by Sony in 2010. There are no mono versions included, although the original LP was issued in both mono and stereo. The album does really need to be heard in stereo.

The self-titled first album by Procol Harum is on an Esoteric CD (2015) and includes both sides of the group's first two singles (*A Whiter Shade Of Pale* and *Homburg*), which were not on the original LP.

The CD of *Forever Changes* by Love has seven bonus tracks altogether, including the two sides of the single (Warner 2001).

Pink Floyd's *A Piper At The Gates Of Dawn* was issued as a triple CD set by EMI in 2007, comprising the mono version, the stereo version, and a compilation of the first three singles with some alternate takes. The double LP *Ummagumma* becomes a double CD (EMI, 2011) – one disc is live, the other recorded in the studio. For the listener who does not require all of the early albums, the album in between these two is the essential one. *A Saucerful Of Secrets* (EMI, 1994 – originally issued in 1968) is the band's most masterful recording prior to *Dark Side Of The Moon*. The album *More* (the 2016 CD is on Pink Floyd Records), issued immediately before *Ummagumma*, has its imagination curtailed by the demands of the film for which it served as soundtrack and cannot be counted as a proper group album.

Their Satanic Majesties Request by the Rolling Stones is on an Abkco CD (2002).

MUSIC GENRES

David Bedford's *Star's End* is on a Virgin CD (1997). The David Chesky album is on his own Chesky label and includes two other orchestral works in addition to the *Concerto for Electric Guitar and Orchestra*.

The Patrick Gowers *Rhapsody* was included on the LP *John Williams Plays Patrick Gowers* (CBS, 1977). It has not been issued on CD. Gowers wrote the music for the *Sherlock Holmes* TV series starring Jeremy Brett, which is available on CD but does not have any electric guitar playing. John Buller's *Proenca* accompanies another work, *The Theatre Of Memory*, which does not include an electric guitar, on a Unicorn-Kanchana CD (1992).

The William Russo work is paired with *Street Music* on a Deutsche Grammophon CD (2002). The featured blues band is the Siegel-Schwall Band, which made several albums in its own right during the sixties and seventies, without ever managing to achieve the authenticity and conviction of rival concerns like the Butterfield Blues Band or Canned Heat. It is largely unknown in the UK, where none of the albums were issued, apart from the one made by Russo.

Jon Lord's *Concerto For Group And Orchestra* was issued under the name of Lord's group, Deep Purple, which performed the work with the Royal Philharmonic Orchestra conducted by Malcolm Arnold. It was issued on CD by EMI in 2002. A new version of the work was recorded by Jon Lord in 2012, using some well known rock musicians, including Joe Bonamassa, Steve Morse, and Bruce Dickinson. It was issued on the Thompson Music label.

Leonard Bernstein's *Mass*, conducted by the man himself, is on a Sony CD (1997). There are also three other recordings of the work on CD, with different conductors. Karlheinz Stockhausen's *Gruppen*, performed by the Berliner Philharmoniker conducted by Claudio Abbado, Friedrich Goldmann, and Marcus Creed, is included on a Deutsche Grammophon CD (1996, reissued 2012) alongside two much later works by the less celebrated György Kurtág.

There is a long track entitled *The World's Greatest Sinner* available as a digital download from Amazon, Spotify, and elsewhere. This is not the same as the work included on the Frank Zappa *Serious Music* LP, which remains officially unavailable. Bits of the work can be heard within the download, alongside the Zappa-produced song credited to Baby Ray and The Ferns, which is also called *The World's Greatest Sinner*. Most of the download, however, comprises spoken word material from the film. *Serious Music* also includes the otherwise unreleased orchestral version of Zappa's *Sinister Footwear* and is an essential purchase for admirers of the man's music. *Absolutely Free* is on a Zappa Records CD (2012); *Civilization Phaze III* is a double CD on Barking Pumpkin (2017).

The Moody Blues album *Days Of Future Passed* is on a Decca/Universal CD from 2008. It includes several extra tracks taken from singles and alternate takes.

The Nice album *Ars Longa Vita Brevis* is on a Charly CD from 2003. There is also a double CD version on Sanctuary from the same year, where the second disc contains BBC sessions and other live material. *Pictures At An Exhibition* by Emerson Lake and Palmer is on a Sony CD from 2011, which includes some alternative versions recorded over twenty years later. There are also earlier editions on the Castle label, without the bonus tracks. *Works Volume 1* fills a double CD set on Sony (2011).

In The Court Of The Crimson King has been given a few different CD releases over the years. The Original Master Edition on the EG label dates from 2004 and benefits from a 24 bit remaster carried out by Simon Heyworth. The 40th Anniversary Edition on DGM (2009) is available as a 6 disc set. There is room here for the 2004 remaster, a new 2009 remaster, and a 5:1 surround sound version. There are numerous alternate takes and run-throughs, which are interesting but not really essential. There is also a recording of the King Crimson performance in Hyde Park, whose sound quality is not great and which features some dodgy harmony vocals in places, but is a fascinating document, nevertheless, of the original group's live work. An abbreviated double CD version of the set has the 2009 remasters, the surround sound version, and a small number of the out-takes. Some of the BBC session recordings and more live material from 1969 in reasonable quality is available in the *Epitaph* collection, which was issued as a 2 or 4 CD set in 1997, and reissued as two separate 2 CD sets in 2009. All are on Robert Fripp's DGM label.

King Crimson's second album, *In The Wake Of Poseidon*, complete with the reworked interpretation of Holst's *Mars*, was issued by DGM as a remastered 30th Anniversary edition in 1999, with the addition of both sides of the *Catfood* single. In view of the circumstances in which the record was made, with the band in a state of disintegration, it is best viewed as half of a double album, which is completed by the Ian McDonald and Michael Giles recordings that make up their *McDonald and Giles* LP (issued on CD in 2002 by Virgin). At least some of this consists of music that was originally intended to be performed by the whole band.

The key album by the Twenty First Century Schizoid Band is the first (and only studio recording), entitled *Official Bootleg Volume One* (Schizoid Band, 2002). The 2015 King Crimson tour is represented by the double CD, *Live In Toronto* (DGM 2016).

Script For A Jester's Tear by Marillion is on EMI (2012). King Crimson's *The ConstruKction Of Light* is on DGM (2007).

All of Radiohead's music is well-worth investigating. *Ok Computer* is on XL Recordings (2016). *Creep* is included on the first album, *Pablo Honey* (Parlophone 1993). There is a *Best Of Radiohead* available (Parlophone 2008), although this focusses on the band's early years and is inevitably no substitute for the individual original albums.

THE FIRST TIME

Eric Clapton joined the Yardbirds in October 1963, at the age of eighteen, replacing guitarist Top Topham, who had been with the band for less than five months, but was too young to consider becoming a professional musician. Eric Clapton's first recordings are with the Yardbirds. Sonny Boy Williamson had come to the UK for a tour and was given the inexperienced Yardbirds as his backing group. Fortunately, they performed much better than might have been expected. A live album, recorded at the Crawdaddy Club in Richmond on December 8th 1963, was issued later, but two tracks were recorded the day before at a club in Croydon. The first of these, *Take It Easy Baby,* has some good lead guitar playing by Eric Clapton and marks his recording debut. A studio demo, recorded at a similar time by the Yardbirds on their own, *Baby What's Wrong,* is equally impressive. They do not, of course, have the overdriven guitar sound of Clapton's work with John Mayall and afterwards.

The best indication of Eric Clapton's talent in his early career is not on a Yardbirds record, but on a track made by visiting American bluesman Otis Spann. *Pretty Girls Everywhere* is not exactly standard blues material, but in the hands of Spann and his group there is no doubting its authenticity. It was quite a coup for Clapton to be invited on to the session at all, but he is in no way overawed by his good fortune. He plays a solo, but also throughout the song, constructing a melody to complement the one sung by Otis Spann. Buoyed up by a rhythm that is airy and infectious, the guitar melody is such an asset to the song that it would make an interesting instrumental on its own, yet at the same time it allows Spann to deliver the lyrics without his thunder being stolen. It is, in short, a magnificent piece of sympathetic lead guitar playing.

In an interview with *Playboy* magazine in 1980, John Lennon claimed the title of first heavy metal record for the Beatles song, *Ticket To Ride,* issued as a single in April 1965. While the rhythm guitar drone and dominant drum beat that push the song forwards enable one to understand what he meant, the fact of the matter is that, as far as sheer heaviness is concerned, the song was immediately eclipsed by the Who, issuing their single, *Anyway Anyhow Anywhere,* a month later and by the John Mayall/Eric Clapton *I'm Your Witchdoctor* in August, even if neither of those records was as big a hit as *Ticket To Ride.* In any case, the Kinks' single, *You Really Got Me,* was arguably a more powerful performance than any of these and was issued the previous August and got to number one in the UK charts. Despite persistent rumours over the years that the energetic guitar solo on the track was played by Jimmy Page, it has been confirmed during interviews with Ray Davies, producer Shel Talmy, and Jimmy Page himself that the soloist was Dave Davies. It would appear that no interviewer has had the courage to quiz the understandably touchy Dave Davies himself on the matter.

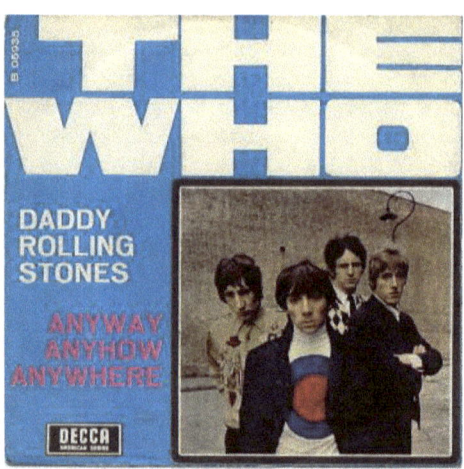

This Italian issue of the Who single switches the A and B sides and decides, wrongly, that the cover of an old Otis Blackwell song, Daddy Rolling Stone, must have been intended as a tribute to the rival group.

21 HEAVY METAL

The album *Cheap Thrills*, recorded by Big Brother and the Holding Company during the summer of 1968, contains a track called *Ball And Chain*. At the start, the lead guitar plays three high climbing notes and a twiddle, then pauses. In silence, James Gurley, the guitarist, turns his volume and tone controls up to maximum. Then, putting fingers to fretboard with an audible click on the amplified strings, he launches into a solo with an attack so vicious as to make the guitar apparently wail for mercy. During the Janis Joplin vocal performance that follows, it merely rumbles crossly, but then, given the chance, Gurley drags it protesting into a second solo, feedback screaming under his fingers and only just under control.

Ball And Chain is a great rock music track, but it becomes particularly interesting when compared with the songs to be found on Big Brother and the Holding Company's debut album, recorded only the previous year. For here, on a collection of fairly routine blues-based material, the lead guitar is unremarkable, low on amplification, and low on emotional impact. James Gurley is not a guitarist with a high reputation as an innovator, indeed the name is hardly likely to mean much to anyone not a fan of the late Ms Joplin. What had happened was, that in the period between the recording of the two LPs, both the Jimi Hendrix Experience and Cream had toured the United States and had attracted widespread attention from fans, critics, and fellow musicians for their revolutionary approaches to the electric guitar. Both Jimi Hendrix and Eric Clapton were concerned with exploring the electronic potential of their instruments and the virtuosity that both men developed to enable them to do this made them crucial figures in the development of rock music.

In common with a number of his contemporaries in the early sixties, Eric Clapton was a keen admirer of the blues and, in particular, the work of guitarist B.B.King. Unlike the situation in America, rock 'n' roll in Britain had caused too small a ripple in chart terms for its appeal to have become exhausted and musicians were only just beginning to delve into its background, of which the blues was very much a part. Initially, Eric Clapton's understanding and ability within the form was no less superficial than that of the Rolling Stones, Manfred Mann, and other blues-inspired groups, who made up with enthusiasm for what they lacked in accuracy. As a member of the Yardbirds, he played a kind of frantic R&B which seldom provided much opportunity for him to do anything other than maintain the excitement with flurries of high repeated notes. But on the occasions when the tempo was slowed a little, it became apparent that he was learning fast. The way in which his fingers tumble over the chords of *Five Long Years*, for example, shows that he had certainly mastered all the clichés, while more significantly, even without extravagant amplification, Clapton was achieving a piercing tone that gave the music a satisfying hard edge. *Got To Hurry*, the B-side of the hit single, *For Your Love*, found him tackling an instrumental in a blues style that emphatically had no resemblance to the Shadows – the biggest influence on guitar playing in Britain up to that time. There is no real melody, just a set of simple, repetitive variations on a sturdy twelve-bar progression, but the guitar tone has become even fiercer and the phrasing more considered.

The Yardbirds' recording of a pop song, *For Your Love*, having nothing to do with the blues, even if a worthy and interesting performance, provided Eric Clapton with the excuse he wanted to leave the group. That he was looking for such an excuse at all was remarkable enough and a significant indication of Clapton's musicianly approach at the time. The contemporary pop music press was amazed at a guitarist who could choose to leave a group just as it was achieving a top five hit single and was inclined to report Clapton as having had a nervous breakdown. His subsequent decision to join John Mayall's Bluesbreakers was a logical one in the circumstances, for Mayall shared his distaste for the commercial and was equally fascinated by the blues. In fact, Mayall's work prior to that time was considerably less specialist than was often suggested. The live album, *John Mayall Plays John Mayall*, is made up almost entirely of his own

THE FIRST TIME

In September 1962, the first Marshall amplifier, named 'Number One', was developed. Jim Marshall, originally a drummer, had opened a music shop in London and was persuaded by guitarist customers, who included session players Big Jim Sullivan and Ritchie Blackmore, to design and build an amplifier to give them the sound and volume they wanted. The Number One fitted their requirements and when placed in the window of the Marshall shop, twenty-three orders were taken on the first day. Eric Clapton asked Jim Marshall to install the amplifier, now called the JTM45, in an amplifier-speaker combo he could easily transport to gigs. He discovered that the output of his Gibson Les Paul guitar would cause the amplifier to distort at high volumes and realised he was on to something. Clapton asked the engineer at the recording sessions for the *Bluesbreakers* album to place the guitar microphone on the other side of the room. Fortunately, producer Mike Vernon was happy to allow Clapton to play as if he was on stage, with the amplifier volume control turned up to full.

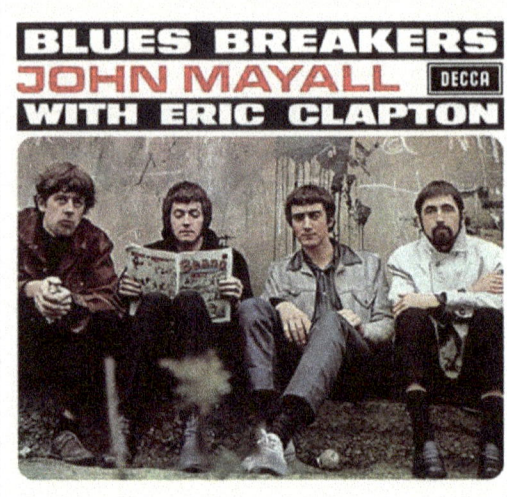

The impetus to build an even more powerful amplifier came from Pete Townshend and John Entwistle of the Who, both of whom were keen to be able to play as loudly as they could, if only to successfully compete with a drummer, Keith Moon, who had the most aggressive playing style of any group of the time. Marshall produced an amplifier rated at a hundred watts and designed to sit on top of two cabinets holding four twelve-inch speakers each – an arrangement that, known as the Marshall stack, became the essential equipment to deliver the powerful sound of not just the Who, but Eric Clapton's Cream and the Jimi Hendrix Experience.

compositions and their sound is the warm organ-based R&B that was commonly associated with London's Flamingo Club and the playing of Georgie Fame and Zoot Money. The one track not written by Mayall himself is a medley of Jimmy Forrest/James Brown's *Night Train* and Little Richard's *Lucille*, both somewhat removed from the music of Chicago. The liaison between John Mayall and Eric Clapton was, therefore, an adventure for both of them, as they influenced each other towards an earthier sound. The immediate result, a song called *I'm Your Witchdoctor*, recorded in August 1965, showed that it was Clapton who initially responded to the challenge most successfully. Though Mayall managed to coax a more ethereal sound from his organ than previously, the song is essentially in the same R&B style as on the live LP. It comes as all the more of a surprise, therefore, when at the end of the first verse, Eric Clapton's guitar suddenly gives forth an intense sobbing wail. The effect is repeated by way of a solo, this time oscillating between two notes in a sustained tone that lasts for well over ten seconds before the plectrum again touches the strings. A guitar part of such tremendous intensity is somewhat at odds with the rest of the song, yet it turns the performance into something approaching the magical.

By the time the newly constituted Bluesbreakers felt ready to record an album, both men had arrived at a fully worked-out sound that marked the successful end product of their joint venture. It is impossible to overestimate the importance of the album *Bluesbreakers – John Mayall With Eric Clapton*, for it represents both the birth of the modern guitar sound and the transition of pop into rock. Although the Americans were not to become aware of it until the arrival of Cream the following year, the revolution that was not only to transform James Gurley's sound, but to carry out a similar make-over for Canned Heat's lead guitarist, Henry Vestine, to change Jefferson Airplane from a gentle folksy outfit into the creators of the powerful *Somebody To Love* and the electric improvisation *Spare Chaynge*, and to encourage the formation of loud guitar-centred groups such as Spirit, SRC, and Quicksilver Messenger Service, had already taken place.

If, in turning his amplifier controls up to full, so that the guitar distorted almost to the point of continuously feeding back, Eric Clapton merely sought to reproduce the excitement in the playing of his blues heroes, then he must have realised that he had actually moved a step further on from their tonal explorations. The point is made obvious by a comparison between the Bluesbreakers' version of *All Your Love* and the original, which is by Otis Rush. Rush's performance is a typical piece of late fifties urban blues, incorporating a wailing saxophone, played with more energy than skill, a hard shouting vocal, and an electric guitar that gives the music its cutting edge, without having very much distortion in its tone. Rush manages to bring an emotional intensity to the music even without distortion. John Mayall and Eric Clapton make little attempt to alter the song's arrangement, for their aim is more for authenticity than for interpretation, although Clapton does allow a little quiet sustain to intrude during the verse, in place of the saxophone of the original. For his solo, Eric Clapton plays the identical lines to those of Otis Rush – a mournful pattern of minor chord notes, followed by a rapid acceleration through four repeated strikes of the plectrum into a rather faster tempo. The valve overdrive of the sound, however, makes his playing so much more powerful than Rush's, that the Bluesbreakers' *All Your Love* becomes wrenched into the late sixties, the performance threatening to make obsolete the version that the group only intended to echo.

This was a studio recording, where the Bluesbreakers felt bound to restrict themselves to relatively short pieces. On stage, they were inclined to use these and other similar songs as the bases for longer improvised solos, which revealed them to be acting as creators rather than mere interpreters of a blues-derived form. Even with The Yardbirds, Eric Clapton had indulged in what the group called 'rave ups', but with his newly discovered guitar tone, these now achieved a magisterial power that made them very exciting indeed. These highly influential and innovatory performances are very nearly lost to history. John Mayall was in the habit of bringing a tape recorder to his live concerts, but the music so preserved was nearly all destroyed during a fire at his Californian home in the seventies. Immediate records were at one time to have released a live album, but apparently decided that its sound quality was too poor for the plan to be followed through. Some of the tracks under consideration, however, have survived and today, their sound quality is irrelevant (and actually not too bad at all), in view of the music's inestimable significance

The Who and Cream in the sixties, with Marshall stacks

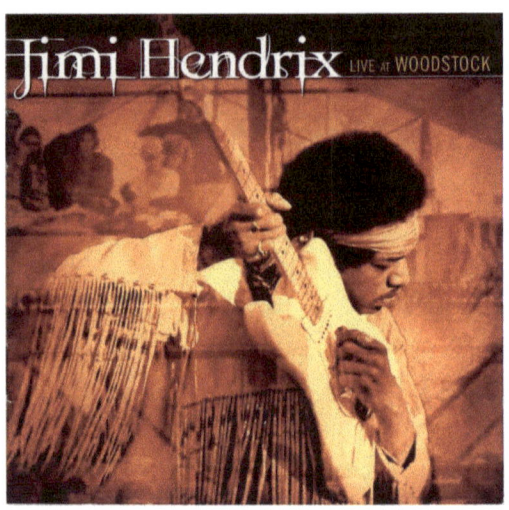

as the starting point for the whole of the heavy rock genre.

Six tracks recorded at the Flamingo Club in London on November 7th 1965 (the date given on Jack Bruce's own website, contradicting later dates given on Decca LP sleeves and CD booklets), during the brief period when Bruce was the bass player with the Bluesbreakers, are included on the two CD deluxe version of the *Bluesbreakers* album. Eric Clapton's playing is exemplary throughout, but he is undoubtedly at his most remarkable on the one track that did manage to be issued on an album in the sixties. Based on a version of *Stormy Monday*, the performance is almost entirely made up of a guitar solo, supported by a full-toned organ over slow blues changes. The solo is not, in fact, complete, as the music fades in with Eric Clapton already in full flight. His playing is rather less fluent than it would become a year or two later, but it is remarkably forceful and, above all, its hyper-amplified tone is a revelation. If *Stormy Monday* is listened to after any other guitar break from 1965, then the push given to rock music by Eric Clapton becomes obvious. Fans at the time thought so as well, and it was while Clapton was playing with John Mayall that the slogan 'Clapton Is God' was spray-painted on a wall in Islington and thereafter in many other London locations too.

As a member of Cream, Clapton did little more than refine his approach and bring it to a wider audience. There is nothing on the group's debut album, *Fresh Cream*, issued in December 1966, that he could not have played earlier, although his solos on songs like *NSU* and *I'm So Glad* do emphasise that his style was essentially melodic even when at its most tonally extreme. These solos derive a considerable strength from the fact that they do contain what are themselves memorable tunes. Although the music on *Fresh Cream* takes the blues as its starting point and includes several cover versions, the musicians succeed in imposing their own signatures on it, so that the album emerges with far less of a purist feel than the John Mayall *Bluesbreakers* LP has. Realistically, this is the first hard rock album.

A brief American tour in the spring of 1967 was not very successful, but following the release of the *Disraeli Gears* album, on which the hard rock approach was applied to a set of post-*Sgt Pepper* songs with great effect, Cream toured America again and made a huge impact. It was the more straightforward music of *Fresh Cream* that the group mostly chose to perform live, but in greatly extended versions in which long improvised sections dominated.

Remarkably, when the Animals' bass player, Chas Chandler, arrived back in Britain in his new role as a manager, his unknown protégé, Jimi Hendrix, already had his skills fully formed and waiting only to be given a push in the right direction. Hendrix had spent his formative years as a musician playing backing guitar to second division soul acts like Lonnie Youngblood, Curtis Knight, Little Richard (whose time had passed), and the Isley Brothers (whose time, a couple of early hits notwithstanding, had yet to come). Seldom was he given much chance to flex his imagination in these circumstances, for no singer struggling to maintain a paying career was likely to want to risk being upstaged by one of his supporting musicians. As a consequence, none of the early recordings featuring Jimi Hendrix in a supporting role is of any more than historical interest. Even the recordings made for contractual reasons with singer Curtis Knight in 1967 provide little indication of the guitarist's talents.

In contrast, the first album made by the Jimi Hendrix Experience, *Are You Experienced*, with the guitarist having acquired a Marshall stack as soon as he arrived in the UK, is a startling compendium of guitar possibilities. It was clear that Hendrix's understanding of his instrument was so complete as to enable him to make it do almost anything he wanted. Jimi Hendrix presented a style in which the electronic potential of the guitar was devastatingly realised. In a very real sense, it might be said that Hendrix's instrument was not so much the guitar itself as the electronics that fed it. On stage, his equipment was boosted to the extent that the road managers could get nothing from it but feedback. Hendrix, however, was able to control this feedback and use it as an integral part of his guitar playing. The film of him playing his chaotic interpretation of *The Star Spangled Banner* at Woodstock is a highly effective demonstration of his abilities in this respect. A maelstrom of sound pours from the loudspeakers and yet the guitarist's hands on the strings seem to be doing comparatively little. The movement of fingers on frets has become just one technique within a repertoire that includes the way in which the guitar itself is positioned and moved and the effects of continual manipulation of volume and tone controls and the tremolo arm. It is significant that Hendrix, as a left-handed player,

THE FIRST TIME

The back cover of the Jeff Beck Group's second album, *Beck-ola,* describing the music to be found on the record, demonstrates the contemporary idea of heavy music well. "Today, with all the hard competition in the music business, it's almost impossible to come up with anything totally original. So we haven't. However, at the time this album was made, the accent was on heavy music. So sit back and listen and try and decide if you can find a small place in your heads for it." It was as though Beck had realised he had managed to miss the boat. As the guitarist to replace Eric Clapton in the Yardbirds, it was Beck's imaginative playing that was responsible for making the group's run of five remarkable singles into classics of a hard rock genre that had barely been invented at the time. His own first album, *Truth,* found a way of playing a blues-rock music that stripped out some of the more arty aspects of Cream, leaving a more straightforward sound, though still with enough virtuosity to impress, ready to take on the seventies. The beginning of the genre known as 'classic rock', in fact. Saddled with an unsympathetic manager, it had become apparent by the summer of 1969, when *Beck-ola* was released, that Led Zeppelin, featuring the guitarist who had replaced Jeff Beck in the Yardbirds, Jimmy Page, had jumped in with the same sound and cornered the market. Jeff Beck's talent and skill ensured that he did all right in the long term – he is playing better than ever today and has been hailed as one of the best guitarists in the world for many years. The lead singer and bass player in the Jeff Beck Group did well too. The bass player, Ron Wood, switched back to his preferred guitar and joined the Faces and the Rolling Stones, while the singer, Rod Stewart, has had some success as a solo artist!

Only the very first UK issues of the Led Zeppelin LP used the turquoise colouring shown. After a few weeks this was replaced by orange – a fact that has delighted collectors of rare LPs ever since.

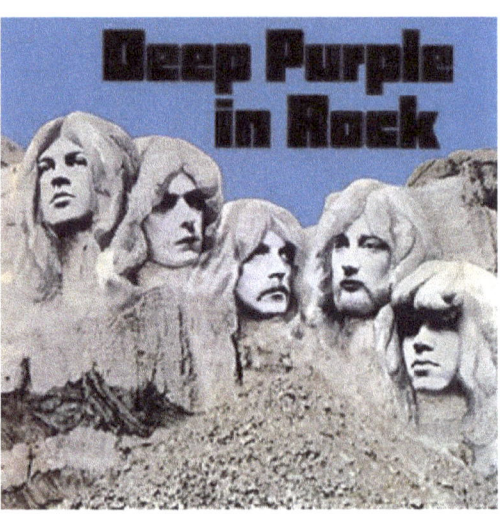

Just as the band calling itself Earth made the decision to change the name to Black Sabbath, in September 1968, Tony Iommi was invited to replace guitarist Mick Abrahams in Jethro Tull, which was rapidly gaining acclaim at the time, with a first album about to be released on the Island label. He lasted less than three months, however, before deciding that he preferred working with his Birmingham colleagues. Iommi can be seen performing with Jethro Tull in the video recording of the Rolling Stones event, *Rock and Roll Circus,* which took place in December 1968, although he is miming the guitar part played on record by Mick Abrahams.

Claims that the Beatles invented heavy metal, if not with *Ticket To Ride*, then with *Helter Skelter*, ignore the fact that the latter track, included on the *White Album*, did not appear until November 1968. By this time, both Jimi Hendrix and Cream had already issued three albums, filled with music considerably more powerful than anything by the Beatles. Paul McCartney has stated that he wrote *Helter Skelter* in response to the Who's psychedelic masterpiece, *I Can See For Miles*, which is an equally 'heavy' piece of music and was released in September 1967.

chose to play a right-handed guitar held upside down and re-strung appropriately, so that the controls were at the top and able to be moved by the side and palm of a hand whose fingers were simultaneously striking the strings. The extreme high level of amplification used, moreover, enabled sound to be generated merely by the placing of fingers on the fretboard, without any need for the strings to be further excited, so that the controls and the tremolo arm could be played in their own right.

The emergence, during 1968 and 1969, of several new bands, for which a sustaining, overdriven guitar, a floor-shaking rhythm section, and a generally high volume were essential, is testament to the enormous influence of both Cream and the Jimi Hendrix Experience. Most had discovered an interest in the blues, even as they endeavoured to find ways of moving beyond it, although one of the most raucous of the bands, the American Blue Cheer, made its reputation with a supercharged version of a rock 'n' roll song, the slightly misleadingly titled *Summertime Blues*. The music of Taste, Ten Years After, Steamhammer, the Edgar Broughton Band, Love Sculpture, Led Zeppelin, and the rest was soon being described as 'heavy', an appropriate adjective for music designed to be crushingly powerful. Jack Bruce used exactly that term, clearly not for the first time, to describe the music of Cream in an interview with *Rolling Stone* published in February 1968. Curiously, the one band to use the word as an album title, Iron Butterfly, (whose album *Heavy* was released in January 1968), was one whose music was least deserving of it, mainly because the guitarist, gaining his tone from a fuzz box rather than from a powerful amplifier, was no more than an adequate player.

During 1970, three albums were released which were welcomed by fans as the heaviest yet, even as the critics, mounting a backlash against the entire approach, were condemning the music with some particularly bad reviews. Lester Bangs, writing in *Rolling Stone* magazine, described Deep Purple, whose fourth album *Deep Purple In Rock*, appeared in June, as a band "who lack both expertise and intuition; plodding along and hanging in there album after album in spite of being such quiet nonentities that they're not even good copy…….The only roots in evidence here are all the clubfooted 'heavy' riffs laid down in the last three years." The Uriah Heep album, *Very 'Eavy…Very 'Umble*, which also appeared in June, was attacked even more viciously in the same magazine by Melissa Mills, who began her review, "If this group makes it I'll have to commit suicide. From the first note you know you don't want to hear any more." It is unlikely that Ms Mills carried through her supposed intention, although Uriah Heep did indeed make it.

Lester Bangs did not like the first of the three albums to be issued either. Reviewing the self-titled album by Black Sabbath in *Rolling Stone*, he writes "the album has nothing to do with spiritualism, the occult, or anything much except stiff recitations of Cream clichés that sound like the musicians learned them out of a book, grinding on and on with dogged persistence. Vocals are sparse, most of the album being filled with plodding bass lines over which the lead guitar dribbles wooden Claptonisms from the master's tiredest Cream days." Clearly Bangs, perhaps unaware or uncaring of the group's vital importance within rock music development, did not think much of Cream either.

Tony Iommi, the guitarist in question, had suffered an industrial accident at the metal works (no pun intended) where he was employed, severing two of the fingertips of his right hand. As a left-handed player, these were the fingers that he fretted with. Determined to carry on regardless, Iommi fashioned himself a set of prosthetic fingertips from plastic bottle tops and strips of leather and lowered the tuning on his guitar to make the strings slacker and more easily pushed on to the frets. In combination with songs played mostly at slow tempo, with bluesy melodies laid over weighty riffs played by guitar and bass in unison, the result was Black Sabbath's signature sound – bass heavy and doom-laden and the antithesis, in terms of mood, of the ecstatic, free flying music of Led Zeppelin, even if both groups liked to play as loudly as possible, with an overdriven guitar at the centre of the stage. Led Zeppelin's lyrics too were all about love and sex: Ozzy Osbourne, Black Sabbath's wild singer, preferred themes of witchcraft, and madness, and death. Released in February 1970, *Black Sabbath* is the first heavy metal record.

Black Sabbath received bad reviews for the album in all the music papers. Listeners who had seen the band play live bought the LP regardless, in sufficiently large numbers to push *Black Sabbath* up to number eight in the UK album charts. Six months later, the group's follow-up, *Paranoid*, did even better, reaching number one in the album charts and

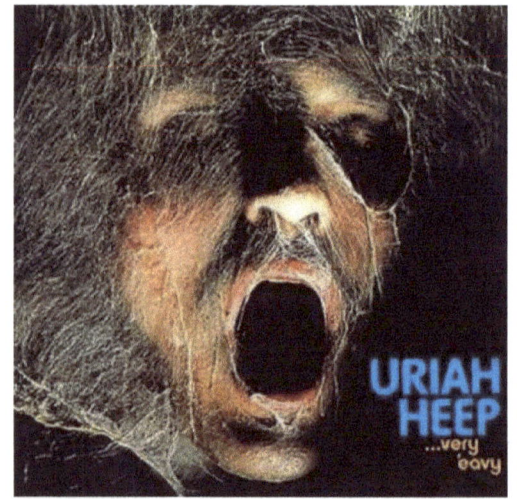 

Black Sabbath's Tony Iommi and Ozzy Osbourne

 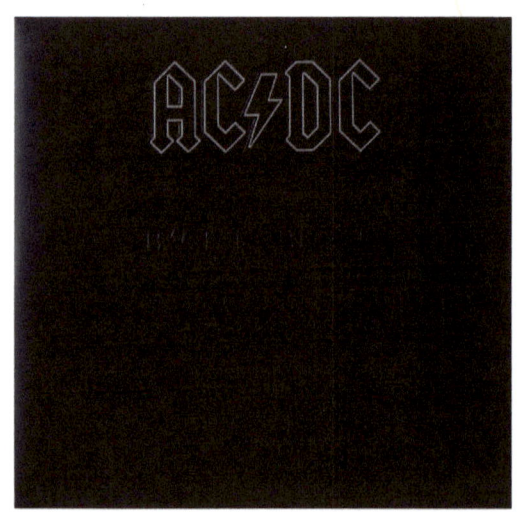

spawning a top five hit single with the title track.

Surprisingly, no-one seems to be able to identify exactly when the term 'heavy metal' began to be used in its modern sense. *Rolling Stone* magazine liked to refer to the music of Black Sabbath as 'downer rock' and it was not until the release in 1973 of the group's fifth album, *Sabbath Bloody Sabbath*, that the magazine felt able to describe Black Sabbath as "the planet's premier heavy-metal band" at the start of a review that, for the first time, was almost complimentary. Two novels by William Burroughs use the phrase 'heavy metal', but as a metaphor for addictive drugs, rather than music. The novels are *The Soft Machine* from 1962 and *Nova Express* from 1964 – both titles being subsequently stolen by music groups, half a dozen times in the case of the latter one. The 1967 album, *Hapshash And The Coloured Coat Featuring The Human Host And The Heavy Metal Kids*, takes the phrase directly from Burroughs. The music comprises a selection of aimless jam-session tracks of the kind that appeared on a few hippy albums of the period. It is not heavy in the Led Zeppelin manner, although the muscular drumming and thick-toned bass guitar actually come courtesy of musicians who would later form Spooky Tooth, which was one of the bands creating powerful, riff-based music, thought of as being 'heavy' at the end of the sixties.

The 1968 song, *Born To Be Wild*, by Steppenwolf, uses the phrase 'heavy metal thunder', but this time the reference is to motor bikes. Sandy Pearlman, manager and producer of Blue Oyster Cult, claims to be the first person to apply 'heavy metal' to rock in 1970. Even if true, the group he supposedly referred to was the Byrds, which matches no-one else's definition of the term. Chas Chandler maintained in a 1995 interview that a New York critic had referred to the music of Jimi Hendrix as being "like listening to heavy metal falling from the sky", which is certainly apposite, except that the review in question has never been discovered. A review by Barry Gifford in the May 11th 1968 edition of *Rolling Stone* describes the first album by the Electric Flag, *A Long Time Comin'*, by writing, "this is the new soul music, the synthesis of white blues and heavy metal rock", which may well be the actual first use of the phrase as a musical term, although again, the soul-blues music of the Electric Flag is still not heavy metal by any modern definition.

Mike Saunders, reviewing a job lot of three albums by Humble Pie in November 1970 (*Rolling Stone* again) describes one of them as being "more of the same twenty-seventh-rate heavy metal crap" and uses the phrase again elsewhere in the same article. The use of 'heavy metal' as a disparaging term occurs again, or almost, in a February 1971 *Rolling Stone* review by John Mendelsohn, who dismisses the Ten Years After album, *Watt*, as "mostly deathly predictable 'heavy' stews of familiar blues phrases" and later refers to the live track, *Sweet Little Sixteen*, as a "leaden-metallic, graceless, horribly engineered atrocity". Mike Saunders uses the actual phrase again in a May 1971 review (in *Creem* magazine this time) of an album by Sir Lord Baltimore, where he writes, absolutely appropriately on this occasion, that the group "seems to have down pat most all the best heavy metal tricks in the book".

Through the seventies, the terms heavy metal and hard rock were used more or less interchangeably, although only Black Sabbath employed classic metal lyric themes with any degree of consistency. In May 1979, a writer for *Sounds* magazine, Geoff Barton, attended a concert at The Heavy Metal Soundhouse in North London. He reviewed the performances by Iron Maiden, Samson, and Angel Witch in *Sounds*, referring to the groups as being at the forefront of "the new wave of British heavy metal" (NWOBHM). The first records to appear from what was effectively an underground movement were the self-produced *Def Leppard EP* from January 1979, Iron Maiden's four track demo tape from November 1978, which finally achieved release on record the following November, as *The Soundhouse Tapes,* and the LP, *Survivors,* by Samson, issued on the Laser label in June 1979. With Metallica in the United States forming to play music inspired by the NWOBHM and Iron Maiden and Def Leppard both achieving huge levels of popularity, the expansion of heavy metal from that time into one of the main genres of rock music, complete with a number of subdivisions to satisfy the tastes of individual groups of fans, was begun.

Arguably, of course, the main catalyst for this, certainly in the US, where metal became widely popular through the eighties and beyond, was not the NWOBHM at all, but the phenomenal success of AC/DC. The Australian hard

Motorhead (often written with an umlaut over the second letter o, to conform with the band's gothic script logo) pioneered the concept of heavy metal played fast, with the first recordings released in 1977, a little before the rise of the NWOBHM. The band's extreme descendent, Napalm Death, released its first album, *Scum*, ten years later. One track on the album, *You Suffer*, has the distinction of being the shortest piece of music ever recorded. The Guinness Book Of Records quotes a length of 1.316 seconds for the song, although this rather depends on when one considers the last reverberations have finally died away. The track was issued as a 7" vinyl single by Earache Records in 1989, with a similar piece by the Electro Hippies, *Mega Armageddon Death Pt.3*, on the B-side. The record labels give the length of both sides as one second, although it sounds as though the Electro Hippies track is fractionally longer. The style of heavy metal played by Napalm Death has been given the genre name 'grindcore'.

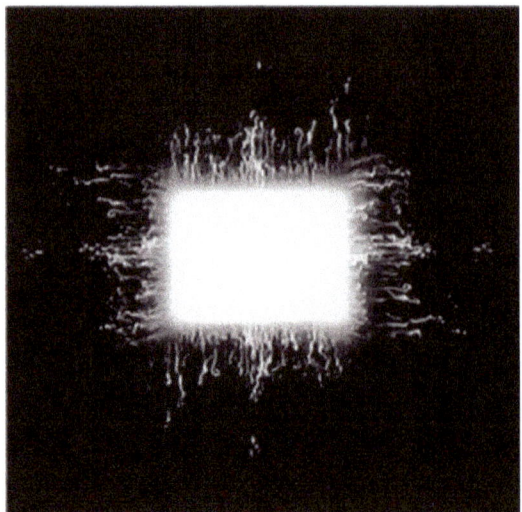

Tool Aenima

You Suffer has made enough of an impact that in 2011, a company called Sirona put together a various artists collection under the name of *Napalm Death You Suffer Tribute Compilation*. A hundred different groups and solo performers were invited to contribute, most of whom made little attempt to replicate the brevity of the original track, since only three of the new ones are as short as one second. One track, credited to Contraband, lasts for over eleven minutes and presents a bleak landscape of droning electronica, with its sound quality gradually degrading. This music makes the whole enterprise worthwhile on its own, although it has nothing to do with any kind of heavy metal. In 2019, Elise Ecklund made a YouTube video of herself creating an answer song to *You Suffer*. *I Suffer More* is only 0.875 seconds long and features her voice, ukulele, hand claps, and kazoo, so is very definitely not heavy metal either.

rock band, with a lead guitarist, Angus Young, cavorting in one of the most improbable stage costumes in the whole of rock, was responsible for a particularly big selling album, the 1980 release, *Back In Black*. Beaten only by Michael Jackson's *Thriller*, the AC/DC record is the first rock album to achieve an estimated fifty million international sales.

During the early eighties in the US, the various British developments to follow in the wake of punk – new wave, goth, new romantic, and so on – failed to gain much popularity. Instead, a number of guitar-centred bands created a kind of uncompromising rock that retained the energy and simplicity of punk, while restoring some of the older acceptance that instrumental expertise was something to value. Bands like Hüsker Dü, Sonic Youth, and R.E.M., all of whom had first studio albums released in 1983, took their guitar playing seriously and understood how the textures resulting from the use of unusual chord shapes could give the music an increase in power. In the process, they laid down the ground rules for the way that mainstream rock music in the US was supposed to sound during the late years of the century, even if the critics insisted on calling the results 'alternative rock'.

Two albums issued in 1991 were so successful and, in consequence, so influential that they could no longer be realistically labelled as alternative. Instead, *Nevermind* by Nirvana and *Ten* by Pearl Jam, both of which used distorted guitars, harsh vocals, and strident rhythms to drive music that was nevertheless very melodic, were seen as the flowering of a genre christened 'grunge'. Grunge had much in common with heavy metal, except that its exponents were likely to be much less theatrical, both in the way they played and in the way they looked. They were less interested in swords and sorcery and grandstand soloing. But Ben Shepherd, bass player with the grunge band Soundgarden, is widely quoted as saying, "We've taken everything we know from Black Sabbath". The two genres were easily united, therefore, and this was definitively achieved by the band Tool, with the album, *Aenima*. It was released in 1996 and eventually achieved triple platinum status.

TRACKING THE TRACKS

The 4 CD set, *The Yardbirds Story* (Charly 2008), is a comprehensive anthology of the group's recordings from the first half of its career and includes the tracks mentioned. The John Mayall with Eric Clapton, Cream, and Jimi Hendrix catalogues are discussed at the end of the chapter on The Electric Guitar. It should be noted that the stereo mixes of the *Fresh Cream* tracks, included on the various CD reissues, are the result of an unsatisfactory attempt to create a stereo sound out of two track master tapes intended to be heard in mono. To properly appreciate songs like *NSU, Sleepy Time Time,* and the single *I Feel Free* as they were intended, it is necessary to combine the left and right stereo channels into a single centre channel, if this is at all possible.

John Mayall Plays John Mayall is on London (1988). Otis Rush *1956-1958 Cobra Recordings* is on Paula Records (1999).

The first and second albums by Big Brother and the Holding Company, where the change in James Gurley's guitar playing can be easily appreciated, are *Big Brother & The Holding Company Featuring Janis Joplin* (Columbia 2003) and *Cheap Thrills* (Columbia 1999). A similar transformation can be heard with the playing of Henry Vestine on *Canned Heat* and *Boogie With Canned Heat* (issued together on one Beat Goes On CD, 2003). Jefferson Airplane's *Somebody To Love* is on *Surrealistic Pillow* (BMG 2003); *Spare Chaynge* is on *After Bathing At Baxter's* (BMG 2003). The first, self-titled album by Spirit is on Repertoire (2004); the following three albums (*The Family That Plays Together, Clear,* and *Twelve Dreams Of Dr Sardonicus* – all Repertoire 2007-8) are just as good. *SRC* is on Microwerks (2010); *Quicksilver Messenger Service* is on BGO (2009), although it is the second album, *Happy Trails,* that attracts all the plaudits (BGO 2010).

During the sixties, the singles by the Who were always the group's strongest tracks. These were collected on an LP anthology called *Meaty Beaty Big & Bouncy*, which has been reissued on CD (US MCA 2012). It includes the Who's hard rock psychedelic extravaganza, *I Can See For Miles*. The most impressive album by the Who is not the over-rated *Tommy*, but rather the early seventies release, *Who's Next* (Polydor 1999), which includes the classic tracks *Baba O'Riley* and *Won't Get Fooled Again*.

Blue Cheer's *Summertime Blues* is on *Vincebus Eruptum* (Sundazed 2012).

Taste by Taste (Spectrum 2000) – the explosive arrival of guitarist Rory Gallagher.*Ssssh* by Ten Years After (EMI 2004) – the playing by Alvin Lee on the live *Undead* (Decca/Universal 2002) is more impressive technically, but this is much more powerful.*Reflection* by Steamhammer (Repertoire 2002). The 1970 follow-up, *Mk.II* (Repertoire 1992), is more inventive and is starting to move almost into jazz-rock territory, but for that reason is not really a heavy rock album. *Wasa Wasa* by the Edgar Broughton Band (EMI 2004) makes rather less impact than did the group's incendiary live performances at this time, but it is good enough.

MUSIC GENRES

The first album by Love Sculpture, *Blues Helping*, is routine British blues, but the second, *Forms And Feelings* (Esoteric 2008), moves more towards hard rock and is much more interesting, if only for its hit single, *Sabre Dance*, where guitarist Dave Edmunds turns a Khachaturian piece into a virtuoso high-energy guitar display.

Led Zeppelin was undoubtedly the biggest band of the seventies in every way, and all their albums are well worth investigating, but the first two albums are the ones that are relevant to this chapter – *Led Zeppelin* (Atlantic 2014) and *Led Zeppelin II* (Atlantic 2014). These most recent reissues have been expanded to double CDs with the addition of live tracks and out-takes.

The essential Jeff Beck release is the live DVD from 2008, *Performing This Week...Live At Ronnie Scott's*, which demonstrates exactly why Beck is so highly rated as a guitarist. The relevant late sixties albums are *Truth* (EMI 2005) and *Beck-ola* (EMI 2004).

Black Sabbath and *Paranoid* (both Castle 1996) are the first two definitive albums by Black Sabbath.

Rock And Roll Circus by the Rolling Stones is on an Abkco DVD (2004).

Very 'Eavy...Very 'Umble by Uriah Heep was on the same Vertigo label as Black Sabbath; the CD is on Sanctuary (2008).

Deep Purple In Rock (EMI 1995). The group's hard rock anthem, *Smoke On The Water*, is on the 1972 album, *Machine Head* (EMI 1997), but is even better when heard as part of the live set on the double CD *Made In Japan* (EMI 1998).

Hapshash And The Coloured Coat Featuring The Human Host And The Heavy Metal Kids is on an Akarma CD (2002) but is not in the least essential.

Hard rock band Steppenwolf has released eighteen albums, not including compilations, but nothing beats their three early tracks, *Born To Be Wild*, *The Pusher*, and *Magic Carpet Ride*, which can be found on any of the various 'Best Of Steppenwolf' albums, such as *The Collection* (Spectrum 2003).

Humble Pie, with both Steve Marriott and Peter Frampton (or later, Clem Clempson) singing and playing guitar, was rather a good hard rock band, even if Mike Saunders did not like them, and they were very successful in the United States. *The Definitive Collection* (A&M 2006) serves the band well.

The Def Leppard EP had four separate issues on vinyl, but was not reissued on CD, although re-recordings of the three tracks are split between the albums *On Through The Night* (the band's first) and *Retro Active*. Def Leppard was phenomenally successful in the United States, less so in the UK, where the album *Vault – Def Leppard Greatest Hits* (Vertigo 1999) serves the band well.

Iron Maiden's *The Soundhouse Tapes* was not reissued on CD either, although two of its tracks were re-recorded for the first LP, *Iron Maiden*. The band has sold almost as many records and CDs as Def Leppard and also has a good compilation CD, *Best Of The Beast* (EMI 1996).

Samson are the poor relatives in this company, although the band managed to release eleven albums before 2002, when the death of guitarist Paul Samson brought the band's career to a close. The lead singer on the second two albums, as well as bonus tracks included on reissues of the first, was Bruce Dickinson, who subsequently joined Iron Maiden. The album *Survivors*, with its bonus tracks, was issued on CD by Sanctuary in 2001, but is not currently available.

The tracks from Metallica's *Garage Days Revisited* are included on a double CD made up entirely of cover versions played by the band, *Garage Inc* (Virgin/EMI 2007). Metallica took heavy metal in a surprising direction with the double CD *S&M* (Universal/Vertigo 1999), recorded live with the San Francisco Symphony Orchestra, conducted by Michael Kamen.

No Sleep 'Til Hammersmith presents Motorhead playing live and is expanded to a double CD on Sanctuary (2008). *Scum* by Napalm Death crams twenty-seven tracks alongside *You Suffer* into a playing time of less than thirty-five minutes. It is on Earache (2012). *Napalm Death You Suffer Tribute Compilation* (Sirona 2011) is available as a free download.

Back In Black by AC/DC is on Columbia/Sony (2009).

The recommended album by Hüsker Dü is *Zen Arcade,* originally issued in 1984. The currently available CD is on SST (1987). Guitarist Bob Mould later formed a group called Sugar, whose excellent album *Copper Blue* (Creation 1992) is in the grunge style he helped to create, and he also made several equally fine solo albums. The recommended album by Sonic Youth is *Daydream Nation,* originally issued in 1988 (Geffen CD 1993). The music made by R.E.M. before the group became an international success is well represented by *The Best Of R.E.M.* (IRS 1991).

Nevermind by Nirvana is on Universal (2011). *Ten* by Pearl Jam is on Sony/BMG (2005). *Aenima* by Tool is on Sony/Volcano (2006).

THE FIRST TIME

The group described in the quote was the Boomtown Rats, performing their first hit, *Looking After Number One,* and the lead singer was Bob Geldof. Ironically, of course, Geldof has become much more famous as a man who has managed to motivate both the music industry and the general public into providing huge amounts of financial help for starving people in Africa. Despite appearances, Bob Geldof on *Top of the Pops* was, after all, acting.

In America, punk often refers to a different music. It is applied to sixties groups like the Seeds, the Standells, and the Thirteenth Floor Elevators – groups that had loved the music of the British beat invasion and wanted to take it a little further, but could not quite manage the leap into uncharted musical territory happily undertaken by Jefferson Airplane and the Grateful Dead.

According to the Allmusic website, Brian Eno once suggested that although hardly anyone bought the LPs by the Velvet Underground when they were first released, almost all those who did formed a band. The Velvet Underground could be included with the six groups mentioned opposite, except that the backgrounds and clear intelligence of Lou Reed and John Cale, the leaders of the Velvets, suggested that they were playing in that way on purpose. The band's use of drones was a particularly striking feature and turned tracks like *Venus In Furs* and *All Tomorrow's Parties* into powerful artistic statements. In later years, Lou Reed produced memorable performances like *Walk On The Wild Side* and *Perfect Day,* but he also created the unrelenting and impenetrable noise celebration that is the double LP, *Metal Machine Music.* John Cale made some striking rock albums, but he also created convincing works to add to the contemporary classical repertoire, such as the vital pieces for strings to be found on his 1991 album *Paris S'Eveille.* It has become clear that the Velvet Underground was, indeed, all about Art. The fact that the hugely influential artist Andy Warhol chose to sponsor the group for its first album makes perfect sense.

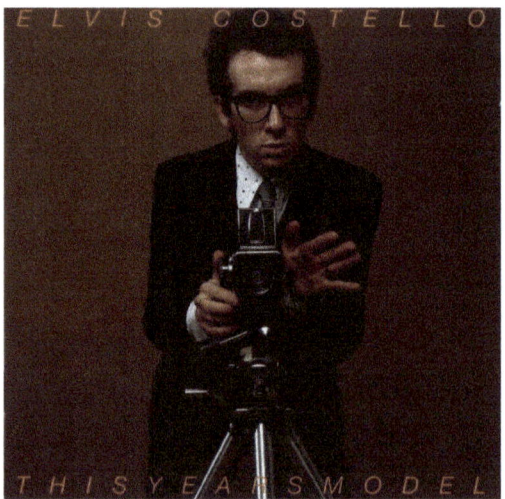

The dismissive attitude towards rock's past that was apparently displayed in the cover versions recorded by the Damned, Siouxsie and the Banshees, and the Dickies was turned to highly creative ends by Elvis Costello. He once remarked that he had already forgotten who Bob Dylan was, yet in reality he possessed a considerable knowledge of sixties music. Realising too that pop music by its very nature tends to unconsciously recycle melodic ideas, Costello decided to make the process a conscious one. Shamelessly plagiarising his predecessors, he created a powerful set of songs in which the sense of style was so well conceived as to make the music far more than simply the sum of its influences. By drawing on a wide range of rock's previous achievements, Costello helped to give the new wave some kind of historical perspective. By channelling these elements into a sound that was unified and distinctively his own, and tying the whole package up in the authoritative title, *This Year's Model,* he reaffirmed the claim for control over rock's destiny that punk sought. Part of the joy of listening to the music lies in trying to identify the origin of its various ideas. The Who and the Beatles and Percy Sledge and the Crystals are conjured up and dismissed; Bob Dylan is merged with the Spencer Davis Group; the Doors are introduced to the rhythms of reggae; and the Rolling Stones are simply re-written. Everywhere, Elvis Costello succeeds in brilliantly reworking his materials to his own ends, giving them new life in these different contexts and making them sound as though he had invented them himself.

The sheer breadth and ambition of the music made by Elvis Costello since *This Year's Model* has few parallels in modern music. In a catalogue stuffed full of highlights, it suffices to mention his supervision of a collection of contemporary jazz performances of his songs by guitarist Bill Frisell (*The Sweetest Punch*), a ballet, based on *A Midsummer Night's Dream*, both composed and orchestrated by Costello (*Il Sogno*), and a sparkling collaboration with legendary R&B veteran Allen Toussaint (*The River In Reverse*).

22 PUNK

> The group that came on first, one *Top Of The Pops* in the summer of 1977, was evidently one of the new punk rock crowd. The music was loud, fast, and brash, and the youngsters miming to it were the same – one of them was even cavorting in a pair of striped pyjamas. For all that, the group would have been nothing without its lead singer. He leered at the camera, making obscene gestures with his fingers. He looked dangerous – a teenage mugger, or worse. And, boasting in his song's lyrics that he "owed nobody nothing" and would step on your face as soon as look at you, he seemed to be for real. "I-I-I don't want to be like you!" went the chorus and, in terms of rock music, Harry knew he meant the Beatles, he meant the progressives, he meant every kind of music made before that moment. Looking at his face on the screen, with his record collection stacked neatly behind him, suddenly, at the age of twenty-six, Harry felt old.   (*Music For A Desert Island* by Nick Hamlyn)

Punk was about fashion – ripped clothing, safety pins, and spiky hair – and it was about attitude. It was much less of a *musical* revolution than it might have seemed to be at the time. Throughout rock music's brief history, there had been numerous examples of young groups playing energetic music with more enthusiasm than competence and many of them had made records. In the sixties, the Kinks, the Troggs, the Deviants, the Monks, Iggy and the Stooges, and the MC5 were six of those that had done that. In the years immediately before the first punk records appeared, several high energy rhythm and blues bands were playing in pubs in the London area. Records by the likes of Dr Feelgood and Ducks Deluxe were labelled pub rock, but sound remarkably similar to punk. All these groups are punk antecedents, but they do not have the style, and they are not punk, although some of the music is exactly the same.

Punk was unique, moreover, in the way that its exponents made a virtue out of their inability to play with any degree of skill. Groups that relied on some technical sophistication or who displayed evidence that they had spent time developing instrumental dexterity were not just accused of being pretentious, but were declared to be irrelevant 'dinosaurs'. Songs had to be short and simply constructed. Singers had to have the kind of voice that any member of a football crowd could match. And guitar solos, if allowed at all, had to be conspicuously anti-virtuosic. The two note siren played by Pete Shelley on the Buzzcocks' *Boredom* represents the ideal – or else the single accelerating crunch chord of XTC's *Love At First Sight*, although that was produced by a group stretching punk's restrictions to the limit.

To emphasise their disdain of earlier rock styles, many punk groups recorded irreverent cover versions. Typical of these were the destruction of the Beatles' *Help!* by the Damned; the similar treatment of *Helter Skelter* by Siouxsie and the Banshees; and the Dickies' ninety miles per hour reworking of the Moody Blues' *Nights In White Satin*. Meanwhile, within the ranks of the Sex Pistols, bass player Glen Matlock was expelled for being too musical and his place taken by Sid Vicious, who could hardly play at all, but who looked exactly right for the part.

The attitude of the punk musicians was reflected and reinforced by the music press, which, in an effort to reverse the decline in its figures, decided to seek the support of the new generation it presumed punk to represent. Accordingly, *Melody Maker* abandoned its status as the music paper of record, scrapping its specialist coverage of folk and jazz. Both it and the *New Musical Express* took on new writers possessing the same combination of inexperience, intolerance, and aggression as the musicians they proceeded to champion. At the same time, John Peel, whose programme on BBC Radio One had for ten years been a showcase for the more adventurous kinds of rock music, announced that, for him, punk provided the kind of challenge he had not heard in rock for a long time. The music of Led Zeppelin and Pink Floyd disappeared overnight from his playlist, to be replaced by the Undertones and the Fall.

The problem with rejecting traditional musical values, however, is that a system of aesthetics based on what is left is at best rather fragile. Certainly, those for whom punk appeared as the only worthwhile kind of music showed every sign of being confused. For some, the chanting anthems of the Clash ("I'm so bor-or-ored with the U.S.A." and

THE FIRST TIME

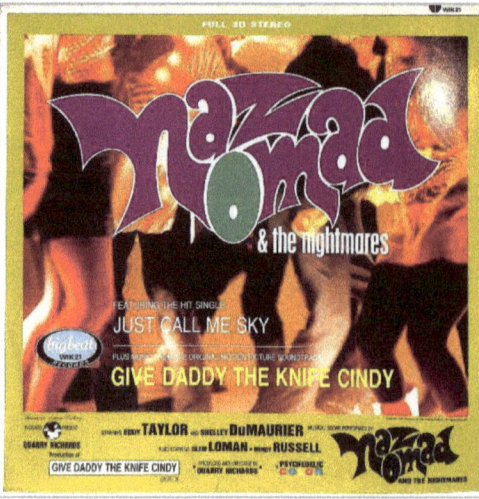

The more melodic exponents of the 'new wave' music that followed in the wake of punk were described as being performers of 'power pop'. Nick Lowe and the Jam in the UK, the Knack and the Ramones in the US, qualified by underscoring catchy tunes with driving guitar chords. The term was originally coined by Pete Townshend during an interview for *NME* in May 1967, applied to the music of the Small Faces and his own group, the Who. On that basis, the first power pop record should be *I Can't Explain*, issued as the debut single by the Who in January 1965, except that many earlier songs by the likes of Buddy Hollly and Eddie Cochran are little different musically.

The punk aesthetic cast a long shadow across the music that followed it. The following review was published in Q magazine in August 1987, when the Genesis back catalogue was being reissued on CD. The writer is David Hepworth.

> "A*nd Then There Were Three* had eleven tracks for a start, so it was clear that noodling was beginning to be frowned upon. The signs of a new group sloughing off the dead skin of the old were there in *Undertow,* a Banks tune with a surging chorus line and lyrics so forthright they would have been considered suspicious in Gabriel's day. *Snowbound* had a similar single-mindedness while *Follow You, Follow Me,* which was coyly dropped in right at the end, was utterly elementary and all the better for that. It had a hook that bore repetition and they didn't stunt themselves; nothing, not even the guitar solo, was allowed to slacken the momentum. It could have been Abba or Cliff Richard; it was a pop record. It was a bloody relief considering how long it had taken them to get there."

There is, of course, nothing wrong in sounding like Abba or Cliff Richard, but they would be the first to admit that, excellently crafted though their material is, it is not art. To argue that the early work of Genesis is not art either is a tenable point of view, but it is sad to realise that such critics would deny the right of rock musicians to even attempt to create art. Ultimately, these critics render their own position useless, since if the highest aspiration for a rock performer is to produce music of sufficient attractiveness to become popular, then the measure of his success becomes merely the music's fortune in the charts. The degree of originality, imagination, skill, and creativity applied in these circumstances matters not at all and no critic is required to point these qualities out. Meanwhile, every time a new group emerges with a sound that could have been produced in the late seventies, the critics, who have carried on regardless, heap extravagant praise upon it, without realising the contradictions involved.

"White riot, I wanna riot") were the epitome of good music. Others claimed the group ceased to be interesting as soon as it signed with the mighty CBS, implying that the actual sound of the music was less important than its political stance. Tony Parsons and Julie Burchill, enfants terribles of *New Musical Express*, came to the conclusion in their book, *The Boy Looked At Johnny*, that the only worthwhile group was the Tom Robinson Band. The opinion was a little surprising then and seems extraordinary now, given the jaunty sing-a-long pop of the band's greatest hit, *2-4-6-8 Motorway*, or the times-should-be-a-changing polemic of, *Glad To Be Gay*, a Bob Dylan pastiche in all but its subject.

John Peel confessed to a particular fondness for the Undertones, but their *Teenage Kicks*, despite having gained extra resonance from its association with the much-missed Peel, has an inept guitar solo that is not so much simple as simple-minded. In contrast, a record widely touted as one of the best of 1977's crop was Television's *Marquee Moon*. It was convenient to pretend that this music was in some way akin to punk, especially since original member Richard Hell had supposedly come up with the idea of tearing his clothes before Johnny Rottten, but in reality it was no such thing. Television certainly had a refreshing new sound, but it was one based around the elegant and lengthy solos of the guitarists, which was the kind of approach that punk was supposed to despise. Even the Stranglers, whose image and attitude made them seem like natural punks, could not hide the fact that their keyboard player was actually a rather skilled musician, even if the group's many fans seemed able to ignore this uncomfortable fact.

The punk aesthetic became even more shaky as the inevitable happened. With constant practice provided by concert and club appearances, the punk musicians simply got better at playing their instruments. As their horizons thereby expanded, so too did their imaginations. The process is as obvious as the difference between the Undertones' *Teenage Kicks* and *Julie Ocean*; between Siouxsie and the Banshees' *Hong Kong Garden* and *Spellbound*; or between the Damned's *New Rose* and *Smash It Up* – an intricately crafted and imaginative piece of music, despite its title.

It was interesting to see too, how many of the erstwhile revolutionaries began to adopt the lifestyles and images of precisely those groups that punk was supposed to have swept away. It became clear that Mick Jones of the Clash was determined to emulate Keith Richards of the Rolling Stones; that the Damned would have loved to have been a sixties psychedelic group (performing faithful re-creations of songs by Jefferson Airplane and Love and adopting an appropriate alter ego, Naz Nomad and the Nightmares); and that Siouxsie and the Banshees, developing a glossy stage show with a piece of classical music to start, apparently saw themselves as heirs to the likes of Yes and ELP.

Of the various punk groups to emerge from 1977 onwards, the Sex Pistols were the spearhead. The Clash and the Buzzcocks, as musical communists, sought to return rock music to the proletariat. Their respective first albums are textbook examples of the required anti-sophisticate stance. The revolution presented by the Sex Pistols' first album, *Never Mind The Bollocks*, is at once less sincere and more profound. In adopting the persona of Johnny Rotten and snarling "I am the antichrist, I am an anarchist," singer John Lydon was creating an image as theatrical in its own way as that of Mick Jagger or Rod Stewart. In ironic contrast to the message of *Anarchy In The UK*, whose lyrics advocate the destruction of our materialist society, Lydon and manager Malcolm McLaren were actually determined to milk the rock business for all they could get. To this end, they devised a strategy whereby their behaviour, in advance of the final signing to Virgin, led to the group's expulsion from two other record companies, but not before they had obtained substantial advance payments, which were not returned. The Sex Pistols were no communists, whether musical or any other kind, but were instead, like Bob Geldof claimed, very much "looking after number one".

Musically, however, *Never Mind The Bollocks* makes *The Clash* or *Another Music In A Different Kitchen* sound almost conservative. With a guitar sounding more powerful than most heavy metal and a lead vocal that sneers and gibbers as though bordering on insanity, Johnny Rotten drags his cohorts through some of the most aggressive music ever recorded. It is no wonder that it was the Sex Pistols, rather than the Clash, who were noticed by the media and treated with the kind of outraged hostility that had previously been reserved for the Rolling Stones. No wonder either that established musicians and critics reacted with initial distaste, for music that so deliberately flouted the accepted standards of excellence was clearly a considerable threat, being too clamouring and strident to be simply ignored.

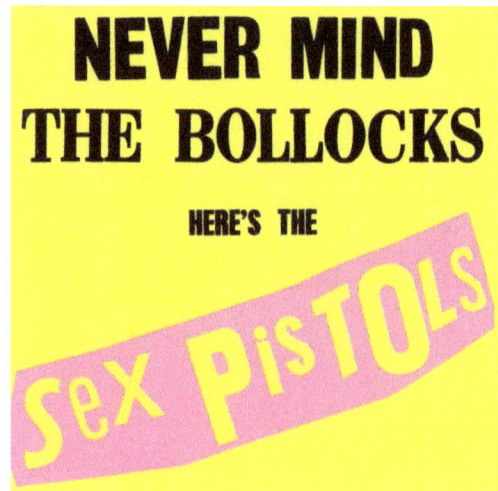

The Kinks' music is always interesting because of the way in which Ray Davies evolved a songwriting style for which the studied amateurism of the group's performances was actually an advantage. There is a toughness behind Davies' wry celebrations of the British way of life that gives the songs an immediately distinctive character. From *Face To Face* to *Preservation Act One,* his touch hardly falters, the result being a body of work whose power of expression transcends the simplicity of its resources. Later on, the high energy music of much of the live *One For The Road,* recorded in 1980, reveals a strong kinship between the Kinks and the Clash, although for Ray Davies, this music is nothing new, but simply rock 'n' roll.

Although formed as a response to seeing the Sex Pistols play live, Joy Division was ultimately not a punk band. Rather than merely trashing rock music's past, Joy Division discovered a genuinely new way of playing the music, in which the bass guitar, played high and with an emphasis on melody as much as on the beat, was elevated to become the lead instrument, the central focus of the music. All the musicians favoured a direct, utilitarian playing style, preferring to leave space in the sound, rather than fill it with unnecessary decoration. Only Ian Curtis's voice, reminiscent of Jim Morrison, provided any link with the legacy of rock 'n' roll, except that even here, Curtis stripped out the warmth and replaced it with a sense of disintegration only just kept at bay. The music looked, not back towards what rock had previously done, but forwards, to the impending agony of 1984, as portrayed by George Orwell, and beyond. Yet emotion seeped through regardless. It was there in the headlong rush of *Transmission,* the helpless resignation of *Love Will Tear Us Apart,* and, above all, in the unbearable sadness of *Atmosphere,* where a synthesizer replaces the guitar (until, that is, a perfectly judged chord comes crashing in near the end) and somehow manages to sound as though the instrument is being heard for the first time.

With Johnny Marr playing some virtuoso rhythm guitar that, paradoxically, owed a little to Roger McGuinn's work with the Byrds, the Smiths invented Britpop during the mid eighties, as another way forward from punk. The group's method of songwriting was unusual, involving singer Morrissey drawing on his stored collection of lyrics in order to improvise melody lines over Marr's completed patterns of chords. It was an approach that worked extremely well, however, and never more so than on the magnificent *How Soon Is Now,* originally issued in 1984 as a single B-side. Recast, with some little alteration, as a piece of US alternative rock, and sounding as fresh as when it was first recorded by the Smiths, the song was performed by Love Spit Love and used as the theme tune for the hit television series *Charmed,* which was first broadcast in 1998. The song has inspired several other cover versions too, appearing as grunge-metal (Quicksand), thrash metal (Elysium), electro-pop (Solar Fake), inventive avant-pop (Snake River Conspiracy), happy hardcore (Inner Sanctum), and whatever genre of pop-rock the Russian girl duo t.A.T.u. is. It has to be said, however, that few of these are as convincing as Morrissey when claiming that they are "criminally" shy! During the nineties, Johnny Marr worked with Bernard Sumner, of Joy Division and its successor, New Order, in a band they called Electronic. Disappointingly, the meeting of key musicians from two important bands produced music that carried no sense of importance at all.

MUSIC GENRES

Technically, the first punk record was *New Rose* by the Damned, beating the first Sex Pistols release by five weeks. The fledgling Stiff Records could move much more quickly than the music industry behemoth, EMI, that had signed the Pistols. The Damned played their first gig just three months previously, in July 1976, when they were the support act for the Sex Pistols, who had been gigging for eight months and had built up a considerable following. Neither band would have been in any doubt as to which was the movement leader. As the group's guitarist Brian James said in a March 2018 interview in *The Guardian*, the Damned simply thought that they were "a fast rock 'n' roll band". Punk begins with *Anarchy In The UK*, by the Sex Pistols, the group that pioneered the style and the attitude. There is no doubt whatsoever.

TRACKING THE TRACKS

Punk antecedents are to be heard on the first albums by The Kinks (*Kinks* – Sanctuary 2008) and The Troggs (*From Nowhere* – BGO 2008 – with the second album, *Trogglodynamite*, included too). Then there is *Ptooff!* by the Deviants (Esoteric 2009), *Black Monk Time* by The Monks (Polydor 2009), *Kick Out The Jams* by the MC5 (Elektra 2000), and *Fun House* by Iggy Pop and The Stooges (Elektra 1987). The Kinks live album, *One For The Road,* has its most recent CD issue on Universal (2010). Dr Feelgood's first album, *Down By The Jetty,* was recorded in mono in 1975 – the CD is on Grand Records (1989). The self-titled first album by Ducks Deluxe was issued in 1974 – on CD it is combined with the second album, *Taxi To The Terminal Zone* (BGO 2002). John Lydon, on the other hand, liked the singing of Peter Hammill, at its most intense on the 1975 album, *Godbluff*, by Hammill's band, Van Der Graaf Generator (Virgin 2005). *The Velvet Underground And Nico* and *White Light/White Heat are* on Universal (2012, 2013). The Lou Reed tracks mentioned are on *Transformer* (RCA 2009). *Metal Machine Music* is on RCA (2000). John Cale's *Paris S'Eveille* is on Yellow Moon (1995). Some prime examples of US punk from the sixties can be found on the compilation CD *Nuggets – Original Artyfacts From The First Psychedelic Era 1965-1968* (Rhino 2012).

The Boom Town Rats' *Lookin' After Number One* is on *Best Of The Boomtown Rats* (Universal 2004). The Buzzcocks' *Boredom* is on the group's first release, a four track seven inch EP entitled *Spiral Scratch*. It was reissued on CD by Mute in 2000, even if the format renders the title nonsensical. The lead singer here is Howard Devoto, who subsequently left to form his own band, Magazine, whose 1978 album *Real Life* (Virgin 2007) represents the first step by a punk musician in the direction of a more consciously arty approach. The Buzzcocks' first album, with Pete Shelley now handling the lead vocals, is *Another Music In A Different Kitchen*. On CD, this is combined with the early singles and the second album, *Love Bites*, which means that the magnificent *Ever Fallen In Love* gets included (EMI 2011).

Love At First Sight is on XTC's rather fine fourth album, *Black Sea* (Virgin 2001) and can also be found on the two CD anthology, *Fossil Fuel The XTC Singles 1977-1992* (Virgin 1996), which provides a splendid overview of the band's career. The Damned are similarly well served by a two CD anthology, *Smash It Up – The Anthology 1976-1987* (Sanctuary 2002), which includes all the tracks mentioned. As further demonstration of the group's move into art-rock territory, the set also finds room for the seventeen minute epic, *Curtain Call*, which was originally included on the Damned's *The Black Album* – issued as a double LP in 1980. *The Best Of Siouxsie and The Banshees* (Universal/Polydor 2002) includes *Hong Kong Garden* and *Spellbound* and another Beatles' cover version, rendered with more respect to the original this time *(Dear Prudence)*. For *Helter Skelter*, it is necessary to go to the group's influential first album, *The Scream* (Universal/Polydor 2006). The Dickies' *The Punk Singles Collection* (Spectrum 2002) includes *Nights In White Satin,* alongside some other well-known songs given the punk treatment, and a rather less interesting selection of group originals.

Elvis Costello's *This Year's Model* adds the single *Radio Radio* for CD (Universal 2007), which does the album no harm at all. It is also available as two different double CDs (Edsel 2002 and Universal 2008), with the sets providing an assortment of out-takes, demos, and live recordings. The newer release offers the most, with the track listing being extended to forty titles overall. *The Sweetest Punch* is on Universal/Decca (1999); *Il Sogno* is on Deutsch Grammophon (2004); *The River In Reverse* is on Verve Forecast (2006).

The first, self-titled LP by the Clash is on Columbia (1999). The music of the Fall is not really punk, being considerably more avant garde in its fondness for broken rhythms and atonal, half spoken vocal lines, although it fits naturally into the musical climate of the times. A six track release, *Slates,* originally issued in 1981 on a 10" record that qualified it as neither LP nor single, provides an ideal point of entry to what another record calls "the wonderful and frightening world of the Fall". It has been issued on CD several times, but the most recent issue – by Sanctuary in 2008 – is not easy to find. There is, however, a reasonably priced official download available. The Undertones have several compilation CDs, but the one to get is *Teenage Kicks – The Best Of The Undertones* (Castle 1993) because it has the best of the late tracks as well as the early singles and it presents them in a sensible, chronological order. Television's *Marquee Moon* adds extra tracks for the CD reissue, including the first single, *Little Johnny Jewel* from two years before, but still not punk (Elektra/Rhino 2003).

Never Mind The Bollocks...Here's The Sex Pistols (Virgin 1993) is not the complete recordings of the group, but it might as well be. Listening to Sid Vicious stumbling through a version of *My Way* the following year makes one realise exactly why John Lydon had decided to move on, to explore altogether more fruitful avenues with his new group, Public Image Ltd.

A good overview of Joy Division's music is provided by *Permanent* (London 1999), combining the best album tracks with the vital singles. *Hatful Of Hollow* by the Smiths (WEA 2011) gathers together some radio sessions with the early singles, including *How Soon Is Now*.

James Brown live in 1973

James Brown in the studio in 1968

> Miles Davis invented the idea of basing jazz improvisations on a single chord, rather than a rapidly moving series of more or less complicated chord changes, and presented an album of pieces like this on *Kind Of Blue,* recorded in March and April 1959, when saxophonist John Coltrane was a member of the group. Coltrane formed his own group in late 1960 and spent most of the rest of his career exploring the possibilities of constructing solos on top of a rhythm section that provided no harmonic development. The results were hugely influential on improvising musicians, whether working in jazz, funk, or rock genres, especially after the release of his album *A Love Supreme* in 1965. This managed the difficult trick of making music that was almost entirely improvised, yet was accessible enough to attract widespread attention and to sell around half a million copies during the sixties – a remarkable figure for a jazz album of any description, let alone one usually defined as being avant garde.

23 FUNK

James Brown scored his first hit with his first record release, in 1956. *Please Please Please* was credited to the Famous Flames, a vocal group whose answering phrases to Brown's urgent lead vocal put them into the role of congregation to James Brown's sermon. The role of gospel preacher was one that Brown never really left behind. Whether singing to a chorus or else calling out instructions to a band, he was always the master of ceremonies, in control of the music. In live performance he developed an act where he would sing as if possessed – having to be draped in a cloak and led off stage, only to break free and continue, as if the notes he had to deliver were simply too powerful to be restrained.

It was two years before Brown gained a second chart success, *Try Me*, but after that he hardly missed at all, with over a hundred single releases through to the nineties. The sales of *Try Me* enabled Brown to form a permanent band. He established himself as a hard taskmaster, turning his band into the tightest of all and insisting on perfection – fining any musician who made a mistake on stage. As he turned from gospel ballads to uptempo pieces like *Think* and *I'll Go Crazy*, this meant that his band was equipped to deliver rhythms that were particularly sharp and compelling.

In February 1965, Brown led his musicians in the recording of a song called *Papa's Got A Brand New Bag*. Although the band was a big one, it does not sound like it. The music has a spacious quality, with the instruments all contributing to the rhythm, rather than providing layers of texture. This is particularly apparent after the song proper is finished, but the band continues to play, with Brown cueing saxophonist Maceo Parker into two separate solos. The song is based on standard blues chords, but for the extended coda, the chord changes are abandoned, as a groove based on just one chord is established. The rhythm is made up of four distinct ingredients, with no one of these predominating. A light, jazz-inflected drum pattern is delivered by Melvin Parker (Maceo's brother), without any particular beat in the bar being emphasised. This is not the backbeat familiar to all rock 'n' roll players, where the second and fourth beats in each bar are stressed. Sam Thomas plays a dancing bass riff, placed in the middle of each bar, while the rhythm guitar strikes a staccato chord, using just two or three strings and placed well back in the mix, so that although Jimmy Nolen does indeed play on the second and fourth beats, he does not succeed in making this the major emphasis in the music. The brass section, playing tightly enough to sound like a single, albeit many-throated musician, compresses a triplet into a single pulse, adding its weight to the guitarist on the second beat of the bar. Maceo Parker solos on tenor saxophone and then on baritone saxophone, and although the one-chord structure he is working with is derived from the work of John Coltrane, whose influential album, *A Love Supreme*, had only just been released, he does not play like Coltrane, preferring to use short notes and brief phrases, so as not to divert attention from the groove. James Brown exhorts and directs the soloist and the other players throughout, to make it clear that what is happening musically is entirely under his command.

The original recording is available in a four CD overview of Brown's career, *Star Time*, but in 1965, it was speeded up slightly for single release, spread over both sides, and trimmed to create tunes short enough for radio. It became Brown's first US top ten entry, hit number one in the R&B charts (staying for eight weeks), and gained a Grammy award for best rhythm and blues record of 1965. The song even scraped into the UK top thirty for the first time, inspiring the influential TV show, *Ready Steady Go*, to present a James Brown special the following March. A live version of the song, at the Paris Olympia in 1967, can be seen on YouTube. Played much faster than the single, it keeps the pace going for a quarter of an hour, as Brown oversees saxophone solos by Maceo Parker and St.Clair Pinckney, dance showcases by the Famous Flames, and a drum solo, performed without breaking the groove by himself. It is interesting to hear the regular drummer, who is presumably Jabo Starks, adopting a much more rock-influenced approach, while the guitarist resolutely hits the first beat of each bar (playing 'on the one'). The rhythm is constructed differently from the original record, but retains its groove, albeit more like that of an express train.

THE FIRST TIME

Local musicians in Brikama, the Gambia

On what was originally side four of the James Brown double album, *Sex Machine*, five songs are presented as a continuous live performance, from a 1969 concert in Brown's home town, Augusta, Georgia. The band makes the change as one man from each song to the next, at the moment Brown gives the cue (which does not appear to be the result of post-production editing). *It's A Man's Man's Man's World* is one of these songs, still a ballad, but delivered in a manner much closer to funk than is the case on the original single. There is an extended pause at one point in the song, ended by a dramatic re-entry by the band that inspires Brown to make a typically theatrical aside to the audience, "Give the band another round of applause, ladies and gentlemen, being so together." He pulls the reins in again soon after, however, with a curt "don't play so much jazz!" directed at the band. It is interesting in this context, to note that the albums made by James Brown bands without the presence of Brown himself, such as those by the JBs, are significantly less rhythmically precise – less funky – than those made by the same musicians when directed by James Brown. This is not the case within the many albums where some of Brown's musicians perform alongside like-minded players, under the supervision of George Clinton. These albums comprise Clinton's P-Funk brand, where the music is usually driven by the bass playing of Bootsy Collins, a key musician in the *Sex Machine* band. For proof, it is not necessary to look any further than the sublime *One Nation Under A Groove*, included in the 1978 album of the same name, and credited to Funkadelic. Clinton is a fascinating figure, whose eccentric and frequently humorous approach, combined with a questing musical ambition, invites an easy comparison with Frank Zappa. He is also responsible for *Chocolate City*, from 1975, a black power anthem making a fine companion to *Say It Loud, I'm Black And I'm Proud*. Clinton picked up on what Jimi Hendrix was trying to do with the Band of Gypsys, as is easily demonstrated by the title track of the 1971 Funkadelic album, *Maggot Brain*, where guitarist Eddie Hazel delivers a long and rather fine guitar solo. The P-Funk music lays the foundation for the funk-rock approach followed several years later by bands like Living Colour and the Red Hot Chili Peppers (whose 1985 album, *Freaky Styley*, was produced by George Clinton).

The success of *Papa's Got A Brand New Bag* was enough to persuade Brown to continue with his new musical direction, the 'brand new bag' of the song's title. Performances like *Cold Sweat* (recorded May 1967), *Say It Loud, I'm Black And I'm Proud* (August 1968), and his masterpiece, *Give It Up Or Turnit A Loose* (January 1969), demonstrate the enormous potential of the style even as they refine and develop it. All are songs based on a rhythmic groove, using a single chord through most or all of the music. The rhythms are all based on four-four time, but vary in terms of which beats are emphasised within the bar. Always the rhythms are constructed using the whole band, with every instrument having a rhythmic role. Rather than using the drums to drive the music, as is the case in all kinds of rock, here the drums are just one component in a tapestry of rhythm. The approach is the same as that employed in African music. In contemporary West African countries like the Gambia, Senegal, and Guinea, a local group formed to play music for dancing is likely to consist almost entirely of drummers. Each musician will be using a different kind of drum and each will be responsible for playing a different pattern of beats within the overall rhythm. For his music, James Brown did the same – making the guitar, bass guitar, and brass play as though they too are different kinds of drum.

Somewhere along the line, the music began to be referred to as 'funk'. A single with the title *Funky Soul #1* was issued in late 1967. It was one of the few James Brown records not to be a hit, but its title shows that the term 'funky' was already in use at that point. This was not the first time that the word, originally a slang term with sexual connotations, had been applied to a kind of music. According to the obituary of drummer Earl Palmer, published in the Guardian in September 2008, Palmer was the musician who first started using the word 'funky' to describe the rhythms he was playing. He was a member of the Dave Bartholomew band, based in New Orleans from the late forties, and responsible for the backing on the hit records by Fats Domino and others. During the fifties, a number of jazz pieces appeared with titles like *Funky Blues* (Johnny Hodges 1952), *Opus De Funk* (Horace Silver 1953), *Barrel Of Funk* and *Funk In Deep Freeze* (Hank Mobley 1957). Organist Johnny 'Hammond' Smith was one of several jazz players to cover the Horace Silver tune and he used it as the title track for an album in 1961. Silver is quoted in Paul De Noyer's *The Illustrated Encyclopaedia Of Music* as explaining "funky means earthy and blues-based. It might not be blues itself, but it does have that down-home feel to it". There is an obvious link here with the music made by James Brown, although the likes of *Opus De Funk* and *Give It Up Or Turnit A Loose* do not otherwise sound very similar.

There are undeniable elements of James Brown influence in the music of other black groups in the late sixties – Sly and the Family Stone, the Temptations, Jimi Hendrix's Band Of Gypsys – but it is impossible to suggest that the music played by these groups is funk, rather than varieties of black rock music. It is striking to realise that it was actually several years after the success of *Papa's Got A Brand New Bag* before other records began to emerge that could be described as funk. Between 1965 and 1972, James Brown achieved a remarkable thirty-seven top ten hits in the US R&B charts, of which thirteen reached number one. Fourteen of the records managed to enter the top twenty in the main national chart – and only one was not a funk record, the gospel-inspired ballad *It's A Man's Man's Man's World*.

When the Beatles started to make an impact on the US charts, a large number of other groups quickly appeared, performing songs in a very similar style. The fact that this did not immediately happen with James Brown can only be because the complex, interlocking rhythms of his music are very difficult to play. This is rather emphasised by the release in 1970 of the first, self-titled, album by Kool and the Gang. Although the group was to become one of the star funk bands of the mid-seventies (and an efficient hit-making unit for a long time after that), it has to be admitted that the first album, whose music sits on the interface between the less dynamic moments of the band Chicago and easy-listening, is not very funky and not very good, although it is clearly trying to be both. The first eponymous album by Earth Wind And Fire, which was released in 1971, is better, if only because the band's leader, Maurice White, is an extremely skilled drummer, but the music still has a much less urgent approach to funk than that of James Brown.

In June 1972, Miles Davis, who had been experimenting with rhythms not previously heard within jazz, turned his attention to the music of James Brown. According to bass player Michael Henderson, whom Davis had recruited from Stevie Wonder's band two years earlier, "Miles just wanted me to be funky and an extended groove – a breakdown – like you get in R&B after you finish the song. Except forget the song and just *start* with the breakdown.

THE FIRST TIME

The reference to the band Chicago is not intended to be a deprecating one, even if Chicago moved very close to easy listening territory itself in later years. The early albums by the band are fine examples of the brass-rock genre and the first album in particular, *Chicago Transit Authority,* is exciting and something of a rock milestone. Kool and the Gang eventually produced their own milestone recording, because that is what *Light Of Worlds* from 1974 definitely is. The album is not entirely a funk record either, but when the band does hit a groove, as on the tracks *Street Corner Symphony, Rhyme Time People,* and *Higher Plane,* it has acquired an authority that it did not have four years previously. The album also includes the much-sampled instrumental track *Summer Madness,* which is too slow and too mellow to be funky, but is a terrific performance regardless.

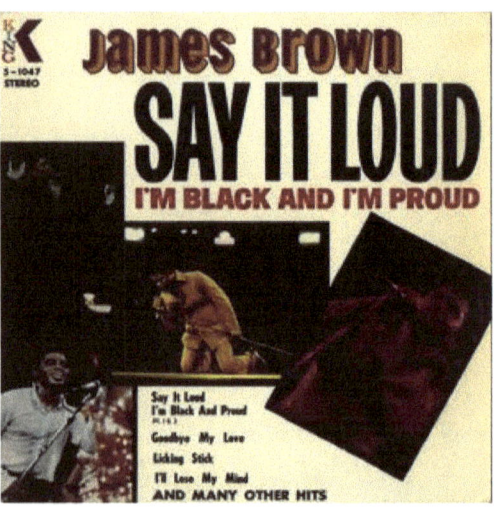 

There are several other jazz albums made during the late sixties and early seventies that use rhythms derived from rhythm and blues styles – such as Herbie Mann's *Memphis Underground* from 1969, which presents jazz versions of some well known Stax soul songs, or Donald Byrd's *Black Byrd* from 1972, which has strong influences from Motown and Philadelphia vocal group soul. Although these records are sometimes described as being funky, they are not funk in the James Brown sense, such as we are discussing here. The instruments all adopt their customary roles, with the drums setting the rhythm, rather than the rhythms being created by a combination of parts from all the instruments. One of these records was actually made by Herbie Hancock – his *Fat Albert Rotunda* from 1969 is typical soul-jazz with appropriately driving rhythms, but it sounds modest in the extreme in its achievements next to what was being played by Miles Davis at this time, or indeed, what was subsequently played by Herbie Hancock himself.

 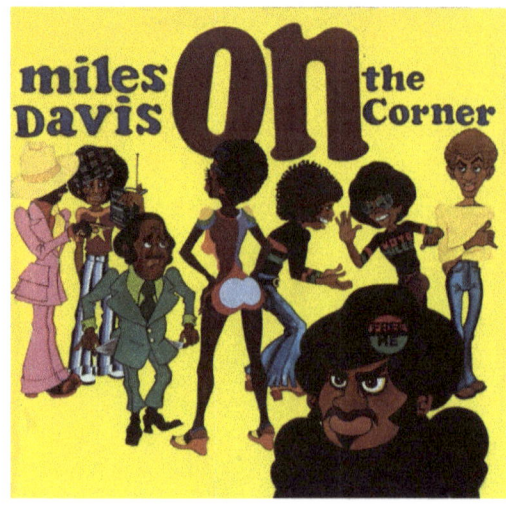

Some members of Miles Davis's seventies band moved into more commercial areas after their years of playing jazz-funk. Mtume became a successful songwriter and producer. His *Juicy Fruit*, credited to a band named after himself, was a number one R&B hit in 1983. Rhythm guitarist Reggie Lucas worked with Mtume and produced the first, self-titled album by Madonna in 1983. Bass player Michael Henderson became a big-selling soul singer, with eight albums released between 1976 and 1986.

He wanted freestyle funk with a little bit of jazz in it and a feel so solid, so intense, people could dance to it a lot easier." Percussionist Mtume added, "We brought a new branch to that tree that's never been explored: improvisational funk." (Both quotes from the sleeve notes to the CD set, *On The Corner – The Complete Sessions*.). The tree that Mtume was referring to was the music dubbed 'fusion', essentially invented on the 1970 Davis album, *Bitches Brew*. The improvisational funk was the music released near the end of 1972, on the album *On The Corner*.

The jazz critics greatly disliked *On The Corner*. They were dismayed by music that showed so little regard for melody, especially when the protagonist was a man who had once been renowned for the exquisite nature of his melodic playing. They did not feel that an intricate mesh of rhythms was at all an adequate substitute. As it happens, James Brown fared little better. The revised *New Musical Express Book Of Rock*, published in the UK in 1977 as a definitive guide, scattered words like 'boring', 'dated', and 'predictable' through its James Brown entry and added a discography that ignored all releases prior to 1972. Of course, Brown himself had sacrificed the intense euphony of his singing on the preaching ballads he had once favoured for the sake of the funk, just as Miles Davis was now doing.

Herbie Hancock, a member of Davis' sixties band, was also one of the musicians to be involved in the June 1972 recording sessions. Fifteen months later, he took a band of his own into the recording studios and created four tracks that presented his own approach to funk. As with James Brown, the rhythms were intricately constructed by all the members of the band, which was only a quintet, except that, with Hancock playing multiple keyboard parts, the effective size was much larger. There was little variation from a single chord in the pieces, but Hancock nevertheless managed to incorporate some memorably melodic material. The music was funky, but it was also very tuneful – making it much more accessible than *On The Corner*. The result, issued on the album *Head Hunters* in October 1973, was an immediate success, with its continued sales in the following years eventually making it into the first platinum jazz album, with over a million copies sold. Numerous other bands began playing similar music as a result, whether they aligned themselves with the jazz or the pop markets, and the emergence of funk as a distinct genre begins here.

TRACKING THE TRACKS

Star Time, a four CD set providing a good and essential overview of James Brown's career, was issued by Universal/Polydor in 2004. A two CD alternative, concentrating on the development of funk, is *Foundations Of Funk – A Brand New Bag 1964-1969* (Polydor 1996). *Sex Machine* was issued on CD by Polydor in 1998. *One Nation Under A Groove* by Funkadelic is a double CD on Charly (2014). *Chocolate City*, credited to Parliament, but featuring many of the same musicians, is on US Mercury (2003). *Maggot Brain* is on Westbound (2005).

There are several albums of West African drumming available – the various artists CD, *A Land Of Drummers* (Village Pulse 1999) is as good a place to start as any. *African Chants and Drums* by Yao Yanaglo Ensemble is on Masso (2002). The CD is impossibly expensive but the album is available as a download. *African Seasonings* by Griot Drum Ensemble is on the band's own label (2008). Much modern West African music has a considerable amount in common with funk – try *Firin' In Fouta* by Baaba Maal (Mango 1994) or *Set* by Youssou N'Dour (Virgin 1990). The music of Nigerian band leader Fela Kuti is a fascinating example of West African musicians stealing the African influenced music back from James Brown. The double CD compilation *The Best Best Of Fela Kuti The Black President* (Universal 1999) presents thirteen prime examples of a music that is essentially an African version of American funk. *Opus De Funk* is on *The Best Of Horace Silver – The Blue Note Years* (Blue Note 2000)

The key albums by Sly and the Family Stone are *Stand!* and *There's A Riot Goin' On* (both Sony/Epic 2007). The sleeve notes to *Stand!* state that the album "virtually invented the 'progressive' funk of the seventies and eighties". The word 'virtually' is used here to obscure the awkward facts that the music is not really funk at all and that, even if it had been, James Brown got there first. The essential Norman Whitfield productions for the Temptations are compiled on the two CD set, *Psychedelic Soul*, (Universal/Motown 2003). *Band Of Gypsys* by Jimi Hendrix is a recording of a concert performed on New Year's Eve 1969-70 (MCA 1997), with the rhythm section of Billy Cox and Buddy Miles giving the guitarist's music a more soulful feel than on any of his other recordings.

Kool and the Gang's first album is *Kool And The Gang* (Polygram/Mercury 1996). The masterpiece *Light Of Worlds* was reissued on CD in 1996 by Polygram/Mercury. Earth Wind And Fire's self-titled first album is on WEA 1996. Miles Davis' *On The Corner* has been issued as a 6 CD box set, *The Complete On The Corner Sessions* (Columbia/Sony 2007). This includes out-takes and extended recordings as they were before being edited for album release, alongside music in a similar style that was originally issued on the albums *Big Fun* (one side of the double LP) and *Get Up With It*. The original *On The Corner* album is included too, or it can be obtained as a separate single CD (Columbia 2000). Herbie Hancock's *Head Hunters* is on a Columbia CD (1997). The soul-jazz albums mentioned are *Memphis Underground* by Herbie Mann (Atlantic 2002); *Black Byrd* by Donald Byrd (Blue Note 1992); and *Fat Albert Rotunda* by Herbie Hancock (Warner Bros 2001).

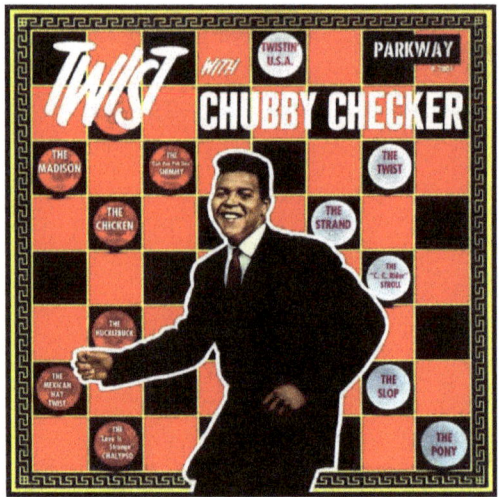

Dancing the twist

Chubby Checker was already a Dick Clark protégé, even before *The Twist*. He had been hired to privately record a novelty song for Clark to use as a Christmas present – this was *The Class*. Born Ernest Evans, the singer was given his stage name by Dick Clark's wife, who was a fan of the similarly named Fats Domino. He gained a few smaller hits after *Let's Twist Again*, many of them including the word 'twist' in the title, and has never succeeded in escaping the sway of a dance he espoused when still a teenager.

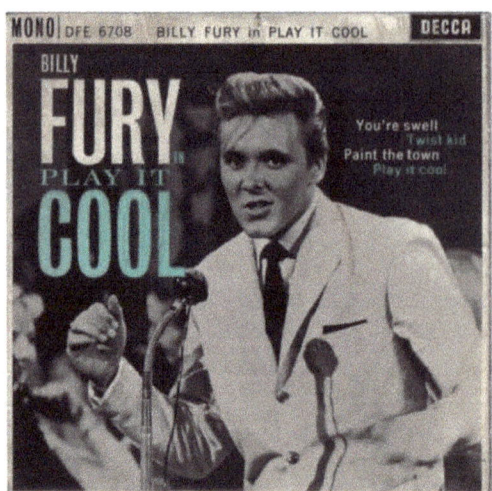

Billy Fury is performing The Twist Kid in this EP cover picture

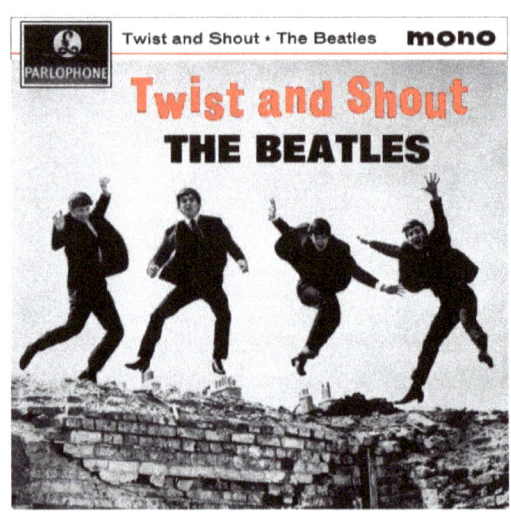

24 DISCO AND DANCE MUSIC

To an extent, music of all genres inspires and encourages people to dance. Much of it is explicitly designed for that purpose. Thus orchestral music has its waltzes and its quicksteps, its ballet; rock 'n' roll has its jiving, English folk its Morris men and country its line-dancing. Meanwhile, in the clubs and discos…

In 1959, Hank Ballard wrote and recorded a song called *The Twist*. Depending on who you believe, the words were inspired either by the moves made by Ballard's own backing singers, the Midnighters, or else by teenagers he had seen dancing in Florida. Either way, the song was placed on the B-side of a single (the A-side was *Teardrops On Your Letter*). After a month in the R&B charts, the single was flipped and the B-side did well in the charts in its own right. A little over a year later, *The Twist* was re-released as the official A-side and this time it did well in the Hot Hundred, reaching number twenty-eight. There are two stories about what happened next, both involving the Dick Clark TV show. In one story, Clark wanted to have the song on his show, but felt that Hank Ballard was too old (he was thirty-two), or too risqué for his teenage audience. He arranged for the young Chubby Checker (nineteen at the time, but with a top forty hit already under his belt, *The Class*) to record a version of *The Twist* and perform it on the TV show. In the other story, Ballard was indeed booked to appear on the show, but failed to turn up. Chubby Checker was persuaded to sing the song in his place and subsequently released it as a single himself. Whatever the truth of the matter, Checker's version of the song became an enormous hit, reaching number one in the Hot Hundred, and then, when re-released with a different B-side the next year, reaching number one again. Bing Crosby's *White Christmas* was the only other record to ever manage this particular chart success.

In the UK and round the rest of the world, the follow up single, *Let's Twist Again*, was the bigger hit. It reached number one in the UK chart, for two weeks, although the Official Charts Company, which uses the Record Retailer listing that the general public never saw, rather than the *NME* or *BBC* charts that everyone did, insists on rewriting history, taking away Chubby Checker's glory and giving him only a number two slot. In any event, the twist caught the public imagination round the world and rapidly moved into a far wider area than the purely teenage culture in which it had started. It even appears in the *Guinness Book of Records* (four thousand people dancing together in Florida, while Chubby Checker sang, as late as 2012). Several other artists tried to hitch a ride on the success of the twist, including Billy Fury (*The Twist Kid* was a highlight of his 1962 film, *Play It Cool*), Sam Cooke (*Twistin' The Night Away* was one of his biggest hits), and the Beatles (*Twist and Shout*, a cover of a slightly earlier hit by the Isley Brothers, was a million selling single in the US, and the title track of the group's first, best selling EP in the UK).

A line dance called the Madison was briefly popular around the same time as the twist. Two records were modest US hits in April – May 1960, *The Madison Time* by the Ray Bryant Combo and *The Madison* by Al Brown's Tunetoppers. Both are essentially jazz records, which easily explains why the Madison did not manage to make the impact that the twist did. The cover of the *Madison* LP by the Tunetoppers makes the target audience for the dance clear and it is not one made up of teenagers. In the UK, a single called *Must Be Madison* was issued by easy listening band leader Joe Loss and reached number twenty in the charts in 1962.

The bossa nova, a relative of the Latin-American samba, was launched at a concert in New York's Carnegie Hall in November 1962, given by saxophonist Stan Getz and a number of Brazilian music stars. Getz recorded several bossa nova albums, some of them in collaboration with the likes of Luiz Bonfa, Joao Gilberto, and Antonio Carlos Jobim. *Jazz Samba* sold a million copies in 1962 and so did a single taken from it, *Desafinado*. The album has the distinction of being the first jazz record to reach number one in the Billboard album charts. The 1963 album, *Getz/Gilberto* generated a second hit single, *The Girl From Ipanema*, which also sold a million copies. The vocals on this song were provided by guitarist Joao Gilberto's wife, Astrud, whose career as a successful singer began here. With the

THE FIRST TIME

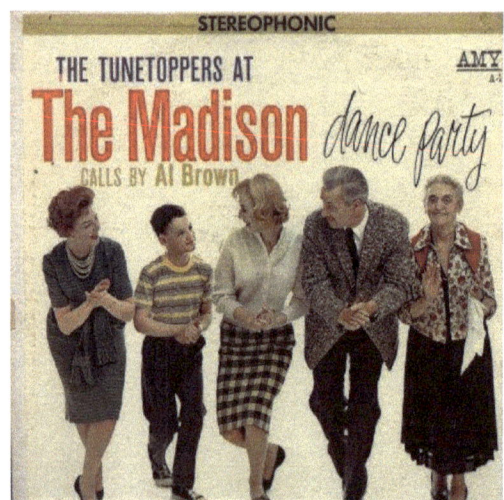
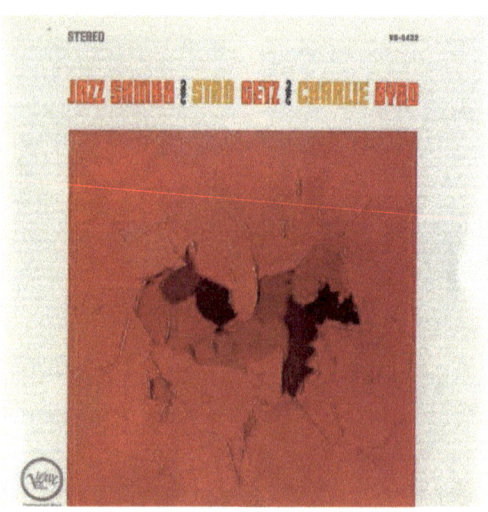

Joe Cocker at Woodstock. The fact that the photograph, reproduced from the booklet of the double Woodstock CD, is a mirror image (unless Cocker is left-handed) seems rather appropriate, given that a mirror image would be the view for many performers on the air guitar!

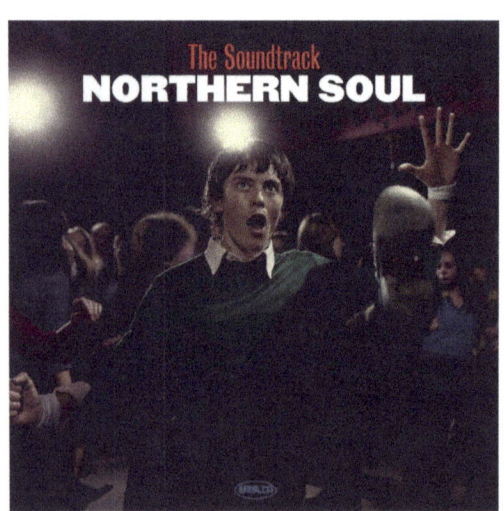

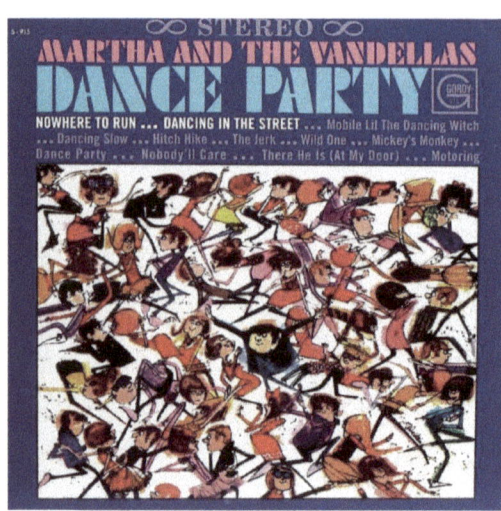

Dancers at the Wigan Casino, as shown in the 2014 film, Northern Soul

dance music delivered by jazz albums, it is clear that the bossa nova was not aimed at a teenage audience either.

Several other dances were tried out with appropriately titled records during the next few years, in an attempt to emulate the success of the twist. These included the hully gully, the mashed potato, the watusi, the swim, the jerk, and several others. James Brown referred to most of them in various of his songs. The hitch-hike was briefly popular when attached to a Marvin Gaye song with the same title. Gaye sang it on television while dancers did the dance and the result was a US hit, but not a big one. The greatest success in terms of it being danced was the shake, although records generating or celebrating the fact were few. The Swinging Blue Jeans nearly reached the top of the UK charts at the end of 1963 with *Hippy Hippy Shake* (kept off the number one spot by the mighty *I Want To Hold Your Hand*) and it was a substantial hit too in the US. A popular EP followed, *Shake With The Swinging Blue Jeans*, adding the hit single to three more songs with 'shake' in the title. Sam Cooke had a posthumous US hit at the beginning of 1965 with *Shake*, a song that was covered by several other people, including Otis Redding, the Small Faces, and the young singer with Steampacket, Rod Stewart. The shake, described at the time as being like an attempt to escape from having one's feet trapped in a block of concrete, rapidly evolved into a dancing style based on free expression, which eventually appeared as the 'idiot dancing' phenomenon of the late sixties. At a time when a new seriousness in rock, typified by the emergence of the progressive genre, had resulted in audiences preferring to sit down at gigs, lone solo dancers, usually male, would rise to their feet to perform extravagant improvisations. They were echoed by the movements of singer Joe Cocker on stage, pretending, like many of them, to play emotional solos on an invisible guitar. (Since the early eighties, actions like this have been referred to as 'air guitar'.)

Through the sixties, a number of records intended for dancing were released, some of them having lyrics about dancing – *Dancing In The Street* by Martha and the Vandellas, *Dance To The Music* by Sly and the Family Stone, *Land Of A Thousand Dances* by Wilson Pickett, *Save The Last Dance For Me* by the Drifters, and many more. The Four Tops single, *Reach Out I'll Be There*, was a dance music song that reached number one in the charts in both the US and the UK in 1966; the Marvin Gaye single, *I Heard It Through The Grapevine*, did the same in 1969; Smokey Robinson and the Miracles did the same in 1970 with *The Tears Of A Clown;* the George McCrae single, *Rock Your Baby*, was a dance music song that did the same in 1974. Arguably, the three Motown hits were good pop songs that were enhanced by a dance beat, whereas the McCrae song was entirely about the dance. These are all soul music records, however, and in the discos at this time it was almost exclusively soul music that was played. The history of the discos is briefly described in the chapter on DJs, with some more information in the chapter on Sampling.

In late 1975, Motown producer Hal Davis chose a song called *Love Hangover* for Diana Ross to record. He installed lights in the studio to give it the feel of a disco, after the arrangers Clay Drayton and Dave Blumberg and he came up with the concept of a song that would start slow and sultry, then shift up several gears for an extended uptempo coda. This fast section has a very specific rhythm – significantly faster than a typical funk or Philadelphia soul track and played with a clearly stated four-four, having no particular emphasis on any of the four beats, like a quick march. Essentially, the genre of dance music known as disco, which is characterised by this same evenly played four-four, begins here. Released as a single in March 1976, in the face of a competing version by the Fifth Dimension (recorded with the same backing musicians), *Love Hangover* climbed to number one in the Billboard Hot Hundred (number ten in the UK). It replaced *Turn The Beat Around* by Vicki Sue Robinson at the top of the Billboard Dance Club Music chart – a record that is close to disco, except that it retains the prevailing dance music approach of emphasising the second and fourth beat of each bar.

The immediate influence of *Love Hangover* was on musicians working in the UK and Europe. In September to October 1976, drummer and producer Marc Cerrone made an LP called *Love In C Minor*, on which the title track filled the whole of the first side. For over a quarter of an hour, Cerrone kept his right foot on the bass drum pedal, maintaining a steady pulse of around two beats a second. Recorded in London, and initially pressed privately, both the album and a single with an edited version of the title track became US hits after becoming popular in the New York discos.

THE FIRST TIME

> Although disco fell quickly out of fashion and became derided by critics who felt that the more important musical phenomenon of the late seventies was punk, the music was nevertheless responsible for several bona fide classic recordings. These include *I Will Survive* by Gloria Gaynor, *I Haven't Stopped Dancing Yet* by Gonzalez, *I Love America* by Patrick Juvet, *I'm Every Woman* by Chaka Khan, *Shame* by Evelyn Champagne King, and *You Make Me Feel Mighty Real* by Sylvester – all of them being issued in 1978 and becoming big hits in the US, the UK, or both.

> *Love Hangover* makes a surprising (if not musically significant) connection between Diana Ross and jazz pioneer John Coltrane. The music for the song was written by Marilyn McLeod, who just happened to be the sister of Coltrane's wife, Alice, a remarkable jazz performer in her own right. The songwriter's grandson is a notable musician too – he is Steven Ellison, who has made a number of adventurous and acclaimed genre-hopping albums under the name of Flying Lotus.

MUSIC GENRES

In July 1977, Italian producer Giorgio Moroder added synthesizers to the disco recipe with *I Feel Love*, recorded by Donna Summer. The result was a second big chart hit for Ms Summer. *Love To Love You Baby* from the year before also employed synthesizers rhythmically, but with a slower beat and a bass line that owed everything to Kool and the Gang – more funk than disco.

In December 1977, the film *Saturday Night Fever* was released. Focussing on a disco as its main location and using a soundtrack comprising disco songs – many of them written and performed by the Bee Gees – the film was a critical and commercial success and made its leading actor, John Travolta, into a star. The soundtrack album, a double LP, was hugely successful too, reaching number one in album charts around the world, and eventually selling an estimated forty million copies. It revitalised the career of the Bee Gees and it had the effect of moving disco music into the mainstream. Through 1978 and much of 1979, disco dominated pop music, to the extent that several established artists felt the need to record disco songs of their own. Rod Stewart was the first, with *Do Ya Think I'm Sexy* – the Beach Boys (*Here Comes The Night*), Blondie (*Heart Of Glass*), and Barbra Streisand (*No More Tears*, in a duet with Donna Summer) followed closely behind.

Hip hop, the music created by New York DJs as a soundstage for rappers to perform, had its first records released in 1979. Breakdancing (whose enthusiasts preferred the term 'b-boying') developed in response to the music's roots during the seventies, both in the clubs where the likes of DJ Kool Herc were working and in the streets. The athleticism and showmanship of the dancing made it an ideal spectator sport. The music is described in this book in the chapters on Sampling and Rap.

In 1983, Frankie Knuckles, DJ at Chicago clubs The Warehouse and his own Power Plant, began using a drum machine to add beats to the records he played. He created his own remixes, often preparing them in advance on reel-to-reel tape. Other DJs in the city became inspired to create similar dance tracks of their own from scratch, using drum machines and electronic keyboards. Jesse Saunders made *On And On* in this way, and issued it at the beginning of 1984 on his own label, effectively launching house music, named after the Warehouse club. House was conceived very much as the dance music equivalent to punk, evolving from disco rather than rock, but where performers with little previous expertise were similarly able to create valid music of their own. Synthesizers and drum machines had become relatively cheap and it was easy to produce interesting results from them. The first major house music hit was *Love Can't Turn Around* by Farley 'Jackmaster' Funk (with lead vocals by Darryl Pandy and co-production by Jesse Saunders), which was a UK top ten hit in the late summer of 1986. In the US, an alternative version, by Steve 'Silk' Hurley, reached number one in the Billboard Dance Club Music Chart. In September 1987, *Pump Up The Volume*, credited to M/A/R/R/S, entered the UK charts and climbed to number one. This time the record was a hit in the US as well, reaching number thirteen in the Hot Hundred. The artist credit disguised the fact that the record was produced in the UK as the result of a collaboration by the electronic group Colourbox and the black experimental duo A R Kane.

A very similar music originating in Detroit was christened techno – essentially house music without the vocals and the soul influence. The founding record was released in 1985 – *No UFOs* by Model 500 (although it did have a few moments of chanting vocals). Techno was particularly influential in the UK, where several electronic music performers presenting themselves as bands issued records from 1988. Model 500 was itself the cover name for a solo artist, Juan Atkins. The first of the UK techno players were 808 State, who recorded the album *Newbuild* at the start of 1988, and Brian Dougans, who achieved a chart hit near the end of the year with *Stakker Humanoid*, credited to Humanoid. He subsequently worked as a half of a duo, Future Sound Of London.

Where mainstream rock and pop have stars, who can vary their sound and approach without audiences thinking they are no longer performing rock or pop, dance, which is largely a music without stars, prefers to designate any change to an existing formula as being a new genre altogether. Following the distinction made between house and techno, a bewildering array of different names has been conjured for slightly different dance music variations, many of

THE FIRST TIME

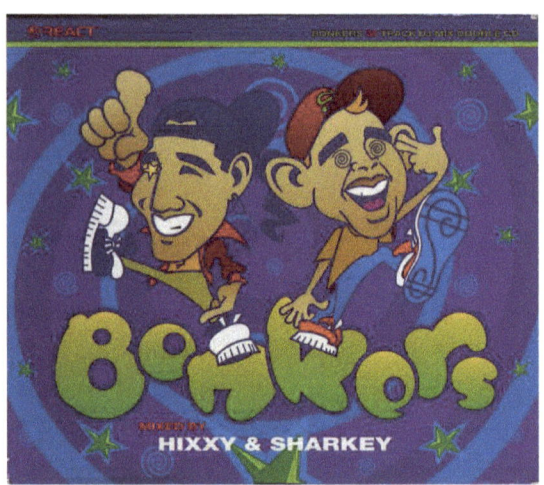

It is unlikely that any of the *Bonkers* performers were aware of the fact, but the Miles Davis track, *Rated X*, recorded as long ago as September 1972, sounds remarkably like a direct ancestor of hardcore. At the time, Davis' dense rhythms with horror movie keyboards but no actual melody appeared to have no influence. Somehow, the music's novelty seemed to permeate through the years regardless. In 1998-9, *Rated X* was treated to three different remixes, on the *Panthalassa* albums supervised by Bill Laswell, making the dance music connection more explicit.

Underworld managed, from a UK perspective, to blend the divergent approaches of techno and hip hop, in so far as it included a twin turntable set-up alongside its synthesizers and drum machines. The band started somewhat differently in 1983, when as a new wave act it achieved a minor hit with *Doot-Doot*. It had come up with the novel marketing idea of making the band name an unpronounceable squiggle. When pressed, the members decided that this should be pronounced 'Freur'. As Underworld, the band achieved the considerable coup of having a track, *Born Slippy NUXX*, prominently included in the hit film *Trainspotting* in 1996. This subsequently reached number two in the UK charts when issued as a single.

On the Panthalassa remixes album, the treatment given to *In A Silent Way* by French producer DJ Cam (Laurent Dumail) turns it into an outstanding demonstration of the art of great remixing. This is despite the fact that the result pushes Miles Davis himself into the background and sounds nothing like a piece that the jazz master would have released himself. DJ Cam's own albums present a similarly rewarding amalgam of trip hop and jazz.

them being exclusive to the UK. These include tech house, acid house, and hard house; trance, big beat, UK garage, and rave; grime, neurofunk, drumstep, techstep, and dubstep; and drum and bass.

A music called hardcore was responsible for a sound that was rather different, by increasing the speed of the beat to levels that made dancing with any degree of subtlety or expressiveness virtually impossible. Once again, slight variations were accorded the status of different genres, such as darkcore, happy hardcore, and gabber. For the birth of hardcore, fans point to an instrumental record called *We Have Arrived* by Mescalinum United (Marc Acardipane), produced in Germany in 1989 and released the following year. This is a loud, raucous affair, using heavy drum beats and blasts of synthesizer sound effects, without a trace of melody, but still paced like a disco or house record. *Toy Town*, produced by DJs Sharkey and Hixxy in 1995 is much faster, but also includes melodic fragments making its 'happy hardcore' label very appropriate. The track kicked off the first in a series of compilation albums titled *Bonkers*, which define the genre.

At the other extreme from hardcore was trip hop, a slower, more reflective kind of dance music, with some of the feel of dub reggae, providing space for invention and the pasting of clever samples. The album *Blue Lines*, issued by Massive Attack in 1991, introduced the genre. Kicking off with a bassline copied or sampled from Billy Cobham's *Spectrum* LP, the music moves through a number of memorable songs and laid-back raps until it reaches the apex of the achingly atmospheric *Unfinished Sympathy*, one of the greatest pieces of music of its era. The term, trip hop, was first used three years later by Andy Pemberton, a writer for the dance music magazine Mixmag, to describe a typical sample extravaganza constructed by DJ Shadow. By the end of 1994, however, with the success of the second Massive Attack album, *Protection*, and the first by Portishead, *Dummy*, the term naturally migrated to them.

The Orb, comprising Alex Paterson and whoever he chose to work with, also issued its first album in 1991, *The Orb's Adventures Beyond The Ultraworld*. Its combination of dance music rhythms with synthesizer riffing in the manner of Tangerine Dream, together with the extensive use of sampling, served to create the novel concept of a dance music album that was intended for listening and not for dancing. Long tracks with several different levels of interest gave the music something in common with the progressive rock of the seventies, and it should have been no surprise that Paterson's collaborators included Steve Hillage and Miquette Giraudy, former members of the progressive group Gong. The album opened the way for techno players like Brian Dougans to make albums reaching the same audience. *Accelerator* by the Future Sound of London also appeared in 1991 and was reissued the year after, following the modest chart success of a single, *Papua New Guinea*. Through the nineties, further music by FSOL, as well as similar works by artists such as Underworld, Leftfield, and Goldie, proved to be a particularly valuable development.

Bjork, leaving the post-punk environment of the Sugarcubes to seek success as a solo artist, issued her first album, *Debut,* in 1993. She had conceived the idea of passing the singer-songwriter approach through the filter of dance music and the skill with which she managed to achieve this was emphasised by the number of different producers who felt inspired to create remixes of her original songs. *Debut* was produced by Nellee Hooper, who had previously produced the albums by Massive Attack and the dance music group Soul II Soul. From the end of 1997 to the beginning of 1999, Bjork, having acquired the status of the premier pop musician of the decade, toured with a band comprising nothing other than eight classical string players and a man (Mark Bell) with a beatbox – a collection of drum machines and sequencers.

TRACKING THE TRACKS

A number of Hank Ballard compilations include *The Twist,* such as *Hank Ballard and the Midnighters – All 20 Of Their Chart Hits (1953-1962)* (King 1995). *The Best Of Chubby Checker* (100% Oldies 2012) includes *The Class, The Twist,* and *Let's Twist Again.* Some compilations by Checker have later versions of the tracks, but these are the originals.

Billy Fury's *The Twist Kid* is included in the bargain priced *Absolutely Essential 3 CD Collection* (Big 3 2016). Sam Cooke's *Twistin' The Night*

The connection between the ambient dance music of the Orb and progressive rock was emphasised by the appearance in 1993 to 1994 of several unofficial remix albums of music by Pink Floyd. It seems likely that Alex Paterson was involved in at least some of these, but neither he nor anyone else was saying.

Acts like Underworld and Leftfield undertook concert tours, at which audiences stood still and listened. The Future Sound Of London carried out its 1994 tour via the internet, uploading its live playing in the studio for audiences to hear on their computers or on the radio. It is likely that few of these listeners danced either.

The embosssed cover of ISDN by Future Sound of London, compiling performances from the group's internet tour

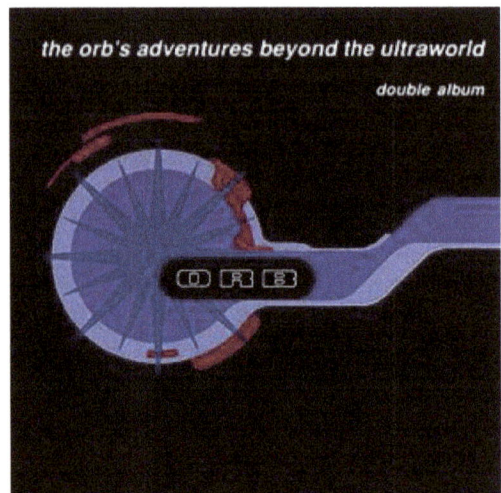

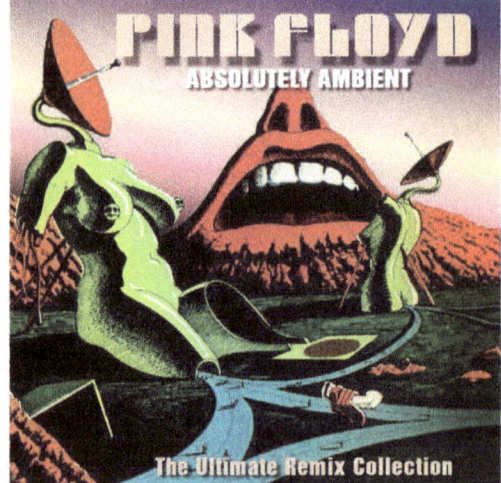

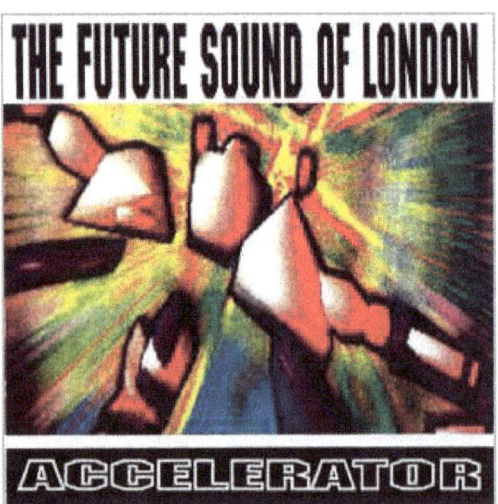

Strictly speaking, *Debut* was Bjork's second solo album. In 1977, when she was just twelve, Bjork recorded an album with the help of her step-father, Saevar Arnason. Mostly comprising cover versions of well-known songs translated into Icelandic, the self-titled LP also included a recorder instrumental composed by Bjork. In 1991, while still a member of the Sugarcubes, she sang on two tracks on the third album by 808 State, *ex:el*, which triggered her interest in dance music.

MUSIC GENRES

Away is included on a number of different compilations, such as *Portrait Of A legend 1951-1964* (Abkco 2003). The Beatles' *Twist And Shout* is on the group's first album, *Please Please Me* (EMI 2015).

The Madison Time is included on a Ray Bryant CD with the same title (Collectables 2003). *The Madison* by Al Brown's Tunetoppers is included on a sixty-three track download compilation, *Let's Soul Dance – Black Dance Crazes from the late 50s & 60s* (History Of Soul 2015) which provides good examples of songs celebrating the Hully Gully, the Mashed Potato, the Watusi, and other dances. Hank Ballard's *The Twist* is also included. *Must Be Madison* is on the three CD set, *Joe Loss & His Orchestra – The Very Best Of 1936-1970* (EMI 2007). *Jazz Samba* by Stan Getz and Charlie Byrd and *Jazz Samba Encore* by Stan Getz and Luiz Bonfa are included together on a single CD (Verve 2012). *Getz/Gilberto* by Stan Getz and Joao Gilberto is on Verve (2005).

Hippy Hippy Shake and the other *Shake* EP tracks by the Swinging Blue Jeans are included on *25 Greatest Hits* (EMI 1998). The Sam Cooke CD mentioned earlier also includes the track *Shake*. Rod Stewart's version of the song is on a bargain priced 4 CD set called *Storyteller* (Warner 2011). This also includes *Do Ya Think I'm Sexy*. The Small Faces version of *Shake* is on the *40th Anniversary Edition* of their first album (Universal/Decca 2006)

Dancing In The Street by Martha Reeves and the Vandellas is on *The Definitive Collection* (Universal 2014). *Dance To The Music* by Sly and the Family Stone is on *Dynamite! The Collection* (Epic 2011). *Land Of A Thousand Dances* by Wilson Pickett is on *The Very Best Of Wilson Pickett* (Rhino 2013). *Save The Last Dance For Me* by the Drifters is on *Up On The Roof – The Very Best Of The Drifters* (Sony 2011).

Reach Out I'll Be There by the Four Tops is on *The Ultimate Collection* (Universal 2014). *I Heard It Through The Grapevine* by Marvin Gaye is on the double CD *The Very Best Of Marvin Gaye* (Universal 2001). The set also includes *Hitch Hike*. *The Tears Of A Clown* by Smokey Robinson and the Miracles is on *The Ultimate Collection* (Universal 2000). *Rock Your Baby* by George McCrae is on *The Very Best Of* (EMI 2001).

Love Hangover by Diana Ross is on *One Woman – The Ultimate Collection* (EMI 1993). The Fifth Dimension version of the song is on a various artists compilation, *Love Hangover* (QED 1998), *Turn The Beat Around* by Vicki Sue Robinson is on *Never Gonna Let You Go* (Gold Legion 2010). *Love In C Minor* by Cerrone is on Malligator (2008). *I Feel Love* by Donna Summer is on *I Feel Love The Collection* (Universal 2013). *Saturday Night Fever* is on Reprise (2007).

The disco version of *Here Comes The Night* by the Beach Boys is on *L.A. (Light Album)* (CBS 1989). *Heart Of Glass* by Blondie is on *Greatest Hits* (EMI 2002). *No More Tears* by Barbra Streisand and Donna Summer is on the Donna Summer compilation mentioned above. *I Will Survive* is on *The Very Best Of Gloria Gaynor* (PolyGram 1993). *I Haven't Stopped Dancing Yet* by Gonzalez is included on *Haven't Stopped* (Thunderclap 2007). *I Love America* by Patrick Juvet is on *Best Of Disco* (Universal 2002). *I'm Every Woman* is on the double CD *The Essential Chaka Khan* (Music Club Deluxe 2011). *Shame* by Evelyn Champagne King is on the double CD *Action* (bbr 2014). *You Make Me Feel Mighty Real* by Sylvester is on *The Original Hits* (Universal 2009). The Chaka Khan, Evelyn King, Gloria Gaynor, and Sylvester tracks are also included on the three CD set *Now That's What I Call Disco* (Universal/Sony 2013).

Eleven different mixes of *On And On* by Jesse Saunders are included on *On & On The Remixes – 20th Anniversary of House Music* (Broken Records 2003). The original track is also included on the double CD *History Of House* (Channel 4 2001) along with *Love Can't Turn Around* by Farley Jackmaster Funk. *Pump Up The Volume* by M/A/R/R/S is on the double CD compilation *Pump Up The Volume – Classic Club Sounds From The Late 80s And Early 90s* (Universal 2001). *Love Can't Turn Around* is included here too.

Classics by Model 500 (R&S 2011) includes *No UFOs*. *Newbuild* by 808 State is on Rephlex (1999). The CD is quite scarce and expensive now but can be heard on YouTube. *Stakker Humanoid* is included on the various artists compilation *Acid In The House* (ZYX 1988).

Rated X by Miles Davis is on the double CD *Get Up With It* (Columbia 2009). *Panthalassa – The Music of Miles Davis 1969-1974* is on Columbia/Sony 1998. *Panthalassa: The Remixes* is on Columbia/Sony 1999. The recommended album by DJ Cam is *Substances* (Columbia 1996). *We Have Arrived* by Mescalinum United is on the album download *The Best Of Marc Acardipane 1989-1998 Vol. 2* (ACA2017 Productions 2006). *Bonkers* (the first of the series) is on Resist Records (2004). The recommended album is Volume 3 (Resist 2004).

Blue Lines by Massive Attack is on Virgin (2015). *Protection* is on Wild Bunch (2000). *Dummy* by Portishead is on Go! Beat (2012). *The Orb's Adventures Beyond The Ultraworld* is on Universal/Island (2006). *Accelerator* by Future Sound Of London is on Jumpin' & Pumpin' (2016). *ISDN* is on Virgin (1995). Underworld's *Dubnobasswithmyheadman* is on Universal (2014). *Born Slippy.NUXX* is on *Trainspotting (Music From The Motion Picture)* (EMI 2003). Leftfield's *Leftism* is on Sony (2007). Goldie's *Timeless* is on FFRR (1999). The album *Doot-Doot* by Freur is on Columbia (2000). *Absolutely Ambient* by Pink Floyd provides a good compilation of the best remixes. It is on New Directions (1994). The CD is hard to find, but some tracks can be heard on YouTube.

Bjork's *Debut* is on Polydor (2008). The self-titled album from 1977 has no official release beyond the original in Iceland, but it can be heard on YouTube. 808 State's *ex:el* is on Salvo (2010). One of Bjork's 1998 performances can be seen on a DVD, *Live in Cambridge* (One Little Indian 2001).

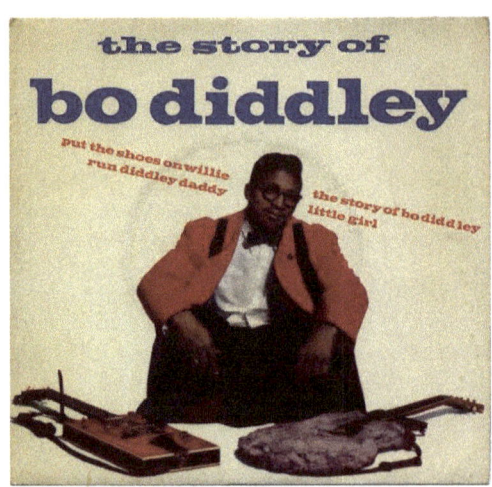

A street recording made by Folkways and issued in 1959 as an album, *Street And Gangland Rhythms – Beats And Improvisations By Six Boys In Trouble,* has been acclaimed in some quarters as a predecessor of rap. Reviewing the album for *All Music*, avant garde guitarist Eugene Chadbourne is inclined to dismiss the whole affair as a put-up job. Certainly, to attempt to assign any kind of artistic or historical significance to the motley assembly of children's chatter and play acting, with someone banging away at a set of bongos in the background, is to considerably overstate the case.

25 RAP

"I said a hip, hop, the hippy, the hippy to the hip, hip hopper you don't stop, the rocker to the bang bang boogie, say up jump the boogie, to the rhythm of the boogiedy beat." (*Rappers Delight*)

With these words, chosen more for their percussive effect than for their poetry, the Sugarhill Gang introduced a new style of music, rap, to the charts in late 1979. The words are not sung, but neither are they spoken naturally – they are delivered rhythmically, to the beat set by the underlying bass riff and handclaps. These are lifted directly from the Chic song, *Good Times*, a hit from a few months earlier. A novelty effect then, rapping has become an essential ingredient within modern R&B, a sound and a style causing no more surprise than a funky drum beat.

The concept of having vocal lines presented in a piece of music, with no clear pitch, derives from much earlier than 1979. Arnold Schoenberg's *Pierrot Lunaire*, composed in 1912, used a style of singing called 'Sprechstimme' (speaking voice), where the pitch is not specific and there is no obvious melody, even though the timbre is that of a soprano rather than simply a female speaker. This is the most well-known piece to feature Sprechstimme, although the technique was invented a few years earlier still, by Engelbert Humperdinck (the composer, not the singer) in his 1897 opera *Königskinder*. On mid-sixties performances like *One Of Us Must Know* and *Rainy Day Women Numbers 12 and 35*, Bob Dylan used this same Sprechstimme style, although he may not have realised that this was what he was doing.

In the blues, there are several performances where the vocals are in the form of a recitation. John Lee Hooker, in particular, made quite a few recordings of this type over the years. *I'm Mad Again, Boogie Chillen*, and *Talkin' The Blues* all have Hooker talking his way through the chord changes, in time with the rhythm. Even when he sings, more often than not it is still close to speech, with any actual melody being extremely hard to distinguish – Sprechstimme, in fact. *Leave My Wife Alone, Boom Boom, One Bourbon One Scotch One Beer, Walkin' The Boogie*, and many more are like this. He is, of course, following a distinct blues tradition. Robert Johnson's *Terraplane Blues, Cross Road Blues, 32-20 Blues*, and many of the other songs he recorded in 1936 to 1937 have little actual melody, being carried along by the rhythm and the blues chords, even if rock groups covering his material thirty years later somehow managed to find a tune. Before Johnson, the work of blues pioneer Blind Lemon Jefferson, playing ten years earlier, is the same. As the blues moves into rock 'n' roll in the fifties, still these half spoken lines can be heard, whether in the form of a novelty hook (as in Eddie Cochran's *Summertime Blues* or the Coasters' *Charlie Brown*) or a complete song (Bo Diddley's *The Story Of Bo Diddley* or *Say Man*).

John Lee Hooker's title apart, the talking blues is a form found within American folk music, which may or may not conform to the twelve bar structure of the blues generally. It was popularised by Woody Guthrie during the forties, but the inventor of the style was Chris Bouchillon, who recorded his *Talking Blues* in 1926. Bouchillon was a contemporary of Blind Lemon Jefferson. Lonnie Donegan recorded *Talking Guitar Blues* in 1959, while *Rock Island Line*, which launched his solo career three years earlier, also includes spoken material. During the early sixties, Bob Dylan recorded several talking blues tracks. Woody Guthrie's son, Arlo, extended the form dramatically, with long monologues related over a musical background. The most successful of these, *Alice's Restaurant Massacree* from 1967, included enough material to enable the song to be made into a film, *Alice's Restaurant*.

This kind of musical narrative is also found in country music. *The Deck Of Cards*, first recorded in 1948 by T. Texas Tyler, but frequently covered by others, or *A Boy Named Sue*, recorded by Johnny Cash in 1969, are well-known examples. One spoken verse by Elvis Presley in his 1960 recording of *Are You Lonesome Tonight* is another. The Shangri-Las, who had nothing to do with either folk or country, used spoken material in many of the hit teenage melodramas that producer Shadow Morton constructed for them (most notably in *Past Present and Future*, which is

THE FIRST TIME

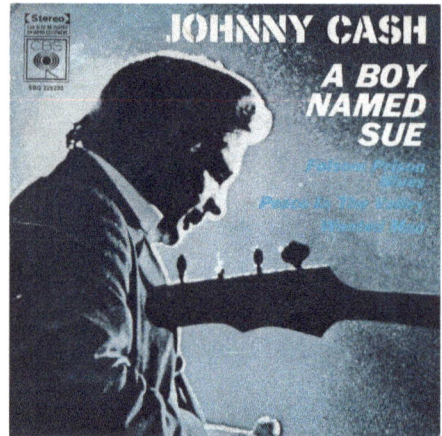

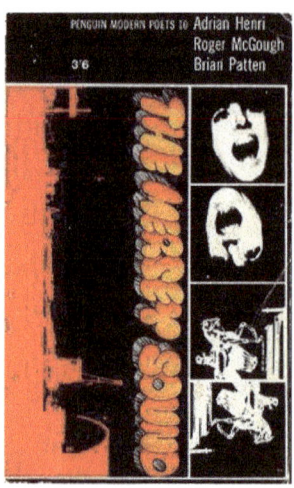

The Liverpool Scene piece, *The Entry of Christ into Liverpool,* is inspired by a painting, *The Entry of Christ into Brussels*, by the proto-Expressionist artist James Ensor. Expressionism was an avant-garde art movement from the beginning of the twentieth century that placed a premium on subjective emotional experience. The repeated cry of "masks!" in the Liverpool Scene track relates to the depiction of the crowd in Ensor's painting. In effect, the group is managing to combine three separate creative arts – painting, music, and poetry – into a single work.

A British equivalent of the Langston Hughes recordings, made in the sixties

To emphasise their wish to be viewed as just a part of the wider Liverpool scene, the band members had their images placed on what was the back of the gatefold album cover for the 1968 LP Amazing Adventures of The Liverpool Scene (with John Peel credited as producer). Guitarist Andy Roberts and bass player Percy Jones, neither of whom was originally from Liverpool, are missing. There is a possible resonance between this cover and that of the Beatles Sgt Pepper album.

entirely spoken).

A set of poems by Edith Sitwell was set to music by William Walton and the resulting work, *Façade*, was first performed in 1922. Unlike other classical works, which use poetry as a libretto to be sung, Façade is designed for the poems to be spoken, but the music is made sufficiently rhythmic to bring out the patterns in the words. Sitwell crams her lines with imagery and rhyme, with the result that *Façade* has much of the character of rap, albeit rap that is transplanted from downtown New York to the genteel gardens of Bayswater.

Ken Nordine attempted a spoken word approach to jazz in the fifties, beginning with an album called *Word Jazz*. Nordine's fluid delivery has much in common with the sound of a jazz soloist, although the accompanying music has more of the quality of flavouring than an essential part of the performance. Black American poet Langston Hughes, whose first collection, from 1926, was titled *The Weary Blues*, was considerably influenced by the rhythms of black music. In 1958, he made a record in which he recited these poems while a jazz group played behind. He managed to achieve a little more integration of the forms than did Ken Nordine.

A yet tighter bonding between poetry and music was achieved when the music started to be rock. The groundwork was done by the publication in 1967 of two poetry anthologies, featuring the work of Liverpool poets Roger McGough, Adrian Henri, and Brian Patten. *The Mersey Sound*, published by Penguin Books as number ten in its series of *Penguin Modern Poets*, achieved a rapid success that must have surprised all concerned, eventually selling around half a million copies. *The Liverpool Scene*, edited by Edward Lucie-Smith, sold much less well, but provided a title and a cover design for an LP, *The Incredible New Liverpool Scene*, in which Henri and McGough were accompanied by the acoustic guitar playing of Andy Roberts. It was Henri who made the most effort to work closely with the guitar playing, with the result that some of his performances have the character of songs, in which the lines just happen to be spoken. Aware of a certain lineage in this respect, Henri presented one of the tracks as a talking blues – *Adrian Henri's Talking After Christmas Blues*.

Soon afterwards, Henri and Roberts expanded their concept and became part of a fully fledged rock group, still called the Liverpool Scene, adding a rhythm section and another poet, Mike Evans, who conveniently played the saxophone. Tracks like *Tramcar to Frankenstein, The Entry of Christ into Liverpool*, and the lengthy suite, *Made In USA*, are highlights of a thoroughly successful blending of spoken word with music. Roger McGough, meanwhile, added his talents to the Scaffold, which mixed poetry and comedy with music. The group achieved a UK number one hit during the Christmas period in 1968, with *Lily The Pink*, although this was definitely a song, with no spoken word element. Brian Patten got into the act a little later on, when he and McGough were involved in an enlarged successor to the Scaffold, called Grimms. No doubt influenced by the Liverpool poets, the Moody Blues included one or two musical poems, written and recited by drummer Graeme Edge, on each of the albums that made the group famous, those recorded between 1967 and 1971.

In the US, Allen Ginsberg allied himself with the burgeoning rock counter-culture based in California, and often performed his poetry while accompanying himself on a harmonium, although he resisted forming a rock group of his own. Ken Kesey, the author of the novel, *One Flew Over The Cuckoo's Nest*, recorded an album with the Grateful Dead in 1965, *The Acid Test*. Poetry, music, and mayhem coexist, but to no great constructive effect, since the participants were tripping on the acid (LSD) of the album's title at the time. The record sold hardly at all.

Canadian poet Leonard Cohen began setting some of his work to music in 1967. The fact that he did not have much of a singing voice forced him, for at least some of the time, to adopt what was essentially another example of the Sprechstimme approach, but it proved to be highly effective.

Cohen's exact contemporary, Leroi Jones, (who eventually changed his name to Amiri Baraka, in line with the aims and attitudes of the Black Power movement), was a generation younger than the great Langston Hughes. Jones/Baraka found in the emotional rush of free jazz a suitable partner for the outpourings of his own poetry. In 1965 and

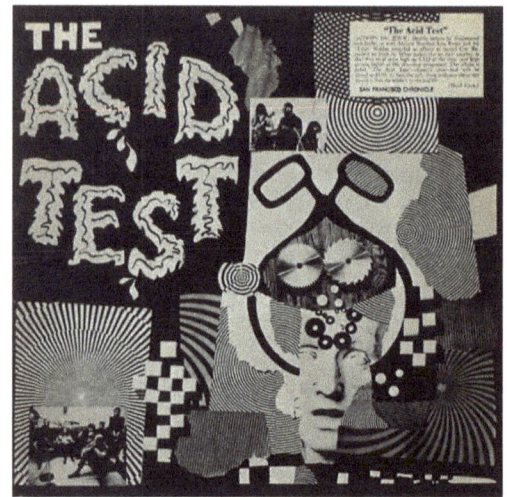

Leroi Jones is in the centre

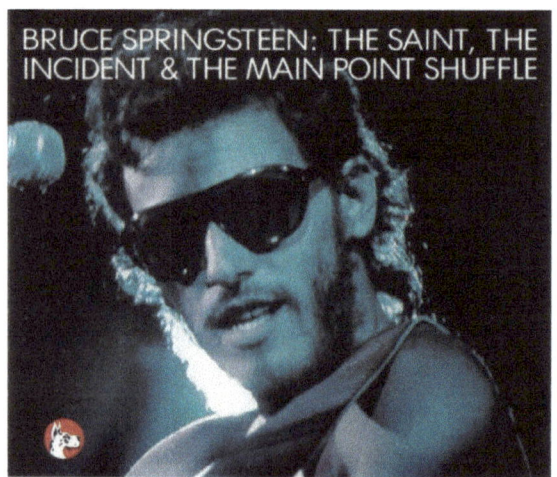

Until Columbia released a recording of Springsteen performing at London's Hammersmith Odeon in 1975, thirty years after the event, bootleg albums like this provided the only way fans could hear tracks such as The E Street Shuffle, transformed into an epic rap in the manner of Isaac Hayes.

1968, Jones performed on three albums – the self titled LP by the New York Art Quartet, *Sonny's Time Now* by Sunny Murray, and *Black & Beautiful.... Soul & Madness* by The Jihad – the last two being issued on Jones' own Jihad label. In between he wrote the words for *A Black Mass*, a theatrical work recorded by Sun Ra, but did not perform on it.

Meanwhile, Muhammad Ali, then known as Cassius Clay and just about to become the world heavyweight boxing champion, released a single in early 1964. On the B-side of a decent cover of Ben E King's *Stand By Me*, Clay delivered the kind of rhyming he was already known for in his interviews, but this time there was a backing track. In effect, *I Am The Greatest* was the first rap record, before there was such a thing.

Gospel music, or rather the sound and style of black preachers during Baptist church services, is another important antecedent for rap. Recordings of the Reverend C.L.Franklin (Aretha's father) in the fifties, or the Reverend J.D.Montgomery in the early seventies, amongst many others, reveal sermons that start slowly and then gradually speed up as the preacher warms to his theme. Eventually, the preacher is delivering short lines in what is very nearly a singing voice (more Sprechstimme), with the response of members of the congregation at the end of each line adding to the rhythmic effect.

In 1969, Isaac Hayes released an album called *Hot Buttered Soul*. There were only four tracks, because Hayes liked to let his music slowly unfold. The longest, at nearly nineteen minutes, was a version of the Jimmy Webb song, *By The Time I Get To Phoenix*. Hayes spent a long time – eight minutes or so – setting the scene for the song proper, with a recitation made to float over the music rather than structured by the rhythm. A few years later, in 1974, Millie Jackson released an album called *Caught Up*. The first track, *If Loving You Is Wrong (I Don't Want To Be Right)* was split in two by a spoken interlude that, in a similar manner to the Isaac Hayes introduction, elaborated the theme of the first part of the song, while setting the mood, raising the temperature, for the song's finale. On this record, the sleeve credits give the middle spoken section a title of its own – *The Rap*. In the years before the Sugarhill Gang, this was what was meant by rapping. When Bruce Springsteen started to add similar spoken passages over the introductory music of some of his songs when performing them in concert, he was said to be rapping. In between Hayes and Jackson, in 1971, Bobby Womack recorded something similar, except that his rapping was performed like a gospel preacher in church. This was on the introduction to *More Than I Can Stand*, given its own title, *The Preacher*.

During the late sixties in Jamaica, single records started being made with instrumental B-sides, known as versions, and DJs at dance halls started to improvise their own rants and recitations over the top. Eventually, the style, known as toasting, made it on to record itself. King Stitt and U Roy (Ewart Beckford) were the first to have records issued in their names. U Roy's *Wake The Town*, recorded by producer Duke Reid in 1970, became a big Jamaican hit. When Virgin records in the UK began issuing reggae albums in the mid-seventies, it was U Roy who was the first to be chosen, with his album *Dread In A Babylon*. There is some similarity between the styles of toasting and rapping, although it is not clear to what extent the first New York rappers were aware of what had been going on in Jamaica. Certainly few reggae records were released in the USA in the seventies. U Roy's *Dread In A Babylon* and *Natty Rebel* would appear to be the only DJ albums. Nothing by the other major toasters of the time – I Roy, Big Youth, Dennis Alcapone – was issued until much later.

Pioneering DJ, Kool Herc, was from Jamaica, but had left the country while still a child. He was far more concerned with tracking down and playing records by James Brown than with referencing the roots he had left behind. The major influence on the Sugarhill Gang and the other early rappers, as with so much funk and soul music, was James Brown. Simultaneously with inventing the rhythmic structure of funk, Brown made his vocals sound closer and closer to speech. Where his early records, like *Please Please Please* and *Prisoner Of Love* were swept along by singing that was almost ecstatic, now he moved from the front of the choir to the preacher's pulpit. With *Say It Loud, I'm Black And I'm Proud* in 1968, Brown delivered lines that were recitation, shaped by the rhythm of the music. In essence, over a decade before *Rapper's Delight*, this too was rap.

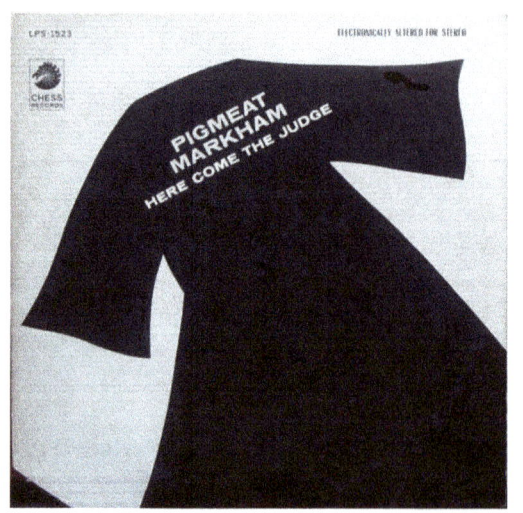
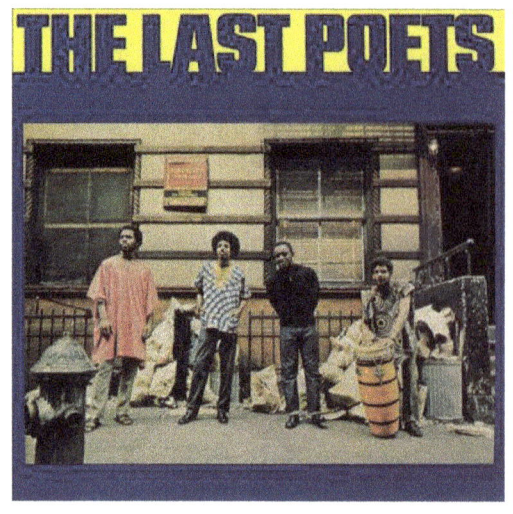

MUSIC GENRES

Comedian Pigmeat Markham enjoyed a hit record in 1968 as well. After forty years in the business, Markham gained his big break, appearing on the popular US television show, *Rowan and Martin's Laugh-In*. His comedy sketch of an irreverent judge presiding over a chaotic courtroom provided the theme for his single, *Here Come The Judge*. Markham rants his way through the song without once singing an actual note, accompanied by a driving soul rhythm track. Like James Brown's *Say It Loud, I'm Black And I'm Proud*, this too is rap. Shorty Long copied Pigmeat Markham's idea for another hit song called *Here Come The Judge* in 1968. This is a different song and Long sings his words, he does not rap.

The album made by Pigmeat Markham, featuring his hit, comprises comedy routines apart from the one song. One of these, *I Got The Number*, performed as a double act with an anonymous stooge, is effectively another rap, delivered in rhythm and rhyme even though there is no music. The following year, Markham and his comedy partner re-recorded the track with a musical background, as *We Got The Number*, although, curiously, the result is rather less effective than the original version.

The first, self-titled album by the Last Poets was released in 1970. The three poets concerned delivered their free-form verse, somewhat in the manner of Leroi Jones, over African-inspired drumming. Most of the poems have black power themes, but they do not use rhyme and in that respect they are very unlike rap. Big Youth and Prince Buster recorded a very loose cover of *When The Revolution Comes* in 1972, but somehow managed to strip out all of the anger. The album, with its anger in place, was a surprise chart hit and several other albums followed, in which only Jalaluddin Masur Nuriddin (or Alafia Pudim, as he sometimes called himself) remained through various changes in personnel. In 1973, Nuriddin made a solo album, *Hustlers Convention*, under the name Lightnin' Rod. The music was much fuller on this, with some tracks being played by Kool and the Gang, and the poetry – used to tell the story of two hustlers, named Sport and Spoon – was much more structured, with short lines that all rhymed. At some point during the sessions for the album, Lightnin' Rod recorded one more piece, *Doriella Du Fontaine*, using as backing an unissued rhythm track played four years earlier by Jimi Hendrix and Buddy Miles. It is attractive to imagine that Hendrix chose to play with a member of the militant Last Poets, but that is not what happened.

The Last Poets were misnamed, because alongside them came Gil Scott-Heron. His first album, the live *Small Talk at 125th and Lennox*, was released in 1970 and sounds very like the work of the Last Poets. Apart from three songs where he is accompanied by a piano, Scott-Heron narrates street poetry with just percussion in support. *Pieces Of A Man* from 1971 introduced the buoyant jazz-funk that Scott-Heron employed for the rest of his career and for the most part he delivered his messages by singing them, although the most powerful track on this album, *The Revolution Will Not Be Televised*, is narrated over a funky drum and bass rhythm in a manner that would be rap, if only the poem used rhyme. Gil Scott-Heron's most powerful recording of all came ten years later, with his anti-Ronald Reagan diatribe, *B Movie*. It is a rap in the Isaac Hayes sense, but its impact, added to the mass of material preceding it, is enough to mark Scott-Heron as an important influence on rap in the Sugarhill Gang sense.

There are conflicting opinions as to who should get the credit for first developing rap in the New York clubs where Kool Herc, Grandmaster Flash, and others were learning how to manipulate records on twin turntables. Afrika Bambaata, who was central to the nascent hip hop scene, has made it clear that, as far as he is concerned, Melle Mel and the Furious Five, the MCs working with Grandmaster Flash, are the ones. (He is quoted in Alex Ogg's history of rap, *The Hip Hop Years*.)

The members of the Sugarhill Gang were very lucky to have been in the right place at the right time, because none of them was performing in the New York clubs. Hank Jackson was working with the DJ Grandmaster Caz, helping to get gigs for him, but earning money in a job in a pizza shop. That was where he was, rapping on his own to fill the time, when Sylvia Robinson, the boss of Sugarhill Records came in. She was looking for someone to make a record and asked Jackson if he was interested. Two of his friends picked this moment to turn up and Ms Robinson held a spontaneous audition. As casually as that, the Sugarhill Gang was formed and was signed.

While DJs like Grandmaster Flash employed separate MCs to do the rapping, Grandmaster Caz carried out both roles himself

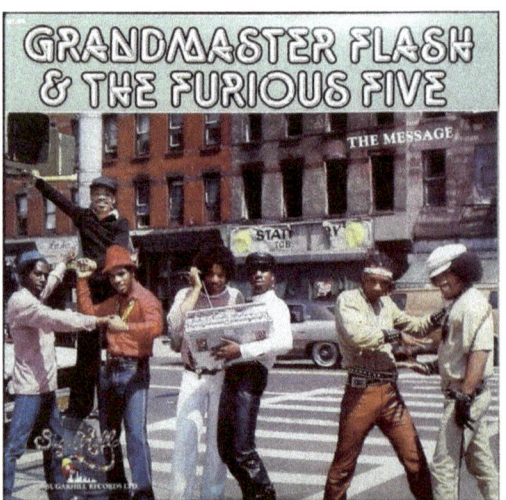

Run DMC broke new ground by collaborating with Aerosmith in 1986, creating a thrilling rap-rock hybrid and inspiring the careers of rap metal bands like Anthrax and Rage Against The Machine.

Public Enemy's second album, issued in 1988, and arguably the greatest/most influential rap album of all.

MUSIC GENRES

Rapper's Delight included part of the routine being used by Grandmaster Caz, who was not best pleased. He complained about the record: "It lowered the standard drastically of what an MC was, and what you had to be to make a rap record. If you never saw nobody play basketball in your life and some knucklehead just played it in front of you – he played terrible but that's what you saw – that's the way you'd think you have to play basketball." (This is from Alex Ogg's book.) He may be right, but the fact remains that the Sugarhill Gang were the first rappers to reach the charts. The group was not quite the first to record a rap record. Opinions are divided as to what that first record was – *Rhymin' and Rappin'* by Paulette and Tanya Winley or *King Tim III (Personality Jock)* by Fatback – but neither candidate was particularly successful. The Fatback recording was originally a B-side, but the single was flipped and re-entered the Billboard R&B charts in October 1979, the week before the Sugarhill Gang's record joined it. Fatback stalled at number twenty-six and made no impact on the Hot Hundred.

Blondie moved rap into the mainstream in early 1981, when the group's single, *Rapture*, climbed to the top of the US charts and was a big hit too in the UK. Debbie Harry performed a rap in the middle of the song, during which she name-checked DJ Grandmaster Flash and rapper Fab Five Freddy. Grandmaster Flash responded by incorporating part of Rapture in his ground-breaking single, *The Adventures Of Grandmaster Flash On The Wheels Of Steel*. The following year, the Furious Five, the rap group that worked with Grandmaster Flash, issued *The Message*, the first rap record to move away from partying in favour of delivering a social commentary. The group so highly rated by Afrika Bambaata had finally got its due and, through it, rap had made its first classic record.

TRACKING THE TRACKS

The double CD *Sugarhill Gang Vs Grandmaster Flash – The Greatest Hits* (Sequel 2000) includes *Rappers Delight* and *The Message*, as well as a second Furious Five classic, *White Lines*.

There are a number of recordings of Arnold Schoenberg's *Pierrot Lunaire* available, such as the one on Naxos (2007), which also includes three other works. There are several recordings of Engelbert Humperdinck's *Konigskinder* too, such as one performed by the Cologne Radio Symphony Orchestra (Gala 2013).

Bob Dylan's *One Of Us Must Know* and *Rainy Day Women #12 and 35* are on *Blonde On Blonde* (Sony 2003).

Unfortunately, there is no one John Lee Hooker compilation that contains all the tracks mentioned. *The Definitive Collection* (Metro 2000) has *I'm Mad Again, Boogie Chillen,* and *Boom Boom. House Of The Blues* (Hallmark 2015) has *Walkin' The Boogie* and *Leave My Wife Alone. Chill Out* (Shout Factory 2007), one of the albums made by Hooker during the period of his greatest success, in his seventies, has *Talkin' The Blues* and *One Bourbon One Scotch One Beer*. The double Robert Johnson CD, *The Complete Recordings* (Sony 2008) means what it says. There are several compilations by Blind Lemon Jefferson, such as *Black Snake Moan* (Snapper 2004).

The double CD *The Best Of Eddie Cochran* (EMI 2005) includes *Summertime Blues*. The double CD *The Very Best Of The Coasters* (Not Now 2014) includes *Charlie Brown*. The double CD *The Story Of Bo Diddley* (Chess/Universal 2006) includes the title track and *Say Man*.

Woody Guthrie's *Dustbowl Ballads* is on Sony (1998). Chris Bouchillon *The Original Talking Blues Man* is on JSP Records (2005). Lonnie Donegan's *Talking Guitar Blues* and *Rock Island Line* are on *The Collection* (Castle 1992). *The Best Of Arlo Guthrie* (Warner 1993) includes *Alice's Restaurant Massacree*. The *Alice's Restaurant* film is available on DVD (20th Century Fox 2003).

T Texas Tyler's *Deck Of Cards* is on *Remember Me* (Gusto 2008). Johnny Cash's *A Boy Named Sue* is on *Johnny Cash At San Quentin* (Sony 2000). *Are You Lonesome Tonight* is on *Elvis 30 #1 Hits* (BMG 2002). *The Best Of The Shangri-Las* is on Spectrum (1997).

Street And Gangland Rhythms – Beats And Improvisations By Six Boys In Trouble was issued on CD in 2007 (Folkways). The brief extracts from each track that can be heard on *Amazon* will be enough for all but the most ardent of collectors.

There are several recordings of *Façade* by William Walton and Edith Sitwell. The ASV CD (1997) has Prunella Scales and Timothy West as the readers.

Ken Nordine's *Word Jazz* is on Hallmark (2013). Langston Hughes reading his poetry to jazz is on the CD *Harlem In Vogue* (Fingertips 2011). *The Weary Blues with Langston Hughes* is on a Polygram CD (1991).

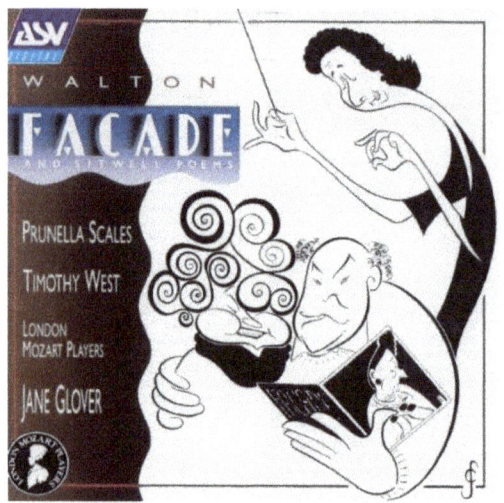
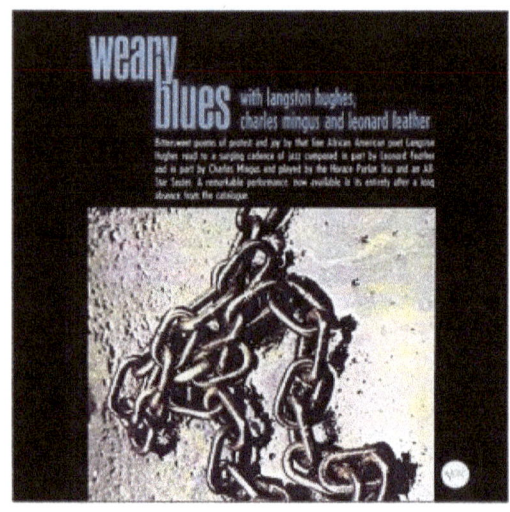
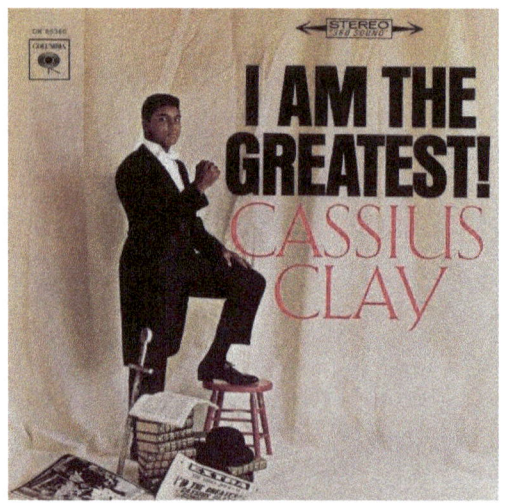
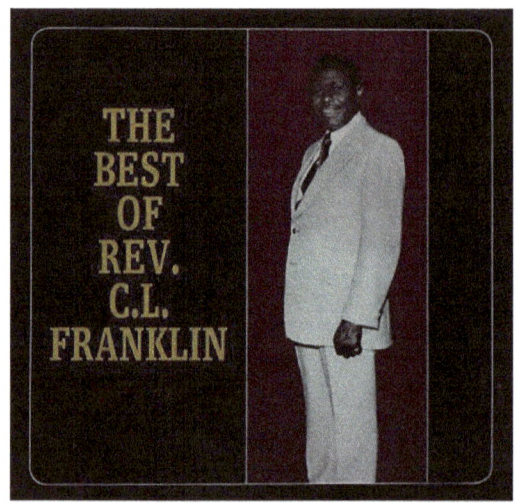

MUSIC GENRES

The books, *The Mersey Sound* by Adrian Henri, Roger McGough, and Brian Patten (Penguin 2007) and *The Liverpool Scene* by Edward Lucie-Smith (Doubleday 1987) are still in print. The Liverpool Scene is well served by a double CD compilation, *The Amazing Adventures Of The Liverpool Scene* (Esoteric 2009). This includes the tracks mentioned. The first album, *The Incredible New Liverpool Scene,* has not been reissued on CD, but it can be heard on YouTube. *Thank You Very Much – The Very Best Of Scaffold* is on EMI (2002). Grimms made three albums, *Grimms, Rockin' Duck,* and *Sleepers.* Brian Patten is not on the third of these, but this is the only one available on CD (Hux 2006). The Moody Blues albums with poems included are *Days Of Future Passed, In Search Of The Lost Chord, On The Threshold Of A Dream, To Our Children's Children's Children, A Question Of Balance,* and *Every Good Boy Deserves Favour.* All are on Universal/Decca (2008).

The Acid Test by Ken Kesey and members of the Grateful Dead in on Acadia (2005) or King Mob (1998), with the earlier issue having over forty minutes of extra material recorded by Ken Kesey a year later.

Leonard Cohen's first album is *The Songs Of Leonard Cohen* (Sony 2007).

The self-titled album by the New York Art Quartet is on ESP-Disk (2008). *Sonny's Time Now* by Sunny Murray is on DIW (1991) – it is a Japanese release and quite expensive. *Black & Beautiful…. Soul & Madness* by the Jihad is on Son Boy (2009). *A Black Mass* by Sun Ra and Leroi Jones is on Son Boy (1999).

I Am The Greatest was originally issued as the title track of a 1963 LP, which comprised spoken word pieces, performed by Cassius Clay in the manner of a comedy routine in front of an invited audience. Here, the track does not have the musical backing. It was reissued on a Columbia CD in 1999. The single version does not appear to be available on CD, but it can be heard on YouTube.

There are several CDs available by Rev C.L.Franklin and there is even a two CD *Best Of* (Fuel 2000), which has three sermons and a few gospel songs. *God's Newspaper*, a recording of a complete service by Rev. J.D.Montgomery, was issued on LP in 1972 by Gospel Truth Records, but has not been reissued on CD.

Hot Buttered Soul by Isaac Hayes is on Universal/Stax (2009). *Caught Up* by Millie Jackson is on Ace (2006). The live version of *The E Street Shuffle* by Bruce Springsteen is included as part of an incendiary set on the double CD *Hammersmith Odeon London '75* (Sony 2006). Bobby Womack's *The Preacher* is on *The Best Of Bobby Womack – The Soul Years* (EMI 2008).

Original DJ (Virgin 1995) is a good compilation by U Roy, but does not include *Wake The Town.* This track is included on the various artists double CD *The Trojan Story* (Metro 2003) alongside much other essential music.

Say It Loud, I'm Black And I'm Proud by James Brown is on Polydor (1996).

Pigmeat Markham's *Here Come The Judge* LP was originally issued on Chess in 1968. It was given a vinyl reissue in 1984. Chess issued the album on CD in 1998, although it is hard to find. *We Got The Number* can be heard on YouTube, uploaded from the original single.

The first two albums by the Last Poets, *The Last Poets* and *This Is Madness*, are available as a double CD on Charly (2012). Two tracks from Lightnin' Rod's *Hustlers Convention* and the track with Jimi Hendrix, *Doriella du Fontaine*, are included as bonus tracks. The Lightnin' Rod album is available in its entirety on Celluloid (1993). The Prince Buster/Big Youth album, *Chi Chi Run*, that includes the track *When The Revolution Comes*, was reissued on vinyl in Jamaica in 2007, but has not appeared on CD. The track can be heard on YouTube, however.

Gil Scott-Heron's albums *Small Talk at 125th and Lennox* and *Pieces Of A Man* are both available on BGP CDs (2015 and 2014). *B Movie* is included on *Reflections* (Sony 2006).

King Tim III is included on the album *Fatback XII* (Ace Records 2013). *Rhymin' And Rappin'* by Paulett and Tanya Winley can be heard on YouTube.

Blondie's *Rapture* is included on *Greatest Hits* (EMI 2002).

Run DMC's collaboration with Aerosmith, *Walk This Way*, is included on *The Best Of Run DMC* (Sony 2007).

Public Enemy's *It Takes A Nation Of Millions To Hold Us Back* is on Def Jam (2000).

Erik Satie

Camille Saint-Saens

The classical music composer responsible for the largest number of film soundtracks was Dmitri Shostakovich. He scored thirty-four films, beginning with *The New Babylon* in 1929.

The first film to have its soundtrack issued on an album (three 78 rpm records) was Walt Disney's *Snow White And The Seven Dwarfs* in 1937. A similar release for *Pinnochio*, two years later, used the phrase 'original soundtrack' for the first time.

The first film to be promoted by its theme song becoming a conveniently timed hit was *High Noon* in 1952. Tex Ritter took the song *High Noon* to number twelve in the US charts, although a cover version by Frankie Laine beat it, reaching number five, and was a UK hit too.

26 AMBIENT AND SOUNDTRACK MUSIC

The idea of performing music intended to be the background to something else, rather than the focus of attention, was first conceived by the composer Erik Satie. In 1917 he described some of his pieces as 'musique d'ameublement' (furniture music), intending that they should be played in the interval of a play or concert, but not closely listened to by the audience. In 1920, two short pieces with the overall title of *Sons Industriels* were played as intermission music to a play by Max Jacob. The audience was supposed to view an exhibition of children's drawings while this was going on, but many of them chose to stay seated in order to listen to the music. An agitated Erik Satie rushed on to the stage, calling for the audience to keep talking.

The birth of the film industry in 1894 created a requirement for music to be composed and played to accompany the otherwise silent films – if only to mask the sounds of the film projectors. Camille Saint-Saens, perhaps best known for his musical portraits from 1886, *The Carnival Of The Animals,* was the first composer commissioned to create music specifically for a film, *The Assassination Of The Duke Of Guise,* directed by Charles Le Bargy and André Calmettes and released in France in November 1908. Two months earlier, a production called *The Fairylogue And Radio-Plays*, based on the Oz stories of L. Frank Baum, also used a specially composed soundtrack, by Nathaniel D. Mann. Its combination of live acting, photographic stills, and film fragments, however, does not conform with most people's idea of what constitutes a film. Mann had previously written a few songs with Baum, for inclusion in a 1902 operetta, *The Wizard Of Oz* (unrelated to the later, better-known film starring Judy Garland).

The first properly synchronised film score, in which the composer watched closely and wrote music to fit the action, was for the film *Entr'acte*, directed by René Clair. Erik Satie composed this in 1924 – the film was shown during the intermission in Satie's ballet, *Relâche*. These were Satie's last works. In 1926, the film *Don Juan,* directed by Alan Crosland, was released. Although there was no dialogue, the film came complete with a recorded soundtrack, the first film to do this. The music was composed by William Axt and David Mendoza. A series of short musical films to accompany *Don Juan* were shown first, beginning with a performance of Richard Wagner's *Overture to Tannhäuser* by the New York Philharmonic.

In 1927, the first film complete with sound was released. *The Jazz Singer,* also directed by Alan Crosland, was a musical, with songs performed by Al Jolson and other soundtrack music written by Louis Silvers. Silvers became head of the Columbia Studio music department and in that capacity he received the first Oscar awarded for a film score, in 1934. The film was *One Night Of Love,* directed by Victor Schertzinger, and the music was actually composed by the director with lyricist Gus Kahn, alongside a number of classical composers, including Donizetti, Verdi, Bizet, and Puccini.

Carl Stalling created an original composing style for his cartoon film soundtracks, beginning with Walt Disney's *The Skeleton Dance* in 1929. To match the rapidly changing action on the screen, he crammed together tiny musical extracts into a sound collage, in which the rhythm and the melody changed with a rapidity that would have been bewildering if listened to separately from the film. He was responsible for several more cartoon soundtracks through to 1958, including the Bugs Bunny and Daffy Duck films, and employed his cut-up technique with all of them. Much later, on a number of records made in 1984 and afterwards, the saxophonist John Zorn was inspired to apply the same methods to jazz, when the resulting music still sounded startlingly innovative. In 1990, Zorn was responsible for the release of a CD compilation of Stalling's music, in an attempt to give the composer increased recognition.

The first library music company, set up to establish a catalogue of music pieces that could be used by film makers, was De Wolfe Music, which began operations in 1909 and started to make recordings in 1927, storing the music on

THE FIRST TIME

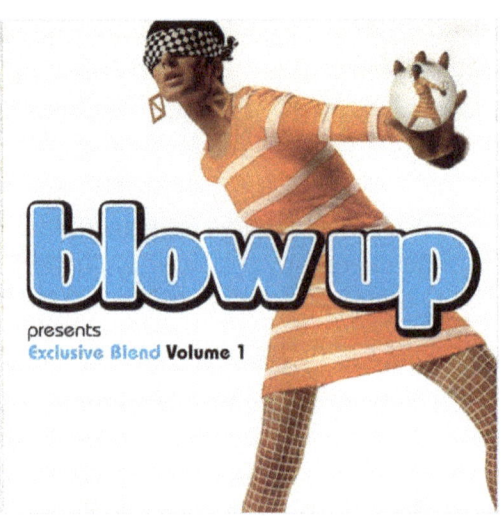

Compilations of De Wolfe and KPM tracks from the sixties and seventies, designed to appeal to sample spotters at the end of the century

Muzak advertising leaflet from 1959

In 1986, heavy rock guitarist Ted Nugent tried to buy the Muzak company, with the intention of closing it down. His offer of ten million dollars was not accepted.

Unlike what has happened with the De Wolfe and KPM catalogues, no compilation CDs of Muzak recordings have been issued.

35mm film (and reel-to-reel tape when this became available). The company provided the soundtrack music for numerous films, including the Pathé and Movietone newsreels that were shown from the thirties onwards. In 1955, De Wolfe provided the music for the first television advertisement in the UK, for Gibb's Toothpaste. In 1962, the company began distributing music on 10" records, with 12" records following soon afterwards. The Pretty Things recorded several tracks for De Wolfe under the pseudonym, the Electric Banana. In 1973, the De Wolfe composition *Eye Level,* played by the Simon Park Orchestra, reached number one in the UK charts. The music was used as the theme for the television series *Van Der Valk* and was the first TV theme to top the charts.

For many years De Wolfe operated without major competition, but in 1956, the publishing company Keith Prowse, then owned by the television company Rediffusion, began making recordings to start a library. In 1959, Keith Prowse merged with another music publisher, Peter Maurice, to form KPM. In 1966, KPM launched a series of LP recordings with *The Mood Modern,* comprising short pieces by five different composers. The majority were by Johnny Hawksworth, a British jazz bass player who had worked for the Ted Heath Orchestra for fifteen years and had also contributed music to the De Wolfe library. Although music created for a specific commercial purpose was never likely to find itself at the cutting edge of innovation, pieces by composers like Alan Hawkshaw and Keith Mansfield, mainstays of the KPM company during the late sixties and seventies, have been extensively sampled more recently. *The Champ,* made in 1968 by the Mohawks, a studio band assembled by Alan Hawkshaw, is one of the most sampled music pieces of all. The website *Whosampled.com* identifies 564 songs, as of late 2016, as having done this. The original track was published by KPM, although actually released on the Pama label. Ironically enough, *The Champ* is itself closely modelled on another piece – the Otis Redding and Carla Thomas song, *Tramp,* although it does not actually sample it.

In the years before radio became established, George Squier registered patents for the transmission of music along telephone wires. In 1934, the Wired Radio company changed focus to concentrate on delivering music to commercial premises – offices, factories, and shops. It changed its name to Muzak, making a sly reference to the successful photographic company, Kodak. Muzak recorded instrumental music, often cover versions of well-known pieces, and was successful enough that its name became synonymous with any light background music played in public. It was used alongside the term 'elevator music'. Often, the muzak description has been used pejoratively, as in the lyrics to the John Lennon song, *How Do You Sleep,* written after his falling out with Paul McCartney.

In 1940, the BBC Home Service began transmitting a programme called *Music While You Work,* which was continued on the BBC Light Programme after this was established in 1945. The light orchestral music that filled the broadcast was anticipated by the music chosen as the theme tune – *Calling All Workers,* which had been composed by Eric Coates in 1940. In contrast to the more recent idea that playing a record on the radio is a good way to advertise it and encourage sales, the Musicians Union in the UK during the forties, fifties, and sixties insisted that the BBC could play no more than five hours of records per day. The result was that live orchestral performances of the kind played on *Music While You Work* were to be widely heard elsewhere on the Light Programme every day. The orchestras made records too, by far the most successful being the one led by a conductor born in Italy, known only by his surname, Mantovani. *Charmaine* crossed the Atlantic and was his first hit in the US, reaching number ten in the Billboard chart at the end of 1951 and eventually selling over a million copies. *The Song From Moulin Rouge* reached number one in the newly established *NME* singles chart in the UK in August 1953. By the time of his last recordings in the mid-seventies, Mantovani had sold thirty-five million records.

In the US, Jackie Gleason, famous as an actor and comedian, conceived the idea of a series of 'mood music' instrumental albums. According to *AllMusic*, Gleason's intention was to "make musical wallpaper that should never be intrusive, but rather conducive". His first album, *Music For Lovers Only,* was released in 1952, went to number one in the Billboard Albums Chart and stayed in the top ten for three years. During the fifties, Gleason made twenty-four of his mood music LPs, all of which reached the top fifty albums, with several getting to number one. Even as late as 1969, a Christmas LP, *All I Want For Christmas,* reached number thirteen.

THE FIRST TIME

The music of people like Mantovani and Jackie Gleason has come to be known as 'Easy Listening' music, although these days the genre has expanded to include any popular music made before the arrival of rock 'n' roll, or made more recently but in a similar style to that. Singers like Frank Sinatra and Tony Bennett are classed as Easy Listening and so is later instrumental music by the likes of Herb Alpert and James Last.

Manfred Eicher

MUSIC GENRES

In 1953, a wealthy New Orleans businessman, Edward B. Benjamin, offered Howard Hanson, the director of the Eastman School of Music in New York, enough money to establish an annual music prize for composition. He had a very specific kind of composition in mind, as was made obvious by the name of the prize – the Edward B. Benjamin Award for Restful Music. The award was discontinued in 1971, and none of the recipients became well-known as composers, but the results were a kind of undemanding classical music that Erik Satie, in his ambient frame of mind, would have appreciated. The first winner was William Pursell, whose gentle work for strings and woodwinds was entitled *Christ Looking Over Jerusalem*. Ten years later, Pursell recorded an easy listening piano piece, accompanied by strings and angelic voices (and, surprisingly, one of Gibson's bass guitars with built-in fuzz-tone, albeit played quietly). *Our Winter Love* was a top ten hit in the US, although UK record buyers were not impressed. Somehow, the record was a hit in the Billboard R&B charts too, although the music can hardly have convinced any listener, even at the time, that it had anything to do with either rhythm or the blues. *Christ Looking Over Jerusalem* was eventually included, along with winning pieces from subsequent years, on an LP called *Music For Quiet Listening*.

The Miles Davis album, *In A Silent Way,* made in 1969, brought the concept of ambient music to jazz, while simultaneously making it seem completely contemporary and cutting-edge. The record turned out to be serving as a bridge between Davis' previous dabbling with R&B and rock influences and the full adoption of them on the landmark *Bitches Brew*, which came next. At the same time, it represented an ambient experiment, presenting a form of improvised jazz that proceeds largely without incident, with no chord changes, and with solos that are essentially decorative. The track titles, *Shhh/Peaceful* and *In A Silent Way,* emphasise the chosen aesthetic. It was notable, moreover, that *It's About That Time*, the only one of the album's three tracks to be included in live performances, was played in a much more muscular way on stage. Nevertheless, like Satie's music before it, *In A Silent Way* does manage to provide plenty to appreciate for anyone who chooses to concentrate on listening.

The debut album by King Crimson, *In The Court Of The Crimson King*, again made in 1969, and important as a milestone in the development of progressive rock, includes one track, *Moonchild,* that is rather different from the epic song structures of the rest of the record. It is the only song that was not part of the band's stage set. In live performance at this time, however, King Crimson did always include an extended passage of free improvisation, leading up to a dramatic version of the Gustav Holst piece, *Mars*. Unlike the jazz groups who employed a somewhat cathartic form of free improvisation, King Crimson tended to prefer a more organic approach, in which unexpected fragments of reggae or light orchestral themes might appear. Much of *Moonchild* is constructed like this too, with the opening verses giving way to an extended improvisation by guitar, percussion, and xylophone. Greg Lake's bass stays silent. The improvisation is gentle, without much in the way of development, and emerges as another adoption of the ambient approach.

In November 1969, the first record on the ECM (Edition of Contemporary Music) label was issued. The company was founded in Germany by jazz enthusiast and bass player Manfred Eicher, who suspected that the market for jazz was about to open up, as a result of the increasing influence of Miles Davis, and his album *In A Silent Way* in particular. That first record was an unspectacular piano jazz recording by the Mal Waldron Trio, *Free At Last*. The subsequent releases were quite varied, but gradually a kind of house style began to emerge. All the records on the label were produced by Manfred Eicher himself. The style that he favoured was one in which great emphasis was placed on timbre and texture, on music that was innovative, but primarily intended to sound beautiful. Writing in the Canadian magazine, *Coda*, in 1971, Jerome Reese described the music issued by ECM as being "the most beautiful sound next to silence". This was adopted by the company as a slogan and, listening to the largely reflective music provided by such early releases as the first solo albums by Terje Rypdal (self-titled), Keith Jarrett *(Facing You)*, and Jan Garbarek *(Afric Pepperbird)* – all of them artists who achieved huge success during decades of recording for the label – one can begin to hear what this means. Keith Jarrett maintained two separate recording careers during the seventies. His solo piano albums, his composed music at the interface between classical and jazz, and his work with Jan Garbarek all appeared on ECM, while his more robust recordings with a jazz group featuring saxophonist Dewey Redman and bass player

THE FIRST TIME

In August 1972, both Tangerine Dream and the group's former percussionist, Klaus Schulze, released albums that finally revealed these artists as breaking away somewhat from the influence of early Pink Floyd. *Zeit* and *Irrlicht* present electronic music that is largely event-free, being primarily concerned with creating a soundscape and moving very slowly within it. They remain, however, altogether too loud and insistent to happily take on the role of ambient music. These are albums that demand to be noticed. Both Tangerine Dream (essentially comprising Edgar Froese and whoever he chose to work with him) and Klaus Schulze have made a large number of albums in the years since. They have been a huge influence on ambient and New Age music, without ever really being a part of it.

The second side of the *Discreet Music* LP finds Brian Eno entering more directly into Steve Reich territory, as he organises a set of unusual interpretations of pieces by the Renaissance composer Johann Pachelbel. These are turned into modern chamber works by the imposition of specific performance rules for the players, such as decreasing the tempo at different rates. The consequence is that the integration of the parts as originally written is lost.

In 1973, King Crimson's guitarist, Robert Fripp, worked with Brian Eno on an LP they called *No Pussyfooting*. The music marked the debut of a style the guitarist subsequently christened 'Frippertronics' – using multiple sound loops to create a version of the minimalist classical music being pioneered by Steve Reich and Terry Riley. Although there are parallels between this and some ambient music, Frippertronics is rather too insistent to comfortably take the role of background music.

Brian Eno was commissioned to write the music fragment played when the Windows 95 operating system was started on a computer – a particularly striking application of the ambient music concept. A YouTube subscriber called bvixer has uploaded a recording of the theme slowed down twenty-three times, thereby creating a piece reminiscent of the Ligeti music used in the film *2001: A Space Odyssey*. Several people have uploaded extended remixes of the theme (the original lasts for less than seven seconds). The most successful are those by Ruler Inc, even if this is also a little short, and DJ Error.

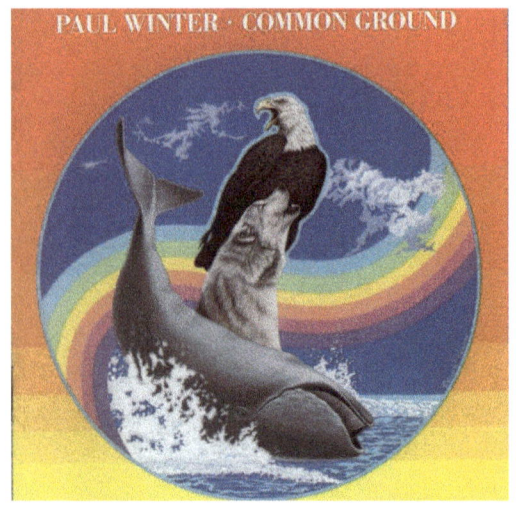

Charlie Haden, closer to the avant garde and not conspicuously 'beautiful' or capable of being employed in any kind of background capacity, appeared on the American Impulse label. The tremendous influence on other contemporary music of both ECM and Keith Jarrett himself was set when an album by the pianist, *The Köln Concert*, was listed by *Time* magazine as a record of the year (1975) and proceeded to become that rare thing, a best-selling jazz album. By 1987, sales were approaching one and a half million. It is interesting to note that Jarrett had been forced to simplify his playing style somewhat during the concert, because he had been given a defective instrument to play.

In 1975, Brian Eno, the former synthesizer player with Roxy Music, two years into an unpredictable solo career, issued an LP called *Discreet Music* as the third release on his own Obscure record label. In the sleeve notes, Eno explained that he had been given a recording of eighteenth century harp music to listen to, while recovering from an accident. After starting the record playing and lying back down, he realised that the volume was set so low that one stereo channel had become completely silent, while the other was so quiet as to make concentrated listening difficult. Being Brian Eno, he decided to make a virtue of the situation and conceived the idea of making a record of his own, using a synthesizer to provide the same kind of listening experience. The result was the first side of *Discreet Music*, the first deliberately ambient piece of original music to be produced since Erik Satie.

Starting in 1978, Eno was responsible for a series of LPs containing music intended to become part of the background when played, yet also having a certain amount of intellectual vigour. He deployed the term 'ambient music' for the first time and in the sleeve notes to the first record, *Ambient 1 – Music For Airports*, set out a rather well-worded manifesto, even if he gets the history of Muzak slightly wrong:

> The concept of music designed specifically as a background texture in the environment was pioneered by Muzak Inc. in the fifties, and has since come to be known generically by the term Muzak. The connotations that this term carries are those particularly associated with the kind of material that Muzak Inc. produces – familiar tunes arranged and orchestrated in a lightweight and derivative manner. Understandably, this has led most discerning listeners (and most composers) to dismiss entirely the concept of environmental music as an idea worthy of attention.
>
> Over the past three years, I have become interested in the use of music as ambience, and have come to believe that it is possible to produce material that can be used thus without being in any way compromised. To create a distinction between my own experiments in this area and the products of the various purveyors of canned music, I have begun using the term Ambient Music.
>
> ………..Ambient Music must be able to accommodate many levels of listening attention without enforcing one in particular; it must be as ignorable as it is interesting.

The piano and synthesizer music on *Ambient 1 – Music For Airports* is exactly that: ignorable but interesting.

Acoustic guitarist William Ackerman, who listed Erik Satie as one influence on his playing, formed a record company, Windham Hill, in 1976 in order to issue his own album, *The Search For The Turtle's Navel*. Later releases included more Ackerman and other guitarists too, but also an album of Satie piano pieces, played by Bill Quist, and several records by George Winston, a pianist whose playing invited comparison with that of Keith Jarrett, although it was simpler and more inspired by folk music than jazz. His impressionist records *December* and *Winter Into Spring*, from 1982, both sold over a million copies and succeeded in defining Windham Hill as an even more ambient version of ECM for people who were not sure if they liked jazz. The label helped to define a music genre known as New Age – music intended to encourage relaxation and meditation, although rather earlier maverick performers like Tony Scott, Paul Horn, and Paul Winter were arguably producing something very similar. Tony Scott played a set of slow, dreamy clarinet improvisations in 1965, on an album called *Music For Zen Meditation*, on which he was accompanied by a pair of musicians playing traditional Japanese instruments. Paul Horn made a number of recordings of his own flute playing inside large buildings that would give the music a spacey, echoing sound. The first, entitled *Inside* when released in 1968, was recorded in the Taj Mahal – later reissues of the LP made this clear with a new title, *Inside The Taj Mahal*. Saxophonist Paul Winter released the first, self-titled album by his group, the Winter Consort, also in 1968.

THE FIRST TIME

Paul Horn's *Inside The Great Pyramid* was released in 1977. In September of the following year, the Grateful Dead played three concerts near to the same Great Pyramid, in Cairo, though not inside it. Some of the Dead's music lends itself to being an accompaniment to meditation of a sort too, although it is far too involving and loud ever to be considered as being any kind of ambient music. When it came to performing at a venue with extreme spiritual connotations, the Dead were preceded by Pink Floyd, who performed in the Roman amphitheatre in Pompeii in 1971, though without an audience. An annual three day concert at the edge of the Sahara Desert in Mali was started in 2001, under the name of Festival in the Desert. The 2003 concert included Robert Plant performing alongside the African groups and it was filmed for release on DVD. Like the Grateful Dead, these are examples of music being given ambience by its surroundings, rather than of music that is itself ambient.

The most commercially successful example of New Age music was undoubtedly that performed and created by the Irish singer songwriter, Enya. Her second album, *Watermark,* was a hit around the world when released in 1988. Similar albums followed and the one she issued in 2000, *A Day Without Rain,* became the best selling album of its genre, with an estimated sixteen million copies purchased.

The best selling video game of 1997, *Riven,* with sales that would have taken it to the top of the charts if it had been an album, had a soundtrack that was issued on CD in 1998. Composed and performed on synthesizers by Robyn Miler, co-creator of the game itself, the various thematically linked pieces are outstanding ambient music as well as a soundtrack. The earlier *Myst,* created by the same team, was the best selling PC game of the nineties and also had a Robyn Miller soundtrack. This was first issued on a CD in 1995, although it works rather less well as a music album. The use of music to accompany video games is as old as the games themselves, although the simple monophonic bleeps of the late seventies would make a poor soundtrack album. The Japanese group, Yellow Magic Orchestra, however, sampled these sounds for inclusion on its first, self-titled LP from 1978, particularly on the two tracks called *Computer Game.*

The Consort played a kind of chamber music version of jazz, with a line-up that included such unlikely instruments as lute, cor anglais, and bass marimba. If it had started playing later, it would have been a natural addition to the ECM or Windham Hill rosters. Winter made an album in his own name in 1978, *Common Ground*, which included his duet work with a timber wolf, a humpback whale, and an African fish-eagle.

New Age music has come to refer to the range of CD albums typically on sale within shops stocking crystals, spices, Celtic jewellery, Tarot paraphernalia, and the like. The New World Company, responsible for the largest number of these ambient recordings, was founded by Colin Willcox, a specialist in alternative medicine, but not a professional musician. The first album issued, on cassette in 1984, was *Crystal Piano* by Phil Wells, who failed to repeat the success of George Winston. Later releases included titles such as *A Concert Of Angels*, *Enchanted Forest*, and *Reverence* (this being one of several recordings made by Terry Oldfield, Mike's brother).

In 1989, Paul Oakenfold, the resident DJ at the Heaven Club in London, had the idea of employing a second DJ who would play relaxing music at the end of an evening, to encourage the dancers to leave the club. Alex Paterson got the job and proceeded to make his Chill Out Room into an attraction in its own right. The imaginative mixes that he created in the club were exposed to a wider audience when Paterson began making records as the Orb. A very long track that may have begun as a remix of the Minnie Riperton song, *Loving You*, but which had ended up by burying the song underneath mellow synthesizer loops and sound effects from nature, was issued as a single with the unwieldy title of *A Huge Ever Growing Pulsating Brain That Rules From The Centre Of The Ultraworld*. It exerted an influence out of all proportion to the tiny impact it made on the singles chart. Successive Orb releases did better, until the second album, *U.F.Orb*, reached number one in the UK album chart in the summer of 1992. During the next ten years, a number of more or less ambient albums were released, by such diverse artists as Anne Dudley, Cinematic Orchestra, Royksopp, and the Aphex Twin, all of whom created music inspired, like the Orb, by dance, yet not actually suitable for dancing. A large number of compilation albums were issued with titles such as *Chill Factor*, *The Chillout Session*, *Serve Chilled*, *Textures*, and *The Best Chillout Ever*. The last named album, an inevitable demonstration of the mighty EMI/Virgin spotting a commercial opportunity, added some rather unlikely material, including ballads such as Elvis Costello's *Allison* and the Beach Boys' *Caroline No*, and even Nat King Cole crooning *Let There Be Love*, none of which had any real connection with the genre initiated by the Orb.

TRACKING THE TRACKS

A Warner/Apex CD (2004) of works by Hindemith and Satie includes the *Entr'acte* music and three musique d'ameublement pieces, though not the *Sons Industriels*. The music is performed by Ensemble Ars Nova, conducted by Marius Constant. The two *Sons Industriels* pieces are included on an Erato CD (2001), performed by L'Orchestre Des Concerts L'amoureux, conducted by Yutaka Sado. Their total playing time is under three minutes.

The music for *L'Assassination De Duc De Guise* by Camille Saint-Saens is included on A Russian Melodiya LP, *Music For French Films,* which was issued in 1984 and has not appeared on CD. The music is performed by the USSR Ministry of Culture Orchestra, conducted by Gennadi Rozhdestvensky. A performance by Ensemble Musique Oblique can be heard on YouTube.

The 1926 *Don Juan* film is available on a Warner Bros region 1 DVD. *The Jazz Singer* is also available on a Warner Bros DVD, and there is a region 2 issue. *One Night Of Love* can be viewed on YouTube, divided into eight parts, or there is an official Sony version that has to be paid for to view.

The complete score that Dmitri Shostakovich composed for *New Babylon* is available on a Naxos double CD issued in 2011. The music is played by Basel Sinfonietta, conducted by Mark Fitz-Gerald.

The soundtrack to Walt Disney's *Snow White And The Seven Dwarfs* is on Walt Disney Records (2006). That for *Pinnochio* is part of the Walt Disney Legacy Collection series of CDs, issued in 2015.

High Noon by Tex Ritter (Bear Family 1992) includes two versions of the title track. The Frankie Laine version is included on the double CD, *The Greatest Hits* (Not Now Music 2010).

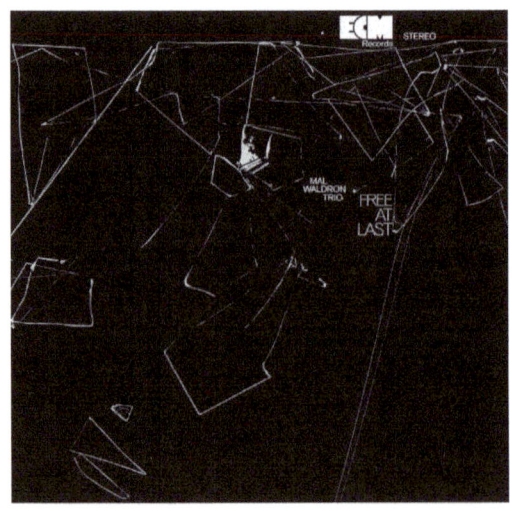

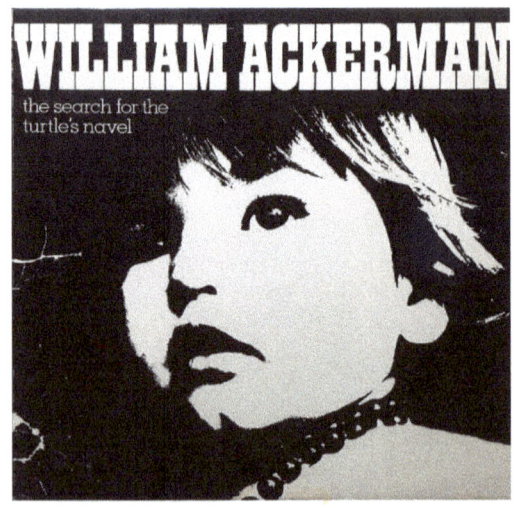

MUSIC GENRES

John Zorn's compilation of music by Carl Stalling is *The Carl Stalling Project – Music From Warner Bros Cartoons 1936-1958* (Warner Bros 1990). Zorn's own first record to include music composed along Stalling's lines simultaneously pays tribute to another film music great – the album is *The Big Gundown – John Zorn Plays The Music Of Ennio Morricone* (Elektra Nonesuch 1998).

The two De Wolfe music compilations shown are *Music De Wolfe Vol.1* (Morphius 2008) and *Bite Harder – The Music De Wolfe Studio Sampler Volume 2* (De Wolfe 2009). *Eye Level* by the Simon Park Orchestra is included on *The Premier Collection Of Instrumental Hits Vol.3* (Disky 2000).

The two KPM music compilations shown are *Music For Dancefloors – The Cream Of The KPM Music Green Label Sessions* (Strut 2000) and *Blow Up Presents Exclusive Blend Volume 1* (Blow Up Records 1996). Copies of *The Mood Modern*, issued by KPM in 1966, turn up on the collectors' market from time to time. It has not been reissued on CD, nor ever given a full commercial release. *The Champ* by the Mohawks is on an album of the same title (Vampi Soul 2015).

John Lennon's *How Do You Sleep* is included on his second solo album, *Imagine* (Universal/Apple 2015).

The Various Artists compilation album, *Music While You Work*, includes the *Calling All Workers* theme tune (Empress 2000). *Some Enchanted Evening – The Very Best Of Mantovani* is a double CD on Decca (1998). *Music For Lovers Only* by Jackie Gleason is on Real Gone Music (2012).

Music For Quiet Listening, performed by the Eastman-Rochester Orchestra, conducted by Howard Hanson, is on Mercury (1994). A Bill Pursell CD, *Our Winter Love – Introducing The Piano Magic Of Bill Pursell,* was issued on the Collectables label in 1997, but has become very hard to find. The title track can be heard on YouTube, however.

Miles Davis' *In A Silent Way* is on Columbia (2010).

King Crimson's *In The Court Of The Crimson King* is on EG (2004).

Free At Last by the Mal Waldron Trio is on ECM (1991). The other albums mentioned, available on ECM CDs, are *Terje Rypdal* (2008), *Facing You* and *The Köln Concert* by Keith Jarrett (2008 and 2005), and *Afric Pepperbird* by Jan Garbarek (1994). The recommended Keith Jarrett recording on Impulse is *Death And The Flower* (MCA/Impulse 1991).

Tangerine Dream's *Zeit* is on Esoteric (2011). *Irrlicht* by Klaus Schulze is on Music On CD (2014)

Brian Eno's *Discreet Music* and *Ambient 1 – Music For Airports* are on EMI (2009). *No Pussyfooting,* with Robert Fripp, is on DGM (2008). This has become a double album, with the inclusion of both original tracks played in reverse and one of them played at half speed.

William Ackerman's *The Search For The Turtle's Navel* is on Windham Hill (1998). *Piano Solos of Erik Satie* by Bill Quist is also on Windham Hill (1986) as are the George Winston albums, *December* (2001) and *Winter Into Spring* (2002).

Tony Scott's *Music For Zen Meditation* is on Verve (2005). Paul Horn's *Inside The Taj Mahal* is on Rykodisc (1987); *Inside The Great Pyramid* is on Kuckuck (1991). *The Winter Consort* has not been reissued on CD, but eight of its eleven tracks can be heard on YouTube at the time of writing. For those that know where to look, the whole album can be downloaded. Paul Winters' *Common Ground* is on A&M(1989).

Crystal Piano by Phil Wells has never been reissued but can be found as an unofficial download.

A Concert Of Angels by Asha (Denis Quinn) (1993), *Enchanted Forest* by David Sun (2003), and *Reverence* by Terry Oldfield (2001) are all available on New World Music CDs. *Watermark* and *A Day Without Rain* by Enya are on WEA (2001 and 2000).

A Huge Ever Growing Pulsating Brain.... is on the first Orb album, *The Orb's Adventures Beyond The Ultraworld* (Universal/Island 2006). *U.F.Orb* is also on Universal/Island (2007).

Anne Dudley's *Seriously Chilled* is on EMI (2003); Cinematic Orchestra's *Man With The Movie Camera* is on Ninja Tune (2003); Royksopp's *Melody A.M.* is on Wall Of Sound (2001); Aphex Twin's *Selected Ambient Works 85-92* is on Apollo (2013).

Chill Factor is on Rhythm Chamber (2000); *The Chillout Session* is on Ministry Of Sound (2001); *Serve Chilled* was given away free with an edition of *Later* magazine in 2000 – secondhand copies are reasonably common; *The Best Chillout Ever* is on EMI/Virgin (2002). *Textures* is a double CD presenting two megamixes, by Alex Paterson and by Darren Emerson (of Underworld) (Vital Distribution 1996).

Riven – The Soundtrack by Robyn Miller is on Virgin (1998). *Myst – The Soundtrack* is also on Virgin (1998). *Yellow Magic Orchestra* is on Restless Records (1992).

THE FIRST TIME

KEY FILM AND STAGE MUSICALS UP To 2000 (credits are for composer and lyricist)

1927	Show Boat (Jerome Kern & Oscar Hammerstein II)
1927	The Jazz Singer (various)
1928	The Threepenny Opera (Kurt Weill & Bertolt Brecht)
1929	The Desert Song (Sigmund Romberg & Otto Harbach)
1931	Of Thee I Sing (George & Ira Gershwin) first musical to win a Pulitzer Prize for drama
1935	Porgy And Bess (George & Ira Gershwin & DuBose Heyward)
1935	Top Hat (Irving Berlin)
1937	The Cradle Will Rock (Marc Blitzstein)
1939	The Wizard Of Oz (Herbert Stothart, Harold Arlen)
1943	Oklahoma! (Richard Rodgers & Oscar Hammerstein II)
1944	On The Town (Leonard Bernstein & Betty Comden & Adolph Green)
1945	Carousel (Richard Rodgers & Oscar Hammerstein II)
1946	Annie Get Your Gun (Irving Berlin & Dorothy & Herbert Fields)
1948	Kiss Me Kate (Cole Porter)
1949	South Pacific (Richard Rodgers & Oscar Hammerstein II)
1950	Guys And Dolls (Frank Loesser)
1951	The King And I (Richard Rodgers & Oscar Hammerstein II)
1951	Paint Your Wagon (Frederick Loewe & Alan J.Lerner)
1951	An American In Paris (George & Ira Gershwin)
1952	Singin' In The Rain (Nacio Herb Brown & Arthur Freed)
1954	Seven Brides For Seven Brothers (Saul Chaplin, Gene DePaul, & Johnny Mercer)
1956	My Fair Lady (Frederick Loewe & Alan J.Lerner)
1956	High Society (Cole Porter)
1956	Rock Around The Clock (various)
1956	Love Me Tender (various)
1957	Loving You (various)
1957	West Side Story (Leonard Bernstein & Stephen Sondheim)
1957	Pal Joey (Richard Rodgers & Lorenz Hart)original Broadway production was in 1940
1957	Jailhouse Rock (Jerry Leiber, Mike Stoller, and others)
1958	The Duke Wore Jeans (Lionel Bart, Mike Pratt, Tommy Steele)
1958	King Creole (various)
1959	The Sound Of Music (Richard Rodgers & Oscar Hammerstein II)
1959	Gypsy (Jule Styne & Stephen Sondheim)
1960	Oliver! (Lionel Bart)
1960	The Fantasticks (Harvey Schmidt & Tom Jones)
1961	The Young Ones (various)
1964	Fiddler On The Roof (Jerry Bock & Sheldon Harnick)
1964	Hello Dolly (Jerry Herman)
1964	Funny Girl (Jule Styne & Bob Merrill)
1964	A Hard Day's Night (John Lennon, Paul McCartney, George Martin)
1965	Help! (John Lennon, Paul McCartney, George Martin, Ken Thorne)
1966	Cabaret (John Kander & Fred Ebb)
1967	Hair (Galt MacDermot & James Rado & Gerome Ragni)
1970	Joseph And The Amazing Technicolour Dreamcoat (Andrew Lloyd Webber & Tim Rice)
1970	Company (Stephen Sondheim)
1971	Jesus Christ Superstar (Andrew Lloyd Webber & Tim Rice)
1971	Godspell (Stephen Schwartz)
1971	Grease (Jim Jacobs, Warren Casey, John Farrar)
1971	Escalator Over The Hill (Carla Bley & Paul Haines)
1973	A Little Night Music (Stephen Sondheim) – the source of *Send In The Clowns*
1973	The Rocky Horror Show (Richard O'Brien)
1973	That'll Be The Day (various)
1975	Tommy (The Who)
1975	A Chorus Line (Marvin Hamlisch & Edward Kleban)
1975	Chicago (John Kander & Fred Ebb)
1977	Saturday Night Fever (The Bee Gees and others)
1978	Evita (Andrew Lloyd Webber & Tim Rice)
1979	Sweeney Todd – The Demon Barber Of Fleet Street (Stephen Sondheim)
1979	All That Jazz (Ralph Burns & others)
1980	The Blues Brothers (various)
1980	The Great Rock 'n' Roll Swindle (various)
1980	The Jazz Singer (remake) (Neil Diamond) film flop but enormous success on record
1980	Les Miserables (Claude-Michel Schoenberg,Alain Boubil,Jean-Marc Natel,Herbert Kretzmer,James Fenton)
1983	Blood Brothers (Willy Russell)
1986	The Phantom of the Opera (Andrew Lloyd Webber, Charles Hart, Richard Stilgoe)
1989	MIss Saigon (Claude-Michel Schoenberg, Alain Boubil, Richard Maltby Jr)
1994	The Lion King (Hans Zimmer, Elton John, Tim Rice)

27 MUSICAL THEATRE

The Ancient Greeks played music as an accompaniment to drama, although it is unlikely that the inventors of opera, at the end of the sixteenth century, would have been aware of the fact. Musical theatre, comprising dramatic works, performed on the stage or on the cinema screen, in which songs and instrumental playing form an integral part, originated in opera. The first such work, *Dafne*, concerned the Greek god Apollo and his love for the nymph of the title. It was composed by the Italians Jacopo Peri and Jacopo Corsi, using a libretto by Ottavio Rinuccini, and was first performed in Florence in 1598. Although the libretto survives, most of the music has been lost, which probably explains why the work is not at all well known to modern music enthusiasts.

During the late nineteenth century, a number of composers sought to create a popular form of opera. Jacques Offenbach, Johann Strauss II, and Arthur Sullivan (working with librettist W.S.Gilbert) created works that were known as operetta by a classical world that could not bear to consider such light, comedic stuff as being in the same genre as Puccini and Wagner. Franz Lehar's most successful operetta, *The Merry Widow*, was first performed in 1905 and thereby set the stage for the development of musical theatre in the twentieth century.

In 1927, Jerome Kern and Oscar Hammerstein II composed a work called *Show Boat*, which was premiered at the Ziegfeld Theatre in New York at the end of the year. Despite moments of humour, this was no trivial light musical comedy, but a serious dramatic work, concerned with racial prejudice and tragic love, in which the music and the drama were fully integrated. Essentially, therefore, this was the first musical. One song in particular, *Ol' Man River*, remained popular throughout the following decades. It has been performed by artists as diverse as Bing Crosby, Frank Sinatra, Cilla Black, Ray Charles, and the Beach Boys, and has even received a rock interpretation by Rod Stewart, singing with the Jeff Beck Group. The best known version, however, remains the one delivered by Paul Robeson in the 1936 film of *Show Boat*. There are those who make claims for a much earlier production as the first musical. A play called *The Black Crook* was turned into a popular success on Broadway as long ago as 1866 by the forcing of a number of musical items by different composers into the dramatic action, against the wishes of the playwright, Charles M. Barras. There was, in consequence, no real integration of drama and music. A similar performance was carried out six years earlier, but the score and the libretto for *The Seven Sisters* have been lost.

The first full-length film with sound was a musical. *The Jazz Singer*, also made in 1927, starred Al Jolson, who performed six songs during the course of the story. *The Desert Song*, made in 1929, was a stage show transferred to film and was a fully fledged operetta.

The 1937 musical, *The Cradle Will Rock*, composed by Marc Blitzstein, had a pro-union political theme which did not endear it to observers in some quarters. As a result, it had some trouble in getting started as a stage production. Nevertheless, the following year its performance at New York's independent Mercury Theatre was recorded and the resulting album of 78s became the first original cast recording.

The invention of the LP provided a huge benefit for the producers and fans of musicals. The soundtrack album for *Carousel* was the first to gain the number one position in the UK album charts, in August 1956. Through the fifties, of the eighteen LPs to top the UK charts, eleven were soundtracks for musicals. *South Pacific*, which reached number one in November 1958, stayed in that position throughout 1959, as well as much of 1960 and several weeks in 1961. During the remainder of the sixties, two soundtrack albums spent several weeks at number one, *West Side Story* and *The Sound Of Music*, and were amongst the best selling records of the decade. It was a similar story in the US, where *West Side Story* spent fifty-four weeks at number one in the Billboard charts and *South Pacific* achieved thirty-one weeks.

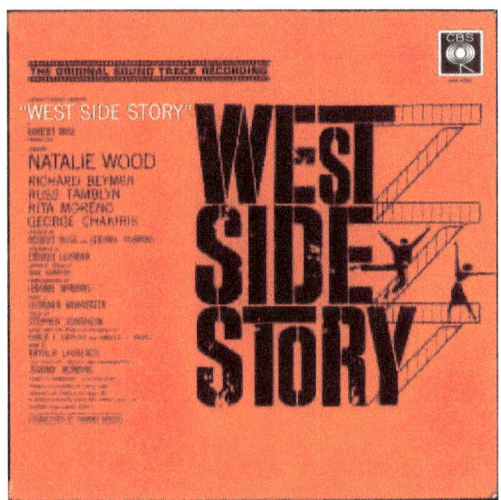

MUSIC GENRES

As popular music developed through the century, musicals took the new approaches on board, even if they were sometimes quite slow in doing this. The songs composed by George Gershwin, Irving Berlin, Cole Porter, Rodgers and Hammerstein, and the rest have come to be collectively referred to as 'The Great American Songbook'. Acquiring a reputation and an impact to transcend that of the musicals in which they first appeared, these songs (with the addition of a few key items from the pens of writers not working specifically in musical theatre, such as Duke Ellington) have provided the repertoire for the greatest singers of the era before rock 'n' roll, including Bing Crosby, Ella Fitzgerald, and Frank Sinatra. Not until the arrival of Lionel Bart towards the end of the fifties did a British songwriter appear to rival the Americans, by which time the whole popular music climate was changing irrevocably. Bart is acclaimed for his production of the music for *Oliver!* but is equally well-known for his rock 'n' roll songs like Tommy Steele's *Rock With The Caveman* and Cliff Richard's *Living Doll*.

Hair, produced in 1967, was acclaimed as the first rock musical, more than a decade after rock 'n' roll had started to dominate the charts. While this was true as far as stage shows were concerned, film musicals had actually used rock 'n' roll almost from the start. *Rock Around The Clock*, made in 1956, attempted to describe the birth of the music, though without worrying overmuch as to the true facts of the matter, and starred Bill Haley and the Comets.

Elvis Presley extended his chart success by starring in several musical films, beginning with *Love Me Tender* in 1956. Bing Crosby had made the same move in 1932, with *The Big Broadcast*, following a few earlier cameo appearances. Frank Sinatra did it too, first starring in *Higher And Higher* in 1944. The move from making music on record to making music on film seemed a natural one. The Beatles did it in 1964 with *A Hard Day's Night*, in which the group members played themselves. Even the Sex Pistols, despite leading what was supposed to be a musical revolution, followed the traditional path and were given a film showcase in 1980, *The Great Rock 'n' Roll Swindle*.

The Who presented a narrative song cycle on record in 1969, *Tommy*, which was described as a rock opera, albeit one in which Roger Daltrey sang most of the parts. A film version, made in 1975, put this right, with important roles being given to Elton John and Tina Turner, alongside Roger Daltrey as Tommy himself. The Pretty Things' *S.F.Sorrow*, issued in 1968, predated *Tommy* and was a similarly constructed album work, but it was never turned into a staged musical. Two albums released before *S.F.Sorrow* also present song cycles telling a story – *Miss Butters* by the Family Tree (1968) and *The Story Of Simon Simopath* by Nirvana (1967). The first rock album to contain music presented as an opera, with different singers being used for the different characters, was *Jesus Christ Superstar* by Andrew Lloyd Webber and Tim Rice, which was released in 1970 and gained its first stage performance in 1971. On the original record, the crucial role of Jesus was sung by the lead vocalist with Deep Purple, Ian Gillan, while much of the music was performed by members of Joe Cocker's Grease Band.

Mark Wirtz produced a song called *Excerpt From A Teenage Opera* for release in July 1967, using members of the group Tomorrow, including the lead singer Keith West. He never completed the entire work, although a CD titled *A Teenage Opera* was compiled in 1996, using Mark Wirtz material that might have ended up in the finished project.

Carla Bley started recording a jazz opera in November 1968, which was eventually completed and released in 1971, as *Escalator Over The Hill*. Jack Bruce, Linda Ronstadt, Paul Jones, and Don Preston were among the singers on a work that is distinctly avant garde, although thrilling and innovative. The work has been treated to a few concert performances, with different singers and musicians, but it has never been staged. Opera has not often featured in a jazz context, given the need to incorporate passages of improvisation, although *Big Man – The Legend Of John Henry* was composed by Cannonball Adderley and released on record just after his death in 1975, while more recently, in 2010, Dutch guitarist Corrie Van Binsbergen was responsible for *Over De Bergen (Over The Mountains – An Opera About Desire)*.

Hip hop, rap music, and salsa finally reached the world of musical theatre in 2005, with the critical and popular success of *In The Heights*, written by Lin-Manuel Miranda. It was followed in 2015 by the equally acclaimed *Hamilton*, a musical about one of the founding fathers of the United States, also written by Miranda. The composer played the lead role in both musicals.

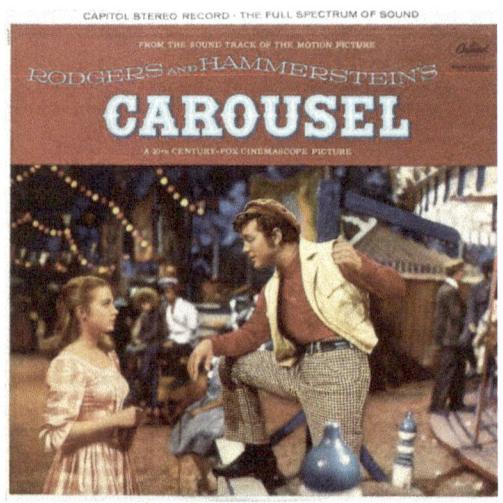
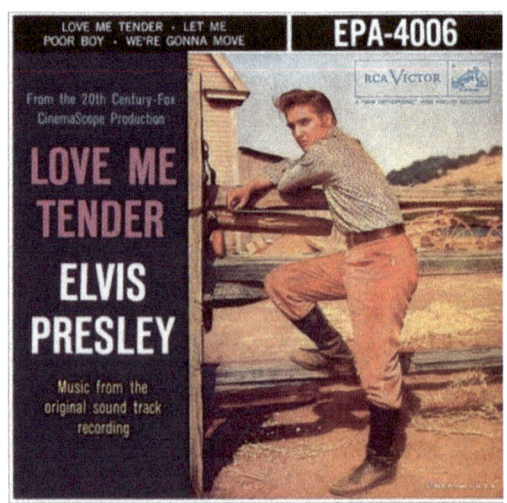

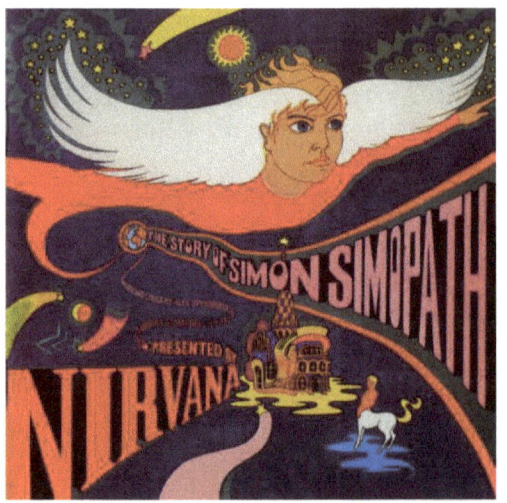

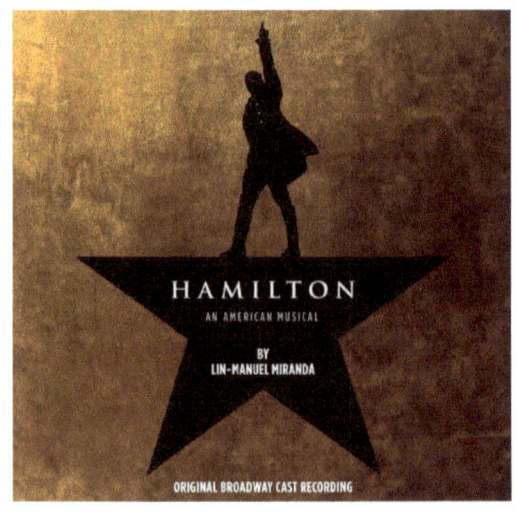

MUSIC GENRES

TRACKING THE TRACKS

CDs of all the key musicals listed at the start of this chapter are available.

There are several recordings of Franz Lehar's *The Merry Widow*, of which the most highly rated is the one that has Elisabeth Schwarzkopf in the title role. It is an elderly recording from 1953 and, being out of copyright, appears on issues from four different companies – EMI (1988), Regis (2003), Naxos (2005), and Opera D'Oro (2013). Three different performances are available on DVD.

A recording of the original version of Show Boat, performed by Frederica Von Stade and other singers with the London Sinfonietta, conducted by John McGlinn, is on a 3 CD set on EMI (2006). The soundtrack of the 1951 film, starring Kathryn Grayson, Ava Gardner, and Howard Keel, is on Hallmark (2005). Paul Robeson sings *Ol' Man River* on *Very Best Of Paul Robeson* (Alto 2014).

The Jazz Singer starring Al Jolson is available on DVD (Warner 2012).

The 1953 remake of *The Desert Song*, starring Kathryn Grayson and Gordon MacRae, is available on a Warner DVD.

Recordings of *The Cradle Will Rock* made in 1960 and 1985 are available on CD (on Line Music and Jay Productions respectively), but not the original 1938 performance.

The soundtrack to *Carousel* is on EMI/Angel (2001); *South Pacific* is on Hallmark (2010); *West Side Story* is on Sony (1997); The Sound Of Music is on Sony (2015). All four films are available on DVD.

The soundtrack of the original Broadway cast production of Hair is on a BMG CD (1993). The musical was not filmed until 1979 – it is available on DVD.

The film, *Rock Around The Clock*, is available on DVD together with a similar film, *Don't Knock The Rock, also* made in 1956, as a sequel.

Elvis Presley's *Love Me Tender* only included four of his songs, but a double soundtrack CD on Follow That Dream/Sony (2014) adds several alternative versions, interview material, and a complete live performance from 1956. The four songs (*Love Me Tender/Poor Boy/ Let Me/We're Gonna Move*) are also included on *Pink Cadillac – 24 Original Recordings Of 1956* (Delta 2007). The film is available on DVD.

Bing Crosby's *The Big Broadcast* is not available on DVD; the soundtrack album was issued on LP in 1974 but is not currently available on CD. Its hit songs *Dinah* and *Please* are, however, included on *The Absolutely Essential 3CD Collection* (Big3 2012).

Frank Sinatra's *Higher And Higher* is available on DVD, together with a second Sinatra film made in 1944, *Step Lively*. The soundtracks to both films are also combined on CD (Great Movie Themes 2001).

The Beatles' *A Hard Day's Night* is available on DVD; the soundtrack, which was the group's third album, is on CD (EMI 2009).

The Sex Pistols' *Great Rock 'n' Roll Swindle* is on DVD; the soundtrack is on CD (Universal 2012).

Tommy by The Who is on a Universal CD (2013). The soundtrack to the film version is on a Polydor double CD (2001). The film is available on DVD.

S.F.Sorrow by The Pretty Things is on Snapper (2008), together with both sides of two singles released later and not part of the song cycle.

Miss Butters by The Family Tree is on a Rev-Ola CD (2007).

The Story Of Simon Simopath by Nirvana is on Island (2003), with both the mono and the stereo mixes included, together with four bonus tracks.

The original studio recording of *Jesus Christ Superstar* by Andrew Lloyd Webber and Tim Rice is on Universal (2012). The film version, with a largely different cast, is on a Universal DVD (2005). The soundtrack is on MCA (1993),

A Teenage Opera by Mark Wirtz is on rpm (1996).

Carla Bley's *Escalator Over The Hill* is on a double CD on ECM (1998). Cannonball Adderley's *Big Man – The Legend Of John Henry* is on Real Gone Music (2015). Corrie Van Binsbergen's *Over De Bergen* is on a double CD on Brokken (2010).

The original Broadway cast recording of *In The Heights* is on a double Ghostlight CD (2008). That for *Hamilton* is on a double Atlantic CD (2015).

THE FIRST TIME

The word 'jazz', or more often 'jass' was originally applied as a euphemism for sex, being related to the similar 'jism', which is still used as a slang word for semen. 'Jazz' appeared as a reference to music in a San Francisco newspaper in 1913, although it was clearly being used in that way in New Orleans considerably before that.

Promotional postcard from 1918

The rhythmic, usually piano-based music known as ragtime was popular for twenty years from about 1895, with Scott Joplin being its most eminent composer and performer. Records of the music were issued from 1897, alongside piano rolls recorded on player pianos by all the major ragtime performers. The music sounds quite similar to early jazz, but differs in the crucial respect that it is entirely composed, with none of the improvisation that is the essential component of jazz.

The edition of *Billboard* dated May 22nd 1961 quoted an article published in the East German newspaper *Freie Walt*. Russian bandleader Alexander Utyosov claimed that Dixieland jazz was played in Odessa for many years before turning up in New Orleans. Accordingly, the official Communist line was that the playing of such music in the USSR was quite acceptable. Utyosov failed to offer any explanation for the absence of suitable Soviet recordings, requiring the import of American records to satisfy the demand.

Kid Ory, Louis Armstrong, Johnny Dodds, Lil Hardin Armstrong, Johnny St.Cyr

Emile Lacoume, known as Stalebread, played a zither with a group of teenagers in New Orleans, calling themselves the Razzy Dazzy Spasm Band. His claim that they invented jazz during the late 1890s has scarcely more credence than that of Jelly Roll Morton. *Jazzways,* a book about the music published in 1946, the year of Lacoume's death, uses the claim to caption his photograph, but makes no further mention of it in an account of the early years of New Orleans jazz.

28 JAZZ

The beginnings of jazz belong to the earliest years of recording or even before its invention. If some nineteenth century trumpeter suddenly decided to create a spontaneous melody while tapping his right foot in a steady beat, we do not know his name and we can never know what he sounded like.

Pianist and band-leader Jelly Roll Morton claimed to have invented jazz in 1902. He also claimed a birth date in 1885 to lend himself credence, although his baptismal certificate was discovered a century later and was dated 1890. Morton would therefore have been twelve at the time he supposedly came up with the idea of jazz. During the eighteen nineties, trumpeter Buddy Bolden led a band in New Orleans which was very successful. Although Bolden was hospitalised with schizophrenia in 1907, died in 1931, and was never recorded, the recollections of other New Orleans musicians who heard him play are clear that his music was jazz. Buddy Bolden must, therefore, be accorded the honour of being the first jazzman whose name we know.

After Bolden's departure from the New Orleans music scene, the younger trumpeter Freddie Keppard was acclaimed as his successor and, by all accounts, had a very similar playing style. In 1915, Keppard was offered the chance of making a record. He turned the offer down, with legend declaring his reason as being that he did not want other people to steal his ideas, although it is just as likely that the Victor record company had simply not offered him enough money. As a result, the first jazz recording was carried out by a group of white musicians, the Original Dixieland Jazz Band, giving listeners of the time a totally false idea as to who were the real innovators. The 78 rpm recording of *Livery Stable Blues/Dixie Jass Band One Step* was recorded by Victor on February 26th 1917 and sold well after being issued soon afterwards. Its success encouraged the recording of several other jazz bands and numerous records were released during the next months of 1917.

The Original Dixieland Jazz Band record was predated by a song recorded in December 1916 and credited to Collins and Harlan. *That Funny Jas Band From Dixieland* is a song *about* jazz, rather than an actual jazz performance, but much of the instrumental accompaniment does sound remarkably like the music the lyrics describe. The claim, therefore, that this release is really the first example of jazz on record is not without merit. Arthur Collins and Byron G. Harlan were a singing duo, well known for their comedy material. One of the voices on *That Funny Jas Band From Dixieland*, however, is clearly a woman and is referred to by name as Mandy. Something is amiss with the label credit.

By general agreement, the most important jazz band of the time was the one led by trumpeter Joe 'King' Oliver, although it did not get to make a record until 1923, by which time it had moved away from New Orleans and had become established in Chicago. Oliver employed as a second trumpeter a young musician by the name of Louis Armstrong. Supremely talented and charismatic, Armstrong soon outgrew the Oliver band, moving on to become a member of the Fletcher Henderson orchestra, before striking out on his own. He became the first big star of jazz and single-handedly shifted the focus of the music away from group improvisation and on to being the vehicle for solo virtuosity that jazz has essentially been ever since. Armstrong's influential recordings with his Hot Five began in 1925. Effectively, therefore, the music of the 'traditional jazz' era, with the bands improvising collectively, which many fans will maintain is the only true jazz, lasted just eight years. By the nineteen sixties, Louis Armstrong had acquired the status of a much loved all-round entertainer. He achieved his greatest successes at this time, with the singles *Hello Dolly* and *What A Wonderful World* earning gold discs, although, ironically, neither had anything at all to do with jazz.

The first big bands arrived only a little after the smaller groups began recording. Paul Whiteman formed his in 1918 and made his first recordings in 1920, as the Paul Whiteman Orchestra (actually an ensemble of eight musicians, with Whiteman conducting). The band became enormously popular very quickly, expanding to as many as thirty-five

THE FIRST TIME

Paul Whiteman Orchestral c.1922

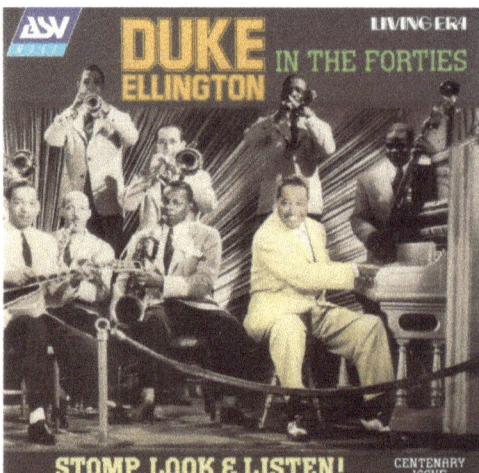

Lester Young, as one of the first hipsters, was the inventor of many word usages that have remained within the jazz world and elsewhere ever since. 'Cool' as a term of approval, 'bread' to mean 'money', and 'dig' to mean 'understand' or 'like' were all his. It is likely that 'axe' to refer to a musician's main instrument (most often applied to a saxophone or a guitar) also originates with Lester Young.

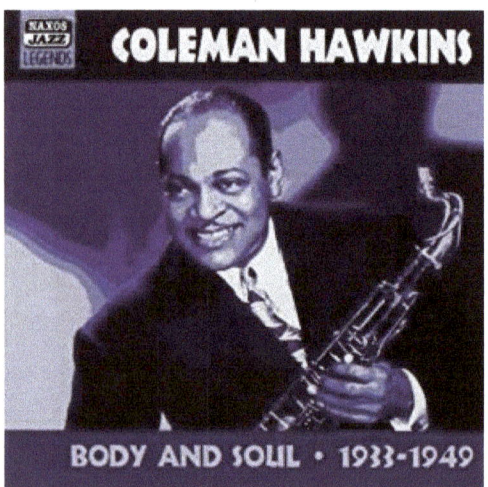

The Benny Goodman Orchestra became the first jazz band to play at the prestigious Carnegie Hall in New York, in January 1938. It is said that when Goodman was asked how long an interval he wished to have in the performance, he replied, "I dunno. How long does Toscanini get?"

'Swing' was a term applied to jazz rhythms some time before 1935. Jelly Roll Morton's *Georgia Swing* was recorded in 1928. Bennie Moten's piece *Moten Swing* was composed in 1932 and was a hit for Benny Goodman in 1938. Duke Ellington's *It Don't Mean A Thing If It Ain't Got That Swing* also dates from 1932. The inspiration for 'swing' as the name for a specific genre doubtless derives from these.

members, and it was claimed that by 1922, Whiteman was earning a million dollars a year. He was helped in this respect by being the organiser of no fewer than fifty-two different orchestras across the Americas and Europe. His recording of *Whispering* backed with *Japanese Sandman*, issued in 1920, became the first million selling jazz record – indeed it was estimated that by the end of the following year, sales amounted to nearly two million copies. Whiteman was dubbed 'The King Of Jazz', although critics have suggested that the amount of jazz content within the elaborate written arrangements that characterised his work was actually rather slight. He did, however, provide a showcase for trumpeter Bix Beiderbecke, the first white jazz soloist to be held in as much esteem as was Louis Armstrong. Beiderbecke came from a well-to-do business family, with parents who did not approve of their son's choice of career. The story goes that, following his death from pneumonia at the age of just twenty-eight, a pile of unopened parcels was found in a cupboard at his parents' house. Bix had been in the habit of sending home a copy of every new record he made, unaware that his parents were not interested.

Edward 'Duke' Ellington, widely regarded as the most important composer within the whole of jazz, also had his first bands at this time. He became leader of the seven-piece Washingtonians in 1924, and made a number of records. At the end of 1927, Duke Ellington and his Orchestra, increased to eleven musicians, became the house band for the Cotton Club in Harlem. Weekly radio broadcasts from the club gave Ellington national exposure. From that time until his death in 1974, Duke Ellington managed to maintain a big band, through the rock 'n' roll years and beyond, and flying in the face of changes in fashion that made big bands generally less than commercially viable.

The Bennie Moten band first recorded in 1923. Operating out of Kansas City, with Fletcher Henderson now employed as an arranger, the band came up with the idea of structuring their music around simple, repeated fragments of melody, known as riffs. The technique enabled a greatly enhanced rhythmic drive and has proved to be highly influential, not least within rock music. Moten died in 1935, following an operation to have his tonsils removed (not usually fatal) and his band was taken over by the pianist, William 'Count' Basie. He became one of the most successful bandleaders of all, managing, like Duke Ellington, to ride the changing fashions in music relatively unscathed. His band, during its most popular years in the thirties and forties, became a showcase for a couple of star soloists, Lester Young and Coleman Hawkins. These men were tenor saxophonists (an instrument not much used in New Orleans jazz) and they succeeded in shifting the primary focus of jazz soloing away from the trumpet and towards the tenor saxophone, where it has stayed. Coleman Hawkins achieved a million selling record in his own right in 1939 (which was more than his erstwhile employer ever managed). *Body And Soul* emerged as a definitive demonstration of how jazz improvisation on a well known theme should be carried out.

Benny Goodman, whose recording debut was in 1926, as a member of Ben Pollack's band, formed his own orchestra in 1934. He was very unusual for the time in frequently having a racially integrated line-up (although his band was not the first in jazz – Jelly Roll Morton, black, recorded with the all-white Rhythm Kings in 1923). Combining the Moten/Basie riff-based music (and employing Fletcher Henderson) with the more fully composed approach of Paul Whiteman, Goodman was successful quite quickly. Metronome magazine nominated the Benny Goodman Orchestra as the best of 1935, with the music being described as 'swing'. The swing era lasted for ten years, although Goodman remained popular for some time after that and was performing right up until his death in 1986. His orchestra was never the *most* popular of the big bands, however. That accolade belongs to Tommy Dorsey, whose band featured the singer Frank Sinatra, or perhaps to Glenn Miller, although Miller was arguably not leading a jazz organisation at all, as there was little improvisation involved in the music.

During 1941, Charlie Christian, the pioneering electric guitarist employed by Benny Goodman, began taking part in jam sessions held at a club in Harlem called Minton's Playhouse (after its founder, a saxophonist and musicians' union official called Henry Minton). Christian's fellow players, including pianist Thelonious Monk, trumpeter Dizzy Gillespie, drummer Kenny Clarke, and, later, alto saxophonist Charlie Parker, were all in their twenties and burning with energy, ambition, and a desire to put their own stamp on jazz. In the competitive environment of the jam session, they were inspired to play with ever increasing virtuosity, which became a qualification for anyone else seeking to join

THE FIRST TIME

"Bebop has set music back twenty years" – band-leader Tommy Dorsey

"This is the sort of bad taste and ill-advised fanaticism that has thrown innumerable impressionable young musicians out of stride" – Downbeat magazine review of Charlie Parker April 1946

"All them weird chords which don't mean a thing… you got no melody to remember, and no beat to dance to… [bebop] is Chinese music" – Louis Armstrong

"Bebop was about change, about evolution. It wasn't about standing still and becoming safe. If anybody wants to keep creating they have to be about change" – Miles Davis

"I say, play your own way. Don't play what the public wants. You play what you want and let the public pick up on what you're doing – even if it does take them fifteen, twenty years" – Thelonious Monk

In his book, *Jazz Modernism*, Alfred Appel describes the occasion in 1951 when Igor Stravinsky was in the audience at Birdland, the jazz club in New York, when the Charlie Parker Quintet was playing. Noting the composer's presence, Parker opened with one of his fastest pieces, *Koko*, and when he came to solo, he played the opening of Stravinsky's *The Firebird*, making it sound as though it had always been a part of the piece. The anecdote emphasises Parker's talent as a musician, especially bearing in mind that *The Firebird* was not a part of his normal repertoire.

Jazz musicians have often used the musical theatre songs from the 'Great American Songbook' as material for improvisation, whether taking only the chord sequence to underpin entirely new melodic themes, or else presenting a version of the complete original song (usually without its lyrics). The Charlie Parker piece *Ornithology*, for example, is based on the chords of the Morgan Lewis song *How High The Moon*, but with a new melody that enabled Parker to claim the writing credit for himself and trumpeter Benny Harris. Parker first recorded *Ornithology* in March 1946, but he also made numerous live performances of *How High The Moon*, with its original melody intact. The first jazz album to comprise nothing but a set of tunes taken from just one musical show was by Shelly Manne and Friends (pianist André Previn and bass player Leroy Vinnegar). This was *Modern Jazz Performances Of Songs From My Fair Lady*, issued in 1956.

in. Tempos were generally fast, with elaborately accented rhythms that broke away from the simple chugging beat of swing. Chordal structures were made deliberately complicated, even if what was being played was really just the blues. Composed melody lines were angular and difficult to play. The resulting music became known as bebop, or just bop, with Gillespie and Parker being feted as the leading players of the style. Ralph Gleason, writing in the Toledo Blade newspaper in February 1959, referred to etymologist Peter Tamony as attributing the word 'bebop' to an onomatopoeic rendering of the sound made by Dizzy Gillespie's trumpet.

Bebop was viewed as being revolutionary and was dismissed by many established musicians and critics as being worthless, in much the same way as was rock 'n' roll a decade and a half later. It has been blamed for diverting jazz away from being a popular music, although in truth the arrival of rhythm and blues and then rock 'n' roll soon afterwards was rather more responsible for this. In any event, the term 'modern jazz' has become established as a serious-sounding description for the improvising, rhythmic music of bop and its subsequent developments, as opposed to the 'traditional jazz' (and swing) of its popular predecessors.

Although the various musicians involved in the Minton's jam sessions made recordings as far back as 1939, they tended to have to compromise their playing in order to fit in with what was expected by the band-leaders employing them. Even the first recordings in Dizzy Gillespie's own name from January and February 1945 are hampered by unsympathetic rhythm sections. The first recording session, therefore, when everything came together was on May 11th 1945. Three tracks – *Salt Peanuts, Shaw Nuff,* and *Hot House* – were completed by a quintet featuring both Dizzy Gillespie and Charlie Parker, with singer Sarah Vaughan added for a fourth, the atypical ballad, *Lover Man*. The tracks were issued on a pair of US 78s on the Guild label in 1945 as the first bebop records. Charlie Parker's own first recordings as leader followed in November, with two new musicians destined to have considerable later success and influence being introduced – drummer Max Roach and trumpeter Miles Davis. The tracks *Billie's Bounce* and *Now's The Time* were chosen for the first release, on a US 78 on the Savoy label.

It was Miles Davis who was responsible for the next development in jazz. As a less skilful player than the older Dizzy Gillespie, he favoured more lyrical lines with fewer notes for his solos. In collaboration with baritone saxophonist Gerry Mulligan, pianist John Lewis, and arranger Gil Evans, he formed a nine-piece band to play music that was less energetic and more thoroughly arranged than bebop. In September 1948, the band played a three week engagement at the Royal Roost club in New York, three sets of which were broadcast on the radio. Enough interest was generated for the band to be given the chance to record a total of twelve tracks in January and April 1949 and March 1950, with ten of them subsequently being issued on 78s by Capitol. The music was eventually dubbed 'cool jazz' and when all twelve tracks were brought together on an LP in 1956, this was given the title *Birth Of The Cool*. Miles Davis himself, however, was unable to immediately capitalise on his original idea as his music began to take second place to a heroin addiction. It was left to Chet Baker (working with Gerry Mulligan) to achieve a measure of stardom in 1952 with a carbon copy of Davis' way of playing the trumpet. The fact that Baker was white, with the looks of a James Dean, was a major factor in his success. He also made several recordings as a singer, revealing himself to have an attractive, if unspectacular singing voice.

Through the fifties, the leading jazz players continued to explore the Charlie Parker legacy. Parker himself died in 1955, a victim of his excessive, chaotic life style, which included being addicted to heroin. The coroner who attended his death estimated Parker's age as being in his fifties – in reality he was just thirty-four. No doubt glimpsing an unpleasant future of his own, Miles Davis opted to end his own addiction by employing a difficult and risky 'cold turkey' cure – simply stopping taking the drug and enduring the consequences. An acclaimed performance at the Newport Jazz Festival in 1955 announced his return to the front line of jazz music making.

The music was now being referred to as 'hard bop', although in essence it was still the bebop of Charlie Parker, albeit slightly less frantic and with a greater number of show tunes being used as source material. Miles Davis formed a new quintet, featuring a previously overlooked tenor saxophonist by the name of John Coltrane. The group

Scott Joplin, who would have considered his own ragtime piano pieces to be a form of classical music, composed an entire opera in 1911, which he titled *Treemonisha*. It included elements of ragtime and other black music styles within music that otherwise followed the European orchestral tradition, but did not receive a performance until 1972, fifty-five years after Joplin's death.

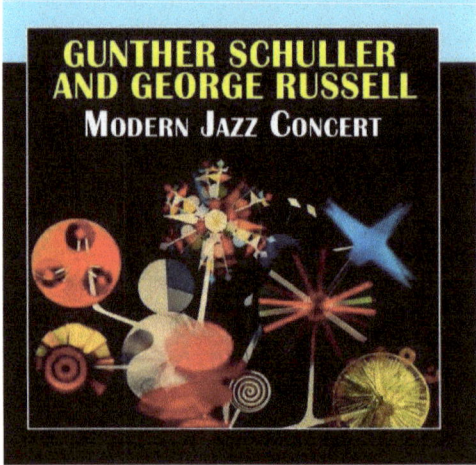

While third stream jazz never quite managed to galvanise the jazz world in the way that the developments pioneered by John Coltrane and Ornette Coleman did, there have been numerous examples over the years of further attempts to integrate jazz and classical music. Various recordings by John Lewis's Modern Jazz Quartet and by Miles Davis in collaboration with arranger Gil Evans are amongst the most notable. The Davis-Evans jazz interpretation of the second movement of Joaquin Rodrigo's *Concierto De Aranjuez* was the highlight of the best-selling 1960 album, *Sketches Of Spain*. As recently as 1997, British composer Mark-Anthony Turnage incorporated improvisation by jazz players John Scofield and Peter Erskine in his orchestral work *Blood On The Floor*.

One of John Coltrane's favourite vehicles for improvisation, a stripped down version of the Richard Rodgers tune, *My Favourite Things*, lasted a little under fourteen minutes in its original 1960 studio recording. By the time of the performance at New York's Half Note in 1965 (issued on the double CD *One Down One Up*) it had become extended to nearly twenty-three minutes. A year later, in the performance issued as the four LP set, *Live In Japan*, the piece had reached nearly an hour. Although there are solos by the other members of the group, the bulk of the length is due to Coltrane's own playing. When working with Miles Davis, the saxophonist had already begun to make his solos longer and longer. He commented to Davis that he had a problem knowing how to stop. Davis is reported to have replied something like, "you could try taking the damn saxophone out of your mouth!"

Alex Ross, in *The Rest Is Noise*, his study of twentieth century classical music, manages to spare a few pages for a solitary jazz composer, Duke Ellington. Ross claims that the Duke invented modal improvisation nearly two decades before Miles Davis, with his piece *Ko-Ko*, which was first recorded in 1940. In truth, however, Davis keeps his reputation. *Ko-Ko* is inventively harmonised, to be sure, but its chord changes are clear. The music does not float on top of one chord: it is a blues.

Milestones was the first jazz performance to eschew chord changes, but it was not the first music to be constructed in this way. In 1950, Muddy Waters recorded a blues, *Rollin' Stone*, which also refused to move away from its root chord (at least until he came to interpolate a one verse instrumental break). A fledgling rock group was later impressed enough by this song to name itself after it. Waters repeated the experiment the next year with *Still A Fool* and again four years after that with a song that became his theme tune, *Mannish Boy*. These tracks are the blueprint for the Jimi Hendrix song, *Hear My Train A-Comin'*, that he recorded several times without ever producing a version he liked, although he frequently performed it live.

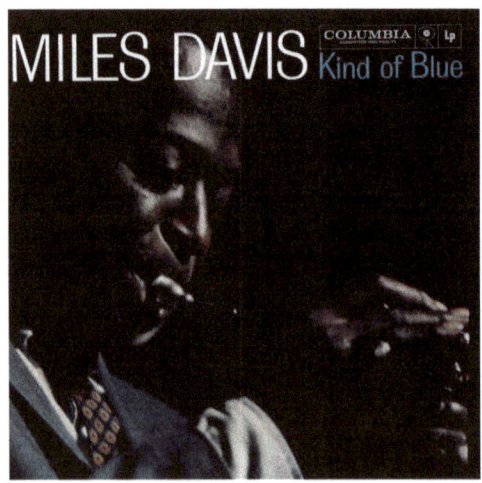

A revealing direct comparison can be made between Jimi Hendrix playing a free version of *Star Spangled Banner* at Woodstock in 1969 and late John Coltrane pieces like *Jupiter* and *Offering*, recorded in 1967. Or the astonishing version of *Leo* played at Newport in July 1966, with Coltrane and his disciple Pharoah Sanders both in particularly fine form. The overall approach of the music and the emotionally charged playing of the star soloists, for all that one is a guitarist and the others are saxophonists, is near identical.

proceeded to record some of the most highly regarded music in the hard bop genre. Keen to take advantage of a lucrative contract offer from Columbia, but still owing Prestige records four albums, Davis simply took his band into the studio on two occasions in 1956, May 11th and October 26th, and played through their entire stage repertoire. As a result, the four albums produced, *Cookin'*, *Relaxin'*, *Workin'*, and *Steamin'*, served as a textbook demonstration of how modern jazz in the mid fifties should be played.

Although the innovations and techniques of bebop have underscored the majority of jazz played since, three different new approaches were tried as a way of moving beyond hard bop. In 1957, composer Gunther Schuller came up with the term 'third stream jazz' as a description of music that tried to combine the techniques of jazz and classical music. His own piece, *Transformation*, issued on an album the same year, alongside similar pieces by George Russell and Charles Mingus (*Modern Jazz Concert*), was designed to demonstrate exactly what he meant. A few classical composers had shown an interest in jazz since the earliest days of the music. Darius Milhaud was the first – his ballet *La Creation Du Monde*, which included some of the sound of jazz if no actual improvisation, was completed in 1923 (clearly a milestone year). George Gershwin, who was a man with his feet in both musical camps, presented his jazz-influenced work, *Rhapsody In Blue*, to Paul Whiteman, who performed it in 1924. Jazz pianist James P Johnson (who invented the Charleston in his 1923 Broadway production, *Runnin' Wild*) and clarinettist/band-leader Artie Shaw both composed jazz-inspired works during the thirties; Igor Stravinsky's *Ebony Concerto* was first performed by Woody Herman in 1945. Extended versions of four of Duke Ellington's pieces were recorded in December 1950 and issued on LP as *Masterpieces* – these were true jazz in that they incorporated improvisation, but had a compositional depth that was new and comparable to classical music. The next year, Stan Kenton recorded *City Of Glass*, composed by Bob Graettinger. The music only very occasionally uses jazz rhythms and sounds generally quite close to the work of someone like Olivier Messiaen. This gives it a distinctly avant garde edge, some years before the term could be applied to anything else played by a jazz band, and prevented the music from being at all influential at the time. Today, it is possible to see the music as an important predecessor to the work of Gunther Schuller. In October 1956, two pieces were recorded by Miles Davis in collaboration with Schuller and issued on an album called *Facets*. They were *Three Little Feelings*, composed by pianist John Lewis, and *Jazz Suite For Brass*, composed by trombonist J.J.Johnson – both men having been involved in Davis' *Birth Of The Cool*. This is essentially where Schuller's third stream jazz begins.

Modern jazz improvisation, as defined by Charlie Parker, involved constructing spontaneous new melodies over the chord pattern set by a written piece of music. On an LP issued in 1958, Miles Davis tried something new. With considerable sleight of hand, or whatever other body parts were involved, Davis managed for the title track, *Milestones*, to create a piece with a highly memorable, melodic theme, that sounds as though it is being propelled forwards by a series of striking chord changes, but which is actually rooted throughout to one A minor chord. The technique was extended on the next LP, *Kind Of Blue*, so that every track required the soloists to improvise over a single chord, if not for the whole piece, then certainly for long periods. It has come to be known as modal improvisation, after the fearsomely intellectual analysis of chromatic scales, or modes, published by George Russell in 1953 as *The Lydian Chromatic Concept of Tonal Organization*. It is doubtful, however, whether the many musicians who followed Davis's lead were particularly aware of Russell's theories. They did not care whether they were adopting a Lydian mode, a Dorian mode, a Mixolydian mode, or something else entirely. The whole point of improvising over one chord rather than being forced to follow a more or less complicated series of chords was the freedom this gave to the soloist to construct whatever melodic lines occurred to him at the time. It was for this reason that the approach was adopted by Miles Davis for the whole of the rest of his career; by his saxophonist John Coltrane for the whole of his, delighting in creating ever longer solo flights in his music through the sixties, and by the huge number of other musicians who took Davis and Coltrane as their primary influence. When rock performers like Cream and Jimi Hendrix started to include improvisation in their playing, this too was usually carried out over a single chord underlay.

Kind Of Blue, issued in 1959, has become one of the best known and most highly regarded of all modern jazz LPs. Selling steadily over the years, it was awarded a quadruple platinum disc in 2008, corresponding to American

THE FIRST TIME

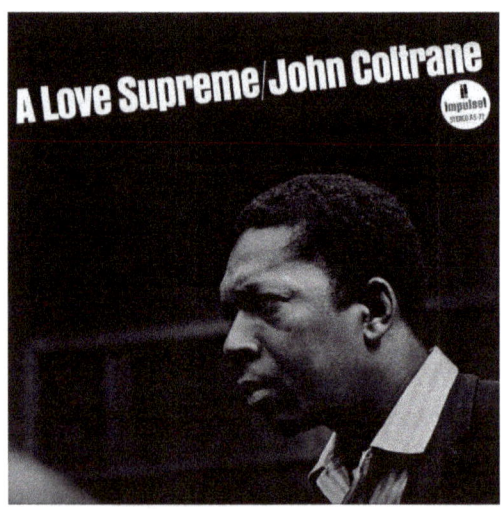

The British obsession with traditional jazz extended back to the late forties and the recordings of trumpeter Ken Colyer, whose band later included Chris Barber as a member. Barber's subsequent role in the creation of skiffle and the elevation of Lonnie Donegan to stardom is covered in the Rock 'n' Roll chapter of this book. Barber is an interesting performer, always as much attracted to the blues as to trad. He added an electric guitarist, John Slaughter, to his own band in 1964 and his album from the next year, *Good Mornin' Blues*, is a fascinating jazz response to the success of blues inspired beat groups such as the Rolling Stones. By the end of the decade and into the seventies he was making adventurous jazz fusion albums like *Battersea Rain Dance* and *Drat That Fratle Rat*, and his live audiences seemed happy to hear this kind of material mixed in with the trad, especially since he always managed to find room in his band for a banjo player. The first British jazz hits were *Experiments With Mice* by Johnny Dankworth and *Bad Penny Blues* by trumpeter Humphrey Lyttelton, in 1956, neither of which were exactly trad.

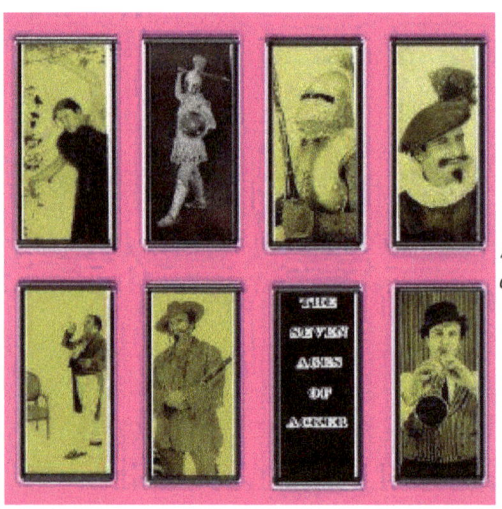

Acker Bilk's top ten album from 1960

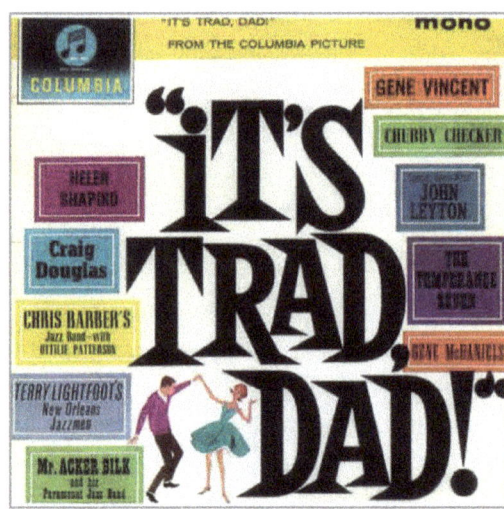

The early careers of some of the jazz-rock musicians tell their own story. Saxophonist Dick Heckstall-Smith made his first recordings with Sandy Brown in 1956, playing trad jazz and blues. From there he moved to Alexis Korner, then Graham Bond and John Mayall, before ending up as a founder member of Jon Hiseman's Colosseum. Drummer Jon Hiseman himself played jazz with Mike Taylor, Howard Riley, and Neil Ardley, blues-rock with the Wes Minster Five, Graham Bond, and John Mayall, as well as completing a session for the Crazy World of Arthur Brown (the hit single *Fire* and its B-side). Bass player Jack Bruce played with Korner, Bond, and Mayall – then Manfred Mann (recording jazz versions of some rock tunes for the EP *Instrumental Asylum*), Cream, and the Tony Williams Lifetime, before running a series of bands of his own. Ginger Baker played with Terry Lightfoot and Acker Bilk, then Alexis Korner and Graham Bond, before co-founding Cream and Blind Faith. Saxophonist Elton Dean played with Long John Baldry's Bluesology (a spin-off from Alexis Korner's band) before joining the Keith Tippett Group and Soft Machine. The pianist with Bluesology, Reggie Dwight, was inspired to take Dean's first name for his own professional name change, coupling it with Baldry's first name. Elton John. Trumpeter Henry Lowther managed to maintain a career in both areas simultaneously, working with Manfred Mann, John Mayall, and Keef Hartley on the one hand, but with Mike Westbrook, Graham Collier, John Dankworth, and many more on the other. Graham Bond himself started off as an alto saxophone player with Don Rendell, then Alexis Korner, before switching to organ and vocals for his own group, playing jazz at first, then pop and rhythm and blues.

During its live performances, Cream used some of its studio recordings as the basis for extended improvisation by the whole band. In a 2000 interview with Barbara Thompson for the BBC (quoted in *A New History of Jazz* by Alyn Shipton), Jack Bruce said "I think you could easily argue that Cream was a jazz band with Eric [Clapton] being Ornette Coleman without knowing it."

sales of four million copies. When a British publisher decided in 2016 to take advantage of a perceived rise of interest in vinyl by issuing a series of records attached to a magazine, for sale in newsagents, it chose to make *Kind Of Blue* the first release. John Coltrane's own *A Love Supreme*, from 1965, follows only a little behind in terms of influence and affection. As a demonstration of the emotional power that modal improvisation makes possible, it is perfect.

Both of these albums are fairly accessible and easy to like. Arguably, the same is not true of the music of alto saxophonist Ornette Coleman. In 1961, Coleman issued an LP called *Free Jazz*, which comprised a single group improvisation by two piano-less quartets playing together, with no theme, no particular key, and only a brief written passage of discordant horn playing to set the music in motion. The music charges along magnificently, driven by two drummers, and is quite gloriously cathartic, although nothing in the way of a conventional melody emerges at any time. Far more revolutionary than the experiments of Miles Davis and John Coltrane up to that point, *Free Jazz* could not match their sales, but proved to be just as influential. Its name was appropriated to describe an entire new genre of improvised music. John Coltrane, for one, was happy to combine the atonality of Ornette Coleman's music within his own explorations. Furious mid-sixties albums like *Meditations*, *Ascension*, and *Kulu Se Mama* are uncompromising and not at all the kind of music one could describe as tuneful (although it definitely has other qualities!)

At the time these various jazz experiments were being carried out, jazz in the UK was centred around something rather different. The chart success of a Chris Barber track, *Petite Fleur*, which reached number three in April 1959, ushered in a period of about five years when traditional jazz – or trad jazz as it was more often called – acquired the status of an alternative pop music. The 1962 film, *It's Trad Dad*, starring Helen Shapiro and Craig Douglas, presented a number of trad jazz bands as being the epitome of early sixties cool. It was retitled *Ring-a-ding Rhythm* in the US, where trad jazz was not popular, although the bands were still there in the film. These players took the old King Oliver band as their model, favouring a collective approach to improvisation, in which trumpet, trombone, and clarinet would decorate and elaborate a theme, all at the same time. This was in contrast to the way modern jazz performers operated, with soloists taking turns to make their statements (some free jazz groups excepted). The most successful trad jazz band was the one led by trumpeter Kenny Ball, who achieved four top ten hits during 1961 to 1963, with some unlikely material chosen to be given a trad refit. This included a tune from the musical *The King And I* (*March Of The Siamese Children*) and an interlude from the John Wayne film *The Alamo* (*The Green Leaves Of Summer*). The biggest hit of all was by Acker Bilk, the clarinet playing leader of the Paramount Jazz Band, whose intensely melodic *Stranger On The Shore* was accompanied by orchestral strings and was scarcely jazz at all, yet became the chart sensation of 1962. It reached number one on both sides of the Atlantic, the first number one hit in America by a British artist.

With the growing credibility of rock during the sixties as a music to be taken seriously, it was inevitable that the two genres would begin to influence each other. In the UK, for jazz musicians who did not particularly want to play trad, the market for their music was tiny. Session or film-score work was available for some (Ronnie Scott, John Dankworth), but many of the young jazzmen playing in the sixties preferred to find work playing with blues or beat groups. Eventually, these musicians became key players in the more jazz-oriented of the new progressive rock bands – such as Colosseum, If, the Keef Hartley Band, and Soft Machine. Tracks like *Those About To Die* on Colosseum's first LP from 1968, or *Hibou Anemone And Bear* from Soft Machine's 1969 LP *Volume Two*, or *Konekuf* from the 1969 LP by Manfred Mann Chapter III were labelled 'jazz-rock' and are a true hybrid, with jazz-like themes and improvised saxophone solos, but more robust rhythms than jazz was hitherto accustomed to. The origins of this hybrid go back to the pioneering work of the blues bands – Alexis Korner's Blues Incorporated, the Graham Bond Organisation, and John Mayall's Bluesbreakers – all of which included improvised solos and were the bands where many of the progressive jazz-rock musicians first played. Much of the music on Alexis Korner's 1964 album *Red Hot From Alex* or the 1963 recordings included on Graham Bond's *Solid Bond* is far closer to the hard bop jazz of people like Charles Mingus or Art Blakey than it is to the Beatles or the Rolling Stones.

In America, where the market for jazz was much bigger, there was little tendency for jazz players to join rock bands, although saxophonist David Sanborn and drummer Philip Wilson (subsequently a founder member of the Art

THE FIRST TIME

The appearance in 1969 of one of the finest jazz-rock albums of all, Frank Zappa's *Hot Rats,* came as a surprise to all those who had become convinced that Zappa's music was no more than a comical sideshow to meaningful progress within rock music. The clues to Zappa's interest in the blending of improvised and composed musics were, however, very numerous within the various records issued under the Mothers of Invention name. Subsequently, the approach became the defining characteristic of Frank Zappa's music, even if his genius has only become more widely appreciated since he became an untimely victim of cancer in 1993.

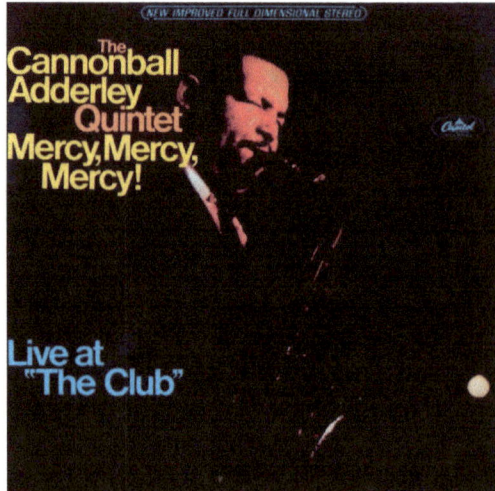

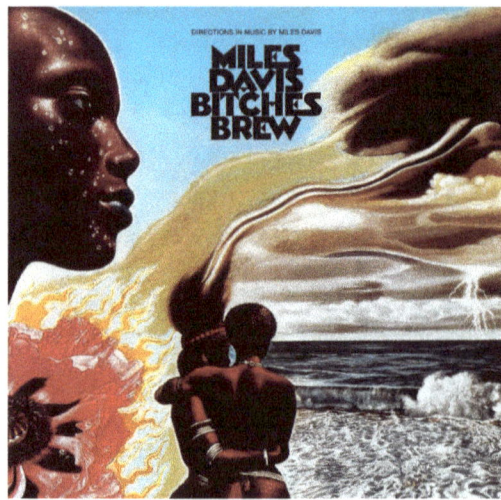

It is worth noting that Miles Davis' influences at this time were not necessarily found within the highest profile rock groups. In the summer of 1970, he was invited to jam along with the likes of Eric Clapton and Jack Bruce at a New York rock festival. He declined, saying "I don't want to be a white man. Rock is a white man's word". When explaining to his drummer, Jack DeJohnette, how he wanted the rhythms to sound on *Live-Evil,* he referred to Buddy Miles' work with the Jimi Hendrix Band Of Gypsys. As quoted in the sleeve notes to the CD set *The Cellar Door Sessions* (which comprised the complete live performances that were edited for *Live-Evil*), DeJohnette said, "I get it, you want a Buddy feel with my technique". Miles smiled and replied, "Yeah, that's it". Michael Henderson, who was now employed as Davis' bass guitarist, had previously worked with Aretha Franklin and Stevie Wonder – soul performers. One of the key pieces on *Live-Evil, What I Say,* took both its title and its inspiration from Ray Charles.

Guitarist John McLaughlin and bass player Dave Holland, both of whom played on *Bitches Brew* and other Miles Davis records, were from the UK. British trumpeter Ian Carr formed his own jazz fusion band, Nucleus, and issued its first album, *Elastic Rock,* in 1970. Acclaimed performances at the Montreux and Newport jazz festivals served to make the point that British jazz musicians had long ago put trad behind them and were capable of making as vital a contribution to jazz as the Americans. Meanwhile, a new specialist jazz label, ECM, was started in Germany in 1969 at exactly the right moment to take advantage of the expanded market for jazz created by jazz fusion. The label chose to feature a rather wider range of music than this, although by the mid-seventies people were referring to ECM music as though it was a genre in its own right. Certainly by then, the label did seem to favour jazz that relied on subtleties of timbre and texture, with a high proportion of composed material, although none of it would ever have been likely to see the light of day had it not been for the music of Miles Davis and Weather Report acting as foundation.

Ensemble of Chicago) did play with the Butterfield Blues Band for a while and some of the members of Blood Sweat and Tears were people with jazz backgrounds. These bands were described as jazz-rock, the same as their British counterparts. Meanwhile, trumpeter Don Ellis and saxophonist Charles Lloyd were interested enough in the rock music world to imagine they could attract some of its audience by playing at venues like the Fillmore. They did not attempt, however, to add actual rock elements to their sound, unless the inclusion of electric piano in Ellis's band, and the addition of electronic effects to the leader's own trumpet are counted. Don Ellis was certainly happy to have the Blood Sweat and Tears founder, Al Kooper, as the producer for his 1968 album *Autumn*.

Alto saxophonist Cannonball Adderley, who had been a member of the Miles Davis *Kind Of Blue* band, played a gritty version of hard bop, after becoming a band leader himself, music that became known as 'soul jazz'. On pieces like the live *Sack O' Woe* and *Mercy Mercy Mercy* from 1966, the straight-ahead rhythms made a comparison with soul music an easy one to agree. The same feel – or even a more soulful one – was achieved by pianist Ramsey Lewis on mid-sixties tracks like *The In Crowd* (a version of an actual soul song) and *Wade In The Water* (with drummer Maurice White, who later formed the successful funk band Earth Wind And Fire). Flautist Herbie Mann produced more of the same on his 1969 collection of jazz versions of soul songs, *Memphis Underground,* and was rewarded with huge sales.

In May 1968, Miles Davis recorded a long track called *Stuff* (included as part of his album *Miles In The Sky*). This was driven by a particularly compelling soul groove, with bass player Ron Carter and pianist Herbie Hancock adding to is effectiveness by using electric instruments. This marked a considerable departure for Miles Davis, if not for jazz as a whole. During the course of the next albums, it became apparent that Davis was gradually feeling his way forward to a new jazz approach. This became gloriously realised on the double album *Bitches Brew*, recorded in August 1969 and released the following March. The music was played by a considerably larger group than Davis' working quintet or even the eight musicians employed on the preceding album, *In A Silent Way*. All the additions were there to add weight and texture to the rhythm section. There were two drummers, two percussionists, two bass players (one a double bass, the other electric), a guitarist (whose role was primarily to play rhythm), two or three electric keyboard players, and a bass clarinet – even this instrument being there for the most part to add riff fragments to the rhythm. Miles Davis himself and Wayne Shorter (using just a soprano saxophone to cut through the dense backing) were the main soloists. Electronic echo was applied to the trumpet in places (and to the keyboards too on the quadraphonic version of the album) and the music was to some extent assembled after recording, through editing and splicing the master tapes, although to be fair, this had been done on several of Davis' previous records too, if less extensively than here. Davis and his producer, Teo Macero, would have argued that making a record is not the same as delivering a live performance, even if this attitude would have run counter to the opinions of many jazz listeners at this time.

There are critics who, nearly half a century after the release of *Bitches Brew*, still maintain that the record proved Miles Davis to be selling out, cynically making music for the sake of money rather than art. A typical example is Bill Cole, the author of *Miles Davis: A Musical Biography*. Curiously, such critics do not seem to direct the same accusations at Herbie Mann, whose *Memphis Underground* has far more of an air of the commercial about it, even with guitarist Sonny Sharrock unleashing one of his characteristic noise-blast solos during the proceedings. Perhaps, however, Mann did not have the weight of expectation heaped on him that Miles Davis seemed to. In truth, there is no resemblance at all between *Bitches Brew* and the two most popular albums of its time, Simon and Garfunkel's *Bridge Over Troubled Water* and the Beatles' *Abbey Road*. If Miles Davis was really trying to capture the market of those artists, he was perhaps not going about it in the right way. For all the emphasis on rhythmic groove that *Bitches Brew* has, it does not sound like a rock music album.

Despite this, however, there is certainly enough in Miles Davis' new music to attract the people who were enjoying the music of the jazz-rock bands. It is, after all, a jazz aesthetic that provides a link between Blood Sweat and Tears, Soft Machine, and *Bitches Brew*, although each of these sounds otherwise quite distinct. Arguably, tracks like *Blues – Part II* (Blood Sweat and Tears) or *Slightly All The Time* (Soft Machine) do not sound like rock music either, if the music of the Beatles or the Rolling Stones is taken as the template.

THE FIRST TIME

The reference to John Coltrane is a good one for fusion in general, but it is reasonable in the case of John McLaughlin's Mahavishnu Orchestra to draw a parallel too with the music of Charlie Parker and Dizzy Gillespie, Both favour the quintet format, though McLaughlin's replaces the saxophone and trumpet with electric guitar and electric violin. Both rely on virtuoso instrumental technique – and like to apply this ability to playing themes that are fast and twisting and difficult to play. Herbie Hancock and Weather Report made much greater use of composed material, although John McLaughlin later followed this path as well for his second Mahavishnu Orchestra line-up and the 1974 album, *Apocalypse*.

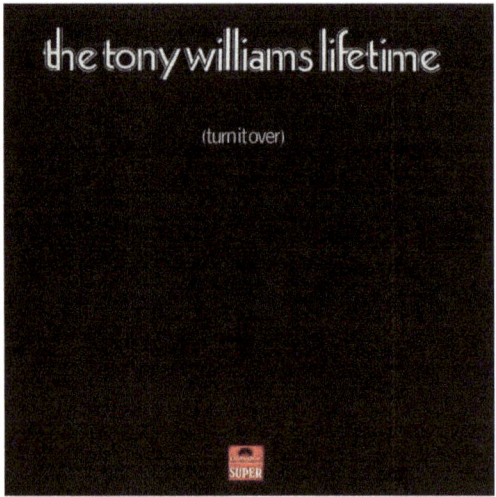 

The names adopted by these fusion bands are as new to jazz as the music they are playing. These are the kinds of name one would expect to see being chosen by rock groups – a year or two previously they would have been the Tony Williams Quartet and the Wayne Shorter – Joe Zawinul Quintet.

Jazz-rock and jazz fusion come together on the 1975 album by Jeff Beck, *Blow By Blow*. The music is entirely instrumental, with electric piano, bass, and drums laying down funk rhythms in support of Beck's fluent electric guitar. An uncredited Stevie Wonder adds his characteristic clavinet sound to one track and producer George Martin adds strings to a couple of others, in a third stream touch reminiscent of his production for John McLaughlin's *Apocalypse* album. It is impossible to say with any conviction whether *Blow By Blow* is a rock album or a jazz album.

While not exactly constituting a genre of jazz, it is very noticeable how, during the last several years, a number of inventive piano trios have attracted much attention. This may have something to do with the fact that in financially constrained times it is easier for a group of just three players to make a living than for anything larger. Medeski Martin and Wood (who first recorded in 1992), E.S.T. (1993), the Brad Mehldau Trio (1996), the Bad Plus (2001), and Go Go Penguin (2012) are amongst the most notable trios.

Meanwhile, Miles Davis moved on. Giving guitarist John McLaughlin a more dominant role (in which he responded by turning up his distortion level) and tightening the rhythms, Davis made albums – *Jack Johnson* and *Live-Evil* (both recorded in 1970 and released in 1971) – which blurred the musical divide even further. Many of the musicians who had played on *Bitches Brew* formed bands of their own, with the result that several other important albums were released in 1970 and 1971. *Turn It Over* by the Tony Williams Lifetime (including John Mclaughlin), McLaughlin's own *Inner Mounting Flame* (credited to the Mahavishnu Orchestra), Herbie Hancock's *Mwandishi*, Joe Zawinul's *Zawinul*, and the self-titled first album by Weather Report (Zawinul's collaboration with Wayne Shorter) presented various aspects of a genre that was being called, since the term jazz-rock was already taken, jazz fusion. For the most part, the solo improvisation that was carried out within fusion was the modal playing familiar to followers of John Coltrane, but the context within which this was done, the harder soul or rock rhythms, an emphasis on variety of timbre, and the widespread use of electric instruments, was new.

The invention of jazz funk (a fusion sub-genre) by Miles Davis and Herbie Hancock during 1972 to 1973 is described in the funk chapter of this book. In 1977, Ornette Coleman presented his own version of jazz fusion on an album called *Dancing In Your Head*. He fronted a band with the same guitars, bass, and drums line-up as a typical rock group. But they played rather differently, apparently all constructing their own busy lines independently, yet somehow managing to slot together. Coleman rode over the top, using his familiar shrill alto saxophone sound to deliver music that has some similarity to the avant garde rock played a few years previously by Captain Beefheart on his album *Trout Mask Replica*. Coleman explored the style further during several subsequent albums and it proved to be a great influence on other musicians working at the interface between free jazz and fusion, some of whom, like Ronald Shannon Jackson, James Blood Ulmer, and Jamaaladeen Tacuma, had worked with Ornette Coleman themselves.

Since then, jazz has largely ceased its forward momentum, its evolution of style after style. Instead, jazz musicians have been content to further explore the various aspects of modern jazz developed in earlier years. Certainly there have been individual innovators. Last Exit was a surprising alliance between two free jazz players with a liking for white noise (saxophonist Peter Brotzmann and guitarist Sonny Sharrock), drummer Ronald Shannon Jackson (who had played on *Dancing In Your Head*), and a bass player producer famous for mixing dance and world musics and reggae, Bill Laswell. The group managed to be every bit as exhilarating as such a musical meeting could have been expected to be, combining particularly ferocious free jazz with driving rhythms, played in time, to create a kind of jazz fusion that is altogether more anarchic than any of the seventies versions. The first, self-titled album was issued in 1986. Miles Davis, still musically restless only months before his death, worked with producer Easy Mo Bee to create a blend of jazz with hip-hop – issued in 1991 on the album *Doo Bop*. Saxophonist Steve Lehman produced a form of jazz he called spectral music, using the minimalist sounds and techniques developed by the composers Steve Reich and Philip Glass as a basis for improvisation. The apex of the approach is the album *Travail Transformation And Flow*, issued in 2009. Although each of these innovations has spawned a handful of like-minded enthusiasts, none has succeeded in galvanising the entire jazz world. They have remained as interesting, but essentially idiosyncratic journeys.

The brief history of jazz firsts that is presented in this chapter makes it very clear that the name of one man emerges as the towering innovator within modern jazz – that of Miles Davis. There is an appropriate quote from him a few pages back, to which could be added the following:

"I'm always thinking about creating. My future starts when I wake up in the morning and see the light. Then I'm grateful."
"Always look ahead, but never look back."
"*So What* or *Kind Of Blue* were done in that era, the right hour, the right day. It's over; it's on the record."
"You know why I quit playing ballads? Cause I love playing ballads."
"You should never be comfortable, man. Being comfortable fouled up a lot of musicians."
"See, if you put a musician in a place where he has to do something different from what he does all the time, then he can do that – but he's got to think differently in order to do it. He's got to play above what he knows – far above it. I've always told the musicians in my band to play what they know and then play above that. Because then anything can happen, and that's where great art and music happens."
"Jazz is the big brother of Revolution. Revolution follows it around."

THE FIRST TIME

TRACKING THE TRACKS

There are several compilations of music by the Original Dixieland Jazz Band available, of which the best value is the double CD *The Essential Collection* (West End 2006). There is perhaps rather more here than many people would wish to hear in one go – for them, both sides of the band's first 78 rpm recording can be heard on YouTube. The Collins and Harlan song can be heard in the same place, along with several recordings from the twenties by Freddie Keppard, who decided too late that making them was, after all, a good idea. His complete works are on a CD called *The Complete Set 1923-1926* (Challenge 2005).

Jelly Roll Morton also has several compilation CDs available. *The Essential Collection* (West End 2006) is a double CD that includes the track *Georgia Swing* and is probably, given Morton's greater significance generally within early jazz, not too much to hear in one go.

King Oliver (and Louis Armstrong) can be heard on a double CD, *The Complete Set* (Challenge 2014). The early recordings by Louis Armstrong with his own band are on *The Best Of Louis Armstrong – The Hot Five And Hot Seven Recordings* (Columbia Legacy 2002). The double CD *At His Very Best* (Universal 2003) provides a good overview of Armstrong's entire subsequent career, including the sixties hit singles.

Paul Whiteman can be sampled on *Greatest Hits* (BMG Collectors' Choice 1998), which includes *The Japanese Sandman* and *Whispering* and also a recording of *Rhapsody In Blue*, with George Gershwin on the piano. Bix Beiderbecke really needs a CD of his own. *The Beiderbecke Collection* (Hallmark 1997) is one of several compilations available. It includes *Cryin' All Day*, the track used as the soundtrack for the James Bolam/Barbara Flynn TV comedy drama series, *The Beiderbecke Affair.*

Duke Ellington needs several CDs to do his career justice. The four CD set, *Masterpieces 1926-1949* (Properbox 2001) covers most of the music that made Ellington great. *Ko-Ko* is included. The single CD, *Masterpieces by Ellington* presents extended versions of four of his compositions, recorded in 1950 (Columbia 2004). Beyond that, anything is worth trying, although the double CD *Complete At Newport* (Columbia 1999), documenting the band's acclaimed performance at the festival in 1956, *Black Brown And Beige*, recorded in 1958 with gospel singer Mahalia Jackson (Columbia 1999), *Such Sweet Thunder* (Columbia 1999), a music suite recorded in 1957 and inspired by Shakespeare, and *New Orleans Suite*, recorded in 1970 and acting as a kind of musical autobiography (Atlantic 2003) are particularly recommended.

Count Basie is well served by the compilation CD, *The Classic Tracks* (Kaz 1996). A live recording, *At The Savoy Ballroom 1937*, provides a wonderful piece of period flavour (and includes some singing by Billie Holiday) (Grammercy 2003). Lester Young needs at least one CD of his own – such as the *Ken Burns Jazz* compilation (Verve 2000), which also has some singing by Billie Holiday. Coleman Hawkins can be sampled on *Body And Soul – Original Recordings 1933-49* (Naxos 2001).

Benny Goodman has a double CD compilation, *Swing! Swing! Swing! – His 48 Finest 1934-1945* (Nimbus 2009). His 1938 Carnegie Hall concert is also available on a double CD (Jasmine 2006).

Jam sessions featuring Charlie Christian and others are on *Live Sessions At Minton's Playhouse* (Jazz Anthology 1989). Dizzy Gillespie's 1945 recordings are on *Shaw 'Nuff* (Musicraft 1992). The essential Charlie Parker recordings can be found on a pair of double CD sets, *The Complete Savoy Masters* and *The Complete Dial Masters* (both Essential Jazz Classics 2015).

As regards Miles Davis, the vital recordings are as follows:

The Complete Birth Of The Cool (Capitol 1998) – the live and the studio recordings.

Volume 1 and *Volume 2* (Blue Note 2001) compile recordings from 1952-4, when Miles had fallen out of the public eye but was still producing some good material. The 4 CD set, *The Legendary Prestige Quintet Sessions*, includes all the material recorded for the *Cookin'*, *Relaxin'*, *Workin'*, and *Steamin'* LPs.

The recordings with Gunther Schuller are included on *Music For Brass – The 1957 Columbia Third Stream Recordings* (Soundmark 2010).

Sketches Of Spain can be found on a 1997 Columbia CD, but two other albums made slightly earlier with Gil Evans demand to be heard as well – *Miles Ahead* and *Porgy And Bess*. These are on 1997 Columbia CDs too.

Milestones is on a Sony CD (2013).

Kind Of Blue is also on a Sony CD (2009), complete with an alternate take.

My Funny Valentine (Sony 2009), a live recording from 1964, includes one track from *Kind Of Blue* and four standards, but these are so stretched out as to effectively become vehicles for modal improvisation. The album also introduces the new, young rhythm section of Herbie Hancock, Ron Carter, and Tony Williams, who were to prove themselves vital in the development that led to *Bitches Brew*. The studio albums made by this group, with Wayne Shorter on tenor saxophone, are some of the finest recordings from the sixties. *ESP, Miles*

MUSIC GENRES

Smiles, Sorcerer, Nefertiti, and *Miles In The Sky* (all Columbia 1998) contain music that is modal bordering on free jazz, but with an emphasis on melody that was seldom free jazz's concern. *Miles In The Sky* includes *Stuff* and one other track, *Paraphernalia*, that has more of a rhythmic groove than jazz was used to, with guest guitarist George Benson playing a vital role. The title track on the previous LP is another rhythm experiment – here it is the drums that improvise throughout, while the horns merely repeat the theme. *Filles De Kilimanjaro* (Columbia 2002) further explores the implications of adding electric instruments to the group, being the work of two different line-ups, as Hancock and Carter were replaced by Chick Corea and Dave Holland. A 6 CD boxed set, *Miles Davis Quintet 1965-68* (Columbia 2004) collects these albums together, along with numerous out-takes.

In A Silent Way (Columbia 2010) added more musicians. There were now three keyboard players, all using electric instruments (Chick Corea, Herbie Hancock, and Cannonball Adderley's pianist, Joe Zawinul), and an electric guitarist, John McLaughlin, instructed for the title track to play as if the guitar was new to him! The groove quota was increased further and much of the music was now based on repeated riffs, despite which, the music managed to retain a considerable ambient feel. A 3 CD set, *The Complete In A Silent Way Sessions*, includes the original tracks that were edited to produce the finished album, alongside numerous out-takes and the two *Filles De Kilimanjaro* tracks that featured Corea and Holland.

Bitches Brew is available in four different forms. A double CD (Columbia 1999) comprises the original double LP plus one later out-take. The fortieth anniversary legacy edition has the original album, together with four tracks surprisingly issued on singles and two alternate takes, but not the previously included out-take. A third CD presents a live set recorded a year afterwards, while a DVD shows a different live set from just three months later. A four CD set, *The Complete Bitches Brew Sessions* (Columbia 1998) adds several tracks recorded a little after the album, two of which had been included on a double LP called *Big Fun*. Annoyingly, the alternate takes included on the legacy edition are not to be found here. A quadraphonic version of the album, with mixes that sound noticeably different in places, was issued on vinyl in 1971, but has not been reissued on CD.

Jack Johnson is on a Sony CD (2005). A five CD set, *The Complete Jack Johnson Sessions*, includes out-takes, one of which is another track from *Big Fun*, and longer versions of pieces that were edited for the original LP.

Big Fun, originally a double LP with four long tracks recorded in 1969, 1970, and 1972, is an essential item for those not choosing to invest in the various 'complete sessions' sets – it is available as a double CD (Columbia 2000) which also includes four of the out-takes from the *Bitches Brew* set.

Live-Evil comprises mostly live recordings from late 1970 and is on a double CD (Columbia 1997). A six CD set, *The Cellar Door Sessions 1970*, has the complete live concerts from which the *Live-Evil* music was taken. Everything selected includes the playing of John McLaughlin, although for most of the Cellar Door music he is not present.

On The Corner, where Miles Davis invented jazz-funk, has also been issued as a six CD box set, *The Complete On The Corner Sessions* (Columbia/Sony 2007). This includes out-takes and extended recordings as they were before being edited for album release, alongside music in a similar style that was originally issued on the albums *Big Fun* and *Get Up With It* (first released in 1974). The original *On The Corner* album is included too, or it can be obtained as a separate single CD (Columbia 2000).

Two live albums, taken from two sets Miles Davis played in Osaka, Japan on the same day in February 1975 represent the pinnacle of his improvised funk style and are high points of jazz fusion generally, even if they provide a far less comfortable listening experience than the majority of the genre. *Agharta* and *Pangaea* are available as double CDs (Columbia 1994).

Following a six year break from performing, Miles Davis' eighties music is less remarkable, with a jazz fusion style that has moved back from the cutting edge. *Tutu*, a collaboration with Marcus Miller, is a blend of jazz with eighties R & B that has its moments. It was issued in 1986 by Warner Bros. *Doo Bop*, Miles Davis' last studio recording, was issued by Warner Bros in 1992.

There are many more recordings available by this remarkable musician, including a large number of live recordings – a number that is continually increasing as more tapes are discovered. One more should be added to this list – the four CD set *Miles Davis At Newport 1955-1975* (Columbia 2015), which includes the acclaimed 1955 performance that re-started his career and otherwise provides a concise demonstration of the way Miles Davis' music changed over the years.

Modern Jazz Performances Of Songs From My Fair Lady by Shelly Manne and his Friends is on Contemporary (2000).

The Best Of The Gerry Mulligan Quartet With Chet Baker is on a Capitol CD (1991). He does not do any singing here, but he does on some of the tracks on his own album, *My Funny Valentine* (Capitol 1994), made soon after leaving the Mulligan group.

Modern Jazz Concert (Stardust 2013), credited to Gunther Schuller and George Russell, includes Schuller's *Transformation*.

La Creation Du Monde is included on a Naxos CD (2005) along with three other works by Milhaud that do not have a jazz influence. Six of James P Johnson's compositions (one of which is *Charleston*) can be found on the CD *Victory Stride* (Nimbus 2011). *The Artie Shaw Collection 1932-54* (Fabulous 2014) is a double CD containing *Interlude In B Flat* and *Concerto For Clarinet*, together with some more

conventional big band tracks. A Phillips CD (1990) has Woody Herman and his Orchestra playing the *Ebony Concerto*, alongside the London Symphony Orchestra playing two other works by Stravinsky with no jazz content. *City Of Glass* is included on a CD with the same title (Capitol 1995) with other music composed by Bob Graettinger and recorded by Stan Kenton.

Much of the music of John Lewis's Modern Jazz Quartet has a chamber music flavour, but the albums *Third Stream Music* and *The Modern Jazz Quartet And Orchestra* (Atlantic 2013 and 2014), both issued in 1960 and both including a work by Gunther Schuller fall entirely within the third stream jazz category. *Blood On The Floor* by Mark-Anthony Turnage is on an Argo CD (1997)

John Coltrane has many more essential albums than just the ones mentioned. In order of recording, these would be *Giant Steps* (1960), *My Favourite Things* and *Africa-Brass* (1961), *Live At The Village Vanguard* (1962), *Impressions* (1963), *Live At Birdland* (1964), *A Love Supreme* and *One Down One Up* (1965), *Ascension, Kulu Se Mama, Meditations, Live At The Village Vanguard Again,* and *Concert In Japan* (1966), and *Expression* (1967). All are on CDs issued between 1999 and 2011, the first two on Atlantic, the rest on Verve/Impulse. A lost studio session from 1963 was issued on Impulse in 2018 as *Both Directions At Once. A Love Supreme* is also available as a double CD deluxe edition, with the second disc containing a live performance of the entire suite, together with four alternate takes. *Offering* is included on *Expression; Jupiter* is on *Interstellar Space (Impulse 2000). Last Performance At Newport*, with *Leo* as the last of three long performances, is on Domino Jazz (2015). The Jimi Hendrix live interpretation of *Star Spangled Banner is on Live At Woodstock* (MCA 1999).

The Muddy Waters tracks mentioned are all on *His Best 1947-1955* (Chess/Universal 1999). The best version of *Hear My Train A-Comin'* is generally held to be the one that Jimi Hendrix performed at Berkeley Community Theatre in May 1970. It is included on the CD *Blues* (Polydor 1994), which also has a version of the song played on a twelve string acoustic guitar, together with group performances of the similarly structured *Catfish Blues* and *Voodoo Chile* Blues and an uptempo version of *Mannish Boy* that has little in common with the Muddy Waters original, except that it is still based on one chord.

Ornette Coleman's *Free Jazz* has gained an extra track with its transfer to CD (Atlantic 2002) – a shorter first version of the piece, which starts in the same way, but then proceeds differently. *Dancing In Your Head* (A&M 2000) has an extra track too, a second version of a meeting between Coleman and the Moroccan Master Musicians Of Joujouka, which already functioned as a bonus track on the original LP, due its different sound from the rest of the music.

As with John Coltrane, there are many other albums that need to be heard by anyone trying to appreciate the music of someone who very much qualifies as a master musician. Coleman made several LPs during the two years prior to *Free Jazz*, all of which have much in common with the bebop of Charlie Parker, albeit delivered with a slightly more wayward approach to tonality. The first was *Something Else* (Original Jazz Classics 2011). The following *Tomorrow Is The Question* (Original Jazz Classics 2003) and *The Shape Of Jazz To Come* (Atlantic 2005) are as remarkable.

The records made by Ornette Coleman in the sixties run with the principle established on *Free Jazz*, although as the different tracks vary considerably in mood, there must have been some kind of planning involved for each one. The two volumes of live recordings *At The Golden Circle Stockholm* (Capitol/Blue Note 2002) are the work of a trio, where every note or beat counts. *Chappaqua Suite* (Cherry Red 2012), commissioned for a film but not used, adds several other musicians to create density in places, but Coleman is the only soloist. *Love Call* (Universal/Blue Note 2014) adds a second saxophonist, Dewey Redman, and John Coltrane's rhythm section, although the result is nothing like Coltrane's music. It has an increased emphasis on melody, making it one of Coleman's most accessible albums of the period.

Skies Of America, which includes a theme subsequently used on *Dancing In Your Head*, is a third stream recording with an added orchestra, although it is a more avant garde version of the approach than anything since *City Of Glass*. Coleman has produced several fully composed, classical works over the years, but most are not easy to listen to. A nice story was quoted in the concert programme for Coleman's appearance in London in 1971, according to which he was at a party where his own composed music was being played on the sound system. Showing his prejudice, and not realising what exactly the music was, another guest (white) commented to Coleman that he supposed the saxophonist found such music hard to understand. Remarkably, Coleman did not own up.

The albums on which Ornette Coleman further explores his *Dancing In Your Head* music include *Of Human Feelings* from 1982 (Antilles 1997 – hard to find, but worth the trouble), *Tone Dialling* from 1995 (Verve), a 1986 collaboration with Pat Metheny, *Song X* (Nonesuch 2005), where the guitarist gives himself completely over to the saxophonist's style, which reverts more closely to what he had been doing in the sixties, and a 1988 album, *Virgin Beauty* (CBS) where, surprisingly enough, guitarist Jerry Garcia does the same.

A live album issued in 2006, *Sound Grammar* (on Coleman's own label, named after the album), manages to act as a concise summary of the saxophonist's entire career. It was awarded the prestigious Pulitzer Prize for Music in 2007.

Chris Barber's *Petite Fleur* is included on the CD *The Best Of Chris Barber* (Sanctuary 2008), which focuses on the trombonist's music from the fifties, when he was at his most traditional and most popular. *Good Mornin' Blues* is available as half of a double CD (BGO 1997) with the earlier *Blues Book Volume One*, which does not include guitarist John Slaughter. *Battersea Rain Dance* was originally issued on the Marmalade and Polydor labels, but has not made it to CD. *Drat That Fratle Rat* (originally on Black Lion records) is not on CD in its own right either, although its tracks are included on the 3 CD set, *The Outstanding Album* (Bell 1996), which also has some live recordings from the seventies.

The soundtrack to the film *It's Trad Dad* is on a Hallmark CD (2013) , which includes a little early sixties pop alongside the trad and, improbably, a performance by rock 'n' roller Gene Vincent. The film itself can be obtained on a US region 1 DVD, which uses the American title, of course.

Kenny Ball's *Greatest Hits* (Sanctuary 2008) means what it says; *The Very Best of Acker Bilk* (One Day Music 2015) squeezes fifty tracks into a double CD and includes *Stranger On The Shore*. For anyone wanting more after that lot, *The Seven Ages Of Acker* has been reissued on CD (Hallmark 2011), although a few of its tracks are on the compilation. *The Best Of Humphrey Lyttelton* (EMI 2002) includes *Bad Penny Blues*. *The Best Of Johnny Dankworth* is a two CD summary of the man's work in the fifties, and includes *Experiments With Mice*, although his later work is generally more ambitious. A double CD combining two early seventies albums, *Full Circle* and *Lifeline*, is as good a place to start as any and includes Dankworth's attractive theme for the *Tomorrow's World* television programme. Ronnie Scott's *Live At Ronnie Scott's* (Sony 2007), recorded in 1968, provides a good showcase for some other eminent British jazz players, as well as Scott himself, and is a reminder of the club that is an even greater legacy of the man than his own music. His best known session appearances are on the Beatles singles *Lady Madonna* and *All You Need Is Love*, both of which are on the CD *1* (EMI 2000).

Colosseum's first album is *Those About To Die Salute You* (Castle 1998). If's first album is *If* (Repertoire 2014). The Keef Hartley Band's is *Halfbreed* (Esoteric 2009). The first four albums by the band, all of which feature Miller Anderson on guitar and vocals, are seriously good – the fifth, a live recording of a bold attempt to create a jazz-rock big band, *Little Big Band* (there were sixteen musicians) has a flat recording quality that makes the music sound much less powerful than it must have been in the Marquee Club. It too is on an Esoteric CD (2009). Soft Machine's *Volume Two* is on a Universal/Polydor CD (2009), *Third* is on a Sony CD (1996). The group's first album is quirky rock music with little apparent jazz input; later albums flip their allegiance – no longer are they any kind of jazz-rock, instead they are unabashed jazz fusion and increasingly influenced by Weather Report.

Manfred Mann Chapter III was another jazz-rock big band, this time one without a guitarist. The music came as something of a surprise for those who had followed the careers of the previous two versions of Mann's group, which was known for playing a series of successful chart singles. The self titled first album is on Creature Music (2013). Actually, Mann and his colleagues had previously shown an interest in jazz as was evidenced by the EP *Instrumental Asylum* and other similar tracks, including a couple of covers of Cannonball Adderley pieces, that were gathered together on a 1967 album, *Soul Of Mann*. This has been reissued as an EMI CD (1999).

Alexis Korner's *Red Hot From Alex* was first reissued in 1969 as *Alexis Korner's All Stars – Blues Incorporated*. This was a bargain price record, so became the Korner album that casual fans were most likely to acquire. The CD is on Sanctuary (2001). Graham Bond's *Solid Bond* is on Sunrise (2004).

The Butterfield Blues Band line-up that included David Sanborn and Philip Wilson recorded the 1967/1968 albums *The Resurrection Of Pigboy Crabshaw* and *In My Own Dream* (issued together in 2004 as a double CD on Warner). The second, self-titled 1968 album by Blood Sweat and Tears, which includes *Blues – Part II*, is on a Columbia CD (2000). *Blues – Part I* can be found on the previous album, *Child Is Father To The Man* (Sony 2013), under the title *Somethin' Goin' On*. This is an interesting LP, if a little less jazzy than its successor. Al Kooper is in charge here – he was effectively fired from his own band after this.

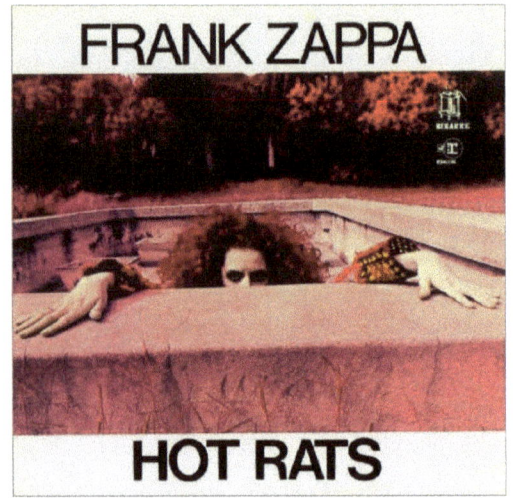

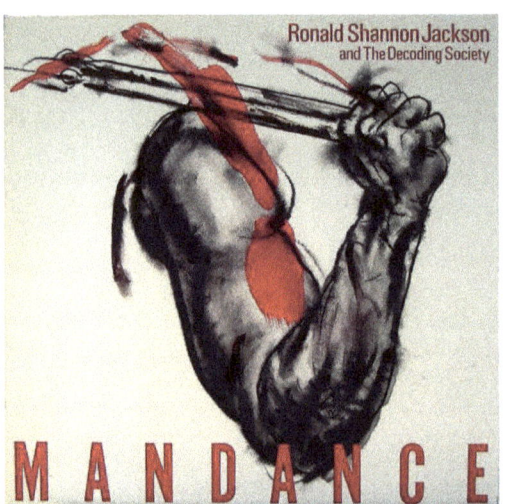

MUSIC GENRES

Frank Zappa's *Hot Rats* is on Zappa Records (2012). *Autumn* by Don Ellis and his Orchestra contains a mixture of live and studio material and is on Sony/Wounded Bird (2007). Charles Lloyd's *Journey Within*, recorded in 1967 at the Fillmore, is packaged with the next year's *Charles Lloyd In Europe* album in a two CD set (Collectables 1998). Keith Jarrett is the pianist.

Cannonball Adderley's *Mercy Mercy Mercy* is on Capitol (1995). Joe Zawinul plays electric piano and wrote the title track, which was also covered by Chris Barber in the seventies. The successful tracks by the Ramsey Lewis Trio are on *The Greatest Hits* (MCA 1997). Herbie Mann's *Memphis Underground* is on an Atlantic CD (2002).

The CD issue of *Turn It Over* by the Tony Williams Lifetime (Verve 1997) adds the Jack Bruce song, *One Word*, to the original album, which is much improved by its inclusion (the song was rather optimistically issued as a single). The Mahavishnu Orchestra album, *The Inner Mounting Flame*, is on a Columbia CD (1998). *Apocalypse* is on a 1990 CD from the same company, when it was still called CBS. Herbie Hancock's *Mwandishi* is on a Warner Bros CD (2001), although a double CD set called *Mwandishi – The Complete Warner Bros Recordings* (1994) is a more useful purchase, as it includes the next album, *Crossings*, which is superior to *Mwandishi*, and also the earlier *Fat Albert Rotunda*, an interesting, though ultimately failed attempt to create a kind of jazz funk before *Bitches Brew* was recorded and before, therefore, Hancock could absorb its lessons.

The Joe Zawinul solo album, *Zawinul* (Atlantic 2013) has brief, but enthusiastic sleeve notes by Miles Davis, who recognises a kindred musical spirit. The first, eponymous, album by Weather Report builds on its achievements (Columbia 1994). Every album made by the group through the seventies is essential – those from the eighties are less so, but still comprise a fascinating body of work. *Mysterious Traveller* and *Black Market* (from 1974 and 1976) are arguably the finest of all, although the group's big hit, *Birdland*, is on *Heavy Weather* (from 1977). All are on Columbia CDs, most recently issued in 2002, 2002, and 1997 respectively.

Elastic Rock by Nucleus is on a Repertoire CD (2005), or it can be acquired as half of a double CD set, with the group's second album, *We'll Talk About It Later* (BGO 1994).

The best selling ECM album is the live *Koln Concert* by Keith Jarrett from 1975. It has sold three and a half million copies, making it one of the most popular jazz records in any category. As a solo acoustic piano performance, however, this cannot be described as jazz fusion and it is not typical of ECM's output. More characteristic of the company's sound are mid seventies albums like *Odyssey* by Terje Rypdal, *The Colours Of Chloe* by Eberhard Weber, or *Arbour Zena* by Keith Jarrett with Jan Garbarek, Charlie Haden, and the Stuttgart Radio Symphony Orchestra. All are on CDs issued in 2008.

Trout Mask Replica by Captain Beefheart and his Magic Band was originally issued in 1969. It is on a Reprise CD (2006). Ronald Shannon Jackson recorded a large number of albums with his own groups, many of them live and many of them, too, quite hard to track down. *Mandance* (Antilles 1986), recorded in 1982 with Vernon Reid on guitar and Melvin Gibbs playing one of the two bass guitars involved (he was previously to be heard driving the avant-funk band Defunkt), is as good a place to start as any. Only the album *Pulse* (also issued as *Puttin' On The Dog*), which is made up of solo drumming, with Jackson sometimes declaiming over the top, should perhaps be avoided. James Blood Ulmer sings as well as playing guitar on many of his albums, making him sound as much like a modern avant-garde blues performer as a jazzman. The stripped down *Odyssey* (Sony 2015), recorded in 1983 with just a violinist and a drummer, sits astride the blues-jazz interface and has the advantage of being the easiest of Ulmer's many recordings to obtain. Bass player Jamaaladeen Tacuma is a less significant artist, often preferring to make records that are closer to disco than jazz, although he shares this tendency with several other jazz fusion players. His *Dreamscape* (DIW 1996) is excellent, however, it's music being neatly summed up by the title of one of its tracks, *Groove With An Attitude*.

The first, eponymous, album by Last Exit is on Enemy (1986). The later *Iron Path* (originally Virgin 1988, latest issue ESP-Disk 2015) is rather easier to find and is almost as impressive. *Travail Transformation And Flow* by Steve Lehman Octet is on Pi Recordings (2009). *Blow By Blow* by Jeff Beck is on an Epic CD (2001).

Recommended albums by the piano trios are: *Uninvisible* by Medeski Martin & Wood (Capitol/Blue Note 2002); *Strange Place For Snow* by E.S.T. (Esbjorn Svensson Trio) (Act/Sony 2002); *Day Is Done* by the Brad Mehldau Trio (Nonesuch 2005); *These Are The Vistas* by The Bad Plus (Sony 2003); *Man Made Object* by Go Go Penguin (Universal/Decca 2016)

As extensive as the above listing may be, it is nevertheless no more than the beginnings of a comprehensive jazz collection. Notable musicians that are missing or almost missing include Art Tatum, Billie Holiday, Thelonious Monk, Sonny Rollins, Oscar Peterson, Art Blakey, Max Roach, Charles Mingus, Dave Brubeck, Stan Getz, Cecil Taylor, Sun Ra, Albert Ayler, Archie Shepp, McCoy Tyner, Mike Westbook, Keith Jarrett, Chick Corea, Anthony Braxton, Carla Bley, and many others.

Bob Dylan strums a G chord while Robbie Robertson plays lead

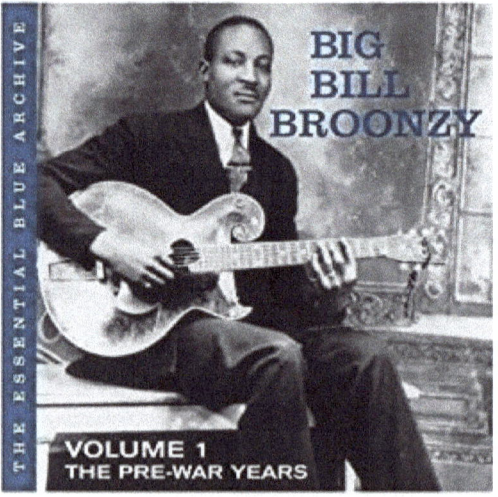

Big Bill Broonzy is quoted as saying, "I guess all songs is folk songs. I never heard no horse sing 'em." (Also attributed to Louis Armstrong).

29 FOLK

Robbie Robertson. guitarist with the Hawks, the rock 'n' roll group that Bob Dylan adopted as his own (and renamed the Band) when he decided to go electric, was quoted by Greil Marcus in his book, *Mystery Train*, as saying,

> He didn't know anything about *music*. He was all folk songs, Big Bill, and we were Jerry Lee. So it'd be, 'Down the streets the dogs are barking' – WHAM!! A huge noise. And Bob would say, 'Hey, that's great, let's do it again, that way.'

On all of his early acoustic songs, Bob Dylan's approach to music is strictly functional. The melodies are entirely subordinate to the lyrics, which are carefully constructed, full of meaning, and frequently poetic. In many cases, Dylan did not even write the tunes himself, but borrowed them wholesale from traditional sources. Thus *A Hard Rain's Gonna Fall* is the traditional song, *Lord Randall,* in disguise, while *Masters Of War* is *Nottamun Town*. Even when the tunes are not those of older songs, they sound as though they are, being continual variations of the same C-F-G chord sequence. In the discography included in his book, *Song And Dance Man – The Art Of Bob Dylan,* Michael Gray states that it would not be a good idea to start listening to Dylan via his *Greatest Hits* LP, though without saying why. The truth is, that abstracted from their original context, though some would consider it almost sacrilegious to say so, even Dylan's best known early songs sound a little dull.

When Robbie Robertson referred to Big Bill, he meant the blues artist Big Bill Broonzy, who made his first recording, *Big Bill's Blues/House Rent Stomp* in 1927, playing his guitar while John Thomas sang. Broonzy often performed with other people – a pianist or even a full jazz group – and in the forties he played lead lines on electric guitar. He was not, therefore, a typical country blues performer and was not the obvious name-check that Robertson could have made. In 1938 Broonzy was asked to be part of John Hammond's influential *Spirituals to Swing* concert at New York's Carnegie Hall, as a replacement for the recently deceased Robert Johnson. During the fifties he toured extensively in the UK and Europe, performing solo and using an acoustic guitar, as he realised that European audiences expected country blues artists to be like that. His material included traditional blues songs, alongside those he had written himself, which were more in the manner of pop songs, albeit structured around the twelve bar form. He also played some traditional folk material, where the connection with Bob Dylan makes sense.

Huddie Ledbetter, who played using the name Leadbelly, was a few years older than Big Bill Broonzy and had a repertoire that mixed blues and folk music even more extensively. Ledbetter served three terms in prison, one of them for murder. According to legend, he managed to win an early release by performing with his guitar for the prison governor. While still in prison, the folk song collectors John and Alan Lomax recorded him for the Library of Congress. The eleven songs completed on July 16th 1933 at the Louisiana State Penetentiary, beginning with *The Western Cowboy,* are Leadbelly's first recordings. He was a successful club and radio performer through the forties and made many records, though without ever troubling the charts. His first European tour began in 1949, but he became ill during it and died later the same year.

Pete Seeger performed with both Big Bill Broonzy and Leadbelly. He became an expert player of the banjo and used it to perform traditional folk and political songs through the forties, both solo and as a member of a group called the Almanac Singers. Even when serving with the US army during the War, he was employed to entertain his fellow soldiers. Seeger's first recordings were as a member of the Almanac Singers – a set of three 78 rpm discs, issued as an album called *Songs For John Doe* in May 1941. The inclusion of some anti-war songs was a poorly timed move – when in June, Germany invaded the Soviet Union, Seeger's group began supporting calls for the USA to intervene and it withdrew its own album from sale. Pete Seeger and Lee Hays reconstituted the group in 1949 with a new line-up and

THE FIRST TIME

Joe Klein's biography of Woody Guthrie reprints a copyright statement included with the singer's best known song, *This Land Is Your Land*. "This song is Copyrighted in U.S., under Seal of Copyright #154085, for a period of 28 years, and anybody caught singin it without our permission, will be mighty good friends of ourn, cause we don't give a dern. Publish it. Write it. Sing it. Swing to it. Yodel it. We wrote it, that's all we wanted to do". Guthrie believed that folk music meant what it said, that it was the music of the people. He had, in any case, taken many of his melodies from traditional songs. Nevertheless, the official Woody Guthrie website lists details of five publishers, who must be contacted by anyone seeking to use any of the songs.

Between 1998 and 2012, Billy Bragg and the American band Wilco made three albums, under the name *Mermaid Avenue*, in which they set music to unused lyrics left behind by Guthrie after his death. He is a major inspiration too on the music of Bruce Springsteen, which is particularly apparent on the three albums of mostly acoustic material, *Nebraska, The Ghost Of Tom Joad* (referencing a song on *Dust Bowl Ballads*), and *Devils & Dust*. Springsteen has often performed *This Land Is Your Land* in his concerts. Springsteen's earlier records provide an interesting hybrid of Dylan-inspired lyricism and a highly theatrical style of composing and performing. It combines rock 'n' roll (but not folk) with the kind of event-filled songwriting found in musicals. The music was quite unique outside the world of someone like Andrew Lloyd Webber (who worked within a much less ecstatic approach), until songwriter Jim Steinman appropriated the sound for his work with Meat Loaf and Bonnie Tyler, at which point Springsteen himself abandoned it.

Bob Dylan's first recording was as a harmonica player on the title track of the Harry Belafonte album, *Midnight Special*, released in March 1962, at the same time as his own album, but recorded the previous June. The song is a traditional one, but was popularised by Leadbelly. Belafonte's version canters along at a fair rate, somewhere between rock and jazz. The earliest unofficial Dylan recording listed in Paul Cable's exhaustive catalogue, *Bob Dylan – His Unreleased Recordings,* is known as *The East Orange Tape* and comprises a selection of mostly Woody Guthrie songs recorded in a private house in February or March 1961. Some even earlier recordings have appeared since the book was written. The *John Bucklen Tape* has four songs played by Dylan and a school friend in 1958. Though not performed at all seriously, the music is rock 'n' roll.

a new name, the Weavers. This group was very successful for a few years, achieving several chart hits, the first of which, a cover of a song by Leadbelly, *Goodnight Irene,* stayed at number one for thirteen weeks and sold two million copies. The group disappeared from the charts and from radio and television in 1953, the left-wing views of its members making it a suitable candidate for placing on the McCarthy entertainment blacklist. Although the Weavers did manage to organise a sold-out concert at Carnegie Hall at the end of 1955, the group never returned to the charts. Pete Seeger achieved a solo hit in 1963 with *Little Boxes* but he did not return to US television until 1968. The chart success of groups popularising folk music, the Kingston Trio and Peter, Paul, and Mary, at the end of the fifties and beginning of the sixties represented the legacy of the Weavers, but without the politics.

Woody Guthrie was close friends with both Pete Seeger and Leadbelly and was a member of the Almanac Singers. In 1940, he was recorded by Alan Lomax for the Library of Congress and also made an album for RCA Victor, *Ballads From The Dust Bowl* (later reissued on LP as *Dust Bowl Ballads*). Eleven songs were included, written by Guthrie about the Oklahoma drought and farming disaster of the thirties, which he had experienced directly. Linking the songs with a common theme in this way turned *Ballads From The Dust Bowl* into the first 'concept album'. Through the forties Guthrie made a large number of further recordings and became a well-known performer in New York clubs and on the radio. He also wrote a successful novel, *Bound For Glory,* and like Pete Seeger, entertained the troops as a soldier during World War II. Just as happened with the Weavers, who recorded some of his songs, Woody Guthrie was blacklisted in the fifties, but his career effectively came to an end when he was hospitalised in 1954, suffering from a degenerative nerve disease. He died, still in hospital, in 1967. In the film inspired by his son Arlo's narrative song, *Alice's Restaurant,* Pete Seeger and Arlo are shown singing by the bedside of a weak but appreciative Woody Guthrie (played by an actor). The song was originally released a month after Woody's death.

Bob Dylan was one of several folk artists to start recording at the beginning of the sixties, inspired by the music of Pete Seeger and Woody Guthrie, and by the first Newport Folk Festival, organised by Pete Seeger and others in July 1959. Arguably, the star of the festival was Joan Baez, making her first major performance and only there at all because she was a guest of one of the billed artists (Bob Gibson). She was quickly signed by Vanguard who released her first album in October 1960. Judy Collins' first album, *A Maid Of Constant Sorrow,* was issued in November 1961. Both records included the acoustic guitar playing of Fred Hellerman, who was a member of the Weavers. Dylan's first, self-titled, album, was issued in March 1962 and had *Song To Woody* as one of the songs written by Dylan himself (most were traditional or covers of blues songs). Two years later, the Animals recorded rock versions of two of the album's songs (one of them being the sixties classic, *House Of The Rising Sun*), without anyone suggesting that folk rock was being invented. Meanwhile, Bob Dylan himself issued a folk rock song as his first single, in December 1962. *Mixed Up Confusion* was not a hit, however, and many of the singer's fans, especially in the UK, where the single was not released, were probably unaware that the recording even existed.

In March 1965, Bob Dylan released his fifth album, *Bringing It All Back Home.* The protest songs, the political material that had made Dylan's name, were now absent and in their place, a rock group sound was introduced for the whole of the LP first side, using a number of session musicians. For all those who had missed *Mixed Up Confusion,* the change in direction must have been startling. Despite a couple of surrealistic blues songs smacking a little of filler, the performances generally were amongst the singer's most memorable so far. Above all, the album was not dull. A month later, the Byrds issued their own version of one of the acoustic tracks on the LP's second side. The group had added layered harmonies to highlight *Mr Tambourine Man's* melodic strength, had cut some of the verses to give the song more impact when heard on the radio, and had sandwiched the whole thing between repeats of a distinctive twelve string guitar figure, constructed by Roger McGuinn (or Jim McGuinn as he was known then). The record climbed to number one in both the US and the UK charts. Between the Byrds and Bob Dylan himself, a new genre had been established, with the music press in the US referring to 'folk rock' for the first time.

The Byrds consolidated their position as a group to watch with a second folk rock single, this time a version of a Pete Seeger song, *Turn Turn Turn.* Meanwhile Bob Dylan performed as the headline act at the Newport Folk Festival

THE FIRST TIME

The Byrds had an earlier attempt at recording *Mr Tambourine Man*, in which McGuinn's guitar figure hardly featured. The song was also spoilt by a militaristic drum beat that was somewhat less than Mike Clarke's finest hour. Convinced that there was nevertheless a hit song in the making, new producer Terry Melcher hired some of the musicians who played on Phil Spector's records, leaving the Byrds to deliver just the twelve string guitar and the vocals. The group played on all its own recordings after that, but on this occasion, Melcher's decision did the trick.

In a rare example of the Beatles deliberately following the innovations of another group, the song *If I Needed Someone*, included on the *Rubber Soul* LP at the end of 1965, featured George Harrison playing a twelve string guitar figure remarkably similar to Roger McGuinn's. On the same album, *Norwegian Wood* had a discernible Bob Dylan influence (and not for the first time – *You've Got To Hide Your Love Away* on the previous Beatles LP, *Help!*, had it too). Dylan clearly thought so. He stole part of the melody of *Norwegian Wood* for his own song, *4th Time Around*, included on the *Blonde On Blonde* album. John Lennon, fully aware of how the influences were working, chose to ignore the breach of copyright. He was not averse to appropriating lines himself on occasion, such as on another of *Rubber Soul*'s songs, *Run For Your Life*, which stole from *Baby Let's Play House*, an Arthur Gunter song recorded by Elvis Presley.

The Byrds maintained an adventurous approach to music making for several years, long after the point when members moved on, leaving Roger McGuinn as the only original. The highlight in a series of great singles (and albums) released through the sixties was *Eight Miles High*. Written by Gene Clark, David Crosby, and Roger McGuinn and recorded in January 1966, the song transposed John Coltrane's modal lines from saxophone to lead twelve string guitar and from jazz to rock. It emerged as one of the defining tracks of a rock music variant that became known as psychedelic, after its imagined or real inspiration from mind-altering recreational drugs. The next generation of American folk-rock bands, led by Jefferson Airplane, Country Joe and the Fish, and the Grateful Dead, all of whom included improvisation and a psychedelic ambience in their music, took their main inspiration from this one track.

Simon and Garfunkel, who had started out as a rock 'n' roll duo in the late fifties, calling themselves Tom and Jerry, had switched to folk by the time of their first record release for Columbia in 1964, the LP *Wednesday Morning 3 am*. Inspired by the success of Bob Dylan's folk rock, producer Tom Wilson (who had been responsible for *Like A Rolling Stone*) added many of the same rock musicians to the recording of the track *The Sound Of Silence*, without telling Simon and Garfunkel that he was doing this. Released as a single in September 1965, the song reached number one in the US charts and helped make Simon and Garfunkel one of the key acts of the late sixties as well as launching the career of Paul Simon as one of the most highly regarded singer songwriters of all.

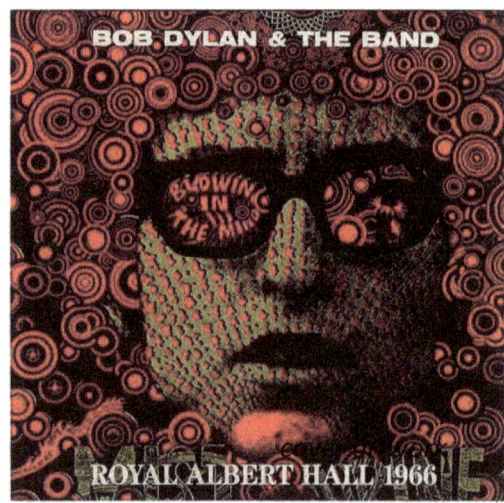

One of the many bootleg issues of Dylan's concert, using a famous poster designed by Martin Sharp in 1967 as the cover artwork

Bob Dylan, equating himself with Jesus by implication, was ignored by the religious bigots who delighted in burning Beatles records in 1966, after John Lennon, quoted out of context, seemed to make a similar comparison for his group.

in July 1965. He was backed by members of the Paul Butterfield Blues Band, to the approval of many members of the audience, but to the dismay of some. They considered folk music to be above such modern inventions as drums and electric guitars and had presumably never heard Dylan's most recent recordings. Festival organisers Pete Seeger and Alan Lomax were displeased too – as they had been earlier on, when the Butterfield Blues Band had delivered its own set. Today, it seems hard to comprehend the divide in opinion that viewed folk music and rock 'n' roll as being polar opposites, as irreconcilable as capitalism and communism. To some, folk rock was not just something they did not wish to hear, it was positively immoral. For them, Bob Dylan was betraying his own roots and offending their entire belief system. (It was as if Beethoven came back to life and, instead of rushing to complete work on his tenth symphony, instead offered his services to a television talent show – or worse, entered it as a contestant.) Only Paul Nelson, writing in *Sing Out!* magazine, showed a little prescience.

> "Make no mistake, the audience had to make a clear-cut choice and they made it. Pete Seeger. They were choosing suffocation over invention and adventure, backwards over forwards, a dead hand instead of a live one. It was a sad parting of the ways for many, myself included. I choose Dylan. I choose art." (quoted in *Dylan – A Biography* by Bob Spitz).

In August, Bob Dylan released his first unequivocal rock album, *Highway 61 Revisited*, preceded by a single with what is probably his greatest song, *Like A Rolling Stone*. Some of the same musicians as on the previous album were used again, but with the crucial addition of bass player Harvey Brooks (later to join Mike Bloomfield's Electric Flag, the rock big band he formed after leaving the Butterfield Blues Band), Bloomfield himself on lead guitar, and Al Kooper, a session musician at the time, who subsequently became a member of the Blues Project (and founded Blood Sweat and Tears after that). Much has been made of the fact that Kooper played organ on *Like A Rolling Stone*, despite being unfamiliar with the instrument. He was a pianist as well as a guitarist, however, so the leap involved was not a very great one. In the event, it is the memorable organ part that is crucial in making a good performance great.

During 1966, Bob Dylan embarked on a world tour, supported by the Hawks, which included two weeks in the UK. Some of the British fans reacted in the same disappointed manner as their American counterparts the previous year, even though Dylan had now had four top twenty hits in his folk rock style (with *Like A Rolling Stone* reaching number four) and the two albums had both spent some time near the top of the album charts. The concert-goers could hardly claim to be surprised if Dylan performed in the same manner on stage. The electric half of the concert at Manchester on May 17th was presented on one of the first rock bootleg LPs, confusingly attributed to the Royal Albert Hall in London. It is apparent that the protesters in the audience were in the minority and the only time that Bob Dylan betrays any anger at the treatment he is receiving from them is when someone shouts "Judas!". "I don't believe you – you're a liar!" Dylan retorts and the band launches into a magnificent version of *Like A Rolling Stone*. At the end of 2016, an enormous thirty-two CD boxed set was issued, comprising all the recorded concerts from Dylan's tour. With the benefit of several years' hindsight, even those who booed in Manchester will have reached the realisation that rock music history had been in the making at the time.

Immediately prior to the tour, Bob Dylan had recorded the music that was released in the summer of 1966 as the double album, *Blonde On Blonde*. Dylan had been persuaded by producer Bob Johnston to carry out the recordings in Nashville, using some of the town's best session musicians, although Dylan took Al Kooper and Robbie Robertson with him as well. The Nashville musicians, used to working quickly and efficiently, were astonished to discover that Bob Dylan expected them to sit around while he wrote the material. He would then emerge with the songs, one at a time, and record them, with the barest of instructions to the musicians and with no rehearsal. Most of the songs on the album are first takes, produced in this way. *Blonde On Blonde* is generally regarded as the pinnacle of folk rock in the sixties, the equivalent in its own genre of the Beatles *Sgt Pepper's Lonely Hearts Club Band* in theirs.

During interviews, Bob Dylan was very good at being enigmatic. "Being noticed can be a burden. Jesus got himself crucified because he got himself noticed. So I disappear a lot," he said on one occasion. Through 1967, Dylan

THE FIRST TIME

Music from Big Pink – cover art by Bob Dylan

Three notable hits were achieved with songs from *The Basement Tapes.* Manfred Mann reached number one in the UK (number ten in the US) with *The Mighty Quinn.* Julie Driscoll with Brian Auger and the Trinity took *This Wheel's On Fire* to number five in the UK. The Byrds did less well in the charts with *You Ain't Goin' Nowhere*, but the song is now numbered among the group's greatest hits regardless. In addition, the Tremeloes scored a small hit with *I Shall Be Released,* although the song has been covered by many different artists since. Sandy Denny's Fotheringay brought Dylan back to the world of British folk rock when the group recorded *Too Much Of Nothing* on its album of 1970.

When Leonard Cohen died in 2016, his legacy of great songs largely derived from the first three albums. There was one, however, that he first recorded in 1984, when the acclaim for his work had considerably diminished. *Hallelujah* has belatedly become Leonard Cohen's greatest hit, with more than two hundred different versions being recorded. Ironically, the reason for the song's popularity lies not with Cohen himself, but with the fact that Jeff Buckley (the son of another adventurous sixties singer songwriter, Tim Buckley) chose to record a memorable cover of the song for his debut album *Grace* in 1994. Buckley, who was being groomed by Columbia records as the next Bruce Springsteen and whose concerts were attracting ecstatic attention, then died and succeeded in proving correct the cynical aphorism that dying is the best career move a rock star can make. (Elvis Presley, to name another example, has generated more income since he died in 1977 than he did during his career, incredibly successful though that was).

Jimi Hendrix declared himself to be a big fan of Bob Dylan and his own lyrics in poetic songs like *The Wind Cries Mary* and *Bold As Love* rather demonstrated this to be the case. Towards the end of 1968, Hendrix issued his own version of the Dylan song, *All Along The Watchtower.* It was not so much a cover as a re-composition and the fact that the song has become a rock standard is due to Jimi Hendrix rather than to Bob Dylan himself. Even Dylan performed the song in a way that acknowledged the Hendrix version during his concerts in the seventies. As he said in the sleeve notes to his *Biograph* anthology, "Ever since he died I've been doing it that way... when I sing it I always feel like it's a tribute to him in some kind of way".

Jimmy Webb's *MacArthur Park,* an elaborate, fully orchestrated composition that moves through several different phases, has the distinction of being the most misunderstood song ever written. The song's central metaphor is of the park in Los Angeles, a place of romantic significance for the singer, yet spoilt since the ending of the romance in question, while having the appearance of an iced cake similarly spoilt, when seen from a distance in the dark. This seemed, however, to present an image too complicated for many listeners to appreciate. Taking the lyrics literally, they could not understand why anyone would choose to leave a cake outside in the rain. Intrigued despite this, or else won over by the majestic sound of the music, they bought the single of *MacArthur Park,* recorded by actor Richard Harris, in sufficient numbers to make it a top ten hit in both the US and the UK, in the summer of 1968.

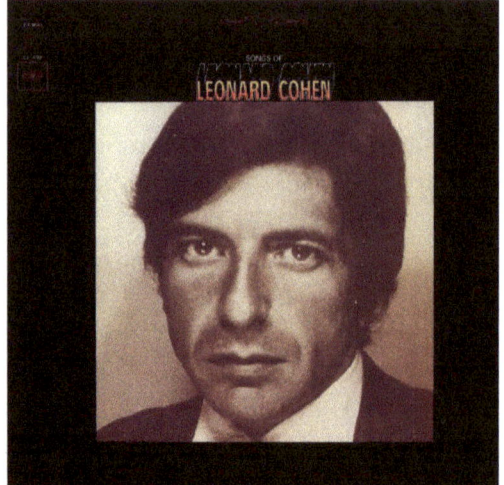

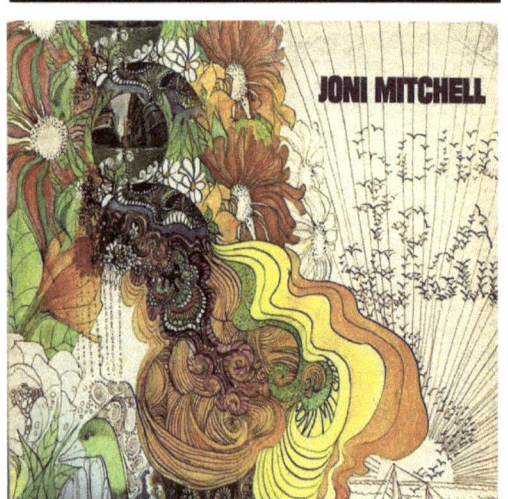

did indeed disappear from the public gaze, supposedly recovering from a serious motorcycle accident. During that time, he recorded a large number of tracks with the Band. The songs trickled out, some being given to other artists, more being included on several different bootleg LPs, before finally gaining an official release in 1975 as *The Basement Tapes*. The music was a different kind of folk rock, in which Dylan dug deeper into the mother lode of traditional American song. The tumbling lyrical imagery of his work on *Blonde On Blonde* and its immediate predecessors, with words seeming to rush out of their author's consciousness too quickly to be properly formed into coherent sentences, was replaced by a simpler kind of songwriting. It was one that succeeded in creating a rock music that appeared to be timeless, imbued with history yet also modern. It was a style that was continued by the Band, without its patron, on a number of albums released during the next decade and in particular on the two made at the end of the sixties, *Music From Big Pink* and *The Band*. Eric Clapton for one, who had been a fan of Big Bill Broonzy in his early days, but whose extrovert lead guitar represented a very different approach to the song-centred playing of Robbie Robertson, declared himself very impressed by *Music From Big Pink*. So much so, in fact, that he resolved to bring his group Cream to an end, although he never did fully explore the roots music that lay behind the Band's recordings.

At the end of 1967, an album called *The Songs Of Leonard Cohen* appeared on the market. At the age of thirty-three, Cohen presented a music that was clearly made possible by the innovations of Bob Dylan, but he did not have a background in folk music. Instead, he was a published poet who had decided that he was more likely to make his fortune if he set some of his poems to music. He was a less accomplished singer than even Bob Dylan, whose voice alone would never have won him any prizes. The strength of the lyrics in Cohen's mournful songs, however, was enough to make a huge number of friends. Although Cohen made little attempt to capture the singles market, his album, and the two that followed it in fairly quick succession, were substantial hits in the LP charts in both the US and the UK. A new kind of pop music artist, the singer songwriter, had arrived.

Leonard Cohen did at least adopt the essential calling card of the folk singer, the acoustic guitar. Laura Nyro, who wrote songs for the Fifth Dimension and Barbra Streisand and played the piano to accompany her own soulful vocals, did not even do that. Her own first record was the LP, *More Than A New Discovery*, which was issued in January 1967, although it did not sell particularly well. She was a singer songwriter with no links to the world of folk music, even if her album did appear on the Verve Folkways label. She was supposedly in the running for lead singer with Blood Sweat and Tears, she became friends with Miles Davis, and eventually recorded a covers album of her favourite teenage songs, which all turned out to be from the Motown stable.

Jimmy Webb was an artist who had much in common with Laura Nyro. He wrote songs for several other people before recording anything himself, with his first big success being the song *By The Time I Get To Phoenix*, a hit for Glen Campbell at the end of 1967. Webb's first record, *Jim Webb Sings Jim Webb*, issued in August 1968, comprised a selection of demos, orchestrated without his agreement. He was happy to assume the mantle of singer songwriter, however, for the album *Words And Music*, released in November 1970. Influenced far more by country music and by the writers of show tunes like Richard Rodgers and George Gershwin than by anything in the folk music world, Webb nevertheless shared the same kind of oblique imagery as Bob Dylan in some of his most remarkable songs. These included *Wichita Lineman*, *A Tramp Shining*, and *MacArthur Park*.

Joni Mitchell, a singer songwriter who did have a folk background, moved from her native Canada (the home country too of four fifths of the Band) to begin working in the American folk clubs in 1965. She was armed with an unusual guitar playing style for the time, in which she retuned her instrument in various ways in order to remove a sense of certainty from her songwriting. One of her songs in particular, *Both Sides Now*, had 'classic' written all over it. The song was taken up by several other artists too and was turned into a hit single by Judy Collins, after she recorded it for her 1967 LP, *Wildflowers*. Joni Mitchell herself waited until her second album before recording the song. Her first album, *Song To A Seagull*, was issued in March 1968. It was produced by David Crosby, who had recently left the Byrds. He decided that his best policy as producer of the record was to do as little as possible and simply let Joni Mitchell's voice and guitar win listeners over. Only one track bore any resemblance to folk rock, *Night In The City*

THE FIRST TIME

Cover artwork for her three albums shown by Joni Mitchell herself

The way in which the aging Joni Mitchell was able to achieve a greater effect with a voice that had become technically less fluent has everything in common with the singing of the great jazz singer, Billie Holiday, on her 1958 album, *Lady In Satin*, recorded near the end of the singer's life. The two women emerge as artists of equal greatness, giants of twentieth century music.

Chris Hillman of the Byrds is quoted in a 2015 Vanity Fair article by Lisa Robinson as saying, while recalling the late sixties music scene in Laurel Canyon, "What Joni Mitchell did was way far and above what most of the guys, myself included, could do as a songwriter or guitar player".

The only cover song recorded by CSN&Y was *Woodstock* by Joni Mitchell. They had been at the festival, although Ms Mitchell had not. She had managed to compose a perfect encapsulation of the event's spirit regardless. Another version of the song became a number one hit in the UK in October 1970 (and a chart success too in the US), played by the British country rock band, Matthews Southern Comfort.

Of the many recordings made over the years by the members of CSN&Y individually and in various combinations, both the best and the worst have been made by Neil Young, sometimes on the same album. The ragged electric guitar histrionics of his work with the group Crazy Horse turns the live album *Weld,* from 1991, into a celebration of the man's wayward genius. Raucous rock music almost completely overpowers the folk, until that is, Young delivers a version of Bob Dylan's anthem, *Blowin' In The Wind,* complete with war sound effects and a lead guitar line that takes on the role of a trumpet last post, and reminds us of the strong tradition lying behind his music. But then, the bonus album *Arc,* included with early issues of *Weld,* presents a noise-fest made up of the ecstatic closing bars of numerous live songs, joined together in an extended piece that is less a medley than a melee. A different kind of awfulness is presented by Young's 2014 album, *A Letter Home.* This comprises a selection of well-known songs by other writers, recorded, for some reason, in a refurbished home recording booth from the forties. These were designed to provide musical mementos of no great sound quality, which is what this one does here. The studied artlessness of Neil Young's playing is presumably intended to be appropriate for the musical letter home concept, but does not make anyone else want to hear it more than once. On the other hand, there are marvellous records like *After The Goldrush, Zuma, Rust Never Sleeps,* and *Silver And Gold...*

During the sixties, Carole King was a prolific co-writer of hit songs (with her then husband, lyricist Gerry Goffin) for artists like the Shirelles (*Will You Love Me Tomorrow*), the Drifters *(Up On The Roof),* Billy Fury (*Halfway To Paradise*), Bobby Vee (*Take Good Care Of My Baby*), Aretha Franklin (*You Make Me Feel Like A Natural* Woman), and the Monkees (*Pleasant Valley Sunday*). She even managed one hit for herself, *It Might As Well Rain Until September,* in 1962, although she was not able to repeat this success at the time. None of these songs had anything to do with folk, but seeing an opportunity, Ms King decided to try and rebrand herself as a singer songwriter at the start of the seventies. Her second attempt, the album *Tapestry,* released in 1971, became the best selling record of the genre, staying at or near the top of the US album charts for nearly six years. One of its songs, *You've Got A Friend,* was a number one hit for another singer songwriter, James Taylor, who had made a rare decision to cover a song written by someone else. His own *Sweet Baby James* album, sounding much closer to country than the records of his contemporaries, was a huge hit in 1970, though not quite in the league of *Tapestry*. The 1996 film, *Grace Of My Heart,* written and directed by Allison Anders, was inspired by Carole King's career, although it did not include any of her music.

being a feature for Ms Mitchell's uptempo piano playing, with Steve Stills adding a fluent bass guitar line.

On the many albums that Joni Mitchell recorded from *Song To A Seagull* to *Shine* (issued in 2007 and likely to be her last), she revealed herself to be a poet of the highest order, on a par with both Bob Dylan and Leonard Cohen. She was also musically restless, tackling approaches to songwriting and performance that ranged much more widely than did her contemporaries. For the first few albums, she gradually added extra instrumentation until, when *Court And Spark* employed a full soft rock band with hints of jazz, in 1974, it sounded as though she had freshly invented the folk rock genre. The jazz influence increased during the next few albums and she worked with some very well known names, including Wayne Shorter, Herbie Hancock, Pat Metheny, Charles Mingus, and Jaco Pastorius. The Weather Report bass player delivered some of his most sublime playing on the 1976 *Hejira*, whose sparse version of jazz rock was more or less unique. At the other extreme, *Paprika Plains*, on her 1977 album, *Don Juan's Reckless Daughter*, was an orchestral extravaganza worthy of a progressive rock band, while some of the tracks on *Wild Things Run Fast*, from 1982, were close to being hard rock, albeit of a particularly subtle kind. For the 2000 album, *Both Sides Now*, Joni Mitchell reinvented herself as a torch singer, performing masterful versions of some jazz standards, alongside two of her own, *A Case Of You* and the title track. With a voice coarsened by a lifetime of smoking, she still managed to deliver an emotional power that gave the song *Both Sides Now* a depth of meaning and an impact that no other version, including her own original, had managed to achieve. The recording was used to highlight a particularly poignant moment in the 2003 film *Love Actually*, directed by Richard Curtis, to the credit of both film and song.

Crosby Stills and Nash, named like a firm of solicitors, was a group (or supergroup, as such meetings of musicians with a previous history were called at the time) made up of three singer songwriters. It was the first such to be formed in the US. David Crosby had been a member of the Byrds, Steve Stills had been with Buffalo Springfield, another similarly inventive folk rock band, while Graham Nash was from the Hollies. During the beat group years, the Hollies had laboured under the shadow of the Beatles. They had been inspired to progress in the same manner as the more successful group (and they achieved several hit singles and albums too). The LP *Evolution*, issued in June 1967, was a response to *Revolver*, while *Butterfly*, from November of the same year, was like a *Lance Corporal Pepper's Lonely Hearts Club Band*. The next album was *Hollies Sing Dylan*, but by then Graham Nash had jumped ship. Following the release of the Crosby, Stills & Nash album in May 1969, which was distinguished by gorgeous three-part harmony vocals on every track, a fourth singer songwriter was invited to join as well. Neil Young had been a member of Buffalo Springfield, alongside Steve Stills, and had already released two acclaimed solo albums. As Crosby, Stills, Nash and Young, the group gave concerts divided into an acoustic set and an electric set, in the manner of Bob Dylan in 1966. The electric sets revolved around lengthy lead guitar duels between Stills and Young, in an approach not previously associated with any music described as folk rock (although the reconstituted Byrds were also playing lengthy improvised versions of the song *Eight Miles High* at the time).

In the UK and in Europe, composers like Ralph Vaughan Williams, Joseph Canteloube, and Bela Bartok incorporated folk music themes into the music they produced during the early decades of the twentieth century. The English Folk Dance And Song Society was formed in 1932 by the merger of two earlier organisations, with Vaughan Williams as president. It has its headquarters in Cecil Sharp House in London, named after the man who did much to revive the traditional folk music and the morris dancing of England. In 1934, the EFDSS was responsible for the first traditional folk song record, comprising two songs performed by an unaccompanied singer. They were *Down By The Riverside* and *The Pretty Ploughboy*, sung by Harry Cox and issued on the Decca label.

Topic Records was formed in 1939, as an outlet for music promoting communism, sponsored by the Workers' Music Association. The first release was *The Man That Waters The Worker's Beer* by Paddy Ryan. After the war, the label began to shift towards traditional folk music generally and in 1950, it issued the first record by Ewan MacColl, a 78 including *The Asphalter's Song* and three other songs. MacColl and A.L.Lloyd were responsible for starting the revival

Ewan MacColl was the writer of two classic songs in the folk tradition. Both *Dirty Old Town* and *The First Time Ever I Saw Your Face* have been performed and recorded by numerous other artists. The second of these, written for MacColl's third wife, Peggy Seeger (a successful folk singer in her own right and half-sister to Pete Seeger), was turned into a number one hit in the US in March 1972 by Roberta Flack. Few purchasers of that record would have been aware of the song's origins. The singer songwriter Kirsty MacColl was Ewan MacColl's daughter. Her best known song was not written by her. *Fairytale Of New York*, made in 1987 with the Pogues (a group that found a kinship between Irish traditional music and punk), has become a perennial Christmas favourite.

During the thirties, Willie Kemp recorded a number of his narrative ballads for the specialist Scottish music label, Beltona. Kemp copied the style of the bothy (farm labourer) ballads collected by Francis James Child in the latter part of the nineteenth century, accompanying himself on the piano. To modern ears, his performances sound rather closer to music hall than any kind of traditional folk sung and played more recently.

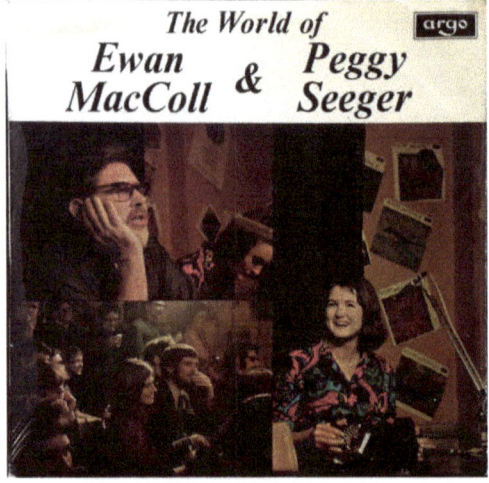

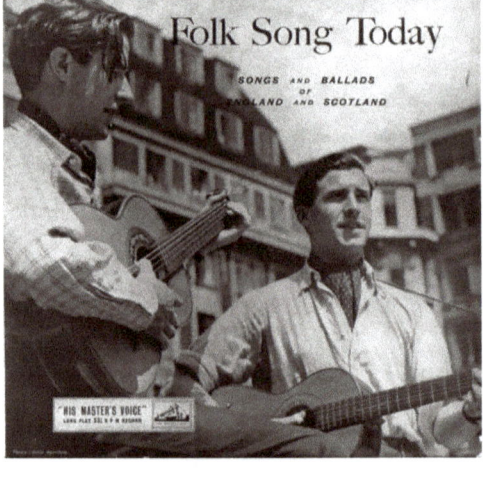

LP cover shows Rory and Alex McEwan

Shirley Collins made some major folk rock records in the seventies, following her marriage to the founder of Steeleye Span, Ashley Hutchings. In 2016, at the age of eighty-one and after a long absence, she made a new album, *Lodestar*. Her exact contemporary, Peggy Seeger, made a record two years previously, *Everything Changes*. Both albums, by these matriarchs of the traditional folk music world, were greeted with enthusiastic reviews.

Joni Mitchell's use of alternative guitar tunings does not appear to have been inspired by Davy Graham. Indeed it is likely that she was not familiar with his playing at all, when developing her own skills in Canada. As described in Karen O'Brien's biography, she was aware of the open chord tunings favoured by slide guitarists playing the blues and expanded the technique from there.

of interest in traditional folk music in the fifties. Lloyd's first record was *Lord Bateman/The Shooting Of His Dear*, issued on HMV in 1953. The definitive collection of the music, *The Penguin Book Of English Folk Songs*, was compiled by A.L. Lloyd with Ralph Vaughan Williams and published in 1959. Meanwhile, the first LP compilation of traditional folk music, *Folk Song Today*, was issued as a ten inch LP by Decca in 1955. The ten tracks included one by Harry Cox and one each by Bob and Ron Copper and Shirley Collins, who became significant folk singers in the years following.

In April 1962, the first record by acoustic guitarist Davy Graham was released. *¾ A.D.* was an EP comprising three instrumental tracks, one of them featuring Alexis Korner on second guitar. It was followed the next year by an LP, *The Guitar Player*, again made up of instrumentals, with Graham's playing this time being supported by a drummer. Although some of the music is based on the blues, Davy Graham's music was classified as folk by default, because acoustic guitars had become associated with that music. In truth, the music is closest to jazz, where the American Charlie Byrd, playing in a very similar manner, had made a number of albums from 1957. Regardless, Graham had a huge influence on guitarists like Bert Jansch and John Renbourn, who were presented as folk players. Both of them issued first LPs in 1965, with skilful, intricate acoustic guitar playing being applied to traditional folk and blues, and with vocals too in the case of Bert Jansch. Graham's tune, *Angi*, included on the first EP, and sounding a little as though it needed to be played by two guitarists, became a test piece for acoustic players. Bert Jansch, Paul Simon, and Gordon Giltrap passed with flying colours; Stan Webb did not. Meanwhile, Davy Graham himself recorded an unequivocal folk album, *Folk Roots New Routes,* with singer Shirley Collins. It is not clear whether Graham actually invented an alternative tuning for the guitar, whereby the bottom string and the top two strings were lowered in pitch by a tone (the DADGAD tuning), but he certainly used it and became associated with it. Bert Jansch and John Renbourn acknowledged the jazz aspect of their music when they combined forces in 1967 with Alexis Korner's most recent rhythm section to form a jazz folk group, the Pentangle. Singer Jacqui McShee had previously performed with Renbourn. The group's third album, *Basket Of Light*, was a top five album in the UK at the end of 1969.

During the early weeks of 1965, the UK television programme, *Ready Steady Go*, gave a regular slot to a folk singer by the name of Donovan. The fact that he looked and sounded rather like Bob Dylan would not have been lost on the programme's producers. He played a guitar emblazoned with the legend 'This Machine Kills' – a shortened, sanitised version of the one that Woody Guthrie had on his guitar, 'This Machine Kills Fascists'. Signed to the Pye record label, Donovan gained the first of a series of top ten UK singles in April with his song, *Catch The Wind*. Although he resisted the Dylan comparison, he nevertheless issued an EP of Dylan-like 'protest songs' in August. *Universal Soldier* effectively became Donovan's third hit single, although three of the four songs, including the title track, were not written by Donovan himself. One was by Bert Jansch, while *Universal Soldier* was composed by the native American singer songwriter, Buffy Sainte-Marie. In time for the 'summer of love', 1967, Donovan made a number of recordings that applied to folk music the same kind of imagination and inventiveness as shown in the music of the Beatles. Introduced at the end of the previous year by his biggest hit of all, *Sunshine Superman*, the best of the recordings were issued in the UK in June on an album named after that hit. The LP was actually a hybrid of two American releases, from September 1966 and March 1967. Three tracks were dropped from the US *Sunshine Superman* and replaced by five tracks (half the LP) taken from the following *Mellow Yellow*. Even though the result was a stronger album, the decision to delay the UK release (unrelated to a label dispute in the US, which was resolved earlier in 1966) robbed the record of some of its impact. It appeared to be in the shadow of *Sgt Pepper*, whereas in reality most of its music was made before the Beatles record.

A Scottish folk duo, the Incredible String Band, provided a rival to Donovan's *Sunshine Superman*, with a suitably mystic LP, *The Five Thousand Spirits Or The Layers Of The Onion*, issued in July 1967. Less elaborately arranged than Donovan's record, the Incredible String Band's LP maintained its finger on the contemporary musical pulse by incorporating some judiciously exotic instrumentation to match the band's chosen name. The album was actually the second release by Mike Heron and Robin Williamson – the previous year's *Incredible String Band* was the work of a trio, with banjo player Clive Palmer added, but it lacked the psychedelic quality of its successor.

THE FIRST TIME

The Strawbs, led by singer songwriter Dave Cousins, soon became very successful themselves. Keyboard player Rick Wakeman joined the line-up in 1970, en route to his tenure with Yes, and the band moved rapidly into progressive rock territory. At the beginning of 1973, the Strawbs had a surprise number two hit in the UK singles chart with *Part Of The Union*, very much a modern folk song, in a style that had by then become atypical of the band.

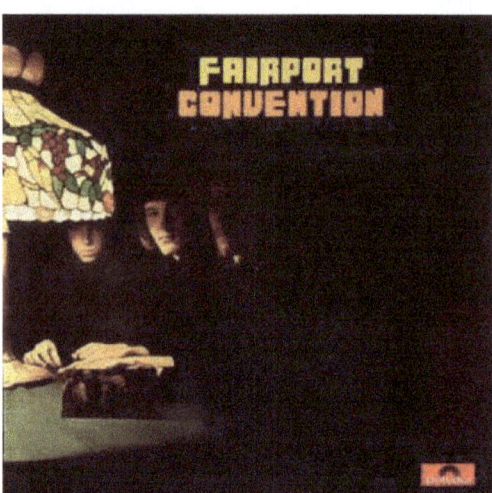

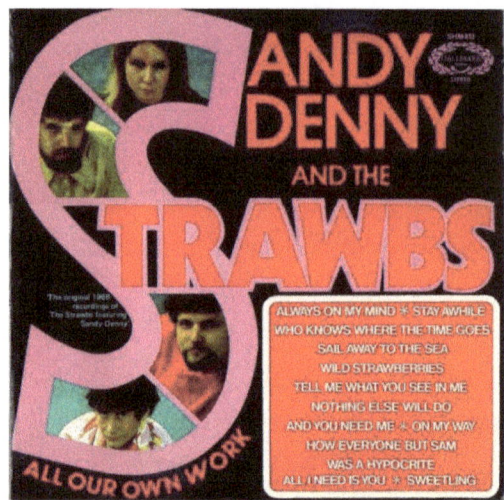

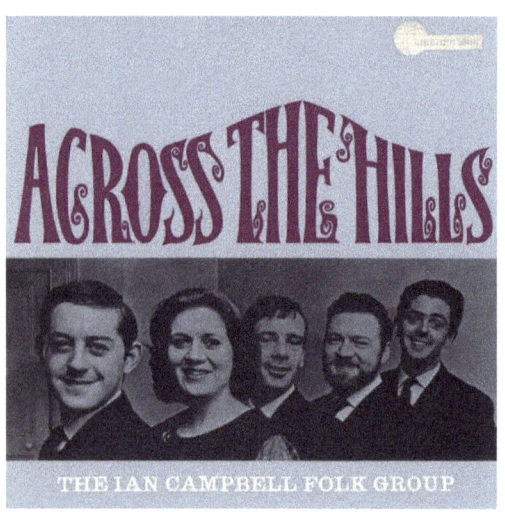

Dave Swarbrick is on the left of this 1964 group portrait. Ian Campbell is second from the right. Some fourteen years later, Campbell's sons were founder members of the group UB40.

Fairport Convention Unhalfbricking

Martin Carthy established himself as the head of a folk-singing family when he married Norma Waterson, whose own family group, the Watersons, made several folk records from 1965. Their daughter, Eliza Carthy, became a notable folk violinist and singer songwriter, with a first solo album, *Heat Light And Sound*, issued in 1996. Mother, father, and daughter made several family records too, as Waterson-Carthy. It was Martin Carthy who conceived a distinctive guitar accompaniment for the traditional song, *Scarborough Fair*, borrowed without acknowledgement by Paul Simon, for the song that became one of his signature pieces.

The first LP by a group calling itself Fairport Convention was issued in June 1968. The music was folk rock in the American manner, having much in common with Jefferson Airplane and similarly featuring a male and female pair of lead singers. Covers of songs by Joni Mitchell, Bob Dylan, and the less well-known Emitt Rhodes were included alongside the band's own material. The record introduced the work of its young lead guitarist, Richard Thompson, already a distinctive and fluent player. Following the release of the first record, Fairport Convention began a series of personnel changes which have been a feature of the band ever since. Some later line-ups have included none of the original members. For the second LP, *What We Did On Our Holidays*, released in January 1969, singer Judy Dyble was replaced by Sandy Denny. She was already established as a performer in the folk clubs and had recorded with the traditional singers Alex Campbell and Johnny Silvo as well as with another nascent folk rock band, the Strawbs. She brought to Fairport Convention a song she had written while with the Strawbs, *Who Knows Where The Time Goes* quickly achieving the status of a modern folk classic. It was recorded by Judy Collins as the title track of her own acclaimed 1968 album, where it took its place, as an equal, alongside memorable interpretations of the work of such luminaries as Bob Dylan, Leonard Cohen, and the Incredible String Band. Sandy Denny kept her own version for Fairport Convention's third LP. In the meantime, she introduced two traditional songs to the group's repertoire. *Nottamun Town* and *She Moved Through The Fair* were given a full rock band treatment, much as Judy Collins had done with the song *Pretty Polly* on her LP, *Who Knows Where The Time Goes*.

For the third Fairport Convention LP, *Unhalfbricking*, released in July 1969, violinist Dave Swarbrick was added as a guest musician on four of the eight tracks. Swarbrick had previously been a member of the traditional Ian Campbell Folk Group, which made several records from 1962, and he also worked with guitarist Martin Carthy. The duo recorded five albums of traditional material between 1965 and 1969. For the Fairport Convention album, Swarbrick was featured most strongly on a long version of the traditional song, *A Sailor's Life* (included in A.L.Lloyd's Penguin anthology). The recording, with its determined two-step rhythm sounding like a suitable accompaniment for a morris dance, opened the way to a whole album celebrating, Judy Collins notwithstanding, a peculiarly British approach to folk rock. It was one that married traditional material with rock group instrumentation, while stripping away any blues influences. Dave Swarbrick was invited to join the band on a permanent basis. His decision to accept the invitation and to play an electrically amplified violin was rather to the consternation of some of the traditionalists. He was quoted in Robin Denselow's portion of the folk music history book, *The Electric Muse*, as wanting to make a distinction between the folk singers who were passing songs from father to son (such as the Copper Family) and the revivalists who learned the songs from the folk clubs or from records. He maintained that the real traditional singers did not worry about what was truly ethnic and had no problem with those who sought to amplify the music. *Liege And Lief* became Fairport Convention's third LP release of 1969. Most of the music comprised traditional material arranged for a rock group to play, including a medley of violin reels. The three tracks composed by members of the group were constructed in a traditional style, making them sound like old songs revived.

The album succeeded in becoming the blueprint for the British folk rock explosion that followed. Fairport Convention based its entire subsequent career on the record's innovations, even if the musicians involved were not often those who had played on *Liege and Lief*. Sandy Denny, who viewed the album as a one-off project and was rather more interested, in the long term, in showcasing the songs she had written herself, left to start her own group, Fotheringay. Her husband Trevor Lucas, who had previously been a member of Eclection, worked with her in the group. Bass player Ashley Hutchings started a traditional folk rock group, Steeleye Span, with the duo Tim Hart and Maddy Prior and only a little later, the guitarist Martin Carthy. He was replaced in Fairport Convention by Dave Pegg, who had previously worked with Swarbrick in the Ian Campbell Folk Group. The pair of them steered Fairport Convention through the production of a narrative song cycle, *Babbacombe Lee*, which was issued on record in November 1971. This was in the days when such works were referred to as 'rock operas' and it was as one of those that *Babbacombe Lee* took its place as the first folk equivalent of the Who's *Tommy*, although in sales terms it was very much less successful.

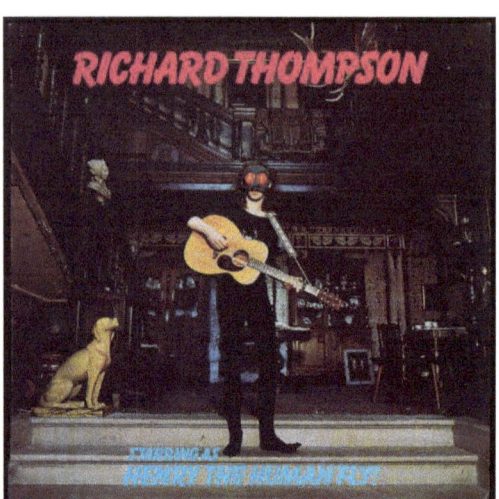 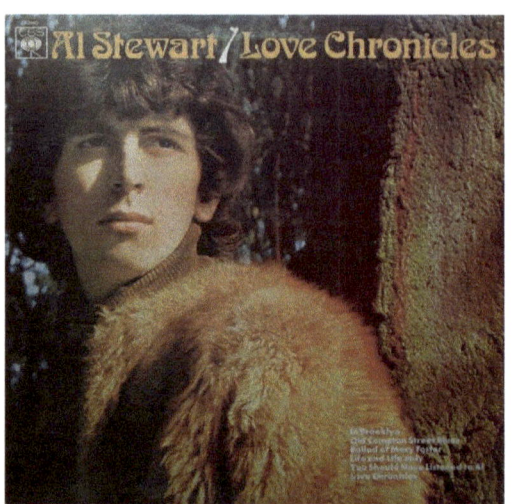

Pete Brown, like Leonard Cohen, was a published poet who decided to become a songwriter and he established a fruitful partnership with Jack Bruce. Starting with songs for Bruce's band, Cream, and continuing through numerous solo albums, the Bruce-Brown team produced some scintillating music. Only the first album, *Songs For A Tailor,* however, managed to enter the charts, in September 1969. Although one later track was titled *Folk Song*, there was no discernible folk influence in the music. Brown also attempted to present his poetry as a lead singer himself, despite having one of the worst voices in the whole of rock music. His Battered Ornaments was made up of musicians who outclassed him, with the result that he found himself eventually being sacked from his own band.

Richard Thompson, reborn as a singer songwriter, made his first solo album, *Henry The Human Fly* in early 1972 and followed it with an album recorded jointly with singer Linda Peters, who had become his wife. *I Want To See The Bright Lights Tonight* was issued in April 1974. Gradually, from album to album, Thompson established himself as one of the finest and most respected singer songwriters of all. His knowledge of traditional folk forms and subject matter gave his songwriting a unique edge as he deliberately made them his underlying influence, in place of the blues-inflected structures that informed almost all of the rest of rock music. As a guitarist too, whether delivering long electric solos or providing a fluent acoustic accompaniment to his own singing, the different aesthetic basis of his playing, together with his keen melodic imagination, made him stand out.

Other British singer songwriters languished a little in the shadows cast by the big names in America. Al Stewart employed guitarist Jimmy Page and members of Fairport Convention (disguised by pseudonyms) to support his tales of the ups and downs of love. The title track of *Love Chronicles*, issued in September 1969, was an eighteen-minute marathon, although it broke down into shorter segments, giving the song the character of a medley. His song *Manuscript*, included on the album *Zero She Flies* in April 1970, introduced some historical story telling that Stewart made a valuable part of his work from then onwards.

John Martyn was one of the first artists, not of West Indian origin, to record for the Island record company. His *London Conversation* in 1967 was the first album to be issued with the distinctive Island pink label. He gradually introduced a jazz element into his songwriting, most notably on the 1973 album, *Solid Air*, which had an improvised feel, with vibrant double bass playing from Danny Thompson (free to play live with John Martyn since the collapse of his group, the Pentangle) and solos by saxophonist Tony Coe and by Martyn himself. John Martyn developed an approach to guitar playing that made extensive use of electric effects, but applied to the playing of an apparently acoustic guitar. He was able, as a solo artist in concert, to fill a hall with sound, using a tape echo device to create multiple loops and delay textures.

The title track of *Solid Air* was dedicated to Martyn's friend and label-mate, Nick Drake. His first album, *Five Leaves Left*, issued in July 1969, was a masterpiece of attractively melodic songwriting, based on an assortment of different guitar tunings, and enhanced by some very skilful arranging. Richard Thompson and Danny Thompson both featured, as did some moving writing for strings, done by a university friend of Drake's, Robert Kirby. Although *Five Leaves Left* and its two following records were not big sellers, they have been actively retained in the Island catalogue ever since. Drake died at the age of twenty-six from an overdose of anti-depressant tablets, without ever becoming more than a cult success, but during the twenty-first century his music has been very frequently employed as background for radio and television programming. The March 2018 issue of *Mojo* magazine had Nick Drake as its cover star, to commemorate what would have been the singer songwriter's seventieth birthday.

Cat Stevens, previously a pop singer with two top ten hits to his name, took advantage of the popularity shift towards folk based material by making an album in that style himself. *Mona Bone Jakon*, issued in July 1970, was a very modest success, but it led to a series of best selling albums, through to the middle of the decade. The first albums by Elton John, *Empty Sky* in June 1969, *Elton John* in May 1970, and several made after that, appealed to the same market, although his background, like that of Cat Stevens and like Jimmy Webb in the US, had nothing to do with folk music. His career continues, the most successful singer songwriter in a crowded field, albeit one who works with a lyricist, Bernie Taupin, rather than doing everything himself. The duo's reworking of their song, *Candle In The Wind*, as a tribute to Princess Diana in September 1997, is the second best selling single ever made (after Bing Crosby's *White Christmas*).

The Irish fiddler, Michael Coleman, made his first recordings for the specialist Shannon label in the spring of 1920 (according to music historian Gearóid Ó hAllmhuráin), before being taken up by various other record companies.

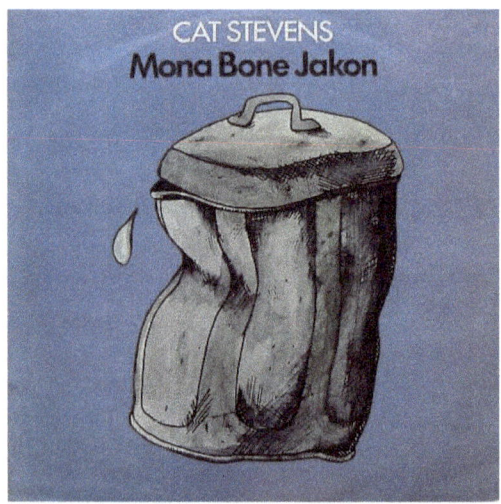 

The Clancy Brothers and Tommy Makem were successful in the US, performing Irish songs with acoustic guitar accompaniment to emulate the sound of the other popular folk groups of the time. The first album, *The Rising Of The Moon – Irish Songs Of Rebellion,* was issued in 1956. The group became big record sellers and the first album recorded for Columbia, in 1961, with Pete Seeger employed to play banjo, was nominated for a Grammy award. Subsequently, the group became popular in its native Ireland. The Dubliners, formed in 1962 to sing in the same style, gained a surprise top ten hit in the UK in 1967 (*Seven Drunken Nights*) and followed it with two top ten albums, *A Drop Of The Hard Stuff* and *More Of The Hard Stuff.*

 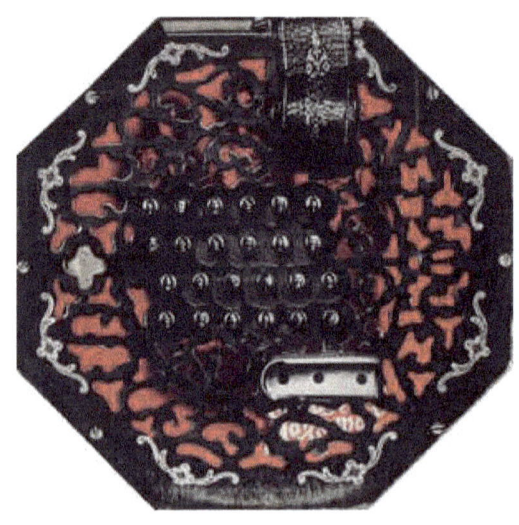

Working in America during the twenties and thirties, he was a major influence on country and folk violin players alike. A number of Coleman's reels can be heard on YouTube, accompanied by a pianist. A comparison with the playing of Dave Swarbrick or with a contemporary virtuoso like Liz Carroll, nearly a century later, reveals them to be closely similar.

The composer Seán Ó Riada incorporated traditional Irish themes in his music through the fifties. In 1960, he formed a band, Ceoltóirí Chualann, in order to play Irish music using the traditional instruments. These included the drum, the bodhran, which Ó Riada played himself, but which had fallen out of favour. The band performed right through the sixties, but some of the original members formed a separate group in late 1962. This was the Chieftains, who made their first recording, *The Chieftains*, in 1963 and have played ever since, with piper Paddy Moloney presiding over changes in personnel. The Chieftains have largely resisted any attempt to introduce rock music elements to their music, although they did team up with singer Van Morrison in 1988 for an album of mostly old tunes, *Irish Heartbeat*. Ciarán Ó Braonáin was drafted in from Clannad to play the bass, and harpist Derek Bell played keyboards on some tracks, but the overall feel of the music remained traditional. A version of Irish music sounding more familiar to fans of groups like Steeleye Span was provided by Planxty, initially formed in early 1972 to provide an accompaniment for the singer Christy Moore. The group still preferred to use a bodhran to drive the rhythms, however, rather than a drum kit. A full integration of Irish music with rock was provided by Horslips, whose first album, *Happy To Meet – Sorry To Part*, was issued in 1972 in a sleeve shaped like the end of a concertina.

TRACKING THE TRACKS

The Bob Dylan albums mentioned are currently available as follows: *Bob Dylan* (Sony 2005); *Bringing It All Back Home* (Sony 2004); *Highway 61 Revisited* (Sony 2004), *Blonde On Blonde* (Sony 2004); and *The Basement Tapes* (Sony double CD 2009). The Manchester concert is on *The Bootleg Series Vol.4 – Live 1966*. This is a double CD with the acoustic set on one disc and the electric set on the other. The three albums between *Bob Dylan* and *Bringing It All Back Home* are also available on Sony, or one can make do with the six tracks included on *Greatest Hits* (Sony 1997), Michael Gray notwithstanding. *Mixed Up Confusion* is included on the three CD set *Biograph* Sony 2011), where a live version of *All Along The Watchtower* from the seventies can also be found. Dylan's harmonica playing with Harry Belafonte is on *The Midnight Special*. This is scarce and expensive on CD, but it is available as a cheap vinyl reissue or as an official download via Speakers Corner Records.

Big Bill Broonzy's first recordings are included on *Big Bill Broonzy Vol.1 1927-1932* (Document 1991). There is also a good double CD compilation of his music, *The Anthology* (Not Now Music 2011). *The Definitive Leadbelly* is a double CD compilation on Not Now Music (2008). *The Western Cowboy* is included on the various artists compilation, *Field Recordings Volume 5 – Louisiana, Texas, Bahamas* (Document 2009).

The Almanac Singers CD, *Talking Union – Original 1941-1942 Recordings* (Naxos 2001) means what it says. *The Ultimate Collection* by the Weavers is on Prism (2003). Pete Seeger's *Greatest Hits* is on Sony (2001). Woody Guthrie's *Dust Bowl Ballads* is on Sony (1998). Some of the tracks are also included on the double CD set, *The Ultimate Collection* (Not Now Music 2007). Arlo Guthrie's *Alice's Restaurant* is on Reprise (1989). The film is available on a Twentieth Century Fox DVD (2003).

Mermaid Avenue by Billy Bragg and Wilco is on Warner (1998). Volumes 2 and 3 are also available. The Bruce Springsteen albums mentioned are *Nebraska* (Sony 2015), *The Ghost Of Tom Joad* (Columbia 2000), and *Devils And Dust* (Columbia 2005). The definitive early Bruce Springsteen album (and still the best music he has ever produced) is *Born To Run* (Sony 2015).

The first, self-titled LP by Joan Baez is on Hallmark (2012). *A Maid Of Constant Sorrow* by Judy Collins is on Hallmark (2015). *Wildflowers* and *Who Knows Where The Time Goes* were issued together on a Rhino CD in 2006.

The Best Of The Animals (EMI 2000) includes the group's versions of *House Of The Rising Sun* and *Baby Let Me Take You Home*. (Dylan's version was called *Baby Let Me Follow You Down*).

The Very Best Of The Byrds is on Sony (2006). The Beatles *Rubber Soul* is on EMI (2009). *The Essential Simon & Garfunkel* is a double CD on Sony (2010). *Greatest Hits* by Manfred Mann (Polygram 1996) includes *The Mighty Quinn*. *A Kind Of Love In 1967-1971* by Julie Driscoll, Brian Auger & The Trinity is on Raven Records (2004) and includes *This Wheel's On Fire*. The Tremeloes *Ultimate Collection*, which includes *I Shall Be Released,* is on Castle Communications (1991).

THE FIRST TIME

All Along The Watchtower by Jimi Hendrix is on *Electric Ladyland* (Sony 2012). *Experience Hendrix* (Sony 2010) is a decent enough collection of the man's hits, including *All Along The Watchtower,* but is not in itself an adequate summary of his music.

Music From Big Pink and *The Band* have been packaged together as a double CD on EMI (2000), together with several out-takes.

The Essential Leonard Cohen is a double CD on Sony (2010). It includes four tracks from *The Songs Of Leonard Cohen.* The complete album is on Sony (2011).

Laura Nyro's *More Than A New Discovery* is on Rev-Ola (2008), although her next album, *Eli And The Thirteenth Confession* (Columbia 2008) is more remarkable. Jimmy Webb is best represented by the compilation CD, *And Someone Left The Cake Out In The Rain* (Debutante 1998), which includes the best known versions of his songs recorded by other people. *Archive* (WEA 1993) is a reasonable compilation of Webb's songs sung by their composer. *Jim Webb Sings Jim Webb* has been issued on CD only in Japan (Sony 1997).

Joni Mitchell's *Song To A Seagull* (Reprise 1988) is the first of twenty-one original albums, all of which are essential for anyone interested in following the career of one of the most significant artists of the twentieth century. With regard to the albums mentioned, *Court And Spark* is on Rhino (2004), *Hejira* is on Asylum (1992), *Don Juan's Reckless Daughter* is on Rhino (2005), *Wild Things Run Fast* is on Polydor (1999), *Both Sides Now* is on Warner Bros (2000). The first version of the song *Both Sides Now* is on *Clouds* (Reprise 1988); Joni Mitchell's own recording of *Woodstock* is on *Ladies Of The Canyon* (Reprise 1988), the album that also includes her biggest hit, *Big Yellow Taxi.* Her most popular album is *Blue* (Reprise 1988). There are three compilation CDs of Joni Mitchell's work available, *Hits* and *Misses* (both Warner 1996) covering the first half of her career and *Dreamland* (Rhino 2004) covering the second half, but, as with Jimi Hendrix, such anthologies are not adequate summaries of her music.

Crosby Stills & Nash is on Atlantic (1994). *Déjà Vu* by Crosby, Stills, Nash & Young is also on Atlantic (1994). *4 Way Street* is a recording of a live performance on a double CD (Atlantic 1992). *Retrospective – The Best Of Buffalo Springfield* is on Rhino (1988). The three Hollies albums mentioned are included with two later releases in a bargain priced five CD set, *Original Album Series Vol.2* (Parlophone 2016). The hit singles are on *20 Golden Greats* (EMI 2000). The Byrds issued five albums while David Crosby was a member, all of which are well worth investigating. The last of the series, *The Notorious Byrd Brothers* (Columbia 1997) is particularly fine. A live version of *Eight Miles High* is included on the double CD, *Untitled/Unissued* (Columbia 2000). Neil Young's *Everybody Knows This Is Nowhere* (Reprise 2009) provided the template for the electric music played by CSN&Y. The Young albums mentioned are *Weld* (Warner Bros 1991), *A Letter Home* (Warner Bros 2014), *After The Goldrush* (Reprise 2009), *Zuma* (Reprise 1993), *Rust Never Sleeps* (Reprise 1993), and *Silver And Gold* (Warner Bros 2000). The version of *Weld* complete with the bonus *Arc* CD is also on Warner Bros (1991).

Carole King's *Tapestry* is on Sony (2009). *The Essential Carole King,* a double CD on Sony (2010), provides a good selection of her own recordings and also of the hit songs she wrote in the sixties, including most of those mentioned. Billy Fury's *Halfway To Paradise* is on *His Wondrous Story – The Complete Collection* (Universal 2008). James Taylor's *Greatest Hits,* which includes *You've Got A Friend,* is on Warner (2005). *Sweet Baby James* is on Warner (1984). *Grace Of My Heart* is on an Odyssey DVD (2015).

The most celebrated examples of the use of folk themes by Vaughan Williams are his *Norfolk Rhapsody No.1* from 1906 (revised in 1914) and his *Fantasia On Greensleeves* from 1934. Both are included on a double CD of his orchestral works, performed by the Academy of St.Martin in the Fields and the New Queen's Hall Orchestra (Decca 1999). Canteloube's *Chants D'Auvergne,* sung by Victoria De Los Angeles, are on EMI (1999). Bartok produced his own settings of a large number of Hungarian folk songs, such as those included with his ballet, *The Miraculous* Mandarin, on a Phillips CD (2000), where the performances are by the Budapest Festival Orchestra, conducted by Ivan Fischer.

There are two currently available CD compilations of songs by Harry Cox, on the Topic and Rounder labels, using recordings made in the fifties. A version of *The Pretty Ploughboy* is included on both. The original 78 rpm record – both songs – can be heard on YouTube. Several recordings by Willie Kemp can be heard on YouTube, mixed in with clips of a basketball player with the same name.

The Paddy Ryan song is included on a seven CD set that celebrates the seventieth anniversary of Topic Records – *Three Score & Ten – A Voice To The People – 70 Years Of The Oldest Independent Record Label In Great Britain* (Topic 2009). It can also be heard on YouTube.

Black And White – The Definitive Collection (Coooking Vinyl 2010) is a good compilation of songs by Ewan MacColl and includes both *Dirty Old Town* and *The First Time Ever I Saw Your Face. The Asphalter's Song* does not appear to be currently available.

England And Her Traditional Songs (Fellside 2003) is a collection of songs by A.L.Lloyd taken from *The Penguin Book Of English Folk Songs* and made in 1960. Both sides of his first record are included with other recordings he made in the fifties on the double CD, *Bramble Briars And Beams Of The Sun* (Fellside 2011). *Folk Song Today* has not been reissued on vinyl or CD. The Shirley Collins track is included on the double CD, *Two Classic Albums Plus Bonus Tracks* (Real Gone 2012).

Fairytale of New York by Kirsty MacColl and the Pogues is included on many of the contemporary Christmas compilation albums. It is also on *A New England – The Very Best Of Kirsty MacColl* (Union Square Music 2013) and on the double CD by the Pogues, *30:30 – The Essential Collection* (Rhino 2013).

MUSIC GENRES

Lodestar by Shirley Collins is on Domino (2016). *Everything Changes* by Peggy Seeger is on Signet (2014).

Davy Graham's *The Guitar Player* is on Castle Music (2003), with *Anji* included in the bonus tracks. An earlier CD issue, *The Guitar Player...Plus* on See For Miles (1992) added the whole of the ¾ *A.D.* EP. The album with Shirley Collins, *Folk Roots, New Routes* is on Fledg'ling (2005). Bert Jansch's version of *Anji* is on his first album, *Bert Jansch* (Sanctuary 2001). Paul Simon's is on Simon & Garfunkel's *Sounds Of Silence* (Sony 2001). Gordon Giltrap's is on *Janschology* (La Cooka Ratcha 2000). Stan Webb's is on the Chicken Shack album, *100 Ton Chicken* (Talking Elephant 2012). John Renbourn's first album, *John Renbourn,* is on Sanctuary (2015). *Basket Of Light* by the Pentangle is on Sanctuary (2006).

Donovan's late sixties music is very well served by a four CD set, *Breezes Of Patchouli – His Studio Recordings 1966-1969* (EMI 2013). *Catch The Wind* and the four *Universal Soldier* songs are included on *The Very Best Of The Early Years* (Sanctuary 2005).

The first, self-titled album by the Incredible String Band and *The 5000 Spirits Or The Layers Of The Onion* are both on Fledg'ling (2010).

The first, self-titled album by Fairport Convention is on Polydor (2003). *What We Did On Our Holidays* is on Island (2003). *Unhalfbricking* is on Island (2003). *Liege And Lief* is on Island (2012), with a second CD of out-takes and BBC sessions. *Babbacombe Lee* is on Island (2004). The first four albums, together with the fifth, *Full House,* are assembled on a bargain priced box set, *5 Classic Albums* (Universal 2015). *Sandy Denny and the Strawbs – All Our Own Work* is on Witchwood (2010). *Part Of The Union* is on the Strawbs album, *Bursting At The Seams* (Universal 1998).

The original albums by the Ian Campbell Folk Group are deleted on CD and hard to find. There is a reasonably priced four CD boxed set, however, *The Complete Transatlantic Recordings* (Cherry Tree 2016). Several albums by Dave Swarbrick and Martin Carthy are available on CD. All of them are excellent, but perhaps *Byker Hill* (Topic 2008) has the edge. *Scarborough Fair* is included on Martin Carthy's self-titled debut album (Topic 2000). Eliza Carthy's *Heat Light And Sound* is on Topic (2000). Norma Waterson's self-titled album from 1996, recorded for Hannibal with her family and friends, was nominated for a Mercury Music Prize.

Fotheringay is on Fledg'ling (2004). *The Best Of Steeleye Span* is on EMI (2002). *The Lark In The Morning – The Early Years* (Sanctuary double CD 2003) provides an essential companion for it.

Richard Thompson's *Henry The Human Fly* is on Fledg'ling (2004); *I Want To See The Bright Lights Tonight* is on Island (2004). Of the many Thompson albums issued after these, none is less than excellent. *Amnesia* (EMI 1988) is particularly recommended and is a good place to start an appreciation of the man's work. Remarkably, his 2015 album on the Proper label, *Still,* which reveals his songwriting talent burning as brightly as ever, reached number ten in the UK album charts, making it his most successful release to date.

Al Stewart's *Love Chronicles* and *Zero She Flies* are included in the five CD set, *Original Album Series* (Parlophone 2014), together with the original version of his first album, *Bedsitter Images*, and two later albums, *Year Of The Cat* and *Time Passages. May You Never – The Essential John Martyn* (Universal Island 2016) provides a good overview of Martyn's career on three CDs. Two thirds of the *Solid Air* album is included – the whole thing is also on Universal Island (2000). *Live At Leeds*, presenting the work of a trio, John Martyn on acoustic guitar plus electric effects, Danny Thompson on double bass, and jazz player Jon Stevens on drums, and originally issued as a limited edition LP available by mail order from John Martyn himself, is on a Snapper double CD (2006) with numerous bonus tracks. *A Treasury* (Universal Island 2012) is a good compilation of Nick Drake's music. The three albums he released during his lifetime are *Five Leaves Left* (Universal Island 2013), *Bryter Layter* (Universal Island 2004), and *Pink Moon* (Universal Island 2004). *The Very Best Of Cat Stevens* is on Universal Island (2006). *Mona Bone Jakon* is also on Universal Island (2000).

Elton John is overdue for an updated overview of his music on CD. *Greatest Hits 1970-2002* is a double CD on Virgin/EMI (2002). *Empty Sky* is on Mercury (1995); *Elton John* is on Mercury (2008), with a bonus CD of demos and BBC sessions. *Candle In The Wind 1997* is still available as a CD single (Mercury 2007).

Sunshine Of Your Love – A Life In Music is a double CD compilation by Jack Bruce on Universal Polydor (2015). *Songs For A Tailor* is on Polydor (2003). Of his many other albums, *Harmony Row* (Polydor 2003) and *Monkjack* (a duo recording with organist Bernie Worrell) (CMP 1995) are particularly recommended. *Living Life Backwards – The Best Of Pete Brown* (EMI 2006) is a good compilation of Brown's work with Battered Ornaments and the band he formed subsequently, Piblokto!

Michael Coleman 1891-1945 is a package of two CDs with a book on Gael Linn (2011). Liz Carroll has made several albums. *Liz Carroll* is on Green Linnet (2008). *The Best Of The Clancy Brothers And Tommy Makem* is on Sony (2002). *The Very Best Of The Dubliners* is on Universal Decca (2009). *The Essential Collection* (Gael Linn 2011) is a three CD set by Seán Ó Riada, including music by Ceoltóirí Chualann. *The Best Of The Chieftains* is on Sony (2002). The first album is on Claddagh (2000). *Irish Heartbeat* is on Polydor (1999). *The Planxty Collection* is on Shanachie (2000). *Treasury – The Very Best Of Horslips* is a double CD on Horslips Records (2010).

THE FIRST TIME

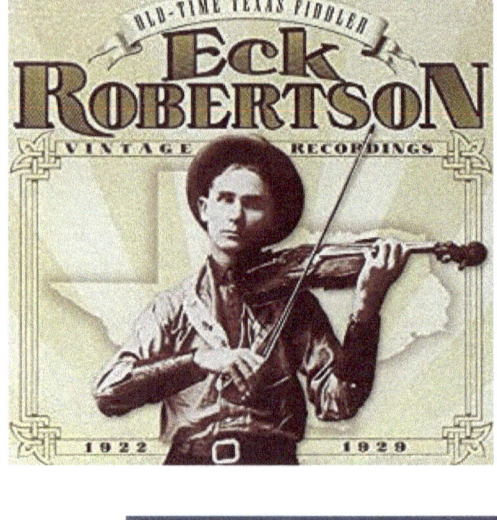

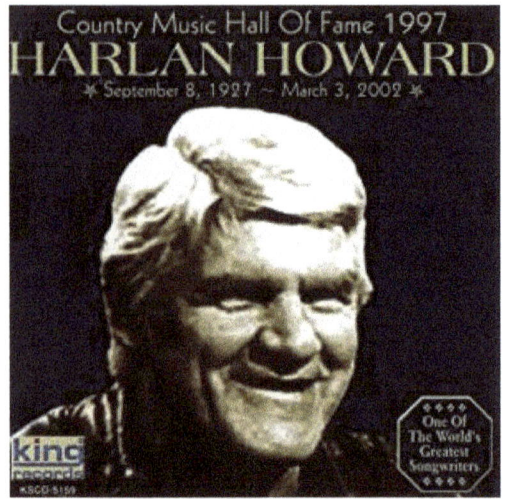

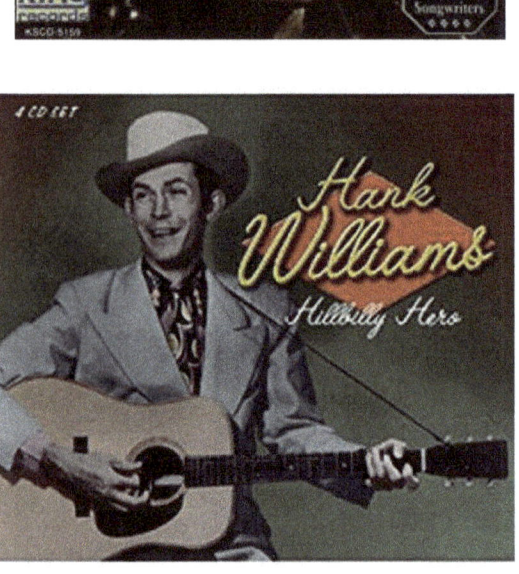

The first musician to play at the Grand Ole Opry, the week that the show was announced with that title, was the black harmonica player DeFord Bailey. Unusually for a concert venue in the South at that time, the Opry was clearly not racist, although on tour elsewhere, Bailey had to pretend to be the servant of singer and banjo player Uncle Dave Macon, one of the biggest stars of the time, in order to avoid trouble. The same motivation applied in the case of the Charlie Parker Quintet, playing modern jazz over twenty years later. Red Rodney, who was employed to play trumpet after Miles Davis left the band, had to pretend to be an albino Negro when touring in the Southern states. To add credence to the masquerade, Parker persuaded Rodney to sing a blues during each set.

Ryman Auditorium, home of the Grand Ole Opry from 1943 until 1974

30 COUNTRY

"There is hidden among the mountains of Kentucky, Tennessee, and the Carolinas a people of whose inner nature and its musical expression almost nothing has been said. The music of the Southern mountaineer is not only peculiar, but, like himself, peculiarly American. Nearly all mountaineers are singers. Their untrained voices are of good timbre, the women's being sweet and high and tremulous, and their sense of pitch and tone and harmony remarkably true. The fiddler or the banjo-player is well treated and beloved among them, like the minstrel of feudal days."
(Emma Bell Miles, *Harper's Monthly Magazine* June 1904)

"You've got to have smelled a lot of mule manure before you can sing like a hillbilly."   (Hank Williams c. late 1940s)

"Country is a music which was bred in poverty and violence, and is the polar opposite of the Broadway philosophy that everything will come out all right at the end. Baseless optimism is not on the agenda."
(Brian Hinton, author of *Country Roads – How Country Came To Nashville*)

"What do you get when you play a country song backwards?
— You get your house back, your wife back, your dog back, your truck back..." (joke, unknown origin)

"The best country music is incredibly simple, yet very poignant and moving."   (Emmylou Harris)

"Country music is three chords and the truth."   (Harlan Howard)

In essence, country music is to white America what the blues is to black America – indeed much of the music even shares the same three chord structure that defines the blues, as the Harlan Howard quotation above acknowledges. Like the blues, the origins of the music lie hidden, back in the time before there were recordings to capture the sound. The first country record, made by a country musician, living and working in Texas, was *Sallie Goodin/Arkansaw Traveler*, by fiddler Eck Robertson, with a second fiddler, Henry Gilliland, joining in on the B-side. This was released by Victor in 1922. Clearly the music is descended from the playing of Gaelic reels, the folk music of parts of the UK and Ireland, but Robertson uses a drone technique that takes the music into a territory that is distinctly American. At this time, he would not have heard any of the contemporary fiddlers from Ireland playing – Michael Coleman's career in the US had not yet started. As with the blues, there are earlier recordings than this of music taken from country sources, but performed by people who were not themselves country musicians. Len Spencer recorded a comedy routine based around *Arkansaw Traveler* in 1902, in which a fiddler can be heard playing the tune itself, but the record is *about* country music rather than being a genuine example of it. Similarly, the Victor Military Band recorded a country tune called *Soldier's Joy* in 1917.

On November 28th 1925, George D. Hay, working as a presenter on the Nashville, Tennessee radio station WSM, made the first broadcast of a live concert he called the WSM Barn Dance. The performer on this occasion was an elderly fiddler by the name of Uncle Jimmy Thompson, with his niece Eve accompanying him on the piano. The broadcast became a regular weekly feature and, following a throw-away remark by Hay in December 1927, that the concert, which followed a programme of opera music, was not so much grand opera as "grand ole opry", it became known ever after as the Grand Ole Opry. The programme is still broadcast today and is the longest running radio show in the US.

Hay had strong views as to what was acceptable to be played on his shows. Drums were not, brass instruments were not, and neither, when first introduced by Sam McGee at the start of the forties, was the electrically amplified guitar. In September 1967, *Billboard* reported that a full drum kit was used for the first time when Jerry Reed

Roy Acuff and band

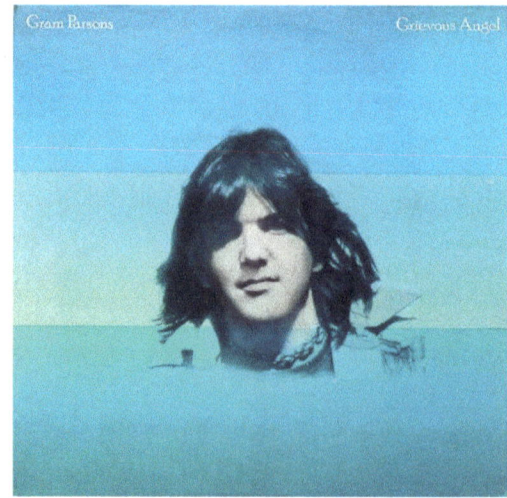

Note guitarists in both bands pictured on this page playing with their instruments held flat and their left hands moving a metal slide on the fretboard

Dolly Parton at the Grand Ole Opry in 2005

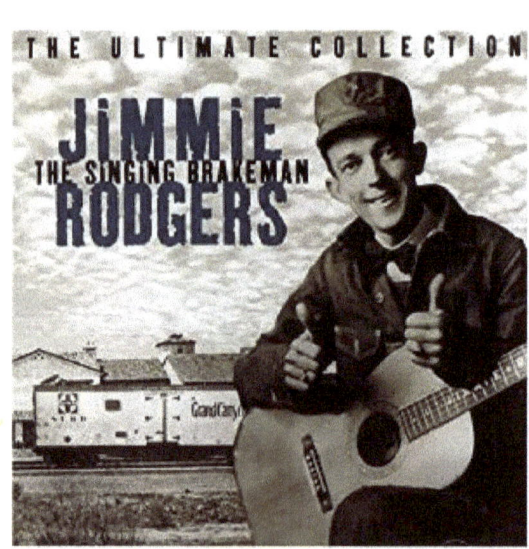

Emmett Miller

performed. Several other artists over the years have also claimed to have used drums, however, the first being Bob Wills in 1944. Some sources claim that Wills used only a snare drum and that this was hidden behind a curtain, but Wills' biographer, Charles R. Townsend, who spoke with the musician himself, is adamant that the drums were on show. Ernest Tubb appeared at the Opry in 1943 with a band that included an electric guitar, after which several other artists did the same. In March 1968, the Byrds played at the Opry, as the first band lacking a country background to do so. They did not go down well with the audience, which heckled the group's long hair and did not appreciate the last minute switch from an announced Merle Haggard cover to a song of their own, *Hickory Wind*. The version of the song recorded by former Byrd Gram Parsons on his solo album *Grievous Angel*, made in 1973, which has disturbingly loud audience noise added to a studio performance, is perhaps a sly reference back to the Opry experience. In January 1973, Jerry Lee Lewis went much further than this when he greatly exceeded his allotted performance time and included several of his rock 'n' roll hits, which he had been asked not to do. According to legend and to *Rolling Stone* magazine, when instructed beforehand that he must play only country music, he replied, "What country?" To underline his rebellion, Lewis also broke the rule that no four letter words should be uttered on stage.

Although singers did perform on occasion in the early days, the focus was very much on instrumental music, until Roy Acuff, who first sang at the Opry in 1938, started a general move towards a song based approach. Acuff achieved a million selling hit in 1942 with *Wabash Cannon Ball* and became known as the 'king of country music'. He founded the Acuff-Rose music publishing company in Nashville in 1942, with songwriter Fred Rose. This eventually became the most successful publisher in country. It was the combination of Acuff-Rose with the Grand Ole Opry that made Nashville into the spiritual and the actual centre of country music.

The first million selling country records came early – *Wildwood Flower* by the Carter Family, issued in 1928, and three songs by Jimmie Rodgers – *Blue Yodel* and *Brakeman's Blues*, also from 1928, and *The Soldier's Sweetheart*, the first recording made by Rodgers, in 1927. It was not until January 1944, however, that Billboard introduced a country music chart, the confusingly named (for modern listeners) 'most played jukebox folk records'. A chart relating to record sales followed four years later, with a radio play chart appearing the year after that. In 1958, these were all combined into a single 'Hot C&W Sides' chart. The first number one, in 1944, was a country song, but not a country performance – *Pistol Packin' Mama* by Bing Crosby and the Andrews Sisters – although it was followed to the number one slot by the version recorded by Al Dexter, the song's composer. Dexter's record also reached number one in the national charts, the first country record to achieve this. It eventually sold a million copies (as did the Bing Crosby recording). The first number one in the 1948 country records chart was *Anytime* by Eddy Arnold, while the first in 1958 was *Bird Dog* by the Everly Brothers. The fact that this record, by a duo that is usually considered to be a rock 'n' roll act, also reached number two in both the national chart and the R&B chart serves to emphasise the crucial role played by country music in the development of rock 'n' roll. This is explained in full in the Rock 'n' Roll chapter in this book.

Jimmie Rodgers was the first major star of country and he created the blueprint for the subsequent development of the music, not least by including a Hawaiian guitar in his backing band. The instrument gave birth eventually to the pedal steel guitar, first built in 1939, whose sound has become the defining characteristic of country. Writer Nick Tosches proposes an alternative name for the true founding master of country music, that of Emmett Miller. Despite gaining little popular success with his records, Miller invented the bluesy yodelling singing style that Jimmie Rodgers made his own and was also the first country musician to record with brass instruments and with drums – with a jazz band, in fact. He performed in blackface because his background was in the minstrel shows where this was commonly done. He first recorded in 1924. Writing in 1977, for the first edition of *Country – The Twisted Roots Of Rock 'n' Roll*, and leaving the paragraph unchanged for the revised edition in 1996, Tosches could say that he had never heard the October 25th 1924 recording of *Anytime* and that he did not know of anyone who had. In 2010, the song was uploaded on to YouTube, where anyone can hear that the claims made by Tosches for Emmett Miller's innovations are completely accurate. The song is the same as the one that provided a hit for Eddy Arnold twenty-four years later.

THE FIRST TIME

Bob Wills and the Texas Playboys in 1944

The Four Aces of Western Swing. Bill Haley is third along

Bill Monroe and the Blue Grass Boys c.1945

A version of the Light Crust Doughboys is still performing, making it the longest-lived band in recording history. Unsurprisingly, none of the current members were in the band at the start, but banjo player Marvin 'Smokey' Montgomery performed from 1935 until his death in 2001. The gospel group, the Blind Boys of Alabama, was formed in 1939, with original member Jimmy Carter still singing in 2018. The Dixie Hummingbirds was formed even earlier, in 1928, and is still performing, albeit with no original members. Only in recent years, however, has a group of singers with no musicians been considered to be something we can call a 'band'. Of course, many classical music orchestras still performing today have been in existence far longer than these. The Royal Danish Orchestra traces its origins back to 1448 and is probably the oldest of all.

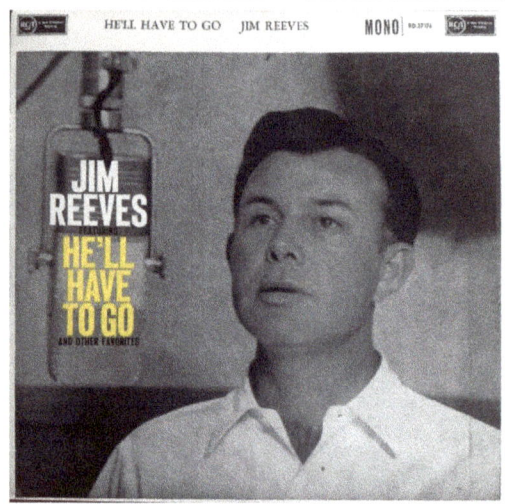

Other early country artists followed Emmett Miller's example in borrowing elements of jazz for their music. Carson Robison's Kansas Jack-Rabbits, with a piece called *Nonsense* recorded in 1929, were a genuine hybrid, proceeding from verse to verse as though the band could not decide whether it was playing jazz or country. Violinist Bob Wills formed the Wills Fiddle Band in 1930, with singer Milton Brown. It had no brass instruments, but a distinct New Orleans jazz feel to the rhythms. The band became the Light Crust Doughboys in 1931, after receiving sponsorship from the Burrus Mill company in Saginaw, Texas, a flour producer, although Brown left in 1932 and Wills was fired by the manager a year later. Both formed new bands to continue playing in the same style – Milton Brown's Musical Brownies and Bob Wills and his Texas Playboys. By the early forties, the music played by these bands was being described as 'Western swing'. During 1944, *Billboard* used the term a number of times, in reference to the similar sounding music of Spade Cooley, and in September 1945 a short documentary film titled *Spade Cooley: King of Western Swing* was released. It was Bob Wills, however, who scored the biggest hit. His *San Antonio Rose* was issued in 1940 and went on to sell a million copies. Western swing had a major part to play in the development of rock 'n' roll – Bill Haley started his career within the genre, leading a band called the Four Aces of Western Swing, while the bands led by Milton Brown and Bob Wills were also home to some significant electric guitar pioneers.

The instrumental country music favoured by the Grand Ole Opry in its early days was not jazz influenced – it did not, after all, include drummers. In 1939, mandolin player Bill Monroe formed the Blue Grass Boys, named after a region in Kentucky, to revive a style of music that was in danger of dying out. The band played at the Opry and was given an encore, which was the first time this had happened at the venue. The music, relying on the virtuosity of its players to delight audiences, especially after banjo player Earl Scruggs joined the band in 1945, became known as bluegrass. Scruggs and guitarist Lester Flatt achieved considerable success as a duo after leaving the Blue Grass Boys in 1948.

Hank Williams, regarded as the most important artist in the whole of country music, had his first record, *Never Again*, issued in January 1947, after being signed by Fred Rose. Contracted to the newly formed MGM record company shortly afterwards, Williams scored his first hit later the same year, with *Move It On Over*, a song whose rhythm and structure anticipated Bill Haley's *Rock Around The Clock*, despite its reliance on traditional country instrumentation. The first of several million selling records, *Lovesick Blues*, followed in 1949. This was one of the few songs recorded by Williams that he did not write himself. On New Year's Day 1953, Hank Williams died of a heart attack. He was just twenty-nine. He had been fired from the Grand Ole Opry for unreliability and drunkenness, but this was forgotten after his death as he rapidly acquired legendary status. His rise from rags to riches epitomised the country music dream, especially when his rowdy behaviour was interpreted as a sign that he had always stayed true to his roots. In 1975, when Waylon Jennings wanted to draw attention to the fact that, in his opinion, country music had become too much a part of showbiz, it was the legend of Hank Williams that he chose to draw on for the words of his song, *Are You Sure Hank Done It This Way?*

In the UK, artists like Elvis Presley, Jerry Lee Lewis, and the Everly Brothers were big stars, as they were in the US, but they had moved beyond their country roots into rock 'n' roll. The first successful singer performing country music straight was Jim Reeves. A star in the US since 1953, when his second single, *Mexican Joe*, was a country chart number one, he scored his first hit in the UK in 1960, with *He'll Have To Go*. In 1966, when the beat groups were supposed to be reigning supreme, Reeves gained a number one hit with *Distant Drums*. Paradoxically, the other big country success in the UK was Ray Charles, who had made a surprising change of direction with his 1962 album, *Modern Sounds In Country and Western Music*, and achieved a number one hit with a song taken from it, *I Can't Stop Loving You*.

The beat groups, though happy to cover songs by the rock 'n' roll artists, largely stayed clear of country. The Liverpool group Sonny Webb and the Cascades, however, included country material in its act and made a single, *You've Got Everything*, in 1963, although this was not successful. The song is more pop than country, but the B-side, *Border Of The Blues*, is a cover of a Hank Locklin song. In 1964, the group changed its name to the Hillsiders and

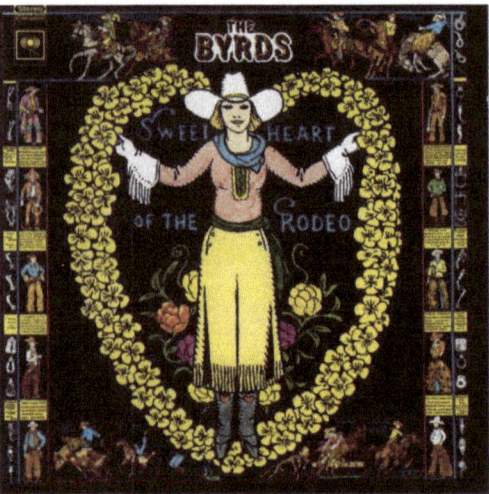
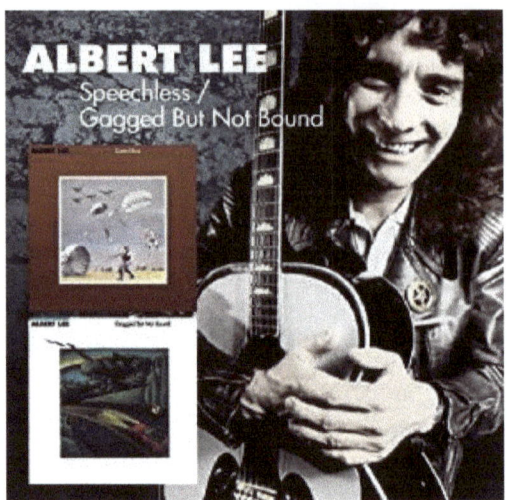
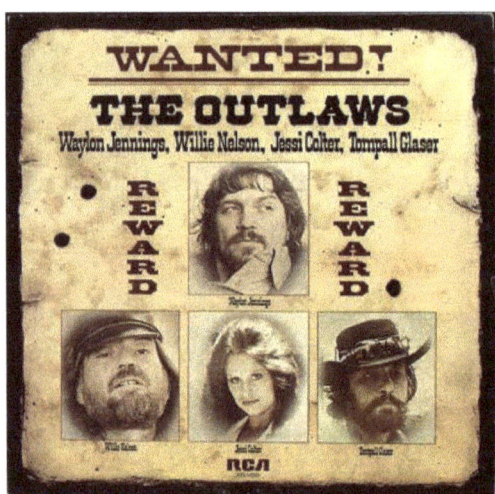

What has become known as alternative country was introduced by the band Uncle Tupelo, whose first album, *No Depression,* was issued in 1990. Essentially, the genre is a development of country rock rather than anything to do with Nashville, although it does emphasise the extent to which the musical vocabulary of country has become a standard resource for rock musicians. Uncle Tupelo broke up in 1994, but two notable bands emerged from the ashes – Son Volt and Wilco.

concentrated on playing just country music. An album, *The English Country Side,* recorded with Bobby Bare and produced by Chet Atkins, reached number 17 in the US country albums chart in 1967, and the group was invited to appear at the Grand Ole Opry. The Beatles played country on occasion, such as the Buck Owens cover, *Act Naturally,* included on the *Help!* LP, or *What Goes On,* a group composition in the same style, included on the *Rubber Soul* LP. Both of these songs were sung by Ringo Starr. After the break-up of the Beatles, he made a whole album of country music, *Beaucoups Of Blues,* issued in September 1970. At the end of 1966, Tom Jones scored a number one hit with *The Green Green Grass Of Home* and the next year Engelbert Humperdinck reached number two with *There Goes My Everything.* Both had been country hits in the US, by Porter Wagoner and Jack Greene respectively, but the UK cover versions were not marketed as country. The British guitarist Albert Lee, who first gained a measure of fame with the band Heads Hands and Feet, moved to the US in 1974. Beginning as a member of Emmylou Harris' band, he built a reputation as one of the great country guitarists – a reputation in no way tarnished by his five year stint in Eric Clapton's band.

An album made by the Byrds in 1968, *Sweetheart of the Rodeo,* has been much lauded as inventing a genre known as country rock. Realistically, country rock was invented in the fifties when it was called rock 'n' roll, but what the Byrds album did do was to bring back to rock the traditional country instruments – steel guitar, mandolin, and banjo – that had been abandoned by the country musicians who played rock 'n' roll. More to the point, the Byrds did this from the position of being one of the most respected rock groups of the time, whose move to a new direction was likely to be very much noticed. New member Gram Parsons had previously produced something very similar with his International Submarine Band, whose album *Safe At Home* was recorded the year before. *Sweetheart of the Rodeo* was not a huge success in chart terms in either the US or the UK, but its influence definitely was huge. Numerous other groups were formed during the next years to play country rock, the most successful of them being the Eagles.

The outlaw movement, spearheaded by Waylon Jennings and Willie Nelson, was to some extent a response from the world of country to the appropriation of its music by rock. Adopting a suitably hirsute appearance and playing music that was noticeably tougher than country had generally become at the time, Jennings and Nelson, together with Tompall Glaser and Jessi Colter laid out their musical manifesto on a 1976 album titled *Wanted! The Outlaws.* The immediate result was sales of nearly five million copies – the first country album to achieve this level of success. One song, *Honky-Tonk Heroes* by Waylon Jennings, had previously been the title track of a Jennings album issued in 1973, which was effectively the first outlaw record.

The rise to success of Linda Ronstadt and Emmylou Harris was even more remarkable, with the singers managing to appeal equally to the rock and country markets. Linda Ronstadt made her first record in 1967, as a member of the Stone Poneys. Her first solo album followed in 1969, *Hand Sown…Home Grown.* Her career continued to build slowly, until 1975, when her album *Heart Like A Wheel* succeeded in reaching number one in both the pop and country album charts. Her version of *I Can't Help It (If I'm Still In Love With You),* originally a hit for Hank Williams, gave her a Grammy award for best female country vocal performance. Emmylou Harris attracted little attention with her 1969 album, *Gliding Bird,* but she sang with Gram Parsons in 1973 and relaunched her solo career with *Pieces Of The Sky,* issued in 1975. (She was able to give this a boost by performing as second singer on Bob Dylan's *Desire* album, the following year). The two women collaborated with each other and with the legendary Dolly Parton for the album *Trio.* This was released in 1987, although it had been created over several years previously. The album was an enormous pop and country success, reaching number six in the Billboard album chart, number one in the country chart, and selling over four million copies altogether. The assimilation of country into the popular music mainstream that this success represented was underlined in later years by the similar achievements of Shania Twain and Taylor Swift – and by the tumultuous reception given to Dolly Parton – now a venerated veteran performer – at the Glastonbury Festival in the UK in 2014.

Garth Brooks produced nothing new when he issued his self-titled first album in 1989. Nevertheless, it launched the career of a performer who has gained unprecedented success in both country and the wider music arena. As

THE FIRST TIME

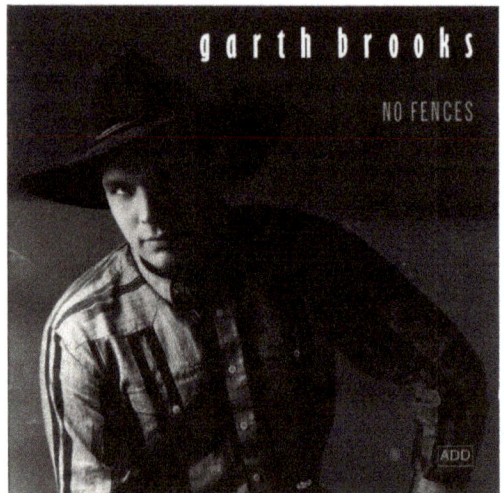
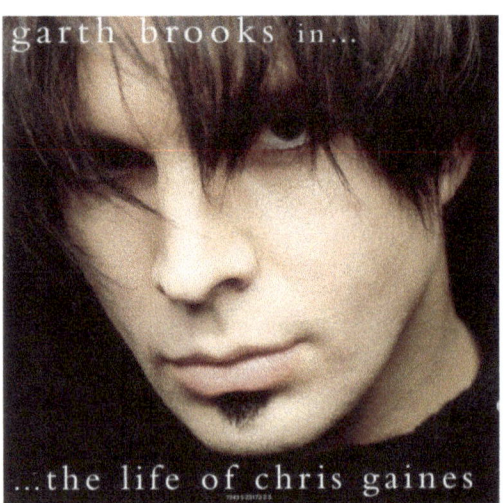

Garth Brooks' biggest selling album (and the only one to enter the top ten album chart in the UK)

American III: Solitary Man

Having revitalised the music of Johnny Cash, Rick Rubin was called on to do the same for Neil Diamond. *12 Songs* was issued in 2005 and fulfilled its brief. The album entered the top five in both the US and the UK charts, which Diamond had not managed since his 1980 album, *The Jazz Singer*. It also succeeded in extending interest in Neil Diamond beyond his accustomed easy listening audience, probably for the first time. Amongst Rubin's other successes were the six albums he produced for the funk-rock band Red Hot Chili Peppers during the nineties and the noughties, music which included the hugely influential single, *Under The Bridge*, in 1992. This has nothing to do with country, of course.

An equally unlikely, but equally effective collaboration was that between bluegrass singer and fiddle player Alison Krauss and the former lead singer with Led Zeppelin, Robert Plant. Their album, *Raising Sand,* was issued in late 2007 to considerable commercial success and critical acclaim. The pair toured in support of the album in 2008, but further recording sessions were left unfinished.

The Country Music Association Awards (CMAs) were first presented in 1967. There were five categories, with the accolade of 'Entertainer of the Year' being presented to Eddy Arnold. The following year, the event was hosted at the Grand Ole Opry and televised – as it has been ever since. Glen Campbell was Entertainer of the Year on that occasion.

reported in *Rolling Stone* magazine, at the start of 2015, Garth Brooks was the best selling solo artist of all time in the US, ahead of Elvis Presley. The Beatles were the only music act of any kind ahead of him. In 1999, Brooks took the extraordinary step of adopting the role of a fictional rock singer, Chris Gaines, and recording the greatest hits compilation that would have been made if the character had been real. The result, presumably intended to demonstrate Brooks' ability to create other kinds of music apart from country, was a very good folk rock album indeed. Brooks proved his point, although the album sales of two million, which would have been considered an enormous success if achieved by anyone else, resulted in the album, *Garth Brooks In The Life Of Chris Gaines*, being counted a failure.

Johnny Cash was signed to Sun records in 1955, but did not become a rock 'n' roller. His big hit of 1957, *I Walk The Line*, was very much a country tune and reached number one in the country charts. During the sixties he performed at a number of prisons in the US and his two best-selling albums from that time were live recordings from those venues – *Johnny Cash At Folsom Prison* and *Johnny Cash At San Quentin*. With his tough image, he was able to convince the long-term inmates that he was the same as they were. He married June Carter, daughter of Mother Maybelle of the Carter Family, in 1968. June Carter had written the biggest hit of Cash's career, *Ring Of Fire*, to describe her feelings of falling in love with him. During the last decade of his life, he confirmed his status as one of the greats of country music with a series of five albums, *American Recordings I – V*, made in an unlikely collaboration with producer Rick Rubin, the co-founder of hip hop's premier label, Def Jam. Earlier artists, the Electric Flag (with little country input), the Flying Burrito Brothers (formed by Gram Parsons), and Steve Stills' Manassas, had created music intended to describe what it meant to be American. Arguably, Johnny Cash, with his stately covers of songs from such diverse sources as Tom Petty, Neil Diamond, Hank Williams, and Odetta, was the first person to really achieve this.

TRACKING THE TRACKS

Eck Robertson can be heard on *Old Time Texas Fiddler – Vintage Recordings 1922-1929* (County 1998).

Len Spencer's *Arkansas Traveler* can be heard on YouTube.

The various artists CD, *Nashville – The Early String Bands Volume Two* (County Records 2015) includes three tracks by Uncle Jimmy Thompson, four tracks by DeFord Bailey, and two tracks by Uncle Dave Macon.

Grievous Angel by Gram Parsons is on Rhino (2008).

The Essential Recordings is a double CD by Roy Acuff (Primo 2016) and includes *Wabash Cannon Ball*.

The Best Of The Carter Family (Prism 2003) includes *Wildwood Flower*.

Jimmie Rodgers The Singing Brakeman – The Ultimate Collection (Platinum 2002) includes all the tracks mentioned.

The Essential Collection by Bing Crosby and the Andrews Sisters (MCA Coral 1999) includes *Pistol Packin' Mama*. The Al Dexter version is on a CD named after it (ASV 1999).

Eddy Arnold's *Anytime* is included on *Complete Original #1 Hits* (Real Gone Music 2013). *Bird Dog* is on *The Very Best Of The Everly Brothers* (Rhino 2014).

The Minstrel Man From Georgia (Columbia 1996) contains the recordings made by Emmett Miller for the Okeh label in 1928-29. Other Miller recordings can be heard on YouTube. Carson Robison's *Nonsense* is on YouTube.

The earliest recordings by the Light Crust Doughboys date from 1933, after Milton Brown and Bob Wills had left the band. *Roll Up The Carpet – Recorded 1933-1940* is on BACM. The work of Milton Brown and his Musical Brownies is given a comprehensive overview on a four CD boxed set issued by Proper Records, called *Daddy of Western Swing* (2003). A similar Proper Records set is devoted to Bob Wills and his Texas Playboys – *Take Me Back To Tulsa* (2001). *The Essential Recordings* by Spade Cooley is a double CD on Primo (2015). A Proper Records four CD set by Bill Haley, *From Western Swing To Rock* (2013), has fifteen tracks by the Four Aces Of Western Swing.

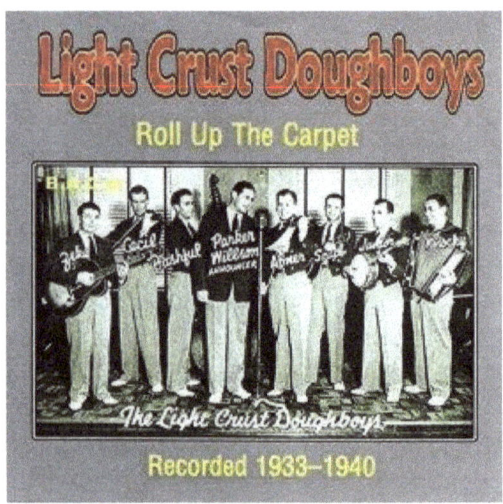
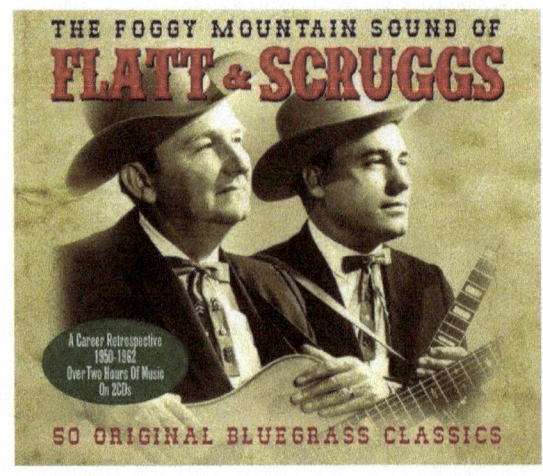

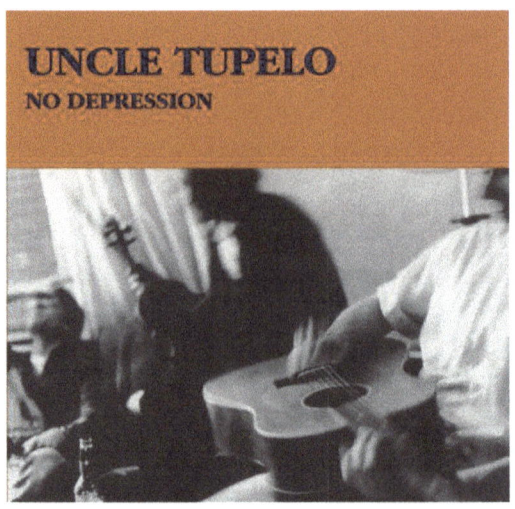
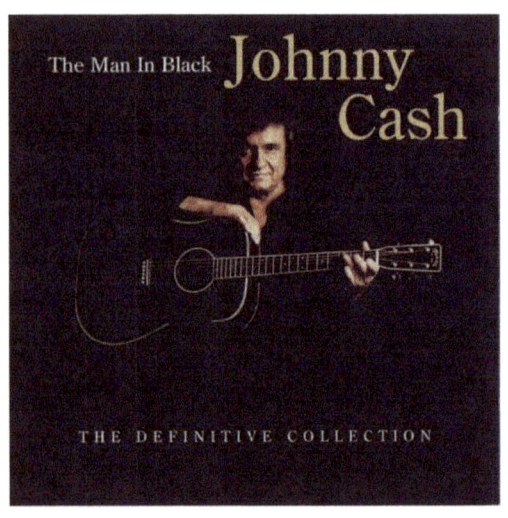

MUSIC GENRES

A four CD set by Bill Monroe – *All The Classic Releases 1936-1949* – is on JSP rather than Proper (2003). Flatt and Scruggs are well represented by the double CD, *The Foggy Mountain Sound Of Flatt and Scruggs* (Not Now Music 2013).

The Very Best Of Hank Williams is a double CD on Not Now Music (2013). *Never Again* is included on the four CD set, *The Complete Singles As & Bs 1947-55* (Acrobat 2016). *Are You Sure Hank Done It This Way* is on *The Essential Waylon Jennings* (Sony 2011).

The Very Best Of Jim Reeves is on Sony (2009). *Mexican Joe* is on *The Absolutely Essential 3 CD Collection* (Big 3 2011).

Modern Sounds In Country And Western Music by Ray Charles is on Hallmark (2014).

Sonny Webb and the Cascades have not made it to CD. Various tracks, including both sides of the single, can be heard on YouTube. The LP by Bobby Bare and the Hillsiders is not on CD either. Nine of its eleven tracks are on YouTube, however.

The Beatles LPs *Help!* and *Rubber Soul* are on EMI (2009). *Beaucoups Of Blues* by Ringo Starr is on EMI (1995).

The Green Green Grass Of Home is on *Tom Jones Greatest Hits* (Polygram 2003). *There Goes My Everything* is on *Release Me – The Best Of Engelbert Humperdinck* (Universal/Decca 2012).

Albert Lee has made a large number of records over the years, both in his own name and with other people. *Like This* from 2008 (Heroic Records) is a good place to start.

Sweetheart Of The Rodeo by the Byrds is on Columbia (2008). Numerous bonus tracks, including some by the International Submarine Band, have expanded the album to a double CD. The complete *Safe At Home* album is on Gonzo (2016).

The various artists compilation *Wanted! The Outlaws* is on RCA (1996). *Honky Tonk Heroes* by Waylon Jennings is on Buddha (1999).

Hand Sown... Home Grown by Linda Ronstadt is on Capitol (2004). *Heart Like A Wheel*, which includes *I Can't Help It,* is on Capitol (1996). *Gliding Bird* by Emmylou Harris is not on CD, but all of the tracks can be heard on YouTube. *Pieces Of The Sky* is on Rhino (2004). Bob Dylan's *Desire* is on Columbia (2004). *Trio* by Linda Ronstadt, Emmylou Harris, and Dolly Parton is on Warner Bros (1987).

No Depression by Uncle Tupelo is on Columbia (2003). A double CD version including numerous out-takes was issued by Sony in 2014.

Garth Brooks *The Ultimate Hits* is a boxed set comprising two CDs and a DVD (Sony 2014). *In The Life Of Chris Gaines* is on Capitol (1999).

The prison concerts by Johnny Cash are *Johnny Cash At San Quentin* (Columbia 2001) and *At Folsom Prison* (Columbia 1999). *Ring Of Fire* and *I Walk The Line* are included on *The Man In Black – The Definitive Collection* (Sony 2006). The five volumes of *American Recordings* were issued separately on Sony between 1994 and 2006.

Raising Sand by Robert Plant and Alison Krauss is on Rounder Records (2007).

Almost Blue by Elvis Costello is on Hip-O Records (2007). The double CD edition of *My Aim Is True*, issued by Universal in 2007, includes *Stranger In The House* on its second disc.

When Elvis Costello was recording the songs for his first album, *My Aim Is True,* released in July 1977, he included one called *Stranger In The House.* Composed and performed as a country song, it was left off the album by a record company (Stiff) clearly concerned that the music was not cool enough for an artist they were determined to present as a part of the nascent punk rock movement. At the time, country music, as typified by the number two hit, *The Most Beautiful Girl,* by Charlie Rich, or the number one hit, *Stand By Your Man,* by Tammy Wynette, was generally perceived in the UK as being a variety of easy-listening. Four years later, Elvis Costello had become a successful and established rock artist; he decided to make his sixth album a collection of country song covers. *Almost Blue* was issued with a red-bordered warning sticker, as though anticipating the Parental Advisory labels that would appear on some records and CDs in 1985 (in the US; 2011 in the UK). It read, "Warning! This album contains country and western music and may produce radical reaction in narrow minded people". *Almost Blue* reached number seven in the UK album charts and was awarded a gold disc.

THE FIRST TIME

Before ska, before rhythm and blues, the dominant popular music of Jamaica was a local version of calypso known as mento. Calypso, still the most widely played style of music in the Caribbean, is a kind of folk music flavoured by a large dash of Latin American rhythm. It continues today, in a modernised form, as salsa. Mento records began to be made in the early fifties, when the locally produced master tapes were sent to the UK to be pressed on to 78 rpm records. The first of these was *Don't Fence Her In,* recorded in 1951 by Harold Robinson and the Ticklers. As the interest in mento began to wane, the first recordings by a vocal duo, Bunny and Scully, were made. They were heavily influenced by the sound of the American singers, Shirley and Lee, known as the 'Sweethearts of the Blues', who had a big R&B ballad hit in 1952 called *I'm Gone*. Bunny and Scully's *Till The End Of Time,* also a ballad, was issued as an acetate in 1954, but *Silent Dreams* was given a full release. The singers, whose career began when they were the winners of two talent contests, were still recording into the twenty-first century, having switched to reggae a long time previously. A delightful interview with the duo was uploaded on to YouTube in 2011.

Coxsone Dodd at the controls of Studio One, which he built in 1962

Clue J and his Blues Blasters

Byron Lee

What is referred to as an offbeat is strictly speaking an afterbeat – an extra beat inserted in between each beat played in four-four time, giving the music a bouncy, sprung quality. This is the same rhythmic device as employed by jazz drummers, enabling them to play with a quality referred to as 'swing' (whether or not they are actually playing the jazz style with the same name). Jazz players do not, however, emphasise the afterbeat in the manner of reggae players.

31 REGGAE

The Caribbean island of Jamaica has a population numbering just a third that of London, spread across an area a little less than that of Yorkshire. Thanks to the country's links with the United Kingdom, however (and until 1962 Jamaica was a British colony), the impact of its music has been enormous.

During the fifties, a number of sound systems – discos – became popular. These provided the music at dances, with three operators dominating – Clement Dodd (known as Coxsone), Arthur 'Duke' Reid, and Vincent 'King' Edwards. A fourth followed just a little later, at the end of the decade – Prince Buster. The music they played comprised American rhythm and blues, with a preference for obscure tracks that could be made exclusive. Coxsone Dodd and his rivals would scratch out the label credits to prevent anyone knowing what the records were and would give them names of their own. Thus Willis Jackson's *Later For The Gator* became *Coxsone Hop*, while Harold Land's *San Diego Bounce* became *Coxsone Shuffle*. These were instrumental pieces in the style of saxophonist (and singer) Louis Jordan, who had been enormously successful in the US through the forties and whose records were much played in Jamaica too. Neither of the Coxsone records was a hit in the US, but they became very popular in the Jamaican dancehalls, even if no record sales were generated. Both tracks had a repetitive piano stab on the offbeat, pushed to the back of the mix, but noticeable.

With the supply of rare American records becoming increasingly difficult to maintain, the sound system operators began to record local musicians, who played their own versions of rhythm and blues. The results were pressed on to a very limited number of acetates. The first, produced by Coxsone Dodd in 1957, was *Shufflin' Jug* by Clue J and his Blues Blasters. The first Jamaican record companies started in 1958. Edward Seaga (later the Jamaican prime minister) founded West Indies Records and issued *Manny Oh* by Higgs and Wilson, while Chris Blackwell founded a label called R&B and issued *Boogie In My Bones* by Laurel Aitken. It was Aitken who scored the first locally produced hit in the newly established Jamaica Broadcasting Corporation chart in August 1959, with *Boogie Rock*. The title became the first Jamaican record to be issued in the UK, on the Blue Beat label founded in 1960.

There are a few contenders for the first ska record. The name itself is derived from the sound made by the guitar as it delivers the distinctive stabbing offbeat. This, at least, is the theory offered by guitarist Ernest Ranglin, who should know, as he played on most of the early sessions. In the UK, the music was referred to as Blue Beat, after the label that issued it. A favourite choice as first ska record is *Easy Snappin'* by Theo Beckford with Clue J and his Blues Blasters, which was issued in 1959 and became a big hit. This track greatly emphasises the piano offbeat of the earlier rhythm and blues records, but only a little more than the same group's *Shufflin' Jug* of two years previously. Neither record finds much for a guitar to do, which is doubtless the reason for Prince Buster making the claim for his own record, *They Got To Go,* as the first recorded example of ska. This was produced late in 1960, but has a guitar delivering the strong offbeat throughout, played by Jah Jerry. Meanwhile, Byron Lee and the Dragonaires released a cover of a US rhythm and blues record, Ernie Freeman's *Dumplins*, on Seaga's label in 1959 and employed the same guitar offbeat. Lee is widely accused of being a plagiarist, copying a sound that he heard in the dance halls and not being truly a part of the local music scene. He had a working band, performing in hotels, and did not record for the sound systems. With no other record having the guitar sound in 1959, however, it is not clear what exactly he was supposed to be copying. It may not be entirely irrelevant that Lee had a comparatively privileged background, having been brought up in the well-to-do Mountain View Gardens area of Kingston. Nobody has ever denied Lee's primary innovation, however. As a bass player, he was the first Jamaican musician to play the electric Fender bass – an instrument that before long became the most essential ingredient of the country's music.

THE FIRST TIME

Prince Buster

A studio version of *Humpty Dumpty* was included as one of four tracks on a Georgie Fame EP issued in 1964 – *Rhythm And Blue Beat* (and was re-recorded in German for release in that country!) One of the other tracks was *Madness*, a Prince Buster song that several years later had its title appropriated for the name of a rather successful UK group. The previous year, Fame issued two ska singles for Chris Blackwell's R&B label. *J.A. Blues* and *Stop Right Here* were credited to the Blue Fames, with Fame playing organ and not singing.

Duke Reid

In 1959, Prince Buster recorded a song for the Folkes Brothers, *Oh Carolina*. The percussion was provided by a group, led by Count Ossie, who lived in a Rastafarian community on the East side of Kingston. A mento tune, *Ethiopia* by Lord Lebby, had sung the praises of the movement's spiritual home, but the first records to explicitly promote the Rastafari beliefs were *Mount Zion* by Desmond Dekker, released in 1965, followed by *Lion Of Judah* by Delroy Wilson and *Rasta Shook Them Up* by the Wailers (fronted by Peter Tosh) in 1966. The movement eventually became such a dominant influence within the music that Velma Pollard could refer to reggae as being "music written essentially by Rastafari" in her 1994 study, *Dread Talk*. The first mention of 'herb' (marijuana), the smoking of which is central to Rastafari, was *Cool Collie*, included on the LP, *Take It Easy*, issued by Hopeton Lewis in 1967, to consolidate his introduction of rocksteady.

Reggae in the UK was adopted as its own in 1969 by an emerging group of teenagers known as skinheads. Their very short hair and utilitarian clothing, complete with braces, was designed to be a polar opposite to the appearance of the hippies who had dominated youth culture during the previous two years or so. The British reggae band Symarip gained a very small hit at the start of 1970 with the appropriately titled *Skinhead Moonstomp*. Neither reggae association – as music for skinheads or as music promoted by dodgy bargain basement LPs – did much to promote the genre to the rock audience, even after Paul Simon employed Jamaican musicians to play on the first track of his keenly anticipated 1971 solo album. The members of Slade re-branded themselves as skinheads in 1969, but did not play reggae. By the time the group had begun its highly successful chart career in 1971, it was no longer attempting to appeal to the skinhead market.

Trojan was part sponsored by Island records, which had been formed as an independent record company in Jamaica by Chris Blackwell in 1959, and in the UK in 1962. During 1967, Island began issuing records by UK artists who played rock or folk, the first being the LP *London Conversation* by John Martyn. By the end of 1968, the label had stopped issuing any reggae at all, although some of the music did creep back into the catalogue a few years later.

MUSIC GENRES

Cluett Johnson (Clue J) took up a job playing in a hotel band in Montego Bay, Jamaica's prime tourist location. Many of his previous colleagues were involved in the formation of a new studio band, the Skatalites, who became the musicians of choice on a large number of ska records made during the first half of the sixties. A number of these tracks were put together on an LP, *Ska Authentic,* in 1964. This was the sixth LP issued by Coxsone Dodd – the first appeared in 1961, another various artists compilation called *Jamaican All Stars,* issued in a plain sleeve. The first LP by a single artist was the third to be issued by Coxsone, in 1962. This was *I Cover The Water Front* by the Cecil Lloyd Group, which was a modern jazz quintet, including saxophonist Roland Alphonso and trombone player Don Drummond, both members of the Skatalites.

In January 1964, Georgie Fame's first LP, *Rhythm And Blues At The Flamingo*, included a ska performance, *Humpty Dumpty*. The original version, by Eric Morris, with production by Prince Buster, had been the biggest Jamaican hit of 1961. The track was reprised on another British LP released at the end of the year, when a verse was included within a cover of the Isley Brothers song, *Respectable,* already being delivered with a heavy offbeat on *Five Live Yardbirds*. In the spring of 1964, the Jamaican singer Millie Small achieved the first international ska hit, *My Boy Lollipop*. It was arranged by Ernest Ranglin and recorded in London by Chris Blackwell, with a harmonica solo played by one of the members of the Five Dimensions – either Jimmy Powell or Pete Hogman or Rod Stewart, depending on who one believes.

During 1967, there were a number of small ska chart hits in the UK – *Train To Skaville* by the Ethiopians, *Guns Of Navarone* by the Skatalites, and, as the first in the series, *Al Capone* by Prince Buster. Back in Jamaica, however, the music had changed – as a fourth hit, *007(Shanty Town)* by Desmond Dekker, made clear. The rhythm was slowed down, with the bass delivering syncopated repeated patterns across the beat. Hopeton Lewis set the style in late 1966 when he asked the musicians, led by guitarist Lyn Tait, to play slower behind his song *Take It Easy*. Pianist Gladstone Anderson remarked that the beat was "rock steady" and the phrase became adopted as the name for the music, cemented by the Alton Ellis song, *Rocksteady*. In the process, Coxsone Dodd was dethroned as the number one producer, in favour of Duke Reid and his Treasure Isle label.

In 1968, the Maytals made a record called *Do The Reggay*. The music was faster than rocksteady, with an even more insistent bass figure and three guitar parts, one to deliver the offbeat, though mixed further back than previously, while the other two found repeated riff fragments to make the rhythm more intricate. The move to a faster beat had been made earlier, at the start of the year, by a record called *Pop A Top,* made by Lynford Anderson (also known as Andy Capp). 'Reggae' became adopted as the name for the new style and although the music changed again in later years, reggae stayed in place as the general name for Jamaican popular music of all kinds.

During 1969, several reggae records became chart hits in the UK, led by Desmond Dekker's *The Israelites,* which was issued in March and reached the number one position. The records were all released or distributed by the specialist Trojan record company, which was established in 1968 (and named after a make of truck used by Duke Reid to carry his sound system). Keen to break through into the increasingly lucrative LP market, Trojan began producing bargain priced compilations of reggae tracks, with covers intended to radiate sex appeal. First into the shops, in 1969, was a record called *Tighten Up,* which soon developed into a series.

The July 1973 issue of the influential UK magazine *Let It Rock* carried a major feature promoting the merits of a Jamaican group by the name of the Wailers, who were described as playing "rebel music". In April, an album by the group, *Catch A Fire,* had been issued by Island records (established by then as the home of the most vital new rock acts) in an attention-grabbing sleeve constructed like a giant cardboard cigarette lighter. The front line of the Wailers had been recording in Jamaica since 1963 and had issued two albums produced by the revered Lee Perry. Only now, however, did the group, turned into a self-contained unit by the addition of a rhythm section, start to generate interest outside Jamaica. In order to make the music of *Catch A Fire* more appealing to rock music listeners, extra keyboards and a lead guitar were overdubbed on some tracks, although the original, unadulterated recordings were retained for the Jamaican version of the album.

THE FIRST TIME

The 1972 film, *The Harder They Come*, did much, for music fans in the UK, to smooth the way for the launch of the Wailers the following year. The film starred Jimmy Cliff, who had scored two top ten hits, and it was set in Jamaica, with a reggae music soundtrack. In addition to several songs by Jimmy Cliff, the accompanying album included a definitive performance by the Maytals, *Pressure Drop,* and a song by the Melodians that was later turned into a pop hit by Boney M, *Rivers Of Babylon.* The album was influential on at least one other major performer – *Johnny Too Bad* by the Slickers was given a dub treatment eight years later by John Martyn, for whom the sounds and procedures of dub reggae and those of his own guitar, treated with echo and delay, had much in common. He also collaborated with Lee Perry in Kingston, on a track called *Big Muff,* although Perry had not been involved in *The Harder They Come.*

The Wailers with Bunny Livingston, Bob Marley, and Peter Tosh

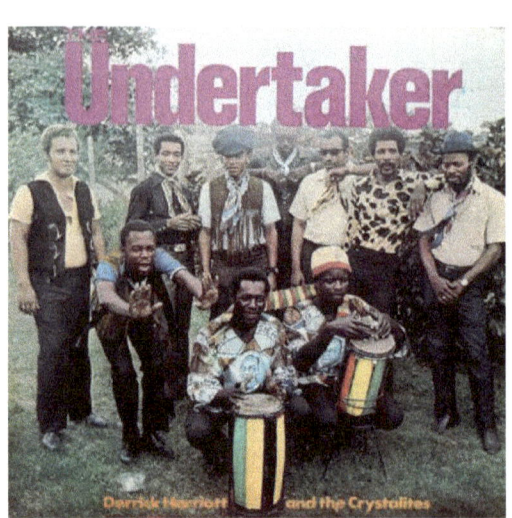

The following year, Eric Clapton drew attention to the work of the Wailers when he recorded a version of the group's song, *I Shot The Sheriff*. Retaining the reggae feel of the original, the single became a top ten hit in the UK, and reached number one in the US.

In July 1975, the group now known as Bob Marley and the Wailers (founder members Peter Tosh and Bunny Livingston having left to begin solo careers) performed for two nights at the Lyceum Theatre in London. The recorded legacy of what was reported as being a pair of incendiary concerts was issued as an LP, *Live!*, with an edited version of one track, *No Woman No Cry*, being issued as a single. This was a top ten hit in the UK and it was from this point that Bob Marley began to be spoken of as an international star, the first such to have emerged from the Developing World.

There are two stories about the evolution of the 'version', the instrumental B-side included on reggae singles during the late sixties and afterwards. Sebastian Clarke, writing in his study of 'the popular Jamaican song', *Jah Music*, claims that a number of records released by Coxsone Dodd towards the end of 1965 were lacking the planned horn solos, due to the non-arrival of the relevant musician at the studio. The records made do with an instrumental break regardless, which became known as a 'rhythm solo'. *Girl I've Got A Date* by Alton Ellis, mentioned by Clarke, has a rhythm solo like this, although the music is rocksteady and must have been made later than 1965. The B-side of the Treasure Isle single, credited to Alton and the Supersonics, is a fully fledged instrumental. An organ takes the lead role so that there is no suggestion of a horn or anything else being missing. The track is, however, labelled as a 'version'.

According to the second story, in late 1967, the sound system operator Ruddy Redwood, who worked closely with Duke Reid, was given an acetate on which the vocal track had been inadvertently left off. Redwood played the record anyway, to great acclaim, so asked Reid's engineer, Byron Smith, to make more acetates in the same way. The record involved varies according to who is telling the story – perhaps it was *On The Beach* by the Paragons or perhaps it was *Ain't Too Proud To Beg* by Slim Smith and the Uniques. Either way, the fact is that there is a third possibility. The year before, the backing track for *Put It On* by the Wailers was re-used by the producer Lee Perry for his own *Rub and Squeeze* (credited to King Perry and the Soulettes), which was issued a little later. This was effectively a version, even if not used as a B-side.

In 1970, a collection of instrumental tracks, many of which used the rhythms recorded for hit records produced by Derrick Harriott, was issued as an LP titled *The Undertaker* and credited to Derrick Harriott and the Crystalites. Subsequently, various producers began to play games with their instrumental tracks, adding effects like reverb and delay and dropping instruments out of the mix at different times, creating the music that became known as 'dub'. King Tubby was the most highly rated sound engineer to do this (using tracks that had been produced by others) and when, in the spring of 1973, Lee Perry produced an album called *Upsetters 14 Dub Black Board Jungle* (later reissued as *Blackboard Jungle Dub*), King Tubby worked with him on it. This was the first LP to be made up entirely of dub music. It was, perhaps, a measure of how thoroughly dub had become assimilated as an essential part of reggae, that when Island issued the 1975 first LP by Burning Spear, *Marcus Garvey*, it was followed by an LP comprising dub versions of all the tracks, *Garvey's Ghost*. A linguistic game was being played here – in Jamaican, a ghost is a 'duppy' (as in the Bob Marley song, *Duppy Conqueror*) and it is thought by many that the word 'dub' derives from 'duppy'. Winston Rodney, who performed under the name Burning Spear, was promoted by Island as a star to rival Bob Marley. This did not quite happen, although the singer released many successful records up to 2008 and has won several awards.

Although Lee Perry produced, over thirty years later, a dub version of the LP he made with Bob Marley in 1971, *Soul Revolution Part 2*, the star's Island recordings have generally been subjected to remix treatment rather than being made into dubs. This no doubt reflects Marley's acceptance into the wider community of dance music, where the remix is the standard approach. It involves replacing entire elements of original recordings with new ones, rather than treating what is already on the master tape in the manner of dub. The Danish house music producer known as Funkstar De Luxe, who was born in the year that *Catch A Fire* was released, created an extended dance remix of the

THE FIRST TIME

Through the seventies, the white British ex-bouncer, Alex Hughes, performing under the name Judge Dread, managed to score a number of top twenty hits. The Judge's idea of a good reggae track was to chant crudely lascivious nursery rhymes over a rocksteady or reggae rhythm. Although the use of rude imagery was something of a Jamaican tradition, Judge Dread's version of the approach avoided the poetic entirely and never sounded anything other than puerile. Amazingly, however, his first UK hit, *Big Six*, from 1972, was also a chart success in Jamaica.

Lee Perry at the desk

The distinction between the remix and the dub is muddied by Lee Perry's *Super Ape* LP, from 1976, for one. The track *Black Vest* uses the rhythm track from Max Romeo's *War Ina Babylon*, produced by Perry in the same year. The original single had a version on the B-side titled *Revelation Dub*, which undoubtedly was constructed by removing most of Max Romeo's vocals and treating what was left. *Black Vest*, however, does rather more than this. It adds a brass section and other instrumentation that was not on the original recording. In effect, therefore, *Black Vest* is a remix, despite being included on an LP whose cover announces 'Dub it up – blacker than dread'. In this case, the only thing preventing *Black Vest* – and the other tracks too – from being described as a remix is the fact that the original source is not identified.

As a Rastafarian, Winston Rodney (Burning Spear) was naturally interested in making the name of Marcus Garvey more widely known. Garvey was a Jamaican political leader, devoted to promoting solidarity between all people of African descent. Working mainly in America, it was Garvey's dream that all black people would one day be able to return to Africa. He died in 1940 at the age of just fifty-two, without seeing his dream become a reality. Red, gold, and green, as displayed on the Lee Perry and Bob Marley album covers shown on page 348 and serving as the title of one of the songs on Burning Spear's *Marcus Garvey* LP, are the colours of the flag of Ethiopia, the African country that has been adopted as the focus for Rastafari. 'Ras' is an Ethiopian title with the literal meaning of 'head', while Tafari is the first name of the man who became the Ethiopian emperor in 1930, Haile Selassie I. The fascination with the North East African country is curious, given that the Jamaican ancestors would all have come from the other side of the continent, from the Mandinka people in West Africa. As far as music is concerned, it is perhaps equally curious that, while Bob Marley and Peter Tosh are still held in very high regard in modern West Africa, Jamaicans are not at all interested in the work of important African musicians like Baaba Maal and Ali Farka Touré – or even that of people like Alpha Blondy, playing an African form of reggae with great success in both Africa and Europe. Blondy's 2007 album, *Jah Victory,* did, however, include the playing of the always open-minded Sly and Robbie.

The two UK hits by Dave and Ansil Collins in 1971, *Double Barrel* and *Monkey Spanner*, featured vocalist Dave (whose surname was actually Barker) interjecting a series of excited one-liners. He was not toasting, however, his vocals having more in common with what James Brown had been doing on his funk records for a few years.

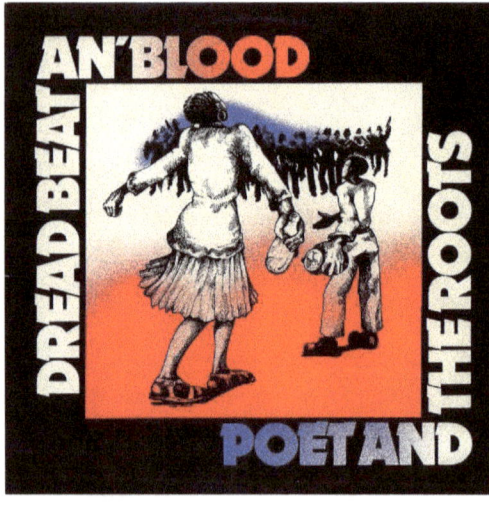

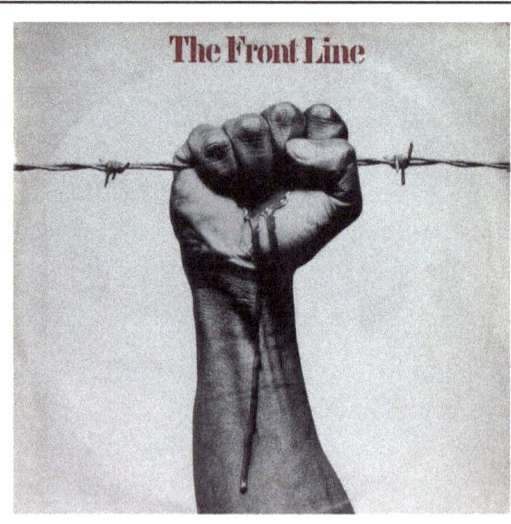

Bob Marley song, *Sun Is Shining*, in 1999 and proceeded to enjoy an enormous hit with it. Two years previously, Bill Laswell produced an entire remix album of Bob Marley songs, *Dreams Of Freedom*, although his intent was to emphasise the psychedelic aspects of the songs rather than turn them into house music. A 2012 album, *Bob Marley & The Wailers In Dub Vol.1*, did present a set of dub versions of variable quality, although, with the exception of one track credited to Scientist, nobody was admitting to having produced them.

At the dance halls, the DJs in charge of the proceedings would often add their own rants over the top of the records being played, especially when these were the instrumental versions. (The person who actually played the records was called the selector and generally remained silent). Winston 'Count' Machuki, who worked with Coxsone Dodd in the fifties, was the first DJ to do this and, although he made no records himself, his voice can be heard, uncredited, on the otherwise instrumental *Alcatraz* by trumpeter Baba Brooks, issued in 1965. King Stitt was the first DJ to issue records in his own name, with several singles made in 1969 by producer Clancy Eccles, beginning with Fire Corner. U Roy (Ewart Beckford) refined the style, to the point where he was able to keep his vocals going throughout a track, as if he was the singer. In 1970 he recorded *Dynamic Fashion Way* with producer Keith Hudson (as the B-side to a Ken Boothe release) and three singles, *Wake The Town*, *Rule The Nation*, and *Wear You To The Ball*, with producer Duke Reid. The Reid tracks became Jamaican hits. So successful were they, in fact, that during one week, the three singles filled positions one, two, and three in the Jamaican chart. Later the same year, the third single was included on *Version Galore*, U Roy's first album and the first to showcase toasting, as the style was now called.

Big Youth's toasting on his 1972 hit single *S90 Skank* achieves a first of sorts in that it includes a recording of a Honda motorbike (the S90) revving its engine, having been brought into the studio for the purpose. The point is hidden on the many pressings of the record that call the track *Ace 90 Skank* (phonetically identical when spoken with a Jamaican accent). The skank was a dance and the way that the bass struts across the Keith Hudson rhythm that underlies Big Youth's performance makes the music seem much slower than the music that preceded it, even if the beats-per-minute measure is the same. The term did not manage to replace reggae as a name for the music, however. *Ire Feelings (Skanga)* which was taken to the top of the UK charts at the end of 1974 by Rupie Edwards has the same rhythm and a spacious mix, giving it the feel of a dub record, though with vocals. The single's B-side, *Feeling High*, presented a dub version, without most of the vocals.

Inspired by the poetry he heard in the work of the DJ toasters, Linton Kwesi Johnson – born in Jamaica but living in the UK from the age of eleven – began publishing his own poetry, with his first collection, *Voices Of The Living And The Dead*, appearing in 1974. During 1978, Johnson collaborated with the musician and producer Dennis Bovell, a founding member since 1971 of one of the first touring reggae bands in the UK, Matumbi. The initial results were released on an album called *Dread Beat An' Blood*, credited to Poet and the Roots. Although the sound of the music would have been familiar to fans of the DJs, it was produced differently in that the music was created to accompany previously written verse, rather than the other way round. The album did not sell well and Johnson was dropped by Virgin, the record company involved. Subsequent LPs were issued by Island in Johnson's own name – *Forces Of Victory* from 1979 and the two albums that followed it scraped into the bottom end of the UK album charts.

Virgin had been issuing reggae records in the UK since 1974, when the LP *Dancing Shoes* by the singer B.B.Seaton was added to the company's mid-price Caroline catalogue. In 1978, Virgin started a dedicated label, called Front Line, and promoted it with a compilation album housed in a striking cover, aligning the music with struggle, and retailing at a bargain price. *Dread Beat An' Blood* was part of the Front Line series, though not represented on the compilation, but the first album was *Heart Of A Lion*, by the third great toaster, I Roy. He also had the first single, *Fire Stick*. The label's emphasis was on what had come to be called roots reggae, concerned with spiritual and social matters, in the manner of both Bob Marley and the DJs, and often associated with the Rastafari movement.

When punk arrived in the UK in 1977, it became clear that some of the performers were very fond of reggae. The Clash played a rather lumpy version of Junior Murvin's *Police And Thieves* on their debut album, but had improved

THE FIRST TIME

Some years after the heyday of the Specials and the Beat, the Jamaican community in the UK got its musical own back when the Easy Star All-Stars issued *Dub Side Of The Moon*, a reggae reworking of the classic Pink Floyd album with a similar title. This 2003 recording was followed by albums of Radiohead and Beatles songs treated in the same way. The albums work, not just for their amusing irreverence, but because the resulting music is simply very good!

In 1974, a failed attempt to promote the teenage Sharon Forrester as a reggae equivalent of Diana Ross was made in the UK. Her album, *Sharon*, was recorded in London with a substantial orchestra playing in support of her gentle vocals. The musicians included some well-known British jazz names, although they were given no chance to show what they could do. Only a year later, a similar soft soul vocal sound with a reggae rhythm became popular in the UK under the name of lovers rock. Janet Kay eventually (in 1979) achieved a number two chart hit with *Silly Games*, performed in lovers rock style – and produced by Dennis Bovell. It was strictly a British phenomenon, although in Jamaica, smooth vocalists like Dennis Brown and Gregory Isaacs, singing more or less romantic songs, were popular at this time.

their playing skills by the time they recorded *Revolution Rock* and *Armagideon Time* two years later. The Slits managed to persuade Dennis Bovell to produce their 1979 debut album, *Cut*, and proved themselves to be highly adept at blending a studied punk amateurism with spot-on reggae beats. And John Wardle, adopting the tongue-in-cheek name of Jah Wobble, proceeded to place thrilling reggae bass lines all over the music of John Lydon's Public Image Limited. During the same time, the Police, though hardly punk, used reggae stylings to underscore everything they played. One of the group's biggest hits, *Walking On The Moon*, positioned multiple accents from the three instruments with the intuitive skill of a Lee Perry. It emerged as a particularly memorable British reggae creation and was included on an album whose title translated as *White Reggae*. It established the Police as the creators of a valid original approach to a borrowed music form, just as John Mayall had managed to do with the blues a decade earlier, at the time of the British blues boom.

The British reggae boom of the late seventies and early eighties was carried along, the Police apart, by groups made up of a mixture of black and white musicians. It was this that inspired the formation of a specialist record label called Two Tone, founded by Jerry Dammers, keyboard player and songwriter with the Specials. Different groups within the movement favoured different aspects of reggae's history. For the Specials, for Madness, and for many others, it was ska, even if they moved forward from that point later on. The Beat (renamed the English Beat in the US and including the veteran Jamaican horn player Saxa in its line-up), preferred from the start a high energy version of later styles, adding dub mixes to many of their songs, although these were generally delivered at a headlong tempo, in marked contrast to the laid-back cool of Jamaican dub. UB40 preferred to use mainstream reggae rhythms to underscore what was essentially easy-listening pop. All of these groups enjoyed considerable chart success – in contrast with established reggae acts like Steel Pulse, Aswad, and Misty In Roots, which were formed within the West Indian community, were particularly inspired by Bob Marley and roots reggae, and attracted rather less notice.

Back in Jamaica, the rhythm team of Sly Dunbar and Robbie Shakespeare started playing together, during the mid seventies, in the Revolutionaries, the studio band at Joseph Hookim's Channel One. Always interested in trying something new, the duo added elements of disco to its playing and when the electronic syndrums became available at the end of the decade, Dunbar added those to his kit. Becoming full members of Black Uhuru at this time, the duo helped to make a series of cutting edge reggae albums during the early eighties. In 1985, Black Uhuru won the newly introduced Best Reggae Recording category in the Grammy Awards, with the album *Anthem*. In 1987, the duo, moving beyond music that could easily be defined as reggae, was incorporated into one of Bill Laswell's cross-cultural projects. The resulting album, called *Rhythm Killers* and credited to Sly and Robbie, was supplied with a cover sticker proclaiming 'File Under Funk'. That is undoubtedly what the album was, albeit funk of a particularly heavy-duty kind, with the bass and drums very much in the driving seat. In 1993, the duo produced and played on the album *Tease Me*. Apparently nobody had thought of pairing a singer with a toaster before and Chaka Demus and Pliers were awarded with a UK number one album, together with a flurry of hit singles, using tracks taken from the album. In 1998, Sly and Robbie were still experimenting. The album *Drum & Bass Strip To The Bone* meant what it said, with very little apart from some minimal synthesizer being added to the masterful playing of the drums and the bass guitar. Producer Howie B was given equal star billing on the CD artwork, but the music was very much a Sly and Robbie showcase.

In 1985, producer Prince (later King) Jammy made a record with singer Wayne Smith, called *Under Me Sleng Teng*. The accompaniment was played by a cheap Casio keyboard (the MT40), using one of its preset rhythm patterns in place of a bass line. The keyboard was owned by Noel Davy, a friend of Smith's, who discovered how the preset could be relocated to a reggae track. It was actually intended to be used within a rock setting and was copied from an unspecified seventies British rock recording, according to Hiroko Okuda, the Casio engineer who created it. *Under Me Sleng Teng*, the Jamaican equivalent of a techno recording, launched a new kind of reggae techno known as ragga (from 'ragamuffin', applied to ghetto youth in Kingston). DJ Shabba Ranks emerged as the premier ragga performer, having made his first record, *Original Fresh*, in 1987, produced by Prince Jammy. Signed to the Epic label, he achieved considerable international success, including scoring a number three hit in the UK in 1993 with *Mr Loverman*.

THE FIRST TIME

In 1991, when Arista was putting together an all-star tribute album to the Grateful Dead, Burning Spear was asked to record an interpretation of the Dead song, *Estimated Prophet*. It was an inspired choice. The meeting of rock and reggae, on a song that seems purpose-built for the task, succeeds in paying great respect to both sides. It becomes the standout track of the album, issued as *Deadicated*.

Albums focussing on just one rhythm track, used as the basis for every song, became popular during the late eighties. The first LP like this, however, was released much earlier, in 1974. A various artists compilation called *Yamaha Skank* and subtitled *My Conversation Stylee – 12 Original Cuts* presented twelve variations (versions in effect) of a hit single by Slim Smith, *My Conversation*. All were produced by Rupie Edwards. As an experiment, this cannot have been considered a success, since no more one-rhythm albums were issued until the eighties.

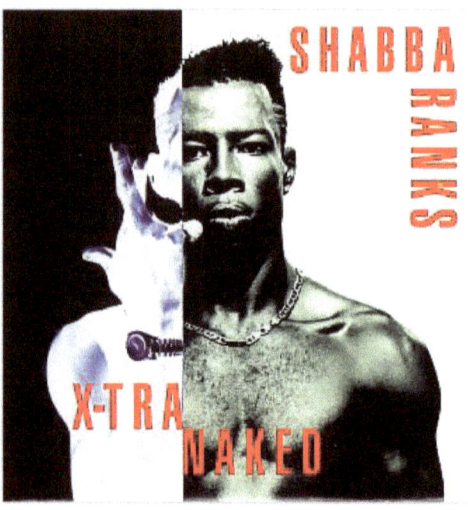 

The addition of a reggae beat to a 1991 recorded live version of *Love Rears Its Ugly Head* by Vernon Reid's coolest of hard rock bands, Living Colour, seems as natural as it is effective. It is also a very interesting black American response to the influence of Jamaican music, that has nothing to do with R&B, but it is not one that Reid chose to explore further.

The author, in his capacity as a guitarist, was involved in a short-lived attempt to fuse reggae with free jazz improvisation, in a band called Six Bop Drop. By the time that the band was recorded, however, for the 1997 album, *Four Bop Drop*, the reggae element, in the person of singer and rhythm guitarist Glenroy Grant, had moved on (and so had the drummer). Grant has a few records of his own, without the jazz element, including a lovers rock LP, *There Goes My Everything*, and a couple of twelve inch singles in a more roots reggae style.

MUSIC GENRES

Shaggy took the music more decidedly into the territory of modern R&B, an easy move to make, given the frequent adoption by that genre of displaced rhythms ultimately inspired by dub. Shaggy's songs added samples to the mix, such as the Marvin Gaye fragment (from *Let's Get It On*) used during the opening of the 1995 hit (number one in the UK), *Boombastic*. His songs were treated to multiple remixes, as was the norm in R&B, and the vocals owed as much to rap as they did to toasting, even with the Jamaican accent sounding clear. Shaggy's first big hit, however, seemed chosen to reveal his awareness of his roots, being an updated version of the old Folkes Brothers classic, *Oh Carolina*.

The assimilation of twenty-first century reggae into American R&B, while just about managing to hang on to some Jamaican identity, was emphasised by a remix of *Breathe* by the American singer Blu Cantrell, which made a contribution from Jamaican vocalist Sean Paul into an essential ingredient. The song did well in the US and became a UK number one hit in 2003.

TRACKING THE TRACKS

All of the key tracks mentioned can be heard on YouTube.

Trojan Presents Mento & R&B (Trojan 2011) is a two CD compilation that does what it says. It includes *Ethiopia* by Lord Lebby, *Boogie In My Bones* by Laurel Aitken, and *Dumplins* by Byron Lee and the Dragonaires.

Willis Jackson's *Later For The Gator (Coxsone Hop)* and Harold Land's *San Diego Bounce (Coxsone Shuffle)* are included on the three CD set, *Jumping The Shuffle Blues* (Fantastic Voyage 2011) alongside many other American R&B tracks that were played on the sound systems in Jamaica.

Mash It! More Jamaican R&B And The Birth Of Ska (Fantastic Voyage 2013) includes *Manny Oh* by Higgs and Wilson and *Boogie Rock* by Laurel Aitken on a two CD set. *Down Beat Shuffle – The Birth Of A Legend* (Sunrise 2013) is a three CD set, including *Shufflin' Jug* by Clue J and his Blues Blasters and *Easy Snappin'* by Theo Beckford. The three CD set, *Blue Beat* (Music Digital 2014) includes *Boogie Rock, Dumplins, Mary Oh,* and *Easy Snappin'* and also has *Oh Carolina* by the Folkes Brothers and *Humpty Dumpty* by Eric Morris.

The Blue Beat Explosion! The Birth Of Ska (Sunrise 2013) comprises early tracks by Prince Buster, including *They Got To Go*. *Prince Buster Fabulous Greatest Hits* (Diamond Line 1998) includes *Al Capone*.

Ska Authentic by the Skatalites is on Studio One (1999). *I Cover The Water Front* by the Cecil Lloyd Group has not been issued on CD, but is available as a vinyl reissue or on YouTube.

One Step Beyond – 45 Classic Ska Hits (Virgin 2003) has Jamaican ska (and some rocksteady) on the first disc, British ska and reggae revival from the early eighties on the second. The first disc includes *Train To Skaville* by the Ethiopians, *Guns Of Navarone* by the Skatalites, *007* and *The Israelites* by Desmond Dekker, *My Boy Lollipop* by Millie, *Madness* by Prince Buster, and *Skinhead Moonstomp* by Symarip. The second disc includes the best known tracks from the era by the Specials, Madness, the Beat, UB40, and others. *Club Ska '67* was a definitive compilation of the music when first issued in the UK in 1970 and it still is. The CD on Island (1998) adds a Prince Buster track and retitles the album accordingly, as *Whine And Grine Club Ska '67*.

Rhythm And Blues At The Flamingo by Georgie Fame is on Universal (2016). A six CD set of Georgie Fame's music, *Survival – A Career Anthology 1962-2015* (Universal 2016) includes the B-sides of the two early singles and two of the four tracks from the EP *Rhythm and Blue Beat*. The other two tracks are only available via YouTube. Both sides of the early singles are included on a download album, *Blue Flames Ska* (Rhythm & Blues 2014). The other tracks are taken from little known singles where the Blue Flames played the backing. Despite the album title, the songs are rhythm and blues rather than ska, even with Fame's Hammond delivering a stabbing offbeat on *Little Gloria* by Clive and Gloria and *Comin' Home* by Ronnie Gordon. *Five Live Yardbirds* is on Repertoire (2007).

Duke Reid's Rock Steady is a double CD on Trojan/Sanctuary (2007) and includes *Rocksteady* and *Girl I've Got A Date* by Alton Ellis and *On The Beach* by the Paragons. *Take It Easy With The Rock Steady Beat* by Hopeton Lewis, which includes both the title track and *Cool Collie*, is on Dub Store Records (2015).

There are several compilations of songs by Toots and the Maytals, such as *Pressure Drop* (Universal 2012), which includes *Do The Reggay*. There are also several compilations of songs by Desmond Dekker, such as *Israelites* (Trojan/Sanctuary 2008)., which includes the title track, *007 (Shanty Town), It Mek,* and *Mount Zion*. *Tighten Up Volumes 1 and 2* are combined on a single CD on Trojan (1996).

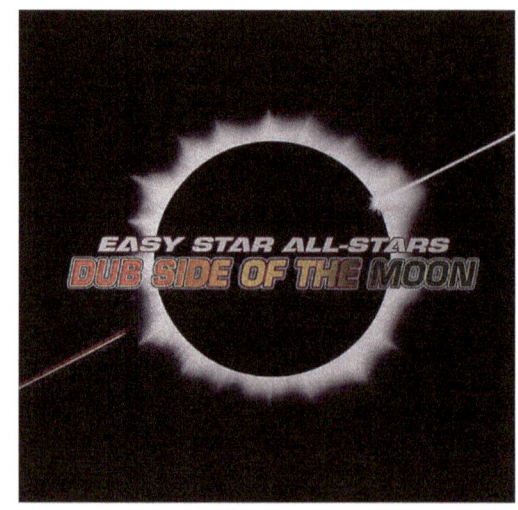

MUSIC GENRES

The Harder They Come soundtrack album is on Universal/Island (2001). John Martyn's *Johnny Too Bad* is on *Grace And Danger* (Universal/Island 1989). *Big Muff* is on *One World* (Universal/Island 1990). Paul Simon's self-titled album, including *Mother And Child Reunion,* is on Sony (2004). *The Best Of Judge Dread* is on Trojan (2017).

The double CD, deluxe edition of *Catch A Fire* by the Wailers (Universal/Island 2002) includes both the UK and the Jamaican versions of the album. *Bob Marley And The Wailers Live!* is on Universal/Island (2001). *Soul Revolution Part II* (Universal 2004) includes *Put It On* and early versions of *Duppy Conqueror* and *Sun Is Shining*. *Soul Revolution Part II Dub* is a vinyl only issue from 2014 on Cleopatra Records. The Funkstar De Luxe remix of *Sun Is Shining* is on Club Tools (1999). The Bill Laswell produced *Dreams Of Freedom* is on Island (1997). *Bob Marley & The Wailers In Dub Vol.1* is on Universal (2012). *Rasta Shook Them Up* is included on *The Toughest,* credited to Peter Tosh (Heartbeat 1996). Eric Clapton's version of *I Shot The Sheriff* is included on *461 Ocean Boulevard* (Polydor 1996).

Lee Perry is well served by a three CD compilation, *Arkology* (Island 1997). It includes *War Ina Babylon* by Max Romeo and its version, *Revelation Dub*. It also has the original version of *Police And Thieves,* by Junior Murvin. *Rub And Squeeze* is included on *Club Dread* (Sanctuary 2004), which purports to be the soundtrack album for the film *To Die For*. *Blackboard Jungle Dub* is on Get On Down (2010). *Super Ape* is on Mango (1990). Derrick Harriott's *The Undertaker* has been reissued as *For A Fistful Of Dollars* (Crystal 2013) with some extra tracks. Despite its recent release date, the CD is hard to find, but a download is readily available.

Marcus Garvey and *Garvey's Ghost* by Burning Spear are combined on to a single CD on Universal/Island (1990).

Reggae Fire Beat (Jamaican Gold 1996) is a good compilation by King Stitt and includes *Fire Corner*. Annoyingly, there is no single U Roy CD with all his early hits. *Original DJ* (Virgin 1995) has *Rule The Nation, Wear You To The Ball,* and some great tracks from later in the seventies. *Your Ace From Space* (Trojan 1995) has *Wake The Town* and *Wear You To The Ball* and includes all the tracks originally issued on the *Version Galore* LP. *Super Boss* (Nascente 2001) includes *Dynamic Fashion Way* and *Rule The Nation*. The double CD set, *Ride Like Lightning – The Best Of Big Youth 1972-1976* (Sanctuary/Trojan 2003) includes *S90 Skank*.

The bargain priced five CD set, *Total Reggae Party* (Universal 2010), includes the hits by Rupie Edwards, Dave and Ansell Collins, and Janet Kay, alongside many other popular reggae tunes. *Best Of Alpha Blondy* is a double CD on Wagram (2017). *Jah Victory* is on Utopia (2007). *Dread Beat An' Blood,* now credited to Linton Kwesi Johnson, is on Virgin (2000). *Forces Of Victory* is on Universal/Island (1991). *The Front Line*, now expanded to a three CD box set, is on EMI (2009).

The Clash, which includes *Police And Thieves,* is on Sony (1999). *Revolution Rock* is on *London Calling* (Sony 1999). *Armagideon Time* was originally included on a ten inch LP called *Black Market Clash,* but for some reason the expanded version of this on CD manages to leave off the track. It is included on the double CD, *The Story Of The Clash Volume 1* (Sony 2004), which also includes *Police And Thieves*. *Cut* by the Slits is on Universal/Island (2000). The first album by Public Image Ltd, with Jah Wobble on bass, is *Public Image* (Virgin 2012). *Reggatta De Blanc* by the Police is on A&M (2003).

Dub Side Of The Moon by the Easy Star All-Stars is on Easy Star Records (2003). *Sharon* by Sharon Forrester has made it to CD, but only in Japan (Production Dessinée 2013). The Grateful Dead tribute album, *Deadicated,* is on Arista (1991).

Anthem by Black Uhuru is on Mango (2003). *Rhythm Killers* by Sly and Robbie is on 4th & Broadway (1989). *Drum And Bass Strip To The Bone By Howie B* is on Palm Pictures (1999). *Tease Me* by Chaka Demus & Pliers is on Mango (1993).

Under Me Sleng Teng by Wayne Smith (Greensleeves 2004) includes the original single, a version, and a remix, alongside other tracks by the same artist. *Greatest Hits* by Shabba Ranks is on Sony (2003). *The Boombastic Collection – Best Of Shaggy* is on Universal/Island 2008. *Bittersweet* by Blu Cantrell, including the remix of Breathe with Sean Paul, is on Arista (2003). *Yamaha Skank* is not available on CD in its original form, but the download album, *Conversation Riddim* (Tad's Record 2016) has many of the same tracks and a few more besides.

The live reggae-influenced version of *Love Rears Its Ugly Head* by Living Colour was included on the CD single release of *Cult Of Personality* (Epic 1991). The *Soul Power Mix* of the song, included on the 2014 reissue of *Time's Up* (Music On CD), is quite similar. The self-titled album by Four Bop Drop (which has nothing to do with reggae) is on Slam (1997). The Glenroy Grant records mentioned are not available on CD, but *No Babylon* can be heard on YouTube.

THE FIRST TIME

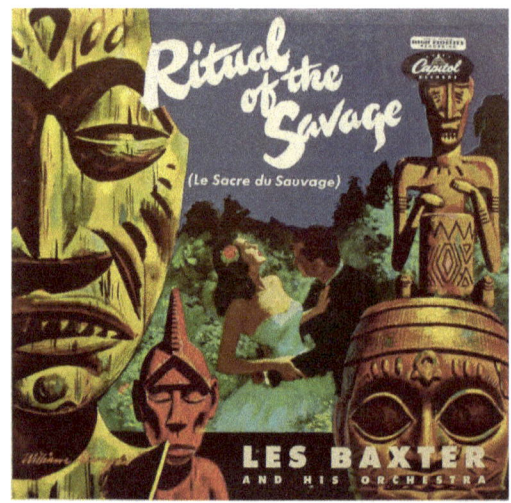

32 WORLD MUSIC

During the early decades of the twentieth century, a number of European stars made successful records in their own languages. Marlene Dietrich made her first record in 1928, *Wenn die beste Freundin* being extracted from the stage revue, *Es Liegt in der Luft* (*It's In The Air*) and sung with the stars of the show, Margo Lion and Oskar Karlweis. Edith Piaf made her first record in 1939, *Les Trois Cloches*. Following the introduction of a best selling chart in the UK, the first foreign language hit was the original Italian version of *Volare*, which was taken into the top twenty by Domenico Modugno in September 1958. In the US, the record reached number one, becoming the first foreign language song to achieve this. The first hit sung in a language that was not European was *Sukiyaki* by Kyu Sakamoto, which reached number six in the UK in August 1963 and number one in America. The title, deemed to be sufficiently memorable for people wanting to buy the record, was the name of a Japanese food that did not actually feature in the lyrics.

The Beatles recorded their two biggest hits of 1963 in German at the beginning of the following year. *Sie Liebt Dich* and *Komm, gib mir deine Hand* were combined on a German single, with the A-side also being issued in the US. It was common at this time for British and American hits to be translated into the local language in Europe, sometimes with very different lyrics to the original. The French media used the refrain from *She Loves You* as a catch-all name for the teenage fans of beat music. The first home-grown star of 'les Yé-Yés' was Françoise Hardy. Her song, *Tous Les Garçons et les Filles*, achieved some success in the UK too, especially when included as part of a hit 1964 EP, *C'est Fab!*, although the actual music had far more in common with what Cliff Richard had been doing than with the Beatles.

The Gramophone Company was established in London in 1898 and made recordings throughout Europe during the next years. In 1902 to 1903, it expanded into Egypt and into Asia. The recordings were sold to the local markets, with little or no attempt being made to interest UK music buyers in what would have seemed to be outlandish exotica. It was not until 1951, that American composer Les Baxter made the first of what became a series of LPs, in which he adopted a flavour of the Far East, the jungle, and the desert within his light orchestral compositions. *Ritual Of The Savage* was the first in a genre of music that has come to be called exotica. This was not exactly world music in the true sense – it was an impressionistic interpretation of far countries rather than any attempt to employ their actual music. Nevertheless, it definitely opened listeners' minds to the possibilities of music that was not Western.

The Decca West Africa series was established in 1948, with the first LP, by Ghanaian star E.T.Mensah, appearing in 1952. Mensah was regarded as the 'King of Highlife', the dance music style dominating West African music from the thirties until the sixties. *Missa Luba*, a recasting of the Catholic mass using the traditional singing styles of the Congo, was released in 1958. It achieved some considerable success, especially when part of it was incorporated in the soundtrack music for Lindsay Anderson's influential 1968 film, *If*.

The self-titled album by the Jazz Epistles was issued in 1959 as the first jazz record to be made in South Africa. Subsequently, the group's leading musicians, Hugh Masekela and Dollar Brand, left their home country and established themselves as significant jazz performers in the US. Both incorporated riffs and rhythms derived from African music into their jazz, while Masekela gained extra kudos by performing with the Byrds. The trumpet playing on the 1966 recording, *So You Want To Be A Rock & Roll Star*, is his and the African influence in the song's rhythm (especially Chris Hillman's bass part) is apparent in retrospect, although this was not commented on at the time. South African singer Miriam Makeba also moved to the US, before either of the jazz players, in 1959. She made numerous recordings through the sixties and beyond, employing a style that was crammed full of references and influences from her home country. She became in the process the first African international music star.

The sitar master, Ravi Shankar, first toured in the UK, Germany, and the US in 1956, and recorded his first LP,

THE FIRST TIME

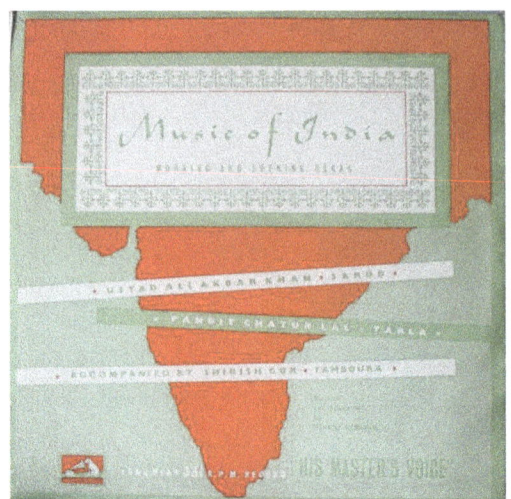

George Harrison's fascination with Indian music reached its apex on the soundtrack album he recorded in 1968 for the film *Wonderwall*. Indian and British rock musicians are both involved, although for the most part they perform separately. In truth, there is nothing here as remarkable as the Indian infused music that Harrison made with the Beatles.

The British-based jazz big band, Chris McGregor's Brotherhood Of Breath, whose core membership comprised South African expatriates, released its first, self-titled album in 1971. The music presented a more aggressively rhythmic version of the African jazz pioneered by Hugh Masekela and Dollar Brand and was clearly taking advantage of the eclectic music tastes encouraged by the success of progressive rock. It was even released on RCA's specialist progressive label, Neon. Two earlier recordings by smaller versions of the band have fewer African influences and are far less inspirational. The 1968 session was issued as *Very Urgent,* the 1969 session was unreleased at the time and hard to find now.

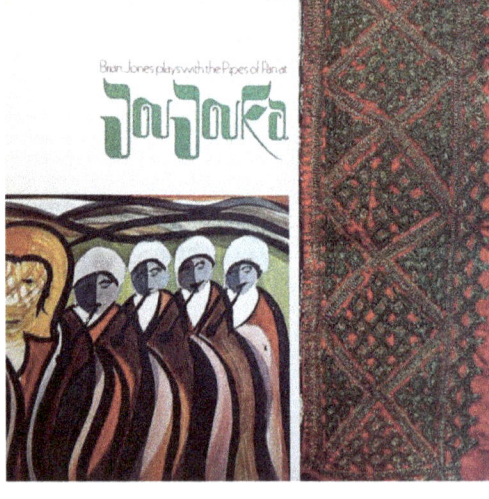

Three Ragas. He had been invited to play in the US the previous year, but had recommended Ali Akbar Khan to play instead. Khan played another Indian stringed instrument, the sarod. His album, *Morning And Evening Ragas*, released in 1956, a little before Shankar's record, was the first classical Indian music to be issued in the West. Indian violinist John Mayer worked with the London Philharmonic Orchestra from 1953. His groundbreaking fusion of Indian and Western classical traditions, *Raga Jaijavanti*, was performed by the LPO, conducted by Sir Adrian Boult, in 1958. His collaboration with Jamaican saxophonist Joe Harriott resulted in three albums recorded from 1966 to 1968 in which a hybrid between jazz and Indian music was explored. *Dream Sequence*, an album released on the Regal Zonophone label in 1972 and credited to Cosmic Eye, was a further extension of the Indian-jazz fusion approach, with John Mayer continuing his involvement, and marketed this time as progressive rock. An album made by Ravi Shankar in 1962, *Improvisations*, included contributions from four American jazz musicians, although Shankar's controlling hands ensured that the music remained predominantly Indian, with a little jazz flavouring, rather than a complete fusion.

John Coltrane demonstrated an Indian influence on the music he played during 1961, most obviously on a track actually called *India*. Playing this live at the Village Vanguard in New York, he added what was supposed to be an Indian flavouring by featuring Ahmed Abdul-Malik as a guest performer. In fact, Abdul-Malik played the Arabic stringed instrument, the oud, claiming to be of Sudanese descent. He made a number of jazz albums himself where the music was combined with a notable North African element, beginning with *Jazz Sahara* in 1958.

As described in the chapter on World Instruments, the sitar made its debut in rock music when played by George Harrison on the Beatles song, *Norwegian Wood*, in 1965. Harrison became an enthusiastic supporter of Indian music and incorporated its sounds and modal structure into several of the songs he recorded with the Beatles during the next couple of years. *Love You To*, from 1966, then *Within You Without You*, *The Inner Light*, and *Blue Jay Way*, all produced in 1967, are fully integrated amalgamations between rock and Indian music. Not wanting to be outdone, the Rolling Stones produced their own Eastern-inspired track, *Gomper*, which utilised the multi-instrumental abilities of Brian Jones to the full. Jones had previously played the sitar on the Stones' hit, *Paint It Black*, issued in May 1966.

The American group Kaleidoscope, whose lead singer Solomon Feldthouse had spent six years living in Turkey, introduced a pronounced Middle Eastern flavour to rock music. *Egyptian Gardens*, the opening track of the group's first album, *Side Trips*, issued in June 1967, is as startling a world music fusion as was the Beatles' *Love You To*, released the previous August. Long, partly improvised tracks (*Taxim* and *Seven-Ate Sweet*) on the group's next two LPs continued the approach highly successfully. In late 1969, the group Quintessence made its first LP, *In Blissful Company*, which maintained a style of rock infused with Indian music throughout. Osibisa did the same thing with African music on its first, self-titled, LP from 1971, while the Third Ear Band allowed the world music influences to overwhelm the rock on its first album, *Alchemy*, released in June 1969.

In 1971, the misleadingly titled LP, *Brian Jones Plays With The Pipes Of Pan At Joujouka*, was released as the first record on the Rolling Stones' own label. The music was performed by the Moroccan Master Musicians of Joujouka in 1968 and was recorded by Brian Jones, although he did not actually play along with the group. For subsequent issues of the record, the wording 'plays with' was replaced by 'presents'. Although this was not the first recording by third world musicians to be released in the West, the association with Brian Jones and the Rolling Stones meant that it received far more attention than would otherwise have been the case. Jazz saxophonist Ornette Coleman made a recording with the same musicians for inclusion on his 1977 album, *Dancing In Your Head*.

During 1971 and 1972, Ginger Baker performed and recorded with the Nigerian band leader Fela Ransome-Kuti (who later, having become inspired by the American Black Power movement, traded the Ransome part of his name for Anikulapo). Kuti's music was already something of a hybrid, in which African polyrhythms were blended with the funk approach of James Brown. Through the seventies, it seemed probable that he would become a major third world star, to rival Bob Marley, but somehow this never happened. Baker, meanwhile, continued with his interest in African music. *Horses And Trees*, released as a come-back album in 1986, featured African players, working alongside musicians

A similar, but more ambitious project than *One World One Voice* was carried out in 2001 by Jamie Catto (previously a member of the dance music band Faithless) and Duncan Bridgeman, who recorded and filmed numerous musicians around the world, then created a set of songs out of their contributions. They were included within a multimedia presentation, under the name *One Giant Leap*.

 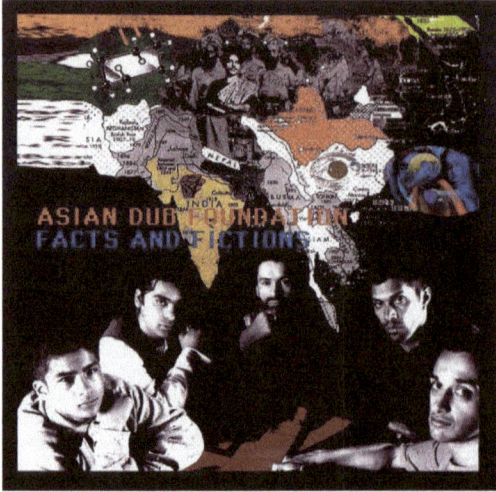

from India, South America, and the USA. Produced by Bill Laswell, the album functioned as the first of Laswell's world music projects, deliberately mixing together instrumental sounds and techniques from different parts of the world. Paul Simon followed a similar approach with his 1986 album, *Graceland*, employing South African musicians to blend their playing styles with his own contemporary folk-rock music. Simon was much criticised for flouting the prevailing cultural boycott against South Africa, although the musicians concerned expressed their gratitude for theexposure they were given as a result. The singing group Ladysmith Black Mambazo became internationally successful in their own right, following their contributions to *Graceland*.

Through the eighties, a number of attempts were made by Western record companies to turn various African artists into international stars, in an attempt to fill the considerable gap left by the death of Bob Marley in 1981. The Nigerian King Sunny Ade was the first. He was signed to Island records (Marley's record company too), which released the album *Juju Music* in 1982. Ade had already made a huge number of records, going back as far as 1967, but none had appeared outside West Africa. It was the Senegalese musician Youssou N'Dour who achieved the chart success, however. *Shakin' The Tree*, recorded in collaboration with Peter Gabriel, was a minor UK and US hit in 1989; then *7 Seconds*, made with Neneh Cherry, reached number three in the UK charts in 1994.

Peter Gabriel started the Real World record label in 1989, specifically to produce world music recordings. The first release was his own *Passion*, originally conceived as a film soundtrack, but turned into a world music extravaganza, using a large number of musicians from different countries, rather in the manner of a Bill Laswell album. This was followed by *Shahen-Shah*, by the Pakistani devotional singer Nusrat Fateh Ali Khan. In 1990, Kevin Godley, former member of Ten cc, conceived the idea of a musical chain letter – a piece of music that would travel around the world, being added to by various musicians receiving the master tape in turn. *One World One Voice*, produced by Rupert Hine, emerged as a masterpiece of world music composition and performance, climaxing with a highly moving, if surprising, meeting between singer Salif Keita from Mali and the Leningrad Symphony Orchestra.

Middle Eastern and Asian musicians living in the UK found that the dance music of the nineties lent itself particularly well to incorporating elements of their own popular music. Trans-Global Underground, whose first album was released in 1993 (*Dream Of 100 Nations*), and Asian Dub Foundation, with a first album in 1995 (*Facts And Fictions*) were the pioneers. The former group served as springboard for the solo career of singer Natacha Atlas, who has made several albums through to the present day. The biggest international star in this area, however, is Khaled. His 1996 album, *Sahra*, was the first of several multi-million selling records in a genre of Arab music known as 'raï'. His records have been successful throughout the Arab world and Europe, though not particularly in the UK.

Japan gifted the Western world with karaoke (empty orchestra), allowing amateur singers to make fools of themselves in public with the aid of pre-recorded backing music. The activity is usually credited to band manager and drummer Diasuke Inoue in 1971, although there are rival claims. It spread to the US and UK during the late eighties and has never looked back. The first Japanese rock band to achieve some success in the West was the Sadistic Mika Band, whose first, self-titled album was issued in 1973. The band's drummer later became a member of the electronic Yellow Magic Orchestra, the first Japanese group to gain major success in the West. The first, self-titled album was issued in 1978. The group Samurai, whose first LP was issued in Germany in 1970, had some Japanese members, including bass player Tetsu Yamauchi, who subsequently played with both Free and the Faces, although these groups could not be truthfully described as playing any kind of world music. The same is true of Yoko Ono, whose first avant garde album with John Lennon, *Unfinished Music No.1 – Two Virgins*, was issued in 1968. Paradoxically, the British group Japan, whose members were not actually Japanese, played music on the 1981 album, *Tin Drum*, that does sound like a convincing oriental-rock fusion, albeit using Chinese music textures, rather than Japanese.

K-pop, centred on the boy band BTS, became internationally successful during 2016. It is a dance-pop sound not markedly different from other chart music produced in the previous twenty years, but just happens to originate in South Korea. K-pop, however, is devoid of any Asian musical influence.

THE FIRST TIME

TRACKING THE TRACKS

Marlene Dietrich's earliest recordings are included on the double CD, *La Blonde Venus 1928-1948* (Varese Sarabande 2000). Edith Piaf's are on the double CD, *Je Ne Regrette Rien* (Not Now Music 2011). There are several compilations by Domenico Modugno and all of them include his hit – such as the CD actually called after it, *Volare* (MCP 2013). *Sukiyaki* is included on a Japanese CD by Kyu Sakamoto, *Golden Best* (Universal 2002). It is also on some sixties compilations, such as the double CD, *BBC Radio 2 Sounds Of The Sixties* (EMI 2011).

The German language versions recorded by the Beatles are on the double CD *Past Masters* (EMI 2009).

The two CD set, *The Vogue Years* (BMG 2001) provides a good overview of Françoise Hardy's sixties recordings, although it is missing one track from the *C'est Fab!* EP.

Some of the earliest world music recordings issued by the Gramophone Company are included on *Sprigs Of Time – 78s from the EMI Archive* (Honest Jon's Records 2008). Les Baxter's *Ritual Of The Savage* is on a scarce Rev-Ola CD (2006) and is also included on the cut-price four CD set, *Les Baxter Vol.1 – Eight Classic Albums* (Real Gone Jazz 2013). There is an excellent double CD overview of Baxter's music, *The Exotic Moods Of Les Baxter* (Capitol 1996).

E.T.Mensah gets the four CD box set treatment on *King Of Highlife Anthology* (RetroAfric 2015). The original recording of *Missa Luba* is on Hallmark (2013).

The recordings by the Jazz Epistles are on CD as *Jazz In Africa Volume 1* (BMG 1998) but this is hard to find. All the tracks can be currently heard on YouTube, however. Eight tracks are also included on the Dollar Brand CD, *Dollar Brand Plays Sphere Jazz* (Phono 2015). Brand (or Abdullah Ibrahim as he is now called) has made numerous recordings over the years. His best-selling album from 1980, *African Marketplace* (Discovery 1995) is as good a place as any to start. There are a few CD compilations by Hugh Masekela, but his best album is *Home Is Where The Music Is*, recorded in 1972 (Decca/Universal 2008), His contributions to the music of the Byrds are on *Younger Than*

MUSIC GENRES

Yesterday (Sony 1996). A double CD compilation by Miriam Makeba, *The Sweet Sound Of Africa,* is on Not Now Music (2011).

Ravi Shankar's *Three Ragas* is on Angel (2000). There is also a good double CD compilation of his work, *The Very Best Of Ravi Shankar* (EMI 2010). Two of his daughters are successful recording artists – Anoushka Shankar plays the sitar like her father; Norah Jones doesn't.

Ali Akbar Khan's *Morning And Evening Ragas* fill the first disc of the double CD set, *Then And Now* (AMMP 1995).

John Mayer's orchestral music is not well served on record or CD. His *Shanta Quintet for Sitar and Strings* was issued on a Columbia LP in 1967; his Flute Concerto and other flute music was issued on a RCA LP in 1981, recorded by James Galway. Neither have made it to CD. The three albums that John Mayer made with Joe Harriott are *Indo-Jazz Suite* (Atlantic 2014), then two volumes of *Indo-Jazz Fusions*, which are combined on a Universal CD (1998). *Dream Sequence* by Cosmic Eye is on Silva Star (2002). *Improvisations* by Ravi Shankar is on EMI (1999).

Jazz Sahara by Ahmed Abdul-Malik is on Universal/Riverside (2009). Four versions of John Coltrane's *India* are included on the 4 CD set, *The Complete 1961 Village Vanguard Recordings (Universal/Impulse 1997).*

Norwegian Wood is on the Beatles' *Rubber Soul*. *Love You To* is on *Revolver*. *Within You Without You* is on *Sgt Pepper's Lonely Hearts Club Band*. *The Inner Light* is on *Past Masters*. *Blue Jay Way* is on *Magical Mystery Tour*. All are EMI 2009. The Rolling Stones' *Gomper* is on *Their Satanic Majesties Request* (Abkco 2002). George Harrison's *Wonderwall Music* is on Apple (2014).

The first four albums made by Kaleidoscope are combined on the three CD set, *Pulsating Dreams – The Epic Recordings* (Floating World 2010). A UK group called Kaleidoscope recorded slightly psychedelic Beatle-inspired music during the same period. The music is well worth hearing, but it has nothing to do with the theme of the present chapter.

In Blissful Company by Quintessence is on Repertoire (2004). The second album by the group, *Quintessence* (Repertoire 2004) is even better. *Osibisa* is also on Repertoire (2008). The group's second album, *Woyaya* (Repertoire 2008) is just as good. *Alchemy* by the Third Ear Band is combined with the second album, *Elements,* on CD (BGO 2009).

Brian Jones Presents The Pipes Of Pan At Joujouka is on Point Music (1999). Ornette Coleman's *Dancing In Your Head* is on Verve (2000).

Chris McGregor's Brotherhood Of Breath is on Repertoire (2011). *Very Urgent* is on Fledg'ling (2008).

Fela Ransome-Kuti and the Africa '70 with Ginger Baker Live! is on Wrasse (2005). *Stratavarious*, issued in Ginger Baker's name, but also including Fela Kuti, was issued on LP in 1972 but has not been reissued on CD., although the entire album can be heard on YouTube. *Fela – The Best of the Black President* (Knitting Factory 2013) provides a good overview of Kuti's music on two CDs and a DVD.

The Ginger Baker/Bill Laswell collaboration, *Horses And Trees* is on BCD (2015). Paul Simon's *Graceland* is on Sony (2012). *The Star and the Wiseman – The Best of Ladysmith Black Mambazo* is on PolyGram (1998).

Juju Music by King Sunny Ade is on Island (2000). *The Best Of Youssou N'Dour* includes *7 Seconds* and is on Sony (2004). *Shakin' The Tree* is included on *The Lion* (Disky 2001) and it can also be found on the Peter Gabriel compilation, *Shaking The Tree – Sixteen Golden Greats* (Real World 2014).

Peter Gabriel's *Passion* is on Real World (2011). Gabriel followed this up with a second album, *Passion – Sources* (Real World 1989) which comprises various world music recordings which Gabriel claims as his inspiration. *Shahen-Shah* by Nusrat Fateh Ali Khan is on Real World (2012).

One World One Voice is on Virgin (1990). *One Giant Leap* is on Palm Pictures (2001) but is better experienced with its visuals on the DVD version (Palm Pictures 2002).

Dream Of 100 Nations by Trans-Global Underground is on Nation Records (1993). *Facts And Fictions* by Asian Dub Foundation is also on Nation Records (1995). *The Best Of Natacha Atlas* is on Mantra (2005) – she has made some fine albums since then too. *Sahra* by Khaled is on Barclay (1997).

Sadistic Mika Band is on EMI Japan (2006). *Yellow Magic Orchestra* has been expanded to a double CD, with a set of alternate versions, on Music on CD (2015). *Samurai* is on USM Japan (2007). A progressive rock group called Samurai and recording a year later is not related and had no Japanese members. This Samurai has its CD issued on Esoteric Recordings.

Unfinished Music No.1 – Two Virgins by John Lennon and Yoko Ono is on Rykodisc (1997). *Tin Drum* by Japan is on Virgin (2013).

The most successful BTS album to date is *Love Yourself 轉 'Tear'* (Big Hit Entertainment 2018).

THE FIRST TIME

Top Composers by Event	Most Performed Works
1 Mozart	1 Symphony 5 (Beethoven)
2 Beethoven	2 Messiah (Handel)
3 J S Bach	3 Violin Concerto (Sibelius)
4 Brahms	4 Symphony 5 (Tchaikovsky)
5 Tchaikovsky	5 Violin Concerto (Mendelssohn)
6 Schubert	6 Symphony 7 (Beethoven)
7 Haydn	7 Symphony 1 (Brahms)
8 Ravel	8 Symphony 6 (Beethoven)
9 Sibelius	9 Eine Kleine Nachtmusik (Mozart)
10 Schumann	10 Violin Concerto (Brahms)

charts for 2015, published on website bachtrack.com

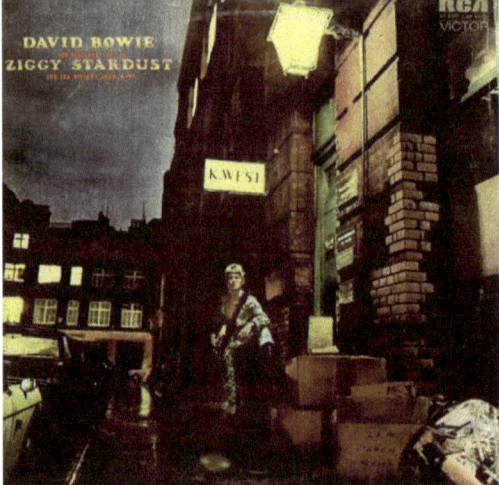

There are, of course, differing opinions as to what exactly a memorable melody is like. Chuck Berry, in the lyrics he composed for his song *Rock And Roll Music,* suggested that the ultimate example of music abandoning "the beauty of the melody" was the classical symphony. The seventies and eighties BBC television rock music show, *The Old Grey Whistle Test,* was titled after a supposed method adopted by American songwriters in the early years of the twentieth century for establishing the effectiveness of a melody – whether an elderly listener would be inclined to whistle it after a first hearing. A symphonic composer like Ralph Vaughan Williams would be unlikely to pass such a test, although realistically, his music is an outstanding example of twentieth century classical composition that does place a high premium on powerfully melodic writing.

33 CLASSICAL

During the first quarter of the nineteenth century, Ludwig Van Beethoven developed the orchestral concerto, the string quartet, and the symphony, among other structures, starting from musical ideas pioneered by Wolfgang Amadeus Mozart and Joseph Haydn during the previous twenty-five years or so. Nearly two hundred years later, Beethoven's forms remain the essential templates for music intended to be included within the genre known as classical. Even the composers of such determinedly contemporary works as the *Low Symphony* (published by Philip Glass in 1992 and incorporating themes taken from David Bowie's *Low* album) or the *Concerto for Turntables and Orchestra* (making its performance debut at the 2011 BBC Proms, five years after its completion by Gabriel Prokofiev, a man with a very famous grandfather) – even these chose titles to make their ancestry clear.

The performers, listeners, and reviewers of a music with such a long lineage feel justified in adopting a second genre title, that of 'serious' music, in order to make a distinction between the stuff they prefer and all the other kinds of presumably frivolous music. The definitive history, *The Larousse Encyclopaedia of Music*, first published in 1971, had no problem with devoting just one chapter out of eighty to jazz and none at all to pop and rock. *Settling the Score*, based on a series of BBC radio programmes made in 1999, and subtitled *A Journey Through The Music of the 20th Century*, has just one chapter out of twenty concerning itself with jazz, pop, and rock. Robert P. Morgan's authoritative *Twentieth-Century Music* from 1991, with a summary on Amazon stating that "all musical genres are represented", can nevertheless manage barely three pages out of five hundred to discuss rock and jazz. Even Alex Ross's acclaimed *The Rest Is Noise – Listening To The Twentieth Century*, published in 2007, has hardly anything to say about rock and jazz (Duke Ellington apart), other than to describe a handful of examples where the author can detect some influence from contemporary classical music. At least Morgan does admit that the influences run the other way too.

This attitude would be understandable if the classical music of the twentieth century had made a huge cultural impact. The fact of the matter, however, is that, with a few exceptions in the case of composers working in the first decades, it has not. The website *bachtrack.com* publishes a variety of classical music articles and reviews. Its summary of the year 2015 includes a list of the top ten most performed works and the top ten composers 'by event'. The most recent of the performed works dates back to 1905 (the Sibelius *Violin Concerto*). Only Ravel and Sibelius, in the list of top composers, worked into the twentieth century – Sibelius composed nothing after 1926, Ravel's last composition was in 1932.

Certainly, a number of composers working more recently than this have created some remarkable music. They have not often, however, succeeded in persuading the general listening public that this is the case. The deaths of rock musicians Lemmy and David Bowie in a two week period at the end of 2015 and the beginning of 2016 generated an enormous amount of public grief. These two musicians were perceived as having created music that made a difference to people's lives. The reactions to the deaths of two eminent 'serious' music composers during the same period and slightly afterwards – Pierre Boulez and Peter Maxwell Davies – were strikingly different, in so far as the deaths were hardly noticed.

It can easily be argued that key works by these musicians, *Pli Selon Pli*, *The Rise and Fall of Ziggy Stardust and the Spiders from Mars*, *Eight Songs for a Mad King*, and *Ace of Spades*, are nevertheless equally innovative and important within the history of music. They are equally effective in highlighting different strengths, whether it is memorable melody, rhythmic power, or intricate, mathematical construction. The decision as to the cultural significance of these works rather depends on how important each of these various qualities is considered to be. Classical music development through the twentieth century is only sometimes concerned with memorable melody and hardly ever concerned with rhythm, whether powerful or not. (It is often fascinated by metre, to be sure, but can provide no equivalent to the

THE FIRST TIME

Clearly, rock musicians do sometimes perform their own interpretations of music originating with other people. Joe Cocker, on one relevant occasion, produced his own version of a *Sgt Pepper* track, *With A Little Help From My Friends*. It was radically different from the Beatles' recording because he imposed his own musical personality on the song. Generally speaking, classical musicians do not behave like this. The many recordings and performances of Beethoven's *Symphony No.5*, for example, are not seeking to introduce a personal slant like Joe Cocker. Rather, they are attempting to reach ever further into the mind of Beethoven himself. They use the written score as the instruction manual, even while recognising that the process by which a composer translates the music in his head into a version that can be written down is not a completely exact one.

Apart from the neglect of the electric guitar by classical music, as described in the chapter on Progressive Rock, a good example in support of Zappa's attitude regarding the classical world's ignorance of developments elsewhere is provided by the reception accorded to Jonathan Harvey's *Madonna Of Winter And Spring*. The work was given a first performance at the BBC Proms in 1986, with a television documentary being shown at about the same time. The programme made much of Harvey's use of sampling keyboards in the work, indicating that this was a new technological advance. In reality, the group Landscape had used the same kind of keyboards on a hit album made some six years previously – a long time in the fast moving world of electronics. The Harvey work is certainly interesting, but it does not represent a musical first.

"I occasionally play works by contemporary composers, and for two reasons. First, to discourage the composer from writing any more, and secondly to remind myself how much I appreciate Beethoven."
Jascha Heifetz, virtuoso classical violinist.

Michael Gray writes in his book about Frank Zappa that the conductor Kent Nagano attended his first ever rock concert – a Zappa performance – prior to recording his music with the LSO. Shockingly unfamiliar with the entire genre, Nagano admitted to being "*really* surprised" by the level of musicianship on display. James Thomas, an American professor of English, is quoted in the special *Harry Potter* edition of *Time* (published in June 2017) as saying, with regard to his praise of J.K. Rowling's books: "They're easy to underestimate because of what I call the three Deathly Hallows for academics – they couldn't possibly be good because they're too recent, they're too popular, and they're too juvenile." It would appear that the same quote would work equally well for the typical attitude of trained classical musicians towards rock music.

Arnold Schoenberg

Claude Debussy

Berg 12 tone row notated by American composer Andy Brick

complicated interlocking beats and riffs of, say, a James Brown piece.) Its proponents do not view these things as being particularly important. Others would disagree.

Of course there are exceptions, but it rather seems to be the case that the primary concern of classical music through much of the twentieth and into the early twenty-first century is to maintain interest in the established repertoire. Every year, yet more performances of the same works are recorded and released on CD – with the intention, it can only be assumed, of providing more exhibits for the classical music museum (as well, no doubt, as selling the product to an audience of listeners whose tastes are established and certain, since classical is affected by the same commercial considerations as any other kind of music). Composers of new works frequently struggle to achieve even one recording. If rock music worked in this way, then we would expect a number of groups each year to be recording new versions of *Sgt Pepper's Lonely Hearts Club Band*. Certainly, tribute bands, including a number attempting to impersonate the Beatles, are a popular feature at many live venues. They seldom get to make records, however, and nobody believes that they are anywhere near the cutting edge of music innovation and development. Most of the orchestras and smaller units performing music by Mozart, Beethoven, and the rest do get to make records, but they are nowhere near the cutting edge either and are essentially taking on the role of tribute bands. Or, as Frank Zappa puts it in his autobiographical collection of essays, *The Real Frank Zappa Book:*

> When a guest conductor comes to town, he is not usually giving a performance of something by a living composer. He's doing Brahms; he's doing Beethoven; he's doing Mozart – because he can warm it up in one afternoon and make it sound okay. This makes the accountants happy, and allows the audience to concentrate on his *choreography* (which is really why they bought the tickets in the first place). Why is that any better than a bunch of guys in a bar band jamming on *Louie Louie* or *Midnight Hour*?

Never afraid to be outspoken in interview, Mr Zappa lamented the classical world's ignorance with regard to the various recording and music composition techniques developed by the performers of different kinds of popular music. He had little patience with musical snobs, who, despite such ignorance, would seek to claim moral superiority for the genre they happen to prefer, by using terms like 'serious' to describe it. In the sleeve notes for his album, *The Perfect Stranger*, where a number of quite difficult modern classical pieces were conducted by no less a figure than Pierre Boulez, the composer, Frank Zappa himself, writes, "all material contained herein is for entertainment purposes only, and should not be confused with any other form of artistic expression". Frank Zappa, at least, never forgot what the primary function and the point of music really is – to communicate with an audience, to entertain.

In 1899, the Austrian Arnold Schoenberg composed a work, inspired both by a poem of Richard Dehmel and by his love for the woman he would later marry, and titled, after the poem, *Verklarte Nacht (Transfigured Night)*. The work is a romantic one, with powerful, memorable melodies, but with harmonies that stretched the contemporary ideas of what sounded right to the limit and a little beyond it. The work was scored for a string sextet, but Schoenberg arranged it for a string orchestra in 1917 and revised this again in 1943. Clearly he was fond of what was, for him, an early composition. In view of its original composing date and its 1902 first performance date (when many of the audience apparently found its harmonies unpleasant), *Verklarte Nacht* acts as a neat dividing line between the procedures and achievements of nineteenth century classical music and the more testing methods of the twentieth century.

During 1907 and 1908, Schoenberg worked on his second string quartet. It was unusual in including a part for a soprano singer during the last two movements (inspired, no doubt, by his hero Gustav Mahler's similar use of singers in some of his symphonies, beginning with his second, premiered in 1895). More significantly, however, Schoenberg rendered the whole question of harmony irrelevant by writing the last movement in no fixed key at all, creating the first 'atonal' composition.

Eventually, Schoenberg decided to invent a system to give structure to music that was atonal, and in 1921 he

THE FIRST TIME

Charles Ives

The first recording was a classical music piece – a performance of Handel's choral work *Israel in Egypt* carried out in 1888. The following year, the composer Johannes Brahms was recorded playing one of his *Hungarian Dances* on the piano. The first opera recording was of Verdi's *Ernani* in 1903. The first LPs, issued by Columbia in 1948, included a number of classical music recordings. The first of these was Mendelssohn's *Violin Concerto* (composed between 1838 and 1844), performed by Nathan Milstein and the New York Philharmonic Orchestra. Seventeen years earlier, RCA Victor issued a number of records that played at thirty three and a third rpm but were made of shellac, like 78 rpm recordings. The first of these was a recording of Beethoven's *Fifth Symphony* (composed between 1804 and 1808) performed by Leopold Stokowski and the Philadelphia Orchestra.

Igor Stravinsky

Constant Lambert also wrote in *Music Ho!* – "Atonalism, though plastic in minor details of texture, is in fact the least flexible and most monotonous of media, and for that reason alone it is unlikely to play much part in the music of the future". Lambert expected that classical music would aim to retain some kind of popular following. He could not have predicted the arrival of rock music, and the consequent acceptance by classical composers of a much lower profile than that enjoyed by their predecessors. Atonalism has turned out to be the normal mode for the majority of cutting-edge classical composers through the rest of the twentieth century.

Karlheinz Stockhausen

Olivier Messiaen with Myung-Whun Chung. Yvonne Loriod, the pianist on this album, was Messiaen's wife; Jeanne Loriod, the ondes martenot player, her sister.

Walt Disney's film, *Fantasia,* released in 1940, directly focussed on its classical music. Only one of the pieces chosen was from the twentieth century. Ironically enough, this was Stravinsky's *Rite Of Spring,* the music originally heard as extreme now being considered as a suitably popular companion for works by Tchaikovsky, Beethoven, and Ponchielli.

Cellist Laura Moody prepares to play Stockhausen

came up with the idea of twelve-tone composition, or serialism. At the start of a piece of music, all twelve notes of a chromatic scale are placed in a particular order, according to the decision of the composer. The music then proceeds by playing games with the note order chosen – reversing it, turning it upside down, transposing the whole thing upwards or downwards, and so on. Schoenberg applied the method to his *Variations for Orchestra* of 1928, after which many other composers tried it for themselves. Serialism is a difficult technique to use for the generation of memorable melody, a point that was proved over and over again by the many composers who tried it. Alban Berg's *Violin Concerto* of 1935, however, which was subtitled *To the Memory of an Angel*, showed that it could be done. The angel in question was the young daughter of Alma Mahler, the former wife of Gustav Mahler, who had died of polio.

The intellectual challenge provided by serialism made the system hugely influential for other composers, but it was not the only innovation to find a way forward from the procedures of nineteenth century classical music. In 1905, French composer Claude Debussy created a musical portrait of the sea, which he logically titled *La Mer*. He piled notes upon notes, harmony upon harmony, to create a work that had a chromatic density quite different from anything composed in the previous century, but was still very melodic and accessible. The music, described as 'impressionistic', in a deliberate reference to the visual art movement that also demanded positive interaction from the senses, has ultimately proved to be much more influential than serialism, on all kinds of music.

In 1906, the American Charles Ives composed two short pieces that have more in common with Debussy than Schoenberg, though somewhat different in conception from either. They are strikingly modern in the way that they sound. *Central Park In The Dark* portrays a walk through that park, and just as the walker would simultaneously hear different natural sounds, people talking, and music playing from two or three different sources, so Ives puts all these elements into his piece, playing at the same time. *The Unanswered Question* is altogether more abstract. Long slow chords create a mood of mystery in which instrumental timbres are as important as the actual notes. It is the same kind of music that synthesizer artists like Klaus Schulze were performing in the seventies, but decades earlier and with no electronics.

Just before the first world war, in 1913, the Russian composer Igor Stravinsky unveiled his ballet, *Le Sacre Du Printemps (The Rite Of Spring)*, at the Théatre des Champs-Élysées in Paris. For the first time, a work based on insistent rhythms pushing dissonant riffs and chords was being presented to the public, who were not at all sure that they liked what they heard. Some of the more rowdy members of the audience were thrown out of the theatre and afterwards, the music critic in the French newspaper, *Le Figaro*, described the work as a "laborious and puerile barbarity". Even twenty years later, Constant Lambert, in *Music Ho!*, his study of what was, for him, recent music, could still somewhat condescendingly describe *The Rite Of Spring* as "barbaric music for the supercivilized, an aphrodisiac for the jaded and surfeited".

The rhythmic emphasis introduced by Stravinsky did not, in the end, inspire many other composers to produce anything similar. Gustav Holst used a powerful five-four riff to underscore *Mars*, from his suite, *The Planets* (composed in 1914 to 1916); Arthur Honegger emulated a moving steam train with his *Pacific 231* (composed in 1923); and Maurice Ravel used an annoyingly insistent six-beat side drum pattern for his *Bolero* (composed in 1928). By that time, however, jazz had arrived. This music presented rhythm as an essential part of its structure and the classical composers preferred, on the whole, to leave further explorations to it. Those few exceptions, like George Gershwin, who embraced jazz as an inspiration for their own creations, are covered in this book within the chapter on jazz. *Ionisation*, a piece composed by Edgard Varèse between 1929 and 1931, and scored entirely for percussion, is not actually concerned with rhythm at all, but rather with the sounds and the textures of the instruments employed.

A number of new, electronic instruments were invented during the twentieth century, as described in the chapters devoted to keyboard and to electronic instruments. A few composers responded to the challenge by writing music for them and one unqualified masterpiece was produced, featuring the ondes martenot. This was the *Turangalila Symphony*, composed by the Frenchman Olivier Messiaen between 1945 and 1948. Messiaen had previously started to

THE FIRST TIME

The Aeolian harp is a real instrument, in which strings attached to a wooden soundbox are intended to be played by the blowing of the wind. A thirty-foot-tall example was built in Vermont in 1971 by Ward McCain. The following year it was recorded by Chuck Hancock and Harry Bee and the resulting sounds were edited into a set of compositions on a double LP entitled *The Wind Harp – Song From The Hill*. If one did not know, it would be assumed that the eerie music was electronic in origin. It sounds nothing like Henry Cowell's piece. A large wind harp built by Sverre Larsen in Norway was used on three tracks of the Jan Garbarek album, *Dis*, recorded in December 1976. In Zadar, Coatia, pipes have been built underneath large concrete steps in the sea wall, to create a sea organ, which is played by the movement of the waves. Several YouTube clips of its ethereal sounds have been uploaded.

LaMonte Young wrote a piece for David Tudor to perform in 1960 that turned the aesthetic of Cage's *4'33"* into an event. Tudor was required to bring a bucket of water and a bale of hay to the stage in order to attempt to feed the piano. The piece was determined to have been completed when the piano had either been fed or had decided not to eat. Young created a number of compositions of a similar nature to this, but is primarily remembered for his use of drones in various pieces, some of which were of marathon proportions. John Cale, later a founding member of the Velvet Underground, was one of his early students and proved it by playing drones on songs like *Venus In Furs*.

John Cage

Several anti-war songs by Bob Dylan and a few by Donovan are roughly contemporaneous with the *War Requiem*. They achieve their effect through powerful lyrics rather than with the music, which is very simple and has the main purpose of enabling the lyrics to be easily heard and appreciated. Perhaps the first rock music to deal with war and to achieve the impact of the Britten and Penderecki works is to be found in two fairly short pieces recorded by Jimi Hendrix in 1969 – *Machine Gun* and *The Star Spangled Banner*. Jazz, meanwhile, can offer two extended works, also recorded in 1969 – Mike Westbrook's *Marching Song* and Charlie Haden's *Liberation Music Orchestra*, although the latter does not seem entirely sure whether it is condemning war or celebrating it.

The third piano concerto by Hungarian composer Bela Bartok, from 1945, employs an arresting theme, angular yet fluent, played by woodwind instruments over a rippling piano underlay, as the central apex of the first movement. It sounds remarkably like something written by Frank Zappa or the Soft Machine some twenty-five years later. A number of twentieth century composers are name-checked as influences in the sleeve-notes to Zappa's 1966 album with the Mothers of Invention, *Freak Out*, but the list does not include Bartok. During a 1967 interview with *Hit Parader* magazine, however, quoted on the website *globalia.net*, Frank Zappa did recommend all three of Bela Bartok's piano concertos. During its 1988 tour, Zappa's band performed a brief *Theme From The Bartok Piano Concerto #3*, but it was re-orchestrated with the effect of making the music hard to identify.

The British composer John Tavener first appeared on record due to the benevolence of the Beatles. His uncompromising avant garde work, *The Whale*, which has no discernible rock influence at all, was nevertheless released on the Beatles' own Apple label in 1970. Just over twenty years later, a Tavener work of a markedly different character, a meditative composition for cello and string orchestra, *The Protecting Veil*, was a surprise commercial success. It was a rare classical music nominee for the Mercury Music Prize in 1992, although it did not win.

The various directors of the many films to incorporate Samuel Barber's moving, though not conspicuously modern work, *Adagio for Strings*, managed to avoid royalty issues by waiting until after the death of the composer and the moving of the music out of copyright. *Adagio for Strings* was composed in 1936.

use carefully notated bird song as source material for his music and he continued to do so for many years. He first employed the technique during his long organ work from 1935, *La Nativité du Seigneur*. The Italian composer Ottorino Respighi incorporated a recording of an actual nightingale in his 1924 work, *Pines Of Rome*. Finnish composer Einojuhani Rautavaara took the idea a little further in 1972, with his *Cantus Arcticus*, which includes contributions from a flock of birds and is subtitled *Concerto for Birds and Orchestra*. In 2016, Nitin Sawhney composed an *Animal Symphony*, incorporating melodic ideas taken from bird song and other animal sounds and intended, as the ultimate novelty (and a certain amount of scientific enquiry), to be appreciated by those birds and animals, as well as humans!

The chapters covering keyboard and electronic instruments also describe the invention and development of music that is entirely, or almost entirely, electronic. Reference is made to the first acclaimed masterpiece in the genre, which is Karlheinz Stockhausen's *Gesang der Jünglinge* from 1955-6. The work combines the sound of children's voices with electronics. Stockhausen retained an experimental approach throughout his career. His orchestral pieces, *Gruppen* and *Carré*, from 1955-7 and 1958-9, employ three and four separate orchestras respectively and explore their positioning with regard to the audience as an important part of the music. During the seventies, the alto saxophonist Anthony Braxton, who also composed avant garde orchestral works, described his intention to write music for orchestras positioned on different planets. Stockhausen, content to operate more practically, though with only a little less eccentricity, published a string quartet in which the four musicians played from within four airborne helicopters. The *Helicopter String Quartet* was recorded in 1996, with the engine noise and rotor sound becoming an inevitable addition to the music.

In 1923, the American Henry Cowell explored new ways of playing the familiar acoustic piano in his piece titled *Aeolian Harp*. The pianist was required to pluck the strings directly with his hands, inside the piano, in order to create sounds that were indeed very like those of a harp. John Cage went further by inventing what he called the 'prepared piano' in 1940 – attaching bolts and clips to various of the piano strings, in order to drastically change its sound and response to what was played on the keyboard.

It was Cage who conceived the controversial piece, 4'33", which was originally included as part of a piano recital by David Tudor in August 1952. At the start, he lifted the piano lid; at the end he closed it again. In between he played nothing. Several pieces of music before this had included passages of silence, but this was the first time a piece was presented that was apparently made up entirely of silence. In reality, this was not quite the case, because Cage intended that the music should consist of the tiny ambient sounds that would inevitably occur during the four and a half minute duration. Nevertheless, in 2002, Mike Batt (the creator of the Wombles as a musical act) agreed to make a substantial out of court settlement after a piece included on one of his records, *One Minute Silence*, caused Cage's publisher to sue for plagiarism. A silent piece on John Lennon's *Mind Games* album from 1973, *Nutopian International Anthem*, avoided any such action, but then Lennon was not foolish enough to credit John Cage as a co-composer. Cage's idea was extended a little further by Luc Ferrari in 1970. *Presque Rien No.1* consists entirely of ambient sounds recorded at the seaside (at Vela Luka in Yugoslavia, modern-day Croatia, as it happened).

With rhythm and blues and rock 'n' roll not yet having sufficient artistic gravitas to tackle the subject, it was left to classical composers to commemorate the second world war, although they took their time to do this. Benjamin Britten's *War Requiem* was published in 1962. It is a striking and monumental work, if not an overly modern sounding one. The first recording of it supposedly sold two hundred thousand copies during 1963, remarkable for a classical album, although if this is true, then it somehow achieved these sales without ever troubling the album charts. *Threnody for the Victims of Hiroshima* by the Polish composer Krzysztof Penderecki is an altogether more disturbing piece, from 1960. Originally given the more prosaic title *8'37"*, it was renamed by the composer after he heard it performed for the first time and realised the emotional impact of what he had written. The work uses discordant sounds and advanced playing techniques to deliver a very powerful message. If Britten's work mourns the futility of war, then Penderecki's describes its horror.

THE FIRST TIME

Terry Riley with the Kronos Quartet

Terry Riley collaborated with John Cale in 1971 for an album, *Church Of Anthrax,* which found common ground between minimalist classical music and improvising rock. The record is a worthy effort, although the incorporation of Riley's approach by Soft Machine into compositions such as *Out-Bloody-Rageous* from 1970, is rather more interesting. The group was the first act, categorised as rock, to be invited to play at the Proms, also in 1970. The techniques of minimalism were employed in a record made by a nineteen year old guitarist in 1973 and turned into a surprising multi-million seller. This was *Tubular Bells* by Mike Oldfield.

Caroline Redman Lusher founded Rock Choir in 2005, in Farnham, Surrey, offering amateur singers the chance to perform contemporary, usually pop material in a choral context. She initiated a revival of interest in choral music. This was extended further by the work of Gareth Malone, who made the business of amateur singing in a choir a subject able to attract large television audiences. A Rock Choir album was issued in 2010, while a choir led by Gareth Malone followed suit in 2013. Both albums were very successful in the charts. The Rock Choir album, featuring nearly a thousand singers, also earned itself an entry in the Guinness Book of Records, for the largest musical act ever to release an album.

Robert John Godfrey in 1974

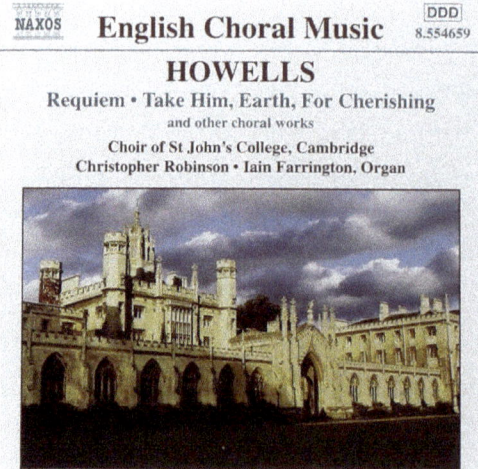

It was Lesley Garrett who, during the early years of her career, made some quite unnecessary remarks about the quality of Madonna's singing voice, compared to her own. One is reminded of similar remarks made by establishment critics in the sixties and directed at the Beatles. It turns out, however, that great art can in fact be made by people whose technical ability is not the greatest, while the converse is also true. The argument that Garrett's *From The Heart* has made as big a contribution to modern culture as Madonna's acclaimed *Ray Of Light* is not tenable.

Gustav Mahler supposedly believed, on little more evidence than the example of Beethoven, that no composer could survive long enough to compose more than nine symphonies. To cheat fate he attempted to pass off his set of orchestral songs, *Das Lied Von Der Erde (Song Of The Earth),* composed between 1906 and 1908, as a symphony. After finishing a genuine ninth symphony in 1909, he began work on a tenth, but died two years later, before he could complete it. The British composer Havergal Brian had no such superstition. Having composed a gargantuan first symphony in 1927, he had still only managed as far as symphony number five by the time he reached retirement age in 1940 (he had worked as a musical journalist). Now able to devote all his time to composing and undaunted by the fact that none of his music was recorded during his lifetime (in line with what was said earlier in this chapter about the difficulties experienced by composers of new works), he had completed no fewer than thirty-two symphonies by the time of his death in 1972, at the age of ninety-six. Meanwhile, the American composer Alan Hovhaness completed an astonishing sixty-seven symphonies by the time of his death, at the age of eighty-nine, in 2000. The work of both men is original and of a high quality, modern but accessible.

The soundtrack from a film released in 1968 did much to draw attention to the world of modern atonal classical music. The powerful music that plays during the opening sequences of *2001: A Space Odyssey* is the beginning of a piece composed by Richard Strauss in 1896, *Also Sprach Zarathustra*. In this context it is made to sound like a much more recent piece, but the complete work is in reality something of a let-down after this and never manages to regain the sense of awe inspired by its dramatic start. This is not, after all, a modern work, nor even a modern-sounding work. No more is the music used in a spaceship docking sequence, *The Blue Danube*, composed in 1866 by an older, unrelated Strauss, Johann II. Much of the film, however, employs music by the Hungarian composer György Ligeti, most notably his *Atmospheres*, from 1961, and the choral work *Lux Aeterna*, from 1966. Both of these are highly evocative, slow moving works, like descendants of the Ives composition, *The Unanswered Question*. Dense clusters of notes abandon any pretence of melody in favour of, well, atmosphere. Astonishingly, director Stanley Kubrick neglected to obtain Ligeti's permission for the use of his music, so that the composer had to sue for compensation.

In 1964, the American composer Terry Riley published a work he called *In C*. The music starts with a rapidly repeating C note, played percussively, high on a piano, like a fast pulse. The note is expanded to a chord, which gradually becomes denser, before shifting slowly into other chords. There is no melody, just texture and the pulse, yet *In C*, surprisingly, emerges as easy on the ear. It was the first in a genre that came to be called minimalism, by critics who perceived parallels with a similarly event-free movement in visual art. Minimalist works constructed around slowly evolving patterns of chords and melodic fragments became increasingly adept at producing an emotional response during the succeeding years. A number of bona fide masterpieces were published and recorded, including *Tabula Rasa* by Arvo Pärt (1977), *Shaker Loops* by John Adams (1977-8), *Koyaanisqatsi* by Philip Glass (1982), *Different Trains* by Steve Reich (1988), and *Concerto for Piano and Orchestra* by Michael Nyman (1993), using themes taken from his soundtrack for the award winning film, *The Piano*. Many of the composers formed permanent groups of musicians to perform their music and went on tour, exactly as if they were leading rock bands. Steve Reich was the first to do this, in 1966.

The Kronos Quartet behaved in much the same way a few years later, making a point of playing music by the composers it felt were closest to the cutting edge, while allowing itself to be marketed in the same way as a star rock group. The quartet's first album was *In Formation*, released in 1982, although the breakthrough album was the self-titled one issued in 1986, the first on a major label. It gleefully put Jimi Hendrix alongside the likes of Philip Glass and Conlon Nancarrow (famous for player piano pieces where his prepared paper tapes enabled techniques that would have been impossible for a human performer).

The interaction between the members of real rock bands and classical music is described in this book in the chapter on progressive rock. To the names mentioned there should be added that of a group formed specifically to play the classically-inspired compositions of its keyboard player, Robert John Godfrey. The Enid made its first album, *In The Region Of The Summer Stars*, in 1976, while Godfrey's early masterpiece, *Fand*, was included on the 1977 second album, *Aerie Faerie Nonsense*, and revised several times afterwards. *Fand* has a pastoral, folky influence, with state-of-the-art electric keyboards emulating an orchestra. They make the music sound a little like something Ralph Vaughan Williams might have composed a few years earlier, but with the surprising addition, in some places, of drums and an electric guitar.

Glenn Branca preferred to use the energy and abrasiveness of punk as the starting point for a synthesis of rock and classical music. He issued his first recordings in 1980, two pieces on a mini-album named after one of them, *Lesson No 1*. The music is dissonant and avant garde, occupying a middle ground that is not quite either genre. A second album in 1981 included *The Ascension* as its title track, a work composed for massed guitars, which became Branca's signature sound. A succession of long works were given the titles of symphonies, but were structured in a similar minimalist manner to Terry Riley's *In C* and were delivered by orchestras of guitars (usually modified or specially hand-built). The music is relentless and loud but remarkably cathartic. The guitarists – numbering a hundred in the case of his Symphony No 13 – sometimes included Lee Ranaldo and Thurston Moore, who founded the group

THE FIRST TIME

TRACKING THE TRACKS

Most of the works mentioned in this chapter are available on CD as several different recordings. Many of the recommendations given below could just as easily be replaced by other CDs.

Philip Glass's *Low Symphony* – his first if he were to put a number on it – is played by the Brooklyn Philharmonic Orchestra conducted by Dennis Russell Davies on Point Music (1993). Gabriel Prokofiev's *Concerto for Turntables and Orchestra* has not been recorded at the time of writing, but the Proms performance can be seen and heard on YouTube.

The *Violin Concerto* by Jean Sibelius, played by Anne-Sophie Mutter with the Staatskapelle Dresden, conducted by André Previn, is on Deutsche Grammophon (1995).

Pli Selon Pli by Pierre Boulez is included with two other key works on a double CD (Warner 2000), played by the BBC Symphony Orchestra conducted by Boulez himself. *Eight Songs for a Mad King* by Peter Maxwell Davies was released on vinyl in 1971. It has not been reissued or re-recorded on CD, but the original recording can be obtained as a legal download via Treasure Island Music. The music is sung by Julius Eastman and played by the Fires of London, conducted by Peter Maxwell Davies. *The Rise and Fall of Ziggy Stardust and the Spiders From Mars* by David Bowie is on Parlophone (2015). *Ace of Spades* by Motorhead is on Sanctuary (2015).

The Perfect Stranger by Frank Zappa is on Rykodisc (1995). The music is performed by the Ensemble InterContemporain, conducted by Pierre Boulez and by the Barking Pumpkin Digital Gratification Consort – which is, in reality, Frank Zappa himself playing his synclavier.

Jonathan Harvey's *The Madonna Of Winter And Spring* is performed by the Netherlands Radio Philharmonic, conducted by Peter Eötvös, on a Nimbus CD (1999), together with two other works by the composer.

The 1888 performance of Handel's *Israel in Egypt,* the piano playing of Johannes Brahms, and one song from the 1903 recording of Verdi's *Ernani* can be heard on YouTube. The Mendelssohn *Violin Concerto In E minor*, played by Nathan Milstein with the New York Philharmonic conducted by Bruno Walter, is on Dante Productions (1998). Later recordings of Beethoven's *Symphony No.5* by Leopold Stokowski conducting different orchestras are available on CD, but not the 1931 recording.

The string sextet version of Schoenberg's *Verklarte Nacht* is played by LaSalle Quartet with extra members on Deutsche Grammophon (1988). The final string orchestra version, played by the Berlin Philharmonic conducted by Herbert Von Karajan is also on Deutsche Grammophon (1998). The CD also includes another early Schoenberg work, *Pelleas und Melisande.* Schoenberg's *String Quartet No.2* is included on a Naxos CD (2005) with two other works and is played by the Fred Sherry String Quartet. *Variations for Orchestra,* performed by the City of Birmingham Symphony Orchestra conducted by Simon Rattle, is on EMI (1995) with two other major Schoenberg works. The Berg *Violin Concerto*, played by Isabelle Faust with Orchestra Mozart conducted by Claudio Abbado is on Harmonia Mundi (2012), paired, surprisingly, with the Beethoven *Violin Concerto.*

La Mer is included with three other works by Debussy on Deutsche Grammophon (2002), played by the Cleveland Orchestra, conducted by Pierre Boulez. A three CD set on Sony (2002) includes all four of the Ives symphonies, as well as *Central Park in the Dark* and *The Unanswered Question*, played by the Chicago Symphony Orchestra, conducted by Michael Tilson Thomas.

The Rite Of Spring is coupled with a slightly earlier Stravinsky work, *The Firebird,* and played by the Philharmonia Orchestra, conducted by Esa-Pekka Salonen, on a Sony CD (2002). *The Planets* by Gustav Holst is combined with two major works by Ralph Vaughan Williams on a BMG CD (1994) and played by the Philadelphia Orchestra, conducted by Eugene Ormandy. Honegger's *Pacific 231* is included on a double CD on Apex (2006) along with another short work, *Rugby,* and the five symphonies, all played by the Bavarian Radio Symphony Orchestra, conducted by Charles Dutoit. *Bolero* and some other works by Ravel are on a Deutsche Grammophon CD (2010), played by the Boston Symphony Orchestra, conducted by Seiji Ozawa.

Ionisation by Edgard Varèse is included on the double CD, *The Complete Works* (Decca 2004), played by the Asko Ensemble, conducted by Riccardo Chailly. Messiaen's *Turangalila Symphony*, performed by L'Orchestre de L'Opéra Bastille, conducted by Myung-Whun Chung, is on Deutsche Grammophon (1991). *La Nativité du Seigneur,* played by Jennifer Bate, is on Regis (2001). Respighi's *Pines Of Rome* is available via several different recordings, such as one by the London Symphony Orchestra, conducted by Istvan Kertesz (Decca/Eloquence 2013). The CD includes a 1928 work, *The Birds,* where Respighi presented musical portraits of various birds, though without attempting to properly notate their song as did Messiaen. Rautavaara's *Cantus Arcticus,* performed by the Royal Scottish National Orchestra, conducted by Hannu Lintu, is on Naxos (1998), together with two other works by the composer. Nitin Sawhney's *Animal Symphony* was given its own documentary on Sky television in 2016, but has so far not been issued on CD.

Stockhausen's Gesang der Jünglingen is not currently available on CD, but can be heard on YouTube or as a download from Puzzle Productions. *Gruppen* and *Carré* are on a Stockhausen Verlag CD (1992), but this is hard to find. Several performances can be found on YouTube. *Gruppen* is also included, with some works by György Kurtág, on a Deutsche Grammophon CD (2012). Members of the Berlin Philharmonic are used to form all three orchestras, which are conducted by Friedrich Goldmann, Claudio Abbado, and Marcus Creed. *Helikopter-Streichquartett,* played by the Arditti String Quartet, is on Montaigne (1995).

MUSIC GENRES

Sonic Youth after playing together on some of Branca's earliest recordings.

In the US, Billboard published classical music charts in the forties. In the UK, the classical artists album chart was started for the week beginning October 17th 1999. The number one album was by the popular soprano singer Lesley Garrett, presenting a selection of defiantly unmodern operetta and show tunes, under the title *From The Heart*. Shortly afterwards, Charlotte Church began an eleven week run at number one, with her self-titled second album, presenting a similar selection to that of Ms Garrett, though with a slightly Welsh slant. The first twentieth century composer to enter the chart was the English church music specialist, Herbert Howells, whose album of choral music from half a century earlier, performed by the Choir of St John's College Cambridge, was at number eight in the first week.

Cowell's *Aeolian Harp*, performed by the composer, is included on *Piano Music* (Smithsonian Folkways 1993). *The Wind Harp – Songs From The Hill* has not been reissued on CD, but two short extracts can be heard on YouTube. *Dis* by Jan Garbarek is on ECM (2008).

Some of John Cage's music for prepared piano can be heard on *Sonatas and Interludes for Prepared Piano* (Naxos 1999), played by Boris Berman. *4'33"* is included on the double CD, *A Chance Operation – The John Cage Tribute* (Koch International Classics 1993). The piano was supervised by Frank Zappa on this occasion. Mike Batt's *One Minute Silence* is on the album *Classical Graffiti* by the Planets (EMI 2002). John Lennon's *Nutopian International Anthem* is on *Mind Games* (EMI 2010). As it is only three seconds long, it is difficult to distinguish from the normal gap between tracks. *Presque Rien No.1* by Luc Ferrari is included with other similar works by the composer on *Presque Rien* (INA 2004).

The piece composed by LaMonte Young for David Tudor has not been recorded, for some reason, although short versions for piano and for guitar can be seen in YouTube video clips, courtesy of Karen Thompson and Cherry McDonald, respectively. A drone performance by LaMonte Young, with John Cale and others, can be found on *Inside The Dream Syndicate – Volume 1 Day Of Niagara 1965* (Table Of The Elements 2008). A very short piece is included on the double CD *The Roots Of Drone* (Chrome Dreams 2012). *Venus In Furs* is included on *The Velvet Underground & Nico* (Universal 2012).

The original recording of Benjamin Britten's *War Requiem*, performed by the London Symphony Orchestra and soloists, conducted by the composer, is on a double CD (Universal/Decca 2006). Penderecki's *Threnody for the Victims of Hiroshima* is included with other works by the composer, including his third symphony, on a Naxos CD (2000). The performances are by the National Polish Radio Symphony Orchestra, conducted by Antoni Wit.

The Bob Dylan songs, *Blowin' In The Wind, Masters of War, A Hard Rain's A-Gonna Fall,* and *Talking World War III Blues* are on *The Freewheelin' Bob Dylan* (Columbia 2003). The Donovan songs *Universal Soldier, Do You Hear Me Now,* and *The War Drags On* (actually written by Buffy Sainte-Marie, Bert Jansch, and Mick Softley) were originally included on an EP titled *Universal Soldier*. The songs are currently available on *The Very Best Of The Early Years* (Sanctuary 2005). *Machine Gun* is on the Jimi Hendrix album *Band Of Gypsys* (Sony 2010); *The Star Bangled Banner* is on the double CD *Live at Woodstock* (Experience Hendrix 2010). *Marching Song Vol 1 & 2* by the Mike Westbrook Concert Band is on a double CD (Righteous 2009). *Liberation Music Orchestra* by Charlie Haden is on Impulse (1996).

The three Bartok *Piano Concertos*, played by Vladimir Ashkenazy with the London Philharmonic Orchestra, conducted by Sir Georg Solti, are on Decca (1996). A more recent double CD combines the same performances with the Bartok *Violin Concerto* (Universal/Decca 2003). Frank Zappa's *Theme From The Bartok Piano Concerto #3* is on the double CD *Make A Jazz Noise Here* (Zappa Records 2012).

The soundtrack album from *2001: A Space Odyssey* is on Sony (1996). Walt Disney's *Fantasia* is available on a DVD (Walt Disney Studios 2011). Samuel Barber's *Adagio for Strings*, played by the Detroit Symphony Orchestra, conducted by Neeme Järvi, is included on a Chandos CD (1998).

John Tavener's *The Whale* is on Apple (1992). A 2010 issue on Apple finds room to include the composer's second recording for the label as well, *Celtic Requiem*. The London Sinfonietta plays both works, with Tavener himself on keyboards. *The Protecting Veil*, played by cellist Steven Isserlis with the London Symphony Orchestra, conducted by Gennadi Rozhdestvensky, is on Virgin (2006).

In C by Terry Riley is on Sony (2009). *Tabula Rasa* by Arvo Pärt is included on an ECM New Series CD (2010), performed by the Lithuanian Chamber Orchestra and soloists, conducted by Saulus Sondeckis. Another Pärt work on the same album, *Fratres*, finds pianist Keith Jarrett stepping out of his accustomed jazz role. *Shaker Loops* is included with other works by John Adams on a Naxos CD (2004), performed by the Bournemouth Symphony Orchestra, conducted by Marin Alsop. *Koyaanisqatsi* by Philip Glass is on Island (1995), performed by Philip Glass Music, conducted by Michael Riesman. *Different Trains* by Steve Reich, performed by the Kronos Quartet, is on WEA (1989). Michael Nyman's *Piano Concerto,* performed by John Lenehan with the Ulster Orchestra, conducted by Takuo Yuasa, is on Naxos (1998).

THE FIRST TIME

In Formation by the Kronos Quartet is on Reference Recordings (1990). It comprises ten short works by some lesser known names – David Keshley, Ken Benshoof, Derek Thunes, Hunt Beyer, Alan Dorsey, John Whitney, and John Geist. The self-titled album is on Nonesuch (1986). It moves up a league or two, with works by Peter Sculthorpe, Aulis Sallinen, Philip Glass, Conlon Nancarrow, and Jimi Hendrix.

Church Of Anthrax by Terry Riley and John Cale and performed by them, with the addition of a drummer and, on one track, a singer, is on Esoteric Recordings (2014). The Soft Machine's performance at the Proms is on *Live at the Proms 1970* (Reckless 1988). *In The Region Of The Summer Stars* by the Enid is on Operation Seraphim (2010). The most satisfying version of *Fand*, lasting just under thirty minutes, is on the Mantella issue of *Aerie Faerie Nonsense* (1994) or the Inner Sanctuary issue (2002). The whole album was re-recorded for these – the original recording, with a much shorter version of *Fand*, is on Operation Seraphim (2010).

Glenn Branca's *Lesson No 1* (complete with two extra tracks) and *The Ascension* are on Acute CDs (2008) but are expensive. *Symphony No 1 (Tonal Plexus)* is on Roir (2007); *Symphony No 13 (Hallucination City)* is on Atavistic (2016). Perhaps the best starting place for Branca's music is *Symphony No 3 (Gloria)* (Atavistic 2011). *From The Heart* by Lesley Garrett is a double CD, on Silva Treasury (1999). *Charlotte Church* is on Sony (1999). The album of Herbert Howells music recorded by the Choir of St.John's College, Cambridge, is on Naxos (1999). Madonna's *Ray Of Light* is on Warner (2001). *Rock Choir Vol.1* is on Universal/Decca (2010). *Voices* by Gareth Malone is also on Universal/Decca (2013).

Mahler's *Das Lied Von Der Erde*, performed by the Royal Concertgebouw Orchestra of Amsterdam, conducted by Bernard Haitink, with singers Janet Baker and James King, is on Philips (1991). His *Symphony No.9*, perormed by the Berlin Philharmonic, conducted by Herbert Von Karajan, is on Deutsche Grammophon (2003). The *Symphony No.10*, completed from the composer's rough draft by Deryck Cooke, in collaboration with Berthold Goldschmidt, Colin Matthews, and David Matthews, is on EMI (2000) in a performance by the Berlin Philharmonic, conducted by Simon Rattle. The *First Symphony 'Gothic'* by Havergal Brian is on Naxos (2004), performed by the CSR Symphony (Bratislava) and the Slovak Philharmonic, conducted by Ondrej Lenard, together with several choirs. The number of people required to perform the work exceeds those on Mahler's *Symphony No.8*, which was subtitled *Symphony of a Thousand*. All of Brian's symphonies have been recorded in recent years. The best selling CD on Amazon combines symphonies 2 and 14 on one disc. They are performed by the Royal Scottish National Orchestra, conducted by Martyn Brabbins (Dutton 2016). A CD combining Symphony No. 50 (Mount St. Helens) and Symphony No. 22 (City Of Light) provides as good an introduction to the music of Alan Hovhaness as any. The performance is by the Seattle Symphony Orchestra, conducted by Gerard Schwarz (Delos 2001).

BIBLIOGRAPHY

25 Years Of Rock by John Tobler and Pete Frame (Hamlyn Publishing Group/W.H.Smith 1980)

500 Albums You Won't Believe Until You Hear Them by Neil Nixon with Thom Nixon (Gonzo Multimedia 2014)

Abbey Road by Brian Southall, Peter Vince, and Allan Rouse (Omnibus Press 1997)

The Ambient Century by Mark Prendergast (Bloomsbury 2000)

The Autobiography Of Malcolm X (Penguin 1968)

Bass Culture by Lloyd Bradley (Penguin 2001)

The Beatles Recording Sessions by Mark Lewisohn (Hamlyn/EMI 1988)

The Beatles: The Authorised Biography by Hunter Davies (Heinemann 1968)

The Beatles Tune In by Mark Lewisohn (Little, Brown 2013)

Becoming Elektra by Mick Houghton (Jawbone 2010)

The Big Book Of Blues by Robert Santelli (Pavilion Books 1994)

The Billboard Book Of American Singing Groups – A History 1940-1990 by Jay Warner (Billboard Books 1992)

Bird Lives! – The High Life And Hard Times Of Charlie 'Yardbird' Parker by Ross Russell (Quartet Books 1973)

A Black Manifesto In Jazz Poetry And Prose by Ted Joans (Calder & Boyars 1971)

Black Music by Leroi Jones (Amiri Baraka) (W. Morrow 1967)

Black Nationalism And The Revolution In Music by Frank Kofsky (Pathfinder 1970)

Blues-Rock Explosion edited by Summer McStravick and John Roos (Old Goat Publishing 2001)

Bob Dylan – His Unreleased Recordings by Paul Cable (Scorpion Publications 1978)

The Book Of Golden Discs by Joseph Murrells (Barrie and Jenkins 1978)

The Book Of Rock Lists by Dave Marsh and Kevin Stein (Sidgwick & Jackson 1981)

The Boy Looked At Johnny by Julie Burchill and Tony Parsons (Pluto Press 1978)

British Hit Singles And Albums edited by David Roberts (Guinness World Records 2004)

Brother Ray by Ray Charles and David Ritz (Futura 1980)

The Byrds by Bud Scoppa (Scholastic 1971)

Collectable 45's Parts 1-2 (Vintage Record Centre 1981)

Collectable EPs Parts 1-3 (Vintage Record Centre 1982, 1983, 1985)

Complete British Directory of Popular 78/45 rpm Singles 1950-1980 Volumes One and Two by Paul Pelletier (Record Information Services 1986,1987)

Continuum Encyclopaedia Of Popular Music Of The World Volume 2 Performance and Production edited by John Shepherd, David Horn, Dave Laing, Paul Oliver, Peter Wicke (Bloomsbury 2003)

Conversations With Eric Clapton by Steve Turner (Sphere Books 1976)

Country: The Twisted Roots Of Rock 'n' Roll by Nick Tosches (DaCapo 1996)

Country Roads – How Country Came To Nashville by Brian Hinton (Sanctuary 2000)

The Crack In The Cosmic Egg by Steven Freeman and Alan Freeman (Audion 1996)

Crossroads: The Life And Music Of Eric Clapton by Michael Schumacher (Little, Brown 1995)

Detroit '67 – The Year That Changed Soul by Stuart Cosgrove (Clayton 2015)

Dread Talk – The Language Of Rastafari by Velma Pollard (Revised edition McGill-Queen's University Press 2000)

Duke's Diary Part Two – The Life Of Duke Ellington 1950-1974 by Ken Vail (Scarecrow Press 2002)

Dylan – A Biography by Bob Spitz (Norton 1991)

From Edison To Marconi: The First Thirty Years Of Recorded Music by David J. Steffen (McFarland & Co. 2005)

Electric Guitars – The Illustrated Encyclopaedia by Tony Bacon (Merchant 2000)

The Electric Muse – The Story Of Folk Into Rock by Dave Laing, Karl Dallas, Robin Denselow, and Robert Shelton (Methuen 1975)

Encyclopaedia Of Albums edited by Paul Du Noyer (Parragon 1999)

The Faber Companion To 20th Century Popular Music 2nd ed. by Phil Hardy & Dave Laing (Faber and Faber 1995)

Fuzz, Acid And Flowers by Vernon Joynson (Borderline Productions 1996)

The Gimmix Book of Records by Frank Goldmann and Klaus Hiltscher (Virgin 1981)

Goldmine Price Guide to 45 rpm Records 2nd edition by Tim Neely (Krause Publications 1999)

Goldmine Record Album Price Guide 3rd edition by Tim Neely (Krause Publications 2003)

Goldmine's Price Guide to Collectible Jazz Albums 1949-1969 by Neal Umphred (Krause Publications 1992)

The Gramophone Guide to Classical Composers and Recordings by Lionel Salter (Salamander 1978)

The Great White Wonders – A History Of Rock Bootlegs by Clinton Heylin (Viking 1994)

The Guinness Book of Records (Guinness World Records, annually from 1955)

The Guitar – The History The Music The Players by Allan Kozinn, Pete Welding, Dan Forte, Gene Santoro (Quarto 1984)

He's A Rebel – Phil Spector: Rock & Roll's Legendary Producer by Mark Ribowsky (Da Capo Press 2007)

Here There And Everywhere: My Life Recording The Music Of The Beatles by Geoff Emerick and Howard Massey (Gotham Books 2006)

The Hip Hop Years – A History Of Rap by Alex Ogg with David Upshal (Macmillan 1999)

The History of Rickenbacker Guitars by Richard R. Smith (Centerstream 1987)

Hit Singles – Top 20 Charts From 1954 To The Present Day by Dave McAleer (Carlton Books 2003)

In The Court Of King Crimson by Sid Smith (Helter Skelter Publishing 2001)

Incredibly Strange Music Volumes I and II by Andrea Juno and V.Vale (Re/Search Publications 1993/1994)

The Illustrated Encyclopaedia Of Music by Paul De Noyer (Flame Tree 2003)

An Illustrated History Of Gospel by Steve Turner (Lion Hudson 2010)

The Illustrated New Musical Express Encyclopaedia Of Rock by Nick Logan and Bob Woffinden (Salamander 1976)

Jah Music – The Evolution Of The Popular Jamaican Song by Sebastian Clarke (Heinemann 1980)

The Jazz Book by Joachim Berendt (Hart-Davis, MacGibbon 1976)

Jazz Modernism – From Ellington & Armstrong To Matisse & Joyce by Alfred Appel Jr (Yale University Press 2002

Jazz Records 1897-1942 (2 volumes) by Brian Rust (Arlington House 1978)

Jazz Records 1942-1962 (11 volumes, some extended to 1965 or 1969) by Jorgen Grunnet Jepsen (Knudsen 1963-9)

Jazzways edited by George S. Rosenthal and Frank Zachary (Musicians Press 1946)

Keith Jarrett – The Man And His Music by Ian Carr (Grafton 1991)

Killing Floor by Lee Child (Transworld 1998)

The Larousse Encyclopaedia of Music edited by Geoffrey Hindley (Hamlyn 1971; latest edition Smithmark 1997)

Last Night A DJ Saved My Life – History Of The Disc Jockey by Bill Brewster & Frank Broughton (Headline 1999)

Lennon Remembers by Jann Wenner (Penguin 1973)

The Liverpool Scene edited by Edward Lucie-Smith (Donald Carroll 1967)

London American Recordings Complete Singles Catalogue 1949-1982 by Paul M.Pelletier (Record Information Services 1982)

Making Music Modern – New York In The 1920s by Carol J. Oja (Oxford University Press 2000)

Miles Davis: A Critical Biography/The Definitive Biography by Ian Carr (Quartet 1982; 2nd ed HarperCollins 1998)

Miles Davis: A Musical Biography by Bill Cole (W. Morrow 1974)

Miles The Autobiography by Quincy Troupe and Miles Davis (Picador 1990)

Milton Brown and the Founding of Western Swing by Cary Ginell (University of Illinois Press 1994)

Modern Jazz – The Essential Records by Max Harrison, Alun Morgan and others (Aquarius 1975)

Modern Music – The Avant Garde Since 1945 by Paul Griffiths (Dent 1981)

Mojo Risin' – 1600+ Bite-sized Album Reviews by Alexander Rez (Createspace 2018)

Mother! The Frank Zappa Story by Michael Gray (Plexus 1993)

Motown – The History by Sharon Davis (Guinness Publishing 1988)

Multi-Track Recording For Musicians by Brent Hurtig (GPI Publications 1988)

Music For A Desert Island by Nick Hamlyn (Createspace 2015)

Music Ho! by Constant Lambert (Faber & Faber 1934; The Hogarth Press 1985)

Mystery Train: Images Of America In Rock'n'Roll Music by Greil Marcus (Omnibus Press 1977; sixth revised edition Plume Books 2015)

The New Book Of Rock Lists by Dave Marsh and James Bernard (Sidgwick & Jackson 1994)

A New History Of Jazz by Alyn Shipton (Continuum 2007)

The New Musical Express Book Of Rock 2 edited by Nick Logan and Bob Woffinden (W.H.Allen 1977)

New Sounds – The Virgin Guide To New Music by John Schaefer (Virgin 1990)

O'Brien Pocket History Of Irish Traditional Music by Gearoid O hAllmhurain (O'Brien Press 2012)

The Penguin Encyclopaedia of Popular Music edited by Donald Clarke (Viking 1989)

Penguin Modern Poets 10 – The Mersey Sound by Adrian Henri, Roger McGough, Brian Patten (Penguin 1967)

The Penguin Price Guide For Record & CD Collectors by Nick Hamlyn (Penguin 1997)

Play It Loud – An Epic History Of The Style, Sound, And Revolution Of The Electric Guitar by Brad Tolinski and Alan di Perna (Doubleday 2016)

Playing The Band – The Musical Life Of Jon Hiseman by Martyn Hanson (Temple Music 2010)

Rare Classical Record Price Guide 2004 by Barry Browne (Silverwood 2003)

The Real Frank Zappa Book by Frank Zappa with Peter Occhiogrosso (Picador 1989)

The Record Producers by John Tobler and Stuart Grundy (BBC 1982)

Reggae – The Rough Guide by Steve Barrow and Peter Dalton (Rough Guides 1997)

The Rest Is Noise – Listening To The Twentieth Century by Alex Ross (Fourth Estate 2007)

Revolution In The Head – The Beatles' Records & The Sixties by Ian MacDonald (Fourth Estate 1994)

The Road To Rock – A Zigzag Book of Interviews edited by Pete Frame (Charisma 1974)

Rock File 2 edited by Charlie Gillett (Panther 1974)

Rock Hardware by Paul Trynka and others (Balafon 1996)

The Rock Primer edited by John Collis (Penguin 1980)

Rock Record 7 by Terry Hounsome (Record Researcher 1997)

RockTalk edited by Joe Kohut and John J.Kohut (Faber and Faber 1994)

The Rolling Stone Record Guide edited by Dave Marsh and John Swenson (Virgin 1980)

The Rolling Stone Rock 'n' Roll Reader edited by Ben Fong-Torres (Bantam 1974)

San Antonio Rose – The Life and Music of Bob Wills by Charles R.Townsend (University of Illinois Press 1986)

San Francisco Nights: The Psychedelic Music Trip 1965-68 by Gene Sculatti & Davin Seay (Sidgwick & Jackson 1985)

Savannah Syncopators – African Retentions In The Blues by Paul Oliver (Studio Vista 1970)

'Scuse Me While I Kiss The Sky: The Life Of Jimi Hendrix by David Henderson (Bantam 1981)

Settling The Score – A Journey Through the Music of the 20th Century edited by Michael Oliver (Faber & Faber 1999)

Shadows And Light – Joni Mitchell – The Definitive Biography by Karen O'Brien (Virgin 2002)

Single File by Terry Hounsome (Record Researcher 1990)

Song And Dance Man – The Art of Bob Dylan by Michael Gray (St Martin's Press 1981)

The Soul Book by Ian Hoare, Clive Anderson, Tony Cummings, Simon Frith (Methuen 1975)

The Sound Of The City: The Rise Of Rock And Roll by Charlie Gillett (Souvenir Press/Sphere 1971; revised edition DaCapo 1996)

The Story Of The Blues by Paul Oliver (Barrie and Rockliff 1969; revised edition Pimlico 1997)

Stranded – Rock And Roll For A Desert Island by Greil Marcus (Alfred A.Knopf 1979)

The Symphony by Ralph Hill (Penguin 1949)

Talking Guitar – Conversations With Musicians Who Shaped Twentieth-Century American Music by Jas Obrecht (University Of North Carolina Press 2017)

The Tapestry Of Delights by Vernon Joynson (Borderline Productions 1996)

Top R&B Singles 1942-1995 by Joel Whitburn (US Record Research 1996)

Twentieth-Century Music by Robert P.Morgan (Norton 1991)

The Top Twenty Book by Tony Jasper (Blandford sixth edition 1994)

Turn It Up – I Can't Hear The Words by Bob Sarlin (Coronet 1975)

Twilight Of The Gods – The Beatles In Retrospect by Wilfrid Mellers (Faber and Faber 1976)

The Ultimate Guitar Book by Tony Bacon (Dorling Kindersley 1991)

Wax Trash & Vinyl Treasures – Record Collecting As A Social Practice by Roy Shuker (Ashgate 2010)

The Who And I by Tony Klinger (Gonzo Multimedia 2017)

The Wit & Wisdom Of Music edited by Nick Holt (Prion 2011)

Woody Guthrie: A Life by Joe Klein (Dell Publishing 1980)

Young Gifted And Black – The Story Of Trojan Records by Michael de Koningh & Laurence Cane-Honeysett (Sanctuary 2003)

The Gramophone, Let It Rock, Melody Maker, Mojo, New Musical Express, Q, Rolling Stone, Sound On Sound, Vox back issues.

The booklet notes attached to the CDs listed in the discographies at the end of the chapters have also been invaluable.

The following websites were useful sources of information:

1001hifi.blogspot.co.uk / 120years.net / 4thefirsttime.blogspot.co.uk / 78records.wordpress.com / 8dio.com / aitstudy.com / alchetron.com / anarchistnews.com / archive.knoxnews.com / archive.nationaljazzarchive.co.uk / arhoolie.org / bachtrack.com / billhamlights.com / bloggerhythms.blogspot.co.uk / blogs.loc.gov / books.google.co.uk / centraldelawareblues.com / childrensmusic.org /cyberneticserendipity.net / daelectronicmusic.wordpress.com / daily.redbullmusicacademy.com / data.bnf.fr / dcc.newberry.org / dereksmusicblog.wordpress.com / digital.livesoundint.com / discography of American historical recordings / en.wikipedia.org / encyclotronic.com / entertainment.howstuffworks.com / equipboard.com / exspectingrain.com / forums.stevehoffman.tv / gizmodo.com / globalia.net / gloriousnoise.com / hammondorganco.com / hitcovers.weebly.com / indianapublicmedia.com / jazzwisemagazine.com / kglteater.dk / levonhelm.tumblr.com / library.syr.edu / listverse.com / mainlynorfolk.infomelodicas.com / marshall.com / mentalfloss.com / mgthomas.co.uk / moogarchives.com / moogfoundation.org / museumofmagneticsoundrecording.org / musicweird.blogspot.co.uk / news.google.com / noisey.vice.com / oneweekoneband.tumblr.com / publicdomainreview.org / rootstrata.com / rutherfordchang.com / secondhandsongs.com / sheffieldlab.com / sondahl.com / soundcloud.com / soundofthehound.com / teamrock.com / thebeatlesgear.com / top5000-rocketman5000.blogspot.co.uk / tutmarc.tripod.com / UCSB cylinder audio archive / uk.businessinsider.com / uniqueguitar.blogspot.com / web.archive.org / wiki.killuglyradio.com / www.1001hifi.com / www.1960sailors.net / www.45cat.com / www.45worlds.com / www.aes.org / www.allmusic.com / www.amazon.co.uk / www.ambisonic.net / www.americanradiohistory.com / www.apmmusic.com / www.archive.org / www.atsf.co.uk/elektra / www.bateristars.com / www.bbc.co.uk / www.beatlelinks.net / www.billboard.com / www.bluesinbritain.org / www.bobmarley.com / www.bsnpubs.com / www.capsnews.org / www.cashboxmagazine.com / www.centuryoldsounds.com / www.chicagosouthsidepiano.com www.classicfm.com / www.columbia.edu/~brennan/beatles / www.columbusmusichistory.com / www.covermesongs.com / www.criterionforum.org / www.cubby.net/worldofcubby/rcr /www.culturekiosque.com/ www.dawsons.co.uk / www.davemcaleer.com / www.dewolfemusic.com / www.digitalviolin.com / www.discogs.com / www.djhistory.com / www.downbeat-special.co.uk / www.dubwisefestival.com / www.duduki.net / www.dustandgrooves.com / www.earlyblues.com / www.electricearl.com / www.electricprunes.com / www.elektra60.com / www.electrotheremin.com / www.engadget.com / www.englishclub.com / www.factmag.com / www.fame2.com / www.fenderrhodes.com / www.fretlessbass.com / www.frets.com / www.fultonhistory.com / www.funtrivia.com / www.gibson.com / www.globaldogproductions.info www.gracesguide.co.uk / www.grahamlees.co.uk / www.gridface.com / www.grunge.com / www.hallofelectricpianos.co.uk / www.harkitrecords.com / www.henrydoktorski.com / www.hitsofalldecades.com / www.ididj.com.au / www.indiana.edu / www.irishcentral.com / www.jackbruce.com / www.jasobrecht.com / www.jazzdisco.org / www.ksanti.net / www.largeup.com / www.lionelhampton.nl / www.lukedanielsmusic.com / www.marcodi.com / www.marmalade-skies.co.uk / www.marshallamps.com / www.mellotron.com / www.melvinleedavis.com / www.merseybeatnostalgia.co.uk / www.midnightflyerblues.com / www.musicals101.com

www.musicradar.com / www.mustrad.org.uk / www.namm.org / www.obsoletemedia.org / www.officialcharts.com / www.old-charts.com / www.patmissin.com / www.philips.com / www.philsbook.com / www.pinterest.co.uk / www.planetchocko.com / www.pong-story.com / www.popsike.com / www.popvortex.com / www.pri.org / www.progarchives.com / www.prosoundweb.com / www.psychemusic.org / www.punkhart.com / www.quora.com / www.radioechoes.com / www.radiomuseum.org / www.radiorewind.co.uk / www.record-information-services.info / www.recording-history.org / www.redbullmusicacademy.com / www.reddit.com / www.redhotjazz.com / www.riaa.com / www.rickenbacker.com / www.rickresource.com / www.rockabillyhall.com / www.rollingstone.com www.scaruffi.com / www.singers.com / www.soulmusic.info / www.sixtiescity.net / www.songkick.com / www.soundonsound.com / www.spaceagepop.com / www.spillersrecords.co.uk / www.startribune.com / www.statista.com / www.staxrecords.com / www.stick.com / www.stomping.nl / www.straightdope.com / www.synthmuseum.com / www.synthtopia.com / www.talkbass.com / www.telegraph.co.uk / www.theartsdesk.com www.theengineer.co.uk / www.theguardian.com/ www.thereminsound.com / www.thevinylfactory.com / www.thewhitealbumproject.com / www.thewho.info / www.thewhothismonth.com / www.thomasbloch.net / www.thomholmes.com / www.topicrecords.co.uk / www.uaudio.com / www.ukmix.org / www.valueyourmusic.com www.vintageguitar.com / www.vinylengine.com / www.whosampled.com / www.woodyguthrie.org / www.youtube.com (with a special mention for the Tim Gracyk and Scott Hoyt channels)

PHOTO CREDITS

Every effort has been made to contact the copyright holders of the photographs used in this book, but some were unreachable. The author would be grateful if the photographers concerned would contact him.

The record companies issuing the various covers shown through the book are given due credit in the discographies at the end of each chapter. Other pictures derive from websites listed above. In particular:

Page 4   Rickenbacker guitar from 1931 Rickenbacker catalogue. Lloyd-Loar electric harp guitar from www.gibson.com
Page 6   Milton Brown and his Musical Brownies from Proper Records CD set, *Daddy of Western Swing*. Perry Botkin from 1935 Rickenbacker catalogue.
Page 8   Merle Travis from Deke Dickerson archive. Slingerland Songster from www.retrofret.com.
Page 12 B-bender courtesy of Stephen Antonucci at ChasingGuitars.com. The Yardbirds from Rhino double CD *The Yardbirds Ultimate!*
Page 14 Eric Clapton from Universal CD *Bluesbreakers John Mayall with Eric Clapton*.
Page 16 Larry Coryell from JCOA CD *The Jazz Composer's Orchestra*. John McLaughlin from Polydor LP *Extrapolation*.
Page 18 Jimmy Bryant from See For Miles LP *Guitar Take-Off*. George Harrison from EMI/Universal double CD *The Beatles Anthology 1*.
Page 20 Meshuggah from Shadowgate, Wikimedia Commons. Jordan Rudess courtesy of Jordan Rudess YouTube channel. Hans Reichel from Virgin/Caroline LP *Guitar Solos 2*.
Page 24 Vernon Alley courtesy of AB Fable Archive/Metronome magazine. Gibson bass courtesy of National Music Museum, University of South Dakota. Mark Allen from 1936 Rickenbacker catalogue.
Page 26 Monk Montgomery from Estrad magazine Sweden, Wikimedia Commons. Joel Price from the Gainsville Times. Paul McCartney from EMI/Universal CD *Beatles For Sale*. John Entwistle from Polydor CD *The*

Page 28   *Singles* by the Who. Larry Graham from Sony CD *There's A Riot Goin' On* by Sly and the Family Stone. Anthony Jackson courtesy of Louis Obbens. Tony Levin from Thomas Ceddia, Wikimedia Commons. Rick Danko from Heinrich Klaffs, Wikipedia Commons.

Page 32   Roman water organ from Jerzy Kociatkiewicz, Wikimedia Commons.

Page 34   Mike Ratledge from Cuneiform CD *Noisette* by Soft Machine.

Page 36   Ray Manzarek/Jim Morrison from Warner CD *Live At The Bowl '68* by the Doors. Ondioline courtesy of Hans Kockelmans.

Page 38   Chamberlin courtesy of Rafi Sofer at Q Division Studios. Moody Blues from Universal CD *In Search Of The Lost Chord*. Moog synthesizer courtesy of the Stearns Collection, University of Michigan.

Page 40   Robert Moog from Finnianhughes101, Wikimedia Commons. Keith Emerson from Surka, Wikimedia Commons.

Page 48   Leon Theremin from Wikimedia Commons. Barbara Bucholz from Barbara Bucholz/Gregor Hohenberg, Wikimedia Commons. Ondes martenot from 30rKs56MaE, Wikimedia Commons. Lothar from Capitol LP *Presenting Lothar and the Hand People*.

Page 50   Trautonium from Wikimedia Commons. Magnetophone tape recorder from 1935 Berlin Radio Fair catalogue.

Page 52   EMS VCS3 synthesizer from The Standard Deviant, Wikimedia Commons. Computer performance from Delia Derbysire YouTube channel.

Page 54   Rhythmicon courtesy of Andrey Smirnov.

Page 58   Gene Krupa from Slingerland Drum Company advert. Ginger Baker from artwork in Universal 4 CD set *Those Were The Days* by Cream.

Page 60   Mothers of Invention from Universal CD *Burnt Weeny Sandwich*. Airto Moreira from Airto CD *Best Picks #2*.

Page 62   Moody Blues artwork from Decca LP *Every Good Boy Deserves Favour*.

Page 64   Simmons Drums from Wolfgang Stief, Wikimedia Commons. Bill Bruford from DGM CD *Vrooom Vrooom*. Neil Peart from www.roland.co.uk

Page 72   Taj Mahal from Sony CD *The Real Thing*.

Page 74   Andy MacKay from Jean-Luc, Wikimedia Commons. Jethro Tull from Chrysalis/Island LP *This Was*.

Page 78   George Harrison and Ravi Shankar from Babaimage. Gimbri player from Ahron de Leeuw, Wikimedia Commons.

Page 80   Vess Ossman from Wikimedia Commons. Luna Lee from Luna Lee YouTube channel.

Page 82   Washington Phillips from Wikimedia Commons.

Page 84   Roland Kirk courtesy of Heinrich Klaffs. Charlie McMahon from Arc Music Productions YouTube channel. Kathryn Tickell from Maelor, Wikimedia Commons. Pete Hampton & Laura Bowman from WKU Libraries, Wikimedia Commons. Ocarina from 0x010C, Wikimedia Commons.

Page 86   Joseph Falcon from Columbia 4CD set *Roots n' Blues – The Retrospective 1925-1950*, second disc.

Page 90   1920 pa system from Wikimedia Commons. Beatles from www.beatlesource.com. Grateful Dead courtesy of Richard Pechner, www.rpechner.com. Bill Hanley courtesy of Hidden Years Music Archive Project/3rd Ear Music/David Marks.

Page 94   Edison phonograph from Norman Bruderhofer, Wikimedia Commons. Thomas Edison from Wikimedia Commons. Columbia cylinder courtesy of UC Santa Barbara Cylinder Audio Archive. Samuel Holland Rous from Wikimedia Commons. His Master's Voice painting from Wikimedia Commons.

Page 104   Wurlitzer jukebox from Arnaud 25, Wikimedia Commons. Luke Daniels from Gael Music CD *Revolve and Rotate*.

Page 108   Slade from Polydor LP *Sladest*.

Page 120   Rock Factory recording studio from Mike Logan, Wikimedia Commons.

Page 122   Amy Slattery courtesy of Amy Slattery YouTube channel.

Page 124   Christopher Stone courtesy of Radio Luxembourg, Photo Aloyse Anen, © RTL Group. Martin Block courtesy of Joel Block.

Page 132   Led Zeppelin from Warner Music Group CD *Led Zeppelin*.

Page 134   Jack Jackson courtesy of greatentertainersarchives.blogspot.com. James Tenney from Mode CD *Melody, Ergodicity and Indeterminacy*.

Page 140   Kool Herc murals courtesy of www.planetchocko.com.

Page 142   Double Dee and Steinski from DJFood double CD *Now We Come To The Payoff*. Akai S900 sampler from Shawn Rudiman's Studio, Pittsburgh PA, Wikimedia Commons.

Page 150   Eclection from Warner Music CD *Eclection*. Dorris Henderson from Fledg'ling Records CD *Watch The Stars*.

Page 156 Spillers Records black and white photo from www.spillersrecords.co.uk. Spillers Records colour photo from O.Trevino, Wikimedia Commons. Record fair courtesy of VIP Record Fairs.
Page 160 Jimi Hendrix poster from Track LP *Axis: Bold As Love*.
Page 164 Elvis Costello from Universal CD *My Aim Is True*.
Page 166 Paganini lithograph from Hetty Krist, Wikimedia Commons.
Page 184 Peter Green and Willie Dixon from Sony CD *Blues Jam In Chicago Volume 1*.
Page 190 Berry Gordy from Classic Motown.
Page 194 Stax Record Company – photograph by Ronnie Booze, courtesy of Stax Museum of American Soul Music. Otis Redding still from Criterion DVD set *The Complete Monterey Pop Festival*.
Page 218 Mick Jagger & Alexis Korner from Sanctuary CD *R&B From The Marquee* by Alexis Korner's Blues Inc.
Page 220 Pink Floyd equipment from Harvest LP *Ummagumma*.
Page 228 Clapton is God from Roger Perry.
Page 230 The Who from Polydor CD *A Quick One*. Cream from Polydor CD *Live Cream Volume II*.
Page 234 Tony Iommi & Ozzy Osbourne from Padgett22, Wikimedia Commons.
Page 246 James Brown live in 1973 from Heinrich Klaffs, Wikimedia Commons. James Brown in the studio from Polydor CD *Foundations Of Funk*.
Page 248 Brikama musicians courtesy of Nick Hamlyn.
Page 252 The twist from Knoxville News Sentinel.
Page 254 Joe Cocker from Warner Music double CD *Woodstock*.
Page 274 Erik Satie from Sonia y natalia, Wikimedia Commons. Camille Saint-Saens from Wikimedia Commons.
Page 278 Manfred Eicher from ECM Records.
Page 292 ODJB from Wikimedia Commons.
Page 294 Paul Whiteman Orchestra from advert for Buescher saxophones.
Page 312 Bob Dylan and Robbie Robertson from robbie-robertson.com.
Page 332 Ryman Auditorium from Ryan Kaldari, Wikimedia Commons.
Page 334 Dolly Parton from Tech.Sgt. Cherie A.Thurlby, USAF, Wikimedia Commons.
Page 336 Bob Wills & the Texas Playboys courtesy of bobwills.com. Four Aces of Western Swing from Proper Records CD set, *Bill Haley – From Western Swing to Rock*. Bill Monroe courtesy of Bluegrass Unlimited.
Page 344 Byron Lee from Trojan LP *Sparrow Meets The Dragon*.
Page 346 Prince Buster from cover of Blue Beat LP *Prince Buster On Tour*. Duke Reid from cover of Planet Vibe CD *Hog In A Cocoa* by the Skatalites.
Page 348 The Wailers from booklet for Universal/Island CD *Catch A Fire*.
Page 350 Lee Perry from Metro CD *Lee Perry The Upsetter – Essential Madness From The Scratch Files*.
Page 368 Arnold Schoenberg from cover of Deutsche Grammophon LP *Das Klavierwerk* by Maurizio Pollini. Claude Debussy from Wikimedia Commons. Berg 12 tone row from Professor Andy Brick's class notes for the Contemporary Music Theory course on the Stevens Institute of Technology website, personal.stevens.edu.
Page 370 Charles Ives from Columbia LP *Symphony No.2* by Leonard Bernstein and New York Philharmonic. Igor Stravinsky from Naxos CD *Stravinsky Conducts Stravinsky*. Karlheinz Stockhausen from Deutsche Grammophon LP *Drei Lieder-Sonatine-Spiel-Schlagtrio*. Helicopter from theartsdesk.com.
Page 372 John Cage from ECM New Series CD *The Seasons*.
Page 374 Terry Riley and the Kronos Quartet from Gramavision CD *Cadenza On The Night Plain*. Robert John Godfrey from Charisma LP *Fall Of Hyperion*.

INDEX OF FIRSTS

A.I. composition 122
Accordion recording 87
Acetate 100
Acuff-Rose publishing company 335
Aeolian harp 372
African music 359,360,361,363
Air guitar 255

Album charts 111
Alternative country 338
Alternative guitar tuning 319,322-3
Alternative rock 237
Ambient dance music 259,260
Ambient music 274 et seq
Ambisonic recording 101
American Music Award 115

American number one by British artist 301
Amplified guitar 9
Amplified violin 69
Appalacian dulcimer 83
Artificial double tracking 122
Atonal music 369,370,375
Audiobook 99

Autoharp 83
Auto-Tune 122
Avant garde jazz 299,301
B-bender 12
B-boying 257
Backwards recording 122
Bagpipes 83
Balalaika 81
Banjo 81
Barbershop quartet 189
Bass guitar 24 et seq, 345
Bass guitar recording 27
Bassoon 73
BBC chart 109
Beatboxing 63
Bebop 295-7
Benjamin Award for Restful Music 279
Big band 293
Billboard album chart 111
Billboard chart 106,107
Billboard magazine 107
Bird song 373
Black American to be recorded 111
Black music chart 106,169
Blue Beat label 345
Blue Horizon records 183
Blue-eyed soul 197
Bluegrass 337
Blues 178 et seq
Bodhran 329
Boogie woogie 167,181
Bootleg record 161,317
Bossa nova 253-5
Bouzouki 79,81
Breakdancing 257
Brit Award 115
British Blues 183,184,218,219
British group to play in Hamburg 205
British record reaching no.1 in US 119
Britpop 244
Buchla synthesizer 53
Cajun music 87
Cashbox chart 10
Cassette 103
Cassette single 103
CD 103
CD single 105
Cello 69

Celtic harp 83
Chamberlin 37,38,39
Chapman stick 20,21,28,29
Charisma records 216
Charleston 299
Chillout music 283
Choral music 374
Clarinet 73
Classic rock 232
Classical 366 et seq
Classical music charts 377
Classical themes in pop/rock 133
Clavioline 37
Club DJ 127
Collectors' record price guide 157-9
Collectors' record shop 157
Coloured vinyl 97.98
Columbia records 95
Compact disc 103
Computer music 53
Concept album 315
Cool jazz 297
Country 332 et seq
County Music Association Award 340
Country music chart 335
Country rock 339
Cover version albums 100
Crooning 117
Crumhorn 73
Cuban percussionist in jazz 61
Cylinder recording 95
Dance music 252 et seq
Danelectro Bellzouki 19
De Wolfe music 275-7
Decca records 96
Decca West Africa Series 359
Deutsche Grammophon 95
Dial records 96
Diamond award 113
Didgeridoo 85
Digital audio tape 103
Digital compact cassette 103
Digital recording 102
Disc jockey 125
Disco 255-7
Disco mix 152
Discography 157
Discotheque 127

DJ on record 127
Doo-wop 190,191
Double bass drum set 59
Double LP 98
Double-tracked vocal 117
Download million seller 105
Download number one hit 105
Download-only single 105
Drum battle 59
Drum kit 59
Drum machine 55
Drum solo 59
Dub 349,350
DVD 105
Easy listening 278
Ebay 161
ECM 278,279,281,302,310
Eight string guitar 19
Eight-track recording 121
Eight-track tape cartridge 103
Eko ComputeRhythm 55
Elcaset 103
Electric bass 24,25,30
Electric guitar 5 et seq
Electric guitar at Grand Ole Opry 5
Electric guitar blues recording 9
Electric guitar concerto 221
Electric guitar hit recording 9
Electric guitar in classical music 222
Electric guitar jazz recording 9
Electric guitar recording 5
Electric harp 83
Electric harp guitar 4
Electric instrument 33
Electric organ 33,34,35
Electric piano 35,36,37
Electric violin 68
Electrical recording 117
Electro-theremin 49
Electronic drums 63
Electronic instrument 49
Electronic masterpiece 51
Electronic pop music 51
Electronic rock album 51
Elevator music 277
Embassy Records 100
EMI 97
English Folk Dance And Song Society

387

321	Grunge 237	Krautrock 220
EP 99	Guitar effect units 11 et seq	Latin jazz 61
Eurovision Song Contest 115	Guitar feedback 16,17	Library music 275-7
Exotica 359	Guitar fuzzbox 13	Light show 222
Fairlight CMI 43	Guitar synthesizer 17	Lindy-hop 166,167,169
FAME studio 195	Guitar tremolo arm 11	Linn LM-1 drum computer 55
Fantasia 370	Guitar whammy bar 11	Liquid light show 222
Farfisa organ 35	Guitorgan 18	Long playing record 95,97,370
Fender Bassman amplifier 13,25	Half-speed mastered recording 101	Long song (over 10 mins) 218,219
Fender Broadcaster 10,11	Hammond organ 33,34,35	Longest-lived band 336
Fender guitars 8	Happy hardcore 259	Loudspeaker 91
Fender Precision bass 25	Hard bop 297,303	Lovers rock 352
Fender Rhodes electric piano 36	Hard rock 231	Lowrey organ 35
Fender Stratocaster 11	Hardcore 258,259	LP 95,97,370
Fender Telecaster 11	Harlem Hit Parade 106,169	LP to sell 100,000 in UK 206
Film industry 275	Harmonica 85	LP to sell a million in UK 206
Film with sound 275	Harmonium 33	Lyricon 53
Flexi disc 100	Harpejji 20,21	Madison 253,254
Flute 75	Harvest records 216	Maestro Fuzztone 13
Folk 312 et seq	Heavy metal 226 et seq	Make Believe Ballroom 125
Folk rock 315 et seq	Hip hop 257,305	Mandolin 81
Foreign language UK & US hit 359	Hitch-hike 255	Marshall amplifier 13,228
Forty-five 97,99	Hot Hundred 107	Marshall stack 17,228
Four-track recording 121	House music 257	Mash-up 127,153,154,155
Freakbeat 218	Ibanez Universe 19	Megamix 141,143
Free jazz 301,305	Idiot dancing 255	Mellotron 37,38,39,223
French horn 71	Impressionistic music 371	Melodica 43
Fretless bass guitar 27,30	Indian instruments 13,79,360,361	Melodeon 87
Frippertronics 280	Indian music 360,361	Melody Maker 107,108
Front Line label 351	Industrial music 42	Memphis recording studio 195
Funk 246 et seq,353	Irish music 327-9	Mento 344
Fusion 251,302-5	Island pink label 327	Mercury Music Prize 115
Fuzz Face 17	Island records 346	Merseybeat 205
Gatefold sleeve 98	Japanese rock 363	Microphone 91,117
Gayageum 81	Jazz 292 et seq	Million selling country record 335
Gibson EB-OF bass guitar 13,279	Jazz-funk 249,250,251	Million selling download 105
Gibson ES150 9	Jazz fusion 251,302-5	Million selling jazz record 293
Gibson guitars 4	Jazz opera 289	Million selling record 111
Gibson Les Paul 11	Jazz recording 292,293	Million selling rockin' record 169
Gimbri 78,79	Jazz-rock 300-303,321	MiniDisc 103
Gold disc 111,113,205	John Peel Festive Fifty 115	Minimalism 305,374,375
Gospel 189	Jukebox 104	Minimoog 41
Grammy Award 113,115	K-Tel 100	Mixing with two turntables 141
Gramophone Company 95,359	Karaoke 363	Mod groups 195
Grand Ole Opry 332-5	Kazoo 82	Modal improvisation 246,298,299
Great American songbook 289,296	Kora 83	Modern jazz 297,305
Greatest hits album 100	Koto 81	Mood music 277,278
Grindcore 236	KPM 276,277	Moog synthesizer 39,40,41

Moon Dog House   125
Motown   190-3,196-9
Mouth organ   85
Mp3 file format   105
Multiple sleeve LP   159
Music chart   106 et seq
Music festival   90
Music lasting one second   236
Music magazine   106
Music While You Work   276,277
Musical chain-letter   362,363
Musical theatre   286 et seq
MusicStack   161
Musique concrète   51,135
Musique d'ameublement   275
Muzak   33,276-8,281
New Age music   281-3
New Musical Express   108,109
New wave of British heavy metal   235
New World Company   283
Newport Folk Festival   315
Nine string guitar   19
Nobel Prize for literature   115
Northern soul   127
Northumbrian pipes   83,85
Nose flute   83
Nova records   216
Novelty record   94
Now That's What I Call Music   100
Number one in Harlem Hit Parade   9
Oberheim polyphonic synthesizer   43
Oboe   73
Ocarina   84
Octavia   15
On-stage monitoring   90
Ondes martenot   48,49,371
Ondioline   37
Opera   287,370
Operetta   287
Orchestral instruments   69   et seq
Organ with paper tape control   51
Original cast recording   287
Oscar for film score   275
Oud   78,79
Outlaw country   338,339
Overdubbing   116,117,122
PA system   91
Parody mass   133

Pedal steel guitar   8,18,335
Pepe   45
Phasing   122
Philadelphia soul   198
Phonograph   95
Piccolo bass   29,30
Pick Of The Pops   109
Picture disc   158,159
Pipa   81
Pirate radio ships   125
Platinum disc   113
Plunderphonics   150,153,154
Poetry and music   264,265,269,351
Polar music prize   115
Polyphon   105
Polyphonic synthesizer   41,43
Power pop   242
Prepared piano   373
Pro Tools   145
Prog term   220
Progressive rock   216 et seq, 301,375
Psychedelic music   218,316
Pub rock   241
Pulitzer Prize   115
Punk   240 et seq,351,352
Quadraphonic recording   101
Race Records chart   106
Radio broadcast   125
Radio jingles   125
Radio One   125,126,127
Radio station   125
Radios as instruments   137
Ragga   353
Ragtime   292
Rai   363
Rap   125,262 et seq
Rastafarian music   346,350
RCA Victor   95
Real World label   363
Record   94
Record collectors' fair   157
Record player   95,96
Record producer   119,121
Record shop   157
Recording   95,133,370
Recording sold for $2 million   158
Recording effects   117
Recording studio   117

Reel-to-reel tape   103
Reggae   344 et seq
Remix   150 et seq, 349-51
Resonator guitar   6
Reverberation (Reverb)   117
Rhythm and blues chart   106
Rhythmicon   54,55
Rickenbacker 12 string guitar   19
Riffs   295
Rock acclaimed as Art   205,207,211
Rock festival   90
Rock musical   289
Rock 'n' roll concert   171
Rock 'n' roll LP   176
Rock 'n' roll on Ed Sullivan show   171
Rock 'n' roll radio show   171
Rock 'n' roll record   164 et seq
Rock 'n' roll UK   174
Rock opera   289,325
Rockabilly   173
Rocksteady   347
Roland TR-808 drum machine   55
Sampling   131 et seq,368
Saxophone   73
Scratching   140
Serialism   368,371
Seven inch EP   99
Seven inch single   97,99
Seven string guitar   19
Seventy-eight   95
Shakuhachi   83
Shake   254,255
Shaped picture disc   159
Shortlist Prize For Artistic
          Achievement In Music   115
Silver disc   113
Simmons electronic drums   63,64
Singer songwriter   319-21,325-7
Single   97,99
Sitar   78,79
Six string bass guitar   27,29
Sixteen rpm record   99
Sixteen-track recording   121
Ska   344-7
Skank   351
Skiffle   174
Slap bass guitar playing   27
Slide guitar   4,179

Snake mixing desk cables   91
Solid electric guitar   9
Solo bass album   28
Solo drum recording   61
Solo plectrum guitar recording   6
Song called *The First Time*   1
Soul   188 et seq
Soul jazz   303
Sound systems   345
Sound Tools   145
Soundtrack album   274
Soundtrack music   274 et seq
Spirituals   189
Sprechstimme   263
Stax   194,195
Steel drums   63
Stereo recording   99,101
Stylophone   38,39
Sun Records   172
Super Audio CD   105
Supergroup   321
Surround sound live   221
Swing   294,295
Synclavier   43
Syndrum   63
Synthaxe   18
Synthesizer   39-43,51-53
Synthpop   43
Talking blues   263
Tamla   191-3
Tamla Motown   192,193

Tannerin   49
Tape recorder   50,51.117
Tape recording   51
Tascam Portastudio   121
Techno   257
Telharmonium   32,33
Theremin   48.49
Third stream jazz   298,299
Toasting   267,351
Tone Bender   13,14
Top Of The Pops   109
Topic records   321
Traditional folk   321-5
Traditional jazz   293,300,301
Trautonium   49,50
Trip hop   259
Trojan records   347
Trombone   71
Trumpet   71
Tuba   71,73
Turntables   51,135,140,141
Twelve inch single   103,153
Twelve string guitar   19
Twelve-tone composition   368,371
Twin-necked guitar   19
Twist   252,253
Two Tone   353
Two-handed guitar tapping   21
Two-track recording   121
Uillean pipes   85
Ukulele   81

Univibe   17
Vacuum cleaners in music   2
Varitone   53
VCS3 synthesizer   52.53
Version   267,349,354
Vertigo records   216
Vibraphone (Vibes)   61,62,63
Video game music   282
Vinyl   97 et seq
Viola   69
Violin   69
Vocal percussion   63,65
Vocal quartet   188-191
Vox Continental   33
Vox Guitar Organ   18
Vox wah-wah   13
Wah-wah pedal   14,15
Water organ   32,33
Wax cylinder   95
Western swing   337
Windham Hill   281
Windows 95 music   280
Woodstock festival   90-1,320
World music   359 et seq
World Music Award   113
Wurlitzer electric piano   35,36.37
Wurlitzer Sideman   54,55
Yodelling   335
Your Hit Parade   109
Zither   83
Zydeco   87

INDEX OF NAMES

808 State   257,260.261
A R Kane   257
Abasi, Tosin   21,23
Abba   103,115,143,242
Abbado, Claudio   67,225,376
Abdul-Malik, Ahmed   79,88,361,365
Abrahams, Mick   232
Abse, Danny   264
AC/DC   234,235,239
Acardipane, Marc   259,261
Ackerman, William   281,284,285
Acuff, Roy   334,335,341
Adam And The Ants   115

Adams, John   375,378
Adderley, Cannonball   289,291,302,
    303,307,309,311
Ade, King Sunny   362,363,365
Adler, Larry   84,85,89
Aerni, Dave   137
Aerosmith   149,273
Aiken County String Band   81,88
Aitken, Laurel   345,355
Albarn, Damon   45
Albert II   113
Alcapone, Dennis   267
Alexander, Arthur   194,195,202
Alford, Clem   88

Ali, Muhammad   267
Allen, Henry Red   63,67
Allen, Mark   24,25,29
Alley, Vernon   24,25
Allison, Jerry   204
Almanac Singers   312,315,329
Almond, Johnny   217
Alpert, Herb   70,71,76,278
Alphonso, Roland   347
Alsop, Marin   378
Altman, Peter   212
Alwyn, Kenneth   56,101
Amazing Blondel   73,77
AMM   16,23,136,137,147

Ammons, Albert   167,168,175,188
Anders, Allison   320
Anderson, Gladstone   347
Anderson, Ian   75,81
Anderson, Laurie   68,75
Anderson, Leroy   99
Anderson, Lindsay   359
Anderson, Lynford   347
Anderson, Miller   309
Anderson, Stig   115
Andrews Sisters   166,335,341
Andrews, Ed   179,180,185
Angel Witch   235
Anglos   196,203
Animals   34,35,45,85,89,231,315,330
Animals As Leaders   23
Anthrax   270
Aphex Twin   283,285
Appel, Alfred   296
Arden, Suzi   19
Arditti String Quartet   376
Ardley, Neil   300
Ardoin, Amede   87,89
Argent   1
Arlen, Harold   286
Armstrong, Lil Hardin   292
Armstrong, Louis   59,65,184,185,292, 293,295,296,306,312
Arnold, Billy Boy   183
Arnold, Eddy   335,340,341
Arnold, Malcolm   2,69,75,85,89,225
Arnold, P.P.   47
Arnold, William S.   104
Arnason, Saevar   260
Arrau, Claudio   103
Art Ensemble of Chicago   301
Asha   285
Ashby, Harold   77
Ashby, Irving   6
Ashkan   216
Ashkenazy, Vladimir   377
Asian Dub Foundation   362,363,365
Asko Ensemble   376
Assia, Lys   115
Association   75,77
Astaire, Fred   6
Aswad   353
Atkin, Pete   154
Atkins, Chet   15,22,339

Atkins, Juan   257
Atlas, Natacha   363,365
Auger, Brian   318,330
Austin, Lovie   179
Automatic Man   63,67
Avakian, George   98
Avalanches   145,149
Axis Of Awesome   154,155
Axt, William   275
Ayers, Kevin   221
Ayler, Albert   85,89,184,186,187,311
Ayres, Mitchell   106
B, Howie   353,359
Babbitt, Milton   51,52,57
Baby Ray and the Ferns   225
Bach, Johannes Sebastian   40,41,46, 97,133,223,366
Bad Plus   304,311
Baez, Joan   101,132,315,329
Bagdasarian, Ross   118
Bailey, DeFord   85,89,332,341
Baker, Chet   297,307
Baker, Ginger   17,58,59,61,231,300,360, 361,365
Baker, Janet   378
Baldry, Long John   300
Ball, Kenny   301,309
Ballard, Florence   190,191
Ballard, Hank   253,259,261
Baltan, Kid   51,57
Bambaata, Afrika   55,149,269,271
Band   27,31,35,45,86,87,89,161,313, 318,319,330
Bangs, Lester   233
Banks, Tony   242
Banton, Hugh   35,45
Bar-X Cowboys   7
Baraka, Amiri   265
Barbarin, Paul   63,67
Barber, Chris   174,183,300,301,308, 309,311
Barber, Samuel   372,377
Barclay James Harvest   37
Bare, Bobby   338,339,343
Bargeron, Dave   73
Barnard, Junior   22
Barnes, George   9,22
Barnet, Charlie   106
Barras, Charles M.   287

Barraud, Francis   94
Barry, John   71,76
Barson, Mike   35
Bart, Lionel   286,289
Barth, Paul   5
Bartholomew, Dave   249
Bartok, Bela   321,330,372,377
Barton, Geoff   235
Basel Sinfonietta   283
Basie, Count   8,9,167,188,295,306
Bate, Jennifer   376
Batt, Mike   373,376
Battered Ornaments   326,331
Baum, L.Frank   275
Bavarian Radio Symphony Orchestra 376
Baxter, Les   358,359,364
BBC Radiophonic Workshop   51,56,57, 129
BBC Symphony Orchestra   376
Beach Boys   39,46,49,55,56,57,62,67,91, 121,123,133,138,146,165,190,191, 202,211,214,215,257,261.283,287
Beat   352,353,355
Beatles   15,17,19,23,27,31,35,37,39,41, 45,47,51,68,69,71,73,74,77,79,81, 88,89,90,91,109,110,111,113,115, 119,121,122,123,125,127,128,133, 137,138,139,144,146,147,150,151, 152,153,155,158,159,160,165,181, 193,194,196,197,200,202,203,204- 215,217,218,219,224,226,231,232, 240,241,245,249,252,253,252,262, 264,289,291,301,303,309,316,319, 321,323,325,330,339,341,343,352, 359,360,361,364,365,368,369,374
Beau Brummels   196,203
Beau Dommage   49,56
Beauchamp, George   5
Beautiful People   144,149
Beaver, Paul   39,41,47
Bechet, Sidney   116,117,121,188
Beck, Jeff   12,13,14,22,79,85,89,133,153, 197,203,217,232,238,239,287,304,311
Beckford, Ewart   267,351
Beckford, Theo   345,355
Bedford, David   129,130,220,221,222, 225
Bee, Harry   372
Bee Gees   55,103,211,215,256,257,286

Beecham, Thomas 101
Beefheart, Captain 8,73,77,90,122,123, 184,187,305,311
Beethoven, Ludwig Van 97,101,103,133, 317,366,367,368,372,374,376
Beiderbecke, Bix 71,77,294,295,306
Belafonte, Harry 111,314,329
Belar, Herbert 51
Bell, Alexander Graham 51,91,95
Bell, Derek 329
Bell, Mark 259
Bell, Vinnie 19
Bellotte, Pete 43
Bellson, Louis 59,65
Benedetti, Dean 161
Beneke, Tex 128
Benjamin, Arthur 85,89
Benjamin, Edward B. 279
Bennett, Boyd 174
Bennett, Tony 133,146,278
Benshoof, Ken 378
Benson, George 307
Berg, Alban 63,67,368,371,376
Berlin Philharmonic 103,225,376,378
Berlin, Irving 286,289
Berliner, Emil 91,94,95
Berlioz, Hector 101
Berman, Boris 376
Bernstein, Leonard 101,222,225,286,288
Berry, Chuck 133,134,135,146,164,165, 167,170,172,177,181,184,185,191, 211,366
Berry, Dave 15,22
Berry, Jan 46
Best, Pete 205
Beyer, Hunt 378
Beyoncé 200,201,203
Big Brother & the Holding Co. 196,203, 226,227,237
Big Youth 267,269,272,273,351,357
Bigsby, Paul 8, 9,11
Bilk, Acker 72,73,77,119,123,300,301, 309
Bishop, Elvin 183
Bizet, Georges 275
Bjork 259,260,261
Black Sabbath 232,233,234,235,237, 239
Black Uhuru 63,67,353,357

Black, Bill 25,34,173
Black, Cilla 287
Black, Jimmy Carl 60,65
Black, Matt 143
Blackburn, Tony 125,126,127,129
Blackmore, Ritchie 228
Blackwell, Chris 196,345,346,347
Blackwell, Ed 61
Blackwell, Otis 226
Blades, James 60
Blakey, Art 61,301,311
Bley, Carla 286,288,289,291,311
Bley, Paul 41,46,47
Blind Boys Of Alabama 336
Blind Faith 300
Bliss, Philip 189
Blitzstein, Marc 286,287
Block, Martin 124,125,128
Blondie 257,261,270,271,273
Blondy, Alpha 350,357
Blood Sweat and Tears 73,77,303,310, 317,319
Bloomfield, Mike 11,22,37,46,183,218, 219,224,317
Blue Cheer 233,237,238
Blue Flames 346,355
Blue Grass Boys 336,337
Blue Men 118,123
Blue Oyster Cult 235
Blues Brothers 286
Blues Project 69,75,218,219,224,317
Bluesology 300
Blumberg, Dave 255
Blythe, Jimmy 180,185
Bocelli, Andrea 146
Bock, Jerry 286
Boettcher, Curt 39
Bogart, Humphrey 141
Boggs, Noel 170
Bolam, James 306
Bolden, Buddy 293
Bon Jovi 113
Bonamassa, Joe 183,187,225
Bond, Graham, Organisation 17,23,39, 46,59,65,71,76,183,300,301,309
Boney M 348
Bonfa, Luiz 253,261
Bonham, John 59
Bonzo Dog Doo-Dah Band 183,187,210, 211,215

Booker T & MG's 22,35,45,194,195,202
Boomtown Rats 240,241,245
Booth, Johnny 40
Boothe, Ken 351
Borden, David 41
Borodin, Alexander 133
Bostic, Earl 176
Boston Symphony Orchestra 88,376
Boswell Sisters 168,175
Bothy Band 85,89
Botkin, Perry 6
Boubil, Alain 286
Bouchillon, Chris 263,271
Boulez, Pierre 362,367,368,369,375,376
Boult, Adrian 361
Bournemouth Symphony Orchestra 67, 378
Bovell, Dennis 351,352,353
Bow Wow Wow 102,103
Bowie, David 38,39,46,81,88,105,366, 367,376
Bowman, Laura 84
Bown, Alan, Set 70,71,76
Boyd, Bill, Cowboy Ramblers 7
Boyd, Jim 7
Boyle, Gary 67
Boys, Jerry 210
Brabbins, Martyn 378
Bradford, Perry 178
Bradley Brothers 37,39
Bradshaw, Tiny 170,176
Brady, Victor 63, 67
Bragg, Billy 314,329
Brahms, Johannes 366,368,376
Branca, Glenn 375,377,378
Brand, Dollar 359,360,364
Branson, Richard 146
Braxton, Anthony 311,373
Breaux, Clemo 86
Brecht. Bertolt 286
Bredin, Patricia 115
Bredon, Anne 132
Brenston, Jackie 165,169,170,172,175
Brett, Jeremy 225
Breuer, Harry 99,100
Brewer, Gage 5
Brewer, Theresa 139
Brian, Havergal 374,378

Brick, Andy   368
Bridgeman, Duncan   362
Britten, Benjamin   372,373,377
Bronski Beat   150
Brooker, Gary   221,222
Brooklyn Philharmonic Orchestra   376
Brooks, Baba   351
Brooks, Garth   113,339,340,341,343
Brooks, Harvey   317
Broonzy, Big Bill   9,22,188,312,313,319, 329
Brotherhood Of Breath   360,364
Brotzmann, Peter   305
Broughton, Edgar, Band   233,237
Brown, Al, Tunetoppers   253,254,261
Brown, Charles   98,106,119,123
Brown, Clarence Gatemouth   184
Brown, Dennis   352
Brown, Jake   98
Brown, James   139,143,185,192,193, 195,198,199,202,229,246-251,255, 267,268,269,273,361,369
Brown, Les   128
Brown, Michael   69
Brown, Milton   6,7,21,337,341
Brown, Nacio Herb   286
Brown, Pete   326,331
Brown, Roy   170
Brown, Sandy   300
Browne, Barry   159
Brubeck, Dave   311
Bruce, Harvey   122
Bruce, Jack   17,23,27,31,69,218,219, 231,233,289,300,302,311,326,331
Bruford, Bill   64,65,67
Bruner, Cliff   7
Bryant, Jimmy   18,19,23
Bryant, Ray   253,261
Bryars, Gavin   140,148,149
BTS   363,365
Buchanan and Goodman   135,147,148
Buchholz, Barbara   48,49
Buchner, Milton   176
Buchla, Donald   53
Buckley, Jeff   318
Buckley, Tim   318
Buckley, William F.   204
Bucks Fizz   222
Budapest Festival Orchestra   240

Buff, Paul   137
Buffalo Springfield   91,219,321,330
Bull, Sandy   78,79,88
Buller, John   222,225
Bunny and Scully   344
Burchill, Julie   243
Burdon, Eric   85,89
Burgess, Richard   43
Burke, Solomon   197
Burlison, Paul   13,22
Burnette, Johnny, Trio   12,13,22
Burning Spear   349,350,354,356,357
Burns, Ralph   286
Burroughs, William   235
Burtin, Jacques   83,88
Burton, Gary   17,23,62,63,67
Burton, James   11,22
Burton, Richard   127
Burton, Sybil   127
Buschmann, Christian   85,87
Bush, Kate   43,44,47,85,89
Bushell, Garvin   73
Buskin, Richard   173
Buster, Prince   269,273,345,346,347, 355
But, Rosalind   89
Butterfield, Paul, Blues Band   22,71,76, 77,183,187,218,219,224,225,303, 309,317
Buzzcocks   241,243,244,245
bvixer   280
Byas, Don   22
Bygraves, Max   108
Byrd, Charlie   254,261,323
Byrd, Donald   250,251
Byrds   12,19,41,47,71,76,90,211,215, 218,235,244,315,316,317,318,320, 321,330,335,338,339,343,359,364
Byrne, David   138,139,147,154
Byrne, Ossie   151
Cable, Paul   314
Cage, John   134,135,137,140,145,147, 372,373,376
Cahill, Thaddeus   33
Cale, J.J.   55,57
Cale, John   69,240,245,372,374,378
Callas, Maria   145
Callender, Red   71,72,77
Calloway, Cab   168,169

Calmettes, André   275
Calvert, Eddie   99
Camardese, Vittorio   21
Cameron, Basil   89
Cameron, John   217,224
Campbell, Alex   325
Campbell, Clive   140,141
Campbell, Glen   319,340
Campbell, Glenn   18
Campbell, Ian, Folk Group   324,325,327, 331
Campbell, Muryel 'Zeke'   9,22
Can   55,57,139
Canned Heat   184,225,229,237
Cannon, Freddy   204
Canteloube, Joseph   321,330
Cantor, Eddie   6
Cantrell, Blu   355,357
Capp, Andy   347
Caravan   216
Cardew, Cornelius   136,147
Carey, Mariah   113
Carib Tokyo   63,67
Carlos, Walter (Wendy)   40,41,47,53
Carney, Harry   73,77
Carr, Ian   302
Carré, Benoît   122
Carroll, Liz   329,331
Carroll, Ted   157
Carson, Bill   10,11,13
Carter Family   82,83,88,335,341
Carter, Goree   169
Carter, Jimmy   336
Carter, June   341
Carter, Maybelle   83,341
Carter, Ron   29,31,303,306
Carthy, Eliza   324,331
Carthy, Martin   324,325,327,331
Caruso, Enrico   110,111,116,125
Casady, Jack   27,31
Case, Russ   97
Casey, Howie and the Seniors   204,205, 215
Casey, Warren   286
Cash, Johnny   130,263,264,271,340, 341,342,343
Casher, Del   15
Catto, Jamie   362
Cauty, Jimmy   143

Cecil, Malcolm 41
Cedrone, Danny 169
Ceoltoiri Chualann 329,331
Cerrone, Marc 255,256,261
Chadbourne, Eugene 262
Chailly, Riccardo 89,376
Chaka Demus and Pliers 352,353,357
Chamberlin, Harry 37,39,55
Chandler, Chas 231,235
Chandra, Sheila 66,67
Chang, Rutherford 150,155
Channel, Bruce 87,89
Chaplin, Saul 286
Chapman, Emmett 20,21,29
Charlatans 222
Charles, Ray 36,37,46,192,193,198, 202,287,302,337,343
Checker, Chubby 98,139,252,253,259
Chenier, Clifton 86,87,89
Cher 122,123
Cherry, Don 83
Cherry, Neneh 363
Chesky, David 222,225
Chess, Leonard 132
Chic 141,263
Chicago 71,77,139,147,249,250
Chicago Symphony Orchestra 99,376
Chicken Shack 183,187,331
Chieftains 84,85,89,328,329,331
Child, Francis James 322
Child, Lee 182
Chkiantz, George 122
Choir of St.John's College Cambridge 374,377,378
Chopin, Frederic 97,103
Christian, Charlie 6,8,9,22,188,295,306
Christie, Agatha 99
Christiensen, Axel 181
Chung, Myung-Whun 56,370,376
Church, Charlotte 377,378
Cinematic Orchestra 145,149,283,285
City of Birmingham Symphony Orchestra 376
Civil, Alan 71,209
Clair Brothers 91
Clair, René 275
Clancy Brothers and Tommy Makem 328,331
Clannad 329

Clapton, Eric 11,14,15,16,17,22,23,35, 45,112,133,180,183,184,185,186, 187,210,213,218,219,226,227,228, 229,231,232,233,237,300,302,319, 339,349,357
Clare, Kenny 61
Clark, Buddy 128
Clark, Dave, Five 35,45,138
Clark, Dick 115,252,253
Clark, Gene 316
Clark, Louis 221
Clark, Petula 20400000000000000
Clarke-Boland Big Band 61,65
Clarke, Kenny 22,61,65,295
Clarke, Mike 316
Clarke, Sebastian 349
Clarke, Stanley 29,30,31
Clash 242,243,244,245,352,353,357
Clay, Cassius 267,272,273
Clayton, Buck 188
Cleese, John 146
Clempson, Clem 239
Cleveland Orchestra 376
Cliff, Jimmy 348,356
Clinton, George 248
Clive and Gloria 355
Clooney, Rosemary 108
Clough, Tom 85,89
Clovers 190
Cluster 220
Coasters 119,190,263,271
Coates, Eric 277
Cobham, Billy 61,65,66,259
Cochevelou, Alan 83
Cochran, Eddie 242,263,271
Cocker, Joe 196,203,254,255,289,368
Cockney Rebel 121
Coe, Tony 327
Cohen, Leonard 265,273,318,319,321, 325,326,330
Cohn, Nik 212
Coldcut 129,142,143,146,147,149
Cole, Bill 303
Cole, Cozy 59,65
Cole, Nat King 110,111,283
Coleman, Michael 328,329,331,333
Coleman, Ornette 61,65,298,300,301, 305,308,309,361,365
Collier, Graham 300

Collins and Harlan 107,292,293,306
Collins, Albert 184
Collins, Arthur 107,293
Collins, Bootsy 248
Collins, Dave and Ansil 350,357
Collins, Judy 315,321,325,329
Collins, Mel 222
Collins, Shirley 322,323,330,331
Cologne Radio Symphony Orchestra 271
Colosseum 17,91,216,218,300,301,309
Colourbox 257
Colter, Jessi 338,339
Coltrane, Alice 256
Coltrane, John 37,53,61,73,77,184,187, 211,219,246,247,256, 297,298,299, 300,301,304,305,308,309,316,361,365
Colyer, Ken 183,300
Comden, Betty 286
Como, Perry 97,113
Conniff, Ray 101
Constant, Marius 283
Contraband 236
Conway, Russ 113
Cooder, Ry 83,88,90,102
Cooke, Deryck 378
Cooke, Sam 192,193,195,199,202,253, 255,259,261
Cooley, Spade 96,97,170,336,337,341
Coolio 149
Cooper, Lindsay 73
Cooper, Ray 61,67
Copper Family 323,325
Cordet, Hélène 127
Cordet, Louise 126,127
Corea, Chick 61,67,307,311
Corsi, Jacopo 287
Coryell, Larry 16,17,23
Cosey, Pete 14,23
Cosgrove, Stuart 190
Cosmic Eye 79,88,361,365
Cosmic Sounds 40,41,46
Costello, Elvis 35,45,164,240,245,283, 343
Cotton, James 13,220
Cotton, Mike, Sound 71,76
Coulthard, Alan 141,149,150
Country Joe and the Fish 316
Coupleaux, Edouard 51
Cousins, Dave 324

Cowell, Henry   54,55,57,372,373,376
Cox, Billy   251
Cox, Harry   323,330
Cox, Michael   119,123
Craine, Don   83
Crawford, Alan   100
Crawford, Big   169
Cray, Robert   183,187
Crazy Horse   320
Crazy World Of Arthur Brown   217,300
Cream   14,15,16,23,27,31,59,65,71,76,
   183,210,211,215,217,221,224,227,
   228,229,230,231,232,233,237,299,
   300,319,326
Creed, Marcus   225,376
Cribbins, Bernard   119,123
Cricket, Jimminy   81
Crickets   204
Crombie, Tony   174
Crompton, Tom   160
Crook, Max   37
Cropper, Steve   11,22
Crosby, Stills, and Nash   320,321,330
Crosby, Bing   6,106,108,133,171,253,
   287,289,291,327,335,341
Crosby, David   316,321,330
Crosland, Alan   275
Crudup, Arthur   96,97,170,173,175
Crystals   119,191,202,240
CSR Symphony (Bratislava)   378
Culbertson, Bob   20
Culture Club   141
Curtis, Colin   129
Curtis, Ian   244
Curtis, Richard   321
Curved Air   130,159
Cyrille, Andrew   61,65
Czukay, Holger   138,139,140,147
D'Oyly Carte Opera Company   97
Da Bologna, Bartolomeo   133,146
Da Teramo, Antonio Zacara   133,146
Daffan, Ted   7
Dallas String Band   81,88
Daltrey, Roger   195,289
Dammers, Jerry   353
Damned   240,241,243,245
Daniels, Luke   104,105
Danko, Rick   27,28,86
Dankworth, John   126,129,300,301,309

Darin, Bobby   37,113
Dave Dee,Dozy,Beaky,Mick & Tich   79,88
Davies, Dave   226
Davies, Dennis Russell   376
Davies, Hunter   204
Davies, Ray   43,47,226,244
Davis, Chuck   190
Davis, Hal   255
Davis, Josh   145
Davis, Miles   14,17,23,29,31,61,65,79,
   88,122,152,153,155,184,187,206,
   246,249,250,251,258,261,278,279,
   285,296,297,298,299,301,302,303,
   304,305,306,307,310,311,319,332
Davis, Spencer, Group   12,22,35,45,69,
   76,196,203,219,240
Davy, Noel   353
Dawson, Dinky   91
Day, Doris   108
De Los Angeles, Victoria   330
De Noyer, Paul   249
Dean, Elton   300
Dean, Farmer Carl   129
Dean, James   297
Debain, Alexandre   33
Debussy, Claude   53,368,371,376
Dee, Simon   125
Deep   218,224
Deep Purple   69,75,216,225,232,233,
   239,289
Dees, Abby   31
Def Leppard   234,235,239
DeForest, Lee   91
Defunkt   311
Dehmel, Richard   369
Deiro, Guido   86,87,89
DeJohnette, Jack   302
Dekker, Desmond   346,347,355
Delaney, Eric   59
Delaunay, Charles   157
Delius, Frederick   81,88
Denny, Sandy   318,324,325,331
Denselow, Robin   325
DePaul, Gene   286
Depeche Mode   43,45,47,153,155
Derbyshire, Delia   50,51
Derry and the Seniors   205
Desprez, Josquin   133,146
Destination Tokyo   63

Detroit Symphony Orchestra   377
Deutsch, Herbert   39,41,46
Deviants   241,245
Devoto, Howard   245
Dexter, Al   7,22,335,341
Dexys Midnight Runners   196,203
Diamond, Neil   286,340,341
Dickens, Little Jimmy   25,26,29
Dickies   240,241,245
Dickins, Percy   109
Dickinson, Bruce   225,239
Dickinson, Jim   173
Diddley, Bo   12,13,22,181,185,262,263,
   271
Dietrich, Marlene   359,364
DiFranco, Douglas   141
Dik Mik   53
Dimeola, Al   31
Dinwiddie Colored Quartet   189,201
Dion   154
Dion, Celine   113,222
Dire Straits   6,103,104,105
Disney, Walt   143,274,275,283,284,372,
   377
Dissevelt, Tom   51,57
Dixie Hummingbirds   336
Dixon, Willie   132,133,181,183,184,187
Dizzy Trio   85,89
DJ Cam   258,261
DJ Error   280
DJ Shadow   129,144,145,148,149,259
Dobell, Doug   157
Dodd, Coxsone   344,345,347,349,351
Dodds, Baby   58,59,61,65
Dodds, Johnny   292
Domino, Fats   100,168,169,175,177,
   249,252
Donegan, Lonnie   119,174,177,263,271,
   300
Donizetti, Gaetano   275
Donovan   87,89,211,215,217,223,322,
   323,325,331,372,377
Doors   35,36,41,45,90,102,159,218,224,
   240
Dopyera Brothers   6
Dorsey, Alan   378
Dorsey, Jimmy   106
Dorsey, Thomas A.   188,189,201
Dorsey, Tommy   106,107,295,296

Double Dee & Steinski 141,142,143,148,149
Double Exposure 103,152,153,155
Dougans, Brian 257,259
Douglas, Alan 152,155
Douglas, Craig 301
Dowd, Tom 121
Downliners Sect 83,88
Down Homers 172
Dr. Feelgood 165,241,245
Drake, Nick 326,327,331
Dransfield, Barry 89
Drayton, Clay 255
Dream Theater 21
Drifters 190,191,201,221,255,261,320
Driscoll, Julie 318,330
Drummond, Don 71,77,347
Dubliners 328,331
Duchin, Peter 127
Ducks Deluxe 241,245
Dudley, Anne 283,285
Dudley, S.H. 94,95
Dudley, Sherman Houston 94
Dukes Of Dixieland 99
Dumail, Laurent 258
Dunbar, Aynsley Retaliation 160
Dunbar, Sly 63,353
Dundees 190
Dunn, Bob 6,7,9,11,13,21
Durante, Jimmy 81
Durham, Eddie 5,6,7,9,21
Durham, Topsy 9
Dutoit, Charles 376
Dvorak, Antonin 99,221
Dwight, Reggie 300
Dyble, Judy 325
Dylan, Bob 8,86,87,89,115,158,160,161,182,197,209,218,219,224,240,243,262,263,271,312,313,314,315,316,317,318,319,320,321,323,325,329,330,339,343,372,377
E.S.T. 304,311
Eagle, Roger 126,127
Eagles 85,102,113,339
Earth 232
Earth Wind and Fire 249,251,303
Earthworks 65,67
East Of Eden 217

Eastman-Rochester Orchestra 278,285
Eastman, Julius 376
Easy Mo Bee 305
Easy Star All-Stars 352,356,357
Ebb, Fred 286
Eccles, Clancy 351
Ecklund, Elise 236
Eclection 71,77,150,151,155,325
Eddy, Duane 27,31
Edge, Graeme 63,265
Edison, Thomas 91,94,95
Edmunds, Dave 237
Edwards, Cliff 81,88
Edwards, King (Vincent) 345
Edwards, Rupie 351,354,357
El-Dabh, Halim 51,57
Eicher, Manfred 278,279
Einstürzende Neubauten 2
Electric Banana 277
Electric Flag 41,47,71,77,139,147,235,317,341
Electric Light Orchestra 73,77,212,214
Electric Prunes 15,22
Electro Hippies 236
Electronic 244
Elen, Richard 100,101
Ellington, Duke 8,36,37,46,58,59,73,77,139,167,289,294,295,298,299,306,367
Elliot, T.S. 131
Ellis, Alton 347,349,356
Ellis, Don 303,311
Ellison, Steven 256
Elysium 244
Emerick, Geoff 71
Emerson Lake And Palmer 41,47,133,146,222,223,225,243
Emerson, Darren 285
Emerson, Keith 35,40,41,45,47,133,221,223
Eminem 104,105
English Beat 353
Enid 375,378
Eno, Brian 53,138,139,140,147,154,240,280,281,285
Ensemble Ars Nova 283
Ensemble InterContemporain 376
Ensemble Musica Negativa 135,140,147
Ensemble Musique Oblique 283

Ensor, James 264
Entwistle, John 26,27,70,71,228
Enya 282,285
Eötvös, Peter 376
Epstein, Brian 204
Eric B and Rakim 143,146,149
Ertegun, Ahmet 79
Ethiopians 347,355
Evans, Bill 122,123
Evans, Gil 297,298,306
Evans, Mike 265
Everett, Kenny 125
Everly Brothers 22,154,335,337,341
Ewing, Tom 213
Fab Five Freddie 271
Fabric, Bent 115
Faces 232,363
Fairport Convention 87,89,151,324,325,326,327,331
Faith, Adam 1
Faithless 362
Falana, Mike 71,76
Falcon, Joseph 86,87,89
Fall 184,241,245
Fame, Georgie 34,35,45,229,346,347,355
Family 63,67,211,215
Family Tree 289,291
Famous Flames 246,247
Fanny 1
Farmer, Art 25,29
Farrar, John 286
Fatback 271,273
Fatboy Slim 145,149
Faust, Isabelle 376
Feaster, Patrick 94
Feather, Leonard 272
Feldthouse, Solomon 79,361
Fender, Leo 9,10,11,13
Fenton, James 286
Ferrari, Luc 373,376
Fessenden, Reginald 125
Fields, Dorothy 286
Fields, Herbert 286
Fifth Dimension 255,261,319
Fine, Robert 117
Fires of London 376
Fischer, Ivan 330
Fisher, Eddie 99

Fisher, Vivian   65
Fisk Jubilee Singers   188,189,201
Fite, Buddy   102,103
Fitz-Gerald, Mark   283
Fitzgerald, Ella   106,191,289
Five Dimensions   347
Five Royales   180,181,185
Flack, Roberta   322
Flamingos   190,201
Flanders, Michael & Donald Swann   119, 123
Flatt, Lester   337,342,343
Fleetwood Mac   22,91,102,183,187
Fleetwood, Mick   115
Flowers, Herbie   71,73
Flying Burrito Brothers   341
Flying Lotus   256
Flynn, Barbara   306
Fogerty, Tom   63,67
Folkes Brothers   346,355
Folmann, Troels   105
Foo Fighters   67
Forbes, Rand   27
Ford, Mary   22,116,117,123
Foreigner   222
Formby, George   81,88
Forrest, Jimmy   229
Forrester, Sharon   352,356,357
Forte, Dan   5
Fortunes   128
Fotheringay   318,327,331
Four Aces Of Western Swing   172,336, 337,342
Four (Six) Bop Drop   354,357
Four Freshmen   190,202
Four Seasons   103,191,202
Four Tops   191,198,255,261
Fox, Michael J.   164,165
Fox, Samantha   115
Frampton, Peter   239
Frankie Goes To Hollywood   150,151, 153,155
Franklin, Aretha   177,184,187,194,195, 203,267,302,320
Franklin, Rev.C.L.   195,267,272,273
Fransen, Bill   37
Free   363
Freed, Alan   125,128,164,170,171,172
Freed, Arthur   286

Freeman, Alan   125,204,205
Freeman, Ernie   345
Fresh, Doug E.   64,65,67
Freur   258,261
Fripp, Robert   38,220,222,225,280,285
Frisell, Bill   240
Frith, Fred   21,23
Froese, Edgar   280
Fugs   218,224
Fullerton, George   11
Funk, Farley 'Jackmaster'   257,261
Funkadelic   248,251
Funkstar De Luxe   351,357
Furious Five   269,270,271
Furtwangler, Wilhelm   103
Fury, Billy   252,253,259,320,330
Future Sound Of London   257,259,260, 261
G, Kenny   73
G.L.O.B.E. and Whiz Kid   141
Gabler, Milt   170
Gabriel, Peter   43,242,363,365
Gaines, Chris   340,341,342
Gallagher, Rory   237
Galway, James   365
Gamble and Huff   198
Gang Of Four   45,47,184
Gant, Cecil   106,170
Garbarek, Jan   279,285,311,372,376
Garcia, Jerry   309
Gardner, Ava   291
Gare, Lou   136
Garfunkel, Art   190,201
Garland, Judy   90,275
Garnett, Carlos   29,31
Garrett, Lesley   374,377,378
Garrick, Michael   264
Garson, Mort   41
Garthwaite, Paul   18,19,23
Garvey, Marcus   349,350,356
Gaye, Marvin   192,193,198,199,202, 203,255,261,355
Gaynor, Gloria   152,155,256,261
Geesin, Ron   129
Geist, John   378
Geldof, Bob   240,241,243
Genesis   21,23,37,201,217,220,222,242
Gentle Giant   73,77
Geometro   29

Georgia Tom   188,201
Gerry & the Pacemakers   73,77,207,221
Gershwin, George   33,286,289,299,306, 319,371
Gershwin, Ira   286
Gerzon, Michael   101,161
Getz, Stan   61,65,253,254,261,311
Gibb, Robin   54,55,57
Gibbons, Walter   153
Gibbs, Melvin   311
Gibson, Bob   315
Gibson, Orville   4
Gifford, Barry   235
Gilbert and Sullivan   97,287
Gilberto, Astrud   61,253
Gilberto, Joao   61,65,253,261
Gilels, Emil   101
Giles, Michael   222,225
Gillan, Ian   289
Gillespie, Dizzy   22,61,65,295,296,297, 304,306
Gillham, Art   117,123
Gilliland, Henry   69,333
Gilmour, David   10,29
Giltrap, Gordon   323,331
Ginell, Cary   7
Ginsberg, Allen   265
Giraudy. Miquette   259
Girls On Top   155
Givelet, Armand   51
Glaser, Tompall   338,339
Glass, Louis   104
Glass, Philip   83,85,88,89,305,367,375, 376,378
Gleason, Jackie   277,278,285
Gleason, Ralph   297
Glennie, Evelyn   60,63
Glitter, Gary   113
Gnarls Barkley   105
Go Go Penguin   304,311
Godin, Dave   127
Godfrey, Robert John   374,375
Godley, Kevin   363
Goffin, Gerry   320
Golden Gate Quartet   189,201
Goldie   145,149,259,261
Goldkette, Jean   69,75
Goldmann, Friedrich   225,376
Goldschmidt, Berthold   378

Gomelsky, Giorgio 79
Gondwanaland 85,89
Gong 259
Gonsalves, Paul 77
Gonzales 256,261
Goodman, Al 97
Goodman, Benny 8,9,22,59,65,188, 294,295,306
Gor, Shirish 360
Gordon, Ronny 355
Gordy, Berry 52,190,191,193,197,199, 202
Gordy, Gwen 191
Gore, Lesley 198,203
Gorecki, Henryk 133
Gorillaz 47
Gosdin Brothers 39,46
Gould, Glenn 204
Gould, Morton 89
Gowers, Patrick 222,225
Graas, John 71
Gracie, Charlie 174,177
Graettinger, Bob 299,308
Graham, Davy 322,323,331
Graham, Larry 26,27
Grand Mixer D.St. 140
Grand Wizard Theodore 140
Grandmaster Caz 269,270,271
Grandmaster Flash 51,129,140,141, 143,145,149,269,270,271
Grant, Glenroy 354,357
Grant, Gogi 173
Granz, Norman 59
Grateful Dead 27,31,61,65,71,75,90,91, 154,155.165,240,265,266,273,282, 316,354,357
Graves, Milford 60,61,65
Gray, Elisha 33
Gray, Michael 313,329,368
Grayson, Kathryn 291
Grease Band 289
Grebs 138
Green, Adolph 286
Green, Al 198,199,203
Green, Peter 11,16,22,122,183,184, 187,219
Greene, Jack 339
Greene, Richard 69
Grimms 265,273

Griot Drum Ensemble 248,251
Grofé, Ferde 63,67
Grohl, Dave 67
Groove Armada 116,123,145,149
Groves, Brian 63
Gruppo Di Improvvisazione Nuova Consonanza 65,67,136,147
Gryce, Gigi 25
Gryphon 73,77
Gulland, Brian 73
Gunter, Arthur 135,316
Gunter, Hardrock 170
Gurley, James 227,229,237
Guthrie, Arlo 263,271,315,329
Guthrie, Woody 262,263,271,314,315, 323,329
Guy, Buddy 13,22,184,219
Hackett, Steve 21
Haden, Charlie 281,311,372,377
Haggard, Merle 335
Hagstrom, Marten 20
Hai, Liu De 81,88
Haile Selassie I 350
Haines, Paul 286,288
Haitink, Bernard 378
Haley, Bill 25,165,168,169,170,171, 172,174,175,176,177,191,289,336, 337,342
Hall, Marie 111
Ham, Bill 222
Hamilton, Bruce 157
Hamilton, Chico 69,76
Hamlisch, Marvin 286
Hamlyn, Nick 81,158,159,354,368
Hammer, Jan 41,47
Hammerstein, Oscar 110,286,287,288, 289,290
Hammill, Peter 245
Hammond, John 167,188,189,195,313
Hammond, Laurens 33
Hampton, Lionel 9,24,25,29,63,67
Hampton, Pete 84,85,89
Hancock, Chuck 372
Hancock, Herbie 39,43,44,46,47,55,57, 61,83,88,140,148,149,199,250,251, 303,304,305,306,307,311,321
Handel, George Frederick 95,101,125, 135,145,366,368,376
Handy, W.C. 178,179,185

Hang-hai, Wai 89
Hankinson, Mike 52,53,57
Hanley, Bill 90,91
Hansen, Cecilia 68
Hansen, Jack 152,155
Hanson, Howard 278,279,285
Hanson, Martyn 59
Hanton, Colin 214
Hapshash & the Coloured Coat 235,239
Harbach, Otto 286
Hardin, Louis 172
Hardy, Françoise 358,359,364
Hare, Pat 13,22
Harlan, Byron G. 107,293
Harley, Rufus 84,85,89
Harmonicats 117,123
Harmonium 49,56
Harnick, Sheldon 286
Harriott, Derrick 348,349,357
Harriott, Joe 78,79,88,264,361,365
Harris, Benny 296
Harris, Eddie 53,57
Harris, Emmylou 22,332,333,338,339, 343
Harris, Erline 169
Harris, Jet 26,27,31
Harris, Richard 318
Harris, Rolf 39,85,89,119
Harrris, Wynonie 168,169,170,175
Harrison, George 18,19,20,41,78,79,81, 122,207,209,210,212,213,214,215, 316,360,361,365
Harrison, Lou 81,88
Harrison, Patti 210
Harrison, Wilbert 123
Harry, Debbie 271
Hart, Charles 286
Hart, Lorenz 286
Hart, Mickey 65
Hart, Tim 327
Hartley, Keef 122,217,300,301,309
Harvey, Jonathan 368,376
Harvey, Morton 179
Hawkins, Adrian 160
Hawkins, Coleman 72,73,77,294,295,306
Hawks 313,317
Hawkshaw, Alan 277
Hawksworth, Johnny 277
Hawkwind 53,57

Hay, George D.   333
Hayden, Victor   73
Haydn, Joseph   216,366,367
Hayes, Isaac   196,203,266,267,269,273
Hayne, Joe   168
Hays, Lee   315
Haza, Ofra   143
Hazel, Eddie   248
Heads Hands and Feet   339
Heath, Ted   277
Heavy Jelly   160
Heckstall-Smith, Dick   218,219,300
Heifetz, Jascha   368
Heil, Bob   91
Hell, Richard   243
Hellerman, Fred   315
Henderson, Doris   150,151
Henderson, Douglas 'Jocko'   124,125,128
Henderson, Ella   1
Henderson, Fletcher   73,293,295
Henderson, Michael   249,250,302
Hendrix, Jimi   8,11,14,15,16,17,21,23,
    55,57,62,75,77,90,104,122,123,
    127,136,144,145,152,155,159,160,
    165,183,184,187,197,200,202,203,
    211,215,219,221,224,227,228,230,
    231,232,233,235,237,248,249,251,
    269,273,298,299,302,308,318,330,
    372,375,378
Henley, Don   85,89
Henri, Adrian   264,265,273
Henry Cow   73,77
Henry, John 'Shifty'   25,26,27
Henry, Pierre   56,57,147
Henze, Hans Werner   61,67
Hepworth, David   242
Herman, Jerry   286
Herman, Woody   299,308
Herman's Hermits   15,81,88
Heron, Mike   79,325
Herrmann, Bernard   29
Herrold, Charles   125
Herth, Milt   32,33
Heyward, DuBose   286
Heyworth, Simon   225
Higgins, Billy   61
Higgs and Wilson   345,355
High Numbers   194,203
High Tide   68,69,75

Hill, Ralph   216
Hill, Walter   166
Hillage, Steve   259
Hiller, Lajaren   53,57
Hillman, Chris   320,359
Hillsiders   337,338,339,343
Hindemith, Paul   51,56,87,89,283
Hine, Rupert   363
Hines, Earl   9,22
Hinton, Brian   333
Hiseman, Jon   59,300
Hitchcock, Alfred   49
Hitler, Adolph   159
Hixxy & Sharkey   258,259
Hodges, Johnny   249
Hodgson, Brian   51
Hoffnung, Gerard   2
Hogan, Carl   170
Hogman, Pete   347
Hohner, Matthias   85
Holdsworth, Allan   18,23
Holiday, Billie   306,311,320
Holland-Dozier-Holland   198
Holland, Dave   302,307
Holland, Jools   21
Hollies   63,67,194,202,211,215,321,330
Holly, Buddy   11,22,25,68,69,75,152,
    155,164,204,214,242
Holmes, Jake   132
Holst, Gustav   133,137,146,222,223,
    225,279,371,376
Holy Modal Rounders   218,224
Holzmann, Jac   41
Honegger, Arthur   371,376
Hooker, Earl   132,146,184
Hooker, John Lee   166,167,169,177,
    182,183,184,185,186,262,263,271
Hookim, Joseph   353
Hooper, Nellee   259
Hoopii, Sol   5
Hopkins, Lightnin'   170,184
Hopper, Hugh   67
Horn, Paul   281,282,284,285
Horse   158
Horslips   328,329,331
Hot Butter   42,47
Houghton, Mick   96
Houghton, Richard   160
House, Simon   69

House, Son   184
Houston, Whitney   104,105,155
Hovhaness, Alan   374,378
Howard, Adina   155
Howard, Harlan   332,333
Howells, Herbert   374,377,378
Howlin' Wolf   14,23,132,170,182,183,
    184,185,186,219
Hudson, Garth   35,45,86,87
Hudson, Keith   351
Hughes, Alex   350
Hughes, David Edward   91
Hughes, Langston   264,265,271,272
Hulbert, Maurice 'Hot Rod'   125,128
Human League   43,47,155
Humanoid   257,258,261
Humble Pie   86,235,239
Humes, Helen   188
Humperdinck, Engelbert (composer)
    263,271
Humperdinck, Engelbert (singer)   339,343
Hunter, Alberta   179,185
Hunter, Long John   170
Hurley, Steve 'Silk'   257
Hüsker Dü   237,238,239
Hutchings, Ashley   89,322,327
Hutchison, Frank   4,5,21
Hütter, Ralph   47
Hyman, Dick   41,42,47,54,55,57
I Roy   267,351
Ibrahim, Abdullah   364
If   301,309
Ifield, Frank   87,89,206,207
Iggy and the Stooges   241,245
Il Gruppo   136,147
Impressions   191,199,202,203
Inagaki, J.   102
Incredible String Band   78,79,88,159,
    324,325,331
Incubus   81,88
Ink Spots   191,201
Inner Sanctum   244
Innes, Neil   210
Inoue, Diasuke   363
International Submarine Band   339,343
Iommi, Tony   232,233,234
Iron Butterfly   233
Iron Maiden   234,235,238,239
Isaacs, Gregory   352

Isaacson, Leonard 53
Isley Brothers 200,203,231,253,347
Isserlis, Steven 377
Ives, Charles 370,371,373,376
J, Clue & his Blues Blasters 344,345, 347,355
Jackson Five 199,203
Jackson, Anthony 28,29,31
Jackson, Hank 269
Jackson, Jack 134,135,147
Jackson, Mahalia 188,201,306
Jackson, Michael 55,1100,113,153,198, 199,201,203,207,215,237
Jackson, Millie 266,267,273
Jackson, Milt 62,63,67,98,99,193
Jackson, Ronald Shannon 16,305,310, 311
Jackson, Wanda 71,76
Jackson, Willis 345,355
Jacob, Max 275
Jacobs, Dick, Orchestra 69,75
Jacobs, Jim 286
Jacobs, Little Walter 86,87,89,104,181
Jagger, Mick 218,243
Jah Jerry 345
Jakszyk, Jakko 222
Jam 242
James, Brian 245
James, Dick 119
James, Elmore 184,187
James, Tommy & Shondells 37,46,134
JAMMS 142,143,148
Jammy, Prince 353,355
Jan And Dean 39,46
Jan Dukes De Grey 79,88
Jansch, Bert 323,331,377
Japan 363,365
Jarrett, Keith 63,67,278,279,281,285, 311,378
Järvi, Neeme 377
Jasini, Viram 88
Jazz Composers Orchestra 16,17,23
Jazz Epistles 359,364
JBs 257
Jefferson Airplane 27,31,75,77,90,222, 229,237,240,243,316,325
Jefferson, Blind Lemon 4,21,180,181, 183,185,263,271
Jennings, Waylon 25,337,338,339,343

Jenny, Georges 37
Jensen, Edwin 91
Jesus 319
Jethro Tull 74,75,77,81,88,232
Jets 205
Jihad 266,267,273
Joans, Ted 72
Jobim, Antonio Carlos 253
Joel, Billy 102,103
John, Elton 61,67,113,115,286,289, 300,327,328,329,331
Johns, Glyn 122
Johnson, Cluett 347
Johnson, Eldridge 95
Johnson, George Washington 111
Johnson, Howard 73
Johnson, J.J. 299
Johnson, James P. 188,299,307
Johnson, Johnnie 167
Johnson, Linton Kwesi 351,357
Johnson, Lonnie 6,179,184
Johnson, Marv 191,202
Johnson, Pete 167,188
Johnson, Robert 165,166,167,177,181, 183,184,185,263,271,313
Johnson, Roy 25
Johnston, Bob 317
Jolson, Al 274,275,287,291
Jones, Brian 75,81,83,183,360,361,365
Jones, Elvin 61,67
Jones, Howard 141
Jones, Jo 188
Jones, Leroi 265,266,267,269,273
Jones, Mick 243
Jones, Norah 364
Jones, Paul 289
Jones, Percy 264
Jones, Philip 209
Jones, Quincy 25,198,199
Jones, Tom (lyricist) 286
Jones, Tom (singer) 165,339,343
Joplin, Janis 100,101,196,227,237
Joplin, Scott 292,298
Jordan, Louis 27,170,177,345
Jordan, Stanley 21,23
Joy Division 129,244,245
Judge Dread 350,357
Juicy Lucy 18,23
Justified Ancients Of Mu-Mu 142,143, 149

Juvet, Patrick 256,261
Kahn, Gus 275
Kaleidoscope (UK) 365
Kaleidoscope (US) 79,88,360,361,365
Kamen, Michael 239
Kamin, Wally 24
Kander, John 286
Kansas City Five 9,21
Karas, Anton 83,88
Karloff, Boris 49
Karlweis, Oskar 359
Katz, Fred 69,70,76
Kaufman, Murray 125
Kauffman, Doc 11
Kavina, Lydia 49,56
Kay, Janet 352,357
Keane, Shake 264
Keegan, Pierce 81
Keel, Howard 291
Keita, Salif 363
KeKuKu, Joseph 4
Kelly, R. 200,201,203
Kemp, Willie 322,330
Kennedy, Will 99
Kenton, Stan 61,65,190,299,308
Keppard, Freddie 293,306
Kern, Jerome 286,287,288
Kershaw, Nik 141
Kertesz, Istvan 376
Kesey, Ken 265,266,273
Keshley, David 378
Khachaturian, Aram 238
Khaled 362,363,365
Khan, Ali Akbar 359,360,361,365
Khan, Chaka 31,256,261
Khan, Nusrat Fateh Ali 363,365
Kimmel, John J. 87,89
King Crimson 29,31,37,38,53,57,65,66, 67,73,77,136,137,146,147,201,220, 222,223,225,279,280,285
King Jammy 353
King Sisters 8
King Tubby 349
King, Albert 184
King, B.B. 170,172,181,182,183,184,185, 187,227
King, Ben E. 267
King, Carole 320,330

King, Evelyn Champagne 256,261
King, Freddie 184
King, James 378
King, Jonathan 154,155
King, Martin Luther 139
Kingston Trio 315
Kinks 47,226,241,244,245
Kinn, Maurice 109
Kinobe 145,149
Kirby, Robert 327
Kirk, Andy, Clouds Of Joy 9,21,71,77, 106,169
Kirk, Roland 73,74,75,76,77,84,85,89
Kirkman, Terry 75
Kirkpatrick, John 86,87,89
Kitchener, Lord 63,67,119,123
Kives, Philip 100
Kizart, Willie 169,172
Kleban, Edward 286
Klein, Joe 314
Kletzki, Paul 99
KLF 143
Kluster 42,43,47,220
Knack 242
Knapp, Orville Orchestra 5,21
Knight, Beverley 200,203
Knight, Curtis 231
Knight, Jesse Jr 24
Knight, Peter 221
Knuckles, Frankie 256,257
Kool & the Gang 198,203,249,250,251, 257,269
Kool Herc 129,140,141,257,267,269
Kooper, Al 22,37,46,218,219,224,303, 310,317
Korner, Alexis 182,183,185,187,218, 219,224,300,301,309,322,323
Kraftwerk 42,43,47,155,220
Krasnow, Bob 122
Krause, Bernie 41,47
Krauss, Alison 340,342,343
Kretzmer, Herbert 286
Kreutzmann, Bill 65
Krips, Henry 101
Krist, Hetty 166
Kronos Quartet 57,374,375,378
Krupa, Gene 58,61,65,66
Kubrick, Stanley 375
Kurtág, György 225,376

Kuti, Fela 251,360,361,365
Kyser, Kay 106
L.A. Express 55,57
Lacoume, Emile 292
Ladd's Black Aces 81
Ladnier, Tommy 188
Ladysmith Black Mambazo 361,364
Laine, Denny 69,75
Laine, Frankie 108,274,283
Lake, Greg 222,279
Lal, Pandit Chatur 360
Lamb 133,146
Lambert, Constant 370,371
Land, Harold 345,355
Landford, Bill & the Landfordairs 130
Landscape 43,47,63,64,67,368
Lane, Noi, Hawaiian Orchestra 5,21
Lang, Eddie 68,69,75
Lanson, Snooky 109
Lanza, Mario 110,111
Larsen, Sverre 372
LaSalle Quartet 376
Last Poets 268,269,273
Last Exit 304,305,311
Last, James 278
Laswell, Bill 139,141,147,258,305,351, 353,357,363,364
Lateef, Yusef 72,73,77
Lawson, Steve 28
Le Bargy, Charles 275
Leadbelly 19,174,312,313,314,315,329
Lebby, Lord 346,355
Led Zeppelin 59,65,113,115,132,133, 146,154,159,204,210,232,233,235, 237,241,340
Ledbetter, Huddie 313
Lee, Albert 338,339,343
Lee, Alvin 237
Lee, Byron and the Dragonaires 344, 345,355
Lee, Laurie 264
Lee, Luna 80,81
Left Banke 68,69,75
Leftfield 259,260,261
Lehar, Franz 287,291
Lehman, Steve 305,310,311
Leiber, Jerry 26,118,119,123,286
Leibert, Dick 97
Leibrook, Min 71

Lemmy 367
Lenard, Ondrej 378
Lenehan, John 378
Leningrad Symphony Orchestra 363
Lennon, John 16,35,37,45,87,89,122, 133,134,151,165,174,209,212,213, 214,215,226,277,285,286,316,363, 365,373,376
Leonard, Herbert 85
Leonard, Mike 222
Leoncavallo, Ruggero 111
Lerner, Alan J. 286
Lesh, Phil 27,31,71,154
Lester, Ketty 102
Levidis, Dimitrios 49,56
Levin, Tony 21,28,29
Levine, Ian 129
Levy, Morris 134
Lewis, Edward 96
Lewis, Hopeton 346,347,356
Lewis, Jerry 25
Lewis, Jerry Lee 5,167,313,335,337
Lewis, John 297,298,299,308
Lewis, Meade Lux 166,167,181,188
Lewis, Morgan 296
Lewis, Ramsey 303,311
Lewisohn, Mark 71,137,210
Ligeti, György 280,375
Light Crust Doughboys 9,22,336,341,342
Lightfoot, Terry 300
Lightnin' Rod 268,269,273
Lindbergh, Charles 186
Linhart, Buzzy 62
Lintu, Hannu 376
Lion, Margo 359
Liszt, Franz 88
Lithuanian Chamber Orchestra 377
Little Richard 25,141,167,170,192,193, 202,229,231
Little Sister 55,57
Little Walter 86,87,89,104,181
Littlefield, Little Willie 119
Liverpool Scene 129,183,187,264,265, 273
Living Colour 16,248,354,357
Livingston, Bunny 348,349
Livingstone, Theodore 140
Lloyd Webber, Andrew 1,286,289,291, 314

Lloyd, A.L.   323,325,330
Lloyd, Cecil, Group   347,355
Lloyd, Charles   303,311
Loar, Lloyd   4,24,35
Locklin, Hank   337
Lockwood Jnr, Robert   184
Lodge, Oliver   91
Loesser, Frank   286
Loewe, Frederick   286
Lohmeyer, Aletta   160
Lomax, Alan   178,179,185,313,315,317
Lomax, Jackie   160
Lomax, John   179,185,313
London Philharmonic Orchestra   361,377
London Sinfonietta   291,377
London Symphony Orchestra   67,89, 101,130,146,308,368,376,377
Long, Shorty   269
Lookofsky, Harry   69
Lopes, Joseph   5,9
Lord, Jon   69,75,222,225
Loriod, Jeanne   56,370
Loriod, Yvonne   56,370
Loss, Joe   137,253,261
Lothar and the Hand People   48,49,56
Louis, Joe Hill   172
Louisiana Five   181,185
Louisiana Sugar Babes   73,77
Love   71,75,159,211,215,218,220,221, 224,243
Love Sculpture   233,237
Love Spit Love   244
Love, Mike   48,49,214
Lovin' Spoonful   83,85,88
Lowe, John   214
Lowe, Nick   242
Lowther, Henry   69,71,76,300
Lucas, Nick   6,21
Lucas, Reggie   250
Lucas, Trevor   327
Lucie-Smith, Edward   264,265,273
Ludwig, Leopold   101
Lully, Jean-Baptiste   1
Lunceford, Jimmie   7,9,21,22
Lusher, Caroline Redman   374
Lydon, John   243,245,353
Lyle, Will   81,88
Lynn, Vera   108,166
Lynne, Jeff   212

Lythall, Rob   157
Lytle, Marshall   169,171
Lyttelton, Humphrey   119,123,300,309
M People   200,203
M/A/R/R/S   257,258,261
Maal, Baaba   251,350
MC5   159,241,245
McAuliffe, Leon   7,8,9,22
McCain, Ward   372
McCarthy, Joseph   315
McCartney, Linda   122
McCartney, Paul   26,27,31,39,51,61,75, 115,122,123,205,213,214,215,232, 277,286
McClune, Harry   91
MacColl, Ewan   322,323,330
MacColl, Kirsty   322,330,331
McCoy, Clyde   14
McCrae, George   255,261
McCreary, Joseph 'Foley'   29,31
MacDermot, Galt   286,288
McDonald, Cherry   377
McDonald, Ian   222,225
McEwan, Rory and Alex   322
McFerrin, Bobby   64,65,67
McFly, Marty   165
McGee, Dennis   87
McGee, Sam   4,5,333
McGhee, Stick   169
McGlinn, John   291
McGough, Roger   264,265,273
McGregor, Chris   360,365
McGuinn, Roger (Jim)   19,244,316,317
Mackay, Andy   73,74
McLaren, Malcolm   243
McLaughlin, John   14,16,19,23,302, 304,305,307,310
McLeod, Marilyn   256
McMahon, Charlie   84,85
McNeeley, Big Jay   176
McPhatter, Clyde   190,191,201
McPhee, Tony   16
MacRae, Gordon   291
McShee, Jacqui   323
McTell, Blind Willie   19,23
McVie, Christine   187
Macero, Teo   122,303
Machito   61,65
Machuki, Winston 'Count'   351

Mack, Craig   106
Macon, Uncle Dave   332,341
Maddox Brothers and Rose   169
Madness   35,346,353,355
Madonna   31,55,113,207,250,374,378
Maelstrom Percussion Ensemble   147
Magazine   245
Maggio, Anthony   178,179,185
Magic Carpet   79,88
Magic Sam   13,22
Mahal, Taj   63,67,72,73,77
Mahavishnu Orchestra   23,47,304,305, 311
Mahler, Alma   371
Mahler, Gustav   1,101,216,217,371,374, 378
Makeba, Miriam   359,360,364
Makhonine, Ivan   68
Malcolm X   167
Male, Kerrilee   150,151
Malone, Gareth   374,378
Maltby Jr, Richard   286
Mamas and Papas   75,77,185
Manassas   341
Mancini, Henry   113
Mandingo Griot Society   83,88
Manfred Mann   39,41,46,71,75,76,77, 146,227,300,309,318,330
Manfred Mann Chapter III   301,309
Manfred Mann Earth Band   133,146
Mangione, Gap   29,31
Mann, Herbie   17,23,250,251,302,303, 311
Mann, Nathaniel D.   275
Mann, William   204,205,207
Manne, Shelly   296,307
Mansfield, Keith   100,101,277
Mantovani   101,277,278,285
Manzarek, Ray   35,36
Maphis, Joe   76
Mar-Keys   71,77,195,202
Marathon Dance Orchestra   98
Marcels   190,201
Marclay, Christian   142,143,145,149
Marcus, Greil   160,180,313
Marcus, Steve   102
Mardi Gras Sextette   81
Margouleff, Robert   41
Marillion   222,225

Marino, Frank   16
Markham, Pigmeat   268,269,273
Marley, Bob   348,349,350,351,357,361, 363
Marr, Johnny   244
Marriner, Neville   89
Marriott, Steve   195,239
Marshall, Jim   13,15,17,228
Marshall, Maithe   191
Martenot, Maurice   49
Martha and the Vandellas   254,255,261
Martin, Constant   37
Martin, Dean   25
Martin, George   118,119,121,123,126, 129,207,210,212,213,215,286,304
Martin, Giles   210,213
Martin, Grady   13
Martin, Ray   98,99,108
Martin, Sara   179,185
Martino, Al   108,109
Martyn, John   326,327,331,346,348,357
Marvelettes   191
Marvin, Hank   11,22,117
Mascara Snake   73
Masekela, Hugh   359,360,364
Masked Marauders   160
Mason, David   71
Massive Attack   258,259,261
Material   139,147
Mathis, Johnny   100,103
Matlock, Glen   241
Matsui, Kazu   82,83,88
Mattacks, Dave   89
Matthes, Johann Nikolaus   140
Matthews Southern Comfort   320
Matthews, Austin   158
Matthews, Colin   378
Matthews, David   378
Matumbi   351
Maxwell Davies, Peter 61,67,366,367, 376
May, Brian   16,23,81
Mayall, John   15, 19,22,35,45,50,57,69, 71,75,77,122,123,133,183,186,187, 196,204,211,215,217,218,219,224, 226,227,228,229,231,237,300,301, 353
Mayer, John   78,79,88,361,365
Mayer, Roger   17

Mayfield, Curtis   184,198,199,202,203
Mayorga, Lincoln   102,103
Maytals   347,348,355
Me Myself & Me Again   65,66,67
Meaden, Peter   194
Meat Loaf   165,314
Medeski Martin & Wood   304,310,311
Meehan, Tony   27,31,126
Meek, Joe   118,119,123
Meeks, Tim   21
Mehldau, Brad   304,311
Meisels, Saul   97
Mel, Melle and the Furious Five   269
Melanie   139,147
Melcher, Terry   316
Mellers, Wilfred   205,207
Melodians   348
Melvin, Harold and the Blue Notes   198
Memphis Jug Band   81,88
Mendelsohn, John   235
Mendelssohn, Felix   96,97,366,368,376
Mendoza, David   275
Mensah, E.T.   358,359,364
Mercer, Johnny   286
Mercury, Freddie   130
Merrill, Bob   286
Mescalinum United   259,261
Meshuggah   19,20,23
Messiaen, Olivier 49,56,299,370,371,376
Metallica   235,238,239
Metheny, Pat   57,309,321
Meyers, Augie   35
Midnighters   176
Milburn, Amos   106,119,169
Miles, Emma Bell   332,333
Miles, Buddy   17,251,269,302
Milhaud, Darius   299,307
Miller, Emmett   334,335,337,341
Miller, Glenn   8,49,106,111,128,295
Miller, Jack   5,7,9
Miller, Jacob   152
Miller, Jimmy   196
Miller, Marcus   307
Miller, Mitch   82,177
Miller, Rice   168
Miller, Robin   73
Miller, Robyn   282,285
Miller, Roger   103
Milli Vanilli   115

Millie   346,347,355
Mills Brothers   188,189,191,201
Mills, Melissa   233
Milstein, Nathan   96,97,368,376
Minevitch. Borrah   85
Mingus, Charles   198,272,299,301,310, 321
Minster, Wes Five   300
Minton, Henry   295
Mintz, Leo   171
Miracles   190,191,192,193,198,202, 255,261
Miranda, Lin-Manuel   289,290
Misty In Roots   353
Misunderstood   18,23
Mitchell, Adrian   264
Mitchell, George, Minstrels   206
Mitchell, Guy   108,174
Mitchell, Joni   27,31,83,88,318,319,320, 321,322,325, 330
Mitchell, Ollie   71
Mitchell's Christian Singers   189
Mizzy, Vic   15
Mo, Keb   183,186,187
Mobius, Dieter   42
Mobley, Hank   249
Moby   130,131,145,149
Model 500   257,261
Modern Jazz Quartet   67,98,99,298,308
Modugno, Domenico   113,358,359,364
Mohawks   277,285
Moloney, Paddy   85,329
Money, Zoot   229
Monk, Thelonious   22,295,296,311
Monkees   41,47,320
Monks   241,245
Monro, Matt   119
Monroe, Bill   336,337,343
Montero, Andre   49,56
Montgomery, Marvin 'Smokey'   336
Montgomery, Monk   25,26,29
Montgomery, Rev.J.D.   266,267,273
Monty Python   94
Moody Blues   37,38,39,46,62,63,67, 69,75,77,204,211,215,217,220, 221,223,225,241,265,273
Moody, Laura   370
Moog, Robert   39,40,41
Moon, Keith   26,59,228

Moondog   172,177
Moore, Christy   329
Moore, Gary   150,184
Moore, Scotty   173
Moore, Thurston   375
Moore, Wild Bill   169,176,177
Morcheeba   145,149,200
More, Jonathan   143
Moreira, Airto   60,61,65,67
Morgan, Robert P.   367
Morgan, Sunny   60,61,65
Morissette, Alanis   112
Moroccan Master Musicians of Joujouka   308,360,361,365
Moroder, Giorgio   43,257
Morphine   21,23
Morricone, Ennio   136,149,285
Morris, Eric   347,355
Morrison, Jim   36,244
Morrison, Van   85,89,196,197,203,328,329
Morrissey   244
Morse, Steve   225
Morton, Jelly Roll   65,181,292,293,294,295,306
Morton, Shadow   263
Moss, Jerry   71
Moten, Bennie   294,295
Mother Mallard's Portable Masterpiece Co.   41,47,138,139,147
Mothers Of Invention   46,60,61,65,73,77,135,136,147,218,224,302,372
Motorhead   236,239,366,376
Mould, Bob   239
Moulton, Tom   152
Move   98,127
Mozart, Wolfgang Amadeus   216,366,367
Mr. Scruff   172
Mtume   250,251
Mulligan, Gerry   297,307
Munchinger, Karl   97
Mundi, Billy   60,65
Muni, Scott   204
Munro, Ronnie   97
Murad, Jerry   123
Murray, Ruby   99
Murray, Sunny   267,273
Murray The K   124,125,128
Murvin, Junior   353,357

Musical Brownies   6,7,21,337,341
Mussorgsky, Modest   223
Mutter, Anne-Sophie   376
Mystic Moods Orchestra   102,103
N'Dour Youssou   251,363,364,365
Nagano, Kent   368
Naïve, Steve   35,45
Nancarrow, Conlon   375,378
Napalm Death   236,239
Narell, Andy   62,63,67
Narell, Jeff   63,67
Nash, Graham   321
Natel, Jean-Marc   286
Nathan Syd   193
National Polish Radio Symphony Orchestra   377
Neely, Tim   98
Nelson, Nate   190
Nelson, Paul   317
Nelson, Ricky   22,107
Nelson, Sandy   59,65
Nelson, Willie   338,339
Netherlands Radio Philharmonic   376
New Order   45,47,55,115,244
New Riders Of The Purple Sage   63,67
New Vaudeville Band   115
New York Art Quartet   267,273
N.Y. Philharmonic   96,97,101,368,376
Newby, Ray   125,127
Newton, Wayne   106
Nice   35,45,133,146,223,225
Nichols, Roger   55
Nightingale, Annie   127
Nikolais, Alwin   39
Nirvana (UK)   289,290,291
Nirvana (US)   67,236,237,239
Noble, Ray   128
Noel, Terry   126,127
Noelani's Hawaiian Orchestra   5
Nolen, Jimmy   247
Nomad, Naz, & the Nightmares   242,243
Nordine, Ken   264,265,271
Norris, Al   9,22
Northern Sinfonia Orchestra   130
Nova Express   235
Nucleus   302,311
Nugent, Ted   278
Numan, Gary   43,44,47,155
Nuriddin, Jalaluddin Masur   269

Nyman, Michael   375,378
Nyro, Laura   318,319,330
O Braonain, Ciaran   329
O hAllmhurain, Gearoid   329
O Riada, Sean   328,329,331
O'Jays   31,198
O'Brien, Karen   322
O'Brien, Richard   286
Oakenfold, Paul   283
Oasis   45,47
Oberheim, Tom   43
Odetta   341
Offenbach, Jacques   287
Ogg, Alex   269,271
Oja, Carol J.   57
Okuda, Hiroko   353
Oldham, Andrew Loog   22,121
Oldham, Spooner   35
Oldfield, Mike   130,146,221,374
Oldfield, Terry   282,283,285
Oliver, King   65,293,301,306
Oliver, Paul   179,185
Olson, Harry   51
Omartian, Michael   139
One Giant Leap   362,365
Ono, Yoko   363,365
Orb   144,145,149,259,260,261,283,285
Orchester Musikhochschule Karlsruhe   56
Orchestra Mozart   376
Orchestre de l'Opéra Bastille   56,376
Orchestre des Concerts L'amoureux   283
Organisation   47
Original Dixieland Jazz Band   58,59,65,82,89,292,293,306
Orioles   191,201
Ormandy, Eugene   96,101,376
Orwell, George   244
Ory, Kid   292
Osborne, Jerry   157
Osbourne, Ozzy   204,206,233,234
Osibisa   361,365
Ossie, Count   346
Ossman-Dudley Trio   81
Ossman, Vess L.   80,81,88,95
Oswald, John   138,153,154,155
Otis, Johnny   119
Owens, Buck   165,339
Ozawa, Seiji   88,89,376
P-Funk   248

Pablo, Augustus   44,45,47,155
Pachelbel, Johann   280
Pachet, François   122
Packard, Vance   177
Paganini, Niccolo   166
Page, Hotlips   188
Page, Jimmy   13,14,79,132,133,204,
   226,232,327
Page, Patti   116,117,121
Palmer, Clive   325
Palmer, Earl   249
Pandy, Darryl   257
Pankow, James   71
Paragons   349,356
Park, Simon, Orchestra   277,285
Parker, Charlie   61,65,96,139,161,172,
   184,295,296,297,299,304,306,308,332
Parker, Colonel Tom   173
Parker, Evan   73,76,77
Parker, Junior   22
Parker, Maceo   138,139,147,198,203,247
Parker, Melvin   247
Parks, Van Dyke   67,81,88
Parliament   251
Parsons, Alan   120,121,123
Parsons, Gene   12
Parsons, Gram   334,335,339,341
Parsons, Tony   243
Pärt, Arvo   375,377
Parton, Dolly   153,334,338,339,343
Passport   130
Pasternak, Michael   125
Pastorius, Jaco   27,30,31,321
Patchen, Kenneth   134,135
Paterson, Alex   259,260,283,285
Patten, Brian   264,265,271,273
Patton, Charley   180,181,183,185
Paul, Les   4,8,9,11,22,24,116,117,119,
   121,122,123
Paul, Sean   355,357
Pauling, Lowman   181
Paxton, Gary   39
Peacock, Annette   41,47
Pearl Jam   237,239
Pearlman, Sandy   235
Peart, Neil   64,65,67
Peatman, John G.   107
Peel, John   115,125,126,127,128,129,
   196,223,241,243,264

Pegg, Dave   327
Pemberton, Andy   259
Penderecki, Krzysztof   84,89,372,373,377
Penguins   160,161
Pennsylvania Melody Syncopators   98
Pentangle   183,322,323,327,331
Pere Ubu   184
Perfect, Christine   187
Pergolesi, Giovanni   131
Peri, Jacopo   287
Perkins, Carl   135,181
Perrey, Jean Jacques   37,41,47,101
Perry, King and the Soulettes   349
Perry, Lee   347,348,349,350,353,356,357
Pet Shop Boys   5,154,155
Peter, Paul, and Mary   315
Peters, Linda   327
Peterson, Oscar   311
Petrucciani, Michel   31
Pettiford, Oscar   69,76
Petty, Norman   152
Petty, Tom   341
PFM   222
Philadelphia Orchestra   96,101,368,376
Philharmonia Orchestra   99,101,376
Phillips, Barre   28
Phillips, Sam   172,173,174
Phillips, Washington   82,83,88
Piaf, Edith   49,56,359,364
Piblokto!   331
Picasso, Pablo   131
Pickett, Wilson   195,202,255,261
Pigbag   153,155
Piltdown Men   102
Pinckney, St.Clair   247
Pinder, Mike   38,39
Pink Floyd   10,27,31,35,42,43,45,51,65,
   67,102,113,115,121,130,136,138,
   146,147,211,215,220,221,222,224,
   241,260,261,280,282,352
Pinkerton's Assorted Colours   83,88
Plagenhoef, Scott   213
Planets   376
Plant, Robert   282,340,342,343
Planxty   81,85,88,329,331
Platt, Lew   171
Platters   190
Poet and the Roots   350,351
Pogues   322,330,331

Police   159,160,352,353,357
Pollack, Ben   295
Pollard, Velma   346
Pomona Valley Symphony Orchestra   221
Ponchielli, Amilcare   372
Poniatoff, Alexander M.   121
Ponty Jean Luc   79
Poole, Brian and the Tremeloes   204
Port Of Harlem Jazzmen   168
Porter, Cole   286,289
Portishead   259,261
Powell, Jimmy   347
Pozo, Chano   61,65
Pratt, Mike   286
Presidents of the USA   21,23
Presley, Elvis   22,25,26,34,73,77,100,
   111,113,130,133,135,146,153,164,
   168,170,172,173,174,175,177,191,
   201,205,207,263,271,289,290,291,
   316,318,337,341
Preston, Denis   118,119
Preston, Don   41,47,289
Preston, Jimmy   168,169
Pretty Things   219,277,289,291
Previn, André   296,376
Prevost, Eddie   136
Price, Alan   35
Price, Joel   25,26
Pridham, Peter   91
Primal Scream   115
Primes   191
Primettes   191
Prince   55,114,199,200,201,203
Prince, Tony   141
Princess Diana   329
Princess Margaret   39
Principal Edwards Magic Theatre   129
Prior, Maddy   327
Proby, P.J.   13,22
Procol Harum   35,45,115,217,221,222,
   224
Prokofiev, Gabriel   367,376
Prokofiev, Sergei   367
Public Enemy   145,149,270,273
Public Image Ltd   245,353,357
Puccini, Giacomo   275,287
Pudim, Alafia   269
Pulitzer, Joseph   115
Pursell, William (Bill)   279,285

Putnam, Bill   117
Qiang, Wu Zu   81,88
Qiao, Wang Yan   81,88
Quarrymen   174,214,215
Queen   16,23,81,88,114,115,130,143
Queen Elizabeth II   115
Queen Victoria   189
Quicksand   244
Quicksilver Messenger Service   229,237
Quinn, Denis   285
Quintessence   361,364,365
Quist, Bill   281,285
R.E.M.   45,47,237,239
Raaijmakers, Dick   51
Race, Steve   177
Rachel and the Revolvers   121
Radiohead   49,56,222,225,352
Rado, James   286,288
Raelettes   193
Rage Against The Machine   270
Ragni, Gerome   286,288
Rainey, Ma   188
Ramey, Hurley   9,22
Ramones   242
Ranaldo, Lee   375
Ranglin, Ernest   345,347
Rare Bird   216
Ratledge, Mike   34,35,45
Rattle, Simon   130,145,376,378
Rautavaara, Einojuhani   373,376
Ravel, Maurice   366,367,371
Raven, Mike   185
Ravens   190,191,201
Ray, Johnnie   108
Ray, Laverne   170
Razzy Dazzy Spasm Band   292
Reagan, Ronald   269
Red Hot Chili Peppers   248,340
Redding, Otis   12,77,90,194,195,196,
    202,255,277
Redman, Dewey   279,308
Redwood, Ruddy   349
Reed, Jerry   333
Reed, Jimmy   184
Reed, Lou   240,245
Reese, Jerome   279
Reeves, Jim   336,337,343
Reich, Steve   45,47,50,57,130,153,280,
    305,375,378

Reichel, Hans   20,21
Reid, Duke (Arthur)   267,345,346,347,
    349,351,356
Reid, Vernon   16,23,311,354
Reilly, Tommy   85,89
Reiner, Fritz   99,101
Reinhardt, Django   6,7
Reisner, Louise   87,89
Relf, Keith   133,146, 158
Remains   91
Renaissance   133,146
Renbourn, John   323,331
Rendell, Don   300
Residents   138,139,147
Respighi, Ottorino   101,373,376
Return To Forever   61,67
Revere, Paul and the Raiders   15
Revolutionaries   353
Rey, Alvino   5,8,22
Reynolds, Debbie   181
Rhodes, Harold   36
Rhodes, Emitt   122,123,325
Rhodes, Red   13
Ribowsky, Mark   120
Rice, Tim   286,289,291
Rich, Buddy   61,65,66,67
Rich, Charlie   343
Richard X   155
Richard, Cliff   98,117,126,127,152,
    155,174,204,242,289,359
Richards, Emil   38,39,41,46
Richards, Keith   12,13,19,243
Richardson, Mark   213
Rickenbacker, Adolph   4,5
Ricks, Jimmy   191
Riesman, Michael   378
Righteous Brothers   197,203
Riley, Howard   300
Riley, Terry   280,373,374,375,377,378
Rimsky-Korsakov, Nikolai   96,101
Rinuccini, Ottavio   286
Riperton, Minnie   283
Ritchie, Jean   82,83,88
Ritenour, Lee   18
Ritter, Preston   15
Ritter, Tex   274,283
Roach, Max   59,65,297,311
Roach, Rod   160
Robb, Morse   33

Robbins, Marty   13
Roberts, Andy   264,265
Roberts, Kenny   172
Robertson, Eck   69,75,332,333,341
Robertson, Robbie   28,312,313,317,319
Robeson, Paul   188,189,191,201,287,291
Robins   119,123
Robinson, Bob   168
Robinson, Harold and the Ticklers   344
Robinson, Lisa   320
Robinson, Smokey   190,198,202,255,
    261
Robinson, Sylvia   269
Robinson, Tom, Band   242,243
Robinson, Vicki Sue   255,261
Robison, Carson   337,341
Robson, Jeremy   264
Rock Choir   374,377
Rockmore, Clara   49
Rodgers, Jimmie   94,158,159,334,335,
    341
Rodgers, Richard   110,286,288,289,290,
    298,319
Rodney, Red   332
Rodney, Winston   349,350
Rodrigo, Joaquin   298
Roedelius, Hans-Joachim   42
Rogers, Jimmy   181
Rolling Stones   12,13,15,22,27,31,41,47,
    49,56,75,77,81,83,88,102,109,111,
    121,123,160,183,187,194,202,204,
    211,215,216,217,218,219,221,223,
    224,227,232,239,240,243,245,298,
    300,301,303,361,365
Rollins, Sonny   311
Romberg, Sigmund   286
Romeo, Max   350,357
Ronettes   119
Ronstadt, Linda   289,338,339,342,343
Rose Royce   63,67
Rose, Fred   335,337
Rosen, Mike   71
Rosko, Emperor   125
Ross, Alex   298,367
Ross, Diana   41,47,115,190,255,256,
    261,352
Ross, Pipe Major Willie   85,89
Rotations   137,147
Rothenberg, Ned   83,88

Rotten, Johnny   243
Roulettes   1
Rous, Samuel Holland   94
Rowan and Martin   269
Rowe, Dick   204
Rowe, Keith   16,23,136
Roxy Music   53.57,73,77,222,281
Royal Concertgebouw Orchestra   89,378
Royal Danish Orchestra   336
Royal Philharmonic Orchestra   69,75,89, 101,130,146,225
Royal Scottish National Orchestra   376, 378
Royksopp   283,285
Roza, Miklos   48,49
Rozhdestvensky, Gennadi   283,377
Rubin, Rick   340,341
Rudess, Jordan   20,21
Ruler Inc   280
Run D.M.C.   149,270,273
Rush   65,66
Rush, Otis   184,219,228,229,237
Russell, George   298,299,307
Russell, Luis   63
Russell, Willy   286
Russo, William   87,89,222,225
Rust, Brian   27
Rutles   210
Ryan, Paddy   323,330
Rypdal, Terje   279,285,311
Saddler, Joseph   141
Sadistic Mika Band   362,363,365
Sado, Yutaka   283
Sagittarius   39,46
Saint-Saens, Camille   274,275,283
Sainte-Marie, Buffy   53,57,101,323,377
Sakamoto, Kyu   358,359,364
Sala, Oskar   56
Sallinen, Aulis   378
Salonen, Esa-Pekka   376
Sam the Sham & the Pharoahs   34,35,45
Samson   235,238,239
Samurai   363,365
Samwell, Ian   126,127
San Francisco Symphony Orchestra   89, 239
Sanborn, David   301,309
Sanders, Pharaoh   298
Sandman, Mark   21

Sands   137,147
Sanny X   141,149
Santamaria, Mongo   61,65
Santana   60,61,63,65
Sargent, Malcolm   99
Satie, Erik   274,275,279,281,283,285
Satintones   191,202
Satriani, Joe   16
Saturnalia   158
Saunders, Jesse   257,261
Saunders, Mike   235,239
Savile, Jimmy   127
Savoy Brown   217
Sawhney, Nitin   373,376
Sax, Adolphe   73
Sax, Doug   102,103
axa   353
Scaffold   265,273
Scales, Prunella   271,272
Schaeffer, Pierre   50,51,56,57,135,137, 147
Schertzinger. Victor   275
Schiller, Friedrich   94
Schillinger, Joseph   49,56
Schleman, Hilton R.   157
Schlosser, Pieter   105
Schmidt, Harvey   286
Schneider-Esleben, Florian   47
Schnitzler, Conrad   42
Schoenberg, Arnold   145,262,263,271, 368,369,371,376
Schoenberg, Claude-Michel   286
Schubert, Franz   205,366
Schuller, Gunther   298,299,306,307
Schulze, Klaus   220,280,284,285,371
Schuman, William   115
Schumann, Robert   366
Schwartz, Stephen   286
Schwarz, Gerard   378
Schwarzkopf, Elisabeth   291
Scott, Cyril   85,89
Scott, John   75
Scott de Martinville, Edouard-Léon   95
Scott, Raymond   52,57
Scott, Ronnie   174,301,309
Scott, Tom   55,57
Scott, Tony   281,284,285
Scott-Heron, Gil   269,270,273
Scruggs, Earl   337,342,343

Sculthorpe, Peter   378
Seaga, Edward   345
Seal   200,201,203
Seasick Steve   21,23
Seaton, B.B.   351
Seatrain   69
Seattle Symphony Orchestra   378
Sebastian, John   83,85
Sebastian, John Snr   85
Seeds   15,218,224,240
Seeger, Peggy   322,331
Seeger, Pete   312,313,315,317,322,328, 329
Sellers, Peter   119,123
Sembello, Mike   199
Sex Pistols   165,210,241,243,244,245, 289,291
Shabba Ranks   353,354,357
Shadows   11,22,27,113,117,123,227
Shaggy   354,355,357
Shakespeare, Robbie   353
Shakespeare, William   26,306
Shamblin, Eldon   9,13,22
Shangri-Las   133,146,263,271
Shank, Bud   75
Shankar, Anoushka   364
Shankar, Ravi   78,359,359,365
Shannon, Del   37,46
Shapiro, Helen   13,22,301
Sharp, Cecil   321
Sharp, Martin   316
Sharrock, Sonny   16,17,23,303,305
Shaw, Artie   299,307
Shaw, Sandie   114,115
Sheen, Celia   56
Shelley, Pete   241,245
Shepard, Bert   111
Shepherd, Ben   237
Shepp, Archie   184,187,311
Sheridan, Mark   94
Sheridan, Tony   205
Sherry, Fred, String Quartet   376
Shimabukuro, Jake   81
Shipton, Alyn   300
Shirelles   191,202,320
Shirley and Lee   344
Shkreli, Martin   158
Shorter, Wayne   303,304,305,307,321
Shostakovich, Dmitri   274,283

Showard, Derek   140
Shrieve, Michael   63
Shuker, Roy   157
Shulman, Phil   73
Sibelius, Jean   99,366,367,376
Siegel-Schwall Band   87,89,225
Sigur Ros   114,115
Silhouettes   190,201
Sir Lord Baltimore   235
Silver Apples   137,147
Silver, Horace   139,249,251
Silvers, Louis   275
Silvo, Johnny   325
Simon & Garfunkel   41,47,144,152, 155, 211,215,303,316,331
Simon, Bobby   7
Simon, Paul   316,323,324,331,346,357, 363,364
Simon, Winston, Spree   63,66
Sinatra, Frank   6,96,97,100,107,110,111, 175,207,221,278,287,289,290,291, 295
Sinfield, Peter   53,222,223
Singer, Hal   176
Siouxsie & the Banshees   240,241,242, 243,245
Sir Douglas Quintet   35,45
Sister Sledge   141
Sitwell, Edith   265,271
Six Boys In Trouble   262,271
Skatalites   70,71,77,346,347,355
Skip Bifferty   160
Sky   73,77
Slack, Freddie   9,181
Slade   108,346
Slattery, Amy   122,123
Slaughter, John   300,309
Sledge, Percy   35,45,240
Slick, Grace   75
Slickers   348
Slits   353,357
Slovak Philharmonic   378
Slovak Radio Symphony Orchestra   56
Sly and Robbie   350,352,353,357
Sly and the Family Stone   27,31,55,57, 196,197,200,203,249,251,255,261
Small Faces   122,123,133,146,195,203, 242,255,261
Small, Heather   200,203

Small, Millie   346,347
Smart, Terry   126
Smee, Phil   218
Smith, Alan   212
Smith, Arthur   168
Smith, Bessie   178,179,185
Smith, Byron   349
Smith, Clara   85,89
Smith, Clarence 'Pinetop'   167,181
Smith, Ethel   34,35,45
Smith, Floyd   9,21
Smith, Jimmy   34,35,45
Smith, Johnny   23
Smith, Johnny 'Hammond'   249
Smith, Kenny   91
Smith, Mamie   178,179,185
Smith, Mike   35
Smith, Patti   115
Smith, Slim   349,354
Smith, Stuff   69,75
Smith, Trixie   168,175
Smith, Wayne   353,354,357
Smiths   244,245
Snake River Conspiracy   244
Snowden, Shorty   166
Socarras, Alberto   74,75,77
Soft Cell   43,47,115,153,155
Soft Machine   35,45,67,128,206,207, 215,235,300,301,303,309,372,374, 378
Softley, Mick   377
Solar Fake   244
Solti, Georg   377
Son Volt   338
Sondahl, Brad   5
Sondeckis, Saulus   378
Sondheim, Stephen   286,288
Sonic Youth   237,239,377
Sonny and Cher   73,77
Soul II Soul   259
Soul Stirrers   193,201
Soundgarden   237
Sousa, John Philip   88
Southern, Taryn   122
Spann, Otis   181,184,187,226
Specials   352,353,355
Spector, Phil   119,120,121,123,197,213, 316
Spencer, Jeremy   187

Spencer, Len   333,341
Spirit   229,237
Spitz, Bob   317
Spivakovsky, Michael   85,89
Spooky Tooth   159,160,235
Springfield, Dusty   194,202
Springsteen, Bruce   103,266,267,273, 314,318,329
Spyro Gyra   63,67
Squier, George   277
SRC   229,237
St.Cyr, Johnny   292
St.John, Bridget   129
Staatskapelle Dresden   376
Stafford, Jo   108
Stalling, Carl   274,275,285
Standells   240
Stanley, Owsley   91
Stansfield, Lisa   143
Stanshall, Vivian   146
Starks, Jabo   247
Starr, Ringo   158,207,338,339,343
Starrett, John D.   21
Status Quo   165
Steamhammer   233,237
Steampacket   255
Steel Pulse   353
Steele, Tommy   119,174,177,286,289
Steeleye Span   322,327,329,331
Steely Dan   55,57,138,139,147
Stefani, Gwen   104,105
Stein, Steve   141
Steinman, Jim   314
Steppenwolf   235,239
Stevens, Cat   79,88,154,155,327,328,331
Stevens, Jon   331
Stewart, Al   326,327,331
Stewart, Rod   113,232,243,255,257, 261,287,347
Stilgoe, Richard   286
Stills, Steve   22,218,219,224,321,341
Sting   85,89,130,146
Stitt, King   267,351,356,357
Stitt, Sonny   52,53,57
Stivell, Alan   82,83,88
Stockhausen, Karlheinz   50,51,57,222, 225,370,373,376
Stokowski, Leopold   97,368,376
Stoller, Mike   26,118,119,123,286

Stone Poneys 339
Stone, Christopher 124,125,127,128
Stothart, Herbert 286
Stowe, Harriet Beecher 188,189
Strang, Gerald 53,57
Stranglers 243
Strauss II, Johann 83,88,145,287,375
Strauss, Richard 99,101,103,375
Stravinsky, Igor 130,131,133,145,296, 299,308,370,371,372,376
Strawberry Alarm Clock 40
Strawbs 46,324,325,331
Streisand, Barbra 257,261,319
Strickland, William R. 217
Strong, Barrett 191,202
Stuttgart Chamber Orchestra 97
Stuttgart Radio Symphony Orchestra 89, 311
Styne, Jule 286
Subotnick, Morton 50,53,57
Sugababes 155
Sugar 239
Sugarcubes 259,260
Sugarhill Gang 141,149,262,263,267, 269,271
Sullivan, Big Jim 13,15,228
Sullivan, Ed 171
Sumlin, Hubert 182,184
Summer, Donna 43,47,256,257,261
Sumner, Bernard 244
Sun Ra 36,37,40,41,45,46,47,267,273, 311
Sun, David 285
Supertramp 103
Supremes 41,47,141,190,191,193,196, 198
Suso, Foday Musa 82,83,88
Swanson, Chris 41
Swarbrick, Dave 324,325,327,329,331
Sweet Marriage 129
Swift, Taylor 112,339
Swinging Blue Jeans 254,255,261
Sylvester 256,261
Symarip 346,355
t.A.T.u. 244
Tacuma, Jamaaladeen 305,311
Tait, Lyn 347
Takemitsu, Toru 67
Talking Heads 139

Tallis Scholars 146
Talmy, Shel 226
Tamony, Peter 297
Tampa Red 6,21,188,201
Tangerine Dream 43,47,220,259,280, 285
Tanner, Paul 49
Taste 233,237
Tatum, Art 311
Taupin, Bernie 329
Tavener, John 374,377
Taylor, Cecil 311
Taylor, Dick 219
Taylor, James 320,330
Taylor, Johnnie 113
Taylor, Mike 59,65,300
Taylor, Montana 167,175,181
Tchaikovsky, Peter 87,89,97,101,366,372
Television 243,245
Temperance Seven 119
Tempo, Nino and April Stevens 115
Temptations 63,136,137,147,193,196, 197,200,203,249,251
Ten cc 363
Ten Years After 233,235,237
Tenney, James 134,135,147
Terminator X 145
Terrade, Mathieu 20
Terry, Clark 53,57
Texas Alexander 179,185
Texas Playboys 7,9,21,336,337,341
Texas Wanderers 7
Tharpe, Sister Rosetta 189,201
Them 61,65,197
Theremin, Leon 48,49,55
Third Ear Band 129,361,365
Thirteenth Floor Elevators 218,224,240
Thomas, Carla 195,277
Thomas, Evelyn 150
Thomas, John 313
Thomas, Michael Tilson 376
Thomas, Ray 75
Thomas, Rufus 195,202
Thomas, Sam 247
Thomason, Jimmy 7
Thompson, Barbara 300
Thompson, Carl 29
Thompson, Danny 327,331
Thompson, Karen 377

Thompson, Linda 327
Thompson, Richard 87,89,325,326, 327,331
Thompson, Scott 91
Thompson, Uncle Jimmy 333,341
Thorne, Ken 286
Thornhill, Claude 71,77
Thornton, Big Mama 119,123
Three Degrees 198
Thunes, Derek 378
Tickell, Kathryn 84,85
Tillotson, Johnny 204
Tippett, Keith 300
TLC 155
Toch, Ernst 51,56
Tom and Jerry 316
Tomita 53,57
Tomorrow 289
Tonto's Expanding Head Band 41,42,47
Tool 236,237,239
Toots and the Maytals 355
Topham, Top 226
Tornados 36,37,46,119,123,204
Torok, Mitchell 161
Torrence, Dean 46
Tortelier, Paul 99
Toscanini, Arturo 294
Tosches, Nick 7,9,335
Tosh, Peter 165,346,348,349,350,357
Touch 217
Toure, Ali Farka 178,179,185,350
Toussaint, Allen 240
Townsend, Charles R. 335
Townsend, Ken 122
Townshend, Pete 16,195,223,228,242
Traffic 211,215,221,224
Trans-Global Underground 362,363,365
Trautwein, Friedrich 49
Traveling Wilburys 212
Travis, Dave Lee 125
Travis, Merle 8,9
Travolta, John 257
Tremeloes 318,330
Trenet, Charles 37,46
Treniers 25,29
Tripp, Art 60
Tristano, Lennie 122,123
Troggs 84,89,241,245
Trower, Robin 16

Tubb, Ernest   335
Tubby, King   152,155
Tubeway Army   43,47
Tudor, David   372,373,377
Turbans   190
Turnage, Mark-Anthony   298,308
Turner, Ike   24,25,172,177,184
Turner, Ike and Tina   120,192,193,202
Turner, Joe   171,188
Turner, Ruby   105
Turner, Steve   189
Turner, Tina   289
Tutmarc, Bud   25
Tutmarc, Paul   24,25
Twain, Shania   339
Twentieth Century Steel Band   62,63,67
Twenty-First Century Schizoid Band   222, 225
Tyler, Bonnie   314
Tyler, T.Texas   263,271
Tyner, McCoy   311
Tyrannosaurus Rex   129
U2   1,85,89
UB40   324,353,355
U Roy   140,149,267,268,273,351,357
Ukulele Ike   81,88
Ulmer, James Blood   305,310,311
Ulster Orchestra   378
Ultravox   43,47
Umphred, Neal   159
Uncle Tupelo   338,342,343
Undertakers   160
Undertones   241,243,245
Underwood, Ian   73
Underworld   258,259,260,261,284
Unique Quartette   189,201
United States Of America   27,28,55,57
University of Pennsylvania Mask and Wig Glee Chorus   117,123
Upsetters   348,349
Uriah Heep   233,234,239
Us3   144,149
USSR Ministry of Culture Orchestra   283
Utyosof, Alexander   292
Vagabonds   7
Vai, Steve   16,19,23,166
Valli, Frankie   202
Van Binsbergen, Corrie   289,291
Van Der Graaf Generator   5,35,45,129, 245
Van Eps, Fred   88
Van Eps, George   19,20,23
Van Halen, Eddie   21,23,165
Van Vliet, Don   122,184
Vance, Tommy   125
Vanilla Fudge   196,197,203
Varèse, Edgard   50,57,371,376
Vaughan Williams, Ralph   111,323,330, 366,375,376
Vaughan, Sarah   297
Vaughan, Stevie Ray   183,187
Vee, Bobby   154,204,320
Vega, Suzanne   105
Velvet Underground   68,69,75,240, 245,372,377
Ventures   13,22
Venuti, Joe   68,69,75,107
Verdi, Giuseppe   275,368,376
Vernon, Mike   122,228
Vestine, Henry   184,229,237
Vicious, Sid   241,245
Vickers, Mike   41,75
Victor Military Band   179,333
Villa-Lobos, Heitor   85,89
Vincent, Gene   309
Vinnegar, Leroy   296
Vipers   119
Vivaldi, Antonio   216
Vollenweider, Andreas   83,88
Von Karajan, Herbert   103,376,378
Von Stade, Frederica   291
Voorhaus, David   51
Wagner, Richard   275,287
Wagoner, Porter   339
Wailers   346,347,348,349,351,357
Wakeman, Rick   40,41,47,324
Waldron, Mal   279,284,285
Walker Brothers   103
Walker, T-Bone   6,7,9,22,181,184,185
Waller, Fats   32,33,45,77
Walter, Bruno   96,97,376
Walters, John   43
Walton, William   265,271,272
War   115
Ward, Billy and his Dominoes   176
Ward, Ed   180
Wardle, John   353
Warhol, Andy   68,240
Washingtonians   295
Waters, Muddy   14,23,87,89,132,146, 167,169,177,181,182,183,184,185, 186,219,298,308
Waters, Roger   29
Waterson-Carthy   324
Waterson, Norma   324,331
Watersons   324
Watkins, Charlie   90,91
Watkins, Julius   70,71,77
Watts, Charlie   219
Waxman, Franz   56
Way, Darryl   130
Wayne, John   301
Weather Report   27,31,43,47,61,65, 302,304,305,309,311,321
Weaver, Sylvester   4,21,179,180,185
Weavers   315,329
Webb, Jimmy   267,318,319,327,330
Webb, Sonny and the Cascades   337,343
Webb, Stan   323,331
Weber, Eberhard   28,311
Weill, Kurt   145,286
Weindorf, Hermann   130
Welch, Chris   217
Welk, Lawrence, Orchestra   37
Wells, Mary   193
Wells, Phil   283,285
Wesley, Fred   139
West, Keith   289
West, Speedy   19,23
West, Timothy   271,272
Westbrook, Mike   300,311,372,377
Westminster Philharmonic Orchestra   56
White Noise   51,57,129
White, Clarence   12
White, Jack   100
White, Josh   119,123
White, Maurice   249,303
Whiteman, Paul   293,294,295,298,299, 306
Whitfield, Norman   63,137,147,197, 203,251
Whitney, John   378
Whitsell, Bob   49
Whitter, Henry   85,89
Who   16,23,27,31,35,45,58,59,71,77, 102,103,194,195,203,217,223,226, 228,230232,,237,240,242,286,288,

289,291,327	Wincott, Terence Alan 73	Wynette, Tammy 343
Wilco 314,329,338	Winding, Kai 37,46	Wyper, Peter 87,89
Willcox, Colin 283	Wing, Paul 97	XTC 241,245
Williams, Big Joe 19,20,23	Winley, Paulette and Tanya 271,273	Yamash'ta, Stomu 60,61,63,67,102
Williams, Clarence 75,77,179	Winston, George 280,281,283,285	Yamauchi, Tetsu 363
Williams, Hank 169,170,332,333,336, 337,339,341,34300	Winter, Paul 280,281,285	Yao Yanaglo Ensemble 248,251
	Winwood, Muff 196	Yardbirds 12,13,14,15,22,79,88,133,151, 152,153,155,182,183,187,217,218, 224,226,227,229,232,237,347,355
Williams, Jan 147	Winwood, Stevie 35,45,62,196,211,219	
Williams, John 225	Wirtz, Mark 289,291	
Williams, Ken 15	Wit, Antoni 377	Yazz and the Plastic Population 143
Williams, Larry 177	Witherspoon, Jimmy 119	Yellow Magic Orchestra 282,285,363,365
Williams, Paul & Hucklebuckers 171,176	Wobble, Jah 353,357	Yes 40,216,217,222,224,243,324
Williams, Tony 306	Wolverines 71	Young, Angus 237
Williams, Tony, Lifetime 17,23,300, 304,305,311	Womack, Bobby 267,272,273	Young, LaMonte 372,377
	Wombles 373	Young, Lester 188,294,295,306
Williamson, John Lee 'Sonny Boy' 168	Wonder, Stevie 21,43,47,149,197,198, 199,203,249,302,304	Young, Neil 91,320,321,330
Williamson, Robin 79,325		Youngblood, Lonnie 231
Williamson, Sonny Boy 168,182,183, 184,187,226	Wondermints 215	Yuasa, Takuo 378
	Wood, Chris 62	Zappa, Frank 40,41,47,61,65,73,77,79, 88,102,135,136,137,147,218,220, 221,222,224,225,248,302,311,368, 369,372,376,377
Wills Fiddle Band 337	Wood, Ron 232	
Willis, Betty 121	Wood, Roy 73,212	
Wills, Bob 7,9,22,335,336,337,341	Woodson, Craig 55	
Wilson, Allan 56	Woodyard, Sam 58,59	Zawinul, Joe 43,45,47,304,305,307,311
Wilson, Brian 1,39,49,121,123,133,190, 214,215	Worrell, Bernie 331	Zentner, Si 99
	Wray, Link 13,22	Zimmer, Hans 286
Wilson, Delroy 346	Wright, Rick 45	Zinovieff, Peter 52,53,57
Wilson, Jackie 69,75,191,202	Wu-Tang Clan 158	Zombies 211,215
Wilson, Philip 301,309	Wuorinen, Charles 53,57	Zorn, John 52,143,148,149,275,285
Wilson, Tom 135,152,316	Wyman, Bill 27,30	
Winchell, Walter 125	Wyman, Loraine 83	

ABOUT THE AUTHOR

The first record that Nick Hamlyn bought with his own money was Chubby Checker's *Let's Twist Again*, just after his tenth birthday. His interest in music grew, proceeding in a very similar manner to the experiences of Harrison Ashby, the hero of Nick's 2015 novel, *Music For A Desert Island*. As a student at UEA, with limited funds, Nick often had to choose between buying records and buying food. He ate a lot of bread and margarine, but his record collection was larger than anyone else's he knew. Some years later, realising that he had thousands of records but was playing only hundreds, he opened a record shop to get rid of the surplus. With his surname, there was only one possibility for the name of the shop. It was *Pied Piper Records*. After twenty-four years, when Nick transferred his energies to the internet, he had to admit that his original strategy had not worked – his personal music collection had become many times larger.

In 1990 he decided to draw on nearly thirty years of music collecting knowledge by publishing his first Collectors' Record Price Guide. During the next decade and a half, the Guide moved through six editions, the later ones published by Penguin Books, and selling well enough to appear, from time to time, in the top ten non-fiction chart (yes, there was one!). During this time he also wrote regular articles for *Music Collector* magazine and contributed to

Vox. His first appearance in print had come rather earlier than this, when he won second prize in a music writing competition organised by *Melody Maker* in 1980.

Nick has played guitar in several bands over the years. The first, a poetry and music collective called Paris Green (well it was the late sixties) also included the future writing star, Douglas Adams. Much later, Nick was delighted to find himself playing in the same band as a former member of the progressive rock group, Solstice. Another later band, called Four Bop Drop, released a CD of relentlessly uncommercial improvised music on the Slam label in 1997. In live performances on different occasions, this band accompanied trombonist Paul Rutherford and baritone saxophonist George Haslam, alto saxophonist George Khan, and drummer Charles Hayward. Most recently, Nick has appeared on several occasions in a duo with his sister, Cathy, performing songs written by both of them.

In 2017, Nick published a collection of his short stories, under the title *The Tunnel Of Worlds*.

If you have found this book to be interesting and useful, please take the time to write a review of it on Amazon.

Harrison Ashby is a music fan. 'Obsessed' is how his wife Carole would have described him. Born at the start of the nineteen fifties, Harry finds his teenage years underscored by the music of The Beatles and Jimi Hendrix. He also finds his life unexpectedly entwined with that of a successful folk singer by the name of Jed Brandt. As though he were a guest on the long-running BBC radio show, Desert Island Discs, Harry chooses eight pieces of music that seem to represent different areas of his life particularly well and describes how this works for him, as he tells the story of his life. It is an account that is part love story, part teen memoir and coming of age narrative, and part musical discussion. It will interest anyone else who loves music, whether or not they are as overwhelmed by it as much as Harry is, and anyone who remembers the sixties and seventies as he does, or who is drawn to finding out what those decades might have been like for a music fan. In addition, Music For A Desert Island is probably the only novel to include a discography at the end.

A collection of 53 short stories and one short play by the author of the Penguin Price Guide for Record & CD Collectors and the novel Music for a Desert Island. Like the novel, many of the stories are music based, if only as regards the title. Some are science fiction, many are not; some are happy, some are sad; some are intriguing, a couple try to be scary.

Both books available from Amazon as paperback or e-book editions.

THE FIRST TIME

www.ingramcontent.com/pod-product-compliance
Lightning Source LLC
Chambersburg PA
CBHW042034100526
44587CB00030B/4424